CURRICULUM-BASED EVALUATION FOR SPECIAL AND REMEDIAL EDUCATION

A Handbook for Deciding What to Teach

Kenneth W. Howell
Arizona State University

Mada Kay Morehead
Kyrene School District
Tempe, Arizona

Merrill Publishing Company
A Bell & Howell Information Company
Columbus   Toronto   London   Melbourne

Published by
Merrill Publishing Company
A Bell & Howell Information Company
Columbus, Ohio 43216

This book was set in Quorum.

Administrative Editor: Vicki Knight
Production Coordinator: Constantina Geldis
Cover Designer: Cathy Watterson

Library of Congress Catalog Card Number: 86–63862
International Standard Book Number: 0–675–20397–X
Printed in the United States of America
1 2 3 4 5 6 7 8 9—91 90 89 88 87

Photo credits: pp. 2, 304, © Harvey R. Phillips/PPI; **p. 12,** Merrill Publishing/Bruce Johnson; **p. 24,** © Ruth Durrie/PPI; **p. 50,** Merrill Publishing/Kevin Fitzsimons; **pp. 72, 140,** Celia Drake; **pp. 98, 332, 366,** Merrill Publishing/Lloyd Lemmermann; **pp. 112, 162,** Merrill Publishing/Jean Greenwald; **p. 196,** Edgar Bernstein; **p. 236,** © Rocco Sorentino/PPI; and **p. 272,** Strix Pix/David S. Strickler.

To Yakutat, Fox Lake, Disenchantment Bay, and points north
K. W. H.

To my family
M. K. M.

Situations, or tasks, rather than people, should be the basic units of analysis.
E. Brunswick

Preface

We have written this book for use as the basic text in a first course on the evaluation of exceptional children. The idea for the book grew out of our frustration over the lack of straightforward, classroom-oriented texts on evaluating children. True, the literature for practitioners is filled monthly with the business of assessment—journal articles with baseline and intervention data; task analyses; statistical operations of all sorts; critiques; and defenses of one or another of the seeming hundreds of tests used to identify, label, place, or program for handicapped children. But nowhere could we find a text that truly integrated the basic concepts and issues in assessing handicapped children, that offered a teachable format for deciding what to teach, and that gave preservice or practicing teachers a useful set of tools for measuring a child's progress from day to day.

Not surprisingly, those three needs have dictated the plan of this book. Part One consists of eight chapters on the basic models of evaluation and the corresponding concepts and terminology associated with each. Part Two consists of seven chapters that explain, demonstrate, and encourage practice in the task-analytic, or curriculum-based, model of evaluation across academic and social skills content. This part concludes with a discussion of the continuous measurement of pupil progress. Finally, four appendices are included. Appendix A addresses the common issues confronting teachers/evaluators, and Appendix B is a source of support for teachers who want a quick, understandable guide to the statistics and content they often face in evaluation activities. Appendix C lists tables of specifications for content areas, while Appendix D provides answers to Study Questions that appear at the end of each chapter. A reference list and glossary complete the book.

RATIONALE FOR OUR APPROACH

The majority of special/remedial students (sometimes called the mildly handicapped) receive services because of their failure to learn the academic and/or social curriculum presented in regular classes. The special programs developed to combat this failure, including not only special and remedial education programs, but also migrant education, bilingual education, and those for low economic status students, share many commonalities (Wang, Reynolds, & Walberg, 1986). Each program's primary goal is to raise students to the same level of curricular skill as students in regular classes. Students who are behind in the curriculum are placed in special programs, and those who catch up are removed from them. Therefore, by its very nature, special education is *curriculum-based.*

Curriculum-based evaluation draws much of its strength from the *principle of alignment.* This principle states that greater learning will occur in programs that ensure that evaluation and instruction are both aligned with the curriculum. In other words, students will learn more if teachers use materials and activities which cover the curriculum and make decisions from tests which measure the curriculum. This "test what you teach" and "teach what you test" orientation makes common sense and has been found to be very effective.

Curriculum-based evaluation is not new (Carroll, 1963). However, in the past it has lost the competition for coverage in journals and texts in special education and educational psychology. While the rest of education has been acutely interested in curriculum-based issues, such as *mastery learning, outcome-based instruction,* and *teacher effectiveness,* special/remedial education has often shown more interest in the characteristics of its students than in the activities of teaching. This failure to focus on curriculum, not the absence of technology, has led to the current developmental lag in educational psychology and special/remedial evaluation.

Curriculum-based evaluation is no less complex, theoretical, or sophisticated than student-based evaluation. While it does involve some different procedures and techniques, its main distinction is one of focus: what teachers and evaluators do—not who they do it to.

From any perspective, educational evaluation is a difficult, time-consuming business. Lack of time, skills, support, or knowledge often hinders the process. Our goal is to see that you are never prevented from doing the job you want to do because you don't know how! Although our techniques may not save you time or effort, they will afford you the chance to feel good about time well spent.

ACKNOWLEDGMENTS

This text is an extension of two previous books: *Evaluating Exceptional Children* and *Diagnosing Basic Skills.* Much of the material presented here is drawn directly from the valuable work of Joe Kaplan and Theresa Serapiglia. Dr. Kaplan's orientations to education and his conceptualization of evaluative practice are as much a part of the work as those of the current authors. We wish to thank those who reviewed the text: Sandi Cohen, University of Virginia; Nancy Cooke, University of North Carolina, Charlotte; Harry Dangel, Georgia State University; Stephen Isaacson, State University of New York, Geneseo; Jill McCollum-Gahley, Arizona State University; Gail Mindes, Loyola University; and Owen White, University of Washington. In particular, the comments and suggestions of Kay Stevens (University of Kentucky) are greatly appreciated. We are also grateful to Sue Sharkey, Kathy Lorson, and Joyce Howell for their efforts in preparing and organizing the manuscript. Finally, our special thanks to Susan Bigelow for her attention to detail, intelligent analysis of text, and tolerance.

Kenneth W. Howell
Mada Kay Morehead

Contents

APPENDIXES

PART ONE

EVALUATION STRATEGIES

Chapter 1

Principles of Curriculum-Based Evaluation

This chapter provides a preview of topics covered in the rest of the text and explains, very broadly, where evaluation fits into education. In order to do this, we must make some general statements about what education is, what special/remedial education is, and what evaluation has to do with each of them. Because our goal here is to preview, much justification, documentation, and logical support will be left for later.

WHAT IS EDUCATION?

Formal education is planned and carried out by our society at great public expense. If you ask people why we do this, you're apt to get a lot of different answers. One of the most common answers is "to help students learn." Learning is a complex phenomenon; rather than try to explain what it is, for now we will simply acknowledge its complexity and go on to say that it is best indicated by changes in student behavior. That is to say, students who leave class doing (overt behavior) or thinking (covert behavior) different things from when they entered class have learned.

The exact products of education and their value are frequently debated, but most of us would probably agree that they fall into the areas of (a) promotion of knowledge, (b) promotion of skill, (c) certification, and (d) custodial service (Boulding, 1972). Teachers focus on products a and b. Certifications (in the form of degrees, credentials, and transcripts) are supposed to document the knowledge and skills students have acquired. And while it is a painful realization for many professional teachers, it is simply a fact of modern economic and social reality that schools provide a custodial service by occupying student time (Glass, 1974).

The Curriculum and Student Progress
Again, teachers tend to focus on the promotion of skills and knowledge. For them the purpose of education is to prepare people to be socially competent members of society by teaching them things needed to participate in society. These "things" are the skills and knowledge formally articulated in a school's *curriculum*. A curriculum is a structured set of learning outcomes (objectives) resulting from instruction (Johnson, 1967). It is pivotal to all instructional activities, including evaluation. The curriculum tells us what we teach and when we teach it.

Because all the things in the curriculum cannot be taught at the same time, the curriculum must be subdivided so that different objectives can be assigned to different grades, classes, and times of the year. Therefore, a complete curriculum does not specify only what will be learned, but *when* it will be learned. For example, most school districts expect students to have learned multiplication facts by the end of third grade.

Figure 1.1 shows a line of expected student progress. The line is determined by noting the intersections of time spent in school and various levels of curriculum. This line indicates that a student is expected to have learned one year's worth of curriculum in one year's time. Students whose progress falls above the line are working above their expected level; students below the line are below expectation.

Special and remedial students have trouble moving through the curriculum at the expected rate. For example, the student shown in Figure 1.2 is not progressing as he should. The student was expected to learn 5 years of objectives in 5 years of school. However, he has only learned about 2.5 years worth of curriculum. Therefore, he is only progressing at 50% of the expected rate. This failure to progress typically prompts teachers or parents to seek special help for their students. This help commonly involves attempts to alleviate whatever condition is preventing the student from learning adequately in the regular class, move the student through the curriculum faster in order to catch up, or both. To accomplish these changes a decision-making process must be set in motion.

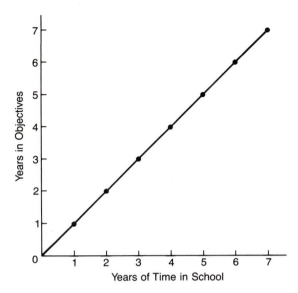

FIGURE 1.1
Expected course of student learning

INSTRUCTIONAL DECISION MAKING

To help students who are behind we must make changes in their educational programs. Because continuing to use techniques that have failed in the past is a waste of student and teacher time, we must modify our instruction by applying exceptional evaluation and teaching techniques. In other words, we must do something *different*, or *exceptional*, for the child if he or she is to catch up. We must decide which of many options to take when selecting objectives, settings, facilities, groupings, materials, and staff. If we make the correct decisions and carry them out effectively, the student's progress and performance will be improved. Figure 1.3 shows the progress of a student before and after an educational decision was made. Before the decision was made, the student was not progressing adequately; after the decision was made,

he was. It is important to know (and to believe strongly) that you can make this kind of positive effect on student learning. You are more likely to have a positive effect if your educational decisions are guided by appropriate evaluative information.

Let's take a quick look into the box in Figure 1.3 labeled "Decision Making." As educators we make two types of decisions about students: placement decisions and treatment decisions. Placement decisions deal with the assignment of the student to a particular school setting or category, while treatment decisions relate to what will be done to the student in that setting.

Placement Decisions

Placement decisions concern grouping, grading, retention/promotion, screening, and the determination of eligibility for remedial or support services.

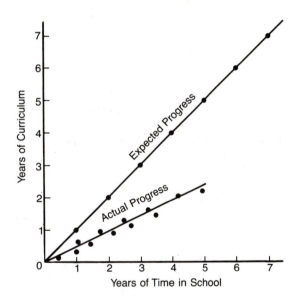

FIGURE 1.2
Actual course of learning of special student

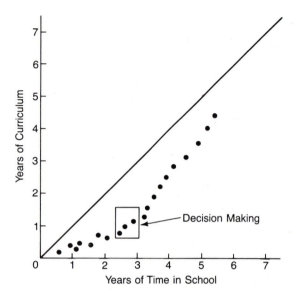

FIGURE 1.3
Effect of decision making on educational progress

They also include decisions about the duration of service; the service model to be employed; and the district, school, and teacher to be used. These placement decisions pertain to students' movement within the schooling system and are essentially classificatory in nature. That is, they involve sorting activity through which students are classified into general categories—for example, "students needing to be retained versus students not needing to be retained."

Because most schools handle large numbers of students, these classificatory decisions are usually normative. That is, they are based on the comparison of students to each other. These comparisons require the use of measurement instruments, such as achievement tests, designed to clarify achievement differences between students. By using a few items that range from very easy to very hard, these normative instruments cover a wide range of content and highlight students' relative achievement. While the institutional nature of schooling requires administrative policies and organizational strategies for students who work at different levels of

achievement, it is an error to assume that these policies (or the tests used with them) say anything that is useful about how individual students should be taught. The issue of classification, particularly classification into various handicapping conditions, is elaborated on in Appendix A.

Treatment Decisions

Treatment decisions deal with two things: *what will be taught* and *how it will be taught*. These decisions include the specification of objectives, materials, time, instructors, and many other instructional variables. Treatment decisions about what to teach and how to teach it are based on different information than are placement decisions. The normative standards and global measures used in placement are not functional for guiding treatment. There are two reasons for this. First, the variables measured during placement evaluations (e.g., intelligence, general achievement, cognitive processing, chronological age, and class standing) are chosen because they are stable (resistant to change through instruction). (You might teach a kid for a year and see terrific academic progress but her score on the IQ test wouldn't change much. It isn't supposed to.) If they were not stable, the student body would have to be sorted and reclassified after each period of instruction. Second, as mentioned above, the placement instruments used to classify students sample very large domains of curriculum or ability. Consequently, they produce results that lack the specificity and focus needed to guide daily instruction. In other words, if somebody hands you a copy of a kid's scores on the *California Achievement Test*, tells you his IQ is 85 and he's in the bottom 10% of his grade, you still don't know whether or not he knows his vowel teams and long division. To start treatment (teaching), you need different information.

For these reasons it is best to keep placement and treatment clearly separated in our thought and practice. The placement criteria developed to move students through the school system, and to hold the entire system accountable, reflect policies that vary from state to state, year to year, and district to district. These criteria are often determined as much by funding, political, and administrative trends as they are by sound educational practice. For example, in the mid-1960s when learning disabilities (LD) was being defined as a condition excluding mental retardation (MR), the definition of retardation most commonly applied was an IQ below 80. Therefore, an LD student became anyone who could not learn *and* who scored over 80 on an IQ test. Later many states changed the maximum IQ for MR to 70 but left the lower limit of LD at 80. This happened because two different committees set the two definitions. As a result, a large group of slow learners with IQ scores between 70 and 80 were left without any available category—a situation that still exists in some school districts. Because these non-LD and non-MR students need special/remedial instruction as much as their formally classified peers, they are often called the "slow-lows" and treated under the table by special/remedial teachers.

In contrast to placement criteria, the proficiency criteria for task performance and the prerequisite skills students must master to succeed in their work are determined by the tasks making up the curriculum. A child labeled mentally retarded in New Jersey may not be labeled mentally retarded in California. But a child who doesn't know her math facts in California still won't know her math facts when she gets to New Jersey. These subskills and proficiency levels, which do not vary from district to district, are easily altered through instruction and should be reflected on the tests used to guide treatment.

As shown in Figure 1.4, treatment decisions fall into two categories: what to teach and how to teach. Both of these categories are directly tied to the curriculum, just as the whole concept of treatment is tied to moving the student through it. The purpose of treatment is to produce desired changes in the student's social, language, or academic skills. When these desired changes do not take place, the student is not progressing. This lack of progress can be attributed to ineffective instruction.

Before anyone gets nervous, let us be quick to assert that ineffective instruction does not necessarily mean bad teaching. Ineffective instruction simply means that the treatment is not producing the desired learning (change). There are many types of treatment decisions, some of which are listed in Table 1.1, and the teacher must select the best one for each student. This selection, when based on good evaluative information, can have the effect of increasing the student's progress.

THE TEACHING/LEARNING INTERACTION

Learning is interactive. It arises from the interchange of many factors that can be grouped under the headings of Student, Curriculum, and Instruction (see Figure 1.5). Because it is interactive, learning will not take place if one of the factors is missing. A teacher with no material to present and no one to present it to will not produce learning, just as a student without instruction (of some sort) will not learn. Therefore when learning occurs we must be willing to give some credit to each of the three elements: instruction (evaluation and teaching), student, and curriculum. Similarly, when learning fails to occur we must consider each element. Most importantly we must consider each element not in isolation, but in interaction with the others.

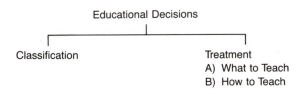

FIGURE 1.4

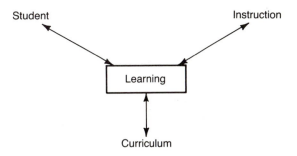

FIGURE 1.5

TABLE 1.1
Educational decisions

A. *What-to-Teach Decisions*
   A.1 No instruction required

   A.2 Instruction required
      A.2.1 Build accuracy
      A.2.2 Build fluency
      A.2.3 Build automaticity

B. *How-to-Teach Decisions*
   B.1 Curriculum decisions
      B.1.1 Stay with current level and/or context
      B.1.2 Change level
         B.1.2.a   Move to a more complex objective
         B.1.2.b*   Move to a simpler objective (only when no corrects have occured
                    after several sessions)
         B.1.2.c   Adjust aim date
      B.1.3 Change context
         B.1.3.a   Teach the objective in context
         B.1.3.b*   Teach the objective in isolation (only when tests of context
                    knowledge are failed)

   B.2 Instructional decisions
      B.2.1 Stay with current format, incentive, and delivery
      B.2.2 Change format of instruction
         B.2.2.a   Use acquisition procedures
         B.2.2.b   Use fluency procedures
         B.2.2.c   Use generalization procedures
         B.2.2.d   Use maintenance procedures
      B.2.3 Change incentives
         B.2.3.a   Change type or schedule of consequences
         B.2.3.b   Provide meaning
      B.2.4 Change delivery of instruction
         B.2.4.a   Change how information is given
         B.2.4.b   Change length of lesson
         B.2.4.c   Change group size or composition
         B.2.4.d   Change use of questions
         B.2.4.e   Change pace of lesson
         B.2.4.f   Change feedback given
         B.2.4.g   Change materials used
         B.2.4.h   Change other high impact variables

*Employ these decisions only when others have failed.

All of us have encountered material that was easy for us to learn but hard for someone else—or teachers under whose instruction we seemed to learn easily while the person next to us sweated out the course in near-despair. These different interac- tions resulted from the relative influences of vari- ous student, instruction, and task characteristics. These interactions cannot even occur if one of the elements is isolated. A student's reading problem, for example, cannot be identified if he is not given something to read, and the kind of reading problem he appears to have will depend in large part on the kind of material we ask him to read.

The interactive nature of learning means that evaluations designed to guide instruction must focus on interactions themselves, not on individual components of interactions (Eisner, 1982). The point of all of this is simple. The solution for a student's failure to learn will not be found by looking just at the kid. This is critical to understand because the traditional procedure for evaluating special/remedial students has been, and unfortunately continues to be, to examine their personal characteristics such as IQ, learning style, cerebral dominance, perceptual ability, and more recently, preferred mode of information processing. This tendency to "blame" the student for the failure has a long history and is deeply entrenched in our thinking about success and failure in school and life. This issue is discussed under the heading "Causation" in Appendix A, which deals with a variety of topical issues related to evaluation.

Obviously we are proposing a shift away from our preoccupation with student characteristics. This is hardly a new proposal, but it remains timely. Consider the following example, which is a logical extension of our discussion of progress and decision making. In that presentation, data were presented (in Figures 1.1, 1.2, and 1.3) showing the learning of a student who was falling behind in

school. Does this mean that there was something wrong with the student? Consider for a moment that the whole idea behind special/remedial education is that instruction can alter the rate at which students learn. This premise is basic to the entire teaching profession. What it means can be seen in Figures 1.6a and 1.6b. In Figure 1.6a the student is moving across time but is functioning below expected levels. Then that student is placed into special education. As a result of the placement, the student ends up progressing faster.

Even if every child placed in special education does not always make that much progress, it is imperative that educators think they will. This is the most basic premise of all formal education: *Instruction matters.*

The solution in Figure 1.6b is only slightly different. In this case the student has received appropriate instruction all along and as a result has never fallen behind. This illustration is not intended to build a case for early intervention. Instead, it is intended to make the point that if a student can catch up with special instruction, then the lack of it can make a student fall behind. We can't have it both ways. If the pupil has not learned, the teacher has not taught.

Once again, if instruction can help a student change, the student has failed to change because instruction has been inappropriate. It is interesting to note that talking about inappropriate instruction

FIGURE 1.6

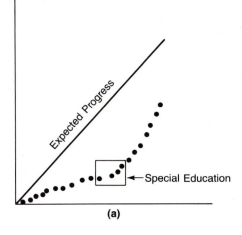

(a)

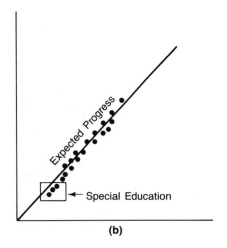

(b)

tends to alienate some teachers much faster than talking about the problems of students. And it is true that while a teacher may reassure parents that the substandard performance of their child isn't anything to feel angry or guilty about, the same teacher will probably feel guilty and ashamed if the source of the substandard performance is somehow traced to him or her.

But "inappropriate instruction," as pointed out earlier, is not synonymous with bad teaching. Inappropriate instruction is instruction that didn't work. It means that, for some reason, the variables that influence learning were not arranged to that student's benefit. The teacher, of course, has the primary responsibility for arranging these variables.

SUMMARY

In this chapter we have introduced the topic of evaluation and described its interaction with instruc-tion. In the following chapters we will present a model of evaluation, and the information necessary to employ it, that does not focus exclusively on student characteristics. As a result it will focus to some extent on instructional characteristics and curriculum. Thus there will be times when the discussion may seem more appropriate for an instructional methods book or for a curriculum development guide. That is because we have tried to present material on functional assessment and *at the functional level, teaching, curriculum, and evaluation are inseparable.*

Underlying this discussion, and often paralleling it, will be extensive presentations on the nature and technology of evaluation. These presentations—on topics like test construction, statistics, scoring, and error analysis—will look more "evaluative," but we will try to retain an interactive orientation and always tie the topics back to instruction, curriculum, and students.

Study Questions

1. Define the following terms as they are used in this text.
   a. Curriculum
   b. Decisions: placement and treatment
   c. Objective
   d. Norm-referenced tests
2. Placement decisions use
   a. stable tests that are insensitive to instruction.
   b. normative measures that compare students to one another.
   c. general tests that sample large domains of behavior.
   d. all of the above.
   e. a & b.
3. Which of the following is not part of a curriculum?
   a. Materials and methods
   b. Objectives
   c. Sequenced learning outcomes
   d. The skills the students are expected to master
4. If a student isn't learning, it is probably because
   a. something is wrong with the student.
   b. something is wrong with the task.
   c. something is wrong with the instruction.
   d. something is wrong with the interaction.

5. Students are placed in special education because
   a. they are handicapped.
   b. they need one-to-one attention.
   c. they are behind in the curriculum.
   d. they cannot learn the same material that regular kids learn.
6. The *most important* goal of special education is to
   a. discover the child's strengths.
   b. increase the student's learning rate and catch up in the curriculum.
   c. provide individual attention to student needs.
   d. build self-esteem.
7. Why is it important to examine our views about "handicaps" *before* conducting an evaluation?
8. Decide whether a placement decision or a treatment decision can be made from the following statements:
   a. Kathy can land an airplane better than Bud can.
      1. Placement?
      2. Treatment?
   b. John can land a plane with 50% accuracy. He needs to land it with 100% accuracy to fly his first solo.
      1. Placement?
      2. Treatment?

Chapter 2

Systems and Models of Evaluation

The first chapter presented a general discussion of expected educational progress and the effect decision making can have on actual progress. We went on to point out that the best treatment decisions are based on good evaluative information. In this chapter we will present some background information about evaluation and some basic schemes for employing it.

WHAT IS EVALUATION?

Evaluation is a thoughtful process we use to help us understand things. Evaluation has been defined in a variety of ways, all of which have at their core the idea of comparison. When we evaluate we make comparisons between things, note any differences we find, summarize our findings, and draw conclusions about our results.

A basic model can be used to represent the evaluation process. This model is shown in Figure 2.1. In the model, a sample of student behavior is compared to a standard and the discrepancy (difference) between the two is noted (Deno & Mirkin, 1977; Yavorsky, 1977). The behavior represents what the student is doing; the discrepancy represents how much the student's behavior must change to match the standard. For example, if a student is expected to read 140 wpm but only reads 35 wpm there is a 105 wpm discrepancy in reading speed (behavior).

The comparison of a student's behavior to a standard is central to the process of evaluation. The process is complete when the evaluator makes a judgment about the significance of any discrepancy and, based on that judgment, decides how to treat the student. Therefore, to understand evaluation we must know about taking behavior samples, establishing standards, summarizing discrepancies, and judging significance.

Measuring Behavior

Measurement has been defined as the assignment of numerical values to objects or events according to rules (Campbell, 1940). Measurement is a tool used to summarize the behavior of a student in manageable terms (scores) so that evaluation can take place. But keep in mind that it isn't possible to sum up a person with scores. Measurement is limited to the characteristics of things. People have physical characteristics and behavioral characteristics investigated and measured for various reasons. However, you should never assume that scores based on even the most thorough evaluation can actually summarize the total person. We are making this point at the outset to promote a realistic understanding of the limitations of all evaluation, not simply to document a commitment to human individuality (the same statement applies equally well to trout and car transmissions). What it means is that the results of every measurement should be interpreted not only in terms of what is summarized, but also in terms of what is *not* summarized. In most cases educational evaluators measure behavior and that behavior only *indicates* learning. It isn't learning itself.

Thorndike and Hagan (1969) have outlined three steps common to all types of measurement.

1. Identify the characteristic to be measured.
2. Devise a procedure to make the characteristic observable.
3. Devise a numerical system for summarizing the observations.

Davies (1973) has suggested another essential step. If the results of educational measurement are to be of practical use, this fourth step should be included.

4. Ensure that the measurement procedure corresponds to reality.

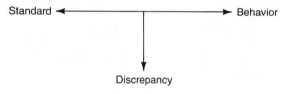

Standard ◄─────────────► Behavior

Discrepancy

FIGURE 2.1

These four steps can be followed no matter what is being measured. For example, suppose the teacher wants to measure a student's computational skills. The heading "computation" includes a number of operations, so the teacher must first identify which ones to measure (step 1). If the teacher identifies working multiplication facts as the characteristic to be measured, he or she must next think of a way to observe the student multiplying. The obvious procedure is to supply the student with a sheet of multiplication problems and a pencil. The student's behavior on the task can be observed by checking the written responses on the worksheet (step 2). The number of responses completed correctly and incorrectly can be counted to numerically summarize the work done (step 3). If the teacher ensures that the problems on the worksheet are similar to multiplication problems found on class assignments, then the results of the measurement can be applied in the classroom (step 4).

Educational evaluators are primarily interested in measuring children's skills, knowledge (thought processes), and attitudes. Although none of these is directly observable, we can draw inferences about them from the way students behave. Many behaviors are observable and are assumed to be brought about by things like skill, knowledge, and attitude. Because of our dependence on observed behavior to make these inferences, our conclusions will always be threatened by the imperfect correspondence between behavior, actual knowledge, and the occasional reluctance of students to display what they know (Fuchs, Fuchs, Dailey, & Power, 1985).

We can tell that knowledge is more than any one behavior by noting that many different behaviors may indicate the same thought process. For example, Figure 2.2 shows that a student's knowledge of addition may be indicated by several behaviors: writing answers, selecting answers, saying answers aloud, or circling answers. While a student who can only perform one of these responses is assumed to know less than a student who can carry out all four, that student has still indicated that he or she has some knowledge of addition.

Just as many behaviors can indicate the same thought process, many thought processes can result in the same behavior. This means that there is more than one way to get the correct answer on a test. For example, suppose a test requires two students to solve this problem:

$$\begin{array}{r} 50 \\ + \ 43 \\ \hline \end{array}$$

One student might work the problem out by following the standard addition algorithm (0 + 3 = 3, 5 + 4 = 9, so 50 + 43 = 93). The other, realizing that both numbers together will approach 100, could solve it this way: 43 is 7 less than 50, 50 + 50 = 100, 100 − 7 = 93. These two students both have the same answer and engage in the same "writes 97" behavior, but they have arrived at the answer by applying very different problem-

FIGURE 2.2

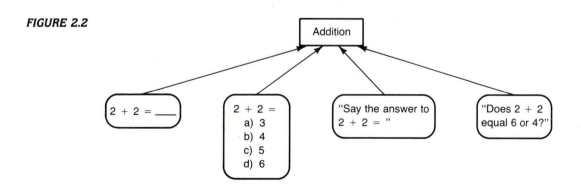

solving strategies. While both students probably know the addition algorithm, it is possible that only the second student knows how to solve problems by rounding and subtracting. Because there are different ways to arrive at answers, *scores from the same tests do not always summarize the same thought processes* and may not mean that the students know the same things (Frederiksen, 1986).

Sampling Behavior

Some domains of knowledge, ability, or attitude are so large that it is impossible to pick every behavior that indicates the student's status. For example, there are so many elements in the domain of mathematics that any attempt to test all of them would take so long that the student would die of old age long before the measurement was complete. For this reason it is necessary to *sample* behaviors.

Sampling involves selecting a few behaviors from the domain of interest. The procedure used to select these behaviors has a lot to do with the usefulness of a measure. The behaviors sampled must represent the domain about which conclusions will be drawn. Several behaviors may indicate knowledge or ability in an area, but some are better indicators of that knowledge than others. For example, supplying the names of coins and stating their value are both indicators of knowing about money. However, stating value is probably a more meaningful behavior than supplying names. There are two ways to get a sample of a student's behavior. One way is to *test* the behavior and the second is to *observe* it.

Observations of behavior are made when the behavior occurs naturally in the environment. Testing elicits behavior under what may be artificial conditions. All things being equal, observation is superior to testing because it supplies information about behavior that may be less strongly influenced by the evaluator or the evaluation process itself. However, some things are not conveniently observed. A teacher who is interested in a student's knowledge of the Civil War, for example, might observe the student for some time before the student happens to start chattering about the Civil War with friends. If the teacher needed to judge that knowledge at a

particular time, say the end of a history unit, then he or she would probably be forced to elicit the behaviors that indicate Civil War knowledge. This procedure of manipulating the environment to elicit behaviors at particular times, or under particular conditions, is called *testing*.

Tests are constructed by developing items that sample behaviors reflecting the things in which the evaluator is interested. As already mentioned, these items must be representative of the domain if the test is to be useful. Observations sample time intervals as well as particular behaviors. If these time intervals are not representative, the usefulness of the observation is decreased.

Think about different times during your typical day and imagine the different conclusions an evaluator might reach about you if you were observed for only a 10-minute period. If you happen to be arguing with someone during that period you might complain that the 10-minute sample wasn't really representative of your whole day and put you in a negative light. This could be corrected by lengthening the interval to allow measurement of a wider range of behavior or by breaking the interval into 10 one-minute samples taken at 10 different times. Either technique, or both, would make the observation more representative of your typical day.

If a student does well on a test or during an observation, the evaluator infers that the student will do well within the domain from which the sample was taken. For example, in Figure 2.3 four items have been sampled and an eighth-grade student has passed only two. This leads to the inference that the student knows only half of what she should know about math. To accept that this conclusion based on four items applies to the thousands of math items an eighth grader is expected to have learned, but which are not on the test, is to place great faith in the representativeness of the four items. However, evaluators do this sort of thing all of the time when they give achievement tests that include only a few items at each grade level.

The number of items required to represent a domain adequately depends in part on the cohesiveness or *consolidation* of the domain from which the

FIGURE 2.3

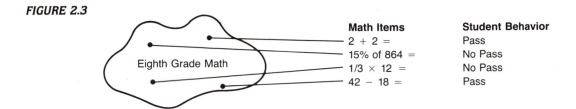

	Math Items	Student Behavior
	2 + 2 =	Pass
Eighth Grade Math	15% of 864 =	No Pass
	1/3 × 12 =	No Pass
	42 − 18 =	Pass

Inference: The student knows 50% of what he or she is supposed to know.

sample is taken. If the domain is composed of items that are very dissimilar from one another (e.g., match states to their capital cities), the student's response on one item will say little about the likely response on another. However, if the items in the domain share many stimulus and response properties, or if completion of the items depends on a common set of underlying strategies, or rules, generalizations are easier to draw. In cases where the domain is consolidated (such as multiplication), fewer items are needed as a basis for making an inference. If, however, the domain is filled with dissimilar materials, many items will be necessary to obtain a representative sample and make accurate predictions from a test. This point will be elaborated on in chapter 4.

A Special Note about Observation

The difference between testing and observation is that in testing we elicit responses and in observation we deal with whatever occurs "naturally." That sounds simple enough but there's one little hang-up: Whenever we measure something we change it. This doesn't just mean we interpret it in some novel way or misrepresent it in our summary (though that happens too). It means we actually change it. (This line of discussion gets metaphysical quickly. If a child miscues in the forest where no one can hear, is there an error? In physics this is called "Schrodinger's cat" dilemma. It states that nothing is resolved until we measure it [Zukav, 1979].) Once the evaluator enters the scene, things are changed. In fact everything is changed. Of course, this is just as true of achievement testing as

it is of observing but people seem to accept the impact of 16-page computer response forms more easily than the effect of strange adults with clip boards and stop watches lurking around in the back of classrooms.

Formats

The term *format* refers to the way a question is presented. The best formats for collecting behavior are those that are most representative of the domain from which the question is being drawn. In other words, the best test doesn't test only what a person knows, it also tests it the way a person will use it in real life. While the content of two items may be the same, the format or conditions imposed by the items may vary. Figure 2.4 shows items with different formats for four domains of content.

There are many different types of item formats and each has its particular disadvantages. These will be elaborated on in chapter 5. Frederiksen (1962) has ranked item types according to their "fidelity," or degree of realism. These levels are shown in Table 2.1. The least realistic format calls for the teacher to solicit the student's opinion about his or her own skill. The next calls for assessment of the student's attitude toward the task in question, and the third calls for a measure of the student's knowledge. This third format is the most common one used in schools; it typically comes in the form of an "objective test." Notice that formats that call for the performance of related behavior, the use of simulations, and lifelike behavior (the highest fidelity category) are seldom used. This is probably because these formats, while more realistic, are diffi-

FIGURE 2.4

Addition

a) $\begin{array}{r} 2 \\ +\ 2 \\ \hline \end{array}$ b) 2 + 2 =

Geometry

a) Define the term *triangle*.

b) Which of the following is *not* a triangle?

Spelling

a) Spell the word "analytical."

b) Circle the misspelled word:
  —antilytical
  —sequences
  —computation
  —components

Phonics

a) What sound do these letters make? *oo*

b) Circle the word that rhymes with *oo*.
  —dome
  —run
  —some
  —tune

cult to arrange and score. The need to use formats of higher fidelity increases as the importance of the measurement increases. A low fidelity format may be adequate for spot checking a student's learning, but higher fidelity formats must be used before making important treatment decisions such as movement to a new objective or assignment to a skill group.

While test items can be categorized in many ways it is common to group them by formats such as *identify* (select the answer) and *produce* (provide the answer) (Table 2.2). While identify and produce items both indicate knowledge, they too

TABLE 2.1
Formats of measurement

High Fidelity

↑

Lifelike behavior
Simulated behavior
Related behavior
Knowledge
Attitude
Opinion

Low Fidelity

Source: Drawn from N. Fredericksen, "Proficiency Tests for Training Evaluation." In R. Glaser (Ed.), *Training Research and Education.* Pittsburgh: University of Pittsburgh Press, 1962.

TABLE 2.2
Item formats

Identify Formats	Produce Formats
True/False	Fill in the Blank
Multiple Choice	Short Answer
Matching	Essay
Select Procedure	Apply Procedure

have certain advantages and disadvantages. For example, produce items, such as fill-in-the-blank or short answer, are often more analogous to what students will do with content in real life. Identify items, such as matching and multiple choice, are easier to score and are less ambiguous because the responses are limited to the alternatives supplied. This is why group tests are almost invariably composed of identify items while individual "diagnostic"[1] tests are commonly composed of production items. The need to trade ease of scoring for usefulness of results is a constant problem for test authors and users.

---

[1]*Diagnosis* is a medical term that means a description of an individual's physical status. Educators have adopted the term for their own use and as a result have changed its meaning. Typically educators call a procedure *diagnostic* when it has some treatment implications. Probably the best way to clarify the term *diagnosis* would be to give it back to the medical profession.

TESTING AND EVALUATION

Once a student's behavior has been summarized, it must be compared to a standard before evaluation can take place. This is an important point. Testing and observing are only efforts to see what a person is doing. Behavior samples mean little without an expectation, or standard, for comparison. Evaluation is more than testing. This point is made clear in the American Psychological Association's guidelines for the ethical use of educational and psychological tests (American Psychological Association, 1983).

- *Evaluation is not the same as testing.*
- *Testing is simply collecting behavior.*
- *Evaluation is comparing a behavior to a standard and rendering a judgment based on that comparison.*

Testing should never be piecemeal. Unfortunately, this is characteristically the case in special education. As Deno (1971) has pointed out, some educators judge the quality of a testing program by the number of tests routinely given. It is not uncommon to find special education programs that subject all referred students to a standard battery of tests regardless of their needs. This is not evaluation—it is called *fishing.*

Standards

It is not enough to know a person's current status; we must know if that status is adequate. To make this determination we must compare the status to some kind of standard. These standards are extremely important because an inappropriate standard can lead to inappropriate decisions. Just as a testing format that inaccurately represents a student's knowledge is of limited value, a standard that inaccurately represents what that student's knowledge should be is of limited value. In general the standards used in education are in such poor shape that they deserve cynicism. Because of this, whenever someone tells you that they know of a student who is unusual or special you should get in the habit of responding, "Compared to what?"

Types of Standards

Most of us are familiar with two types of standards: norms and performance criteria. Normative standards are used when we are interested in the way a student's status compares to that of other students (e.g., above average, below average, *really* below average). Performance criteria are used when we are interested in the way a student's status compares to the requirements of a particular task (e.g., can he read the directions well enough to assemble the class's new microcomputer?). These task requirements are called *criteria.* The terms *norm-referenced test* (NRT) and *criterion-referenced test* (CRT) mean that scores obtained from the tests are compared (referenced) to either norms or criteria. If norms or criteria are not available, there is nothing to which the scores can be referenced and they are meaningless. In that case, evaluation is impossible. Criteria and norms must be formally established and their relationship to decision making validated for them to be useful. This is done through a process called *standardization* that will be discussed in chapters 5 and 8 and Appendix B.

The term *standardized test* can have two meanings. One is that the test was developed to be administered in a standard fashion. In such cases a manual with administration guidelines must be available. The second meaning is that standards have been established following some type of standardization activity. In this case technical information must be available describing the procedures followed to set the standards. There is a tendency to use the term *standardized test* as if it were synonymous with published or norm-referenced tests. This is a mistake. Many published tests lack established standards; criterion-referenced tests need to be standardized just as much as norm-referenced tests.

THE EVALUATION FORMAT

The evaluation model shown in Figure 2.1 represents what evaluation is. Another model,

Fact → Assumed Cause → Test → Decide

provides us with the basic format we use to actually carry out an evaluation. The F.A.C.T. format (we left the D out because it doesn't spell anything, not because it's unimportant) should be followed regardless of the type of student or content with which you are working. The format is expanded in Table 2.3.

Fact Finding (Survey Level)

When following the format you first collect some information about the student, usually through a *survey* procedure, the purpose of which is to determine the student's general status. This survey procedure may include the use of achievement tests, interviews, or class assignments. Survey procedures uncover "facts" about the student. These facts are hardly the equivalent of universal truths. More often they are simply lists of errors made in academics, language, or social behavior. For example, a survey-level reading test may require the student to read several passages out loud so that errors can be noted.

Developing Assumed Causes (Hypothesizing)

The next step, developing assumed causes, requires the evaluator to carefully consider the facts revealed by the survey test. The goal of this step is to develop an explanation(s) for the facts. At this point the explanations are only assumed causes or hypotheses to be validated or rejected during testing.

During the assumed-cause step the evaluator sits back in the chair and looks at the facts collected. He or she then tries to figure out where they came from.

The interesting thing about the assumed cause step is that there can be a lot of different assumed causes for the same facts. Which assumed causes a person lists and later attempts to validate will depend on what that person, as the evaluator, *thinks*. This is a good news/bad news situation. The good news is that our judgment as teachers and psychologists is essential. The bad news is that a lot of us have been trained to think incorrectly about the causes of student behavior. While the issue is complex, we can sum up in brief by saying that some people seem to think student errors are the result of various student illnesses, insults, or idiosyncrasies associated with cognitive or perceptual weaknesses; others think errors simply indicate missing skills. Therefore given the same fact—a reversed letter *b*, for example, one evaluator might assume "failure to exercise directionality due to poorly established cerebral dominance," while a second evaluator might assume "lack of knowledge about the formation of *b*'s."

Obviously two different assumed causes like these will lead to the selection of very different tests and the eventual formation of very different conclusions. This is because we are doing the evaluation; our results will say as much about the way we think as they will about our client. Again, the way evaluators think about their clients determines the outcome of their evaluations, and not everyone in special education thinks the same way. Attention to evaluator thought is critical. It is essential to

TABLE 2.3
F.A.C.T. model

Fact	Assumed Cause (Thinking Required)	Test	Decide (Thinking Required)
Find out what it is about the student that is problematic.	Develop a hypothesis that can explain why the fact (problem) exists.	Test your hypothesis (through additional observation or testing) to see if it is correct.	Reach conclusions about the problem based on your attempt to validate the assumed cause.

carefully examine the assumptions professionals carry in to the evaluation. This is why selected issues are covered in Appendix A. Some of these, particularly "Orientation to Special Education" and "Causation," should be examined closely as they are primary determinants of what evaluators do. We encourage you to read the issues-related material in Appendix A.

Testing/Observation (Specific Level)

After developing an explanation for the student's problem, the evaluator must test the hypothesis to see if it is correct. This means that we must select or produce whatever instrumentation is needed to resolve the question. Obviously the resolution will be clearest if the instrument used is a direct measure of the factor suspected of causing the problem. That is why this step is referred to as specific-level testing/observation (sometimes called *probing*). Where the testing/observation in step 1 may have covered a wide range of material, the probing procedures in step 3 are narrowly focused. Ideally specific-level testing/observation will be based on an objective that, if not passed by the student, will be listed as an instructional objective. Often these tests/observations take a minute or less to administer.

Decision Making (Interpretation)

In step 4 the evaluator compares the results obtained to the assumed causes and then *decides*. If he or she decides that the assumed cause was correct it is listed on the student's plan. If it was incorrect or the results are inconclusive, a new assumed cause is developed and the whole procedure starts again. By repeating the survey testing–specific testing cycle the number of explanations for student failure is gradually pared down to an instructionally manageable set. Treatment plans are then developed to counteract the causes for failure that this whole process has revealed. (Decision making and interpretation will be covered in chapter 6.)

SUMMARY

Evaluation is a thoughtful process involving the comparison of the way things are to the way they should be. It requires good measures of the way things are and good estimates of the way they should be. Educational evaluation follows a fixed format of survey testing/observation to collect facts, thinking to develop assumed causes for the facts, specific-level probing to find out if the assumed causes are real causes, and decision making.

Study Questions

1. Define the following terms as they are used in this text. Some of these terms may be review from previous chapters.
   a. Norm-referenced tests
   b. Criterion-referenced tests
   c. Testing
   d. Observation
   e. Measurement
   f. Survey level
   g. Assumed causes
   h. Discrepancy
   i. Probe
   j. Fidelity
   k. Format
   l. Specific level
   m. Consolidated domain
   n. Identify format
   o. Produce format
   p. Standard

2. Which of the following elements is present in *any* model of evaluation?
    a. Noting the student's strengths
    b. The use of criterion-referenced tests
    c. Making a comparison to a standard
    d. Obtaining a large sample of behavior
    e. None of the above

3. A "discrepancy" in this text refers to
    a. how much the student's behavior must change to meet the standard.
    b. a difference between the way two evaluators think about the causes of student failure.
    c. how far the student's level of achievement falls below IQ.
    d. a difference between the information obtained through an observation and the information obtained through a test.

4. Since thought processes themselves are not directly measurable, it is best to
    a. solicit the student's opinion concerning his or her competence at a skill.
    b. assess the student's attitude toward the task.
    c. make all judgments derived from the evaluation process tentative.
    d. indirectly measure the process through a directly observable behavior.

5. To provide the evaluator with useful information, test items must
    a. sample the modality as well as the behavioral components of the task.
    b. be as close as possible to the behavior the student must perform in real life.
    c. be drawn from several domains.
    d. be efficient to score and administer.

6. Which of the following portions of an evaluation is most highly dependent on the way the evaluator thinks about students? (More than one correct answer)
    a. Survey-level testing procedures
    b. Development of assumed causes
    c. Specific-level testing procedures
    d. Rendering judgments from the evaluation

7. Think of formats for measuring the following skills that would have high fidelity.
    a. Reads vowel sounds
    b. Ties shoes
    c. Raises hand in class
    d. Counts money

8. How does the degree to which a domain is consolidated affect the number of test items you need to use to get an adequate sample of that skill?

9. Why isn't evaluation the same as testing? How is it different?

Chapter 3

Evaluation and Curriculum

This chapter is about *curriculum* and tasks. It is about the stuff teachers should be teaching and students should be learning. It may seem out of place in an evaluation text but it isn't. That's because curriculum is an axial element of the learning interaction. Obviously, it isn't possible to do curriculum-based assessment without a curriculum.

In chapter 1 the role of decision making as it relates to instruction and curriculum was briefly outlined. Learning was described as an interactive phenomenon (involving the student, instruction, and the curriculum) which, when effective, results in desired progress. As discussed in chapter 1, treatment decisions are intended to alter the inadequate curricular progress and performance of special/remedial students. In the last chapter we asserted that for treatment decisions to make such alterations the evaluator must focus on causes of student failure and learning that can be altered through instruction. Deciding which of the numerous curriculum tasks a student should be taught, and which of the many instructional approaches will teach it the best, requires the use of evaluative procedures that are themselves sensitive to instruction. Obviously this sort of "curriculum-based assessment" (Tucker, 1985) requires us to pay attention to the curriculum.

Knowledge of the curriculum is an absolute for successful test construction, evaluation, and teaching (Fuchs & Fuchs, 1986; Howell, 1986). You can't evaluate a student's reading unless you know what reading is and what portions of it are essential for students to learn. These are curriculum issues. The illustrations of expected progress in chapter 1 (Figures 1.1, 1.2, and 1.3) presented a picture of a student who had fallen behind in the curriculum. This picture represents the majority of special/remedial students, most of whom are only considered handicapped because of their failure to meet certain academic or social objectives. A student who can read, write, spell, do math, and socialize normally would never be referred for and placed in special/remedial education. And the ones who are placed should be removed from it as soon as they demonstrate adequate curriculum performance/progress. Therefore, curriculum has both definitional and functional implications for special/remedial education. *The term "curriculum-based assessment" describes this relationship well.* This chapter will deal with information pertaining to the curriculum and to *task analysis.* The chapters in Part Two of this text focus on specific content (such as decoding, comprehension, language, and social behavior) and will use the terminology and ideas about to be presented.

WHAT IS A CURRICULUM AND WHAT IS IT GOOD FOR?

The curriculum is a structured set of learning outcomes, or tasks, that educators call *objectives* (Johnson, 1967). This set of objectives is sequenced, calibrated, and organized to facilitate learning. The curriculum is intended to prepare students to succeed in society; consequently the material in the curriculum comes from someone's analysis of what society requires for success. This analysis should include not only the static bits of skill and knowledge currently available, but also the dynamic principles of how to learn new material students will encounter later. Therefore, all students—including special and remedial ones—who are expected to survive in society need to learn the things specified in the curriculum.

To accommodate all students, the sequence of the curriculum may be shuffled, its tasks may be broken into small pieces or combined into larger ones, and its organizational structure may be altered, but the substance of the curriculum is not changed. The idea that special/remedial students need "individualized" programs pertains to the way the curriculum is delivered, not to the curriculum itself. Objectives are matched to society's requirements and are written into curriculum guides before the student even shows up for class. Some of them are well written and others are not. But they are not altered for each special/remedial student—and they shouldn't be as long as we believe that those students deserve a competitive shot at participation.

When it comes to deciding *what* to teach, the evaluator's job is limited to finding the best objective for the student from within the maze of existing outcomes. The best objective is the one the student is currently prepared to learn, as it is not too easy or too difficult, given current knowledge.

What is taught isn't the same thing as *how* it's taught.

Some educators act as if method (treatment) and curriculum were synonymous. You can tell this is happening when you ask a teacher *what* he or she is teaching and the response is the name of a published program (such as DISTAR, Scott Foresman, Spalding, SRA, Merrill, or Addison-Wesley), rather than a skill (such as saying vowel sounds, solving multiplication problems, writing prime factors, or comparing economic systems). Thus confusion is introduced into the curriculum. (Everyone agrees that kids need to be taught to read, but educators have argued for years about how to do it.)

THE TASK ANALYTIC MODEL

The task analytic model assumes that a student must learn the subcomponents, or prerequisites, of a task in order to learn the task. Evaluators using this model attempt to identify these subcomponents and to test the student's knowledge of them

TABLE 3.1
Elements of objectives/tasks

Content—What the student learns
Behavior—What the student does with the content
Criterion—How well the student does it
Conditions—Under what circumstances the student does it

in order to decide what a student needs to be taught.

Tasks

Tasks and *objectives* are the same things. Tasks may vary but they all have defining elements of content, behavior, criterion, and conditions (Mager, 1962). These elements (listed in Table 3.1) define the task. If one of them is missing the objective is not complete; in fact, it isn't even an objective. Varying any one of these elements makes a new objective. By systematically altering the content, behavior, condition, or criterion statements in objectives we can develop a set of objectives that vary in difficulty from easy to hard. For example, as seen in Table 3.2, the objective "Point to the dictated numeral with 100% accuracy" becomes a new task if the behavior is changed to "Circle the dictated numeral with 100% accuracy" or if the criterion is changed to "Point to the correct dictated numeral at a rate of 30 per minute" or if the conditions are changed to "Point to the numeral on the board with 100% accuracy."

TABLE 3.2
Sample objective with modifications

Original Task:	Point to the dictated numeral with 100% accuracy.
Different Behavior:	Circle the dictated numeral with 100% accuracy.
Different Criterion:	Point to the dictated numerals at a rate of 30 correct per minute.
Different Conditions:	Point to the numeral on the board with 100% accuracy.

Subtasks

Tasks (which are defined by their elements) have two components: *subtasks* and *strategies*. A student must have knowledge of both components to do the task. *Subtasks* are simply smaller, or more elementary, tasks required for the performance of an objective. Subtasks and tasks are exactly the same except for their relative positions in some skill *sequence*. If counting is required for addition, then counting is a subtask of addition. If addition is required for multiplication, then addition is a subtask of multiplication. (We suppose this means "one task's subtask is another subtask's task"—bet that cleared it up for you!) Subtasks must have all the same elements (content, behavior, criterion, and conditions) or they aren't complete. Subtasks can be viewed as the stuff (knowledge, facts, vocabulary, skills) students use whenever they try to do something.

Strategies

Strategies are the rules, procedures, and algorithms students follow to combine subtasks into larger tasks. There can be several different strategies for combining a set of subtasks because there is often more than one way to do something correctly. (There are definitely a lot of ways to do things wrong.) If two students with the same subskill competency follow different strategies, one may succeed at the task where the other might fail.

In the task analytic model it is assumed that students fail at tasks because they are missing an essential component of the task. This means that they are either missing a necessary subtask, don't know what to do with the subtasks they have (lack strategies), or both. An evaluator who is working in the task analytic model, when presented with a student who is failing in some area, will set about trying to find the missing subtask or strategy. Once again the subtasks are the building blocks of the task and must be available for task completion. But some students who have all the building blocks still fail because they don't have the blueprint for building the task. Therefore, student failure doesn't necessarily mean that a subskill is missing. It might mean

FIGURE 3.1

the student is prepared to succeed but doesn't know how to go about it. Figure 3.1 portrays strategies as a mechanism found between the subtasks and the task. This mechanism takes the subtasks and produces a larger, more complex, total task.

Computation is one of the easiest basic skill domains for illustrating strategies because mathematics instruction is based on the presentation of algorithms. Algorithms are step-by-step procedures for arriving at the answers to computation problems. Look at the fraction example in Figure 3.2. The task (adding $2/7 + 3/4$) is presented at the top and the subtasks are presented at the bottom. The strategy for combining the subtasks is also presented. As you read the strategy you will notice that it isn't particularly sophisticated; it simply tells what to do first, second, third, and so on. As you can see, a student who can't multiply and divide accurately (subtask 3) will be unable to succeed at this task—even if he or she has memorized the strategy and writes it on the board 50 times every day. That student will fail at the task because he or she lacks the necessary prerequisite subtasks. This student needs to work on multiplication prior to, or along with, fractions.

Guaranteeing that a student can do all subtasks still does not assure success. A student must also know the strategy. Sticking with the problem in Figure 3.2, imagine that a student writes this answer:

$$2/7 + 3/4 = 29/28$$

This answer is wrong because it is not converted to simplest form. This does *not* necessarily mean the student doesn't know how to convert fractions (subskill 5). It could mean he or she forgot the last step in the strategy (step g). Having this student

Task	*Example*

Task
  Add or subtract fractions without common denominators and that *do not* have common factors between denominators. Convert to simplest form.

$$\frac{2}{7} \; + \; \frac{3}{4} \; = \; 1\frac{1}{28}$$

Task Strategy
  a) Decide if denominators are the same.
  b) Find the least common denominator.
  c) Produce the equivalent fractions.
  d) Decide what operation (add or subtract) is called for.
  e) Carry out the operation.
  f) Decide if the answer is in simplest form. If it isn't,
  g) Convert it.

Essential Subtasks

  5   Converting fractions to simplest form

$$\frac{29}{28} \; = \; 1\frac{1}{28}$$

  4   Adding and subtracting fractions that do have common factors

$$\frac{8}{28} \; + \; \frac{21}{28} \; = \; \frac{29}{28}$$

  3   Multiplication and division facts

$$7 \,\overline{)28}^{\;4} \qquad 4 \times 2 = 8$$
$$4 \,\overline{)28}^{\;7} \qquad 7 \times 3 = 21$$

  2   Finding least common denominators

      ⑦14, 21, *28*
      ④8, 12, 16, 20, 24, *28*

  1   Addition facts

      $2 + 3 = 5$

FIGURE 3.2

memorize the strategy might be a good instructional technique (we'd pass on writing it 50 times a day), but working on multiplication would be a waste of time.

    Errors are often produced when a student attempts to solve a new problem by using a strategy that has worked in the past. For example, a student who writes

$$\tfrac{2}{7} + \tfrac{3}{4} = \tfrac{5}{11}$$

has not gotten the "add unlike fraction strategy"

wrong—he or she hasn't used it at all! Errors are not always the result of a flawed strategy; they are often the result of a correct strategy incorrectly applied. In the $\tfrac{2}{7} + \tfrac{3}{4}$ example the student applied the addition strategy for whole numbers to a fraction problem. In one sense what he or she did was right (added correctly). Unfortunately that wasn't what was needed. When students apply strategies they have already learned to new materials, the errors they produce are not the result of missing subskill information but of the attempt to apply their current knowledge in the wrong way.

Types of Strategies

There may be several different strategies for any one task. The fraction strategy presented in Figure 3.2 is one way to arrive at the answer; another way is to ask the teacher. The first strategy (adding fractions without common denominator) is specific to fractions. The second strategy (seeking assistance) is not specific to fractions and may be used in many different situations.

Specific strategies apply to only a limited range of tasks while *general strategies* may be used across several content domains (Frederiksen, 1984; Rigney, 1980; Wagner & Sternberg, 1984). The fraction algorithm in Figure 3.2 is a specific strategy, good for solving only one type of fraction problem. It won't help do long division, it won't help you get a date, and it won't help you find words in a dictionary. Asking for assistance, in contrast, is a strategy that may help you succeed at all of those tasks and many more.

How Strategies and Subtasks Work

To drive a car you have to know how the car works and the rules of the road. Driving to work is a major task composed of many smaller tasks like starting the car, using the clutch, stopping at traffic signals, and parallel parking. The subtasks of traffic signals include color recognition, color meaning, use of brakes, and knowing where to stop. The strategy is something like: watch for lights, check color, determine meaning of color, judge time and distance to stopping point, determine need to stop according to duration of signal, determine braking pressure required, coordinate brake with clutch and gear shift. Now remember the last time you drove a car. Were you aware of thinking about any of those things? Probably not. That's because you have become highly proficient at the strategy. If you had to consider all the subtasks and strategies

while driving you would end up stopping either several blocks past the traffic signal or sooner if something solid got in the way.

When you first learned to drive you occupied your consciousness with the task of driving. You may even have talked to yourself as a device for recalling strategies when you got in difficult situations. But you don't do that now because the strategies for driving have become automatic. Achieving automaticity allows us to employ strategies without allocating any of our awareness to them. If we encounter very different tasks, we may have to resort to conscious problem solving again.

The shift from automatic to problem solving is illustrated with a reading example in Figure 3.3. In that figure (based on a model by Holdaway, 1979), the boxes are words labeled *E* easy or *H* hard. (Difficulty may be the result of novelty, which is the result of each person's background, so what is hard for one person may be easy for another [Chi & Glaser, 1985; Frederiksen, 1984].) The reader (dotted line) is doing fine (not thinking about reading) until he or she hits the first hard word. At that point self-monitoring says that meaning has been lost. As a result the reader drops out of automatic reading and into a zone of problem solving. In the zone of problem solving, the reader has to think (be aware) of the act of reading and solving problems. Once the problem is solved the reader can return to the automatic zone until the next hard word comes along.

One important ramification of this is that conscious problem solving occupies the reader's awareness and therefore competes with the meaning of the passage. For readers with limited prior knowledge of a topic, or of decoding itself, many words seem difficult. Thus much of their awareness must be allocated to problem solving rather than to the meaning of a passage. Of course, students who

FIGURE 3.3

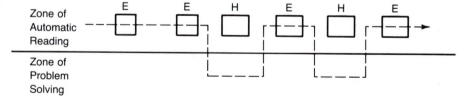

lack knowledge of problem-solving strategies as well as task-specific reading strategies are even worse off. They may have to allocate all of their awareness to simple decoding. These students will understand little of what they read. Another equally disabling problem occurs when a student's self-monitoring skills are so poor that he or she fails even to notice the loss of meaning and simply misreads difficult words without even trying to solve the problems they present. This student may appear to be "impulsive" to an observer.

The model of task performance presented in Figure 3.3 is a reasonable analogy for many tasks. The squares can represent arithmetic problems, social situations, ideas to verbalize, or words to spell. In each case success depends on the proficient use of specific and general strategies to manipulate subtask information. When failure occurs it can be traced to inadequate prior knowledge and proficiency. High levels of proficiency are necessary for students to achieve automaticity. This means that accurate behavior is not sufficient; mastery (fluency) must be obtained for a student to be successful. Therefore, evaluators must use instruments that are sensitive to the various proficiency dimensions and standards that meaningfully represent different levels of proficiency—if they wish to gain insight into strategy use.

CURRICULUM DEVELOPMENT

So far in this chapter we have established that the curriculum is a set of objectives, or tasks, each composed of subtasks and strategies. Next we want to describe how a complete curriculum is developed. We aren't doing this because we think that the average teacher/evaluator will ever sit down and develop a curriculum from scratch, but because it is important to know how it is done. Evaluators must know about curriculum design if they are to appreciate the multifaceted nature of objectives. The complete understanding of objectives is essential for evaluators who use a curriculum-based assessment model. In this section we will explain how to make tasks by working with their elements. The first element we will cover is content.

Content

Content is subject matter. It is history, biology, basic skills, social behavior, and all the other things that show up in the "Table of Contents" in any textbook or the topical outline in any course syllabus. The curriculum is composed of many content domains, each of which may produce many objectives.

As stated earlier, the curriculum is a package of objectives. Each objective has within it a statement of content, which is what the student will learn about. For example, "The student will write three definitions of *learning*." What is the content in that objective? *Learning.*

"Given a list of 60 CVC words, the student will pronounce the words within 1 minute with no more than two errors." What is the content? *CVC words.*

"Given the following list of historical figures, the student will categorize them as either 'friendly' or 'hostile' to the native populations of Alaska." What is the content? *Historical figures.*

The most common way to find content is to ask someone to give it to you or to find it in a published program. However, as consumers we need to learn how to evaluate the programs we are sent because they may be flawed. Do not assume that everything that is published has been validated.

As indicated, few of us will ever be involved in actually developing a complete curriculum sequence. We are more apt to be involved in selecting, elaborating, fine tuning, or polishing someone else's attempts at development. This is all right because it saves us the time we would waste "reinventing the wheel." However, the danger of avoiding reinvention is that we forget how to invent.

Recognizing Content
Recognizing the content elements of tasks is a straightforward, logical, and convergent activity. It begins with a general statement of content from which subtopics are recognized. It is best to generate these lists of subtopics in groups or using reference materials in order to benefit from the thinking of others who know the content area well. Once the subtopics are identified, each item of content should be judged according to the following criteria.

1. *Is it relevant?* Is the main task of value to the student?
2. *Is it complete?* Has any essential content been omitted?
3. *Is it trivial?* Is content included which is too easy for the target student?
4. *Is it necessary?* Is all content necessary to master the main task?
5. *Is it redundant?* Do any of the content statements overlap with other content statements? (Thiagarajan, Semmel, & Semmel, 1974).

For example, one school district includes in its arithmetic domain a kindergarten numeration objective which says

The student will skip count: by 2's to 10; by 10's to 100; by 5's to 100; by 2's to 100.

Does this objective contain content statements which are relevant, complete, trivial, necessary, or redundant? Well, it seems to satisfy the criteria in all aspects except completion. To begin with, skip counting by other numbers may also be needed (Berquam, 1986). More importantly, the objective only specifies counting forward. Students should learn to count backwards as well as forwards in preparation for learning estimation skills, subtraction, and inverse operation concepts. Thus a weakness of this content list is in its "complete" nature.

Sequencing Content

Even though it seems as if critics of education want teachers to teach everything at the same time, they can't. Therefore, once content statements have been identified they must be put into a sequence. Sequencing content allows us to recognize a coordinated series of objectives and the lessons used to teach them. This structure facilitates the who-teaches-what-when decisions that must be made in any school system.

Content of Equal Difficulty.   There are a number of ways to sequence content (Posner & Strike, 1976). If all the topics are of equal difficulty, then the most convenient system should be identified and used. Those systems that do not require ordering content according to difficulty are:

- Logically—Using this system, content is grouped into units defined by some similarity. Animals, for example, can be grouped according to what they eat. But the study of animals that eat grass isn't necessarily easier than the study of animals who eat leaves.
- Chronologically—Time may be used to present tasks as the content itself evolved or as the content was discovered. Even though it may seem obvious to start at the first, that doesn't make the first step easy. In fact, sometimes it's easier to show people where they are going before you get them started.
- According to student interest or teacher priority—This includes such age-old techniques as teaching what you know first so you can study up on something else to teach next. It also includes asking the kids what they would like to know about right away.
- Utility—This means arranging the content according to how the student will use it. This involves a little research into what skills or knowledge the typical kid needs to know first in order to get along. One technique is to ask parents if there is a skill they'd like their kids to start using as soon as possible. Utility is one way of ordering content that will vary a lot from location to location.

Content of Different Difficulty.   If the topics are of different difficulty, it is probably for one of two reasons and the content can be ordered accordingly.

- Functionality—Difficulty may be determined by the way the content functions in the "real" world. This includes complexity, the fact that some things build upon others so that you need to learn the basics first. Constructing a house might be one example.
- Developmentally—Some content may vary in difficulty with the student's changing ability to learn. This developmental approach is based on the idea that kids can't learn certain things until they have reached a certain level of maturity (not necessarily a certain chronological age). Due to the difficulties inherent in *ability* assessment, the

5. CVC words

4. Blending

3. Sound/letter correspondence

2. Letter sounds

1. Letters

Content ↑

FIGURE 3.4

developmental approach rests on largely un-proven assumptions (Arter & Jenkins, 1979). This system seems to work best with physical and perceptual tasks, and is not especially rele-vant to mildly handicapped school-age students.

If content can be sequenced according to diffi-culty or complexity it should be. The obvious thing to do is to put the easiest material in the first les-sons. Prerequisite content relationships (task lad-ders) are occasionally quite clear and easy to find in the literature. If these relationships are not clear, then the sequence should be viewed as a hypothesis to be validated through instruction and evaluation. By convention, lists of content that can be ordered by difficulty start with the easiest (or first taught) content at the bottom and the hardest (last taught) at the top, as shown in Figure 3.4.

Behavior
Every objective, particularly if it is behavioral, will describe what the student must do to show that he or she "knows" the content. How much a person knows is indicated by behavior.

"The student will write three definitions of *learning.*" What is the "know" word in this objec-tive? *Write.*

"Given a list of 60 CVC words, the student will pronounce the words within 1 minute with no more than two errors." What will the student do to demonstrate knowledge in this objective? *Pro-nounce the words.*

"Given the following list of historical figures, the student will categorize them as either 'friendly' or 'hostile' to the native populations of Alaska." What will the student do? *Categorize.*

Remember that *learning* is not directly observed but is indicated by changes in behavior, and that several behaviors can indicate the same knowledge with varying levels of validity. For example, Figure 3.5 shows us that three very different behaviors can be used to draw conclusions about a student's knowledge of reading.

Recognizing Behaviors
As stated earlier, evaluators are interested in ob-serving changes in behavior. Behaviors may change according to proficiency (how well they are carried out) or condition. As educators we recognize that teaching to many different conditions and profi-ciency levels is one way to assure a broader range of learning. The same behavior occurring under dif-ferent conditions (e.g., spelling while writing a let-ter or spelling in a spelling book) or at different proficiency levels (spelling quickly or spelling slowly) may indicate different degrees of knowl-edge. We can list categories, or domains, of behav-ior that indicate when different degrees or kinds of learning have taken place. These categories, which

FIGURE 3.5

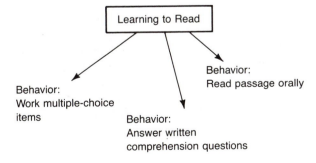

we will refer to frequently from now on, are *not* behaviors such as "touch," "say," "circle," and "write." They are labels applied to the parameters of behavior that indicate different levels of knowledge. These behavior parameters include response type and proficiency level.

Response Type. It is often easier to identify or select a correct answer than to produce the same correct answer. Every college student recognizes this, which is why they ask their instructors what "kind" of items will be on an upcoming test. As shown in Figure 3.6, multiple-choice and matching items are easier than fill-in-the-blank or short-answer items. This is because the response domain "identify" is generally sensitive to lower degrees of learning than is the domain "produce." That is, a student who cannot produce a correct answer may still actually "know" the answer and even demonstrate that knowledge by picking it out. Failure to produce does not always signal a complete lack of knowledge. Conversely, identification of an answer does not signal complete knowledge. Identifying behaviors include pointing to, indicating, selecting, tracing, and crossing out. Producing behaviors include saying, writing, and constructing.

Proficiency Levels. Varying degrees of knowledge may also be indicated by a behavior's location along a proficiency dimension. Two of the proficiency dimensions of interest to educational evaluators are accuracy (the proportion of items done correctly) and rate (the fluency with which items are completed). In general, higher levels of accuracy and higher levels of rate indicate higher levels of knowledge. Accuracy and rate combine within a final proficiency dimension we have labeled *automatic*. Because this dimension is not as widely recognized, it deserves a brief explanation.

Automaticity refers to a student's ability to maintain correct and fluid display of knowledge *under varying conditions*. It is this additional element, the circumstances under which the student works, that distinguishes automaticity from rate. A student who can work well in many situations is assumed to have better knowledge than the student who can only work in one setting. To carry out a task accurately and quickly in many situations you must be able to deal with distractions. When students begin to learn tasks they often must allocate so much attention to the task that even the slightest distraction will affect their accuracy or rate. This is thought to result from the human mind's inability to work with many problems consciously at the same time. For example, one of the authors once went skiing with a Dr. Rutherford. Dr. Rutherford at that point was an accurate skier who could maintain good form on the slopes through constant attention to his skiing. Your author would take advantage of his lack of automaticity by going down the slope ahead of Rutherford to hide behind a tree. When Rutherford came by, the author would shout "Boo!" and Rutherford would immediately fall down.

Automaticity (sometimes referred to as the ability to walk and chew gum at the same time) is an important proficiency dimension that is often ignored by educational evaluators, who tend to test skills in classrooms. Schools are notorious for compartmentalizing content. For example, math is not taught in the context of social studies, spelling, or history; different periods of the day are allocated to those topics. Many math tests even cover the different operations with separate subtests so that students aren't distracted by the operation signs of competing problem types. To find out if a student is

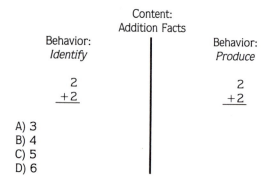

FIGURE 3.6

working at the automatic level, evaluators must provide real-world distractors. For example, educators might test a student's skill at adding coins in a crowded supermarket line in place of having him work addition items on a test.

The proficiency parameters (subdivisions) we will use in this book are accuracy behavior, mastery behavior, and automatic behavior.

1. *Accuracy*—Doing the behavior correctly. Accuracy is usually determined by comparing the number of correct and error behaviors to the total number of behaviors. Accuracy data are most often expressed as percentage (%) data. For example, "Rob got 100% of his spelling words correct."
2. *Mastery* (or fluency)—Doing the behavior accurately and quickly. Mastery is determined by comparing the accuracy of the behaviors to the speed at which they are completed. Mastery is expressed as rate (usually in rate per minute) data. For example, "Linda spelled 14 words a minute correctly with 0 errors."
3. *Automatic*—Doing the behavior accurately and quickly in the presence of relevant distractions. Automatic functioning is determined by having the student do a task in context. Automatic data are usually reported as rate (sometimes only as

accuracy). For example, "Roberto's spelling in his paper about duck hunting was 95% accurate." These levels are illustrated in Figure 3.7.

Conditions

The conditions under which a behavior is carried out also indicate different degrees of knowledge. For example, the automatic level involves accurate and quick response under real-world conditions. These conditions can also be arranged into sequences that make the behavior harder to carry out and indicate that a higher level of learning has taken place (Howell, 1983). Have you ever heard someone say "He can do it on a test but not when it counts"? They were talking about a student who could do a task in the classroom but nowhere else. Remember that an objective includes a statement about conditions for performance. If the conditions under which the behavior occurs change, a new objective is produced even though the content, behavior, and criterion stay the same. Because there is no sense in teaching a student to be able to work only under classroom conditions, we must teach students to transfer and generalize their learning outside of the class and school, as shown in Figure 3.8. This is particularly important for special/remedial students, who, as a group, seem to have trouble

| | Behavior —————————————————————————→ | | |
| | Produce | | |
	Accuracy	Mastery	Automatic
	The student will supply the correct answer at a predetermined percentage level.	The student will supply the correct answer at a predetermined rate.	The student will supply the correct answer at a predetermined rate or percentage level in the presence of distractors.
CONTENT Addition facts	The student will produce the correct answer to addition problems 100% of the time.	The student will produce the correct answer to addition problems at a rate of 40 correct per minute.	The student will balance a checkbook, making no errors in addition.

FIGURE 3.7
Parameters of proficiency

Addition Facts

	Mixed with other problems on worksheet	Making change at supermarket	Keeping score in racquetball game
In isolation on worksheet			
Addition Facts			

FIGURE 3.8
Different addition fact tasks

generalizing what they have learned (Torgesen & Kail, 1980).

The addition example in Figure 3.8 is an academic one. However, conditions are particularly important for language and social behavior objectives (Howell, 1985). For example, "expressing feelings" in a controlled therapeutic setting may be a very different task than at a party among strangers. Similarly, using prepositional phrases in sentences when a teacher prompts their use is not the same as using the phrases spontaneously. The student who displays knowledge in an uncontrolled setting without teacher prompts or cues has learned the task better than the student who must rely on support.

Criterion

The final element of an objective is its criterion. In some ways it is unfortunate that we left it for last as that gives the impression it is of less importance. Actually, the criterion element is absolutely essential for task specific evaluation. Remember the $S \leftarrow \underset{D}{\overset{}{\rightarrow}} B$ model from Figure 2.1? The criterion in an objective is the S (standard) in that model. As you recall, evaluation is a process of comparison and can't even take place if there isn't a standard available to which to compare the kid's behavior.

Task standards or proficiency levels must be established through validation procedures (which will be described in chapters 4 and 6). For now it is sufficient to understand that the student who is 25% accurate has not learned a task as well as the student who is 100% accurate. Accuracy and mastery (as indicated by rate of response) are the two pri-

mary proficiency parameters teachers use. Again, they are summarized in terms of percentage (%) or rate data (count per minute) respectively.

The criterion statement in an instructional objective represents the level of proficiency the student is expected to reach through instruction. Intermediate levels of proficiency may be specified for dates prior to the end of instruction to allow for progress monitoring (White & Haring, 1980). An example of this is shown in Figure 3.9. In that figure, a student is expected to achieve an oral reading rate of 140 words per minute correct within 5 weeks. He is currently reading 60 wpm. Thus, 140 is the mastery criterion, stated in terms of rate per minute (as almost all academic mastery criteria are). The intermediate performance levels marked on the chart each week are not the task criteria but intermediate aims. This is an important distinction. Task criteria are not individualized. They are derived through standardization. If that process is sound the criteria should not be changed, as they should represent competence on the tasks. Aims may be set by teachers at any intermediate point during instruction to represent not competency, but acceptable progress towards competency.

If a student does not meet an aim it probably means the instruction he or she is receiving should be modified and new aims established. If, however, after several such changes the student still has not reached criterion, the criterion cannot be changed. In these cases it is far better to say "This student is not adequately proficient at oral reading" than to drop the criterion for that student and declare a victory by claiming that he or she has "passed" at a rate lower than the functional level. It is tempting to say that "passing" for Sandy is 140 words per minute while "passing" for Joe is only 70 words

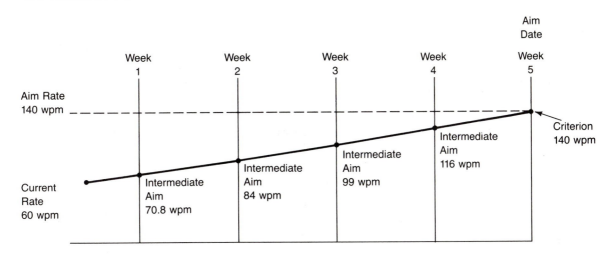

FIGURE 3.9

per minute if you have more trouble teaching Joe. But declaring a victory and stopping reading instruction when a student is failing to learn to read only guarantees that that student will fail on all subsequent tasks for which reading is a subtask.

Because *criterion-referenced* has become an educational buzz word, many tests have appeared with that term in their title. As we have said, a criterion-referenced test is a test that references the student's behavior to a performance standard rather than to a norm. But often these tests would be more appropriately called *content-referenced*; their subtests are linked to clearly defined content domains but they lack the all-important criteria. If criteria statements are included in a test's objectives, a technical manual should accompany the test to explain where the criteria came from and how valid they are.

One so-called criterion-referenced test in wide use today has an objective that calls for students to read words with 70% accuracy at a rate of 5 seconds per word. Because this is the criterion level specified in the objective, a teacher could reasonably decide that a student who is 70% accurate and reading at a rate of 12 words per minute no longer requires instruction on that list of words. Actually this level of accuracy is well below what is com-

monly expected and the rate is 12 times slower. A student reading at 12 words per minute would probably find *War and Peace* a bit tedious and would certainly have trouble filling out a job application.

Tables of Specifications

At this point we will attempt to pull the discussion of task elements together by introducing a tool known as a table of specifications. When the elements of behavior and content are combined they form portions of tasks.

A table of specifications is created by combining behavior and content. This combination is illustrated in Table 3.3. Each place the content intersects with the behavioral sequence a task is created. If an entire content sequence is arranged next to a behavior sequence, the result is a table of specifications (Bloom, Madaus, & Hastings, 1981) or test plan (Gronlund, 1973). Table 3.4 is a table of specifications for addition problems.

If the conditions under which a task will be performed and the criteria for acceptable performance (CAP) for the task are specified as well, then a complete objective is formed. For example, in Table 3.5 the conditions are noted as item formats and the

TABLE 3.3
Table of specifications for two-place addition

	Behavior			
	Identify Accuracy	*Produce Accuracy*	*Produce Mastery*	*Produce Automatic*
	A.1	*B.1*	*C.1*	*D.1*
Content — *Two-place Addition Facts*	"Point to the answer for this problem: 10 + 1 a. 6 b. 7 c. 11 d. 15."	"Write the answers to two-place addition problems without regrouping accurately."	"Write the answers to two-place addition problems without regrouping at the mastery level."	"Quickly balance a checkbook and make no errors in two-place addition without regrouping."

criteria are written in the squares. A table of specifications, therefore, can be used to generate objectives.

The table of specifications is a powerful tool for evaluating and monitoring students. It can also be used to select testing and teaching materials. The use of a table of specifications for test selection will be described in chapter 8.

Conditions

Once again, the evaluative conditions under which a behavior will take place should be similar to the conditions imposed on a student in the real world (assuming there is such a thing). So if the student must work math problems without any tools (calculators, fingers, number lines) in the real world,

then these tools shouldn't be allowed during evaluation. So the objective might be, "Given a sheet of two-place addition problems without regrouping, the student will correctly write answers without the use of study aids."

Content	*Behavior*	*Conditions*	*CAP*
Two-place addition without regrouping	Correctly write answers	Without study aids	

Conditions are things like "in writing," "orally," "from the board," "from dictation," "out of a book," "with references," "with help from a peer," "with distractions."

TABLE 3.4
Table of specifications for addition

		Behavior			
		Identify		*Produce*	
		A	*B*	*C*	*D*
		Accuracy	*Accuracy*	*Mastery*	*Automatic*
Content	5 Two place with regrouping	5A	5B	5C	5D
	4 Two place without regrouping	4A	4B	4C	4D
	3 Addition and equal signs	3A	3B	3C	3D
	2 Number symbols	2A	2B	2C	2D
	1 Number names	1A	1B	1C	1D

TABLE 3.5
Partial table of specifications for addition

| | IDENTIFY | | PRODUCE | |
	A Accuracy Format: Multiple Choice	B Accuracy Format: Write Answer	C Mastery Format: Write Answer	D Automatic Format: Write Answer
5 Two place with regrouping	A.5 CAP: 100%	B.5 CAP: 100%	C.5 CAP: 50 digits per minute correct with 0 errors	D.5 CAP: 100% accuracy
4 Two place without regrouping	A.4 CAP: 100%	B.4 CAP: 100%	C.4 CAP: 50 digits per minute correct with 0 errors	D.4 CAP: 100% accuracy
3 Addition and equal signs	A.3 CAP: 100%	B.3 CAP: 100%	C.3 No test needed	D.3 CAP: 100% accuracy
2 Number symbols	A.2 CAP: 100%	B.2 CAP: 100%	C.2 CAP: 150 per minute correct with 0 errors	D.2 CAP: 100% accuracy
1 Number names	A.1 CAP: 100%	B.1 CAP: 100%	C.1 No test needed	D.1 No test needed

CAP (Criteria for Acceptable Performance)

CAP is how well the behavior must be performed. In the example in the previous paragraph the partial objective has no CAP. Suppose you determine that 100% accuracy is needed for success at basic math. If so, you would place 100% accuracy in the space under CAP.

"Given a sheet of two-place addition problems without regrouping, the student will correctly write 100% of the answers, without the use of study aids."

| Content | Behavior | Conditions | CAP |
| Two-place
addition
without re-
grouping | Correctly
write an-
swers | Without
study aids | 100%
accu-
racy |

Now the table of specifications includes content, behavior, conditions, and CAP. Such a table (Table 3.5, for example) can be used in many ways. It contains all the outcomes for the instructional unit (or

subject area) for which it is designed. Therefore, it can be used as a test plan to guide evaluation. The table says what the student should be able to do at the end of instruction. Square B.4, for example, says "the student will produce (by writing) the answers to two-place addition problems (without regrouping) with 100% accuracy." You can now test the student and find those squares which he or she passes or does not pass. You then teach what is not passed. This is the basic procedure for determining *what to teach*.

Another advantage of the table is that it's sequenced. Remember that when the table was being developed an attempt was made to arrange the content from most to least complex. Also, the behaviors were sequenced from hardest to easiest. This sequence is reflected in the squares of Table 3.5. Square D.5 contains the hardest objective; Square A.1 contains the easiest one. If you want to test a student on addition, you could test each square in the grid, or you could start with D.5 and move across and down towards A.1. If the content is well sequenced, when the student passes an objective you assume he or she will pass all of the easier squares, so you stop testing. If the student passed objective D.5 there would be no need to give the rest of the tests in the table. By using the table to guide your evaluation you can save a lot of time.

One final point about tables of specifications is that many of them already exist. (See Appendix C.) The majority of special and remedial teachers teach the same thing—basic skills. Content sequences (sometimes called scope and sequence charts) are available in all basic skill areas. They need only be combined with a behavioral hierarchy to form a table of specifications. This book will provide sequences for reading, math, handwriting, spelling, and language. However, if you disagree with our content sequences or are obligated to use the one developed by your local education agency, you can easily modify them or use your own.

Time for a quick review: Remember that tasks have subtask and strategy components. Like tasks, subtasks are defined by the elements we just spent considerable time describing. By juggling these elements around, changing their positions in a table of specifications for example, new subtasks will be produced.

TASK ANALYSIS

While it is necessary to understand where tasks come from and to appreciate their multiple dimensions (as assembled in a table of specifications), few of us work at curriculum from the bottom up. More often we are presented with a student who is failing on some task and asked to figure out why. We accomplish this, in part, by engaging in a process called *task analysis. Task analysis is the process of isolating, sequencing, and defining all of the essential components of a task* (Bateman, 1971). Because the task analytic model assumes that failure on a task can be traced to one or more missing subcomponents, the teacher/evaluator working in the model must know how to recognize these subcomponents. This is done from the top down by starting with the problem task and attempting to recognize its subcomponents.

To analyze a task, you must first be able to recognize one. Before you can do this, it helps to know what a task is. Any job or activity that a student engages in during the school day may be referred to as a task. Since we are using task analysis in an evaluative context, we have chosen to define a task as *any behavior or set of behaviors that a child must engage in to demonstrate the acquisition of skill or knowledge.* Therefore, a task, as we've defined it, always includes an element of application.

For example, a teacher may wish to measure a student's knowledge of addition facts. Is it possible to write a task analysis for "knows addition facts"? We doubt it. First of all, "knows addition facts" is not a task; it is a cognitive state. You don't analyze a cognitive state, you analyze a task. A task statement must include a verb that describes some action or observable behavior the learner will perform. These behaviors will, we hope, indicate cognitive states like "knowing." How about "writes the answers to addition problems"? That's more like it. It doesn't describe the state (i.e., knowledge), but rather the behavior that indicates the state. By writing the answers to addition problems, the student is demonstrating whether or not he knows his addition facts. There's only one problem. We would have to know a little bit more about the task before we can analyze it. For instance, is it a see-to-say task, e.g., teacher shows flashcard and student says answer? Is it a see-to-write task, e.g., writing on a ditto? Is it a hear-to-write task, e.g., teacher says "2 + 2 =" and the student writes "4," or is it a hear-to-say task where the student says "4"? Does the student have to copy the problem from a book or a blackboard, or have the problems been written for the student? While all these different behaviors and conditions still indicate the same cognitive state (albeit to different degrees), they each suggest a different task because they each require different test behaviors.

Before you can begin to analyze the task of "writes the answers to addition problems," you will need to know more details. Suppose we told you that the student was given a ditto of 50 simple addition problems with directions to write the correct sums to as many as possible in one minute. Given this additional information, you can now write the task analysis.

To summarize, remember that a task is any behavior or set of behaviors a child must engage in to demonstrate the acquisition of skill or knowledge. Used in the context of evaluation, a task may be defined simply as the behavior required of the learner. It should not be confused with the cognitive state it indicates; it should provide enough information to make an analysis feasible.

The Process

Now that you know what a task is, we can discuss the process of task analysis. Tasks have two types of components: subtasks and strategies. An essential subtask is one that is necessary for the learner to complete the task successfully. A task strategy tells the learner how to combine that subtask with others. To illustrate, we will use the example of a teacher who wants to know if his students have acquired a knowledge of U.S. geography. More specifically, the teacher wishes to determine if they know the capitals of the 50 states.

The teacher gives the students a ditto with the states listed in alphabetical order. Next, the teacher directs the students to write the name of the capital city on the line next to the corresponding state. Conditions for the test include a 30-minute time limit and prohibited use of reference aids such as an atlas or dictionary. What is the task in this example? Is it "knows U.S. geography"? Is it "knows the capitals for each of the 50 states"? Neither is correct. How about "associates capital cities with states"? Much better. But will the association be made by listing, matching, or multiple choice? In this particular case, it happens to be fill-in. Therefore, the best statement of task would be "names the capital city for each of the 50 states, in writing, in 30 minutes." This describes the test behavior and learning required for the student to demonstrate acquisition of the task.

The statement is referred to as a *performance objective* because it describes the behavior required of the learner. It could be stated as "Given a ditto with the 50 states listed in alphabetical order, the learner will correctly write the name of the corresponding capital city next to each state. The task will be completed in 30 minutes without reference aids and with 100% accuracy. A response will be considered correct if it is readily distinguishable as the name of the capital city of the state it is written

next to." Quite a mouthful, isn't it? It's easy to see why it is impractical to actually write out this sort of a statement, though an evaluator should be able to do so in those cases requiring greater clarity. In this example, the subtasks would be (1) writes the names of the 50 capital cities, (2) spells the names of the 50 capital cities well enough so that they can be distinguished as such, (3) writes the names in the correct place, and (4) recalls the capital city for each state.

Our next step is to list these subtasks in order of complexity, if possible, from most to least difficult. The reason for this is that we want to "test down" when testing a student. By testing the student on the most difficult task first, lots of valuable time can be saved. If the student can perform the first or second most difficult task, we can assume (notice we said *assume*) that he or she is capable of performing tasks requiring less complex skills or knowledge. This is the advantage of sequencing the subtasks. Of course, not all subtasks can be easily sequenced. It often depends upon the interdependence of the subtasks. Not all subtasks can be arranged into task ladders; some are more accurately thought of as pies and are complete only if all the pieces are present. Often a group of subtasks resembles a "task tree," with many branches of varying difficulty. In these cases, all subtasks must be tested.

The example task can be sequenced as:

(4) Writes the names of the 50 capital cities in the correct places,
(3) Reads the names of the 50 states,
(2) Spells the names of the 50 capital cities well enough so that they can be distinguished as such, and
(1) Recalls (i.e., can say) a capital city for each state.

Once the subtasks have been isolated and sequenced, it is time for the third step in the task analysis process—describing the subtasks. This is simply a matter of writing a performance objective that, along with directions and test materials, becomes a criterion-referenced test. Since writing performance objectives and criterion-referenced tests are covered in chapter 8, you will not be required to describe any subtasks in this unit. Instead we have described them for you in Table 3.6 so that you may see what a completed task analysis looks like. The task strategy for this one is easy and is written at the bottom.

Is This Trip Necessary?

Suppose you want a child to cut a pattern out of paper with a pair of scissors. You provide the scissors and a piece of paper with the pattern of a triangle drawn on it in ¼-inch solid blue lines and require that the task be completed within one minute without going off the blue lines at any time.

The subtasks essential to the successful completion of this task may be listed:

1. Hold the paper in the nondominant hand.
2. Cut with scissors.
3. Move the paper with the nondominant hand while simultaneously operating the scissors with the dominant hand.
4. Follow a pattern.

Each of these subtasks must be mastered before the learner can successfully complete the task. However, some would argue that the list is not complete. It is possible to add a number of other subtasks distantly related to the terminal task, like being able to open and close scissors and holding scissors properly. These would certainly be necessary for successful completion of the terminal task. However, they are *implicit* in our subtask 2. If it

---

TABLE 3.6
Task analysis for "Identifies in writing the capital city for each of the 50 states"

Task: Identify in writing the capital city for each of the 50 states
Terminal Objective: Given a ditto with the 50 states in alphabetical order, the learner will correctly write the name of the corresponding capital city next to each state. Task will be completed in 30 minutes without reference aids and with 100% accuracy. A response will be considered correct if it is easily distinguishable as the name of the capital city of the state it is written next to.

Subtask 1: Able to recall (i.e., can say) a capital city for each state
Objective 1: Given the name of the state, the learner will say the correct name of the capital city for that state within 5 minutes and with 100% accuracy for all 50 states.

Subtask 2: Able to spell the names of the 50 capital cities
Objective 2: Given the names of each of the 50 capital cities verbally, the learner will correctly spell each within 15 seconds. To be correct, each response when written by the examinee should be distinguishable by a third party as the name of the city it represents.

Subtask 3: Able to read the names of the 50 states
Objective 3: Given the name of each of the 50 states on a flashcard, the learner will correctly pronounce each within 5 seconds and with 100% accuracy.

Subtask 4: Able to write the names of the 50 capital cities in the correct places
Objective 4: Given the task described in the terminal objective and told the correct answer for each item, the learner will write the answer in the correct place for each of the 50 items, taking no more than 15 seconds per item.

Specific Strategy: Read the name of the state (subtask 3), recall the name of the capital (subtask 1), write the name in the proper place (subtask 4) while spelling it correctly (subtask 2).

was found through specific-level testing that the learner was unable to perform subtask 2 (i.e., cut with scissors), it would then be necessary to task analyze it and list "holds scissors properly" and "opens and closes scissors." *The point is you go only as far as you need to in listing essential subtasks.* Try not to get carried away by listing subtasks that are implicit in subtasks already identified, or the task analysis will take too long to complete and be much too unwieldly to be of any real value.

Also, be certain to include only those subtasks that are essential to the completion of the task. For example, is it necessary for the learner to know the name of the object he or she is cutting out of paper? It certainly couldn't hurt, but is it essential to the successful completion of the task? No. Whenever in doubt about the "essential" quality of a subtask, it is a good idea to perform the task yourself and carefully list all your actions. This will help you to separate the essential from the nonessential.

Look at the terminal objective in Table 3.7 and the corresponding list of subtasks below it. Which of these subtasks are essential and which are nonessential to the successful completion of the task? Let's take them one at a time.

1. Is it essential that the learner be able to hold a pencil if he is to write (i.e., copy) his name? Yes.
2. Is it essential that the learner be able to copy letters when he is shown more than one at a time? It sure is. In fact, that's the terminal objective.
3. Is it essential that the learner be able to copy letters when he is shown them one at a time? Sure, if you expect him to be able to copy when more than one letter is shown.
4. Is it essential that the learner be able to copy letters on a line? Yes, if you want him to stay on the line as in your objective.
5. Is it essential that the learner knows the names of the letters in his name? No. Does a kid really have to know the names of the letters in order to copy? You could get the student to copy Russian or Chinese. The names of the letters would

TABLE 3.7
An objective and subtasks

Objective:

Given a pencil, a piece of 8½″ × 11″ ruled paper, and a 3″ × 5″ card with his name written on it in manuscript, Ralph will write (i.e., copy) his name once on the ruled paper, meeting the criterion for acceptable performance, within 60 seconds. To meet CAP, he must have done the following:

1. Formed all letters so that they are legible.
2. Made letters the correct size in relation to one another.
3. Not allowed an inordinate amount of space between letters.
4. Written the letters on one line, not going above or below that line more than ⅛ inch.
5. Put the letters in the proper sequence.

Subtasks:

1. Can hold a pencil.
2. Can copy letters in sequence (i.e., more than one letter shown).
3. Can copy letters in isolation (i.e., one letter shown).
4. Can copy letters in isolation on a line.
5. Knows the names of the letters in his name.
6. Knows the alphabet.
7. Can write letters on a line with the proper space between each.
8. Can read his name.
9. Can copy a triangle, a square, and a circle.

be different and he probably wouldn't know them, but he could still copy them.
6. Is it essential that the learner know the alphabet? No. Letters are no more than squiggly and straight lines at tangents to each other. The objective simply asks that the child transfer these squiggly and straight lines to another piece of paper by means of writing (i.e., copying). A student doesn't have to say the alphabet, or say the names of the letters, to copy them.
7. Is it essential that he write letters on the line with the proper space between each? Sure, otherwise you would have to drop proper spacing as one of the criteria statements in the terminal objective.

8. Is it essential that he read his name? No. We are not requiring that he say the name of the word on the 3 × 5 card but simply that he write (i.e., copy) it, letter by letter, on another piece of paper.

9. Is it essential that he be able to copy a triangle, square, and a circle? No. Although some children learn how to copy triangles, squares, and circles before they learn to write (i.e., copy) their names, countless others were taught to copy letters, numbers, and words before they became proficient at copying simple geometric shapes.

Get the idea about essential and nonessential? If you missed the obvious ones, there are two likely explanations for your trouble: (1) you don't understand the process and need to review this section or (2) you lack the necessary knowledge about handwriting and need to learn about it or (3) you are thinking about your own view of the task "copies name," not the terminal objective.

So far we have discussed only the isolating process in task analysis. Since this is by far the most difficult and most important process, it requires the most attention. Once you have accurately identified all of the essential subtasks, it should require less effort to sequence them. Also, mistakes in sequencing subtasks will not dramatically affect the diag-

nostic process as would errors in isolating and describing them. Therefore, we will not deal with the sequencing process here except to provide you with some examples of subtasks listed both randomly and in sequence according to complexity and operation. (See Table 3.8.)

If you already know how to write performance objectives and you feel confident in your skill at isolating and sequencing essential subtasks, we invite you to try the checkpoints at the end of this chapter.

Learning vs. Doing

We often begin a task analysis by observing an expert working the task, or by doing it ourselves. This is to help recognize the components of task completion that may be considered essential subtasks or strategy steps. There is one thing wrong here: Learning to do something is different than doing it once it has been learned. This is because instruction introduces its own subtasks (Howell, 1983). In other words, learning to add two-place problems in one instructional program is a different task than learning it in another. We are all familiar with nonreading students who fail subject-area courses because they cannot read history or science books. Reading is not a subskill of knowing the causes of

TABLE 3.8
Sequencing subtask

"Writes sums to simple addition problems"	
Listed Randomly	*Sequenced According to Complexity*
1. Writes numbers from memory	1. Reads add sign
2. Reads number	2. Reads numbers
3. Reads add sign	3. Writes numbers from memory
4. Demonstrates comprehension of addition sign	4. Demonstrates comprehension of addition sign
5. Demonstrates knowledge of addition facts	5. Demonstrates knowledge of addition facts
"Ties shoelaces"	
Listed Randomly	*Sequenced According to Operation*
1. Folds one bow under the other	1. Crosses laces
2. Folds one lace under the other	2. Folds one lace under the other
3. Crosses laces	3. Pulls each lace in opposite direction simultaneously
4. Pulls each lace in opposite direction simultaneously	4. Folds each lace into a bow
5. Folds each lace into a bow	5. Folds one bow under the other
6. Pulls each bow in opposite direction simultaneously	6. Pulls each bow in opposite direction simultaneously

TABLE 3.9
Subtasks for "Using a computer to learn to locate words in a dictionary"

Subtask: Locate words in dictionary
Match words
Alphabetize words
Estimate location in dictionary
Use guide words
Use base words

Subtask: Use computer to learn
Turn on computer
Select diskette
Load diskette
Follow commands
Use function keys

the Civil War, but if the only instruction a student receives from the history teacher involves reading assignments, then reading is a subskill of *learning to know the causes of the Civil War* in that teacher's classroom.

Suppose you have a teacher teaching a student to *locate words in a dictionary*. If the teacher decides to use a computer to teach the task, computer control subtasks are added to the dictionary subtasks to form the task of *using a computer to learn to locate words in a dictionary*, as shown in Table 3.9.

Remember that we use task analysis when the student is not learning. While the subtasks of *locating words* are the same for all students (because they are determined by the task), the subtasks of *learning to locate words* vary from class to class (because they are determined in part by the teacher's instruction) and student to student (because they are determined in part by the student's prior knowledge). This is the final reason that task analysis is such an important skill for teachers.

The subtasks and strategies introduced by various materials and classroom techniques need to be examined carefully and probably deserve the same attention we have given here to curriculum development (Gersten, Woodward, & Darch, 1986; Lloyd & Loper, 1986). However, some general advice will have to do for now. The advice is to consider carefully what a student needs to be able to do to benefit from the lesson you are giving. This may include

the needed vocabulary, basic skills, study skills, and knowledge of other tasks imposed by the correction routines, style, and pace of your presentation. Because some students may learn more efficiently if you select a different procedure, requiring different skills and strategies, task analysis gives us guidance in deciding *how* to teach as well as *what* to teach. It is remarkable how many hours teachers have spent analyzing the demands of tasks like spelling and multiplication without paying similar attention to the demands imposed by their own instructional style. A task analysis of *how to learn in my class* would represent time well spent by any teacher, as it would be relevant to all areas of the curriculum.

Before summarizing, here is a checkpoint to allow you to practice task analysis. We strongly suggest that you work the items in this checkpoint; task analyzing is a skill that requires practice.

CHECKPOINT

Directions: Write a task analysis for any *five* of the tasks described below. Isolate, sequence, and describe as many essential subtasks as you can for each task. Take no more than 5 minutes per task.

1. Given a 16-inch playground ball, the learner will bounce the ball on the floor within a 12-inch square target area, catching the ball with two hands after one bounce. The learner will do this for 10 consecutive bounces without missing the target area or failing to catch the ball after each bounce.
2. Given a page of nonsense trigrams (CVC words), the learner will correctly read at least 90 trigrams in one minute with two errors or less.
3. Given 10 pictures of the faces of clocks with hands set at different times (i.e., hour, half-hour, quarter-hour), the student will give the correct time with 90% accuracy, taking no more than 5 minutes per clock.
4. Given 9 different strips of colored paper (i.e., black, white, red, blue, green, yellow, orange,

purple, brown), the student will say the correct color for each with 100% accuracy, taking no more than 5 seconds per color.

5. Given a nail, a hammer, and a piece of wood, the learner will hammer the nail all the way into the wood in 10 seconds without bending the nail.

6. Given a piece of paper with a triangle drawn on it and scissors, the learner will cut out the pattern in 30 seconds without going off the line more than ¼ of an inch.

7. Given a dictionary and a list of 10 unknown words, the learner will locate each in the dictionary and write the corresponding page number next to each with 90% accuracy in 30 minutes.

8. Given a page of short division problems, with no remainder, the learner will correctly write the answer to 50 in 1 minute with no more than two errors.

9. Given a page with 10 fraction problems the student will add fractions without common denominators and simplify the answer with 100% accuracy.

10. Given a reader at grade level, the learner will orally read 100 words correctly per minute with two errors or less.

Apply the criteria in Table 3.10 (which was explained in the text). Check your opinion with other evaluators, students, teachers, or your instructor.

TABLE 3.10
Criteria for a task analysis

1. *Is it relevant?* Is the main task of value to the student?
2. *Is it complete?* Has any essential content been ommitted?
3. *Is it trivial?* Is content included which is too easy for the target student?
4. *Is it necessary?* Is all content necessary to master the main task?
5. *Is it redundant?* Do any of the content statements overlap with other content statements?

Source: Drawn from S. Thiagarajan, D. S. Semmel, and M. I. Semmel, *Instructional Development for Training Teachers of Exceptional Children.* Bloomington, IN: Center for Innovation in Teaching the Handicapped.

Now, for a real piece of excitement, try this one. Analyze this task:

TASK: List and describe the procedural steps of the task analytical (TA) model.

OBJECTIVE: Be able to list in sequence, and then describe by paraphrasing, all of the procedural steps used in the task analytical model.

Given the directions to do so, the learner will list in sequence and accurately describe in writing all of the procedural steps used in the task analytical model. Reference aids may not be used and CAP is 100% accuracy, taking no more than 10 minutes for the task.

The answer is found in Table 3.11.

SUMMARY

This has been a crowded chapter and a review is definitely called for. Tasks have subtask and strategy components. Subtasks (like tasks) are composed of elements of content, behavior, conditions, and criterion. Each of these elements must be present, or the task has not been truly defined. If a change is made in any of the four elements, a new task is produced. By systematically varying the four elements, a sequence of objectives or tasks can be produced for the purpose of planning instruction or evaluation. Content sequences should be relevant, complete, free of trivial material, composed of necessary material, and free of redundancy. Behavior sequences should correspond to the real-world demands of tasks and allow the designation of meaningful proficiency levels. Conditions should also reflect the real world while criteria must accurately indicate functional levels of performance.

There are two kinds of strategies. Task-specific strategies apply to a small particular domain of tasks. General strategies apply to many large domains. Strategy use depends on the proficient levels of prior knowledge, self-monitoring, and problem solving.

Task analysis is a process applied to well-defined tasks. Through task analysis, the essential subtask and strategy components of the task can be identified. When a student is unable to work a task, he or she should be taught any lacking subtask and strategy components.

TABLE 3.11
A task analysis of task analysis

Subtasks	Objectives
1. Recalls procedural steps.	1. Given the directions to do so, the learner will correctly list in writing the procedural steps used in the TA model. All steps must be included, but they do not necessarily have to be in the correct sequence. Reference aids may not be used and CAP is 100% accuracy, taking no more than one minute for this task.
2. Lists procedural steps in sequence.	2. Given the directions to do so, the learner will correctly list in writing the procedural steps used in the TA model. All steps must be included and in the correct sequence. Reference aids may not be used and CAP is 100% accuracy, taking no more than one minute to complete the task.
3. Describes procedural steps.	3. Given each of the procedural steps used in the TA model one at a time, the learner will write an accurate description for each. Reference aids may not be used and CAP is 100% accuracy, taking no more than 7 minutes for the task.
4. Understands procedural steps.	4. Given all of the procedural steps in the TA model in one column and the descriptions or their purpose in another column, the learner will correctly match each procedural step with its corresponding description. CAP is 100% accuracy, taking no more than one minute.
5. Paraphrases procedural steps.	5. Given a written description for each of the procedural steps in the TA model, the learner will write a paraphrased description for each. CAP is 100% accuracy, taking no more than 10 minutes for the task.

Strategy
1. Recall procedural steps.
2. Recall sequence of steps or determine the sequence by asking yourself which steps cannot be carried out until others are completed.
3. Recall the purpose of each step or determine the purpose by considering the overall purpose of task analysis.
4. Select key words in the procedural steps and recall synonyms or alternative phrases which carry the same meaning, or relate the procedural steps to personal experience.

Study Questions

1. Define the following terms as they are used in this text. Some of these terms may be review from previous chapters.
   - a. Objective
   - b. Curriculum
   - c. Calibrate
   - d. Task
   - e. Strategy
   - f. Subtask
   - g. Task analysis
   - h. Content
   - i. Behavior
   - j. Conditions
   - k. Criterion
   - l. Table of specifications
   - m. Accuracy
   - n. Mastery
   - o. Automatic
   - p. Generalize

2. Individualized programs do *not* refer to
   - a. altering the way in which the objectives are taught.
   - b. altering the way the curriculum is sequenced.
   - c. altering the terminal objectives in the curriculum.
   - d. altering the amount of time the student spends in instruction.

3. A curriculum is
   - a. the objectives you teach.
   - b. the methods you use.
   - c. the materials you use.

4. Which of the following lists all the essential parts of an objective or task?
   - a. Behavior, content, materials, method
   - b. Behavior, content, goal, objective
   - c. Behavior, content, conditions, criterion
   - d. Behavior, content, proficiency level, criterion

5. Subtasks are to strategies as
   - a. recipes are to ingredients.
   - b. ingredients are to recipes.
   - c. blueprints are to floor plans.
   - d. bricks are to walls.

6. When a student isn't learning, the task analytical model assumes that it is because
   - a. he or she has a physiologically based learning disorder.
   - b. he or she is being taught in the wrong sensory modality.
   - c. he or she is missing an essential subtask.
   - d. he or she is missing either an essential subtask or an essential strategy.

7. To use a skill efficiently under a variety of conditions, the student must obtain which level of proficiency?
   - a. High degree of accuracy
   - b. Mastery
   - c. Automaticity
   - d. Response frequency

8. Identify the behavior, content, conditions, and criterion for the following objective.

   Given a written sentence containing a series or list, the student will write commas after each item in the series except for the last with 100% accuracy.

9. Which task is the most difficult?
    a. (1) Point to the letter "D."
        (2) Write the letter "D."
    b. (1) Place periods at the ends of sentences when prompted.
        (2) Place periods at the ends of sentences spontaneously.
    c. (1) Read from the third grade reader with 90% accuracy.
        (2) Read from the third grade reader at 140 wpm at 90% accuracy in a noisy class-
            room.
        (3) Read from a third grade reader at 140 wpm with 90% accuracy.

Chapter 4

The Tools of Evaluation

Where the first three chapters were oriented toward the purpose of and rationale for evaluation, chapter 4 turns toward its more technical aspects. This is necessary as we are getting closer to the part of this book that actually tells how to go about conducting an evaluation. Some of this material, particularly the discussion of statistics, has been placed in Appendix B to preserve the flow of the text. We encourage you to read Appendix B, as the statistical tools associated with measurement and comparison are central to an understanding of evaluation. Much of this material is associated with the treatment of groups of scores as required in norm-referenced testing (to be discussed shortly). While the focus of this text is not norm-referenced testing, the majority of testing technology evolved out of its use. So we must discuss normative concepts in order to provide an adequate historical and technical background before we present the treatment-related procedures we will cover later. This isn't an apology for presenting normative material; most teachers will be involved in child study team meetings in which they will help make classificatory decisions based on normative data. But, once again, these placement activities are not our primary focus.

CRTs AND NRTs

Treatment evaluation requires the use of criterion-referenced measures. To understand what a criterion-referenced test/observation (CRT) is, you must know how it differs from a normative test/observation (NRT). We will compare these two types of testing with regard to purpose, construction, and standardization. But first we need a new term: *probe*. A probe is a criterion-referenced test *or* observation procedure. It is the material or time interval used to sample behavior during criterion-referenced evaluation (White & Haring, 1980). It will often be used in place of criterion-referenced test/observation from now on.

Purpose of NRTs

The major purpose of the norm-referenced test/observation (NRT) is to help educators see how a student compares with other students of the same age or class placement. This is accomplished by comparing the student's performance on an NRT to the performance of a peer group (which has been summarized in the form of norms). For example, suppose you teach third grade and 8 ½-year-old Kathy enters your class in the middle of the school year with a note from home explaining that her records have been sent to Whitehorse in the Yukon Territories of Canada and may not turn up for another 2 years. How will you know what kind of a student she is? Is she an average student? Above average? Below? You don't want to waste a lot of time in trial-and-error teaching to identify her approximate level of functioning in each subject area. What do you do? You might give her a norm-referenced achievement test. On this test let's say the average reading score of third graders is 50. Kathy, a third grader, only scores 37. A score of 37 indicates that Kathy is below the other third graders in reading. This information might help you begin to make initial assignments for Kathy. It won't tell you *why* she is functioning below the average third grader (below the norm) in reading; all it tells you is how Kathy compares with her peers. However, since this is what you wanted to know in the first place, the norm-referenced test has served your purpose.

Purpose of CRTs

To find out *why* Kathy is not performing as well as her peers in reading or to find out exactly what skill she needs to be working on, it is necessary to do some further testing. This is where the criterion-referenced test/observation (CRT) becomes useful. Using the task analytic model, the reason for failure can be traced to missing essential task components. The purpose of the CRT, or probe, is to help you find the particular skills or knowledge Kathy lacks. Using CRTs you can compare a student's skills to those specified in the curriculum to find out which are missing. Once you determine what the student should be taught, you can begin instruction. Some

CRTs can also be readministered frequently to determine when to stop instruction on that objective.

Constructing Behavior Samples

Tests and observations are constructed according to the purposes for which they are designed. Because the NRT is used to determine how one student compares with age-mates, it is important that the test contain items from across a wide range of curriculum. If the achievement test given Kathy included only items taught at the third-grade level, she probably would have missed them all. As a result, all we would know from her performance is that she is functioning below grade level in reading. We can only know *how far below* grade level she is working if the test includes items below third grade. To discriminate between students adequately, it may be necessary to include items that cover the range of curriculum from preschool to high school. Figure 4.1, which is the survey computation test of the *Multilevel Academic Survey Test* (Howell, Zucker, & Morehead, 1985), provides an example of the types of progressively difficult items found on typical NRTs. There are a few items on this page that "average" third graders would be working on, but most of the items—probably as many as 80% of them—are either too hard or too easy for a third grader. As a result, a score representing how a student does on the test will not reflect how she is doing on third-grade math. This is why NRT scores aren't of much interest to teachers trying to find instructional guidance. Remember that the NRT was designed this way on purpose to measure a student's academic functioning in relation to peers—not to measure actual skill.

The criterion-referenced test, on the other hand, is designed to measure only one objective and is composed of items that are all at the same level of difficulty. Because this results in less variation in performance, you would not use a CRT to see how Kathy's performance compares with her age-mates.[1] The CRT is used to determine whether or

___

[1] CRTs can be used to discriminate between students in terms of their progress (not performance) by allowing the measurement of time to criterion. This is discussed in chapter 15.

not a student has a particular skill or piece of knowledge, so it includes only those items that measure the skill or knowledge in question. Between-student performance will not vary greatly on the CRT because the item difficulty does not vary. Students either have the skill or knowledge being measured or they do not; they either pass or don't pass the probe. Figure 4.2 provides an example of the kinds of items you might expect to find on a CRT. Notice that they are addition problems involving one- and two-digit numbers. This happens to be first-grade material. If a student passes this test (sometimes called a *probe sheet*), it doesn't necessarily mean that she is working on a first-grade level in arithmetic. There are many other math objectives in first-grade not represented on this CRT. It does tell us, however, that she has the single skill being measured. Since this is all we really wanted to know, it is not necessary to include any other items on the test.

Standardization

To use an NRT to determine how a student compares with her peers, you obviously need a measure of the student's behavior as well as a measure of her peers. The way to obtain those measures is to gather a representative group of the student's peers, test them, and then summarize the performance of the group. This group is called the *standardization sample*. The process of testing and summarizing the scores of the standardization sample is called *norming*. Given this summary of the group's behavior, you can see how any individual's performance compares with the group. In discussions of sampling the key concept is "representative" because it is the selection of the standardization sample that definitionally separates NRTs and CRTs.

A representative sample used in the standardization of an NRT should include a relatively *large* number of individuals (usually at least 100) at each age or grade. To ensure that the sample is representative it may be carefully controlled to assure the appropriate proportion of male/female, majority/minority, high/low socioeconomic status,

1. (A1,1)

$$\begin{array}{r} 2 \\ +3 \\ \hline \mathbf{5} \end{array}$$

2. (S1,1)

$$\begin{array}{r} 8 \\ -6 \\ \hline \mathbf{2} \end{array}$$

3. (A3,2)

$$\begin{array}{r} 3 \\ 6 \\ +2 \\ \hline \mathbf{11} \end{array}$$

4. (A5,2)

$$\begin{array}{r} 39 \\ +4 \\ \hline \mathbf{43} \end{array}$$

5. (S2,2)

$$\begin{array}{r} 46 \\ -3 \\ \hline \mathbf{43} \end{array}$$

6. (S6,3)

$$\begin{array}{r} 51 \\ -28 \\ \hline \mathbf{23} \end{array}$$

7. (A8,3)

$$\begin{array}{r} 601 \\ 39 \\ +427 \\ \hline \mathbf{1067} \end{array}$$

8. (S7,4)

$$\begin{array}{r} 9062 \\ -4185 \\ \hline \mathbf{4877} \end{array}$$

9. (M1,4)

$$\begin{array}{r} 8 \\ \times 9 \\ \hline \mathbf{72} \end{array}$$

10. (M3,4)

$$\begin{array}{r} 47 \\ \times 5 \\ \hline \mathbf{235} \end{array}$$

11. (D2,4)

$$4\overline{)24} \quad \mathbf{6}$$

12. (D3,4)

$$8\overline{)37} \quad \mathbf{4\,r\,5}$$

13. (M7,5)

$$\begin{array}{r} 3075 \\ \times 62 \\ \hline \mathbf{190650} \end{array}$$

14. (D6,5)

$$74\overline{)3061} \quad \mathbf{41\,r\,27}$$

15. (DR% 11,5)

$$\frac{4}{20} = \frac{1}{\mathbf{5}}$$

16. (F11,5)

$$\frac{3}{11} + \frac{2}{11} = \frac{\mathbf{5}}{\mathbf{11}}$$

17. (F16,6)

$$\frac{1}{2} - \frac{5}{18} = \frac{\mathbf{2}}{\mathbf{9}}$$

18. (F20,6)

$$2\frac{3}{4} \times 5\frac{1}{3} = \mathbf{14\frac{2}{3}}$$

19. (F24,6)

$$6\frac{3}{4} \div 3\frac{1}{6} = \mathbf{2\frac{5}{38}}$$

20. (DR% 8,7)

$$\begin{array}{r} 2.43 \\ \times 2.5 \\ \hline \mathbf{6.075} \end{array}$$

21. (DR% 9,7)

$$1.5\overline{)24.39} \quad \mathbf{16.26}$$

22. (M8,8)

$$7^2 = \mathbf{49}$$

23. (D7,8)

$$\sqrt{144} \quad \mathbf{12}$$

24. (DR% 6,8)

$$\frac{7}{8} = \mathbf{87.5}\%$$

FIGURE 4.1

Computation survey (*Source:* From K. W. Howell, S. H. Zucker, & M. K. Morehead, *MAST: Multilevel Academic Skills Inventory: Math, Manual,* p. 40. San Antonio, TX: Psychological Corporation, 1982. Reprinted with permission.)

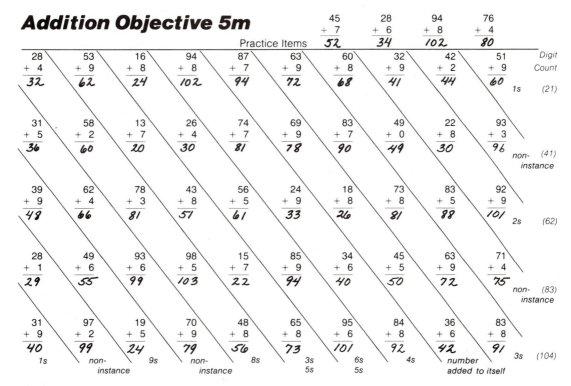

FIGURE 4.2
An addition probe sheet (*Source:* From K. W. Howell, S. H. Zucker, & M. K. Morehead, *Multilevel Academic Skills Inventory: Math Manual,* p. 119. San Antonio, TX: The Psychological Corporation, 1982. Reprinted with permission.)

and urban/rural students. These individuals are selected with no prior attention paid to their skill or knowledge with the tasks being measured. Therefore, with regard to skill, the standardization group for the NRT is chosen at random from the population to ensure an even distribution of skills. For example, if you wanted to standardize a math test for use with *all* college freshmen, you would not go to the Massachusetts Institute of Technology for your norming sample. Average MIT freshmen might have superior interest and training in math. They are a select group (having been screened by the university admittance process) and are not representative of the population who would be taking the test. If your test were standardized on this group, it would have limited value because the norms would describe a special group of students (e.g., engineering, math, and science majors).

In direct contrast, the criterion-referenced sample need only include a *small* number of individuals with no attention to minority status, socioeconomic status, or home setting. These individuals may differ widely according to age or grade; however, they all would have one thing in common—the very thing the NRT tried to avoid. All the people in the CRT sample should have the skill or knowledge being tested. This is important, because a probe is used to assess whether or not a student has a particular skill. A random sample can't be used here because students picked by chance might not have the skill. For example, if we wanted to find out how well a student must know consonant sounds, we would construct a consonant-sound probe and then give it to a group of students skilled at reading consonants. Only skilled readers should be included in the sample. If we chose students at random, we would probably include some who do not know consonants and their performance on consonant sounds would lower the score we eventually came up with. The middle (median) score of this skilled standardization group would become the "criterion for acceptable performance" (CAP). Remember, the CAP is the standard against which other students' scores will be compared.

If students score at least as well as the CRT standard they are thought to have the skill being measured. If not, they are thought to need instruction in the skill. Notice the difference between the standardization samples in the two types of measures. On the norm-referenced math test for all college freshmen, we didn't want to pick a select group of successful math students. We were looking for the typical college freshman. On the criterion-referenced consonant test, we wanted to pick a select group of students—students who had the skill being measured. Remember this, because it is the most basic difference between the two types of tests: NRTs reference student behavior to norms for the purpose of classification; CRTs reference student behavior to behavioral criteria to guide treatment.

MEASUREMENT

Recall that *measurement* has been defined as "the assignments of numerals to objects or events according to rules" (Campbell, 1940). As mentioned in chapter 2, any useful measurement procedure has four components: the definition of the quantity to be measured; a device for making that quantity observable; a mechanism (rule) for assigning different numerals to different magnitudes of the targeted quantity; and a mechanism for summarizing the whole activity (Thorndike & Hagan, 1969). NRTs and CRTs share these four requirements, though they may satisfy them in different ways.

The first component in measurement is definition. NRTs are not really designed to measure curriculum areas like reading and math; they are designed to measure the relative standing of the students in these areas. Therefore, their authors must compromise between the presentation of content and the need to discriminate between people. It all comes down to the need to sacrifice specificity in measuring the curriculum to gain power at discrimination. Specificity is lost three ways. The first is by sampling general domains of curriculum rather than specific ones. This is done to allow all areas of possible student differences to be reflected in the final score. Second, NRTs include items from all difficulty levels to highlight the differences between high and low students; third, they include items selected as much for their ability to trip-up students as for their relationship to content. Each of these problems is magnified by the utilitarian concern for test brevity. A norm-referenced test could be devised that covers specific content at all levels with both curriculum-based and discrimination-oriented items in it, but it would take days or weeks to administer and would require students to attend to masses of material above or below their functional levels. As many teachers and students already think they are being overtested, the likelihood of such a procedure ever being used is deservedly low.

In the case of CRTs, definition is taken care of by the objective. A criterion-referenced probe is composed of two components: a behaviorally stated objective and a procedure for measuring the student's behavior on that objective. This procedure may include the time, materials, and techniques needed to define, observe, and summarize the value of the objective. As we already know, a behavioral objective is composed of four components: content, behavior, conditions, and criterion for acceptable performance (CAP). All four of these components must be present for an objective to usefully describe what is being taught and measured (as was shown in Table 3.1).

The CRT objective is an operational statement representing some skill or concept we want the student to learn. The objective on which the test is based is a short-term instructional objective. This objective is either obtained directly from the school district's curriculum or from a task analysis of an objective found in the district curriculum. Obviously, if the results are to guide instruction, there should be no difference between the content measured and that which is taught. Similarly, behaviors and conditions required by the probe should be as much like the behaviors and conditions specified in the objective as possible. The probe objective and instructional objective are one and the same because at this level of evaluation we are interested only in testing what we teach and teaching what we test.

The more specific and behavioral the objective is, the more clearly it defines some quantity of the concept or skill it represents, thereby making the concept or skill more observable. If the objective calls for a display of knowledge that is expected to occur without the prompt of a test item, then an observation, rather than a test, may be used to measure it. Some examples of unprompted behaviors are "asks questions," "contacts peers," "raises hand to speak." To probe such behaviors a time period will be set aside and the evaluator will watch for the behavior to take place. Observation is commonly used for "social behaviors." (See chapter 14.)

Academic skills are less apt to be spontaneously displayed. No matter how long we watch, we may never just happen to see a student working a long division problem, discussing the powers of the legislative branch, or spelling the word *empathy*. Therefore, testing is necessary. A *test* is simply a procedure for eliciting target displays so that they can be observed. The behaviors are elicited by presenting stimuli (usually in the form of test items) that promote the behaviors indicating knowledge or skill of the content we are trying to teach.

SCORES

A test *score* is a numerical summation of behavior. That testing summarizes behavior is obviously true

FIGURE 4.3
Addition test

of pencil-and-paper tests, but even the measurement of heartbeat and brain activity yields scores of visceral behavior. Scores are useful because they help us compare people to people, or people to tasks. Inherent in the use of scores is the idea that behavior can be segmented and then represented by a number. In educational testing, however, scores seldom represent discrete units of behavior. Remember that measurement involves assigning numerals to objects and events according to rules.

It is important to know the rule because different rules applied to the same event can produce different scores. For example, a math test may have two addition problems, as in Figure 4.3. If a student gets both problems correct, he or she would usually get a score of 2 correct, though in reality, problem b contains five times as much addition behavior as problem a. That's because the rule used for assigning numerals in most tests is "One problem is worth 1 point."

The first question you should ask whenever using a score is "What behavior does this number represent?" With a normative test, the scoring rule illustrated in Figure 4.3 makes sense because the test isn't trying to find out how well the kid can add but how well he or she can add compared to others. But on a CRT each point earned should represent the same amount of behavior. To do that the test designer must slice the behavior into discrete functional units. "Problem" may be too broad a unit of behavior to be functional, but "addition operation" is not. In Figure 4.4 the same problems have been scored according to a different measurement rule. In this case a point is given each time the student

a.
1 point
3
+2
5

b.
1–5 points
838
+ 282
1120

Score = 6

FIGURE 4.4
Addition test

adds one number to another. This measurement (scoring) rule is more sensitive to what the teacher is teaching. The resulting score of 6 describes the kid's addition behavior better than the score of 2 in Figure 4.3.

Scores are needed to make it easier to compare a student's behavior to the criterion found in the objective of a CRT or the norms of an NRT. These scores are arrived at by following the measurement rules established for the test/observation. The rules used to assign numerals to behavior must be carefully established and rigidly applied. Obviously changing the measurement rule for different students could give the appearance of different behavior even if there was none.

Of the many distinctions that can be drawn between CRTs and NRTs, one of the most critical is the distinction in measurement rules. As a group, CRT scores tend to be more sensitive to instruction and to have greater fidelity (Swezey, 1981). However, these are generalities that may or may not be true. Some CRTs and NRTs are more sensitive than others. But when it comes to scores, *all* CRTs should use criterion-related measurement rules, while *all* NRTs must follow normative rules. The exact nature of these measurement rules, along with a discussion of how to treat them, is presented in Appendix B. If you are unfamiliar with the following terms and concepts, you may want to read Appendix B at this point as it covers these topics: *score, distribution, mean, standard deviation, standard score, percentile, gain score,* and *grade equivalency score.* These measurement rules, and the scores they produce, will now be elaborated on.

RELIABILITY AND VALIDITY

Whenever we select a tool we are interested in its quality: If we buy a car we want to know about its security and economy; if we buy a radio we want to know about its reception and sound; if we buy a measure of student behavior we want to know about its reliability and validity. In measurement terms *reliability means consistency.* Knowing that a test is reliable means knowing that it will work the same way every time it is given or on every student to whom it is given. *Validity means goodness.* A valid test is a genuine measure of what it claims to measure; a score from it accurately reflects the student's true level of skill or knowledge.

Given these definitions it should be clear that reliability is easier to document than validity. Proving reliability only requires the test writer to show consistency, not goodness. An automobile that *never* starts in the morning is reliable. It may not take you anywhere but it's consistent. Documenting validity, however, requires the test author to establish a relationship between the test and some real quality such as student skill or knowledge. This "reality," of course, is difficult to pin down. Validating a test can be like interviewing people leaving a Clint Eastwood movie. Opinions vary.

It is possible for a measure to be reliable but not valid; however, it is not possible to have validity without reliability. Therefore reliability is necessary but not sufficient for validity. Many educational tests are reliable because they produce consistent scores, but in some cases these scores are of limited use and therefore of limited validity. These tests are like a compass that consistently points 10 degrees east of magnetic north; it is reliable (because of its consistency) but is not valid. You would not want to use it to chart the route to your destination.

Error

To understand reliability and validity you must understand what makes a measure unreliable, or invalid: error. When it is not possible to measure a concept or behavior directly, evaluators are forced to make inferences from behaviors they *can* measure. Intelligence, for example, cannot be seen or weighed. Its presence is inferred from behaviors such as defining words, solving problems, or tracing mazes. This need to infer introduces error into the measurement. Things that are easy to observe, such as skill at addition, are easier to measure because inferences about them are easier to make. However, because *all* measurement requires some level of inference and contains some degree of imprecision, it is unreasonable to expect any measure to be 100% error-free.

Reliability and validity are desirable qualities that can be contrasted to the undesirable quality known as "error." All obtained scores are composed of two components: truth and error. Figure 4.5 shows the relationship of true and error scores. For the equation to be balanced, any increase in error must be offset by a decrease in truth.

Error is anything that affects a score other than the quality targeted for measurement. Error may arise from many sources, but labeling a thing as error does not mean it is bad or even unimportant. It only means it is *not* what the item (test) in question was designed to measure. For example, suppose a teacher has designed a history test that includes the following item:

Circle the correct letter:
1. The first man on the moon was
    a. John Glenn
    b. Glenn Ford
    c. Jules Verne
    d. Neil Armstrong

This item would seem to be a valid measure of the student's recall of history. However, it also measures the student's skill at reading, following directions, and drawing circles. To the extent that a student cannot perform these tasks, they become sources of error. Does a student need to know how to read to know who the first man on the moon was? No. Therefore, even though reading is an important skill, the dependence of this item on reading makes reading a possible source of error.

If an evaluative instrument is valid, it correctly describes reality. As we have already indicated, validity may be hard to establish when opinions about "truth" vary. It is even harder to establish when truth itself varies. (Just as our opinions about what is happening can change, what is happening can change too.) When reality fluctuates rapidly due to natural changes or the intrusion of observers, validity is even harder to pin down. This is frequently the case when educational evaluators are attempting to get a look at a student's status on a short-term instructional objective. A student's skill and knowledge may vary quickly in the presence of good instruction. One of the biggest problems in educational and psychological measurement is recognizing when changes in a score signal the intrusion of error or an important alteration in the student's actual status.

It Isn't in the Test

Before going any further with this discussion of reliability and validity, an important point needs to be made. People talk about "the reliability and validity of tests" as if those things are characteristics of the instruments themselves. When you hear things like, "the test is valid" or "the test–retest reliability is .89," you can almost imagine that at some critical point in the publishing process someone yells "OK —bring in the validity" and in response someone else (probably a reliable worker) comes running in from the next room with a bucket of validity and pours it into the ink so that it will be permanently infused through every page and word. It isn't that way.

FIGURE 4.5 *The reciprocal* *relationship of true* *and error scores*		True Score		Error Score		Obtained Score
	Test A	.75	+	.25	=	1
	Test B	.60	+	.40	=	1

FIGURE 4.6
Range of correlation coefficients

High Correlation	Low Correlation	No Correlation	Low Correlation	High Correlation

$-1 \quad -.9 \quad -.8 \quad -.7 \quad -.6 \quad -.5 \quad -.4 \quad -.3 \quad -.2 \quad -.1 \quad 0 \quad .1 \quad .2 \quad .3 \quad .4 \quad .5 \quad .6 \quad .7 \quad .8 \quad .9 \quad 1$

Both reliability and validity are determined by having students or experts interact with the tests. Reliability, for example, may be established by having a group of students take the same test twice to see if they get the same score both times. Validity may be established by asking experts to examine the test to see if it is measuring important material. Therefore, our impressions of reliability and validity come from an analysis of how these students or experts behave. The important point (which is often forgotten) is that the resulting statements about reliability and validity say as much about those people as they say about the tests. The results of a validation study done on 8-year-olds may have little similarity to the results of a study using the same test on 10-year-olds. We must always remember that conclusions about reliability and validity cannot be safely generalized (applied) to populations that differ along important variables from those populations used in the validation studies. Some of the variables we should be aware of are handicap, age, sex, race, language status, socioeconomic status, geographic location, and especially differences in educational background that may have influenced prior knowledge of the task.

CORRELATION

To discuss reliability and validity in any depth it is necessary to present a tool used to determine and describe them. This tool is correlation. The terms *reliability* and *validity* refer to certain types of relationships. To summarize these relationships statistical procedures, called *correlational* procedures, have been developed.

A correlation is a relationship usually obtained by applying two different measurements (two test/observations or the same one twice) to one group of students. By giving the same test (or a portion of it) to the same group two times, two sets of scores are obtained. These scores can then be analyzed to

determine the degree to which they seem related. The correlational relationship has two dimensions: magnitude and direction. Both of these dimensions are described with one term—the correlation coefficient. The correlation coefficient is usually expressed as a number between -1 and 1 (Figure 4.6). A correlation of -1 is as powerful as a correlation of $+1$ but the direction of the relationship described is different. A correlation of 0 means that no relationship has been found. A positive correlation between two tests means the higher a student scores on one test the higher he or she will probably score on the other. A negative correlation means the higher the score on one test, the *lower* the score on the other.

Look at the example in Figure 4.7. Suppose John, Jill, Laura, and Sam all take tests A (oral reading) and B (oral reading). If the two tests were positively correlated then a student scoring high on test A would also score high on test B. John scored low (25 points) on both tests, while Sam scored high (100 points) on both tests. Because they each got the exact same score on both tests, the correlation between these tests of oral reading would be $+1$

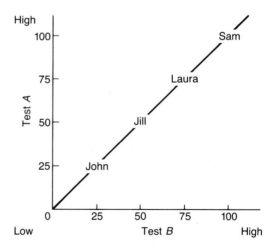

FIGURE 4.7
A positive correlation

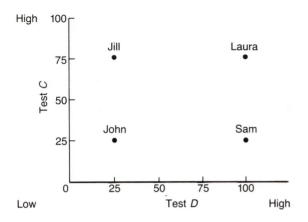

FIGURE 4.8
A 0 correlation

(the highest positive correlation) for these students.

Now suppose they all take two other tests—C (a test of computation) and D (a test of visual perception), as shown in Figure 4.8. In this case, students John and Jill both scored low on test C (25 points), but Jill scored high (75 points) on test C. Similarly, Sam and Laura scored high on test D (90 points) but Sam scored low on test C (25 points) while Laura scored high (75 points). No relationship between tests C and D can be determined or described for this group of students. The correlation is 0.

Next suppose there are two more tests, E and F, as shown in Figure 4.9. In this case, students scoring high on test E have scored low on test F. This is a negative correlation (-1). Because a perfect correlation is rare, most correlations are in the form of decimals (.25, $-.43$, .87). An r is typically used to designate a correlation coefficient. For example, $r = 1$, $r = .23$, $r = -.48$. This small r does not stand for reliability. It originally identified the formula used to arrive at the correlation—the Pearson.

If the test being used is published, then the correlation coefficients pertaining to it should be in the manual. If they aren't, the test should be viewed with some suspicion as it is the professional responsibility of the publisher to supply this information. On the other hand, it is the professional re-

sponsibility of the test user to be able to calculate correlation coefficients whenever using a test on kids who differ from the original norming sample. The necessary calculations are simple, given a hand calculator and a clear set of procedures (for example, Bruning and Kintz, 1968, or Moore, 1985). From this description it should be clear that it isn't possible to correlate students to students, but it is possible to correlate measures to measures. If two groups of students are measured with the same test then what is taking place is comparison, not correlation (Diederich, 1967). This means that it is incorrect to ask "How do the third graders correlate to the second graders?" They don't. You can compare third and second graders but you can't correlate them.

**How Do You Know a Good *r*
If You See One?**

The question of how high a correlation coefficient must be to be "high" is difficult to answer. When r is used to summarize a test's reliability or validity, it is determined by giving the test to students. The test scores are then correlated to something else (other test scores, for example). Because r may be affected by many variables, it should always be viewed as an estimate. Because test reliability and

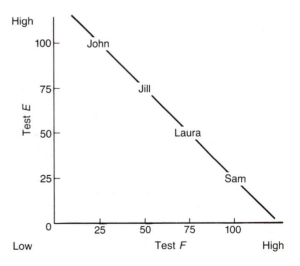

FIGURE 4.9
A negative correlation

validity coefficients are often expressed as *r*, they should also be regarded only as estimates.

The first consideration in deciding how high a correlation coefficient must be is the way it will be used. Higher correlations should be required for more important decisions. A teacher might demand higher correlation coefficients for IQ tests than for tests of bowling skill. The second consideration is who it will be used on. It is easier to make predictions about groups of people than about individuals. The correlation coefficients derived from group studies tell us about groups, not individuals. A reading test might be useful for assigning large numbers of students to programs but it could be nearly worthless in planning instruction for an individual student. Experts have indicated that a correlation high enough to be of any use in predicting about groups must be at least from .3 to .5 (Guilford, 1965; Kelley, 1927). But these correlations are not high enough to use when devising an individualized program. Kelley says that correlations of .94 or above are necessary to make predictions about individuals, while others accept correlations as low as .90 (Arter & Jenkins, 1979).

While it is fairly simple to relate absolute standards like .94, it is difficult to convey a true sense of what .94 means. To do so we will use the example of a prediction task. Let's say you are being asked to predict a student's score on a test he or she is soon to take. The issue is how much knowing a previous test score helps you make this prediction. That will depend on the relationship between the previous test and the one the student is about to take.

If a teacher wants to predict how an individual student will perform on a test, one thing to do is guess. With no other information about the student, the knowledgeable teacher will always assume that the student is average and guess the test mean. (See Appendix B for an explanation of *mean*.) For example, suppose you wanted to predict what a student's IQ score would be next year. If you had no information on the student, you should predict the mean (usually 100). If you predicted the mean, you would be correct a certain amount of time and in error a certain amount of time. The percentage of times you were wrong (which in this case would

still be very high) is called the *error of prediction*. To improve your guess, you must decrease this *error of prediction*. Any useful information you could find out about the student should lower the error of prediction. This information may include test scores.

Suppose you already know the student's score on a spelling test. If spelling and IQ scores from these tests are correlated at .35, knowing the student's spelling score will decrease your error of IQ score prediction by 6.3%. A 6.3% decrease over just plain guessing isn't that impressive, but statistically it is large enough to make you significantly better when making predictions about very large numbers of students. (You may want to take a look at the discussion of statistical significance in Appendix A.) Unfortunately, even though your guessing will be improved for the whole group you're still only 6.3% better at deciding about each individual in the group. This is why lower reliability and validity coefficients may seem adequate for group decisions while being inadequate for guiding the treatment of individual students. Table 4.1 shows the percentage of reduction in error of prediction to be expected for sample correlations (Guilford, 1965). Using this table, we can see that if a teacher knows about a score with a correlation of .45 to the score being predicted, the size of the error of prediction is going to be reduced by only about 11%. That is 11% less error than a prediction made with no previous test information at all.

In using Table 4.1 it is important to remember one thing. If the test doesn't measure anything worthwhile, a prediction made from it will be worthless even if A correlates to B at the $r = 1$ level. Reducing the error of prediction for a nonvalid score from 95% to 75% will not be educationally significant.

Cause and Effect

When two variables are highly correlated an observer should be able to predict the student's behavior on one variable by observing the student's behavior on the other variable. For example, suppose that spelling and math scores are correlated. This means that knowing a student's spelling score

TABLE 4.1
The relationship of r to error of prediction

r	Percentage of error reduction
.00	.0
.05	.1
.10	.5
.15	1.1
.20	2.0
.25	3.2
.30	4.6
.35	6.3
.40	8.3
.45	10.7
.50	13.4
.55	16.5
.60	20.0
.65	24.0
.70	28.6
.75	33.9
.80	40.0
.85	47.3
.90	56.4
.95	68.8
.98	80.1
.99	85.9
.995	90.0
.999	95.5

helps you predict his math score. This correlation does not mean that studying spelling will improve math; it means that math and spelling are correlated due to some other variable (or factor). There is no cause-and-effect relationship between studying spelling and learning math.

Most shark attacks take place in shallow warm water. Therefore, measures of water depth and temperature are highly correlated to the incidence of shark attacks. But lots of sharks live in deep cold water, so why the correlation? A third independent variable, having nothing to do with water or sharks, is the behavior of swimmers. Most people swim in shallow warm water—few swim in the Arctic Ocean. Therefore, most shark attacks take place where the most attackees are available. Warm shallow water does not cause sharks to be hungry.

Speaking of warm shallow water, did you know that sales of ice cream are highly related to the incidence of drowning? As ice cream sales go up, more swimmers go down. Given this relationship, can we assume that when the ice cream vendors go on strike lifeguards can take off too? No. A third factor—warm weather—causes ice cream sales and drownings to change at the same time. They do not affect each other.

One of the biggest errors an educator can make is to confuse a correlational relationship with a cause-and-effect relationship. For example, because scores on tests of student cognitive and perceptual variables (such as the Detroit, ITPA, WISC-R, and K-ABC) are correlated to achievement, many educators have attempted to train cognition and perception to produce achievement. It hasn't worked (Arter & Jenkins, 1979; Glass, 1983; Zigmond & Miller, 1986). Height is correlated to achievement (taller kids read better because they are older and in higher grades), but teachers don't go around stretching kids on the basis of this correlation. Evidence of cause-and-effect relationships is needed before remediation efforts can be justified.

DETERMINING RELIABILITY

Reliability is estimated by correlating the test score to itself. This is done by exposing the same student (or group of students) to the same test twice. There are three methods of doing this: test–retest, parallel forms, and internal consistency.

Test–retest reliability is synonymous with the stability of the test score over time. It is determined by giving the test, waiting, and giving it again. Differences between the first and second test scores may reflect error of measurement or changes in the student. In either case, a low test–retest reliability coefficient limits the use of the test in making decisions over time. This form of reliability coefficient is of interest in cases where the test is designed to identify "types" of students for differential programming. It makes little sense to place a student into a particular program for the whole year on the basis of a test score that may change by accident in a few months.

High test–retest reliability means that a student who is evaluated on a test and scores 23 should score at or near 23 if re-evaluated. The test–retest reliability of a set of calipers measuring a student's head size is high. The test–retest reliability of an instrument designed to measure a student's "good feelings" might not be as high.

The *alternative* (or *parallel*) *form* reliability is determined by giving two forms of the same test to the same group of students. The two scores are then correlated. This method has one advantage in that the student does not take the same test items twice. A disadvantage is that the two forms may not be equally difficult.

Internal consistency reliability can be established through a single administration of a test. This method removes the effect of time found in the first two methods. The internal consistency of a test is often derived by giving the test to a group of students and correlating the even-numbered items with the odd-numbered items. This procedure is sometimes called the *split-half method*. If the odd and even items in the test correlate highly with each other this is a good argument that they are measuring the same things.

If items are found that do not correlate to the total test score, they can be thrown out of the test. Test authors typically develop a pool of items at least 50% larger than needed and then field-test the items to see which ones exhibit internal consistency (high correlations with other items). By throwing out items that don't match they can produce a more consistent test. Because this process of statistically paring down the item pool does not involve giving the test more than once to different groups of students, internal consistency reliability is the easiest type to come up with. You should be suspicious when it is the only type reported in the technical chapter of a test—particularly if you intend to use the test to make treatment decisions that will affect a student over some period of time. In that case test–retest reliability as well as internal consistency is required.

DETERMINING VALIDITY

Validity is determined by correlating the test score to reality. The problem, of course, is that reality is not easily defined. First of all, many (if not most) of the constructs we treat as "real" are actually socially defined or negotiated (Mehan, 1981a, 1981b). This means that as students move from one situation to another (or as the situations they are in change), their appearance of competence may change. A test/observation that reliably captures competence in one setting may be next to useless in another setting or later. A good evaluator understands that because testing/observation procedures are fixed their usefulness will vary in a changing world. *The context in which the test/ observation is employed determines the test's validity—the test does not tell how valid the context is.* When reality and evaluation results seem at odds, it is the evaluation that should be questioned. The authors once read a psychological report that stated that a student who was functioning adequately in all areas but who had gotten a low score on an IQ test was "overachieving." The report advised the teachers to *stop* teaching the student so much material because the test said he could not learn it. This kind of absurd recommendation is the result of a basic misunderstanding of validity. The author of that report reversed the proper role of the test and its context.

A second reason validity is hard to determine is that the process of testing/observing actually changes reality. When the test or evaluator enters the room, the room is changed—some amount of what "really" happens from then on is determined in part by the evaluation process. The evaluation summarizes the interaction between the evaluator and the student. Numerous research studies have shown that changes in evaluator behavior produce changes in student scores (Bradley-Johnson, Graham, & Johnson, 1986; Fuchs et al., 1985), meaning that the validity of the test varies depending on who is giving it.

Because validity is difficult to establish, there is sometimes no mention of it in test manuals. Authors (or publishers) realize that if they produce a reliable test it will be bought because most teachers know very little about validity. Most evaluation texts describe different types of validity and we will present them also so that you can be aware of these terms. However, there is actually only one aspect of validity—the value of the procedure (Messick, 1980). The following "types" of validity are actually the result of *different purposes for evaluating*, not different kinds of validity.

Content Validity

If your purpose is to find out about a student's skill or knowledge of content, you are interested in proof of content validity. A valid spelling test should be made up of items similar to the spelling a student will do in the classroom. Most classroom teachers are interested in content validity as it is necessary to generalize from the test score to classroom practice. Content validity is determined by correlating the test score to the task. Criterion-referenced tests should have high content validity.

Concurrent Validity

If you want to know how a student is doing right now, you want concurrent validity. It refers to a test's ability to describe accurately the student's current level of functioning on certain tasks. To estimate concurrent validity the test score is correlated to other simultaneously administered measures of the student's behavior.

Predictive Validity

Predictive validity is needed when you want to predict the student's functioning in a different setting or at a different time. In establishing predictive validity over time an effort is made to correlate the test score to the student's future. This can only be accomplished by carrying out long-term studies (intervals vary from 6 weeks to years).

Using tests in one area to predict performance in another also requires predictive validity. For example, tests such as IQ tests are designed to predict how the student will do in many situations. In order to have predictive validity, IQ tests sample a wide variety of behaviors. Because these tests are intended to predict performance in all school subjects, their global scores (and even their subtest scores) do not reflect the specificity necessary for guiding treatment. The IQ score does not tell the teacher how or what to teach. Predictive validity should never be confused with the content and concurrent validity necessary for instruction.

Construct Validity

A construct is a theory or idea. Construct validity is the degree to which a test matches the theoretical base from which it was developed. It is of particular interest in special education. Many tests routinely given to special students are based on constructs (theories) of psychological functioning. Naming a test after some type of psychological or perceptual functioning does not make it a test of that function. The Illinois Test of Psycholinguistic Ability, for example, was based on a theory of psycholinguistics developed by Osgood (1953). The test items, however, were not noticeably different from those making up most achievement tests (Waugh, 1975).

Another example is the Kaufman Assessment Battery for Children (K-ABC). The K-ABC is based on a theory of information processing that includes three critical elements for problem solving: awareness, coding, and planning (Das, Kirby & Jarman, 1979). The test itself, however, seems to include only coding tasks and consequently fails to match the idea of information processing upon which it is based. These inconsistencies between a test's theoretical underpinnings and actual structure are threats to construct validity.

Cash Validity

Tests that sell well may have high cash validity (Dick & Hagerty, 1971). It is possible to have cash validity in the absence of any other type of validity. One cannot assume that because a test sells well, it is useful. It is just as likely that a best-selling test has been marketed well or happens to be in style. Cash validity by the way is the only kind that can exist in the absence of reliability.

In the absence of validity data (or even in their presence), a teacher should sit down with the test and carefully analyze it. Look at the items and ask yourself, "Do my students engage in tasks similar to these? Does the test emphasize the same curricular areas I do?" Note if the author tells how the test was validated and on whom.

STANDARD ERROR OF MEASUREMENT

Another way to judge the reliability of a score is to look at the test's *standard error of measurement*. If a student (or group) is given the same test several times and tries equally hard each time, it seems like he should always get the same score, but he won't. When there are differences between the scores, these differences must be attributed to either learning or measurement error. Once learning has been subtracted, all that remains to account for the variability (differences in obtained score) is error. The greater the variability in scores, the greater the standard error of measurement. The standard error of measurement accounts for many sources of score variance because it is calculated from both the reliability and the standard deviation of the test score.

The standard error is used to place an interval around the obtained test score. This interval is conceptualized in terms of the standard deviations found in a normal distribution (see Appendix B). The interval represents the range of scores that a student might get by accident. For example, if a test has a standard error of 5 and a student has a true score of 40, the obtained score may be expected to accidentally range from 35 to 45 (plus and minus one standard error). Assuming the normal distribution, a student's true score will fall between $+1$ and -1 standard error 68% of the time.

The standard error of measurement is a better criterion for judging the test's usefulness than the simple reliability coefficient (Williams & Zimmerman, 1984). There are many sources of error in scores, including fatigue, a broken pencil, bad lighting, and passage of time. While different techniques for determining reliability account for different sources of error variability, standard error tends to reflect them all. When reading a test manual, it is important to notice if the author reports the standard error of measurement as well as reliability.

Imagine that a test is being used to assign students to high and low groups and the cut-off score is 70. Dean gets a score of 69 on the test but the standard error is 2. This means that even though Dean's obtained score is below the cut-off, there is a 68% chance that his true score is between 67 (69 $-$ 2) and 71 (69 + 2). In this situation some other criterion would have to be used to assign Dean to a group as the error in measurement overlaps the critical cutting score. The conversion of the obtained score (69) to an interval (67–71) makes the error in measurement "visible" and easier to understand.

RELIABILITY AND VALIDITY OF CRTS

A CRT is composed of an instructional objective and the materials necessary to carry it out. An objective is composed of elements of content, behavior, conditions, and criterion for acceptable performance (CAP). CAP represents a threshold in task proficiency that corresponds to some type of instructional decision. The idea is that students who don't meet criterion need one type of instruction and those who do meet it need another. How well the CRT indicates task proficiency and aids decision making depends on how reliable and valid it is.

The procedures for determining the reliability and validity of CRTs and NRTs are different. The basis of this difference is the reference. The stability and goodness of an NRT are recognized through calculations that take into account the distribution (variability) of scores in a sample group. One way variability of scores within the group can be assured is to be sure people with varying skills are included in the sample. Another way a large distribution of scores is obtained is by varying the difficulty of items. In either case, statistical procedures sensitive to variability of scores are used in calculations concerning the quality of the NRT.

As we have said, a CRT is standardized not on a population of people with varying skills but on a population of people who are already competent at the task being measured. This procedure is combined with the logical analysis of the task and the experimental use of the test to determine if it is instructionally useful. Because the CRT score is meant to summarize knowledge/skill within a clearly specified domain, the items on the CRT all reflect that single domain. Therefore, there may be very little score variability within the standardization sample (Swezey, 1981).

The validity of a CRT is determined first of all by the value of the objective on which it is based. If the objective does not represent a meaningful learning outcome, the test cannot be valid. The second requirement for a valid CRT is the existence of a meaningful criterion. The ultimate test of CRT validity is its ability to improve educational decision making. If the proficiency level indicated by the criterion signals instructional decisions and if students learn more when these decisions are made, the test seems valid.

Several techniques have been suggested for determining the reliability and validity of CRTs. These suggestions range both in complexity and utility. Because so many of the CRTs used today are teacher-made, it is likely that two sets of procedures will evolve for determining their quality— one set of procedures to meet the accuracy requirements of researchers, another to meet the time requirements of the classroom.

CRT Reliability

One of the most important reliability issues for CRTs is internal consistency. Because a CRT has only one objective, its reliability depends upon the consistency of the items. It has been suggested that variations of the Kuder-Richardson formula used to calculate internal consistency for NRTs be used for determining the reliability of CRTs (Schooley, Shultz, Donovan, & Lehman, 1975). However, the use of techniques that require variability in the test scores is being debated (Berk, 1980; Berk, 1986; Chas & Woodson, 1974; Hambleton & Novik, 1973). At the heart of the issue is the fact that the CRT user isn't interested in discriminating between students. CRT items are not selected for the pur-

pose of producing variability in scores. When variability is small (or restricted), reliability coefficients calculated with NRT statistics will be low. Therefore, some standard statistical procedures underestimate the reliability of CRTs.

Another problem is that CRTs should be timed, or speeded. Depending upon the procedure used, time may either artificially inflate or deflate internal consistency. For example, when the split-half technique is used to calculate internal consistency, the test is either divided by halves or by even and odd questions. If the halves are correlated on a timed test, it is likely that some students will not finish the test and the correlation will be low. If the odd and even items are correlated, the results may be misleadingly high because timing tends to equalize the behavior of test takers, thereby raising the correlation.

In the case of test–retest reliability the specificity of CRTs produces some problems while solving others. Because the tests describe exactly what a student is learning (short-term instructional objectives and CRT objectives are the same), students may quickly learn the objective. Thus the test score appears unstable when the students are retested. However, because the tests should be designed to be readministered frequently, lower levels of test–retest reliability may be allowed because decisions can be double checked almost immediately. Figure 4.10 shows a student's scores on repeated administrations of a CRT measuring vowel sounds read per minute. On the chart the student's behav-

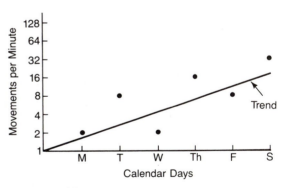

FIGURE 4.10
Minimizing error by determining trend

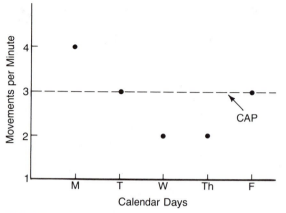

FIGURE 4.11
Ed's scores on the ruler test

ior was different on Tuesday than it was on Monday. If a student takes any test twice, the difference between the two scores is attributed either to learning or measurement error. In this example (Figure 4.10), the difference of 6 per minute does not mean that the student forgot three-fourths of what he had known the day before. In fact, the trend line shows that he is consistently improving. When there is a positive change in the total trend of the data, it is thought of as learning. But the variability, or bounce, seen in the data from one day to the next, is only measurement error. The effect of measurement error can be minimized by giving a CRT several times and determining a trend.

The confidence that can be placed in a test score is related to the number of items the student completes to get the score. Special education teachers will often say things like "Ed is a really unpredictable learner—one day he has it and the next day he doesn't." However, one explanation for Ed's peculiar learning has nothing to do with Ed. Suppose the teacher gives a four-item test with a 75% criterion. Ed could pass or fail the test by getting only one additional problem right or wrong.

In Figure 4.11, Ed passed the test on Monday and Tuesday but did not pass on Wednesday and Thursday. If the test items are specific enough to be educationally useful, then four of them are not enough to compensate for the usual daily score variability (measurement error). In other words, to say that Ed had it and lost it is wrong. He never had it at all. With so few items, the measurement error alone was enough to move him from passing to failing.

Figure 4.12 shows a chart of addition facts. If the criterion for addition facts is 50 per minute, then Ed has not really met criterion until the lower envelope line of his data has passed 50. Even though he first passed 50 on the 11th day, he has not really met criterion until the 15th day. (The use of charting is covered in detail in chapter 15.)

CRT Validity

The score on a CRT provides information as to the student's standing in relationship to a task. A stu-

FIGURE 4.12
Ed's addition facts

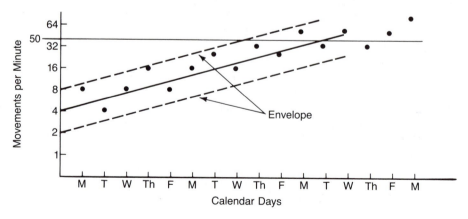

dent who scores above the criterion (CAP) has mastered the task. The test score is valid to the degree that the information it gives is accurate and usable. It must reflect the objective (have content validity) and lead to useful decisions (have instructionally valid criteria).

The content validity of CRTs begins with a well formulated objective and depends on the match between this objective and the test items. This match is facilitated by clarifying the domains of content, behavior, and condition elaborated on in chapter 3. Statements about the content validity of CRTs are often supported with research showing that the content and behavior sequences used are the same as those taught in class and specified in the curriculum. In other instances, judges who are considered to be experts in the target domain are asked to rate the quality of the items.

The validity of the criterion in a CRT is generally supported by describing the standardization procedure or determining the degree to which the crite-

rion separates instructionally different groups of students. The importance of standards (CAP) and how they should be established and employed is highly controversial (Berk, 1986). We believe that it is possible to establish criteria (see chapter 8) that can be used to recognize students who do or do not need instruction on a particular task. Once established, the ultimate validity question is how well the criteria do their job. That is, how well do the criteria help teachers make sucessful treatment decisions?

SUMMARY

This chapter has introduced terminology, tools, and concepts used in evaluation. We began by describing NRTs and CRTs and then followed that discussion with information about reliability and validity. This material will be referred to throughout the remainder of this text.

_____ *Study Questions* _____

1. Define the following terms as they are used in this text. Some of these terms may be review from previous chapters.
   a. Probe
   b. Norm-referenced test
   c. Criterion-referenced test
   d. Standard error of measurement
   e. Scores
   f. Correlation
   g. Mean
   h. Reliability
   i. Validity
2. Norm-referenced tests tell us
   a. which objective the student needs to be working on.
   b. the student's general standing in relation to other students.
   c. which methods will most effectively remediate a student's difficulty.
   d. which curricular changes to implement.
3. Criterion-referenced tests tell
   a. the student's grade-level equivalency.
   b. the student's general standing in relation to other students.
   c. what particular skill or knowledge the student is lacking.
   d. a and c.
4. In scoring a criterion-referenced test, one point should equal
   a. one behavior.
   b. one item.
   c. one problem.
   d. one task.

5. Decide whether each of the following is characteristic of norm-referenced or criterion-referenced tests.
   a. Contains items from across a wide range of the curriculum
   b. Tests only one objective at a time
   c. Items are all at the same level of difficulty
   d. Student performance on the items varies greatly across grade and skill levels
   e. Standardized using a large representative sample of students
   f. Standardized using a small group of students who possess the target skill
   g. Specificity in measuring curriculum is often sacrificed for better discrimination
   h. Used for making treatment decisions

6. A reading test that yields scores that are stable across time but that requires students to do no reading is
   a. reliable, but not valid.
   b. valid, but not reliable.
   c. reliable and valid.
   d. neither reliable nor valid.

7. If test A and test B show a correlation of .85, then
   a. students who do well on test A will do poorly on test B.
   b. students have an 85% chance of getting the same score on test B as they did on test A.
   c. students who do well on test A will probably do well on test B.

8. A reading test is administered to the same group of students twice in 2 weeks, with a resulting correlation of .50. The test is
   a. not reliable enough for use in the public schools.
   b. reliable enough for making decisions about large groups.
   c. not reliable enough for making treatment decisions about individuals.
   d. b and c.
   e. invalid.

9. A valid test is a test that
   a. was standardized appropriately.
   b. is highly discriminative.
   c. accurately measures the real-life skill it is supposed to measure.
   d. has been widely used for a number of years.

10. You have been given a reading test to use in evaluating your students. You have been informed that it is criterion-referenced. Think of five or six things you would look for to decide if this test is reliable and valid.

Chapter 5

Testing

          Setting Standards
- Use Items That Permit Examination of Strategic Behavior
      Solution
      Explanation
          Consolidated Domains
          Evaluating Strategies
          Recognizing a Strategy Problem
             Ask
             Error Analysis
             Strategy-Based Items
- Collect Rate Data
      Solution
      Explanation
          Rate
- A Brief Review/Preview
- Collect an Adequate Sample
      Solution
      Explanation
          Consolidated Domains Revisited
          Strategies Revisited
          Rate Revisited
          Repeated Measures
- Use Appropriate Formats
      Solution
      Explanation
          Fidelity
             Format
             Response Domains
- Use Appropriate Scoring Procedures
      Solution
      Explanation
          Summarizing Behavior
          Sensitivity to Learning

The basic principle of curriculum-based assessment is "test what you teach and teach what you test." As explained in chapter 3, this means that the curriculum must be thoroughly defined. It also means that behavior-sampling devices (tests and observations) must be constructed, or selected, to complement the various aspects of the curriculum being taught. Devices sensitive to content, behavior, conditions, criteria, and strategies must be used. This can be accomplished by assuring that the following 10 guidelines are met. If you are unsure about the meaning of a particular guideline, be patient—each one will be expanded on shortly.

GUIDELINES FOR SELECTING/WRITING BEHAVIOR SAMPLES

1. *Be sure it is easy to use.* Make sure there are directions and scoring procedures. Make it easy to follow, transport, and interpret.

2. *Be sure it has a clearly defined purpose.* Know the purpose and limitations of the instrument being used. Determine if it is a placement or treatment test and if it is norm-referenced or criterion-referenced.

3. *Be sure it measures defined content and behavioral domains.* Be able to cross-reference items and procedures to content and behavioral domains. These may include subskills, theoretical domains, response domains, stimulus-response domains, and proficiency domains.

4. *Be sure the items are keyed to objectives.* Develop a test plan that includes objectives. It may take the form of a table of specifications. Write or select items for each square (objective) in the table and code the items for cross-reference.

5. *Be sure the objectives are standardized.* Decide on the appropriate type of data (accuracy or rate) for the content to be tested. Set standards by reviewing the literature, asking experts, sampling a standardization population, or examining empirical proof.

6. *Be sure to use items that permit examination of strategic behavior.* Decide if product evaluation is sufficient. If not, devise a way to make the strategic process observable, usually by using error analysis or items that test strategy use.

7. *Collect rate data when necessary.* Decide which skills need to be carried out fluently. Use test formats that allow students to work at functional speeds. Collect rate data.

8. *Be sure to collect an adequate sample of behavior.* Decide how consolidated the content is. Write enough items (usually 10) for each strategic element of highly consolidated content or for each instance of unconsolidated content. Avoid ceiling effects.

9. *Be sure to feature appropriate stimulus formats.* Examine the context to which the results will be generalized and be sure the items match that context. Also consider the proficiency dimension. Decide if rate is called for, or if the test will be used for repeated measures.

10. *Be sure to use appropriate scoring procedures.* Use measurement rules that assign points to the smallest educationally relevant unit.

While common sets of criteria for tests/observations and their use have been presented (American Psychological Association, 1983; Brown & Bryant, 1984; Special Education Assessment Coalition, 1981; Taylor, 1984), they have not brought about a uniform style; the production of instruments remains varied and largely undisciplined. Therefore the test consumer (you) must become familiar with each of the guidelines as they are tied to the validity of your assessments.

TESTS/OBSERVATIONS MUST BE EASY TO USE

Solution

Make sure there are directions and scoring procedures. Make it easy to follow, transport, and interpret. At the very least the test/observation should:

1. Be easy for the teacher to administer
2. Be easy for the student to take
3. Have consistent, clearly described directions and scoring procedures
4. Be easily transportable
5. Be easy to interpret
6. Make the trouble of giving it and taking it worthwhile by providing reliable and valid results that can be used to make educationally relevant decisions

Explanation

Directions Supplied

Any published test/observation should be accompanied by a set of directions and technical information. A test/observation that does not have a manual, or two, with directions and a thorough technical rationale should *not* be used. There are plenty of instruments on the market that cover the same things so there's no reason not to pick the ones that do it right. Unfortunately, the directions and technical descriptions are frequently combined, which sometimes smothers the directions or technical issues. This is not necessarily the test publisher's fault; they may be attempting to present the technical limitations of their product "up front," knowing that few users will turn to the back chapters to read the often-dry information there.

Easy to Use

Ultimately, most of us will look for a test that is easy to use, and we (the authors) think that is a legitimate quest. However, there is no value in giving a "quickie" test that gives you zero information. While adminstration time will be an issue, pay attention to things like the ease with which you learn to give it. You are probably going to need to use individually administered tests that take the better part of an hour to give in order to get any useful information. On the other hand, you don't want to get involved with tests that are so complicated that you need weeks to learn how to administer them. If you can't learn to administer a test competently simply by reading the manual and practicing on some friends (what are friends for), you should not consider it for use.

There is some risk in finding a procedure that has been made too easy. One way test authors/ publishers often try to make a test/observation easy to use is to tell you what your results mean. Unfortunately, this practice has great potential for abuse. To make things seem simple, test authors often encourage the application of a "cookbook" approach to interpretation. It essentially says "Kids who score this way need A; kids who score that way need B." These statements make things artificially simple and are more reasonable if the test is designed to pinpoint *what* to teach (which objective) rather than *how* to teach it (which treatment).

The cookbook approach to educational diagnosis is extremely appealing to teachers and evaluators. However, you should be skeptical of programs that try to relate test scores to specific remedial techniques. Such programs place almost absolute faith in the power of the test score. In those cases you should carefully review the test items to see if they seem relevant to what you are teaching. It is also necessary to review the technical data on the test, including the stability of its scores over time.

One other caution about the cookbook method: Many of the tests that lend themselves to this technique are intended to group students into treatment types (e.g., auditory versus visual or sequential versus simultaneous learners). These tests are based on the assumption that predictable, long-term aptitude–treatment interactions (ATI) can be accurately identified and used. Research using existing tests has failed to support this assumption either for groups of students or for individuals. (This is explained in some depth in chapter 15.)

In the end, "ease of use" is a legitimate concern and admirable goal but it must also be subjective. One guideline must surely be "maximum effort for maximum problems," meaning that it is just plain harder to evaluate the most remedial students. You have to be prepared to spend more time and effort with more complex instruments if you intend to help more severely handicapped kids.

TESTS MUST HAVE CLEARLY DEFINED PURPOSE

Solution

Know the purpose and limitations of the instrument being used. Determine if it is a placement or treatment instrument and if it is normed or criterion-referenced.

Explanation

As stated in chapter 1, the reason we evaluate is to make decisions. As a quick review:

1. Educational decisions can be roughly categorized as treatment decisions (about objectives,

materials, lessons, and assignments) and placement decisions (about grading, retention, grouping, and placement).

2. Placement tools are typically normative; they sample global domains of achievement or ability.
3. Treatment tools are typically criterion-referenced and sample specific domains of achievement or ability.
4. It is a mistake to confuse placement and treatment or to try to use placement data for treatment decisions.

Form Follows Function

Placement tests are typically NRTs; as a group they exhibit low test–curriculum match. As you recall, norm-referenced tests are designed to discriminate between students in two ways. First, the tests cover a wider range of content than any one student would be expected to have mastered. If a test is composed of 25 items, instead of providing a cluster of items at one curriculum level to get a thorough picture of the student's skill, the 25 items may be spread over several grade/skill levels. This means that for any given student only 10% to 20% of the test items measure things he or she is currently learning. The rest of the items are too easy or too hard. This spread in item difficulty is intentional because it accentuates the test's discriminative power, which is essential for normative comparison. However, this same spread decreases the test's usefulness for describing a student's actual performance on any skill. We have all been told to teach at the correct level of difficulty. If tests are to help us make decisions to guide our teaching, we must also *test* at the correct level of difficulty. The more a test violates this obvious principle, the less useful it is for making treatment decisions.

Discrimination is also increased by selecting items with high discriminative values (sometimes called *p*-values). If the NRT test authors have two items from the domain of interest, one of which many students pass and the other of which only half of the students pass, they will pick the item half of the students fail to increase the test's discriminative power. Of course, the items most students fail are the ones most teachers do not teach. This means that items teachers spend the most time and effort teaching (and therefore that most students pass) are *less* likely to appear on a placement test. This produces low test–curriculum match. If a test were composed of only the items teachers emphasized, most instructed students would pass all items and most uninstructed students would fail all items, yielding a distribution composed of very low scores and very high scores without the array of scores in between that is needed for normative comparison.

It is not possible to make the statement that for treatment purposes all CRTs are better than all NRTs. Instead it must be said that *good* CRTs are better than NRTs or bad CRTs. It would be easy to develop (and no doubt someone will) a criterion-referenced perceptual-motor test intended to guide the treatment of reading problems even though the relationship of perceptual-motor training to academics is not established. The ability of evaluators to lose the curriculum base and test the unnecessary hasn't done much damage to NRT sales, and it probably won't hurt CRT sales. Still, the treatment superiority of criterion-referenced over norm-referenced measurement will remain theoretically sound even if test developers fail to keep it operationally sound.

Title and Function

Finally, it is important to note that confusion of purpose isn't limited to the classification versus treatment dichotomy we have set up in this discussion. Every once in a while it is a good idea to stop before you use a test and look at its title and the titles of its subtests. Then ask yourself "What can be measured?" (Lennon, 1962). If a teacher reads test catalogs and notes the various titles, he or she might conclude that there are a lot of things that can be measured. For example, a teacher can order tests of auditory discrimination, reading, superego forces, IQ, spelling, self-concept, field dependence, locus of control, addition, information processing, creativity, and even hemispheric dominance (left brain/right brain). In reality, of course, the title of a test tells little about its content. Titles reflect the selective interests of past investigators and the current needs of test buyers. In addition, some things are easier to measure than others, and tests to measure them may develop regardless of interest or need. Well over a decade ago, a comparison of nationally established educational goals to available tests revealed that there are many high priority objectives (ranging from handwriting to the free enterprise system) for which there are few or no published measures (Hoephner, 1974). This still seems to be the case.

The best clue to a test/observation's purpose should be the statement of purpose found in the manual, but these are often vague and sometimes even contradictory. Besides, it is *your* purpose that needs to be specified most clearly. If you know what you are trying to do it is easier to figure what will help you get it done. *For our part, the purpose of this book is treatment evaluation.*

THE TEST SHOULD MEASURE CLEARLY DEFINED CONTENT AND BEHAVIORAL DOMAINS

Solution
Be able to cross-reference items and procedures to content and behavioral domains. These may include content subskills, theoretical domains, response domains, and proficiency domains.

Explanation

Identified Domains
In chapter 3 we stated that a task is more than a statement of content. We introduced response domains (identify, produce) and proficiency domains (accuracy, mastery, automaticity) to make the point that solving a multiple-choice untimed test item on 6×25 is very different than deciding how much six video game tokens will cost before the kid be-

hind you in line steps on your Achilles' tendon. Many, if not most, tests tend either to jumble these domains together to the point that they are inseparable or to use only one regardless of its fidelity.

To relate the results of a test to the curriculum conveniently, you must have a test that allows the scores on items or subtests to be directly keyed to the curriculum. For example, if a student scores low on the addition subtest of a math inventory, it might be interesting to know that several of the items involved addition of fractions and decimals— without knowing that a teacher could erroneously conclude that the student wasn't skilled in addition when the real problem was fractions. The point isn't that fractions don't belong—but that their presence should be clearly acknowledged.

Several years ago the son of Joe Kaplan, the co-author of this text's predecessors, brought home a checksheet from school indicating that he had "mastered computation facts." Kaplan, noting that at the time his son seldom got his homework done without help, double-checked the boy's skills and found his work inaccurate. Given this information, he went to the school where he was told that his son had passed the district's math computation *mastery* test. Kaplan demanded to see the test. When they showed it to him he found that his son had demonstrated "mastery" by successfully working three out of four multiple-choice items in an untimed format. While the content domain (computation) was correctly labeled, the response domain (identify) was not and the proficiency level (untimed—75% accuracy) hardly meets with most people's image of a "master" (which Kaplan told the school principal was closer to being one with the universe than three out of four on a multiple-choice test).

While various domains of content, behavior, condition, and criterion all have their place in teaching and evaluation, they should not be confused. Reading tests that require students to spell and mastery tests that don't include rate (which, as you know, is essential for automaticity) need to have their domains clearly identified so that evaluators do not draw the wrong conclusions from them.

THE TEST ITEMS SHOULD BE KEYED TO OBJECTIVES

Solution

Develop a test plan that includes objectives. It may take the form of a table of specifications. Write or select items for each square (objective) in the table and code the items for cross-reference.

Explanation

Cross-Referencing

Even if the domains the test is sampling are identified, few tests link items, or groups of items, directly to objectives. Table 5.1 is a table of specifications for multiplication. Below the table the accuracy production objectives have been written out. Like most tables, this one is a grid defined by content, behavior, and proficiency dimensions. Figure 5.1 shows the key to a test composed of items from the accuracy column. The number in parentheses above each item can be found in the table of specifications (Table 5.1) and the full objective found below the table. This clear cross-referencing of each item to an objective allows teachers to immediately see in which domains of content or behavior an error has occurred and to select an appropriate objective for the student.

The test shown in Figure 5.1 is a fairly typical survey test (meaning it covers a lot of material). The items are organized from easiest to hardest and rate data are not collected. Figure 5.2 shows a specific-level CRT designed to measure a student's rate at subtraction with borrowing. In this case the diagonal lines, which would not appear on the student's copy, are used to point out items that follow from the same objective. When a test will be used repeatedly for collecting rate data, it is important to group items randomly according to difficulty so as not to distort the student's rate of production. The diagonal grouping technique shown in Figure 5.2 allows an even distribution of items by difficulty, with item types (subtraction from zero, subtraction of a number from itself, borrowing) identi-

fied to allow easy recognition of objectives that are troubling the student (White & Haring, 1980). The diagonal pattern has the additional advantage of being hard to figure out so that the test retains reliability over repeated administrations.

Ideally, all objectives in a curriculum should be numbered and all items that measure that objective given the same number. In this way the curriculum–test match is direct. It would be even better if applicable instructional materials could also be labeled with the same numbers. In that case missing an item(s) would not only key recognition of an objective but selection of a treatment. Obviously such arrangements make a test easier to use. However, few available tests have items cross-referenced to objectives.

TESTS WHICH ARE KEYED TO OBJECTIVES SHOULD BE STANDARDIZED

Solution

Decide on the appropriate type of data (accuracy or rate) for the content to be tested. Set standards by reviewing the literature, asking experts, sampling a standardization population, or examining empirical proof.

Explanation

Standards

While all components are important to a well-written CRT, the criterion is so important that it is definitional. A criterion-referenced test uses a testing procedure to sample behavior and then contrasts, or references, that behavior to a performance criterion (CAP). Obviously, a criterion-referenced test is worthless if the criterion is arbitrarily established or completely missing (the source of CAP and its validity should be supplied in the technical chapter of the test manual). Unfortunately, this is the case for many published tests that claim to be criterion-referenced. Tests that are

TABLE 5.1
Table of specifications for multiplication

	Identify	Accuracy	Mastery	Automatic	MASI Curriculum Level	Local Curriculum Level
Placement Test						
Mixed multiplication problems				9p		
Squaring						
Squares of numbers (0-12)	8i	8a	8m	9p	8	
Regrouping and No Regrouping						
Two or more digits by two or more digits		7a		9p	4-5	
Two-digit numbers by a two-digit number		4a	4m	9p	4	
Place Value						
Multidigit problems with zeros		6a		9p	4	
Multiply by 1, 10, 100, 1000		5a		9p	5	
Regrouping						
Two-digit number by a one-digit number		3a	3m	9p	4	
No Regrouping						
Two-digit number by a one-digit number		2a	2m	9p	4	
Facts						
Multiplication facts (0-10)	1i	1a	1m	9p	4	

Accuracy Production Objectives

8a—Squaring	Produce squares of numbers (0-12). Accuracy CAP 100%.
7a—Regrouping and No Regrouping	Multiply a number containing two or more digits by another number containing two or more digits with or without regrouping. Accuracy CAP 100%.
6a—Place Value	Multiply multidigit problems with zeros as place holders. Accuracy CAP 100%.
5a—Place Value	Multiply 1, 10, 100, 1000. Accuracy CAP 100%.
4a—Regrouping and No Regrouping	Multiply a two-digit number by a two-digit number with or without regrouping. Accuracy CAP 100%.
3a—Regrouping	Multiply a two-digit number by a one-digit number with regrouping. Accuracy CAP 100%.
2a—No Regrouping	Multiply a two-digit number by a one-digit number without regrouping. Accuracy CAP 100%.
1a—Facts	Multiplication facts (0-10). Accuracy CAP 100%.

(Source: From K. W. Howell, S. H. Zucker, & M. K. Morehead, *Multilevel Academic Skills Inventory: Math Manual*, p. 435. San Antonio, TX: The Psychological Corporation, 1982. Reprinted with permission.)

1. (1a)
    2
  ×6
   12

2. (1a)
    9
  ×5
   45

3. (1a)
    8
  ×3
   24

4. (2a)
   64
  × 7
  448

5. (2a)
   24
  × 3
   72

6. (2a)
   91
  × 1
   91

7. (3a)
   18
  × 9
  162

8. (4a)
   22
  ×86
  1892

9. (4a)
   85
  ×63
  5355

10. (5a)
194 × 10 = 1940

11. (5a)
3 × 1000 = 3000

12. (5a)
100 × 74 = 7400

13. (6a)
   102
  × 40
  4080

14. (6a)
   40
  ×31
  1240

15. (6a)
   7005
  × 26
  182130

16. (7a)
   87
  ×25
  2175

17. (7a)
   215
  × 48
  10320

18. (7a)
   5684
  × 39
  221676

19. (8a)
$5^2 = 25$

20. (8a)
$12^2 = 144$

FIGURE 5.1
Test key — *Multiplication accuracy production* (*Source:* From K. W. Howell, S. H. Zucker, & M. K. Morehead, *Multilevel Academic Skills Inventory: Math Manual.* p. 46. San Antonio, TX: The Psychological Corporation, 1982. Reprinted with permission.)

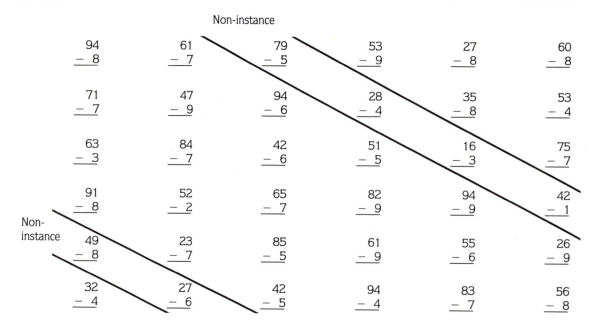

FIGURE 5.2
Error analysis

only keyed to content should be called content-referenced—not criterion-referenced.

As you recall from chapter 2, evaluation cannot even occur without a standard. In the case of CRTs, standards for task proficiency must be established. The CAP is the same criterion found for the instructional objective the test is designed to evaluate. Students who do not meet CAP are thought to need instruction on the objective, while those who do meet it are assumed to require only review or monitoring. As we explained in the last chapter and in Appendix B, the validity of a CRT cannot even be determined without recognizing CAP in order to determine the instrument's threshold loss (Berk, 1986; Haertel, 1985).

CAP can be determined several ways. Most commonly it is determined by guessing (the worst way). For some reason, almost everyone guesses 80% accuracy. If asked to write any objective most teachers will write "Given _____ _____, _____ _____ 80% accuracy." We're not sure, but we think 80% became popular because Gronlund (1973) used it as an example in one of the first books on the subject. It is a nice enough number but it cannot be equally relevant to all areas of curriculum. 80% add facts—80% spell words—80% adjust brakes—80% land airplane? We once read an objective for a high school math class that said "The student will write and read checks with 80% accuracy." That is not a reasonable criterion! Personal experience has taught us that anything less than 100% accuracy in checking can have a profound impact on one's standard of living.

Setting Standards

The best way to establish CAP is to "standardize" the criterion. A standard is defined as something used as a model or criterion. Standards are established by authority, custom, or general consent. In educational literature, you can find criteria that were established in the following ways: (a) by guessing, (b) by asking experts, (c) by sampling techniques, or (d) by experimentally validating the effect of meeting different criteria on subsequent learning. Each technique has advantages and disadvantages (Berk, 1986). For the teacher, the easiest ways to get criteria (next to guessing) are to consult experts and research or to use tests that clearly describe the standardization in their technical chapters. If a school district decides to use CRTs district-wide, the district will typically standardize them through a sampling procedure (as described in chapter 8).

Lesson A	Lesson B
6 + 7 = 13	6 + 7 = 13
$\sqrt{36}$ = 6	4 + 3 = 7
42/9 = 46.67	2 + 7 = 9
2 − 4 − 6 − 8 − ? = 10	8 + 6 = 14

FIGURE 5.3

USE ITEMS THAT PERMIT EXAMINATION OF STRATEGIC BEHAVIOR

Solution
Decide if product evaluation is sufficient. If not, devise a way to make the strategy observable, usually by using error analysis or items that test strategy use.

Explanation

Consolidated Domains
Tasks have various elements of content, behavior, conditions, and proficiency. These elements are considered when articulating curriculum or test objectives. Typically, the objectives specify fairly narrow behavioral outcomes rather than the underlying processes students must follow to achieve these outcomes. For example, an objective may call for a student to write the correct answers to multiplication problems without really specifying the procedure the student should follow to arrive at the answers, even though there may be several ways to do so.

These strategies (both specific and general) are what we actually want students to learn. We teach them by first guaranteeing that students have the necessary subskills to do a task before teaching them how to actually assemble those subskills with a task strategy. Obviously, if strategies are the important things to teach they are also the important things to evaluate. But how?

Before answering that question, we must give a bit more information on strategies and teaching. If a math teacher had the choice of presenting either the four items in Figure 5.3 labeled as lesson *A* or

the four called lesson *B* to a student who couldn't work any of them, which four items would make the most sense? Most of us would agree that lesson B makes the most sense because the teacher would be using only one type of problem. The four items in lesson B can all be worked with the same strategy, where the items in lesson A require four different strategies. Lesson B presents a consolidated domain of tasks.

To review, a consolidated domain contains a group of tasks that share common strategic components. Presenting these tasks together facilitates learning because the solution of any one item points the way to solving the others. If a domain is sufficiently consolidated, a student may learn how to solve problems in it without ever actually being asked to do so. For example, it is completely possible that you have never faced the division problem 333333 ÷ 10101 but you can work it (relax, you don't have to) because you learned the strategy for dealing with items in the domain (division) from which it was drawn. The most rapid learning can be expected in those domains in which the greatest number of items can be approached with the fewest common steps.

Evaluating Strategies
What we are talking about here is a fairly common distinction evaluators draw between product and process evaluation. A *product* is the answer that results from following a *process*. As stated above, the fact of a correct answer (product) is only meaningful in that it indicates that a correct strategy (process) has been employed. There may be many ways to arrive at a particular product (answer), some of which are appropriate and others (such as cheating) which are not. Because different students may

Incorrect Answer	Incorrect Procedure
26	Subtract 6 from 8
− 8	and bring down 2.
22	

Incorrect Answer	Incorrect Procedure
26	Add 2 and 6;
− 8	then subtract 8.
0	

FIGURE 5.4

employ different strategies to work the same problem, their scores actually reflect different thought processes (Frederiksen, 1986). If the goal of instruction is to teach strategies, we need evaluative information that gives us insight into the thought processes students follow as well as the answers at which they arrive.

Figure 5.4 shows two incorrect answers to the same problem. Each answer was arrived at through a logical (if incorrect) attempt to deal with the challenge of subtracting a large number (8) from a smaller one (2). While each answer is wrong, each illustrates the use of a different strategy and points the way to different remediation. This example points out the need to gain insight into the procedures, or strategies, students use. Once again these procedures are often of much greater importance than the simple facts (answers) they lead to. Process (strategy) evaluation is particularly important in cases where an incorrect strategy can be used to arrive at a correct answer on one task but not on subsequent tasks (e.g., using your fists to solve problems when you are young may get you put in jail later on). In such cases students are rewarded for, and practice, erroneous strategies. Later they must spend time "unlearning" these strategies before replacing them with correct ones. A strategic evaluation is required to pinpoint which things they need to unlearn.

Recognizing a Strategy Problem

The easiest way to tell if a student is missing the correct strategy for completing a task is to check subtask skill. If a student fails at a task but succeeds at its essential subtasks, the student must lack the strategy for combining the subtasks. Recognizing this requires the use of CRTs organized into task/subtask hierarchies.

When it is reasoned that a correct strategy is missing, this does not mean that the student should be viewed as a blank slate awaiting the procedural word to be successful. It is more likely that the student is already using an erroneous strategy to attempt the task. Typically this is the result of overgeneralizing the correct strategy for a previously learned task. Some students practice these incorrect strategies so often that they are applied automatically even though they don't work. Appropriate strategic instruction therefore involves three steps: (a) telling the student he or she made an error, (b) disconfirming the incorrect existing strategy, and (c) teaching a correct strategy to take its place. To teach like this a teacher must gain insight into the student's strategy use. There are three ways to do this: (1) ask, (2) use error analysis, and (3) use strategy-based items.

Ask. One very efficient way to find out how someone is doing something is to ask. This usually means encouraging the student to work through a task slowly while verbalizing each step. Sometimes asking a young student to teach you how to do the task will accomplish the same thing. When compared with the elaborate alternatives about to be explained, this technique makes good evaluative, and common, sense (Elliott, 1986).

Error Analysis. Incorrect procedures will eventually lead to incorrect products and patterns in these incorrect products may reveal the flawed processes that produced them. This is known as *error analysis* or *rule assessment* (Siegler, 1983). The idea that error analysis can be used to determine what to teach is common in most basic skills, including reading, where it is sometimes called "miscue analysis." The diagonal item pattern illustrated in Figure 5.2 is one device to help teachers recognize error types because it groups similar problems, allowing for the easier recognition of patterns. Little information is obtained by simply reporting the number of errors a student makes. The knowledge that "Jenny got five wrong" is not particularly valuable. However, hearing that "Jenny made five multiplication errors and they all involved × 8" could lead a teacher to think that she should teach Jenny her 8's.

Errors come in all shapes and sizes. The WISC-R (Wechsler Intelligence Scale for Children–Revised) asks the question, "Why is cotton often used in making cloth?" Invariably students say "because it's soft," which isn't correct, so they get 0 points. When one of the authors recently asked a kid that question, he responded with his own question, "Well, cotton is softer than a brick, and you wouldn't want to sleep with your head on a brick, would you?" That answer is also worth 0 points on the WISC-R, but it's hardly the same as "because it's soft." If you want to do error analysis, you have to make certain assumptions. Let's take a moment to discuss each of them.

Errors Are Not Just the Opposite of Corrects. In education we have a tendency to sort things into two piles: rights and wrongs. We assume that there is only one "right" and that everything else is equally wrong. We don't go in for the idea that something might be kind of right or sort of wrong. But that's the way the world really is—and an error is often not just the opposite of a correct. Here are three reasons why:

1. There's more than one way to be right and more than one way to be wrong.
2. The answer you get depends on the question you ask.
3. Nothing happens by accident.

Let's elaborate on these three reasons.

1. "There's more than one way to be right and more than one way to be wrong." Here is one problem with three answers:

a. $\begin{array}{r} 16 \\ + 5 \\ \hline 21 \end{array}$ b. $\begin{array}{r} 16 \\ + 5 \\ \hline 80 \end{array}$ c. $\begin{array}{r} 16 \\ + 5 \\ \hline 111 \end{array}$

Answers b and c are both errors, but they aren't the same errors. Error b appears to be a wrong operation error (the kid multiplied instead of adding),

and c seems to be a place-value procedural error. When a student makes a mistake, there is information in the error. There is different information in error b than in error c, so it would be a gross oversimplification to report them both as simply "two wrong problems, or − 2." In fact, if they are truly different behaviors, they can't even be added together; to do so would be something like reporting a conviction for jaywalking and one for child abuse as just "two convictions." There are many error responses, and some of them are the result of incorrect procedures. When the errors are viewed carefully, the incorrect procedures from which they result can be recognized and corrected.

2. "The answer you get depends on the question you ask." There is a popular statement attributed to Piaget, which says, "A child never answers his own question wrong." This means that what you think is an error was arrived at by the kid using a process he or she thought was right. Error b (16 + 5 = 80) is a good example. You asked the kid to add, but she multiplied; who's wrong? You think she is wrong because you think you're in charge (haven't you learned by now?). 80 is the *correct* answer to the problem the kid did. You can make it easier to decide what to teach by looking for problems to match students' answers.

3. "Nothing happens by accident." This is probably the hardest of the three ideas to buy. Basically it is the idea that student responses come about through probability. Something causes the answer a student gives to be more acceptable to that student than any other answer. In example c the student responded "111." Why not "10.78?" Why not "1?" Why not "− 47"? Something made the answer "111" seem better than any other answer, so that was the answer the kid gave. By looking for the factors that make the student think one answer is better (or worse) than another, you may find what to teach. You may also find out a few things about how to teach. For instance, some day when a student has just made an error, ask him "Is that the right answer?" Once when we asked that question, the answer was, "No, but I figured you wanted something, so I put down my address." The student's response made it obvious that we had stressed "answering" too much and following the

proper strategy too little. The first assumption is that errors are more than the other side of corrects. Here is a second assumption that is critical to error analysis.

Some Errors Occur in Recognizable and Correctable Patterns. We say *some* errors because while errors aren't truly random, neither are they always predictable. In the example above, the student made a "computational error" when he supplied his address as the answer to a problem. In this case, the error was not random, but it also certainly wasn't predictable. That's because the error response reflected some computation, some student personality, and some misplaced teacher emphasis. Each of those three factors led to the error. As the proportion of computation decreased, so did the ability to predict the error.

If we think that students try to solve problems by using a problem-solving method and if the method they use is wrong, the resulting error reflects that method. These inappropriate methods have been referred to as "failure strategies" (Roberts, 1968) because their use leads to errors. We can recognize these failure strategies and change them into success strategies. The primary source of data that we can use here is the student's error behavior. By observing errors, we can detect patterns that reveal the inappropriate strategies (Ashlock, 1982; Engelhardt, 1977; Enright, 1983; Siegler, 1983).

To find patterns in errors, you must have errors. Some students won't want to make errors so they will omit responses to questionable problems. Others will self-correct and erase information of potential value (removing the erasers from all pencils is a good first step for evaluators). Omissions and erasures can't be analyzed unless you feel comfortable analyzing nothing.[1] An accepting attitude will promote more behavior for you to analyze, so don't do things to discourage the student. And while you're being accepting, don't be teaching. Testing is not teaching. You may do things in the name of assess-

ment you would not do when instructing. For example, in testing you may let responses (correct or error) go by without reinforcing them by commenting on their accuracy.

The most important thing you can do to facilitate error analysis is to be thorough. Remember, you are trying to recognize patterns. Because patterns are made of interrelated data points, the more data you have, the better prepared you'll be to find the pattern. Use every response of the student, not just the answer given. If the student works this problem:

$$
\begin{array}{r}
{\small|} \\
17 \\
+\ 26 \\
\hline
\mathbf{43}
\end{array}
$$

the "1" carried to the tens place is as important as the answer "43."

You should list all responses and have the student do several problems. Because several examples are necessary to recognize any pattern, tests designed for error analysis must provide ample opportunities for error behavior. It is almost impossible to recognize patterns without seeing them occur more than once. This error sample is from Ashlock's (1982) book on error patterns (page 22). What is the pattern?

$$
\begin{array}{r}
46 \\
+\ 3 \\
\hline
13
\end{array}
$$

At first it appears that the student has done the wrong operation and subtracted 3 from 6 and 3 from 4 to get the answer "13." But now look at two other examples of the same failure strategy:

$$
\begin{array}{r}
8 \\
+\ 16 \\
\hline
15
\end{array}
\qquad
\begin{array}{r}
74 \\
+\ 5 \\
\hline
16
\end{array}
$$

What do you think the pattern is now? The wrong operation hypothesis doesn't fit for all of the problems. The additional examples make it clear that the student is not using place value when adding. He is adding all the digits together as if he were doing column addition (the task strategy that worked on all problems until this type.)

---

1. Many tests encourage you to record omissions as errors. This is not a good procedure because any number of factors may cause a student to omit an answer. Therefore, an analysis of omissions cannot be exact enough to lead to a useful conclusion.

One disadvantage of error analysis is that some errors won't occur if you don't happen to promote them. A student who has trouble spelling words with double consonants won't ever demonstrate that problem if you don't put double-consonant words on the spelling test. Similarly, a student who doesn't use past tense could speak correctly throughout an entire evaluation conducted in the present tense.

Strategy-Based Items. Test items can be designed to sample the student's use of the process rather than the construction of a product. In Figure 5.2 notice that while the objective of the test is two-place subtraction with borrowing, some items (labeled "non-instances") do not require borrowing. This is to test the student's skill at deciding what to do as well as skill at doing it. Deciding what to do is one step in all problem-solving exercises; therefore it is considered to be part of a general strategy.

Have you ever had a student borrow when it wasn't necessary, or convert a vowel to the long or short sound without reason, or raise a hand for permission to speak when the situation was too informal? Those students knew what to do—but they didn't know when to do it. The inclusion of non-instances (items of a different type than the type being tested) on tests allows the evaluator to know when students do not have the discrimination strategies needed for deciding when to do something. This is one example of testing strategy usage directly.

Another procedure for testing strategy use is to supply items that require the student to show how he or she would work the task. Several of these items are shown in Figure 5.5; notice that they test the student's knowledge of the process for finding answers and do not even ask the student what the answers are.

COLLECT RATE DATA

Solution
Decide which skills need to be carried out fluently. Use test formats that allow students to work at functional speeds. Collect rate data.

Explanation

Rate
Time is an important concept for educators. How much time it takes to learn something is often used to determine how difficult it is to learn, just as how long something is remembered and how quickly it can be completed indicates how well it has been learned.

Rate is performance divided by time. It is how quickly we use the strategies that combine the subtasks to assemble appropriate behaviors. Rate has functional implications. If two firefighters both put on their uniforms with 100% accuracy, but one does it in one minute and the other does it in ten minutes, which one do you want working in your neighborhood? And rate also seems related to generalization in that it is hard to assemble tasks into a more complex responses if you are slow at all the pieces. If we encouraged our students to disregard any of the other dimensions (like height or width), they would leave school and walk into walls. Similarly, students who are not prepared to work within certain time constraints will not be able to function in the real world. Slower workers are thought to be less proficient workers—and it's true because rate is a proficiency dimension just like accuracy.

But most importantly, rate is related to automaticity. Everything we do without awareness we are doing automatically. Automaticity is the level of task performance above which doing the task does not require the use of working (short-term) memory. We drive cars automatically. If we had to use our awareness pushing in gas pedals and sounding out words, our thoughts would be so filled with minutia that our thinking would become paralyzed. Rate is absolutely important for the recognition of competency—but it is routinely ignored by test authors.

A timed test is not a rate test. Timing is typically added to tests so that administration will be uniform; as a result reliability will be inflated. But the data derived from timed tests are still accuracy data. A rate test yields rate data by timing the student's response to a single item or series of items. The count (number of items completed) is then divided by the time (traditionally in minutes) to ob-

5. There are 40 students. 25% of the students have blue eyes. How many have blue eyes?

a.
```
  40
+.25
____
```

b.
```
.25 )‾40‾
```

c.
```
  40
-.25
____
```

d.
```
  40
×.25
____
```

6. Colleen has 2 crayfish and Gary has 4 crayfish for the science project. On Tuesday, Albert brings them three more. On Wednesday, Robin brings them 5. How many crayfish do they have?

a.
```
 2   6
+4  +5
__  __
```

b.
```
 4   8
×2  ×5    3 )‾40‾
__  __
```

c.
```
 4   6
+2  -5
__  __
```

d.
```
 2   6   9
+4  +3  +5
__  __  __
```

7. There are 40 desks in the 4th grade classroom. 2 desks are loaned to the 3rd grade classroom, 5 desks are loaned to the 6th grade classroom. How many desks are left in the 4th grade classroom?

a.
```
 40   38
 -2   -5
___  ___
```

b.
```
 40   42
 +2   +5
___  ___
```

c.
```
 40   36   34   29   24
 -4   -2   -3   -5   -6
___  ___  ___  ___  ___
```

d.
```
 40   36   33
 -4   -3   -6
___  ___  ___
```

8. There are 4 packages of pencils. Each package contains 5 pencils. There are 8 students, and three are boys. The pencils are to be divided equally among the girls. How many pencils will each girl get?

a.
```
  4    8
 ×5   ×3    20 )‾24‾
___  ___
```

b.
```
  4    8
 ×5   -3    5 )‾20‾
___  ___
```

c.
```
  5    8
 -4   +3    1 )‾11‾
___  ___
```

d.
```
  5
 ×4    8 )‾20‾
___
```

9. There are 30 pairs of scissors in the box. 10 are broken. Fifteen new pairs are given to the class. There are 5 art tables in the room. How many pairs of scissors that are not broken will each table get?

a.
```
 15    30    5
-10   +15  +45    5 )‾50‾
___   ___  ___
```

b.
```
 30
+10    5 )‾40‾
___
```

c.
```
 30    20    35
-10   +15    ×5
___   ___   ___
```

d.
```
 30    20
-10   +15    5 )‾35‾
___   ___
```

10. 2% of the students were absent on Tuesday. 20% of those present brought a sack lunch and 75% of those present bought a hot lunch. The rest of the students fixed a lunch in their classroom. What percent of the students in school fixed a lunch in their classroom?

a.
```
  20%    100%
 +75%   - 95%
_____   _____
```

b.
```
   2%
  20%    100%
 +75%   - 97%
_____   _____
```

c.
```
  .20    .20
 ×.02   ×.75    .040 )‾.1500‾
_____   _____
```

d.
```
  75%    100%
 ×20%   - 15%
_____   _____
```

FIGURE 5.5

Test of mathematics strategies *(Source:* From K. W. Howell, S. H. Zucker, & M. K. Morehead, *Multilevel Academic Skills Inventory: Math, Survey/Placement Booklet.* San Antonio, TX: The Psychological Corporation, 1982. Reprinted with permission.)

tain the rate. If one item is finished in 15 seconds then the rate is $1 \div 0.25 = 4$ per minute. If 80 items are completed in 5 minutes, the rate is $80 \div 5 = 16$ per minute.

Rate could be used to develop norms for classification purposes but it seldom is. More often rate is used to illustrate proficiency on a single skill; as a result it is used almost exclusively for CRTs. The design of rated tests will be presented in chapter 8, which covers specific-level assessment.

If we still haven't convinced you that rate is important try to remember the last time everyone else in class finished a test while you were only halfway through. And if *that* doesn't do it, consider this story. A parent came in to a special education classroom we know of and complained, "Why are you always testing my child with stop watches and telling him to work faster?" The teacher, Linda Levett, looked at the parent a moment and replied, "Do you remember why your child is in this class? He's a slow learner—and the cure for slow is fast."

Because so few tests are designed for collecting rate data or for use in continuous monitoring (which requires giving the same test over and over again), some of us have never seen a rate-formatted test. However, rate data and continuous monitoring are very important when curriculum-based evaluation is employed. Figure 5.6 shows a rate-formatted test and its objective. Notice that there is adequate space to write the answers and that, while the items are organized diagonally by multipliers, they are randomized by difficulty.

A BRIEF REVIEW/PREVIEW

The major quality issue in educational evaluation is curriculum match. If a test does not match the curriculum, it will be insensitive to instruction. Ten recommendations for educational testing are being discussed.

So far we have reviewed these seven:

1. Ease of use
2. Clarity of purpose
3. Definition of content and behavior
4. Items cross-referenced to objectives
5. Objectives standardization
6. Strategy assessment
7. Rate

These recommendations relate primarily to the definition of *what* is being evaluated. Unless the purpose, content, behavior, referencing, standardization, and implications for instruction are clear, test results really aren't worth much and a critic can legitimately wonder if different scores represent different degrees of learning.

A second group of recommendations dealing with fidelity also affects the match between curriculum and the tests/observations designed to assess it. Fidelity is associated more with the way something is tested than with the thing being tested itself (Swezey, 1981). A test is said to have high fidelity if it measures the concept/skill in question with procedures that are similar to the way the concept/skill is naturally used or taught. This point is obvious to anyone; as a result the remaining recommendations will not be covered in great depth. These are:

8. Adequate sampling
9. Appropriate formats
10. Appropriate scoring

COLLECT AN ADEQUATE SAMPLE

Solution
Decide how consolidated the content is. Write enough items (usually 10) for each strategic element of highly consolidated content or for each instance of unconsolidated content. Avoid ceiling effects.

Explanation

Consolidated Domains Revisited
Many tests have a student work only one or two items per objective or domain. This leaves the eval-

Multiplication Objective 1:

Write answers to multiplication facts (0-10).
Mastery criterion: 80 digits correct with zero errors in one minute.

1×6	5×8	8×9	2×2	4×7	0×3	1×1	7×0	4×3	3×7	9×8	5×6	7×7
8×10	3×6	6×8	9×9	7×2	6×7	2×3	4×1	6×4	5×0	8×5	9×10	2×10
3×5	1×10	4×6	7×8	3×9	6×2	5×7	9×3	6×1	5×0	3×4	5×5	3×5
4×4	7×5	0×10	6×6	2×8	6×9	9×2	8×7	7×3	9×3	4×0	9×4	4×4
6×0	5×4	6×5	5×10	7×6	3×8	1×9	5×2	2×7	8×3	9×1	1×0	0×0
2×1	3×0	7×4	9×5	7×10	9×6	8×8	4×9	4×2	7×6	1×7	5×3	3×1

FIGURE 5.6
Rate formatted test (*Source:* From K. W. Howell, S. H. Zucker, & M. K. Morehead, *Multilevel Academic Skills Inventory: Math Manual*, p. 190. San Antonio, TX: The Psychological Corporation, 1982. Reprinted with permission.)

uator with too limited a sample of the student's behavior to allow interpretation. While it is not possible to set an optimal number of items for all objectives, some guidelines are available.

In general, fewer items are needed when the domain being sampled is fairly consolidated and transfer is expected between items. Remember that a curriculum domain is said to be consolidated if it is tied together by a common set of strategies (or rules) that can be successfully applied to most instances within the domain. If a large number of examples can be dealt with reliably by a smaller number of strategic steps, the domain is consolidated. The more instances per strategic step, the more consolidated the material. Phonics is a good example of a consolidated domain. An almost infinite number of phonetically regular words can be written and decoded by using a small (about 40) set of fairly reliable phonetic units. In contrast, the irregular portions of words require a different rule for decoding each instance (word); therefore they do not represent a consolidated body of curriculum. This means that when a student decodes a few regular words the evaluator can assume that he or she can decode the many others not found on the test. However, decoding a few irregular words tells very little about the way a student will read words not found on the test.

Strategies Revisited

The secret to determining item number is to match items to strategic steps. Stated differently, it is better to test the steps of a process adequately than the products derived from the process. Because it is typically recommended that 10 items be written for each element, a test of phonetic decoding would have 10 items for each phonetic rule—not 10 items for each word the rules could produce.

Rate Revisited

When tests are used to collect rate data, students are often told to skip items which they do not know so that their rate of response will not become distorted. For example, suppose a student were reading a selection in which the one word he did not know occurred 10 words into the passage. The student might read the passage at a rate of 100 wpm up to the 10th word and then stare at it for the rest of the allowed time. His rate would then seem to be 10 words per minute rather than the more representative 100 wpm. To avoid this problem, an adequate number of items is provided to allow skipping (usually 50% more than the criterion).

Repeated Measures

If a test is to be used for repeated administrations, enough items must be provided to avoid ceiling effects and prevent rote memorization of the test. Ceiling effects occur when there aren't enough items to allow improvement. If a test has only one item per objective and a student gets it right the first time he or she takes the test, he or she can't do any better no matter how much more is learned about the objective (unless the time required to do the item is recorded—in that case decreases in time can be seen as improvement).

Tests with only a few items may also be memorized after several sessions. Once one of the authors was giving a popular short-form achievement test to some students in a correctional institution. When he paused too long between spelling words, one of the kids in the group supplied the next word —and the exact sample sentence in the manual— from memory.

USE APPROPRIATE FORMATS

Solution

Examine the context to which the results will be generalized and be sure the items match that context. Also consider the proficiency dimension. Decide if rate is called for, or if the test will be used for repeated measures.

Explanation

Fidelity

Occasionally, there is a disparity between the behavior required on a test and the behavior expected of the child in the classroom. We can best describe this with a hypothetical case. Billy was a third grader who, after taking a norm-referenced achievement test, scored at the 3.6 level in spelling. At first glance, there was nothing unusual about this, except that Billy had failed every spelling test given by the teacher that year. Every Friday he brought home an F on his spelling paper. When his parents heard about his achievement scores, they were dumbfounded at first, then angry. They complained to the principal that Billy's teacher wasn't motivating him in school and that was why he wasn't "working up to his potential." His teacher's confusion and frustration were evidenced by contradictory remarks that Billy was both lazy (in class) and lucky (on the test).

Who was right? Billy's parents or his teacher? In this case, neither. Billy's teacher was doing everything he knew how to motivate Billy in school. So it wasn't his fault. But neither was it Billy's. In fact, Billy should have gotten a medal for persevering in the face of failure. However, his teacher was right about his being lucky on the test. You see, the behavior expected of Billy on the spelling section of the achievement test was different from the behavior expected of him on his Friday quizzes. As part of the achievement test, Billy was given a page with rows of words on it. In each row were four words, one of which was the correct spelling of a word dictated to him. The teacher said, "In the first row, underline the correct spelling of the word *enough*." Billy looked at each of the four words in the row and underlined one of them. The same procedure was used for the other items on the page. Sometimes Billy actually recognized the correct word and sometimes he just guessed. Since there was always a 25% chance of guessing the correct answer on this test, it was conceivable that Billy's high score in spelling was as much a result of guessing skill as spelling skill.

The test behavior was in marked contrast to the behavior expected of Billy on Friday's quiz, when his teacher dictated a word and he had to write it from memory. Needless to say, this disparity caused a great deal of confusion, not to mention friction, between school and home, with the child caught in the middle. The confusion is the result of poor curriculum—test match induced by the low fidelity format of the achievement test.

Format. Obviously item presentations should not be so cluttered and confusing that students cannot understand them, but many tests have kids demonstrate knowledge in ways that differ from the ways that knowledge is typically used. This means that relevant content is presented in an irrelevant fashion on the test. This is often done because the test writer is attempting to fit too much material into a small space or is attempting to make a test that can be given to large numbers of students at the same time and that can be machine scored. Obviously item presentations should not be so cluttered and confusing that students cannot understand them.

Remember that a test is composed of items sampled from a curriculum domain. The result of a student's work on the test is supposed to generalize to that domain and to facilitate decision making within the domain. A student who scores well on a math test is thought to be able to do well in math because the high math test score is generalized to the math curriculum. To assure appropriate generalizations, appropriate formats must be used. However, this gets to be a problem in those cases (and there are many of them) where classroom formats differ from real world formats. As an example, consider the two tests shown in Figure 5.7.

The items in test A are all vertical; the largest number in each addition problem appears at the top, and the problems are grouped by operation. Test B, in comparison, presents the same content in vertical and horizontal formats, some larger numbers at the bottom of addition problems, and the two operations are scrambled. Unquestionably, some students who can pass test A will fail test B. Which format is best?

The format of test A is typical of most classroom worksheets and would generalize to most classrooms. However, test B is clearly the better representation of math as it is found outside the classroom. Students who score high on B probably will have less trouble in the everyday use of addition and subtraction than students who can score high

Test A				Test B			
2 +2	8 +6	9 +3	7 + 2	2 + 2 = 8 − 6 =		7 −3	6 +8
8 −6	7 −3	4 −1	5 −2	3 +9	4 −1	5 − 2 = 7 + 2 =	

FIGURE 5.7
Test formats

only on *A*. Test *B* provides better information about everyday use of math than test *A* simply as a function of its format. Another unfortunate aspect of this example is that students who spend much of their time working practice sheets in the test *A* format are likely to fail test *B* because the different format will devastate them. However, unlike the spelling example given earlier, this would *not* be a case of poor *curriculum–test* match; it would be a case of poor *instruction–test* match. Care must also be taken to avoid writing items that match the format of a particular teacher or published program. Formats should be primarily derived from the format constraints of the curriculum, not the instruction used to deliver the curriculum.

Response Domains. Probably the most common format irregularity involves response domains. Many tests adopt an identify (multiple-choice) rather than a produce (complete or fill-in-the-blank) format. Identify formats, like the spelling example, are popular because they make it easier to

give and score large numbers of tests. Unfortunately, the world is not multiple choice. Figure 5.8 shows three formats for testing the same content. These three formats are not equally informative.

USE APPROPRIATE SCORING PROCEDURES

Solution
Use measurement rules that assign points to the smallest educationally relevant unit.

Explanation

Summarizing Behavior
Tests are used to collect samples of student behavior to evaluate a behavior. During the act of evaluation, the student's behavior (where he is now) is compared to a standard (where we want him to be)

FIGURE 5.8
Response domains

1. "Read this word."	"cat"
2. "Circle the word cat."	mat fat (cat) rat
3. "Match the word to the picture."	rat cat —————— sat

and any discrepancy is noted. If the student is not where we want him to be, that information is used to plan instruction.

To facilitate the comparison of the student's behavior to a standard, both the standard and the behavior must be reported in a common language. Usually this language is numerical; both the criterion and student behavior are stated in the form of desired and obtained scores. The discrepancies (if any) between the two are also reported as scores. The direction and significance of a discrepancy leads us to make educational decisions.

There are a lot of tests and measurement procedures available, and they are not all equally important. Therefore, all discrepancies are not necessarily deserving of our attention. Part of teaching is deciding which things deserve our attention and which do not. Information obtained from the comparison of behavior samples and standards must be combined with our judgment about the significance of the discrepancies we discover. From this combination we arrive at decisions—and complete the evaluation process.

"Measurement" is a crucial part of evaluation. As presented in chapter 4, measurement is the assignment of numerals to objects or events according to rules. These measurement rules guide our assignment of numerical values to student behaviors.

Sensitivity to Learning

If the purpose of the evaluation is to guide instruction and facilitate learning, the results of the evaluation must be sensitive to learning. This means measurement rules must be established that will lead to the "best scores." Remember that our purpose for evaluating is to affect educational decision making; therefore the best scores are those which reflect the curriculum and the student's learning of it: These are the things about which our decisions are made. Because learning is operationally defined as behavior change, the measurement rules that result in scores that are sensitive to changes in behavior are the best rules to use. This sensitivity is usually obtained by assigning a number to *the smallest educationally meaningful unit of behavior* on the test. Let's illustrate this point by returning to an example we used back in chapter 4.

Problem		Addition Operations
A.	4 +3 —— 7 = 1 pt.	4 + 3 =
B.	473 ±216 —— 689 = 1 pt.	3 + 6 = 7 + 1 = 4 + 2 =

FIGURE 5.9

During scoring, most tests use the measurement rule "1 point for each problem correct." Using this rule, a student who gets the two problems in Figure 5.9 correct gets 2 points. A student who gets them wrong misses 2 points. However, as seen in Figure 5.9, problem B has three times as many addition operations as problem A. The rule of 1 point for each problem is not as sensitive to learning as a rule that would assign 1 point for each addition operation. That rule would make problem A worth 1 point and problem B worth 3 points. This system is more sensitive to addition learning because it reflects smaller changes in addition behavior. For example, in Figure 5.10 we see the behavior and the pre- and postinstruction addition scores of a student using both measurement rules. While doing problem B on the posttest the student has failed to correctly add 4 + 2, but has added 3 + 6 and 7 + 1. Because of the 4 + 2 error, the student's postinstruction score under the problem rule remains the same as the preinstruction score, indicating *no learning.* The operation rule is more sensitive to learning.

Most tests use a one problem-1 point measurement rule and are insensitive as a result. (A student who is asked to spell *cookies* and misspells it "koukeys" on the pretest and "cookeys" on the posttest doesn't appear to have improved in spelling if the problem rule is used.) A lot of teachers have been frustrated and confused to find that students who seem to have learned a lot do not score higher on tests—because the tests space items far apart in the curriculum and use measurement rules that are insensitive to learning.

FIGURE 5.10

PREINSTRUCTION

Total Score

A	B
4	473
+3	+216
7	798

	A	B	Total Score
Problem Rule	+1	0	1
Operation Rule	+1	0	1

POSTINSTRUCTION

Total Score

A	B
4	473
+3	+216
7	589

	A	B	Total Score
Problem Rule	+1	0	1
Operation Rule	+1	+2	3

SUMMARY

This chapter has pointed out problems with existing behavior samples and elaborated on 10 recommendations for writing good tests. It is particularly important to assure that tests are adequately sensitive to student strategies and that they reflect meaningful conditions and criteria. As you will see in the following chapters, it is not possible to arrive at certain conclusions, or to make certain treatment recommendations, without adequate behavior samples.

Study Questions

1. Define the following words as they are used in this text. Some of these terms may be review from previous chapters.
   a. Curriculum alignment
   b. Content
   c. Domain
   d. Response domain
   e. Proficiency
   f. CAP
   g. Consolidated domain
   h. Error analysis
   i. Strategy
2. If you wish to make treatment decisions, you should select a test
   a. that samples global knowledge domains.
   b. that shows a high degree of test-curriculum match.
   c. that the publisher says is criterion-referenced.
   d. that tests at least five objectives.

3. You have been told that one of your students has "passed" vowel sounds because he was able to correctly point to the word containing the vowel sound the evaluator pronounced. About what should you be concerned?
   a. Whether vowel sounds are a reasonable area of control to study
   b. Whether the response format was appropriate
   c. Whether the proficiency level was appropriate
   d. b and c

4. You have found or written a test that has good content validity and requires an appropriate response format. However, you do not have adequate criteria or standards. What are three things you could do?
   a.
   b.
   c.

5. Examining strategic behaviors allows us to look at
   a. the process by which the student arrives at the answer.
   b. the subtask the student is missing.
   c. the rate at which the student can perform the task.
   d. none of the above.

6. What are three things that you could do to evaluate a student's strategy usage?
   a.
   b.
   c.

7. A student who can do something quickly and accurately is better off than a student who can do something slowly and accurately because
   a. rate is important for developing automaticity.
   b. rate indicates appropriate strategy usage.
   c. the rate at which something is done is important in the real world.
   d. a and c.

8. Teachers often differ greatly in terms of the CAPs they require. What impact could this have on students' educations?

Chapter 6

Making Treatment Recommendations

Chapter 6 is meant to be a bridge between the background and application parts of this book. A person with adequate background who is only interested in the applied material could start the book right here. However, someone not familiar with the concepts and terminology outlined in the previous chapters would probably have difficulty proceeding.

This chapter will be followed by two others (cleverly numbered 7 and 8) that explain the nuts and bolts of test/observation construction and administration. Following those chapters there will be a series of chapters each covering a specific content area such as computation or language. This chapter elaborates on the evaluative process and on educational decision making. Because some educational decisions require the analysis of formative data (data collected over a period of time), a complete discussion of formative evaluation will be presented in chapter 15. The goal of this chapter is to link the foundation arranged in the first of the book to the procedures described in the specific content chapters to follow.

WHERE RECOMMENDATIONS COME FROM

To make a recommendation based on an evaluation you have to conduct an evaluation first. This means taking a sample of student behavior and comparing it to a standard. Assume you've done that with appropriately valid tests/observations and noted the direction and magnitude of any discrepancies. Now what?

Now you get to make decisions.

The next few pages review and link the major types of decisions, and kinds of data, that evaluators combine to make recommendations. The decisions themselves are listed in Table 6.1.

TYPES OF DECISIONS

As shown in Table 6.1, there are two broad categories of treatment decisions: what to teach and how

to teach. Within each category there are more specific decisions, numbered in the table. For instance, how-to-teach decision 2.2.c is "Use generalization procedures."

What-to-Teach Decisions

The first thing a teacher needs to do is decide what to teach the student. This means conducting an evaluation to find out (a) what the student needs to know and (b) which of the things the student needs to know he or she is prepared to learn. In the task-analytic (curriculum-based) model the evaluation begins by finding a task the student can't do and checking skill on the subtask and strategy components of this task. After the evaluator checks a subskill or strategy, he or she makes one of the what-to-teach decisions in Table 6.1. In some cases the evaluator will then discontinue testing. If, however, the decision is that the student is inaccurate (decision 2.1) or not automatic (decision 2.3), additional testing is indicated. This is explained below.

No Instruction Required

This decision means that the student can do the objective accurately, quickly, and under real-world conditions. The decision is indicated by the student having met or exceeded the criterion for acceptable performance established for the skill. For the evaluator, this means the student is already adequately prepared to use this skill and that higher level (more complex) skills should be tested to find the appropriate instructional level. While active instruction is not required in this case, occasional review and monitoring is still a good idea.

Instruction Required

Build Accuracy. If a student makes errors, the evaluator will recommend instruction to build accuracy. This recommendation is also justified when a student seems to be accurate but is *very* slow (less than 25% of the expected rate criterion). Students who are extremely slow are often "inaccurate" though they don't display their errors. These students make errors, catch them, and correct them before making an overt response for the evaluator to grade. They may also avoid errors by skipping items or using functional but inefficient strategies (such as counting on their fingers or repeating the whole alphabet in sequence to recall a particular letter).

The evaluator who finds that a student is inaccurate at a task should check less complex skills (the

TABLE 6.1
Educational decisions

A. *What-to-Teach Decisions*
    A.1 No instruction required

    A.2 Instruction required
        A.2.1 Build accuracy
        A.2.2 Build fluency
        A.2.3 Build automaticity

B. *How-to-Teach Decisions*
    B.1 Curriculum decisions
        B.1.1 Stay with current level and/or context
        B.1.2 Change level
            B.1.2.a   Move to a more complex objective
            B.1.2.b* Move to a simpler objective (only when no corrects have occurred after several sessions)
            B.1.2.c   Adjust aim date
        B.1.3 Change context
            B.1.3.a   Teach the objective in context
            B.1.3.b* Teach the objective in isolation (only when tests of context knowledge are failed)

    B.2 Instructional decisions
        B.2.1 Stay with current format, incentive, and delivery
        B.2.2 Change format of instruction
            B.2.2.a   Use acquisition procedures
            B.2.2.b   Use fluency procedures
            B.2.2.c   Use generalization procedures
            B.2.2.d   Use maintenance procedures
        B.2.3 Change incentives
            B.2.3.a   Change type or schedule of consequences
            B.2.3.b   Provide meaning
        B.2.4 Change delivery of instruction
            B.2.4.a   Change how information is given
            B.2.4.b   Change length of lesson
            B.2.4.c   Change group size or composition
            B.2.4.d   Change use of questions
            B.2.4.e   Change pace of lesson
            B.2.4.f   Change feedback given
            B.2.4.g   Change materials used
            B.2.4.h   Change other high impact variables

*Employ these decisions only when others have failed.

subtasks) to find out what accounts for the current failure. When a point is reached at which the student is inaccurate at a task, but accurate and fluent at its subtasks, the evaluator stops testing and recommends instruction of the task and its strategy.

Build Fluency. Fluency building is indicated when the student is accurate but slow at the task. (Note the discussion of inaccuracy and rate in the last section.) How accurate a student has to be at something before moving into rate-building instruction is debatable, but when deciding to move to a higher level task, estimates range from 80 to 100% with most authors settling for something around 90% (Berliner, 1984; Rosenshine, 1983). The few authors who address the importance of rate set the boundary for shifting the emphasis of instruction on the same skill from accuracy to rate at closer to 80% (Liberty, Haring, & White, 1980; White, 1986).

The evaluator is trying to decide if the student is adequately skilled to use this task to complete other, more complex, tasks. He or she must also decide to continue or discontinue testing once a student is found to be accurate but slow. We believe that rate of correct responding is important to application, so we say that a student who is accurate but slow does need additional instruction. However, the fact that the student is accurate suggests that it is *not* necessary to test the subtasks of this particular skill. In those cases where rate on one task depends on some very basic tool skill, like writing digits or recalling sounds, checking those tool skills may be appropriate.

Build Automaticity. As you may recall from chapter 3, automaticity is the use of a skill in the context of distractions. Often the evaluator will find that students can succeed at a task when it is presented in isolation even though they cannot apply the same skill within other, more complex, tasks. For example, one student may be able to read vowel teams when presented by themselves on flash cards but be unable to use them in words. Another student may accurately work addition and subtraction fact

problems on worksheets but make errors on the same facts during long division.

There are three explanations for the failure to generalize the use of a task to a larger task: (1) inadequate skill (automaticity) on the task to be generalized, (2) inadequate knowledge of the other skills with which the task must be combined to perform larger tasks, or (3) uncertainty about how to do the larger task. To find out which of these applies (they could all apply), the evaluator must check each one. You check for lack of automaticity by examining the effect of realistic distractions on the student's accuracy and rate. Realistic distractions are those imposed by the context in which a skill will normally be used. For example, suppose you are testing a student's skill at driving a car. You could test this skill in an empty parking lot or on a freeway in the middle of high speed traffic. The freeway is a good test of automaticity at driving as it supplies realistic distractors. Testing a student's recall of history vocabulary in the middle of a freeway would not provide a good test of automaticity for vocabulary. The same distractors—speeding semi-trucks and occasional highway patrol cars—that provide realistic distractions for the driving test do not provide realistic distractions for historical vocabulary.

Other explanations for the failure to generalize a skill (inadequate skill on related tasks or lack of knowledge about the actual setting, or task, to which generalization is expected) can be checked the same way other failures are examined. The subtasks and strategies required for success are evaluated and those found to be inadequate are targeted for instruction.

How-to-Teach Decisions

How-to-teach decisions involve both the curriculum *and* instruction. These decisions cannot be made from a single testing session like the what-to-teach decisions just covered. To decide how to teach, one must collect data on two things: (1) the student's current skill performance and (2) how well the student is doing in instruction. The student's current performance can be determined by conducting the sort of task-analytic evaluation already described. However, to form an opinion about how well a student is progressing in a particular instructional treatment, the evaluator must find out how much the student's behavior is changing over time. This involves watching the student for a period of several days or questioning someone who has been working with the student. To be done well, you must use the various monitoring procedures described in chapter 15.

Curriculum Decisions

Curriculum decisions involve the selection of objectives or the context in which objectives will be delivered. Selecting an objective involves choosing the level of complexity at which a student will work. As has been pointed out numerous times by now, that level of complexity should not be too hard or too easy. Objectives are the same as tasks and the correct task is the one a student cannot do but is currently prepared to learn. A student will not be able to do a task if he or she is missing an essential component of that task.

Change Level. Because to some extent the curriculum can be viewed as a sequence of tasks, the decisions a person can make about it are to go ahead, stay, or go back. *Stepping ahead* to the next objective (1.2.a) is indicated when the student has reached criterion. *Staying* with the current objective (1.1) is indicated when adequate progress is being made but criterion has not been reached, or when inadequate progress is being made but the explanation seems to be ineffective instruction rather than a missing task component. *Stepping back* (1.2.b) to an easier objective is indicated when the student is making no progress and lots of errors.

A few points about stepping back merit elaboration. First, no one would have to recommend stepping back unless he or she had previously and erroneously recommended stepping ahead. Second, stepping back is the same as saying "The kid cannot learn this objective under *any available* instructional technique." Third, this is the most dangerous and most common decision teachers make. Stepping back is dangerous because going backwards is the worst way to get ahead. And, while information on teacher decisions is remarkably sparse, it appears that when a student isn't learning, special education teachers are more apt to recommend stepping back than anything else (M. A. Prater, personal communication, 1986). This may be partly due to an overzealous application of the task analytical model, which stresses subtasks as the source of task failure. Those who apply the task analytic model should know that looking for missing prerequisites is not the same as moving to easier objectives. The task analytic model does not suggest abandoning current objectives for easier ones, but rather teaching current objectives by presenting the prerequisite subskills and strategies on which they depend. If a teacher drops back to addition facts every time a kid runs into trouble with two-place problems, the kid is certain to end up (a) hating facts and (b) never working two-place problems. *Endless drilling on subskills will never teach more advanced skills.* Students need to be taught to combine subskills through the use of task strategies to carry out new tasks. Appropriate instruction focuses on the strategies for combining subskills, not on the subskills themselves.

Change Context. You may decide to teach a skill in *isolation* or by *embedding* it within a certain context. For example, some teachers may decide to teach vowel sounds in isolation on flash cards, while others may decide to teach them within the context of whole words. Isolation has the advantage of focusing all attention on the skill in question but it has the disadvantage of making the skill seem meaningless. Things are meaningful as a function of their context (lifeguards have more meaning by the pool than they do on a ski slope; reading skill has more meaning in the context of a library than it does in a game of soccer). It is safe to say that the more meaning a student perceives in a task the easier it will be for him or her to learn it. This is largely because meaning tends to motivate, activate the storage and retrieval mechanisms of memory, and promote early application of skills (Torgeson & Kail, 1980). These advantages justify an initial bias towards teaching all skills within a context that will make them appear meaningful. However, some tasks seem more "naturally" meaningful than others, probably because they are immediately useful or easily related to a variety of contexts.

Learning key phrases in a foreign language is a good example of a task best approached from a meaningful orientation. Learning your social security number is a good example of a relatively non-meaningful activity. The former may be more efficiently taught by using the setting in which the phrase will be used to provide context (e.g., learning how to order dinner by going to a French restaurant). The latter won't be any easier to learn in the social security office than it will be at home. Explaining the social security system and what it will supposedly do for you may raise your interest but will not provide clues to your particular number. Similarly, it may be more meaningful to teach computation in the context of scoring a basketball game or vowel sounds in the context of words.

There are, however, at least two situations where isolation "makes sense." In some cases students may lack the prior knowledge of the context needed to draw meaning from it. For example, a student who doesn't understand basketball wouldn't benefit from a lesson linked to the sport; a student who doesn't understand consonant sounds may not learn vowels surrounded by them. In these cases, which usually occur very early in a sequence of instruction, a teacher may wish to isolate a particular task element because its context only distracts or confuses the student. Similarly, there may be cases where students are so unskilled that they are unable to appreciate the context. In those cases intense isolated practice (drill) may be justified. Whenever a skill is taught in isolation, the teacher should take extra steps to make the exercise seem meaningful and to provide motivation until the skill can be gradually shifted from isolation into its functional context. This "external" approach to motivation may be handled through efforts to link the task to favorite activities, point systems, or other rewards.

Instructional Decisions

Change Format. Lessons fall into various types or formats regardless of the objectives they teach or the context used. These formats have been described under different names by a variety of authors (Haring & Eaton, 1978), but the labels *acquisition, fluency, generalization,* and *maintenance* seem most descriptive. *Acquisition* lessons teach the student to be accurate. They are designed to take a student through the novice phases of task performance. These initial lessons are characterized by elaborate explanations, extensive use of models, correction procedures that focus on accuracy and de-emphasize rate, and reinforcement for accurate performance. For example, suppose you have decided to teach a student "to display knowledge of punctuation by inserting necessary commas in a series or list. Accuracy CAP—100%." In your efforts to teach this skill to accuracy you will need to emphasize procedures for forming commas, the purpose of commas, steps for identifying a list, and how to check work. Some of these might be appropriate for one student but not for another. During acquisition, it is best to emphasize the strategies a student must apply to arrive at an answer—rather than the answer itself. For example, an acquisition strategy might address the steps to be followed when writing a list, or forming a comma, by asking the student to verbalize each step as it is carried out.

Fluency lessons take accurate students and provide them the intense drill and practice they need to add speed to the skills at which they have already become accurate. Fluency lessons are characterized by drill and practice, repetition, minimal teacher talk, heavy external reinforcement, and feedback without correction. (No correction is needed because the student is already accurate and errors are viewed as rate-induced.) *Generalization* lessons teach students to apply skills in a larger context. To teach strategies for problem-solving and synthesizing skills, they involve presentations of novel situations and an emphasis on self-management rather than teacher control. *Maintenance* plans do not involve any active teaching and are usually limited to periodic reviews and monitoring. Table 6.2 shows

TABLE 6.2
Instructional formats and learning outcomes

Format Type	Prerequisite	Lesson	Product
Acquisition	Knowledge of subskills and prerequisite strategies	Elaborate explanation and feedback on strategies for getting correct answers	Accurate behavior
Fluency	Accurate behavior	Drill, practice, and minimal correction to fade conscious use of strategies	Mastery behavior
Generalization	Mastery behavior	Novel context, self-management, and problem-solving strategies	Automatic behavior
Maintenance	Automatic behavior	Periodic review and monitoring	Retention of automatic behavior

the relationship of these instructional formats to various outcomes.

As you can imagine, placing a student who is inaccurate into a fluency format would be a mistake; it would allow the student to practice being inaccurate without any correction procedures. Similarly, an acquisition lesson plan would never allow an accurate student to become proficient; the student would receive constant explanations about how to do things he or she could already do (this may bore the student and actually produce *decreases* in performance).

Change Incentives. Changes in incentives are called for when otherwise sound instructional techniques don't seem to be working. They are particularly called for when a student's interest in a lesson begins to flag. While educators may still debate the application of certain behavior management techniques such as point systems and punishment, everyone recognizes that the presence of some sort of incentive influences student work (Kaplan, 1982). These debates often seem to center on the merits of so-called external and internal incentives. External incentives are those things tacked onto the target task such as points, contingency contracts, and non-task-specific reinforcers such as candy or

happy faces. Internal incentives are more naturally associated with the task itself and may include things like the satisfaction that comes with improvement on, or application of, newly learned skills.

When data indicate that a student is not improving, one explanation may be a lack of incentive to improve. This lack of incentive may be compensated for by tying improvement on the task to various external consequences. In these cases changes in the type and schedule of reinforcement make learning the task seem worthwhile to the student. Similar improvements in learning may be obtained without applying these so-called external consequences by changing the student's perception of the value of the task itself. This is usually done by making the task appear meaningful. This appearance of meaning is developed by showing the student how the target task fits into his or her world and relates to other tasks which the student already values. This is characteristically accomplished by teaching the target task in the context of more advanced tasks (as explained earlier).

Delivery Decisions. In the last decade research on teacher effectiveness has moved away from the examination of teachers and toward the examination

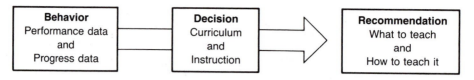

FIGURE 6.1
Systematic
interpretation

of teaching. This emphasis on teacher behavior has led to the recognition of certain teacher-controlled factors that clearly have impact on student learning (Bickel & Bickel, 1986; Brophy, 1983). These delivery factors—pace, group size, lesson length, feedback, use of demonstrations—determine how much students learn. They may be systematically altered to produce the most effective lesson for a particular student regardless of the task being taught, the format being used, and the incentive system being applied. Simply stated, an effective lesson is one that is delivered well. Delivery decisions relate to the quality of instruction and affect how much students learn. This means that regardless of the objective, the use of context or isolation, the selection of an acquisition, fluency, or generalization/maintenance format, teachers can still deliver lessons of varied effectiveness. Finding the right delivery for a particular student and being prepared to alter it when it loses effectiveness is what individualized instruction is all about.

SYSTEMATIC INTERPRETATION

As you recall, evaluation is a thoughtful process. It is during the final step of this process that an evaluator's most sophisticated thinking takes place. After testing/observation, the evaluator either takes the available information and converts it into interpretations or, if he or she doesn't feel adequately prepared to do that yet, sets it aside and continues testing/observation. The move to interpretation follows the sequence illustrated in Figure 6.1. In this sequence behavior summaries are collected, decisions made, and recommendations produced.

We believe that most evaluators can arrive at good functional treatment recommendations if they can confidently answer the six questions presented in Figure 6.2. Notice that we said you have to be able to answer these questions *confidently.* Among other things, this requires the recognition that some of the questions require the use of progress data.

Progress Data

The collection and analysis of progress data (sometimes called *formative* data) will be discussed in depth in chapter 15. The term *progress* was introduced early in the text; it refers to changes in behavior during instruction. Performance data, the kind collected by giving a test once, tell us where a student is on a skill at the time the test is given. Progress data, which are collected by monitoring a skill over a period of time, tell us how much the student's behavior is changing. Because instruction is designed to produce changes in behavior, progress data can tell us if instruction is effective. Consider

FIGURE 6.2

When the student is not learning, ask yourself:

1. Is the objective he or she is trying to learn the right one?
2. Would the task be better learned by isolating it or by presenting it in context?
3. Should I emphasize accuracy, fluency, or generalization?
4. Should I do something to make the lesson more interesting?
5. Should I modify the setting, materials, or instruction I am using?
6. Do I need more information to answer these questions?

this example. A teacher gives Elena and Alan a spelling test and they both get scores of 45. This means they are both performing at the same level. However, a week later when the teacher gives the test again, Alan only gets 50 while Elena gets 75. This means Elena is progressing faster than Alan. It also means that the instruction being used is more effective for Elena than it is for Alan. Information about progress (change) is needed to make certain instructional decisions.

Making Recommendations

Table 6.3 expands on the six questions in Figure 6.2. In the table each question is coded to the how-to-teach decisions originally presented in Table 6.1. The questions are also linked to treatment recommendations and to the type of data (performance or progress) that might indicate the selection of a recommendation. It would be best if you would read through the table now. It might seem better to have made this table into some sort of operations flowchart. However, we decided against a flowchart format because there is *not* a fixed sequence to these recommendations. Although we always recommend beginning by considering the target task (objective), you could start at any point in the table and arrive at an appropriate interpretation because many of the decisions are independent of each other. In fact, several of them may need to be employed at the same time.

The recommendations in Table 6.3 can be applied across all content areas and age groups. Therefore it makes sense to gather all of the information (both performance and progress) that you have and then to ask *each* of the six basic questions. The answers to all questions should then be considered prior to making a final treatment decision. These instructional recommendations are drawn from experience and literature dealing with delivery rather than evaluation. The rationale for many of them can be found in chapter 15. Because the topic of delivery is so large, these recommendations are necessarily general and require you to apply some effort and creativity to make them functional. The secret is to take each recommendation and think what it

means for the content and student with whom you are working.

Suppose you have a student in the 4th grade who decodes with 85% accuracy but *very slowly* (at less than 25% of the expected rate). In Table 6.3 that student would be a candidate for recommendation 2.2.a:

> Use extensive explanations, models, demonstration, guided practice with correction and feedback.

What does that mean? It means you need to show the student how to do the task. An educational psychology student who is very slow at giving IQ tests needs the same thing: demonstrations of test administration. As explained at the first of this chapter, a student who is extremely slow is probably so busy self-correcting or avoiding errors that production rate is suffering. The best instruction for that student is the kind that emphasizes strategies for arriving at correct answers. That is the kind described in recommendation 2.2.a.

Two final comments on the systematic interpretation guide in Table 6.3. First of all, lots of students fail to learn because their instruction fails to teach. For this reason decision E, "modify delivery," should always be the first one tried. The only reason we put it last was to maintain the chapter's structure. In many cases modifications in instructional plans will have been attempted before a student is referred for remedial/special education. If modifications in delivery haven't been attempted *and student progress adequately monitored*, it may be a waste of time to pursue other explanations for failure.

A second point about Table 6.3 is that its structure (the system itself) is *not* a model for learning. We aren't saying that there are students with "step-ahead deficits" or "deficient context-embedding mechanisms." The constructs, categories, and terms in the system are drawn from an analysis of what we do—not who we do it to. It is a system for organizing *our* work—not *their* minds. As such it makes more instructional sense than psychological sense.

TABLE 6.3
How-to-teach decisions

Questions	Decisions	Decisions*	Indicating Data†
Am I working on the correct objective?	B.1.1	Stay with current objective.	Student is not at aim, but *makes some correct responses.*
	B.1.2.a	Move to a more complex objective.	Student is at or above CAP.
	B.1.2.b**	Move back to an easier objective.	Student makes no correct responses and has *made no progress after several sessions.*
	B.1.2.c	Expect faster learning (move aim date forward).	Student is below CAP but *progress is greater than expected.*
Is the context appropriate?	B.1.3.a	Teach the skill in the context of larger tasks. Explain the relevance of the task. Make the lesson "applied." (Ex: Have them do subtraction in a checkbook.)	Student has the necessary background information to derive meaning from the context. (Ex: knows what a checkbook is, what it is used for, but is resisting lessons and seems bored.)
	B.1.3.b**	Teach the largest manageable unit of the objective in isolation. Use "rote" instruction. If student is accurate, employ fast-paced repetitive drill. Set daily performance aims and reinforce improvement. Put the skill in context as soon as possible.	Student is lacking the background necessary to use context, or is confused by context.
Is my instruction appropriate?	B.2.1	Stay with current format, incentive, and delivery.	Student is progressing toward aim as expected.
Should the emphasis be on accuracy, fluency, generalization, or maintenance?	B.2.2.a	Accuracy instruction. Use extensive explanations, models, demonstration, guided practice with correction and feedback. Little independent work.	Student is less than 83% accurate.
	B.2.2.b	Fluency instruction. Emphasize rate. Give extensive drill and practice with frequent timings. Make sure accuracy is maintained.	Student is above 83% accuracy, but is slow.
	B.2.2.c	Generalization instruction. Reduce extrinsic reinforcement,	Student is accurate, or accurate and fast.

TABLE 6.3
(Continued)

Questions	Decisions	Decisions*	Indicating Data[†]
		teach self-monitoring. Present the task in novel contexts; expect student to adjust responses to fit changes in the situation.	
	B.2.2.d	Maintenance instruction. Stop active instruction. Review periodically; monitor retention. Use skill in context of higher skills. Move to variable schedules of reinforcement.	Student is at or above aim.
Should the lesson be made to seem more interesting?	B.2.3.a	Change type or schedule of reinforcement. Use preferred activities or student-selected rewards. Consider increasing or decreasing the frequency of reinforcement. Change when reinforcement is delivered to make it more or less predictable. Change type of reinforcer.	*Was improving, but is getting worse,* or beginning to resist lessons.
	B.2.3.b	Provide meaning. Explain relevance of task. Work skills in the context of higher level skills. Begin and end lessons by explaining how the skill can be used. Allow students input into the kind of instruction they receive. Allow them to chart their own progress. Make lessons "applied."	
Should the delivery be modified?	B.2.4	Change setting, materials or delivery. - Questioning - Feedback - Pace - Explanations - Length of lessons - Size of group - Lesson sequence - Type of practice	Below aim, but seems to have prerequisite skills. *Is making inadequate progress in spite of appropriate objective, context, emphasis, and incentives.*

* Numbers correspond to Table 6.1.
[†] Indications requiring progress data are *italicized.*
**Employ 1.2.b and 1.3.b only as a last resort.

SUMMARY

While all steps in the evaluation process are important, interpretation represents the whole purpose of the activity. It makes little sense to test and compare without a framework for processing the results. This chapter is best summarized by reviewing Table 6.1, which supplies a framework for interpretation.

Study Questions

1. Define the following terms as they are used in this text. Some of these terms may be review from previous chapters.
   a. Formative evaluation
   b. Automatic
   c. Subtasks
   d. Strategy
   e. Fluency
   f. Accuracy
   g. Progress data
   h. Generalization
   i. Maintenance
   j. Acquisition
   k. Format
   l. Decisions
2. What should you always alter first if the student isn't learning?
   a. The level of difficulty
   b. The delivery of the lesson
   c. The incentive
   d. The format
3. You have a student who can complete a task accurately but slowly. What should be your emphasis?
   a. Building accuracy
   b. Building motivation
   c. Building automaticity
   d. Building fluency
4. Which of the following are reasons for failure to generalize?
   a. Uncertainty about how to do the larger task
   b. Inadequate skill on the other tasks with which the task is combined to perform the larger task
   c. Lack of automaticity on the task
   d. All of the above
5. Match the correct decision to the information given about the student
   a. Student has reached criterion.
   b. Student has not reached criterion, but progress is adequate.
   c. Student makes numerous errors; no progress.
   d. Task appears meaningless to student; poor motivation and memory.

   _____Change context
   _____Step back
   _____Step ahead
   _____Stay with current objective
6. What kinds of decisions can be made with progress data that can't be made with performance data?
   a. What-to-teach decisions
   b. Correct-level-of-difficulty decisions
   c. Curriculum decisions
   d. How-to-teach decisions
7. A thoughtful curriculum-based model of evaluation will generate recommendations primarily about which two elements in the learning interaction (student, task, instruction)? Why is this emphasis useful? What are the disadvantages of emphasizing the student?

Chapter 7

Survey-Level Testing

Chapter Outline

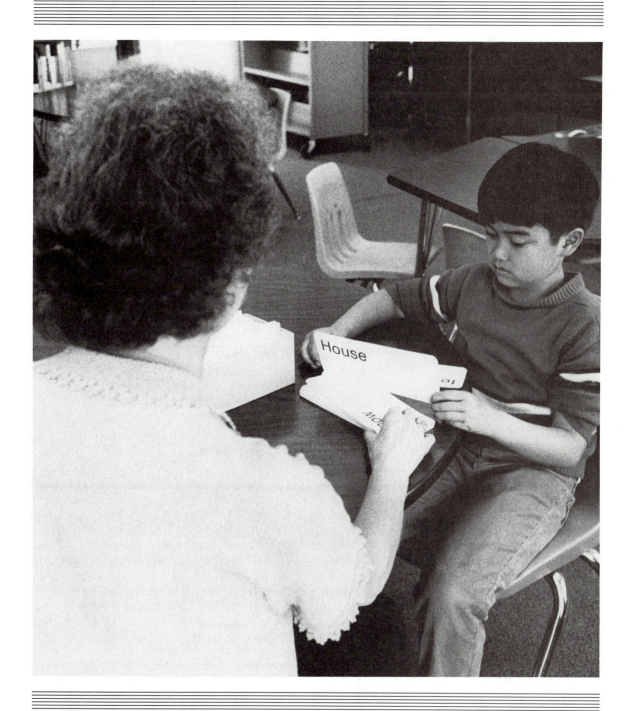

This chapter describes how and why to carry out the first two stages of the task-analytical model of evaluation. These stages follow directly from the format presented in chapter 2, and rereading pages 19–21 might be a good review. As you know, the purpose of the task-analytical model is to provide the evaluator with information regarding what students should be taught. The model includes four stages: fact finding, hypothesizing, validation, and decision making. The entire process is graphically displayed in Figure 7.1. Chapters 7 and 8 are organized in the same sequence as the flowchart for easy reference. These chapters do more than outline what needs to be done. They explain how and why to do it. Because one purpose of these explanations is to instruct you in the procedures and the rationale for them, the descriptions of each step are more complex than actually carrying them out.

THE FLOWCHART

In the flowchart (Figure 7.1), the student's status is represented by a circle, triangles are assessment decisions, and squares are things the evaluator may or may not have to do. There isn't anything in this flowchart that hasn't already been described, but each step will now be explained in order to consolidate the material. The task-analytical model includes two kinds of assessment: the survey level, conducted at the beginning of the cycle, and the specific level. Survey-level assessment relies most heavily on the use of interviews, class assignments, NRTs, achievement tests, and published materials. The purpose of the survey level is to get information from which explanations (assumed causes) for student failure may be generated. This is usually only done once. Specific-level assessment, which

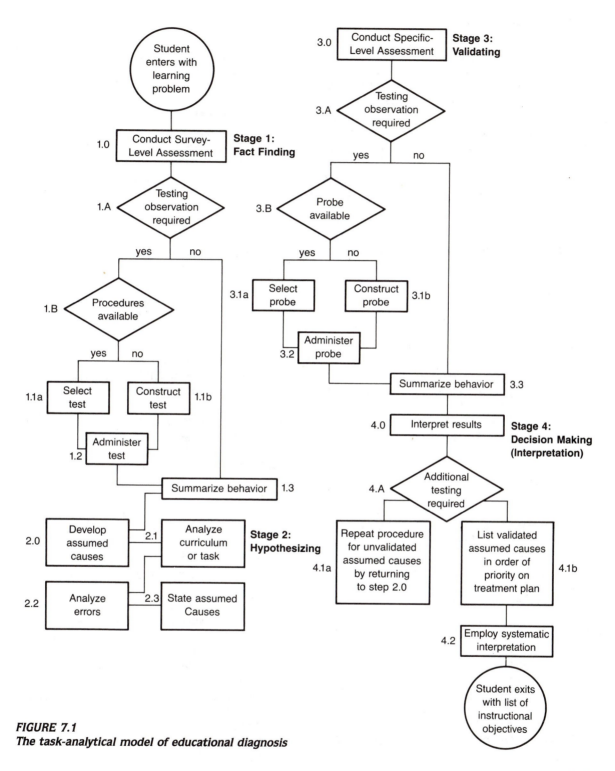

FIGURE 7.1
The task-analytical model of educational diagnosis

will be described thoroughly in chapter 8, is done to determine which, if any, of these explanations are valid. Specific-level probing may be repeated over and over to monitor student progress.

The competencies required of the classroom teacher to conduct survey-level assessment include (1) select published standardized tests, (2) construct teacher-made tests, (3) administer tests, (4) describe student behavior, and (5) make decisions.

1.0 CONDUCT SURVEY-LEVEL TESTING

These activities and decisions take place during the fact-finding stage of the evaluation. They are meant to give the evaluator a general idea about what the student can or can't do.

Question 1 A. Is survey testing/observation required?

Key Consideration: How much you already know.

Explanation: For the purpose of this presentation we will assume that you (the evaluator) have never seen the kid before and have only the most superficial referral to start working from. That's the most difficult situation for an evaluator to be in.

The decision to test/observe depends on your familiarity with the student. The less you know, the more you will need to find out and therefore the more you will need to test/observe. Survey-level assessment might just as accurately be called fishing. It is a process of casting around for hidden information.

Question 1B. Is a testing/observation procedure available?

Key Consideration: Coverage of problematic content.

Explanation: Any referral should at least state an area of concern. Usually these will be academic (e.g., reading, math, written communication) or social (e.g., peer relations, assertiveness, self-control). There are more test/observation procedures available for academics than for social behavior.

The main concern is that you adequately cover the area of the problem. To do this you may wish to use parts of several tests, modify existing tests by adding items, or simply interview other teachers who are more familiar with the student.

1.1a Select Test

This activity, along with *construct test* and *summarize behavior,* is found under both survey- and specific-level assessment but we will describe it here. As just stated, the idea is to select a test that covers curriculum in the area of concern.

While we did say that published standardized tests need not be used in survey-level assessment, we know from experience that many classroom teachers prefer their use over teacher-made instruments or simple classroom observation. For one thing, teachers (as well as the lay public) seem to have more faith in published material than in anything they could design themselves. They believe that the only good test is a copyrighted test. (After all, don't we always call published tests "formal" and teacher-made ones "informal.") Somehow they have gotten the idea that it is illegal to publish a bad test. Their reasoning goes something like this, "How could it be as bad as you say it is and still get published?" The answer is simple—it got put on the market because it looked like it would make money.

Another reason published tests are so popular is that many classroom teachers feel that they have neither the time nor the ability to produce valid tests. We tend to agree with this reasoning. If there already is a test available that is valid and will suit your purposes, it is foolish to spend time writing another. For the iconoclast or do-it-yourselfer, we have provided a lesson on test construction in the chapter on specific-level testing. Meanwhile, you traditionalists who wish to stick to the published tests should attend to the material in this section. If you want to use a published test, you must learn how to choose a good one. All tests are *not* created equal! Get rid of the notion that being copyrighted, published, and marketed automatically makes everything written a worthwhile investment. Educators must become better consumers. While it is popular to criticize test publishers, remember that they sell only what we continue to buy. Years ago, Postman and Weingartner (1969) stated that schools should prepare students to become experts at "crap detecting." One way teachers can do this is to start detecting some themselves. There is a lot of it on the educational assessment market, and you're going to have to learn to be a good detector to sort it all out.

Criteria for Selection

A prerequisite to finding anything is to know what you're looking for. What makes a test acceptable for survey-level assessment? There are four things to consider. The first and most obvious is *accessibility*. If the test is not readily available because it will take too long to get, costs too much, or the district won't let you use it, there is no sense in considering it. You would be wasting a lot of valuable time.

The second consideration is ease of *administration*. If you can't learn to administer a test competently by reading the manual and practicing on some of the neighbor's kids, you should not consider it for use as a survey-level assessment tool.

Third, the test should have *treatment utility* and not be merely an achievement test. Some achievement tests do have the advantage of group administration. These group tests often are composed of select-response (i.e., multiple-choice) items. Conversely, treatment tests require one-to-one administration because they use a supply-response format. The multiple-choice "advantage," however, soon disappears when you discover that the time you save in administering is lost in the laborious process of trying to interpret the results. You literally have to task analyze every item because you have no responses (student behavior) to examine.

Once you have found a test that is readily accessible and easy to administer, you must consider the fourth and most important characteristic of a good survey-level test—*validity*. (In case you forgot what it is, take another look at chapters 4 and 5.) To determine validity, you must identify the material covered on the test and how it is covered. Your next step is to compare these against your instructional objectives and decide how closely the two match. For teachers who have dealt with the curriculum before, this will be relatively simple and straightforward. Because they have taught a particular subject or used a particular set of materials, all they have to

do is go through a test and check those items that match their objectives in terms of material and S-R modes. For lack of a more technical term, we call this process "eyeballing." However, even if you eyeball a test for content validity, we would caution you to make sure you have a thorough understanding of the test items. If it is not immediately obvious what a test item measures, eliminate the item. If this occurs with a number of items on a particular test, throw out the test.

Those of you who are not ready (or willing) to eyeball content validity will need to examine both the curriculum and the test to assure yourselves that the test is, in fact, curriculum-based. This will be easier if the curriculum developers have provided skill sequences or tables of specifications. While tables of specifications may be used for purposes other than determining the content validity of tests, the type of information written in the table and its design seldom change. As you remember, the table always includes two axes. The vertical axis represents the content you want your students to master and the horizontal axis the behavior they must engage in to demonstrate such mastery.

Let's suppose that you want to compare the content validity of two decoding tests. The first step would be to complete the content axis by listing all the material covered in the objectives of the decoding program. The next step is to look at each of the items on test A, and mark the box whenever an item matches both the content (vertical axis) and the behavior (horizontal axis). On tests where items are numbered, you may wish to put the item number in the box. After going through test A item by item and listing the items that match the objectives, you count the items and write in the totals (see Figure 7.2). The entire process is then repeated with a new table of specifications for test B. In looking at Figure 7.2, you can see that the test being examined uses an untimed (accuracy) see-to-say format that does not cover CVCCV and CVCV words, consonant teams, or long vowels. This process is time-consuming but absolutely essential to assure that evaluation is aligned with the curriculum. The good thing about it is that it only needs to be done once. Frankly, we doubt that many teachers will have the time to do this sort of alignment activity on their

Test: "A"

Content \ Behavior	Identifies — e.g., see/hear to point or mark	Totals	Produces — Accuracy	Mastery	See to write	See to say	Hear to write	Hear to say	Totals
Reading from context	– – –	0	✓			LHT LHT LHT /			16
CVCCV, CVCV words	– – –	0							0
Sight words	– – –	0	✓			LHT LHT LHT LHT LHT LHT LHT /			36
Consonant teams	– – –	0							0
CVC words	– – –	0	✓			LHT LHT LHT LHT LHT			25
Vowel sounds	– – –	0	✓			(~) (u) LHT			0 / 5
Consonant sounds	– – –	0	✓			LHT /			6
Letters of alphabet	– – –	0	✓			LHT LHT LHT LHT ////			24
Alphabet	– – –	0	/						1
Totals		0	X	0	0	112	0	0	113

FIGURE 7.2
Table of specifications

own. We recommend that the administration hire experts and/or appoint and support (with extra pay) committees to do this important work in conjunction with curriculum development.

In summary, the criteria for test selection are:

1. Accessibility
2. Ease of administration
3. Treatment utility
4. Validity.

1.1b Construct Test

There are so many published achievement tests, end-of-unit tests, program placement tests, and district skill-level tests that it is unlikely that you will ever have to construct a survey test in any basic skill area. If you need a test in an area of undeveloped curriculum, the best thing to do is to drop back and organize the curriculum (as described in chapter 3). This means:

1. Recognizing the content to be taught/tested
2. Sequencing the content
3. Selecting behavior domains appropriate to the content
4. Recognizing appropriate conditions for the behaviors
5. Locating or establishing CAP
6. Arranging the content, behavior, conditions, and criteria into a table of specifications

7. Selecting a relevant item format
8. Writing items for the most complex squares in the table of specifications

The items taken from the most complex squares (objectives) in the table can be used as a survey test for the whole table. It's a long process but a valuable one for material you find yourself teaching frequently. You can't expect to make a survey test that adequately covers curriculum that is a mystery. Today this type of work is needed most of all at the high-school level and in the area of social behavior (Howell, 1983).

1.2 Administer Test

There is a lot more to administering a test than reading questions from a manual. You must remember that you are interacting with a person, not just pieces of paper. The kid you're testing might be scared or angry or both. He probably hasn't had too much success in school, isn't very good at answering questions, and is wondering why he has to take the 65th test of his young life. At its best, testing is anxiety-producing. At its worst, it can be a devastating experience for the kid as well as the examiner. So if you don't want to be devastated, we suggest that you pay close attention to this section. It is based upon years of experience in education during which time we have tested subjects ranging from 6 months to 60 years old, from handicapped to normal, from cooperative to noncompliant, and even physically aggressive. Over the years we've acquired a few tricks of the trade; and while you probably have seen or used some of them before, we hope there is something in this section you haven't thought about.

Getting Ready

Let's start with the obvious. The first thing to remember in administering a test is how to give it. This means that you should be able to administer the test in a reasonable amount of time without any administrative errors that would invalidate the results. To accomplish this you should study the test manual carefully and practice giving the test to as many people as possible before using it "for real." A word of caution before going on—most of the tests you will give have been designed, for obvious reasons, to be used with nonhandicapped students. The typical test manual doesn't tell you what to do if a student refuses to answer a question or tells you to stuff the test up your nose (or what to do if she tries to stuff it herself). Later on in this section we'll discuss some problems you may encounter, provide some insight into why they occur, and offer some suggestions for dealing with them. In the meantime, here are our general rules of thumb.

1. *Don't try to commit everything to memory.* It is perfectly legitimate to make notations in the margins of the test manual or to highlight certain parts for reference during test administration. If necessary, use 3 x 5 cards with pertinent data (e.g., time, basal, and ceiling limits) on them. Be careful that you make these notations in such a way that reference to it during testing will not interrupt its flow. There is nothing so disconcerting to both student and examiner as those long pauses during a test when the examiner fumbles through the test material trying to find out what to do next.

2. *Have all of the test materials* (e.g., pencils, scratch paper, test booklets, manual, and stopwatch) *ready before the test.* If you know that erasures are not permitted on a particular test or you would like to have errors left intact for subsequent error analysis, do not use pencils with erasers. (Don't always use those fat primary pencils; tear the erasers off the narrow ones the students prefer.) The student has been conditioned to use an eraser and, no matter how many times you tell her not to, she will probably keep on erasing. This behavior is simpler to extinguish if there is no eraser on the pencil. Also pay attention to the size of the pencils. Try to find out about a subject's motor coordination before testing. Look at a sample of written work. If it appears to be immature (for the student's age), use a pencil that will facilitate rather than inhibit her writing on the test. If you don't have access to this information ahead of time, have a number of pencils of assorted sizes available and let the student choose the one she's most comfortable with. Try not to sharpen the pencils too finely beforehand. The anxious student (and who isn't?) tends to push down so hard when writing that she either breaks the point or tears a hole in the paper. This only adds to her anxiety. If the pencil supply is

limited and there is no pencil sharpener in the room, have a pocket sharpener handy just in case.

Provide the kid with scratch paper if the test you are giving permits its use. Write her name or initials along with the date and any other pertinent information on each sheet. This is particularly important when you are testing more than one student during a given day. We would also suggest that you staple or clip all of each student's test materials, including the scratch paper, when the test is finished. Don't stuff little bits of paper inside pockets or purse and expect to remember to whom they belong later. It goes without saying that you fill in all pertinent data regarding the student on the cover of the test. Do this immediately or you may forget it. If you don't know things like dates of birth or age, *don't be sure the kid does.* On several occasions we've asked students their ages and found out later they were wrong.

3. *Get the materials organized.* Aside from having all necessary materials available ahead of time, you should also make sure they are appropriately placed. Place your materials out of reach or be prepared to spend the entire testing session taking things away from the kid. It might be wise to place the test materials on a table behind you with the subject seated across from you. This arrangement requires the child to leave his seat and walk around you to get the materials. Also consider your own needs in the arrangement of materials. Try to have them placed so that they are easily accessible to you and in the proper order for use during the test. If they are laid out on a table, arrange them in sequence of use; if you don't have the table space, pile them in order of use from top to bottom.

If you are planning to use a stopwatch or tape recorder, make sure it works. Remember to wind the watch even if it appears to be working. Stopwatches are notorious for stopping by themselves in the middle of a timed test. Stay away from recorders with built-in microphones since they pick up everything in the room you *don't* want to record (e.g., the buzzing of the lights and the blowing of the heat vent. They'll even pick up traffic noise outside in the street!) Use a directional microphone and tape it to the table to lessen vibration and inhibit the student from picking it up. Our experience has been that kids are seldom neutral when it comes to tape recorders. Put a mike in front of one and he'll either run and hide or begin to perform. Bring along an extra cassette in case the first one breaks or you discover at the last minute it contains the concert you attended last summer. Also make sure that the outlet in the room works. If you are using batteries, have extras available.

4. *Get the setting organized.* Consider which side of the subject you'll sit on if you are not going to sit opposite her. If she is right-handed, you will need to be on her left side so that you may easily observe her written responses. Arrange the environment so that it is comfortable for both of you. Make sure that the lighting and the room temperature are adequate: too warm and you'll both nod off during the test; too cold and you'll each be distracted by the clicking of teeth. Make sure that both seats are the right size: too small and you'll be distracted by cramped muscles; too high and you'll have a kid falling (or diving) off. Physical discomforts of any kind can be very distracting and tend to invalidate a student's performance.

Noise may also invalidate test results. Extraneous auditory stimuli (that's the psychological term for "noise") in the room, the room next door, or outside can be masked with a little gadget called a *white noise machine.* Available from specialty houses for less than $50, it is worth every penny if you are required to do your testing across the hall from the gym or next to the cafeteria. If you can't afford one, tune a radio to a nonstation and adjust the volume for low level static. Recorded instrumental music (especially classical) or electric room air purifiers will also effectively mask noise.

You should be aware of potential visual distractions and limit them before the student arrives. Try to have him facing a direction where there will be no extraneous visual stimuli. Never seat him opposite a door, open or shut. If possible, he should not be facing any of the windows in the room either. As soon as he walks into the testing area, show him where you want him to sit. You should not have to make any adjustments afterward. This doesn't mean that you shouldn't make adjustments during the testing session as they are needed. It means that if you do your homework, you probably won't have to. If others are to be present in the room during testing, try to arrange for a study carrel or screen to obscure any sight of movement. Post a sign on the door of the room in which you are testing.

STOP. TESTING. DO NOT DISTURB.

Most people will respect your privacy. If some curious or inconsiderate souls ignore the sign, pay no attention to them and neither will your student. One last bit of trivia—sit between the student and the door if you can.

5. *Use a checklist.* Many of these preliminary details (e.g., chair size, room temperature, pencil points, white noise machines, and the rest) may seem like so much minutiae to the novice. We're serious about all this. If you want to get valid test results and continue to remain on speaking terms with your students, we urge you to pay attention to

as many of these "minor" details as possible. To make sure you don't forget any, you should use a checklist such as the one in Figure 7.3.

This checklist was based upon the following information received from the student's teacher, an observation by the examiner, and a brief study of the student's written work.

1. Examination of the student's written work indicates poor fine motor control—confirmed by teacher.
2. Teacher reports subject easily distracted by extraneous printed matter—appears to have difficulty focusing on one word at a time.
3. Has speech impediment—difficult to understand.
4. Leaves room without permission—teacher says he does this often.

FIGURE 7.3
Testing checklist

Subject: John   DOB: 8/17/80 CA: 7-2

Dominance: LH   Site: Rm. 108   Date(s): 10/17/87

1. manual   need (1)

2. record booklet   need (2)

3. tape recorder   need (1) with directional mike

4. stopwatch   need (1)

5. pencils   need (2) primary size with erasers

6. scratch paper   --

7. door sign   need (1)

8. extension cord   need (1) 10' length

9. batteries   need (4) "c" cell if no ext. cord

10. cassettes   need (1) 60'

11. rewards   need (1) Spider-Man comic book (unbound)

12. occluders   need (1) 8½ x 11 sheet cardboard; (1) 3 x 5 card with

window cut out

Other   1 pack crayons, clip board, plastic sheet, overhead pens and rag

flashcard for reading test

5. Exhibits anxious behavior, e.g., biting finger nails, chewing gum rapidly, asking questions repeatedly (asked the time 17 times this morning) —teacher confirms this is typical behavior.
6. When not asking time, talks about Spider-Man.
7. Fits comfortably at 24" table and on 18" chair.
8. Counts on fingers.

Given this information the examiner constructed the checklist in Figure 7.3. This plan was based on (a) the test being given, (b) the room where the testing will be done, and (c) the student's characteristics as specified in the this list. As you can see, everything listed was done so for a reason. For those of you who are not familiar with occluders (#12), they are used when the student is exposed to a great deal of printed material on one page. Given what we know about the student, a card with a slit cut in it may be used to focus on one item while masking off the others. If this doesn't work, the examiner has the option of presenting the items separately on individual flashcards (to do so is to violate the norming of the test, which is all right with us as long as the scores you obtain this way aren't reported). The seating arrangement allows the examiner to observe the student's writing (since he's left handed) and block any retreat from the room. The tape recorder will be used to record the subject's verbal responses since he is sometimes inarticulate, and the crayons can be used to help him relax during the testing. The Spider-Man comic book, shown one page at a time, can be used as a reward for on-task behavior. The extra test form can be covered with a plastic sheet for scoring with transparency pens, and the marks can be wiped off later.

6. *Modify standardized measures.* Since the examiner is primarily interested in observing and recording the student's behavior, he or she doesn't have to follow all of the rules of administration exactly as stated in the manual. You only need to do this if you intend to use the test's norms. However, it is bad practice—*if not unethical*—to report scores derived from the nonstandard administration of a standardized test. While modifications in test administration are permissible to get behavior samples, remember that your interpretations cannot follow the standardization guidelines. Modifications may be made during the testing session as the

need arises, but it is better to prepare for them ahead of time so that you can put together all of the materials you may need (e.g., flashcards, occluders, large print test forms, counting beads); this is where the list of the student's characteristics becomes so important. All it takes is a 10-minute question–answer session with the student's current teacher, a brief look at some student work, and a classroom observation to compile a list. (While you're in the room, say "hello" to the kid too so he will meet you before the testing.) Using these characteristics, take a look at the test you are going to use and make any modifications you think necessary. It goes without saying that if these modifications are too drastic or excessive, you would probably be better off using or designing a different test.

Working with the Student During the Test

Checking, Timing, and Taping. Make sure that the student can't see you recording responses. Use a shield or screen between you or a clipboard on your lap; if you are sitting next to the kid, sit a little in back so that she can't easily look at the recording sheet. The test manual will serve as an effective screen if it can stand by itself.

If timing, do not leave the stopwatch where the student can see it or she will pay more attention to the watch than to the test. (Don't take your latest microprocessor watch into the room and let it beep at the kid every half hour—it's bad enough listening to them go off at the movies these days.) You could tape the watch to a clipboard so that you don't have to look back and forth from the test material. This way you can glance quickly at the watch without moving your head. Excessive head movement will make it difficult for you to keep your place and tend to distract the subject. Teachers often report that kids are upset by stopwatches. We find this unusual, because every time we turn our backs the kids take the watches and play with them. If the student is upset by the watch, you must either time covertly (put a clock with a sweep hand where the student can't see it but you can) or desensitize the kid to the watch. One teacher we know had some students complain that a minute was too short a time to do any work. So the teacher started the stopwatch and asked the students to raise their hands when they thought a minute had passed. Most of them had their hands up within 30 seconds. This is a good exercise for kids who are nervous about running out of time.

Tape-record verbal responses that are lengthy or complex whenever possible so that you can double-check the student's work at your leisure after he has gone. The technique is good to use with tests requiring verbal responses that you must score or record during testing instead of afterward. It is especially helpful with reading tests where the student is required to read orally and you have to score responses before deciding to move on to the next level. If you feel that you have missed an item or two while the student was reading, all you have to do is replay the tape. You probably won't lose his attention during this time because most kids like to listen to their own voices. It is improper to have a student reread material because you didn't hear it the first time or he was moving too fast for you to keep up and score too. It's tiring to have to reread this material, and it also may falsely cue the student. He may think you want him to change response(s). Besides, the behavior should be controlled by the student's skill at reading, not your skill at scoring.

Feedback.   Try to limit all distracting movement (i.e., marking or looking up from the test material) unless you are consistent in your behavior. Otherwise, besides distracting the student, you may also cue correct and incorrect responses. If you need to mark test items, mark all of them (not just correct or incorrect ones). By seeing you mark every item, all the kid knows is that the pencil moves when she responds. Because she can't see what you actually write, she doesn't know when she's correct or incorrect. Do the same thing with verbal responses. If you say "good" or "OK" for correct items and nothing for incorrect items, the student will soon know when she's right or wrong. You could say nothing at all or simply repeat the student's response, which, being noncommittal, doesn't cue her. You should also be careful not to cue with tone of voice or facial expression. Sometimes it may be necessary to encourage the kid if she's reticent or reluctant to respond. Even here, try to make your encouragement as noncommittal as possible as you reinforce

working on the test rather than correct performance. Encourage with phrases such as, "You're doing a good job," "Keep up the good work," "Let's try this one," "Do your best," "I like the way you are paying attention," and so on. Once again the idea is to reinforce work on the test, not correct or incorrect responses.

Sometimes students will begin to give *themselves* feedback on the test. They'll say things such as "I blew that one" or "That's another one wrong." This self-defeating feedback can become a vicious circle, particularly if the feedback they give themselves is *wrong.* If you see such a pattern beginning, you may want to break the no-feedback rule and tell the kid that he got the item correct (if he did). It is difficult to decide when this should be done. The purpose is to correct erroneous feedback, not to reinforce correct behavior. This distinction is very subtle. One clue that you can use is the student's statements. "I blew that one!" is an assertion; "I blew that one?" is a question. As a rule you should ignore the questions and correct the assertions if they seem to be part of a self-defeating pattern of feedback.

Rapport.   Every evaluation text tells you to establish rapport. While rapport building is one of the most important aspects of testing, it is also the most difficult to teach. Some say it can't be taught, but we'll give it a try. We have found from experience that the keys to building rapport between student and examiner are empathy and honesty. Always try to put yourself in the student's place. Think about how you would feel if you were being asked to do a lot of things you weren't particularly good at, in front of an adult who may be a total stranger or, worse yet, someone you know and like. Establishing rapport simply means reducing the student's state of anxiety (or hostility) to the point where it no longer interferes with test performance. It doesn't mean you both have to love each other. There are a number of general things you can do to facilitate rapport building. After discussing these, we'll go into the specific behavioral problems we've encountered during testing and describe some interventions we've used successfully.

The first thing you can do to establish rapport is to ask the student personal questions that don't relate to school. Try to show the kid that you have a sincere interest in him as a person as well as a student. Using the tape recorder with younger kids is also recommended. Begin with open-ended questions like "What do you have to say for yourself?" (as you put the mike out) or "What's new?" If this doesn't elicit any spontaneous chatter, ask pointed questions such as what he likes to do after school; what his family is like; whom he plays with; or what shows he likes to watch on TV. If nothing else works, talk about pets or brothers and sisters.

Depending on the subject, we recommend that you discuss what's going on and why she's taking the test. First, ask why she thinks she's being tested. If she is misinformed, tell her the truth. We usually try to get the idea across that the test will help her in school since it will tell us what she needs to be taught. We tell her that we expect mistakes and that this is nothing to feel bad about. If she's afraid to try an item because she thinks she might be wrong, the test won't help her as much because we'll have less of her work to look at. Some of our older subjects tell us that they already know what they can't do. "I can't read, that's what I can't do. I don't need to take a test to know what I can't do." Good point. We reply that we also know that she's having trouble with reading and that our test will help tell us why. We explain each step of the procedure. We ask the student if she has any questions about anything we are doing. If she does, we answer them quickly and in language that she can understand. We also explain to our older students that the material on norm-referenced tests is sequenced from easy to hard, and that eventually they will be exposed to test items that will be too difficult for them. We don't make a big deal about this, but it does help to prepare them for the difficult parts of the test. We also explain about *discontinue rules* so that they understand why we might continue to ask them questions after they've reached material that may be too difficult for them. Students tend to trust you a lot more if you are open with them and encourage them to ask you questions. After a while you'll begin to get "feelings" about some kids, and you'll act accordingly. We have spent upwards of an hour sitting and talking about whatever the kid wanted when we had a feeling that this was not the right time to push testing. At the end of this

rapport-building session, we made a date to come back and in most cases conducted our testing with no problems at all.

Rapport building is especially important when there are sociocultural differences between the examiner and student. This is particularly true where upper- to middle-class Anglo examiners and low socioeconomic status (SES) or minority group subjects are concerned. Many of these students have learned to expect the worst from social institutions such as the schools, police, economic security, and child protective services. They expect to fail at all academic-related activities, including testing. Often they believe their failure is completely beyond their control. Since failure is aversive to them because it makes them feel that they have less value than others and because they don't think they can succeed even if they try, they are not particularly fond of adults who put them into testing situations. How do you establish rapport with a student who has learned to resent and distrust you?

First you need to spend a moment actually considering the problem. When this happened to us, the first thing we did was to ask ourselves why the kid was always so hostile and uncooperative. Since we thought we were such nice, unbiased folks, we couldn't figure out why the two of us were having problems. Then we asked her. And she told us. "You always ask me questions I can't answer. You always ask me to do things I can't do. You're trying to make me feel dumb!" In our narrowmindedness we had been focusing on racial and cultural differences as the cause of the problem. The fact that we were making the student uncomfortable when we were testing her never entered our minds. But once she told us about it, we decided to try giving her questions she could answer and asking her to do things that we knew she could do. We devoted an entire test period to this.

We used items that we were sure she would have no trouble with but which were not obvious giveaways. We gave her lots of verbal praise for effort while being careful never to tie her personal worth to what she did. We made statements like, "You're a good reader" only if they were true. If it wasn't the truth and she knew it (and was aware that we knew it), she wouldn't trust us. So we simply said, "That was a good try," or "You did a good job." We weren't lying when we said this. She knew it and appreciated hearing it. After one or two of these confidence-massaging sessions, we began using heavier test material with which we knew she would have trouble. At this point we found her more willing to try some difficult items. She knew she wasn't dumb, and she knew that we knew it too. Incidentally, some subcultures have a prohibition on physical contact (particularly among males and older students), so watch your use of touching.

Special Problems

Here are some special problems you may encounter when you test handicapped learners. To our knowledge they are not discussed in any test manual you might use.

The Acting-Out Child.   The first one that comes to mind is everybody's nemesis, the *acting-out student.* He may call you names, use profanity, throw the test materials on the floor, scream, or run out of the room. He may attempt to eat the test booklet or make you eat it! This behavior may serve two purposes: first, as a release for the tremendous pressure and tension he feels as a result of the testing; second, as an escape-avoidance strategy. A kid who is asked to read out loud in class may have learned that all she has to do is scream or throw something and most adults will make her stand in the hall. Kids don't have to read when they're in the hall. Make sure you do not let the student's behavior lead to a pay-off by removing him from the testing situation. If you do, you will only reinforce the behavior, and in the future you'll never be able to test him. His behavior may be incompatible with testing, but that doesn't mean he can't stay in the room with you. If he runs away, get him and bring him back. Tell him that you will bring him back again if he runs away again. Ignore the screaming and the verbal abuse as much as you can. Continue with the test in a gentle but *firm* way by asking test questions or giving directions.

When you are only going to be with a student for a short while it is best to state your expectations clearly and simply ignore it when they aren't met. Don't try to be a teacher. You aren't going to make any permanent change in someone's behavior dur-

ing a brief testing session—so insisting on your view of "appropriate behavior" is a bit presuming. Understand that it usually gets worse before it gets better. You know you've got him when he goes from acting-out to quiet noncompliance. At this point, *and not before,* move down to material that he has already mastered and positively reinforce all correct responses. If none of this works, take him back to his room *when he's calm and behaving politely toward you.* Tomorrow is another day!

Test Anxiety.   Students suffering from test anxiety either ask the same questions over and over again—"Is that the answer?" "Was I right?" or they just plain cry. They are fearful of being wrong because someone has taught them that being wrong is followed by rejection and ridicule. Once again it is unlikely that anyone can reverse this sort of pattern during the short duration of evaluation. However, this anxiety reaction often diminishes once they see that people are not going to make fun of them or send them away every time they make a mistake. Try to be as encouraging as you can without committing yourself as to the correctness of their responses or reinforcing the "victim" role they may have negotiated with other adults. Like the rest of us, they usually know when they are right or wrong. What they may really be asking is "Do you still like me?" or "Are you mad at me?"

One technique is to employ counterconditioning whenever possible. Counterconditioning means pairing a rewarding or soothing stimulus with the aversive or anxiety-producing stimulus (i.e., a test). The reward will give pleasure, which in turn reduces tension. The reduction of tension leads to a state of relaxation that inhibits the tension from reappearing. It's hard to be relaxed and anxious at the same time. Making the student relaxed in the presence of the test usually lessens the question-asking behavior or any other anxiety-related behavior that may interfere with the testing. It also makes it easier for the student to respond to test items she is not sure of. Ultimately she may even find that what she feared the most (ridicule and rejection) doesn't have to happen after all. You may be able to reward the student with food, the presence of a friend, the judicious use of physical contact, a favorite toy, or a piece of gum. Be careful, though, that the rewarding stimulus is not so powerful that it distracts the student from the test.

Withdrawn Students. Students who are withdrawn can be more frustrating than acting-out students. They do not speak unless they are spoken to, seldom speak in complete sentences, and then speak only in barely audible tones. Our suggestion is initially to avoid tests with supply-response items unless the responses are written. Nonverbal tests with select-response items (e.g., hear or see, to point or mark) may get them working and can be followed with supply-response items. Another good idea is to bring a friend of the withdrawn student to the session and give bogus items to the friend.

Short Attention. Students who appear to have brief attention spans may have difficulty following directions and remembering test material you present to them. You may wish to give directions and ask questions about the directions themselves. After asking a test question, have the subject repeat it for you before asking for an answer.

Hyperactive. "Hyperactive" students engage in constant and excessive movement such as rocking in place or getting in and out of their seats. The most effective way to deal with hyperactive behavior during the test is to ignore it, as long as it doesn't interfere with the student's performance. Try to introduce frequent breaks into the testing session so that the kid has the opportunity to move about freely. If possible, the breaks should be made contingent upon in-seat behavior. Do not force the student to sit perfectly still with hands folded in the lap. You may be able to confine his or her movement, but you will not be able to limit it. You really wouldn't want to, since this movement may even help the student concentrate better.

Impulsivity. Students with poor impulse control tend to respond before they get all of the stimuli they need to make a correct response. They answer questions before the examiner is finished asking them. They are often automatically employing strategies from other tasks. An effective technique is to require the student to repeat the stimulus (i.e., directions or question) before responding to it. This

forces him to listen to everything you say and tells you whether or not he was paying attention. It also clarifies the task. If you are using a select-response format, do not expose any of the choices until you've finished presenting the stimulus and the subject has repeated it to your satisfaction. A modification of this technique is to expose only one of the possible answers at a time and repeat the stimulus—"Is this the letter *P?*"—for each exposure as you point to the letter in each box. This requires the student to stop and look at each possible choice before responding. Supply-response items are more appropriate for use with the impulsive student than select-response items because, with the former, it is easier to tell if the student is guessing.

Observation

Some of the limitations of observation were discussed in chapter 2. The biggest ones are: (a) observations aren't any good for behaviors that don't occur spontaneously (spontaneous in this case meaning elicited by the kid or environment rather than the teacher); (b) observations of the kid are meaningless without including observations of the environmental context in which behaviors occur (test items provide the context for tests—but observing that a student is "out of seat" without also noting if the behavior occurred during history class or swimming is nonsense); (c) step b is hard to do because the observable geographic environment often has less to do with student behavior than the student's personal psychological environment (we don't behave according to what is going on, but rather according to what we *think* is going on); and finally, (d) when we observe things we change them. These considerations, along with the need to collect adequate samples of time and behavior, dictate the structure of a good observation.

Overt Behaviors. The first thing to do when planning an observation is the first thing to do with any educational assessment: find or write an objective. Next determine if the objective calls for a change in the student's overt behavior, covert behavior, or status.

An overt behavior is traditionally thought of as something involving muscular activity, or movement. To count a behavior you must be able to recognize its beginning and end (White & Haring, 1980). For example, the behavior "writes digit" begins when the student puts pencil to paper and ends when the student stops writing the digit required. The starting and stopping points must be recognizable or an observer won't know when the first behavior ends and the next one begins. Behaviors are best measured through frequency counts to determine their rate of occurrence within a time interval.

Recognition of overt behavior is made easier by applying the concept of a movement cycle (White, 1986). "Movement cycle" is a term applied to overt behaviors. The criteria commonly used to define a movement cycle are:

1. The Dead Man Test. Can a dead man do it? It isn't a movement cycle if the answer is yes.
2. Repeatability. Can you tell when the behavior starts and stops? You need to in order to count it.
3. The Stranger Test. Would someone else see and count the same behavior you see and count? If not, the data lack reliability.

Here are some examples.

- "Student will not interrupt."
  1. Can a dead man do it? Yes—they seldom bother anyone.
  2. Is it repeatable? Not clearly.
  3. Will a stranger agree with your count? Probably.
  Conclusion: It's not a movement cycle as it lacks movement and fails the Dead Man Test.
- "Student out of seat."
  1. Can a dead man be out of seat? Yes.
  2. Is it repeatable? Yes.
  3. Will a stranger agree? Yes.
  Conclusion: It's not a movement cycle because it has no movement.
- "Leaves seat."
  1. Can a dead man do it? No.
  2. Is it repeatable? Yes. (It ends upon returning to the seat.)
  3. Will you and a stranger agree that it happened? Yes.

Conclusion: It *is* a movement cycle.
- "Raises hand."
  1. Can a dead man do it? No.
  2. Is it repeatable? Yes.
  3. Will you and a stranger agree that it happened? Yes.
  Conclusion: It *is* a movement cycle.

Covert Behaviors. Covert behaviors are thoughts and feelings. They are called *covert* because they can't be directly observed. In traditional behavioral or operant circles, concepts such as the movement cycle are considered to be basic. This means that if it doesn't move, it can't be counted. The advantage of this approach is that it makes our observations reliable by excluding data on things that can't be "seen." However, what people see is determined totally by what they are able to see. For example, sometimes teachers get concerned if students move their lips when they read, so they work to have them stop these movements. Actually, all people move their lips when they read; electrical sensing devices have found minute contractions of the throat and facial muscles during reading. These contractions can be "seen" by the electrical sensors but not by the human eye. Our point is that what one can see is influenced by our observational equipment. While some teachers may think they "stopped lip movement," all they really have done is reduce it to a level at which it can no longer be detected with the human eye.

In chapter 14, which concerns the evaluation of social behavior, we will discuss the idea of covert pinpoints. Covert pinpoints cannot be "seen" by observers but can be counted by the students themselves. These pinpoints include such things as thoughts about food or concerns about failure. These covert responses can be recorded by the individuals themselves because they (and only they) are in a position to "see" and count them. When collecting such behavior, it is helpful to explain the Dead Man Test and the Repeatability Test to the student. The Stranger Test is not applicable to coverts, which increases the risk of collecting unreliable data. Obviously, counting coverts raises a variety of measurement and ethical issues. Some of these are covered in chapter 14 and deserve your attention.

Status. The status of a person is not a behavior, but his or her condition or location. Teachers often act as if a student's status were a behavior, but it is important not to confuse the two. A person's status is the condition (physical or psychological) he or she is in. "In seat" is a statement of student status like "in Chicago" or "in a bad mood." "Getting in seat," "going to Maxwell Street," or "complaining about life" are behaviors. We may target overt status (in seat, paying attention, asleep, on time for class) or covert status (happy, angry, depressed, compliant) for data collection. To take data on someone's status, the best procedure is to use duration (length of time) or percentage data. To collect duration data, you time how long the person is in the targeted status. When using status it is a good idea to develop a clear definition of the status—and to share that definition with the student. For example, "at work" might always mean "no talk, work materials out, appearance of attention to materials."

Summarizing Observations

Data Types. If you are interested in changing a student's behavior, you will want to collect rate data by counting how many times he or she engages in the covert or overt target during some time interval (e.g., 50 times in 10 minutes is a rate of 5 per minute). If you are interested in a student's status you will want to collect duration data by timing how long he or she remains in the condition you are concerned about.

Either type of data (rate or duration) can be collected continuously or at certain intervals. If a behavior is very disruptive and overt (e.g., throws chair through window), you might as well count it continuously because you're going to know about it every time it happens anyway. If it is more subtle (makes eye contact with peer), you will want to set aside a certain time (or times) to watch for it so you don't have to try to observe the kid's eyes all day. This is called interval-sampling. Two typical interval-sampling forms are shown in Figure 7.4. In the first case, the "at work" status of the student is observed at certain times; for example, when the signal from a kitchen timer goes off. If the student is in the target status the teacher writes a check; if not, a dash. In this example, no time is spent waiting for the behavior to occur. A check is made only if the student is in the target status at the instant the timer signals the teacher to look up. In other cases the check might be made only if the student maintained the status for a prespecified interval. Both cases would be examples of *interval sampling,* though the interval shown in Figure 7.4 is only an instant in length. This procedure is often called *time sampling* (Kerr & Nelson, 1983).

Expresses opinion (Figure 7.4) is counted every time it occurs during the time the evaluator watches for it. In this example, the evaluator has watched for a total of 30 minutes over 10 separate intervals. During the 30 minutes of actual observation the behavior occurred 8 times, for a rate of .26 (8/30) times per minute. The conversion to rate

FIGURE 7.4
Interval-sampling formats

At Work

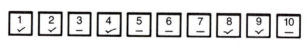

1	2	3	4	5	6	7	8	9	10
✓	✓	–	✓	–	–	–	✓	✓	–

Summary
✓ = 5
– = 5
Total = 10
10 – 5 = 50%

Expresses Opinion

0	1	0	2	0	1	3	0	0	1
1 min.	5 min.	1 min.	1 min.	1 min.	4 min.	1 min.	10 min.	1 min.	5 min.

Total count = 8

Total time in minutes = 30

Rate = .27 per minute

FIGURE 7.5
Recording interactions

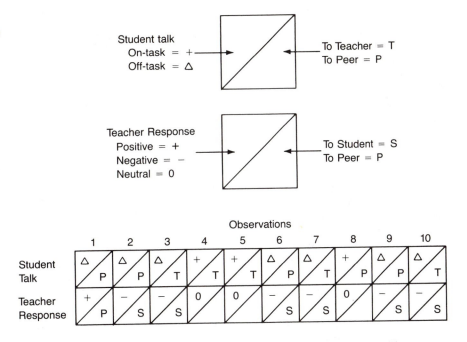

per minute puts the score on a common scale so that the teacher can compare rates across days even if a different amount of observation time was used. Converting the *at-work* data into a percentage (occurrence/opportunity) accomplishes the same thing.

Recording Interactions. Figure 7.5 shows a recording device in which the student's behavior is compared to the teacher's response. Every time the student says something it is coded as + (on task), − (off task), and T (to teacher) or P (to peer). The teacher's responses are coded as + (positive), − (negative), or O (ignore). Positive and negative responses are coded as S (to student) or P (to peer). The data show a pattern in which off-task student talk is preceded and followed by negative teacher comments to the student. Additionally, on-task student talk is always ignored (observations 4, 5, and 8). The implications of these data for treatment (encourage the teacher to attend positively to on-task student talk), while clear, would be completely missing if the only data available were on the student.

Spot Observation. Spot observation (Rogoff, 1978) is a modification of functional analysis (Kerr & Nelson, 1983) and a sort of time-sampling procedure. With it the observer takes a mental snapshot of a moment in the classroom and later follows up on the snapshot with questions. The spot observation begins as the observer briefly notes an event, being sure to include the target student and the surrounding circumstances and people. He or she then turns away and writes down everything he can think of to explain what was seen. Sometimes this is done by "framing" the moment with a brief description of its antecedents and consequences. Figure 7.6 shows a single example, or frame. As you can see, it is hard to reach many conclusions from one frame, but if several are used a total image of the interaction may become clear. This procedure is wordier than the recording systems usually recommended in educational texts but it allows the observer to capture a moment so thoroughly that he can later ask the participants (teacher, student, peers) questions about it. This allows the evaluator to compare what appeared to be going on to him and what the participants thought was

Antecedents	Events	Consequences
History lesson—large group—on Civil War. Many other students confused; Scott asking lots of advanced questions. Teacher responding to all questions.	Scott asks the teacher a question and the other students make fun of him.	Teacher ignores the reaction of the other students and answers Scott's question.

FIGURE 7.6
A snapshot

going on. The differences in perceptions of the event that may be illuminated by a question like "Why did Scott ask questions?" can provide useful evaluative information.

Conducting Observations

Nothing is more obvious than a strange adult lurking around the back of a classroom trying to observe a kid. If the student targeted for observation isn't yours, you may want to prepare the least bothersome observation system you can and then try to get the current teacher to use it. If that doesn't work, walk boldly into the room, get to know *everyone* (not just the target kid), and start collecting data when it seems like they are used to you. This is better than trying to be sneaky. One of the authors once asked a teacher what the target kid was wearing so he'd be able to spot her from a distance at recess. He then went out the back way and walked around the building to make a casual approach from the parking lot. As soon as he leaned against the flagpole and started making notes, one of the other students yelled, "Hey, Bridget! Someone's watching you!" Everybody on the playground froze as Bridget (an 8-year-old) walked timidly over to the evaluator and asked "Are you watching me?" "It's OK," he told her, "I'm paid to do it." Satisfied with that, she shrugged and went back to "punching others" as if he wasn't even there. It's better not to hide—you can look real dumb.

One-way mirrors have their pluses and minuses, depending on which side of them you are on. Videotaping is excellent after the kids have a day or so to get used to it. You do have to leave the TV monitor turned off. One favorite technique for unobtrusive counting is to fill one pocket with coins and then to shift a coin to an empty pocket every time the target behavior occurs. At the end of the day you just count the coins shifted and mark the number in your records—of course, with some behaviors and some kids and some teacher salaries this technique will be impractical.

As a rule, it is better to observe for several short periods spread over the day than one long period. Observation tends to be used for language and social behaviors, both of which are highly sensitive to changes in context. To capture the context, two techniques are available: one is the use of multiple recordings and the other is the use of spot observation. Both involve collecting data on others and therefore both raise some ethical concerns. Primary among these is the idea of consent. If an evaluator must obtain parental permission to observe a student, we can assume you should obtain teacher permission to observe a teacher.

To capture the context in which a behavior occurs, it is sometimes necessary to take data on the student's behavior and the behavior of other important people around her. This is to try to find things that prompt the targeted behavior or reactions that support it. The most important people will be the teacher, close friends, and arch-enemies. If you are an outside evaluator, you can quickly find yourself on shaky ground. Some teachers who refer a student for evaluation won't take kindly to it if they think you're evaluating *them*. Unfortunately, if you explain what you are doing and why, they may change their teaching behavior when you're in the room. This is a real problem as nothing will imperil your status as quickly as the suspicion that you are an undercover agent for the administration.

Again, we are reluctant to advise you to secretly take data on teachers as teachers have the same rights to informed consent kids have. But consider this. Because behavior is interactive, if data are collected on the student only, the interaction is ignored and the essence of behavior avoided. For academics, the other components of the learning interaction may be test items, books, and worksheets. Obviously, these items can be examined closely without a great deal of ethical concern. In the case of language and social behavior, the interactive context includes teachers and peers. To ignore them during data collection is to ignore the heart of the interaction. To change the targeted student's behavior, modifications will have to be employed that affect the teacher and peers. Therefore, a teacher who refers a student for help, particularly in social or language areas, is referring the whole room—including herself. These are important things to talk over with teachers, and the talking should be done *before* anyone is evaluated.

1.3 Summarize Behavior

Survey-level testing collects a general behavior sample. This sample is needed to narrow the range of curriculum so that specific-level testing can follow. The range is narrowed by identifying curriculum areas in which you will need to test further as well as those in which the student is clearly adequate or clearly inadequate. Clearly adequate objectives are marked as passed and set aside with a sigh of relief, while inadequate areas are listed for future instruction. (Some may be far too advanced for current presentation so priorities will still have to be set among these unlearned skills.) Unclear areas will require additional specific-level testing, but to guide this testing you need a clear picture of the student's current performance. This is accomplished by recording both what the student was supposed to do (the stimulus) and what he or she

really did (the response). This has to be done during the test/observation to develop a sufficient context for the hypothesizing step to follow. It is accomplished through note taking.

If you are sufficiently familiar with the content and materials you are using, extensive notes won't be necessary. If you aren't, you may want to use a helpful device for simplifying notes called the *stimulus/response sheet.* Each error a student makes is listed on this sheet. The stimulus is the question the subject was asked, the item given, or the directions read or heard. The stimulus can also include notes about the context in which the student is working. Because the explanation for errors can be traced to either a missing subskill or strategy component of the task, each comment should be a task-specific statement. After the errors have been summarized this way, the subcomponents mentioned most frequently in the comments become the most likely explanations for the student's failure at the task.

If you use the same test frequently, you may wish to make up a scoring form that uses the stimulus/response/comment format. Then you can record the student's work directly onto this form. Figure 7.7 shows an example of such a form. A task-specific comment is written by each error. By task-specific, we mean a comment directly related to what the student probably did or didn't do on that particular item. For example, in Figure 7.7, the student said "lock" for *look* and the comment is about the "oo" sound. Comments about ability such as "not smart enough to read it," "not motivated," "lacks perceptual skills," and "inattentive" are not task-specific and should not be used.

FIGURE 7.7
Comments on survey responses

	Stimulus	Response	Comment
	1. is	—	
	2. come	cōme	Final *e* rule used
	3. the	—	
	4. look	lock	Vowel team *oo* used
	5. up	it	Sight word substitution (initial vowel?)
	6. big	—	
	7. down	done	Vowel team *ow* not used
	8. that	they	Sight word substitution (vowel *a/e*?)
	9. she	—	
	10. on	—	

FIGURE 7.8
Recording a reading passage

Name: ___Patti___   Time: __45 sec.__

Date: ___10/10/87___   Errors: __10__

Book: ___The Wizard of Maldoone___

Page: ___47___

She put her ~~nose against~~ the ~~surface,~~ and tried to ~~peer~~ inside.
(hoose on) *(face)* *(look)*

Her heart leaped ~~with fear~~ as she saw a most ~~horrifying~~ face.
(omitted) *(prompt)*

Going stiff all over she ~~shot~~ away from ~~the sphere~~ a good three
(ran) *(it)*

feet, only to ~~realize~~ it was her own ~~reflection~~ she was seeing.
(really) *(face)*

"Dragons really are scary," she thought.

In the case of reading, many evaluators have the student read a passage while they write in responses above the text. Additionally, many tests supply codes for categorizing errors with circles, slashes, and initials to indicate error types. As seen in Figure 7.8, this is more convenient than recopying behavior to a separate form and is basically the same stimulus/response process.

SUMMARY OF SURVEY-LEVEL TESTING

Remember the purpose of the survey level is to collect "facts" about the student's task-related behavior. The materials used at the survey level may include classroom textbooks and tests. The advantage of class texts is that they have high content validity. However, if they are too difficult the student may not be able to even attempt to work them. Consequently, little useful behavior can be observed.

Because you are trying to collect a representative sample of the student's behavior, you must be a skilled evaluator. This means that you will run the testing session smoothly and reassuringly. If the student is upset by the testing, timing, setting, or you, then the behavior you get will have limited utility.

Finally, remember to take clear and copious notes by using a stimulus/response/comment sheet. Summarize the session so that someone who wasn't even there could interpret the data.

2.0 DEVELOP ASSUMED CAUSES

Once you have some information about what the student is doing you must try to figure out *why* he or she is doing it. This means that you develop some ideas about what skills or strategies the student is missing. These activities take place during the hypothesizing stage of the evaluation. This stage yields possible explanations for the student's poor performance. These explanations, or assumed causes, will be treated as hypotheses to be accepted or rejected through the process of specific-level testing. This stage is either very easy or very hard depending on your own knowledge of the curriculum and the degree to which the curriculum has been adequately organized. We are going to assume the worst case (unorganized curriculum and little prior knowledge) for our explanation. This will make this step seem long and complex; in practice and with knowledge of the curriculum it only takes seconds. Remember the reason you are doing this is to recognize subskills or strategies the student may be missing.

2.1 Analyze Curriculum or Task

If the curriculum is well-organized and sequenced, all you have to do is find a point at which the student fails and work backwards, looking for the point at which he or she succeeds. This is called *testing down*. Table 7.1 is a table of specifications for division. If, on the survey test, the student missed a problem that required her to divide a two-digit number by a one-digit number and get a remainder, she missed square 3m in the table. The as-

sumed cause of this failure is that a more basic objective found to the left of or below square 3m has not been learned. To check this out, you will have to give specific tests of these objectives, but once the lower objectives have been identified step 2.1 is over.

Look at Figure 7.9. This table is a content checklist for summarizing errors a student has made in reading. The checklist is drawn from the content sequence of a decoding table of specifications. To use it, a teacher summarizes the survey behavior by noting each error and then finding its content category. As you can see, most of the errors noted were vowel conversions, CVC + *e*, and vowel errors. Consequently, lack of proficiency in these content areas becomes the assumed cause for the student's reading problem.

Task Analysis

Skill sequences such as the one in Figure 7.9 do not always exist. If every curriculum had already been developed by following the steps outlined in this text, task analysis probably wouldn't be needed. However, the steps outlined are for an ideal situation. There will always be breaks in content sequences and poorly defined behaviors that produce holes in the curriculum. In addition, the calibration of curriculum isn't constant; the ideal distance between tasks varies from student to student and teacher to teacher as it is up to each teacher to slice the tasks into smaller pieces or combine them into larger ones for optimal learning. Finding a relevant task sliced to the optimal size, at the correct level of difficulty, is largely what treatment evaluation is all about. Few evaluators will ever sit down and design a chunk of curriculum from scratch.

Most evaluators will start with whatever information is on the referral form (e.g., fails reading, doesn't concentrate, bad at math) and carry out a task analysis to identify subcomponents. Task analysis was already covered in chapter 3, but we will now review the steps to be followed while using task analysis in the search for useful hypotheses.

Recognize the Target Behavior

This may be done through survey testing or from the referral. The target behavior is a statement de-

TABLE 7.1
Table of specifications for division

	Identify	Accuracy	Mastery
Placement Test Mixed division problems			
Square Root Square root of a number in which the answer is 0-12	7i	7a	7m
Place Value Two- or more-digit number with zero		6a	
Two- or more-digit number by 1, 10, 100, 1000		5a	
Remainder and No Remainder Two- or more-digit number by a one- or two-digit number		4a	
Remainder Two-digit number by a one- digit number (one- or two-digit answer)		3a	3m
No Remainder Two-digit number by a one- digit number (two-digit answer)		2a	2m
Facts Division facts (0-10)	1i	1a	1m

Student ___Chris___
Grade ___4___

Date ___2-17___
Evaluator ___Murray___

	Errors		Total Errors on Each Subtask
8. CVC + e Blending Example: hate, mete, bite, hope, cut	‖‖ ‖‖ ‖‖		12
Sounds			
7. CVC Blending Example: hat, met, bit, hop, cut	‖‖ ‖‖		7
6. Vowel Sounds a, e, i, o, u	‖‖ ‖‖ ‖‖ ‖‖		18
5. Consonant Sounds b, c, d, f, g, h, j, k, l, m, n, p, q, r, s, t, v, w, x, y, z	|||		3
4. Same and different word sounds Directions: Teacher says two sounds and asks if they are the same or different.			
3. Same and different letter sounds Directions: Teacher says two sounds and asks if they are the same or different.			
2. Same and different words Example: "Point to the one that looks like the one in the box." [was] saw mas was wos 1 2 3 4			

1. Same and different letters
Example: "Point to the one that looks like the one in the box." [a]
  o e u a
  1 2 3 4			

FIGURE 7.9
Checklist for reading errors

scribing what you want the student to do—the target *isn't* what the student is doing wrong. Often the referral, or errors on a test, will lead you to target a maladaptive behavior. This is a mistake. In this model it is assumed the kid engages in maladaptive behavior because he or she lacks the essential prerequisites of appropriate (correct) behavior. To find these prerequisites you must identify and focus on a target behavior that is incompatible with the maladaptive behavior. For example:

Maladaptive	*Target*
Makes reading errors.	Reads accurately.
Talks out in class.	Raises hand to speak.
Omits operation signs.	Includes operation signs.

Always focus on and analyze the target task—not the maladaptive behavior.

Specify the Main Task.

Task analysis will be easiest and most useful if the target behavior (main task) can be stated very clearly in behavioral terms. At the very least, the statement must include content, behavior, conditions, and criteria.

Identify Subtasks.

1. Ask "What must a student do to complete this task?"
2. State each subtask in the same behavioral format used for the main task.
3. Keep the distance between subtasks small. As a rule, if the subtasks you list will take more than a week or 2 to learn, you are dealing with oversized chunks of material.
4. List subtasks close to the main task. This is very important. If you find yourself listing subtasks that underpin many tasks (not just the targeted main task), you may want to consider that the main task is stated too generally.
5. Do not list motivation, attention, memory, intelligence, perception, or information-processing abilities as subtasks.

Identify Strategy.

1. Determine rules for task completion.
2. State the simplest procedure for task completion. The simplest procedure is the one with the fewest steps.
3. Determine if a formal algorithm (widely agreed upon step-by-step procedure) is commonly employed by experts for completion of this task.
4. Consider that a general strategy may be required. General task strategies include:
   a. Deciding what needs to be done
   b. Evaluating resources
   c. Selecting a procedure to follow
   d. Carrying out all steps in a procedure
   e. Monitoring work
   f. Checking work
   g. Self-correcting work.
5. Anticipate errors, or examine available incorrect responses, to recognize where a procedural step is needed for accurate performance.

Terminate.

1. Do not overanalyze, as there is some risk of becoming trivial. A good instructor/evaluator constantly balances the need for specificity against the fact that most skills are learned best in context.
2. Initially recognize no more than five subtasks close to the main task.
3. If specific testing indicates that the student can handle (learn) the least complex of these subtasks, then the analysis has been sufficient and can be terminated.

An Example. Here is an idealized example from spelling.

Main Task:	*Behavioral Objective:*
Spell previously misspelled words phonetically.	Given each previously misspelled word by dictation, the the learner will write the word correctly (phonetically) taking no more than 10 seconds per word with 100% accuracy.

Subtasks:

1. Receives dictated word.

2. Isolates syllables.

3. Isolates letters.

4. Spells letters or syllables.

5. Recalls letters/ syllables in sequence.

Behavioral Objectives

1. Given previously misspelled words by dictation, the learner will correctly pronounce each word in 5 seconds.

2. Given each of the misspelled words by dictation, the learner will say each word, with a pause between each syllable. To be correct, the pause must be at least 1-second long and correctly divide the word into morphographic units or phonemic units. CAP will be 100% accuracy, taking no more than 5 seconds per word.

3. The examiner will say a syllable from a misspelled word and the learner will correctly say each sound in the syllable, or the syllable sound if it forms a discrete unit, with a 1-second pause between each sound. This will be done with 100% accuracy, taking no more than 10 seconds per syllable.

4. Given a syllable, letter, or sound (phoneme) in isolation, the learner will write the corresponding letter (grapheme) within 3 seconds and with 100% accuracy.

5. Using the misspelled words, the examiner will say a word by syllable (i.e., with a 1-second pause between each) and the learner will repeat the syllables in the correct order

and with the 1-second pause in the appropriate place. CAP is 100% accuracy, taking no more than 10 seconds per word.

Phonetic Spelling Strategy. Determine correct pronunciation of word, subdivide word into the largest units that make a single sound, spell the units in sequence by recalling phoneme/grapheme correspondence.

This spelling example as presented is quite elaborate. Only text authors would ever go to the trouble to write it all out like that. However, while writing the objectives may seem like a hassle, there are two points to keep in mind. First, once you have analyzed a task thoroughly you won't ever have to do it again, so the effort doesn't need to be repeated for other students with the same problem. And second, when you get to specific-level testing, you are going to need that objective again to select or make up a CRT (specific-level substeps 3.1a and 3.1b).

One last thing about the procedure for task analysis. In the procedure under the heading "Identify Subtasks," Step 4 advises you to stay as close to the original task as possible. For example, in the division example way back in Table 7.1, it would be better to assume the kid can't work two-digit by one-digit division problems without remainders than to jump all the way down to division facts. Always stay as close to the student's expected level as possible; only move backwards if specific testing shows no accurate responses or monitoring fails to show improvement. The skills of remedial/special students are often in a state of regression or disrepair. A student who has been laboring away at two-digit division might well fail rate at basic division facts because he hasn't been using them much. Such a student will perform poorly on a test but can rebound to proficiency with very little practice—*if he wants to.* However, a student who has been taken from fifth grade math all the way back to third grade may look at those fact problems (which he thought he'd seen the last of 2 years before) and just give up. Assume that the reason for failure is a missing subskill, but always start testing and teaching with the highest possible subskill.

2.2 Analyze Errors

Error analysis can be a real short cut. It was explained in some depth in chapter 5 (on page 84). Unfortunately, error analysis is hard to do on many survey tests, especially the ones that use multiple-choice items. Multiple-choice items don't have much that can be analyzed other than the letters or numbers marked for answers. Therefore, you won't know why the student chose the answer she did unless you have her solve the problems for you verbally or in writing at a later date.

To analyze errors, follow these steps:

1. Select a test that provides an opportunity for a variety of errors to occur (borrowing problems are necessary to find borrowing errors).
2. Have the students work the items on the test—encourage them to attempt everything and to show all of their work ("think out loud").
3. Try to get as many examples of errors as possible.
4. Try to gain insight into the student's thought processes by asking "How did you arrive at this answer?"
5. Note patterns, or consistencies, in the errors.
6. Note categories of problems (areas of content) that are always right or always wrong.

2.3 State Assumed Causes

Each subtask of a task analysis, or prerequisite listed on a table of specifications or skill sequence, is a potential cause of student failure. In step 2.3 the evaluator hypothesizes about which of these are the student's most likely problems ("hypotheses" sounds so much nicer than "guess"). There are two ways to narrow the field of possible hypotheses before starting into the specific level.

Comments

With the subtasks in front of you, you may simply review the comments on the S/R form or check-marks on a skill checksheet. You then pick the subskills that seem to be most problematic and list them by priority as assumed causes. It's best to list two or three as a start.

Status Sheet

A simple device for paring down the number of potential specific-level tests is the *status sheet*. All you do with a status sheet is list the prerequisites you found or developed in Stage 2 and then mark them as adequate, inadequate, or uncertain (?). Adequate means there is no doubt that the student has the skill and instruction won't be needed. Inadequate means the student doesn't have the skill and instruction will be needed (though you still don't know which things will need to be taught first). Uncertain means specific-level assessment is needed.

Table 7.2 shows a status sheet on the oral communication component of assertiveness. Language is one area in which survey procedures will often yield enough information to justify skipping most specific-level testing. In this case the evaluator sat down with people who know the student and asked them about her skills. Those marked no will be listed as objectives and taught. For those marked with a question mark, more information is needed.

TABLE 7.2
Status sheet: Assertive oral communication

Prerequisite	Status
Formulates appropriate conclusions/actions	No (Inadequate—teach)
Identifies speaker's assumptions	Yes (Adequate)
Identifies speaker's bias	? (Uncertain—testing required)
Resolves differences	No (Inadequate—teach)
Uses persuasion	Yes (Adequate)
Considers the listener	No (Inadequate—teach)
Explains	Yes (Adequate)
Expresses feelings	? (Uncertain—testing required)
Expresses opinions	Yes (Adequate)
Expresses wants	Yes (Adequate)

SUMMARY

This chapter has explained survey-level testing. The explanation has been more complex than the actual process. Once you have identified some subskills or strategy steps the student seems to be unable to carry out, you have finished the survey procedure. Next it will be necessary to carry out specific testing to see if the hypotheses you have formed are correct. That's what the next chapter is about.

Study Questions

1. Define the following terms as they are used in this text. Some of these terms may be review from previous chapters.
   a. Survey-level
   b. Fact
   c. Assumed cause
   d. Decision
   e. Rate
   f. Specific-level
   g. Tables of specifications
   h. Behavior: overt
   i. Behavior: covert
   j. Status

2. The purpose of a survey-level test is to
   a. help the evaluator to make how-to-teach decisions.
   b. give the evaluator a general idea of what the student can and can't do.
   c. verify assumed causes of student failure.
   d. b and c

3. Indicate which things you should consider in selecting a survey-level test.
   a. Ease of administration
   b. Accessibility
   c. Availability of norms
   d. Treatment utility

4. Which of the following could increase the amount of error in a child's test score?
   a. Test anxiety
   b. Inappropriate feedback given by the evaluator
   c. A distracting environment
   d. Poor academic skills
   e. All of the above

5. Decide whether each of the following is an example of an overt behavior, a covert behavior, or status.
   a. Says vowel sounds.
   b. Writes capital letter "C."
   c. Thinks about rule for capitalizing proper nouns.
   d. Hostile.
   e. Decides which problem is correct.

6. Duration data are best for measuring _____, while rate data are most appropriate for _____.
   a. covert behaviors; overt behaviors
   b. behaviors; status
   c. status; behaviors
   d. status; covert behaviors

7. A survey-level test should
   a. include a few representative items from each target domain.
   b. include items only from one objective.
   c. include "identify" format items only.
   d. include items from reading, math, and written language.
8. Decide on some assumed causes for the facts listed below.
   a. The student missed three of the four long division items.
   b. The student was out of her seat 50% more than any other student in the class.
   c. The student incorrectly read the following words: night   sight   high   right
   d. The student solved this problem as shown.

$$\begin{array}{r} 26 \\ +\ 4 \\ \hline 12 \end{array}$$

Chapter 8

Specific-Level Testing

A BRIEF PEP TALK

In chapters 7 and 8 we are describing what you, as an evaluator, should do and how you might go about doing it. This discussion is long and, at times, complex. It is that way because we are elaborating on each step. In practice, you will never do all of the things we are describing because your understanding of the process will allow you to take short-cuts. The elaborate explanations we are providing now are needed to promote the understanding that will allow efficiency later.

Take a moment to think about where we are in the evaluative process. The format itself is very simple. It has four steps:

1. Find out what the student is doing now.
2. Think of explanations for what he or she is doing.
3. Check and see if these explanations are correct.
4. Decide what to teach.

To explain these steps we must cover topics like error analysis, curriculum development, and test construction. These discussions are presented to assure that you (the reader) will have the extensive prerequisite knowledge required to actually do evaluations.

While the explanations of how, why, and when to carry out each of these steps may get tedious, it is always important to remember that the basic format is simple and logical. So hang in there!

INTRODUCTION

The purpose of specific-level assessment is to verify assumptions formed at the survey level. The boundary between the specific and the survey levels is not always distinct, so let's talk about it for a minute.

The model we are following (Figure 7.1) has four stages:

1. Fact finding
2. Hypothesizing
3. Validating
4. Decision making

At the end of chapter 7 we finished with step 2 by describing how to find task-specific explanations for student failure. Because these explanations may or may not be correct, they are referred to as "assumed causes." The third stage, validating, is intended to find out if the assumptions are correct. This is done through additional specific-level assessment. All steps are briefly summarized in Table 8.1.

SPECIFIC LEVEL

We do specific level-assessment to verify the assumptions made after survey-level assessment and we repeat it frequently to monitor the effectiveness of our treatments. We have to verify the initial assumptions because they are usually based on very general samples of student work and, in the case of NRTs, are calibrated in terms of years (grade levels) rather than weeks, as short-term objectives must be. Because constructing a specific-level test is fairly technical, the discussion of how to do it will occupy a lot of this chapter.

A specific-level test is always a criterion-referenced test. As already mentioned, a criterion-referenced test is composed of two things: (a) a behavioral objective and (b) the materials necessary to implement the objective. Of course these objectives must have statements of content, behavior, conditions, and CAP. And they must be calibrated so that they cover about the same amount of curriculum that the teacher is going to teach. This is because specific-level test objectives are the same as short-term instructional objectives. By "the same" we don't mean similar—we mean they are the *exact* objectives. No difference. This is why failing the test/observation means instruction is needed and why instruction continues (assuming progress is adequate) until the test/observation is passed. It is also why data from readministration of the test (or a form of it) can be used to monitor student learning.

We can repeat specific tests frequently because their finer calibration makes them sensitive to small increments in learning. At the specific level, instruction and evaluation become so tightly meshed that they are difficult to separate—and that's the way it should be.[1]

Question 3A: Is specific-level testing/observation required?

Key Consideration: Do you already have sufficient information to arrive at decisions about treatment?

Explanation: Sometimes the survey procedures and your prior knowledge of the student will provide enough information to begin instruction, so you can go past specific-level assessment directly to

---

1. When we say to test exactly "*what* is taught," you may or may not teach the actual test items. In most cases, a test provides a format for eliciting behaviors that illustrate (or indicate) the application of underlying cognitive activity (strategies). This is particularly true when the test is designed to measure knowledge of a consolidated domain of curriculum.

When a student works the problem

$$\begin{array}{r} 22 \\ +37 \\ \hline 59 \end{array}$$

the hope is that he or she will get the answer by applying the correct problem-solving strategy rather than by guessing, copying, or simply memorizing the "fact" that $22 + 37 = 59$. In most cases an item should indicate the use of a problem-solving strategy, not mere memorization.

What this means is that "teaching to the test" is okay if it involves teaching the targeted strategy (therefore automatically teaching the items) rather than teaching the items themselves (which may or may not affect the strategy). Teaching the items is only a good idea when the items on the test include all of the items in the domain being measured and the items are not consolidated by an underlying strategy.

TABLE 8.1
The task-analytical model of assessment

Stage 1: Fact Finding

1.1 Purpose: To find out what the student is doing now.

1.2 Materials: Classroom work or published tests. A stimulus/response worksheet.

1.3 Procedure: Stimulus and response information is collected on each error.

1.4 Result: The stimulus and response columns of a worksheet are filled out and typical errors are listed.

Stage 2: Hypothesizing

2.1 Purpose: To think of explanations for what the student is doing.

2.2 Materials: Survey-level stimuli and responses.

2.3 Procedure: Each stimulus (task) is analyzed through task analysis or each student response is analyzed through error analysis. *NOTE: An existing table of specifications can be used to replace this step.*

2.4 Result: The subtasks required for successful completion of the survey material are listed. All comments are then reviewed, and general areas of difficulty are recognized and listed as assumed causes for the student's behavior.

Stage 3: Validating

3.1 Purpose: To see if the explanations are correct.

3.2 Materials: Specific-level assessment materials.

3.3 Procedure: Each assumed cause is reworded into a behavioral objective and the student is tested/observed to see if he or she passes or does not pass the objective.

3.4 Results: Conclusions about which task-related subskills the student has or does not have are reached.

Stage 4: Decision Making

4.1 Purpose: To decide what to teach.

4.2 Materials: Specific test results and guidelines for systematic interpretation.

4.3 Procedure: Compare test results to hypotheses and employ interpretation guidelines.

4.4 Results: Recognition of areas where additional testing/observing is required. Statements about what to teach and tentative statements about how to teach it.

interpretation. The status sheet described in step 2.3 (the last chapter) may be helpful here. The only standard for making this decision is your satisfaction that the data you already have provide adequate insight into the student's knowledge of the curriculum.

Question 3B: Is a specific-level test available?

Key Consideration: Correctly calibrated CRT that matches hypothesis.

Explanation: In the analysis stage, objectives were written or identified to correspond to each hypothesis. If a probe (CRT) that matches these objectives is available, it can be used; if not it will have to be made.

3.1a Select Probe
Selecting a specific-level CRT is a lot like selecting any good test or observation procedure. First you make sure it matches your objective and then you check to be sure that it meets the 10 criteria discussed in chapter 5. These guidelines for test selection/construction are shown in Table 8.2. Format is particularly important; specific-level tests should be structured to permit the collection of rate data and for repeated use. Additionally the probe should be calibrated to match short-term chunks of curriculum. These things are explained in great detail in the next section.

3.1b Construct Probe
You are about to find out why it is easier (but not necessarily better) to select a CRT rather than to make one.

Over the next several pages we will focus on calibrating curriculum, planning a test, selecting and writing items, assuring an adequate sample, testing strategies, testing rate, and standardizing criteria. These activities are all necessary in developing curriculum-based measures.

Calibrating Curriculum
Calibrating a test means adjusting its curriculum coverage to complement an interval of instructional time. This is a time-consuming task best accomplished during curriculum development. A CRT

TABLE 8.2
Guidelines for test selection/construction

A Good Test:
- Is easy to use,
- Has a clearly defined purpose,
- Has clearly defined content and behavior,
- Has items or subtests keyed to objectives,
- Is standardized,
- Permits examination of strategy use,
- Allows collection of rate data,
- Collects an adequate sample of behavior,
- Has appropriate formats,
- Has appropriate scoring procedures.

must measure the same slice (portion) of curriculum being taught by the teacher. This is important for two reasons: (1) It assures adequate sampling and (2) it allows repeated measurement and monitoring. Because special/remedial teachers teach in relation to short-term objectives, which by convention take approximately 4 to 6 weeks to teach, specific-level tests/observations should be calibrated at 4 to 6 weeks. (If your idea of short term is 10 to 15 weeks, the principles and procedures we are about to explain will also apply, but the time intervals will be longer.)

Steps.

Step 1. Summarize long-term performance discrepancy. Find the long-term objectives the student has not met. These are specified in some form (usually global) in the school district's curriculum guide. Locate where the student (let's call this kid Vicki) is currently working and where she should be working. Subtract this actual performance from the expected performance. For example, suppose the curriculum indicates that if Vicki is in the fourth grade she should have mastered 78 separate long-term math objectives by this point. If she has only mastered 50, the summary would look like this:

Expected Performance:	78
Actual Performance:	− 50
Discrepancy:	28

Step 2. Decide how long the student will have to make up the discrepancy. Deciding how long it will take to catch a student up is difficult. Usually the duration of service is decided on in a child study team meeting with the input of everyone there. For this example, let's say that the group projects the need for 1 year of resource room math.

Step 3. Find the total. Add to the discrepancy the number of objectives students in regular programs will be expected to learn during the catch-up period. Remember that to catch up a remedial student must actually cover more objectives per time unit than a regular student. Vicki has to make up her discrepancy *and* learn the new stuff that is being presented while she is making it up. She has been given 1 year to catch up. In that year let's assume 20 new long-term objectives will be presented. We now have:

$$\begin{array}{r} 28 \text{ old objectives} \\ +20 \text{ new objectives} \\ \hline 48 \end{array}$$

Vicki's Progress Goal is 48 objectives in 1 year.

Step 4. Calibrate the long-term objectives by weeks. This is done by dividing the number of objectives by the number of weeks available for instruction. Throwing out the first and last weeks plus a couple more for state-mandated achievement testing and parent conferences, let's say that we are going to get 30 weeks of actual instruction during the year. That's 48 objectives divided by 30 weeks or 1.6 long-term objectives per week ($48 \div 30 = 1.6$).

Step 5. Calibrate the long-term objectives by the short-term interval. We (the authors) think a short-term objective takes from 4 to 6 weeks to teach so our short-term interval is 4 to 6 weeks. To allow time for problems to occur and be corrected we'll take the outside time—6 weeks—and multiply it by the weekly factor obtained in step 4 ($6 \times 1.6 = 9.6$) to get a progress expectation of 9.6 original math objectives for each 6-week period. The 48 original objectives can now be clumped into

five groups of about 10 objectives each. The 10 objectives in each group will be taught together.

Step 6. Consolidate the objectives if possible. This means taking each of the objective chunks produced in step 5 and trying to treat them as one task. It may be that this is not possible and Vicki will end up working on 9 or 10 separate tasks, but if the 10 objectives can be merged into two or three related domains it will limit the number of tests Vicki will have to take *and* her teacher will have to write. Consolidation is carried out by examining the content domains in each objective as well as the strategic steps required to carry the objective out. For example, if several of the original objectives cover percents and decimals they can be merged because percents and decimals share the concept of proportion and the application of division. (The calibration steps just explained are listed in Table 8.3 for easy reference.)

Materials. In the example above we used objectives as the basis of calibration. It is also possible to use materials. For example, let's say that Vicki's performance lag has put her one and a half math

TABLE 8.3
Steps in calibrating curriculum

Step 1	Summarize long-term performance discrepancy.
Step 2	Decide how long the student has to make up the discrepancy.
Step 3	Add objectives to be covered by regular students during special services to the discrepancy.
Step 4	Divide the number of objectives found in Step 3 by the number of weeks found in Step 2 to get an objective per week ratio.
Step 5	Multiply the ratio in Step 4 by the number of weeks making up your idea of "short term" (4-6 weeks recommended) to recognize the groups of objectives to be taught at the same time.
Step 6	Attempt to merge or find common elements of the objectives found in Step 5. Task analyze to find short-term objectives and instructional steps.

books behind the other students. If the regular students will cover 1 additional book this year she has a total of 2.5 math books to cover in 30 weeks. If each book has 100 pages, that's a weekly expectation of 8.3 pages (100 pages × 2.5 books ÷ 30 weeks = 8.3 pages a week). 8.3 pages a week is about 50 pages every 6 weeks. To calibrate a probe from materials, you must go to the text pages and see what they are teaching. This means looking at the 50 pages to be covered and devising one or more tests to measure their content. As with the objective method, the aim is to recognize skills that span the entire time period. If four skills are identified you want to produce four 6-week probes—not a series of four covering 1.25 weeks each. *The danger of this system is that it assumes the materials are appropriate and that each page is worth doing.*

Planning a Test

This discussion will describe how to plan a CRT inventory for an entire 4- to 6-week unit of instruction. A unit of instruction may contain several objectives and each one may require its own probe. Each separate probe in the inventory will measure only one objective. The next few pages will elaborate on the following steps.

1. Recognize content.
2. Sequence content.
3. Recognize and sequence behavior.
4. Recognize and sequence conditions.
5. Assemble a table of specifications.
6. Discard nonapplicable objectives.
7. Write items for each square.

Steps.

Step 1. Recognize content.   Once the curriculum has been calibrated, take each short-term objective and decide what content you will teach and test. Obviously the content you test should be the content you teach, but there are two ways to approach content. The content you teach may be *subtask content* or *strategy content*. Perhaps you recall the distinction between these two (presented in chapter 3). Subtask content is vocabulary, facts,

codes, and topic-specific information. Strategy content incorporates the rules, procedures, and algorithms for using subtask content. You may test and teach either or both of these.

In most cases the combined (content and strategies) approach is best. A strategy focus may be indicated if the domain is highly *consolidated* (see chapter 5, page 83). If the curriculum is unconsolidated there is little choice but to emphasize subtasks. A guide for determining if a curriculum domain is consolidated is presented in Table 8.4. It is important to remember that there really isn't a boundary between consolidated and unconsolidated domains. Structure should be viewed as a continuum ranging from high consolidation to low consolidation.

Step 2. Sequence content.   Sequence the content, trying to order it by operation, complexity, or difficulty (see chapter 3).

Step 3. Recognize and sequence behavior. Select a behavior sequence appropriate to the content. It is recommended that you use *accuracy, mastery,* and *automatic* for basic skills and *know, understand,* and *apply* for advanced skills or for strategy content (see pages 33–35).

Step 4. Recognize and sequence conditions. Identify relevant sets of conditions under which the student will be expected to perform the tasks being learned. Usually this will represent a sequence from the teacher-controlled classroom to the student-controlled outside world (see pages 35–36).

Step 5. Assemble a table of specifications. Assemble the content, behavior, and conditions from steps 1–4 into a table of specifications. Table 8.5 is taken from higher level curriculum. Tables for basic skills, decoding, and computation are in Appendix C.

Step 6. Discard nonapplicable objectives.   Look at the table and mark out any squares (objectives) that do not make sense or do not seem to be worth instructional time. These squares are labeled N.A. in Table 8.5.

TABLE 8.4
Guidelines for judging curriculum consolidation

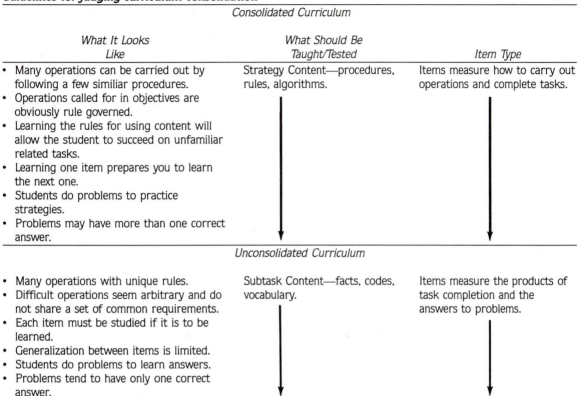

Consolidated Curriculum

What It Looks Like	What Should Be Taught/Tested	Item Type
• Many operations can be carried out by following a few similar procedures. • Operations called for in objectives are obviously rule governed. • Learning the rules for using content will allow the student to succeed on unfamiliar related tasks. • Learning one item prepares you to learn the next one. • Students do problems to practice strategies. • Problems may have more than one correct answer.	Strategy Content—procedures, rules, algorithms.	Items measure how to carry out operations and complete tasks.

Unconsolidated Curriculum

• Many operations with unique rules. • Difficult operations seem arbitrary and do not share a set of common requirements. • Each item must be studied if it is to be learned. • Generalization between items is limited. • Students do problems to learn answers. • Problems tend to have only one correct answer.	Subtask Content—facts, codes, vocabulary.	Items measure the products of task completion and the answers to problems.

Step 7. Write items for each square. The issue of how many items are needed for an adequate sample is a fairly hot one in test development circles. According to Berk (1980), the need for a large number of items decreases with the term and purpose of the decision. That is to say, long-term classification decisions necessitate more items than short-term treatment decisions. Treatment decisions do not obligate you to be as certain because they are backed up with the information supplied by teacher observation and monitoring. For the kind of testing we're talking about here (specific-

TABLE 8.5
Table of specifications for energy

	Uses	Transmission	Storage
Solar			
Electric			
Hydro			
Petro		N.A.	
Muscle		N.A.	N.A.

level probes for short-term objectives), 10 items per objective or strategy step is conventional and probably sufficient. For mastery (rate) objectives, the number of items needs to be increased (or the duration of the test modified, as described below) until the student has the opportunity to do 50% more items than called for in the objective's CAP. (If the CAP is 60, the total number of items should be 90.)

Selecting and Writing Items

The type of item used depends on several factors. Obviously the aim is to select items that are as useful as possible—which means they must be both reliable and valid. An item's goodness is linked to its fidelity, or match with the real world. Swezey (1981) has presented a sequence of item types based on Frederiksen (1962). They range from high to low fidelity: lifelike behavior, simulated behavior, related behavior, knowledge, attitudes, opinions. To assure high fidelity, you should select/ write items that require lifelike behavior, simulated behavior, or behaviors related to those required in actual application. Items can be categorized by content, behavior, conditions, or criteria. They are most often categorized by behavior and condition into select and supply headings (Gronlund, 1973). Supply items are those that require the student to produce an answer and include computation, reading, fill-in-the-blank, cloze, short answer, essay, and project completion. Select items include multiple choice, matching, maze (modified cloze), and true/ false.

While supply items are normally considered to have higher fidelity, they also have functional problems because they do not constrain the student's responses. Consider this example (repeated in the Reading Comprehension chapter). What if you have a student read a story about life in the Yukon Territories and then ask the question, "What is this story about?" If the student replies, "My father's favorite subject," you have no way of knowing if the answer reflects wild guessing or profound insight. Supply items can be improved by developing clear specifications for acceptable responses (e.g., the student's answer must include the location, characters, and principal actions of the story). Conversely, select items have practical (scoring) and technical advantages but they limit student responses and in the process reduce fidelity.

On treatment-sensitive specific-level probes we would expect to find supply items used for most basic skills. Select items are regularly reserved for higher level content or extremely low levels of basic skill knowledge (on which the selection is indicated by pointing, circling, and tracing responses). The best way to choose an item type is to look at the item and ask "Does this item have lifelike stimuli and require lifelike responses, under lifelike conditions?"

Rate Probes

The importance of rate and some general guidelines for writing rated tests have already been given in chapter 5 (pages 87–89). Because the foremost advantage of rate is that it illustrates the automaticity with which the student employs strategies, rate-based tests are characteristically used for relatively consolidated domains of curriculum. Let's take this sample objective:

> Given a sheet of two-place addition problems with regrouping, the student will write the answers to the problems at a rate of 50 digits correct per minute with 100% accuracy.

This objective is so comprehensive that it should not be difficult to match it to materials. First of all, the test will have two-place addition problems. These problems should be randomly distributed in terms of difficulty, meaning the sheet will *not* begin with some easy problems and then move to harder ones. The easy and hard problems should be scattered on the page. Obviously, most of them should require regrouping.

When a written test is used, the problems on the sheet should be legible and spaced to facilitate the student's work. The problems should be written in the same format as those which the student works during class assignments. To make scoring easier, the number of responses possible in each row can be written down the margin, as shown in Figure

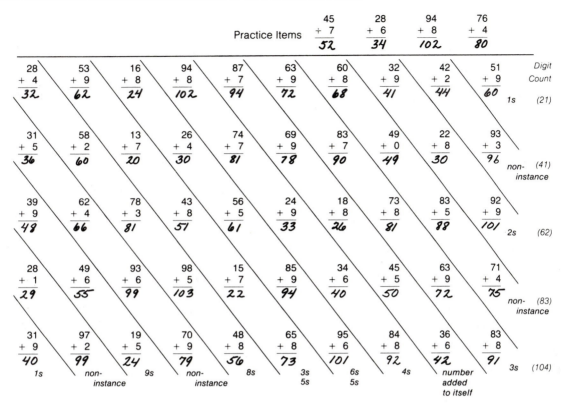

FIGURE 8.1
Sample probe *(Source:* From K. W. Howell, S. H. Zucker, and M. K. Morehead, *Multi-level Academic Skills Inventory: Math Manual*, p. 119. San Antonio: The Psychological Corporation, 1982. Reprinted with permission.)

8.1. Note that some items do not require regrouping; these non-instances are included to test the strategy for deciding when to regroup.

A student's rate of response depends on skill, the number of opportunities, and the time allowed. Because the objective stipulates that 50 digits need to be done in 1 minute, a sufficient number of opportunities must be on the page. Ideally there should be 50% more opportunities than the objective calls for. To get the best idea of student rate, students taking rate tests should be encouraged to skip items they do not know. So the test sheet for this objective should have enough problems (at least 38) to allow 75 digits.

Including 50% more problems means that few students will ever finish all of them. Some kids may become upset when they see all of that work and can't ever seem to get it done. Therefore, you will want to put them at ease by saying "work as fast but as carefully as you can. If you come to one you do not know—skip it. Don't worry about finishing the page. There are more problems here than anyone needs to do."

The prominent consideration when developing rate tests is to avoid anything that artificially reduces or puts a ceiling on response fluency. It is important to allow many opportunities for the behavior to occur. We are trying to evaluate behavior, so the more we have, the happier we are. Remember that one of the greatest weaknesses of published tests is that they encourage teachers to arrive at conclusions from sparse behavior samples. If you find yourself with low frequencies of behavior, you may solve your problem four ways: (a) extend the time interval for the test, (b) provide more opportunities (items), (c) slice the behavior, (d) move to a response class. We will briefly elaborate on each of these.

Time. Time extension is an obvious way to increase the total number of behaviors counted (though not necessarily their rate). Suppose it takes 10 seconds to do a three-place multiplication problem with regrouping. If you allow the students 1 minute, the most problems they can do is six. You can raise this ceiling on their behavior by timing for 2 minutes. In 2 minutes they will have the opportunity to do 12 problems. However, too much time can cause fatigue. Although successful students can write 100 or more digits per minute, they can't keep up this rate for more than a couple of minutes.

Opportunities. Providing more opportunities is also an obvious way to obtain an increase in frequency. If there are only five problems, the ceiling count must be five. Change the number to 20 and you provide the opportunity for more behavior.

Slice. Sometimes you can "slice" a behavior to raise the frequency. When you slice, you segment the behavior and count components. For example, if you want to "stop smoking," you can count (a) packs a day, (b) cigarettes a day, or (c) puffs a day. As a rule, higher frequency behaviors are easier to change than low frequency ones. Therefore, puffs are easier to change than packs, and since decreasing both leads to "stop smoking," it is better to count puffs. Examples of academic slicing include counting digits instead of problems or syllables spelled instead of words.

Classes. The last way to increase frequency is to count an entire class of behavior instead of one member of the class. This is done by first defining a *response class.* A response class is composed of behaviors that are so closely related that changing one raises the probability of changing them all. To illustrate, imagine that you work in a correctional institution, and Margie is sent there for stealing cars. "Steals cars" might be your pinpoint and decreasing "steals cars" your main objective. Unfortunately, there are no cars parked along the hallways of your reformatory, so during Margie's whole stay she never does the pinpoint and is never punished for it. Similarly you may reward her day and night at 10-minute intervals for "not stealing cars," but the treatment may seem somehow peculiar to her. So what do you do? You make up a response class called "respects property of others" and intervene on and count all instances of "property crimes" including stealing extra desserts and entering rooms without permission. You hope that you will ultimately decrease the stealing of cars. By redefining the pinpoint to include all samples of the class "property crimes," you have raised the possible frequency.

Establishing CAP

CAP is the standard of performance specified in the objective. Usually it is assumed that the performance level specified in the CAP represents minimal competency at the skill. Our actual ability to establish these minimal competency levels (or maximum incompetency levels, if you're a cynic) can be questioned. However, most evaluators recognize the need to specify levels of performance that correspond to certain educational decisions. For example, discovering that a student has met CAP typically leads the evaluator to decide that instruction on the skill is no longer needed.

There are at least three reasons why specifying CAP is a good idea. First of all, it provides a target for the student and the teacher, which in turn provides the sort of task and performance focus necessary for good instruction. Second, the CAP specifies levels of task proficiency that, when met, allow the student to learn subsequent tasks in a shorter period of time (Bloom, 1984). Finally, as mentioned above, CAP allows educators to decide when a student is sufficiently proficient at a skill to move on.

Ideally, CAP will have already been established as part of the school program's curriculum development. If not, the burden may fall on the individual evaluator. In this case, you will probably want to follow one of the following procedures. These procedures are not particularly simple—but curriculum-based evaluation is impossible without curriculum expectations.

Academic CAP.   In educational literature, criteria will be found which have been established (a) by guessing (the worst way), (b) by asking experts, (c) by employing standardization techniques, and (d) by using research validating the effect of meeting different criteria on subsequent learning. Each technique has advantages and disadvantages. For the teacher, the best ways to get criteria are to consult experts or to standardize the objective.

Expert Judgment.   One way to determine how well someone should do something is to ask someone who already knows. In many cases, particularly in the basic skills, CAPs have already been established. To find them, you should consult educators, texts, or journals that deal with the content in question. Because opinions will almost certainly vary, some test developers use the levels specified by experts as an initial estimate and then administer the test to see if the standard seems to separate instructed and uninstructed students. This is explained in Appendix B.

Standardization.   When a CRT is standardized, people who are successful at the task are selected. This group is *not* randomly assembled. Only people who are judged by experts to be good at the task and who are in the same grade as the target student are selected for the standardization population. Then they all take the test and their median (middle—not average) score is found. This middle score can then be used as the CAP.

Suppose you are a special/remedial teacher and you have a fourth-grade student named Greg who is doing second-grade work. What is your ultimate

goal for Greg? Placement into the regular fourth-grade curriculum. To meet this goal you must teach Greg to do addition problems like successful fourth graders do them (not necessarily like the *average* fourth grader does them). This means Greg must learn addition facts because they are a subskill of addition problems. So you go to the fourth-grade teacher and ask for the names of students in the class who she believes are successful at addition. You then make up an addition fact probe sheet and give it to those successful students. Next, you arrange the resulting scores from highest to lowest and find the median score of the successful students, as shown in Table 8.6. In Table 8.6, the median of successful students was 59 addition fact problems completed in 1 minute. The average score (norm) for the entire class was only 50. You want Greg to be successful in the fourth-grade class, so you give him a 9-point edge over the average kid and use 59 as your criterion.

The hardest part of the system just described is deciding which students to use for the standardization procedure. We recommend *grade-level peers* rather than *age-level peers*. This means that if a student has been retained, you should compare him to students at his current grade level. We have found that few academic skills vary simply as a function of age; they are more apt to vary as a function of instruction and practice. A student who should be in the eighth grade but who was retained in the seventh grade has only been taught seventh-grade material. Therefore, even though he is older than most seventh graders, they should still be used to establish CAP for him.

As a rule you can accept those selected by the teacher as the ones who have mastered the target skill. Teacher judgment is the ultimate standard to which tests are compared in validity studies, though it is safer to use a few students from several teachers than a lot from one. The teacher's judgment can be improved by making the selection question very specific. For example, "Name the 10 best students at addition—and the 10 worst students at addition." If the teacher can't name a sufficiently large population (at least 10 students), then you may wish to use test scores from a valid standardized

TABLE 8.6
Finding the median score of successful students

	Rate of Addition Fact Problems per Minute	
	Students Selected as Successful	*Students Selected as Unsuccessful*
	87	47
	72	47
	64	47
	64	46
	63	46
	62	45
Median of	60	44
successful ——►	59	44
students	59	39
	57	36
	56	35
	55	35
	48	31
	48	28
	48	27
	Mean (average) of class = 50	

test to find the upper 50% of the class. Although you will lose some content validity, you can assume that the upper 50% of the kids in the class are those most apt to have the skill in which you are interested. Therefore, the median score of the top half of the class will provide a reasonable estimate of CAP.

If the scores of the successful students are extremely variable, you may wish to collect a larger sample. For example, if the scores you got from an addition probe were 94, 92, 73, 70, 60, 55, 40, 35, 22, you wouldn't think that the median (60) was particularly descriptive of the group because the extreme scores, 94 and 22, vary from the median by as much as 273%. The easiest way to tell if a score is descriptive is to rank the scores in a frequency distribution (see Appendix B) and then to look at it. Here is another quick procedure for judging variability. Once the median has been found, multiply and divide it by 1.5. The resulting numbers are then used to form an interval around the median. If your testing produces a large proportion of scores (more than 15%) that fall outside of the 1.5 boundary, you should either increase the sample size or review the way you picked the sample in the first place. Increasing the sample size or improving

the selection procedure should decrease the variability of the sample, which will increase the reliability of the CAP. The median score in Table 8.6 was 59. This means the boundaries around it would be $59 \times 1.5 = 88.5$; $59 \div 1.5 = 39.3$. None of the successful students' scores falls outside the boundaries of 89 and 39, so the median of 59 is accepted as a reliable score. In the case of the scores listed at the beginning of this paragraph, 44% of the scores fall outside the 1.5 interval, indicating that little confidence should be placed in the median score.

The procedure for determining CAP for academic skills is as follows:

1. Devise a test.
2. Select a standardization population of successful grade level peers by using:
   a. Teacher judgment to find students with the target skill or
   b. Test results to find the upper 50% of the class.
3. If the sample is less than 10, locate additional successful students in another class.
4. Administer the test exactly as it will be given to the special/remedial students.
5. Find the median score.

6. Rank order or graph the scores to see if the median score describes the successful group, or multiply and divide the median score by 1.5 to establish a confidence interval around the median score.
7. If most of the scores fall close to the median, accept the median score as CAP.
8. If a large proportion of the sample (more than 15%) falls outside of the confidence interval, double the sample size and repeat the process or review the procedure used to select the sample.

Interestingly, CAPs determined by using this procedure do not vary from class to class as much as class averages do. We have used the procedure with addition and multiplication facts and found that the median score of successful students did not vary as much from school to school as class averages.

Cautions.   Three cautions need to be added to the discussion of standardization. The first is a repeat: The importance of decisions made with a standard determines the rigor of the standardization procedure. If a student is to be placed in a treatment and carefully monitored (see chapter 15), then an incorrect decision will be detected and corrected before any damage occurs. In this case, exact CAP, while ideal, is not absolutely necessary. However, long-term placement decisions that are not followed by monitoring require very high levels of CAP validity (Berk, 1986).

The second caution pertains to the nature of a criterion itself. The standardization procedure just described may be flawed because the level of skill proficiency needed to learn a task may be higher than the level needed to simply be successful at it. This means that the successful students the teacher has identified may actually be less proficient than they were in the past. For example, students just learning math facts often seem better at them than older students or even math teachers. This may be because the high levels of competency reached during active instruction, while necessary to guarantee generalization and maintenance, are not needed for everyday use of math facts. When current experts are used during standardization, you may establish lower-than-necessary levels of competency.

Finally, we should note that ideal proficiency levels undoubtably vary between individuals. This is because any task requires the use of many skills and students who are low at one may simply compensate by being high on another. For example, a student who makes excellent use of passage context when reading may be able to overcome the effect of inadequate phonic skills and therefore read as well as another student who has excellent phonics. The ultimate way to determine a criterion is to find the level of proficiency on skill A that prompts the fastest learning of skill B. For example, White (1986) described a student who needed to obtain twice the fluency level of her normal peers before she could efficiently integrate her skill at "saying sounds" with other tasks.

Taken together, these three cautions tell evaluators that criteria levels are not absolute. If it could be expected that the effects of instructional decisions would be carefully monitored, the need to specify exact task-specific performance levels would be greatly reduced. However, the monitoring procedures needed to provide this reduction (such as the ones discussed in chapter 15) are not widely used and aren't likely to be. So it remains necessary to establish task-specific criteria. In addition, it appears that if errors are to be made in setting CAP, errors that set the standard too high are better than errors that set it too low.

Social Behavior CAP.   The norm (average) is not particularly relevant to academic skills, but it is to social skills. The average has greater relevance to social behavior because in most situations the behavior of others is a primary cue individuals use to decide how to behave. In our culture, while we don't want to be called *average*, we don't like being considered *abnormal* either. The issue of using average behavior as the target for special students is discussed in some detail in chapter 14.

It is as necessary to establish criteria for nonacademic behaviors (such as talk outs or raise hand) as it is for academic behaviors. However, because the appropriateness of behavior varies from situation to situation, absolute criteria cannot be established. The best approach for establishing CAP for social behavior is the ecological approach (Mehan, 1981b;

FIGURE 8.2
A device for collecting an ecological baseline

		Hour 1						Total	Hour 2						Total
Target student Darrell	+	0	0	0	+	+		3	0	0	0	0	+	+	4
Random peer	+	0	+	+	+	0		2	0	+	+	+	0	+	2

+ = In seat
0 = Out of seat

Target's Total __7__
Peer's Total __4__

Moos, 1973; Prieto & Rutherford, 1977; Tuersky & Kahneman, 1973). The ecological model says that a student should be expected to engage in those behaviors that are (a) available in the environment, (b) acceptable to others in the environment, or (c) commonly occurring in the environment. What this means is that kids will act like those around them act (as do adults).

Lack of criteria has always been a problem when evaluating social behavior. To evaluate you must compare. When evaluating the social behavior of students the question becomes "What should we compare this behavior to?" Teachers often compare the behavior of students to their own theories or ideas about what is or is not acceptable. Unfortunately the opinions of teachers vary considerably; one may accept student actions another will not (Walker & Rankin, 1983). In the ecological model, a student's behavior is compared to the environment by asking "Is this behavior acceptable in this context?" to find out if it is necessary to attend to the environment and not just to the student. This is exactly what we do when we task analyze a skill prior to evaluating academics.

One useful environmental observation technique is called an *ecological baseline.* The purpose of the technique is to collect data to which the target student can be compared. Suppose you think a student (Darrell) is out of his seat too often. You could set up an observation form like the one in Figure 8.2. On this form, behavior samples are taken at 10-minute intervals for 1 hour in the morning and 1 hour in the afternoon (for a total of 12 intervals). This is done by setting a timer to signal every 10 minutes. When the timer chimes (vibrator devices can be placed in your pocket if you don't want the class to know about the signal), you mark if Darrell is in or out of his seat. At the same time you also code the behavior of a *random* peer. This means

that for each interval you select at random another student in the class to observe along with Darrell. The selection must be random; therefore, devise a system for picking the other student *before* the signal goes off. Collect the data for three days and summarize it, as shown in Figure 8.3.

As you can see in Figure 8.3, Darrell is out of his seat more often than the random peers. The average frequency of the peers was four. Four, then, becomes the CAP for this behavior.

The CAP tells us how often out-of-seat behavior occurs in the environment. Another way to take the same kind of data is simply to note if *anyone* is out of his seat when Darrell is out of his. If the average student leaves his seat only four times, but there is *always someone* out of his seat when Darrell is, Darrell may believe it is acceptable to be moving

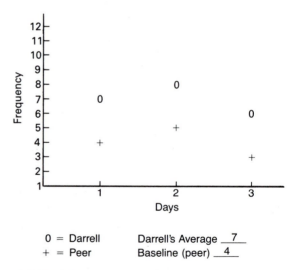

0 = Darrell
+ = Peer

Darrell's Average __7__
Baseline (peer) __4__

FIGURE 8.3
Summary of out-of-seat behavior

around each time he does so. In this case you might want to consider intervening on the class and not Darrell alone.

3.2 ADMINISTER PROBE

Tips for administration were covered in the last chapter under step 1.2 and are not significantly different at the specific level.

3.3 SUMMARIZE BEHAVIOR

Behavior summary was also discussed in chapter 7, but parts of it need to be briefly repeated here. The most important thing to remember is that the summaries of behavior must be reported in relation to the assumed cause (or objective) for which the specific-level test was given.

There are three ways to summarize behavior:

1. Report the actual behavior. This is accomplished with a stimulus/response comment sheet (as described on pages 131–132 of chapter 7).
2. Report discrepancies. At the specific level the scores reported are always direct summaries of accuracy or rate behavior, not normative derivations such as percentiles or grade equivalencies.
3. Reporting status on objectives. This process is very useful and, once again, is simply an extension of a process introduced in chapter 7. Take a sequence of objectives, or even a table of specifications, and for each assumed cause simply mark its status as Pass (adequate), No Pass (inadequate), or ? (uncertain). The table of specifications found in Appendix C can be used this way. An example is shown in Table 8.7.

TABLE 8.7
Behavior summary

Assumed Causes	Content Subskills	Accuracy Test	Fluency Test
	Paragraph reading	NP	NP
	Polysyllabic words	No Test	No Test
	Contractions	No Test	No Test
	Compound words	No Test	No Test
x	Sight words	P	NP
x	Silent letters	NP	NP
	Modifications		
x	Endings (suffixes)	P	NP
x	Clusters	NP	NP
x	*r*-controlled vowels	NP	?
	Teams		
x	Vowel teams	P	?
x	Consonant digraphs	P	NP
x	Consonant teams	P	NP
	Conversions		
x	Vowel conversions	P	P
x	Vowel + e conversions	P	P
	Sounds		
	CVC words	No Test	No Test
	Vowels	No Test	No Test
	Consonants	No Test	No Test
	Sequence	No Test	No Test
	Sounds	No Test	No Test
	Symbols	No Test	No Test

4.0 INTERPRET RESULTS

This is the final stage of evaluation: decision making. The following steps are used to convert the information gathered into treatment recommendations.

Question 4.A Is additional testing required?

Key Consideration: Have you found explanations for the student's failure that can be used to guide treatment?

4.1 Additional Testing

Compare the assumed causes for failure stated in step 2.3 to the summary of specific-level behavior in step 3.3. If the original assumed causes do not prove to be correct you must return to step 2 and develop new ones. This means additional testing may also be required (4.1a). For example, if you suspected that a student could not comprehend a reading passage due to poor vocabulary skills, but specific-level testing revealed that the student's vocabulary was adequate, you would have to come up with a new assumed cause for the failure.

In most cases some of the assumed causes you developed will prove to have been accurate while others will not. Using Table 8.7, we can see that of the content areas originally assumed to be problematic (marked with an X) several specific tests were failed, several passed, and two remain uncertain. These results indicate that all objectives (assumed causes) marked *P* should be dropped from active instruction and simply monitored for maintenance. Assumed causes marked *NP* should be listed as short-term instructional objectives (step 4.1b). Those marked with *?* (fluency of *r*-controlled vowels and vowel teams) will require additional testing (Step 4.1a). If no assumed causes prove to have been valid, the evaluator must return to step 2.0.

4.2 Employ Systematic Interpretation

Decision making was covered to some depth in chapter 6 (it is also presented in chapter 15). As you recall, treatment decisions pertain either to curriculum (what will be taught) or instruction (how it will be taught). Table 8.8 outlines the what-to-teach decision-making process. To carry out the process, look at the test results to determine the student's status and then select the appropriate recommendation. For example, assume that you have conducted a reading comprehension evaluation and obtained the following results:

FACT: Student referred for poor comprehension of science book

Assumed cause	Test	CAP	Behavior on test
1. Slow decoding	Timed reading of grade level passage	140c 5-7e	148c 5e

STATUS: Adequate (at performance aim)
RECOMMENDATION: Decoding instruction isn't needed (1.2a)

Assumed cause	Test	CAP	Behavior on test
2. Poor vocabulary	Select appropriate word definition for a given passage	90%	40%

STATUS: No Pass (partially proficient)
RECOMMENDATION: Teach passage-dependent vocabulary in context (1.1 and 1.3b)

Given these results, it is clear that the student does not need to work on decoding rate, but does need instruction on vocabulary. Because he is partially proficient (40%) at using passage content to identify the meaning of words, it is not necessary to search for additional subskills of that task, but rather to teach the strategy for using passage clues to decide what words mean.

By examining the status of each validated assumed cause, you will be able to make recommendations about what the student should be taught. By readministering specific tests for each objective you will also be able to monitor the effectiveness of treatments and make decisions about how the student should be taught (as explained in chapter 15).

TABLE 8.8
Interpretation guidelines

Possible Curriculum Decisions:
1.1 Stay with current level and context
1.2 Change level
    1.2.a Move to a more complex objective
    1.2.b Move to a simpler objective (only when no corrects have occurred after several sessions)
    1.2.c Adjust aim date forward
1.3 Change context
    1.3.a Teach the objective in context
    1.3.b Teach the objective in isolation (only when tests of context knowledge are failed)

Directions: Ask the following questions about the status of each validated assumed cause and note the appropriate recommendation.

Status		*Recommendation*
A.	Student is partially proficient at the skill or strategy.	1.1 Teach this objective.
B.	Student has reached the performance aim.	1.2.a Instruction isn't needed on this objective. Move to a more complex objective if that is appropriate.
C.	Student demonstrates no (zero) proficiency at a task in spite of instruction on it.	1.2.b Conduct additional assessment and move to a simpler objective.
D.	Student has not reached the performance aim but is closer to it than he was expected to be by this time.	1.2.c Adjust aim date forward.
E.	Student is not adequately proficient at the task but has knowledge of related tasks.	1.3.a Teach the objective in context.
F.	Student is not adequately proficient at the task and lacks the knowledge of related tasks needed to appreciate its purpose or value.	1.3.b Teach the objective in isolation.

SUMMARY

Chapters 7 and 8 have outlined and described the task-analytical system of evaluation. Descriptions of each activity in the system have been presented. At times these descriptions have been elaborate, giving the impression that the system is complex—of course, in some ways it is. To use curriculum-based evaluation, you must clarify the curriculum. If content recognition, specification of behavior/conditions, and development of criteria have not been completed prior to the evaluation, the job of doing them falls—by default—on the evaluator.

Attempting curriculum-based evaluation in the absence of a well-defined curriculum can be like as-sembling a piece of complicated equipment for the first time without any directions. You may know how to use all the tools but be frustrated by the need to puzzle each step out on your own. These chapters have explained each step to help the first-time evaluator.

Once the steps have been followed a few times, these directions may no longer be needed. However, when a particularly difficult student comes along you may want to return to Figure 7.1 and its explanation. You may also need to seek specific help in certain curriculum areas. The second part of this text provides information needed to conduct evaluations in both academic and social skill curricula.

Study Questions

1. Define the following terms as used in this chapter. Some of these terms may be review from previous chapters.
   a. Fact
   b. Measurement
   c. Assumed causes
   d. Specific level
   e. Probe
   f. Standardization
   g. Calibration
   h. Discrepancy
   i. Consolidated
   j. Slice
   k. CAP
   l. Table of specifications
   m. Fidelity
   n. Fluency
   o. Response class
2. Specific-level tests
   a. verify the assumptions made after survey-level testing.
   b. establish grade-level equivalencies.
   c. are synonymous with standardized tests.
   d. obtain general samples of student work.
3. If Candi should have mastered 110 objectives and has only mastered 82, how many objectives must she learn this year?
   a. 28
   b. 192
   c. 28 plus the number of objectives her classmates will cover this year
   d. Not too many, or she will experience excessive stress
4. One good way to avoid administering a separate test for each narrow objective taught is to
   a. test only every third or fourth objective.
   b. consolidate objectives that can be treated as one task.
   c. administer only survey-level tests.
   d. teach only broadly calibrated objectives.
5. Which behavior sequence is most appropriate for the skill "single place addition with regrouping"?
   a. Know, comprehend, apply
   b. Frequency, abstractness, length
   c. Accuracy, mastery, automatic
   d. Content, conditions, criteria
6. Tests used for long-term decisions and very important decisions require
   a. 10 items per objectives.
   b. fewer items than tests used for short-term or less important decisions.
   c. more items than tests used for short-term or less important decisions.
   d. 50% more items than called for in the objective's CAP.
7. Rate probes require
   a. 50% more items than the criterion calls for.
   b. at least 75 items.
   c. few items, since they are generally a subsection of a survey-level test.
   d. few items, since they are only used for short-term discussions.

8. Develop an appropriate specific-level test for the following objective:

   The student will read words containing the vowel team *ea* in isolation at 60 words per minute with 100% accuracy.

PART TWO

EVALUATION OF SPECIFIC CURRICULUM AREAS

Chapter 9

Reading Comprehension

We have subdivided the domain of reading into comprehension and decoding. This chapter is about comprehension, and decoding will be discussed in chapter 10. Before talking about comprehension and decoding, however, we'd like to make the following disclaimer: A domain as complex as reading cannot be adequately addresssed in the few pages we have allocated. Volumes have been written describing reading, reading research, theories of reading, and procedures for evaluating reading (Pearson, Barr, Kamil, & Mosenthal, 1984; Resnick & Weaver, 1979; Singer & Ruddell, 1985). While we do not pretend to discuss all you need to know about reading, we will present a framework for making decisions about where to begin reading instruction for the students you evaluate.

FOCUS: COMPREHENSION

What Is Comprehension?

The reading field has always been characterized by disagreement, even at the definitional level. There is little consensus about what reading is and no consensus about how to teach it, much less how to evaluate it. This is especially true of comprehension. Before the 1980s, arguments about reading focused on whether reading was a *top down* (whole language) or a *bottom up* (skill-based) process (Samuels & Kamil, 1984). Proponents of the *top down* theories focused attention on the meaning-driven integrated process of reading, while *bottom up* advocates noted that reading was comprised of many teachable skills (such as phonics). Top down teachers argued that you cannot break reading into subtasks, while *bottom up* teachers taught students to read by focusing on specific skill acquisition.

Today, while there may be an impression remaining that the disagreement continues unabated, it does finally seem to be giving way to the notion that reading is an interactive process that uses code, context, prior knowledge, vocabulary, and language, along with various cognitive strategies. The recognition that comprehension is an interactive process is a relief to many, but our task of describing how to evaluate it has not been made easier.

By defining comprehension as an interactive process we are agreeing that it is a multidimensional construct, and as such not easily observed. To talk about something that cannot be seen we must rely on inference and on theories. As you recall, in chapter 2 we noted that to evaluate something you

must compare it to a standard. In the case of comprehension the latest theory often becomes the standard. Therefore, a student's behavior may seem typical or atypical, depending on the theory used. In fact, the same student's performance may seem typical when compared to one theory and atypical when compared to another.

Most people would agree that when someone comprehends a passage, he or she understands it. But how do we measure this understanding? Traditionally, we do it by asking questions about the passage after it has been read. This procedure requires the kid to remember what was read. Memory may not even be in the theory, but it becomes part of the *operational definition* of comprehension because it is part of the measurement procedure. Most of the so-called diagnostic reading inventories, for example, are made up of passages followed by questions. The student reads each passage and then answers questions before reading the next passage. In these cases the interval between reading the passage and answering the questions is a minute or two. What if you waited 30 minutes before asking the questions? What if you waited a week? If you did wait longer, the student's score would almost certainly be different (probably lower), because what was once "comprehended" was now forgotten. Therefore, a student's score on postpassage questions depends not only on what he understands but on what he remembers. Many educators seem to accept this even though few of them would agree that memory and comprehension are synonymous.

Is the traditional comprehension test valid? Think about it for a second. Why do you read? Why do you read the newspaper? Why do you read one particular newspaper? Why do you choose *Time* or *Newsweek*, *Rolling Stone* or *People*, *Cognition and Instruction* or *Experimental Education*? Why are you reading this book? There are a lot of answers to these questions. You probably read to get *what you want* from the material. What you want varies from day to day with your mood, purpose, and interest and is determined *before* you read. (Speaking of mood and interest, it is surprising to note that, while most reading teachers extol the virtue of reading for enjoyment, we have never seen a reading test that asks if the kid enjoyed the passage.)

If you were to ask questions a week after the student reads a passage, the student's score would no doubt fall. Now suppose you asked the question *before* the kid read the passage and again after reading, e.g., "Read this paragraph to find out how old Joy is." What would happen? The score on the postreading questions would probably be raised because the student would read to answer the question. Which is the better measure of comprehension—the one that measures what a student happened to retain or the one that measures what information a student can find if directed to look for it? Your answer to that question will reflect what you think comprehension is.

Retention of information (memory), while important, depends on things like motivation and interest that are not really synonymous with comprehension. Instead, we think that comprehension is the act of combining information in passages with prior knowledge in order to construct meaning. Comprehension, therefore, takes place as a person is reading and comprises the set of skills that lets him or her find information and understand it in terms of what is already known. It is a process that depends on the reader's prior knowledge of the content, skill at decoding, knowledge of vocabulary, language proficiency, and application of comprehension strategies. The interactive nature of comprehension requires that each of these elements combines, influences, and at times compensates for each other accurately and fluently.

Text Variables and Their Impact on Comprehension

While our definition of comprehension places great emphasis on what a reader brings to the text, it is important to understand that there are variables outside the learner that influence comprehension. We will discuss one of these variables, text structure, as we refine our definition of reading comprehension. By *text structure* we mean both general organizers and overall structure. Examples of general organizers are abstracts, focus questions, headings, and summaries. Overall structure includes general organizers but is more. It is the way

the "ideas" in the text are related to convey a message to the reader (Meyer & Rice, 1984). The organization of written material can "signal" a reader as to what is relevant. It can either provide cohesion or interrupt and mislead the reader (Armbruster, 1984a; Meyer & Rice, 1984). Text structure influences the quality of comprehension responses we elicit from students during evaluation and contributes to or interferes with the acquisition of adequate reading skills.

Historically, attempts to address text difficulty have not focused on structure. They have focused instead on word frequency, word length, and sentence length. Readability formulas reflect this emphasis. Today we know that text complexity is not solely a function of these factors. Text complexity is linked to organization at the sentence and passage level and to the density of ideas (sometimes called *propositions*) within the text (Kintsch & Keenan, 1973; Meyer & Rice, 1984).

Code-Emphasis Texts

Attempts to develop materials that provide controlled opportunities for students to practice decoding skills may have contributed to the illusion that controlling text difficulty is a solution to reading problems (MacGinitie, 1984). Yes, we should select materials that provide opportunities to practice decoding, but we must also understand that code-emphasis materials may lack certain features. Stories with vague or roundabout language are often created in attempts to control decoding. When used as the sole basis for reading instruction, these stories do not provide appropriate practice for comprehension or opportunities to see known oral vocabulary in text. If the student is forced to practice decoding in the absence of meaning, you can expect it to take him longer to integrate the complex process of reading. We are not suggesting that you discard all material in which stories are controlled for decoding, but we do suggest that you compensate by reading to the students from less controlled books.

Word Difficulty

High interest–low vocabulary texts are often a problem, not a solution. When difficult words are replaced with easier words (a process known as

TABLE 9.1
Word difficulty: Text and student variables

Text Variables	Student Variables
1. Word frequency in text	1. Time spent reading
2. Word frequency in language	2. Knowledge of vocabulary
3. Word fit with phonics rules	3. Knowledge of content
4. Word fit with text context	4. Fluency and accuracy in phonics
	5. Fluency and accuracy in use of context clues

dumbing down the vocabulary), passage meaning may be lost or at least obscured (Bower, 1984). To replace the word "caterpillar" with a phrase such as "a worm with lots of legs" may reduce word-syllable length, but it obscures meaning and does not help improve kids' inadequate vocabularies.

Word difficulty is affected by how frequently a word is encountered in the text, how well the word conforms to phonics rules, the degree to which a passage reveals or contributes to guessing what the word might be, and whether the word is in the student's oral vocabulary. Student variables and text variables related to word difficulty are shown in Table 9.1.

Any evaluation of a student's reading skills should include an evaluation of text readability. Readability cannot be estimated with a formula of word frequency, word length, and sentence length alone. Those who want to become more conversant with text structure should read Armbruster (1984b) and MacGinitie (1984). Those who are interested in developing criteria for evaluating text should read Anderson and Armbruster (1984).

Assumed Causes for Reading Failure

Depending upon your point of view, comprehension either has subtasks or prerequisites. Subtasks are thought of as parts of the task itself, while prerequisites are those things that must be present for the task to take be carried out at all. General and specific comprehension strategies, vocabulary, and language are portions of the comprehension task, and decoding and prior knowledge of context are prerequisites. Comprehension is not as divisible as other skills, but it can still be effectively evaluated with the task-analytical curriculum model. Therefore, while task analysis may do little to explain how comprehension takes place, it can be a big help in discovering what to teach when it doesn't. Both task components and prerequisites can be explanations for a failure to comprehend and thus can be explored as assumed causes. These task components—strategies, vocabulary, and language —and prerequisites—prior knowledge and decoding—will be discussed in the following pages. They are presented by order of probability—meaning the most likely explanations for failing to comprehend will be discussed first.

Prior Knowledge

One prerequisite to comprehension is prior knowledge. In this case we *do not* mean prior knowledge of the necessary language, vocabulary, and decoding skills. We are referring to prior knowledge of passage content. A student who doesn't have some basic core of information about the subject will not be able to comprehend the passage (Gaffney & McCloone, 1984).

Comprehension can, in part, be described as an interaction of the reader's knowledge with the text's content, as well as the anticipation of what the content will be (Palinscar & Brown, 1984). A student's accuracy at comprehension will vary as the content of the text varies. This means a kid may easily comprehend material about which he knows a lot but have trouble with content about which he knows little. For experience in how prior knowledge affects comprehension, work the two paragraphs in Figure 9.1a. The first is based on a later section of this chapter; the second is from an article on cosmic rays. The topic of cosmic rays was selected in the hope that you don't know much about it. As you check your work with Figure 9.1b, you may notice that while you can decode each passage, your understanding of them varies.

Passage 1

"As the teacher you _____ the option of limiting
                          1
_____ vocabulary, but your students _____ necessarily
   2   3
have the option _____ expanding theirs. In addition
                   4
_____ of remedial tests, or _____ reading texts,
   5   6
will intentionally _____ the vocabulary to well _____
                      7   8
the student's speaking vocabulary _____ will seldom
                                     9
include adequate _____ for teaching necessary
                    10
words. _____ failure to provide for adequate _____
          11   12
instruction is also _____ of most basal programs..."
                       13

Answers to Passage 1

"As the teacher you <u>have</u> the option of limiting
                         1
<u>your</u> vocabulary, but your students <u>don't</u> necessarily
    2   3
have the option <u>of</u> expanding theirs. In addition
                    4
<u>authors</u> of remedial texts, or <u>corrective</u> reading texts,
    5   6
will intentionally <u>limit</u> the vocabulary to well
                       7
<u>below</u> the student's speaking vocabulary <u>and</u> will seldom
    8   9
include adequate <u>procedures</u> for teaching necessary
                     10
words. <u>This</u> failure to provide for adequate <u>vocabulary</u>
          11   12
instruction is also <u>typical</u> of most basal programs..."
                        13

Passage 2

"Thus if the critical _____ for galactic confinement
                         1
of _____ protons is 2.6 × 10^{19} electron _____
    2   3
according to certain _____, the critical energy for
                        4
_____ of cosmic-ray iron nuclei _____ to the
   5   6
same model _____ be 26 times less, _____ only 10^{18}
              7   8
electron volts. _____ therefore makes a great _____
                   9   10
of difference whether on _____ one hand the highest-
                            11
energy _____ rays are protons or _____ nuclei or on
          12   13
the _____ hand they have a composition unlike either
       14
of those alternatives."

Answers to Passage 2

"Thus if the critical <u>energy</u> for galactic confinement
                          1
of <u>cosmic-ray</u> protons is 2.6 × 10^{19} electron
    2
<u>volts</u> according to certain <u>model,</u> the critical energy for
    3   4
<u>confinement</u> of cosmic-ray from nuclei <u>according</u> to the
    5   6
same model <u>will</u> be 26 times less, <u>or</u> only 10^{18}
              7   8
electron volts. <u>It</u> therefore makes a great <u>deal</u>
                   9   10
of difference whether on <u>the</u> one hand the highest-
                            11
energy <u>cosmic</u> rays are protons or <u>iron</u> nuclei or on the
          12   13
<u>other</u> hand they have a composition unlike either
    14
of those alternatives."

(a)

(b)

FIGURE 9.1

Cloze paragraphs—Text difficulty and prior knowledge (Source: Passage 2 drawn from J. Linsley,
"The Highest-Energy Cosmic Rays," *Scientific American*, 1978, *239* (1), p. 67.)

"Knowledge" is not a solid thing that can be picked out of the brain. A person is said to have knowledge only after acting knowledgeable. Unfortunately, there aren't "prior knowledge tests" for reading comprehension. If there is a distinction between knowledge and comprehension, it's a temporal one, meaning that what a person comprehends today will be part of his or her knowledge tomorrow.

Decoding

Decoding skill is a prerequisite to comprehending, though this doesn't mean comprehension shouldn't be taught until decoding is mastered. Decoding skill includes both accuracy and fluency. A teacher may justifiably say a student who is extremely slow has not passed comprehension regardless of accuracy on a comprehension test. The rate at which a person comprehends written material is first of all limited by the rate at which he or she decodes it. The person who decodes the fastest is exposed to the most ideas per minute. Therefore, as decoding speed increases, the amount of comprehension increases—up to a point. (That is the point at which the student is no longer able to check each consecutive word to see if it completes a thought [Carver, 1982], and it is *extremely* fast. Few students read too fast to comprehend.) The rate of comprehension is also limited by the number of thoughts per word available in the material. The total amount of understanding per minute is, therefore, the result of a complex interaction between the knowledge base of the reader, decoding skill/speed, and the density of meaning in the material being read (Danks, 1982; Stanovitch, 1983).

In general, reading speed and comprehension are not closely related (Farr, 1969). Both fast and slow readers may be unable to comprehend. And speeding up or slowing down a student will not necessarily alter the quality of comprehension (only the amount). The only instance in which there is a close relationship between speed and comprehension is when the student falls below a minimal level of decoding fluency. In that case, the student must attend so closely to decoding that he cannot attend to the meaning of the passage. Estimates of this critical decoding threshold vary, but 150 to 200 words per minute is probably a good minimal rate after the third grade (Biemiller, 1978; Tenenbaum, 1983).

Automaticity in decoding frees the student's working memory (short-term memory) so that it may interact with comprehension (Samuels, 1983). However, it is impossible to set an aim for the rate at which everyone should read because rate should vary according to the difficulty of the material. And, of course, difficulty depends upon the reader's own knowledge base. Being able to speed up or slow down according to the demands of the material is more important than simply developing speed. This need for flexibility casts serious doubt on the use of reading machines, which impose a rate regardless of the material presented (Spache, 1976). It makes more sense to examine a student's flexibility than maximum rate.

Vocabulary (Semantics)

If a student fails to demonstrate comprehension but passes tests of decoding and prior knowledge, the next most likely cause of the failure is vocabulary. Word meaning may account for up to 70% of the variability between students who do and do not score well on comprehension tests (Farr, 1969; Waugh, 1978).

To find out if a comprehension problem is the result of poor vocabulary, an evaluator must evaluate the student's knowledge of the meaning of the words in the paragraph he or she did not comprehend. Standardized vocabulary tests are not likely to aid in this evaluation. Those tests are composed of words that may or may not be representative of the words in the paragraph the student did not comprehend. The average child enters school with a vocabulary of from 5,000 to 10,000 words. By high school, there are many times more. With all those words to choose from, a standard vocabulary test is not likely to have many words relevant for an individual passage.

When you test vocabulary, you are testing to explain why the student did not understand what was read. Therefore, you test the words from the passage the student did not understand. If the student doesn't know the words, then obviously you should teach them. However, instruction on one set of words won't necessarily generalize to other words. As pointed out earlier, authors of remedial or corrective reading texts intentionally limit text vocabulary to well below a student's speaking vocabulary. Even when the vocabulary is not dumbed down (Bowen, 1984), authors of remedial texts seldom include adequate procedures for teaching necessary new words. This failure to include adequate formats for vocabulary instruction is also typical of most basal programs and has been documented in observations of classroom practice (Anderson, Osborn, & Tierney, 1984). Vocabulary is best learned in a natural reading and speaking environment; however, special and remedial students characteristically lack the skills to derive word meanings from context without direct and explicit vocabulary instruction. Even typical students require repeated exposures before learning new words. The traditional word list–dictionary approach to vocabulary instruction cannot begin to provide kids with the rich knowledge of vocabulary they need if in fact they have inadequate vocabulary (Jenkins & Dixon, 1983). Effective explicit vocabulary instruction requires careful planning, a focus on context, and structured opportunities for practice (Beck, Perfetti, & McKeown, 1982). Recommendations for vocabulary instruction are found in chapter 12 on pages 299–300.

Language (Syntax)

Assume now that you have a student who was given a paragraph he didn't comprehend. You have tested him (using procedures to be described shortly) and determined that he can decode the paragraph fluently. You have also checked his prior knowledge of the content and knowledge of the meaning of the words in the paragraph. You found no problems. What's left?

First of all, a kid who can't tell you what a passage said but can decode the passage, has adequate background information, and knows the meaning of all the words in it is rare. The most likely explanation is a difference between the child's language and the language (discourse style) of the passage. Students who have oral language deficits or bilingual interference generally have difficulty understanding text (Garnett, 1986; Hoffer, 1983; Kintsch & Greene, 1978).

The language of books varies as a result of the same factors that cause the language of people to vary. Primary among these is the background of the author. The same thing is true of television, movie, and radio presentations. It is appropriate, therefore, to give some consideration to reviewing the language of the text to see if it is "user friendly." The failure to comprehend might be traced to a problem of text language, not student language. You may have experienced a text problem yourself if you've ever read a book that was poorly translated from another language.

Comprehension Strategies

The final explanation for a failure to comprehend is that *no one taught the student to comprehend.* We will discuss this assumed cause by describing what comprehension strategy instruction looks like. Our intent is not to describe effective treatments but to highlight variables that may warrant evaluation.

Comprehension can be taught, and there are at least two ways of teaching it. One is with prereading techniques, and the other is with postreading techniques. Postreading techniques are the more commonly used and are, unfortunately, less effective. There is a growing body of literature that indicates that postreading questions as presented in workbook formats seldom promote comprehension and only fill hours of valuable instruction time with tedious or irrelevant work (Durkin, 1978–1979; Johnson, Levin, & Pittleman, 1984; Osborn, 1984). Post-reading questions are usually based on categories such as main idea, sequence, and inference. In a typical postreading exercise, the student reads the passage and then responds to questions (of different types) about the passage. The responses are then graded and feedback is given.

In contrast, a typical prereading exercise begins with the teacher reviewing the content prior to the passage and presenting new vocabulary. Then the student is given questions and asked to read the passage to find the answers. The student may also be given explicit instruction on the use of active-reading, monitoring, problem-solving, and study skills strategies. Once the passage has been read, the teacher checks to see if the student found the answers.

The big differences between the two methods are *when* the questions are asked and *what* instruction is given. If the questions aren't asked until after the reading, the student must read the passage without any goal. The subsequent comprehension test becomes a test of either the student's powers of incidental learning (in which she remembers the entire passage) or luck (in which she happens to remember the part the test was on). At best, success is a measure of whether the student and the teacher thought the same portion of the passage was important. Whichever is the case, praising the student for getting the correct answer does not always reinforce the skills associated with comprehension. It may only be reinforcing guessing.

With the prereading system, the teacher reviews previous content to guarantee that the student has the necessary prerequisite knowledge to comprehend the passage (Langer, 1982). Then the teacher introduces the essential vocabulary to rule out any problems with word meaning. Next he or she asks questions that give the student a specific objective for reading the passage. Finally, the teacher explains or models strategies for finding answers.

Success at finding the answer, therefore, reinforces the student's use of strategies for searching the content and using prior knowledge. If the passage was selected with the student's decoding and language in mind, then success on the passage depends only on comprehension strategies because decoding, language, vocabulary, and prior knowledge were controlled. This system of "guaranteeing" success at comprehension provides experience at comprehending that may "teach" the student (Bereiter, 1985). The review, question, read, and summarize steps of the prereading system are found in many study skills programs, such as the SQ3R method (Robinson, 1946) and *Multipass* (Lovitt, 1984). Coupling prereading activities with comprehension strategy instruction fosters understanding.

EVALUATING COMPREHENSION

Comprehension evaluation (and the rest of this chapter) is outlined in Figure 9.2.

There are many procedures for sampling a student's understanding of print, but each one de-

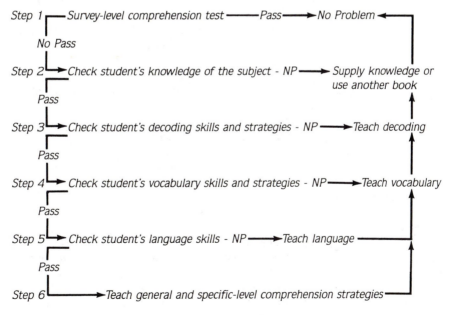

FIGURE 9.2
Reading comprehension evaluation procedures

pends on display skills. This means that the question, "Does he comprehend?" can be subdivided into "Does he know what he read?" and "Can he tell us what he knows?" It is particularly important to remember the second question. Many survey- and specific-level tests require the student to state what he or she knows about a passage of print. However, it isn't uncommon for us to "know" something we can't "tell." This is the result of many things, including our easily exhausted vocabularies.

Step 1 Survey-Level Procedures

To evaluate comprehension you will first need to collect a survey-level sample of the student's comprehension. Because there are so many different definitions of comprehension, there are many different survey-level procedures available. Aside from the "correctness" of these various procedures, they each have particular advantages and disadvantages. We will begin this discussion by *describing* six survey-level formats and their particular characteristics. After we describe all the formats we will provide a step-by-step procedure for using each one. The six formats are questioning, paraphrasing, retelling, cloze, maze, and sentence verification. Table 9.2 summarizes our comparison of these formats. Each should be used with passages of about 250 words.

Questions

As mentioned earlier, the question format is the most popular comprehension survey system for standardized tests. Typically, these tests are composed of a series of paragraphs that vary according to difficulty. Each paragraph is then followed by questions. The usefulness of the questions and categories of questions depends upon a number of considerations. The first is, "Are the categories real?" The answer is, "Nobody knows." We do know the categories don't hold up well under analysis. Scores obtained from the categories are so highly correlated to each other that it is difficult to say if there are any real differences among them. Sometimes students will miss half of the "getting the main idea" and half of the "detecting the sequence" questions, indicating that the total test is hard for them but that no subtest is harder than

another. Rafael and Pearson (1985) have noted that even if questions vary in their cognitive demands, differential levels of difficulty are a function of the question, the learner, and the text—*not* the questions in isolation.

Other problems with the questioning format relate to the number and quality of questions used. Most reading tests ask only a few questions from each category per passage. Worse yet, the questions invariably tap the students' general knowledge, not just their comprehension. To illustrate this, take whatever reading test you are currently using and ask the students some questions without having them read the passage. You will probably find that they will get a lot of questions correct. This is particularly true of questions about word meanings (Pyrczak, 1976).

There is still another problem: scoring. Without knowing how much the student knew about the topic ahead of time, we are unable to separate scores of prior knowledge from scores of information gained from the text. Our assumption is that correct answers are based on the text, yet we know that many questions can be answered without reading text. Establishing a standard of how many correct responses a student should make to demonstrate understanding—setting the criterion—is problematic under these conditions.

While questioning may be the most familiar and most available format for conducting a survey-level assessment, it has serious limitations. It seems that kids who are good at comprehending can answer questions, and kids who aren't, can't. Therefore, questioning may be a good procedure for separating students for additional testing. However, drawing instructional conclusions from categories of questions isn't a good idea (though the practice is common).

Paraphrasing

Another way to determine if the student has comprehended a passage is to ask her to tell in her own words what the passage was about. This is paraphrasing. Suppose you give a student a passage to read and then ask her what she read. If she repeats the passage back to you word for word, you may still not be sure of her comprehension. You would rather she put the passage in her own words. To do so, she needs well-developed vocabulary skills. These skills might include sufficient knowledge of synonyms to replace the original words or sufficient knowledge of the content to reorder the original wording.

One weakness of paraphrasing is that it doesn't tell you if the student can arrive at conclusions about the purpose or intent of the passage. You can find this out, however, by combining paraphrasing with questioning. Another weakness of the technique is that it is difficult to score. Schumaker, Denton, and Deshler (1984) have validated procedures for teaching students to paraphrase and for scoring responses. Deshler (1985) has stated that an adequate paraphrase (a) expresses a complete thought, (b) is totally accurate, (c) provides new information—the information cannot be information for which the student has already been given credit, (d) makes sense, (e) contains useful information, (f) is in the student's own words, and (g) contains only one general statement. The Schumaker, Denton, and Deshler criteria do provide a framework for scoring student paraphrases; however, scoring responses and deciding what the scores mean remain difficult even with these criteria.

Story Retelling

In this procedure students are permitted to repeat exact words found in the story. Like paraphrasing, the development of a scoring procedure and the establishment of criteria are time consuming for the evaluator. Lovitt (1984) has suggested several approaches to solving this problem and provides a step-by-step description of how to proceed. He draws on the work of Kintsch (1974), who noted that text is composed of propositions or idea units. In Lovitt's procedure the evaluator lists the propositions found in a story on a checksheet. The student is asked to read the story and then to retell it. The student's retelling is transcribed and the number of idea units recalled is compared to those on the checksheet. One drawback of retelling is the difficulty of judging if a student who retells a story with exact words has "understood" what he has read. Students need to be taught both to paraphrase and to retell a story. With practice their performance in testing situations improves. An advantage of the paraphrasing and retelling formats is that both may also be used as instructional activities to enhance comprehension (Hansen, 1978; Schumaker et al., 1984).

Cloze

The cloze technique has received a lot of attention as a comprehension measure and as a system for selecting instructional-level reading material (Baker & Brown, 1984; Baldauf, 1982; Berk, 1979; DeSanti & Sullivan, 1984). The basic cloze system starts with choosing a 250-word selection. The first and last sentences of the passage are left intact, while every fifth word in the remaining sentences is blanked out (the blanks should be of equal length regardless of the word removed or you'll end up testing the student's skill at interpreting blanks). The students are asked to read the passage orally and to say (or write) the word that goes in the blank (they *do not* read the unmodified passage first). Most authors require that the students supply the *exact* missing word. This may seem hard but the CAP is fairly low. If a student supplies more than 45% of the missing words, the material is considered too easy for instruction. If he gets between 30% and 45% of the words correct, the material is said to be at the instructional level. A score of below 30% indicates the material is too hard (Pikulski & Pikulski, 1977). Figure 9.1a is an example of a cloze passage.

Cloze is an interesting technique because it seems to challenge the student's skill at using all types of passage information. Cloze performance is closely related to the redundancy of the text as well as to the similarity between the language of the student and the language of the text. One disadvantage, therefore, is that it can't be used with passages that aren't redundant (ruling out particularly descriptive material). Also, students with language problems or native dialects may do poorly on cloze regardless of their comprehension; unfortunately, these same students may do even more poorly on questions and paraphrasing (Propst & Baldauf, 1981).

The primary advantage of cloze is that it is easy to score, unlike the questioning, paraphrasing, and retelling techniques, because corrects and errors are simple to recognize. Scoring is also possible be-

TABLE 9.2
A comparison of six survey-level techniques

Procedure	Example	Advantages	Disadvantages	Type of Data	Criteria	Related Assumed Causes for Failure
1. Questioning	S*: "Who was Ambrose?" R*: "A Civil War author"	1) The teacher can focus on information of particular interest 2) Attempts to test levels of comprehension	1) Hard to score 2) Only a few questions can be written for each paragraph 3) Levels of comprehension may not match types of questions (or even exist) 4) Risk of poorly written questions 5) The student's answer is determined by the question asked	Percent correct	Undetermined	Lack of general knowledge
2. Paraphrasing	S*: "...was fascinated with the human aspect of war..." R*: "...he wanted to know why people decide to fight..."	1) Student responses aren't influenced by the way the questions are asked 2) Supplies an overall impression of the student's understanding 3) Can be used in daily lessons so has fidelity to real life	1) Hard to score 2) Difficult to control sudden responses without questioning, which in turn would negate advantage #1	Percent correct	Undetermined	Poor vocabulary, lack of familiarity with procedure

TABLE 9.2 *(continued)*

Procedure	Example	Advantages	Disadvantages	Type of Data	Criteria	Related Assumed Causes for Failure
3. Story Retelling	S*: "...was fascinated with the human aspect of war..." R*: "...was fascinated with the human aspect of war..."	1) Student responses are not influenced by the way questions are asked 2) Indicates overall number of idea units the student recalls 3) Can be used as a component of daily lessons and therefore has fidelity to real life 4) Can be analyzed for match to text structure or story map	1) Cumbersome to transcribe student responses 2) Analysis of idea units in text to enhance scoring is time consuming 3) May not sample understanding; may only tap recall	Percent correct	Undetermined	Lack of familiarity with procedure
4. Cloze	S*: "...was fascinated with the ____ aspect of war..." R*: "...was fascinated with the *human* aspect of war..."	1) Easy to score 2) Success depends on all types of passage clues 3) Item difficulty is random 4) Large sample of behavior	1) Does not directly test understanding of what you think is the most important part of the passage 2) Can only be used with redundant texts	Percent correct	Instructional level 30-45%; below 30% is no-pass	Discrepancy between student language and text language

TABLE 9.2 (continued)

Procedure	Example	Advantages	Disadvantages	Type of Data	Criteria	Related Assumed Causes for Failure
5. Maze	S*: "...was fascinated with the [technical, geographic, human] aspect..." R*: "...was fascinated with the [technical, geographic, (human)] aspect..."	1) Easy to score 2) Success depends on all types of passage clues 3) Distractors can be used to alter the test difficulty or the focus of the test 4) Large sample of behavior	1) Risk of poorly selected distractors	Percent correct	Instructional level is 60-80%; below 60% is no-pass	Discrepancy between student language and text language
6. Sentence Verification (Original) (Paraphrase)	S*: "...was fascinated with the human aspect of war..." "...he wanted to know why people decide to fight..."	1) Student responses are not dependent on a large store of general knowledge 2) Procedure does not require passage recall 3) Success depends on integration of passage clues: grapho-phonemic,	1) Risk of poorly developed items 2) Requires well-developed student vocabulary skills 3) Time consuming to develop	Percent correct	Undetermined	Poor vocabulary

TABLE 9.2 (continued)

Procedure	Example	Advantages	Disadvantages	Type of Data	Criteria	Related Assumed Causes for Failure
(Meaning Change)	"...was fascinated with the economic aspect of war..."	semantic, and syntax 4) Supplies overall information of student's recognition of new and old information				
(Distractor)	"...was willing to travel to the front to inter-view..."	5) Easy to score				
	R*: "...he wanted to know why people decide to fight ..."					

*S = stimulus; R = response.

cause the procedure of blanking out words distributes item difficulty randomly. This random assignment of difficulty permits the blanks to be treated equally and to be added together without weighting or conversion.

Maze

The maze procedure is similar to the cloze procedure, but the behavior of the student is quite different. In cloze the student recalls and produces the correct response. In maze the student identifies and indicates it. Again, the procedure requires the selection of a 250-word passage. The first and last sentences of the passage are left intact, and a group of words is inserted for every fifth word. The student is asked to select the original word (usually by circling it) from among three or five distractors. Therefore, maze is to multiple choice as cloze is to fill in the blank. Because identification of a correct word is easier than production of a correct word, the criterion for passing is higher. Sixty to 80% correct can be considered instructional level, with scores above 90% indicating easy material; below 55%, material that is too hard.

Just as with all cutting scores (scores used as boundaries for certain decisions), the 60–80% maze criterion is not absolute. The difficulty of maze will vary not only according to the difficulty of the passage but also according to the difficulty of the distractors selected. For example, in Figure 9.3 item *A* is easier than item *B* because the distractors (incorrect choices) are more clearly incorrect. Because you can choose easy or hard distractors,

Item *A*
Just as with all _____
      (volkswagen, trout, cutting)
scores, the 60–80% maze _____
               (criterion, taco, motorcycle)
is not absolute.

Item *B*
Just as with all _____
      (reading, grade level, cutting)
scores, the 60–80% maze _____
               (criterion, procedure, score)
is not absolute.

FIGURE 9.3
Maze formats with choices of varying difficulty

maze is more flexible than cloze. Of course, this also makes it easier to produce invalid items.

One way of controlling for difficulty of the distractors is to have one word that is syntactically correct but semantically incorrect (Type A) and to have another word that is both syntactically and semantically incorrect (Type B). A passage modified in this manner would appear as follows (the distractors are labeled) (Howell et al., 1982).

They felt a soft wind _____
                         walk, little, pass
                          A   B
them by. Then standing _____ the darkness
                       until, little, in
                         A   B
beside them, a strange little man appeared."

The distractors should be drawn from the passage or from word frequency lists to control for complexity and insure that they are words typically taught and used at the passage's reading level. Guthrie (1973) has suggested that distractors also be systematically drawn from categories of word types: noun, verb, modifier, and function. Nouns may include nouns and pronouns; the verbs may include transitives, intransitives, and auxiliaries; the modifier group may include adjectives and adverbs; and the function group may include prepositions, articles, and conjunctions. These distractors would also be selected to be semantically and syntactically incorrect or syntactically correct but semantically incorrect. In the maze example, "walk" and "pass" are verbs and are syntactically correct. "Little" is a modifier and is both syntactically and semantically incorrect. Only "pass" is both syntactically and semantically correct. While some research has suggested that the maze format does not sample comprehension beyond sentence boundaries, the careful selection of distractors appears to influence these findings (Cziko, 1983).

Because the maze format lets students select a response rather than produce one, it is especially appropriate for students with language production problems or students who are acquiring a new language. Even though they may not comprehend well in the second language, the maze format permits them to demonstrate what they do understand (Bensoussan & Ramraz, 1984).

Both cloze and maze formats let the evaluator sample a large number of responses in a single 250-word passage, which certainly is a larger sample than would be obtained using a questions-only format. This large sample size contributes to the reliability of the test scores. In addition, some theorists believe that cloze and maze have superior construct validity for comprehension because both permit readers to look ahead as well as back to previous text to confirm or disconfirm their responses. The use of text *lookbacks* and *lookaheads* seems to be a key self-monitoring strategy used by comprehending readers (Baker & Brown, 1984; Hosseini & Ferrell, 1982). Maze, like cloze, is easy to grade.

One additional advantage of cloze and maze is that the same passage can be used to screen for both comprehension and decoding problems. Scores from these formats appear to be as useful for selecting instructional-level decoding material as the popular graded reading passages.

Sentence Verification

The sentence verification technique is receiving more attention as theorists and evaluators attempt to develop testing procedures that control for prior knowledge (Rasool & Royer, 1986; Royer & Cunningham, 1981). This survey technique, like those previously described, involves a passage of approximately 250 words in length. Royer and Cunningham (1981) have suggested

[prepare] four versions of each of the [target] sentences in a text passage: 1) the sentence as it originally appeared; 2) a paraphrase of the original sentence; 3) a meaning change version of the sentence that preserves as nearly as possible the original wording of the sentence; and 4) a distractor that is similar in length and complexity to an original sentence and is semantically consistent with the topical content of the text passage, but is not semantically similar to any of the original sentences (p. 210).

Have the student read all four sentences and indicate which are new (different from the original) and which are old (mean the same as the original). The example item below is derived from a passage by Palinscar and Brown (1984). (We developed this as a practice example for adults to illustrate the application to complex text.)

Original Sentence. "It is generally agreed that given reasonable facility with decoding, reading comprehension is the product of three main factors: 1) considerate texts, 2) the compatibility of the readers' knowledge and text content, and 3) the active strategies the reader employs to enhance understanding and retention, and to circumvent comprehension failures" (Palinscar & Brown, 1984, p. 118).

Paraphrase—Similar syntax and same meaning. It is usually recognized that, provided modest ease with decoding, reading comprehension is the result of three primary elements: 1) obliging passages, 2) the consonance of the reader's learning and the passage topics, and 3) the dynamic tactics the reader uses to heighten understanding and remembering and to avoid comprehension deficiencies.

Meaning Change—Similar syntax and different meaning. It is generally agreed that given reasonable difficulty with decoding, reading comprehension is the product of three main factors: 1) considerate texts, 2) the compatibility of the reader's knowledge and text content, and 3) the active strategies the reader employs to suppress understanding and retention, and to circumvent comprehension failure.

Distractor—Similar syntax, semantically consistent with topic but different from semantics of sentence. Those who study comprehension-fostering strategies note that immature readers, when they encounter difficult text 1) do not recognize when to employ strategies, 2) often select inappropriate strategies, and 3) fail to use those strategies with ease to construct meaning from grapho-phonemic cues, semantic and syntactic cues, and general prior knowledge.

While the sentence verification procedure samples comprehension at the sentence level, there is evidence it also indicates text comprehension (Royer, Lynch, Hambleton, & Bulgareli, 1984). A limitation is the time it takes to develop alternate sentences and the time it could take to develop standards for passing. Its value as a survey-level test may reside in its sensitivity to particular types of reading problems. Students who rely too heavily on word-by-word analysis of incoming information may indicate that the meaning change sentence is old information and that the paraphrase is new information. Students who are overly reliant on meaning may indicate that the distractor as well as the paraphrase and the original sentence represent old information (Royer & Cunningham, 1981).

Summary of Survey-Level Procedures

The six survey-level procedures we have just presented are summarized and contrasted in Table 9.2. Because the subskills of comprehension are not clear-cut, the best technique is probably to use more than one survey-level procedure. This may include combining procedures. Of the procedures discussed, questioning after passage reading (the traditional procedure) is clearly the worst. Paraphrasing, retelling, and sentence verification, while all sensitive and interesting procedures, are hard to score or develop. Therefore, the survey-level procedure with the greatest utility seems to be a combination of cloze and maze with other techniques (Olson, 1976). The validity of a decision based on maze or cloze can be increased by having the kid complete more than one passage. To control for the effect of prior content knowledge, it is a good idea to have the kid respond to three 250-word passages covering different topics. Since comprehension needs to occur across a number of text styles, you should sample across texts of varying style.

Applying Survey-Level Procedures

This section describes how each of the six survey-level tests can be used (Step 1, Figure 9.2). Because each of the survey-level procedures is described, this will be a long discussion. In practice, you would select and use only one procedure. Directions and interpretation guidelines are provided for each procedure.

Many times the CAP presented is only a recommendation. The CAP could vary according to the text structure and student's knowledge. We have set the CAP high in most cases because it would seem safer to give the student an extra test than to risk missing a problem.

Note: If the student is extremely slow at any of the survey-level tests, consider his performance a no-pass. Because the material you use will vary, you will have to determine the criterion for speed. The most likely explanation for slow performance is slow decoding. See chapter 10 for procedures for checking decoding.

Questions

Directions.

1. Collect passages of varying difficulty from texts used in the classroom or from published tests. The passages should be about 250 words in length (for primary grades 1 and 2, 100 to 200 words is adequate).
2. Construct questions that require interpretation. Also include sequence and fact questions.
3. Say to the student, "Read this part to yourself to find out [state question]. Why are you reading it?" If the student cannot restate the reason for reading, tell him again. (Discontinue if the student fails to repeat with a prompt. Administer a maze test instead.)
4. Have the student read passage sections related to the question.
5. After the student has finished reading, wait for him to tell you the answer to the question.
6. Score responses.
7. Compare the student's scores to the criterion you have established using procedures outlined in chapter 8 or apply our recommended criterion of 95 to 100% accuracy.

Interpretation Guidelines.

If the student no-passes at the level of his current grade placement, administer prior knowledge, specific-level test on page 183. If background knowledge is not the problem, check comprehension strategies, specific-level test on page 187.

Paraphrasing with Questions

Directions.

1. Select passages of varying difficulty from texts used in the school setting or from published tests. The passages should be about 250 words in length (for primary grades 1 and 2, 100 to 200 words is adequate).
2. Develop questions to ask after passage reading and paraphrasing.
3. Set up a recorder to tape student responses.
4. Tell the student that you are going to ask her to read a passage and then tell you in her *own* words what she read. Indicate you will also be asking some questions about the passage.
5. Have her read the passage to herself.
6. Ask her to tell you what she read. Record responses.
7. Ask interpretive questions to verify that the student can derive ideas and draw conclusions from the passage.
8. Score responses using criterion *you establish* or use the criterion suggested on page 173.
9. Compare the student's score to criteria you establish using procedures described in chapter 8. (In step 8 you had criterion for judging *if* responses were correct; in this step you have criteria for *how many* responses must be correct.)

Interpretation Guidelines.
If the student no-passes at the level of her current grade placement, check to see if she can paraphrase sentences, paraphrase phrases, or supply synonyms. Use sentences from the survey-level test she has just failed. The reason you are doing this is to see if the student is so unfamiliar with paraphrasing that she can't pass the test regardless of her comprehension skills.

If the student passes sentence or phrase paraphrasing, this means she can't paraphrase the passage but can paraphrase the sentences in it. Because the student passed this step, you can be sure she does have paraphrasing skills and the original failure to pass wasn't the result of an unfamiliar testing format. Check decoding following the steps

outlined in chapter 10 on pages 204–228. Failure to paraphrase could also indicate that the student lacks sufficient knowledge of the content to tie the paragraph together, so you may wish to check prior knowledge by following the specific-test procedures about to be discussed.

Story Retelling with Questions

Directions.

1. Collect passages of varying difficulty from texts used in the classroom or from published tests. The passages should be about 250 words in length (for primary grades 1 and 2, 100 to 200 words is adequate).
2. Develop interpretive questions to ask after passage reading and retelling.
3. Set up a recorder to tape student responses.
4. Tell the student that you want him to read a passage and tell you what he has read. Indicate that you will also be asking some questions.
5. Have the student read the passage to himself.
6. Ask the student to tell you what he has read. Record responses.
7. Ask interpretive questions to verify that the student can derive ideas and draw conclusions.
8. Score responses using the criterion for response quality you establish or follow the response criterion described by Lovitt (1984, pp. 102-103).
9. Compare the student's scores to criterion you establish using procedures outlined in chapter 8.

Interpretation Guidelines.
If the student fails, check to see if the student can retell sentences or retell phrases. Do this with sentences from the passage the student has just failed to pass. You are doing this to see if the student is so unfamiliar with retelling that he can't pass the test regardless of his comprehension skills. If the student fails passage retelling but passes sentence or phrase retelling, he can't retell passages but can retell sentences or phrases in a passage. Failure to retell larger portions of text may indicate that a

decoding problem is interfering with integration of comprehension processes. Did the student appear to have problems with decoding the survey passage? If so, check decoding, following procedures outlined in chapter 10. Failure to retell large portions of text could also indicate that the student lacks sufficient knowledge of the content to tie the passage together, so you may wish to try the specific-level prior knowledge test outlined in this chapter. It could also be an indicator that he lacks comprehension strategies. Check strategies using the procedures outlined on page 187.

Cloze Procedure with Questions

Directions.

1. Collect passages of varying difficulty from texts used in the classroom or from published tests. The passages should be about 250 words in length (for primary grades 1 and 2, 100 to 200 words is adequate).
2. Leave the first and last sentence intact and omit every fifth word.
3. Prepare interpretive questions to ask to verify that the student can derive ideas and draw conclusions.
4. Tell the student that you are going to have her read a passage in which some words have been omitted. Tell her to fill in each blank with the word she thinks is missing. Have her practice with a sentence such as "Twinkle, twinkle little _____," or "Old MacDonald had a _____."
5. After the student has completed filling in the blanks, ask her the questions.
6. Score the responses. We use "exact word only" for corrects for ease of scoring. Our criterion of 40% is based on this procedure.
7. Compare the student's cloze and question scores to criterion you have established using procedures outlined in chapter 8 or apply our recommended cloze criterion of at least 40% accuracy.

Interpretation Guidelines.
If the student fails at her current grade placement, ask yourself if you have noticed any evidence that

the student has a language problem or unique dialect. If so, you may wish to move directly to language screening, which is described in chapter 12.

If no language problem is evident, check background knowledge using the specific-level test for prior knowledge described on page 183. You may also check her use of comprehension strategies. Use the procedure outlined on page 187.

Maze Procedure and Questions

Directions.

1. Collect passages of varying difficulty from texts used in the classroom or from published tests. The passages should be about 250 words in length (for primary grades 1 and 2, 100 to 200 words is adequate).
2. Omit words and supply choices as illustrated in Figure 9.3.
3. Prepare interpretive questions to ask after the student completes the passage.
4. Tell the student that he is going to select the correct word for each blank. Provide a practice example such as "Old MacDonald had a

   _____."

   farm, TV, running
5. Ask questions after the student has completed the passage.
6. Score responses.
7. Compare the student's maze and question scores to the criterion you have established using procedures outlined in chapter 8 or use our maze criterion of 60% or better. (Criteria do vary as a function of the difficulty of the distractors, so we encourage you to validate your criterion.)

Interpretation Guidelines.
If the student passes the maze but no-passes the questions, check to see if the questions were any good. If they were, check background knowledge using the specific-level test for prior knowledge described on page 183. If the score is about 55% or lower, ask yourself if you have noticed any evidence that the student has a language problem or unique dialect. If so, you may wish to move directly to lan-

guage screening (described in chapter 12). If no language difficulty is evident, you may wish to readminister the maze test with easier distractors. If he still fails, he might be confused by the maze technique itself. If so, you would use at least one other survey-level technique to verify the original no-pass.

Sentence Verification

Directions.

1. Collect passages of varying difficulty from texts used in the classroom or from published tests. The passages should be about 250 words in length (for primary grades 1 and 2, 100 to 200 words is adequate).
2. Follow guidelines for writing passage verification sentences outlined on pages 179–180.
3. Tell the student that you are going to have her read a passage and then read some sentences to see if they contain the same information contained in the passage.
4. Have the student read the passage and select the sentences which match information in the passage.
5. Score the responses.
6. Compare the student's responses to criterion you establish using guidelines in chapter 8.

Interpretation Guidelines.
If the student responds appropriately to an alternative survey-level comprehension test, discontinue testing and continue to monitor student performance.

If the student fails, select the most probable cause of the problem. Decoding is checked easily and may be the easiest specific cause to rule out. See chapter 10 for procedures. If there are no apparent decoding problems, check vocabulary (specific-level test, page 184); prior knowledge (specific-level test, page 183); and comprehension strategies (specific-level procedure, page 187) before assessing language.

Specific-Level Procedures
The purpose of survey-level testing in comprehension is to determine if the student's reading of grade-level passages is acceptable and to identify a level where instruction should begin. When a student fails to demonstrate comprehension of a passage, you then examine assumed causes for the failure. You can simplify your evaluation if you select the most likely explanation for failure.

The steps to follow are shown in Figure 9.2. The available assumed causes are prior knowledge, decoding, vocabulary, language syntax, and comprehension strategies. We will address general evaluation concerns associated with the assumed causes and provide directions for testing them.

Step 2 Prior Knowledge
There are two ways that a deficit in background knowledge can be ruled out as an explanation for failure. The first is to supply the background knowledge and look for a change in comprehension. However, this must be done carefully or the student may end up answering the question from the background rather than the passage; as you can imagine, it isn't easy to use this procedure.

The second way to rule out a lack of knowledge is to test the student on material from several subject areas. In particular, test the kid in areas of personal interest. If the student succeeds at comprehending one passage, failure on another passage of about equal difficulty can be attributed either to lack of background knowledge or motivation. This is one reason why you should have used several passages (at least three of 250 words each) and different techniques (cloze, maze, questions, paraphrasing) at the survey level. In the long run it is often easier to recognize a knowledge deficit by excluding the other explanations for failure (decoding, vocabulary, language, and instruction) than to follow this procedure. Additional procedures for checking prior knowledge are elaborated in Table 9.3.

Directions.

1. Provide the student with background information necessary for understanding the text used in the survey-level test.
2. Administer the survey-level test again.

TABLE 9.3
Assessing prior knowledge—Specific-level testing

Format	Procedure
Questions (oral or written; group or individual; multiple choice or free response)	Develop and ask questions before passage reading that sample the general topic domain but are *not* answered in the text. Avoid text-dependent questions. Score and establish standards for adequacy.
Association-Task (individual or group; written).	Provide a list of key words linked to text topics or concepts and ask students to generate as many associations as they can. Say "Write anything that comes to mind." Count the number of associations and establish standards for judging adequacy.
Association-Task (individual or group; oral)	Same as above except oral.
Scripts or Sequence of Steps (useful when checking procedural prior knowledge).	Provide a list of unordered steps and have students order them or ask them to generate and order steps. Establish standards for adequacy.

Source: From J. Gaffney & B. McCloone, "Prior Knowledge Assessment Procedures." Workshop module presented at the meeting of the Arizona Council for Exceptional Children, March, 1984, Tucson.

Interpretation Guidelines.

Question.   Did the student understand the passage after he was provided with background information?

Recommendation.   If yes, continue to monitor student performance and progress in the daily work that led to initial request for testing. You will need to check to see if the student has sufficient prior knowledge to handle different material.

If no, and the material is sufficiently important, teach the missing background information. *Note*: Remember, checking prior knowledge is difficult to handle well and you may end up distorting your results. In most cases where the text information is not specialized, you should probably skip testing prior knowledge. Check causes such as decoding, vocabulary, and strategies.

Step 3   Decoding Testing
If the student doesn't comprehend the survey-level test, first check her speed; if she is beyond third grade and reads passages at fewer than 140 oral words correct per minute (automatic level), she may need to improve her rate. First graders should be able to read 50 words per minute; second graders, 100 words per minute. If she makes errors,

then you should check accuracy. If she passes accuracy but not mastery (speed), work on her rate. If she no-passes accuracy, work on it before expecting improvement in rate. The procedure for checking decoding fluency and accuracy is found in the Decoding chapter. Remember that speed varies according to content difficulty, and difficulty is influenced by prior knowledge (Carver, 1983).

Step 4   Vocabulary (Semantics)
Most vocabulary tests require the student to supply synonyms for isolated words. Words derive some of their meaning from context; therefore testing word meaning out of context is not ideal. A better procedure is to ask the student to match equally correct synonyms to the sentences in which they make sense.

In Figure 9.4, format A, the synonyms are supplied for the student, as are the sentences. Consequently, this matching exercise tests the student's vocabulary at the identification level. A second example of this is seen in format B. In format C, the student is asked to supply the synonyms with the sentences provided as cues.

When testing word meaning, remember that elementary students (and possibly older special students) prefer to define words by describing how the word is commonly used and by referring to

Format A

Target word: *drill*

Synonyms: A. practice   B. tool

Directions: "Match the synonym to the correct sentence."
1. Hand me the *drill*.
2. We need *drill* on our skills.

Answer(s): Sentence 1 — synonym B.   Sentence 2 — synonym A.

Format B

Target word: *drill*

Directions: "Select the words which make sentence 2 most like sentence 1."
Sentence 1. We need *drill* on our skills.
Sentence 2. If we want to get better at our skills, we should
   ... study them.
   ... put a hole in them.
   ... do them a lot.

Format C

Target word: *drill*

Directions: "Write a synonym for the target word which can be used in each of the following sentences."

Sentence 1. Hand me the *drill*.
Sentence 2. We need *drill* on our skills.

Synonym 1: _____
Synonym 2: _____

Format D

Target word: *drill*

Directions: "Read this sentence — "We need *drill* on our skills." In this sentence, does the *drill* mean to:
a. make a hole in something?
b. work on something over and over again?

FIGURE 9.4
Formats for vocabulary sampling

concrete examples. Older (secondary) students tend to define words with synonyms and to use abstract examples such as classifications (Farr, 1969). The synonym format, therefore, may be unnatural for younger students. In this case, the choices should be more descriptive in nature, as shown in Figure 9.4, format D.

The main point of these examples is that words carry some meaning with them but also obtain some meaning from the text. Comprehension involves understanding context, and word meaning is necessary for this understanding. In a story or an article, comprehension is determined at the passage level (which is why 250-word passages were rec-

ommended for survey testing). However, the meaning of a word is determined by the phrase it is in (i.e., "... we need math *drill*..."), so phrases are all that you need for testing word meaning.

Figure 9.5 may help you organize your vocabulary testing. Notice that there are four levels of complexity translated into test objectives.

Tests for Each Objective.

Test 1   Produces word meaning in context. This objective is tested by underlining important words in the passage and then asking the student to read the passage. When the student comes to an

Behavior (What the student will do)

Content and conditions under which the behavior will occur

	Identify correct synonym or definition	Produce (supply) the correct synonym or definition
Words in context	Test 3	Test 1
Words in isolation	Test 4	Test 2

FIGURE 9.5
Vocabulary specifications

underlined word, have him stop and define it or use it in a sentence. It will be defined correctly if the definition or sentence given follows the context.

Test 2   Produces words in isolation.   This is tested by taking the underlined words from test 1 and presenting them in isolation (flashcards). The student is asked to supply a definition or synonym or use the word in a sentence. In this case, any acceptable definition is counted as correct.

Test 3   Match word to correct context.   This type of test is illustrated in Figure 9.4. Have the student read the passage until he reaches an underlined word. Then supply two definitions and ask him to select the best one. He will be right if the definition (or synonym) selected makes sense in the context of the passage.

Test 4   Match words in isolation to their definitions.   In this test the student is shown the underlined word on a flashcard and given age-appropriate definitions. If the student matches the word to a correct definition (regardless of context), it is correct.

Directions.

1. Construct tests for each vocabulary objective to be sampled.
2. Administer tests in order from 1 through 4. (If the student passes a test, discontinue testing.)

3. Score responses.
4. Compare scores to criteria you establish using procedures outlined in chapter 8 or apply our criteria. We recommend 95–100% accuracy on tests 1 and 2 and 100% accuracy on tests 3 and 4.

Interpretation Guidelines.

Ask yourself the following questions.

Question.   Can the student define the words in context? (test 1)

Recommendation.   If yes, check other causes for comprehension failure—decoding, chapter 10; language, chapter 12; or strategies, p. 187.
   If no, continue.

Question.   Can the student define the words in isolation? (test 2)

Recommendation.   If yes, the student knows word meanings but doesn't adjust them to fit context (as required in test 1), so that's what needs to be taught. This is often referred to as *multiple-meaning* instruction. See the instructional recommendation on pages 300–301.
   If no, continue.

Question.   Can the student match words to correct context? (test 3)

Recommendation. If yes, the student can identify correct definitions by using context clues but can't do so well enough to supply these definitions. Therefore, he must be taught to supply the definitions by instruction that gradually fades out the choices and requires him to provide the definitions.

If no, continue.

Question. Can the student match words in isolation to their definitions? (test 4)

Recommendation. If yes, the student has some knowledge of word meanings but only at the identification level (not production). Previous testing has already indicated that context does not improve his performance. The student needs to be moved from identification in isolation to production with context. Begin by teaching production of correct definitions. Some suggestions for vocabulary instruction are found on page 170 in this chapter and in chapter 12.

If no, before beginning to teach identification of word meanings, consider the possibility of a language (or spoken vocabulary) limitation. If necessary, give an oral language test (described in chapter 12).

Step 5   Language (Syntax)

To see if there is a language difficulty, conduct a survey-level language screening. The procedure we recommend is the oral language sample discussed in chapter 12. Because the techniques for language screening are covered in chapter 12, we will not elaborate here.

Step 6   Comprehension Strategies

Strategy use can best be assessed through direct observation of behavior and interviews with students regarding the procedures they are employing. However, asking a student to tell you what she is doing does not guarantee that she can report accurately, nor does it insure that she will do what she reports. However, it does give you an indication that she knows the components of a procedure and when and why to use it.

If you get all the way to step 6, you have a student who did not comprehend a passage even though she had the necessary prerequisite knowledge to do so. She also could decode the passage well, knew what the words in the passage meant, and had adequate language skills. The only probable explanations for the survey-level failure are 1) a mistake in survey-level testing or 2) a lack of comprehension strategies. If you have ruled out the first explanation (by giving another survey-level test), check the student's use of comprehension strategies. We have developed a checklist, shown in Figure 9.6, that lists indicators of strategy use. The categories are active reading, comprehension-monitoring, problem solving, and study skills. Good readers use them simultaneously.

Directions.

1. Interview and observe the student while she reads, using the strategy checklist shown in Figure 9.6. Ask her to tell you about what she does when she doesn't understand.
2. Rate your estimate of the indicator status.
3. Rate your estimate of the strategy status.

Interpretation Guidelines.

Ask yourself this question.

Question. Does the student use each strategy?

Recommendations. If yes, cease strategy testing. If no, teach the missing strategy using the following recommendations.

Teaching Comprehension Strategies.[1] As you recall, strategies are the task components used by students to coordinate their subskill knowledge. Comprehension strategies include (a) active reading, (b) comprehension monitoring, (c) problem solving, and (d) study skills.

Active reading. Many students who do not comprehend material fail to actively seek clarification even when they realize that it is needed. They seem to think they are meant to be the passive recipients of the author's message and consequently

---

1. Teaching Recommendations listed are used with permission from The Psychological Corporation and are taken from Howell, Zucker, and Morehead (1985).

Strategy	Indicator	Indicator Status			Strategy Status		
		Yes	No	Don't Know	Adequate	Instruction Needed	Additional Testing Needed
A. Active Reading							
1. Recognizes that reading is an active process of combining prior knowledge with text	1.1 Approaches text with questions and attempts to answer questions	____	____	____	____	____	____
	1.2 Seeks to clarify meaning	____	____	____			
	1.3 Uses prior knowledge where appropriate	____	____	____			
	1.4 Evaluates arguments, assertions, and proposals in text	____	____	____			
	1.5 Uses cognitive maps to anticipate and analyze text structure	____	____	____			
2. Understands the purpose(s) of reading and that print can be used to convey information, such as the answers to questions.	2.1 Reads with expression or automaticity	____	____	____	____	____	____
	2.2 Adjusts reading rate for material that is not understood	____	____	____			
	2.3 Does not make frequent whole word substitutions and insertions that seem graphically or phonemically similar to the passage word but violate passage meaning	____	____	____			
	2.4 Is more likely to recall important passage details, not trivial ones	____	____	____			
	2.5 Answers comprehension questions in terms of stated information in passage, not only prior knowledge.	____	____	____			

FIGURE 9.6
Comprehension strategy checklist

Strategy	Indicator	Indicator Status			Strategy Status		
		Yes	No	Don't Know	Adequate	Instruction Needed	Additional Testing Needed
B. Comprehension Monitoring							
1. Monitors own comprehension of the passage by recognizing when the passage does not make sense or is losing understanding of the passage.	1.1 Self-corrects reading errors that violate the meaning of the passage (such as nonmeaningful insertions)	⎯	⎯	⎯	⎯	⎯	⎯
	1.2 Rereads confusing portions of material, or adjusts reading rate on difficult sections	⎯	⎯	⎯			
	1.3 Can predict upcoming events in the passage	⎯	⎯	⎯			
	1.4 Identifies when additional information is needed, or specifically what kind of information is needed to answer questions	⎯	⎯	⎯			
	1.5 Does not make nonmeaningful insertion errors	⎯	⎯	⎯			
C. Problem Solving							
1. Uses problem solving to deal with difficult material.	1.1 "Where did I get lost?"	⎯	⎯	⎯	⎯	⎯	⎯
	1.2 "What kind of information would help me?"	⎯	⎯	⎯			
	1.3 "Where can I find out more?"	⎯	⎯	⎯			
	1.4 "What do the words mean?"	⎯	⎯	⎯			
	1.5 "What relationship has been established?"	⎯	⎯	⎯			

FIGURE 9.6
(continued)

Strategy	Indicator	Indicator Status			Strategy Status		
		Yes	No	Don't Know	Adequate	Instruction Needed	Additional Testing Needed
	1.6 "What information belongs with specific characters or concepts?"	_____	_____	_____			
	1.7 "If I understood this what would I know (or be able to do)?"	_____	_____	_____			
2. Discriminates relevant information in the passage by recognizing portions critical to the central meaning of the passage.	2.1 Answers "best title" and main idea questions accurately	_____	_____	_____	_____	_____	_____
	2.2 Retells story with emphasis on major points	_____	_____	_____			
	2.3 Describes author's purpose for writing	_____	_____	_____			
	2.4 Can locate information in the passage that answers assigned questions	_____	_____	_____			
D. Study Skills 1. Uses active search skills.	1.1 Can describe a search procedure such as multipass	_____	_____	_____	_____	_____	_____
	1.2 Employs a search procedure at an automatic level	_____	_____	_____			
2. Can paraphrase and summarize.	2.1 States key ideas in own words	_____	_____	_____			
	2.2 Follows text structure to restate and summarize	_____	_____	_____			

FIGURE 9.6
(continued)

they do not interact with the passage. Often, these students view comprehension strictly as a memory task—the goal is to try to store for recall the entire passage. This misunderstanding is fostered when the only measures of comprehension they see are postreading questions. This passive view of comprehension is unfortunate for two reasons: (1) It places unrealistic demands on memory, and (2) it rules out the interaction of the student with the text by elevating the message of the text above the interests and prior knowledge of the student. Students who are active readers approach passages with questions and modify their understanding of passages by attempting to answer them. Students who do not do this need to be taught strategies. One such strategy teaches students to recognize that the source of answers may be in the text or in prior knowledge. This strategy is based on Pearson and Johnson's (1978) taxonomy in which questions are viewed in relationship with text and learning and not in isolation. In a cognitive training study, Raphael and Pearson (1985) taught typical and low-achieving students to determine sources of answers using three mnemonics: (1) *Right There*, (2) *Think and Search*, and (3) *On My Own*.

(1) *Right There* meant that words used to create the question and words used for the answer are "right there" in the same sentence. (2)*Think and Search* meant that the answer is in the text, but words used to create the question and those used for an appropriate answer would be found in two or more sentences; you would have to "think and search" for an answer across sentences and paragraphs. (3) *On My Own* meant that the answer is not found in the text; rather you would think to yourself that "I have to find this answer 'on my own'." (pp. 220–221)

Here is an example of their training materials:

"Dennis sat in an old wood rocking chair. He rocked harder and harder. Suddenly he found himself sitting on the floor!"

Right There: What kind of chair did Dennis sit in?
    (old wood rocking chair)
Think and Search: What did Dennis do while sitting in the chair?
    (rocked harder and harder)
On My Own: Why did Dennis find himself sitting on the floor?
    (rocked so hard the chair tipped over)"
(Raphael & Pearson, 1985, p. 221).

Knowledge of sources of answers can be taught and does influence student responses to comprehension questions. Low-achieving students initially seem to be less aware of the relationship of questions and sources of answers. They benefit from explicit instruction in the task demands of questions as they relate to reading.

Here are some other active reading techniques.

1. Semantic webs are described in some detail by Thomas C. Lovitt in his book *Tactics for Teaching* (1984). Semantic webbing is an instructional technique aimed in part at developing knowledge schema. For more information, see the chapter by R. C. Anderson and P. D. Pearson on "A Schema-Theoretic View of Basic Processes in Reading Comprehension" in *The Handbook of Reading Research* (1984).

2. Specific questioning is used to develop active reading and recognition of central and subordinate details in a passage. The student reads specifically to answer a question, so that passage information is interpreted in terms of its relationship to the question asked *prior to* reading. This technique is particulary successful if students can be taught to develop their own questions (Beck & Carpenter, 1986).

3. Carnine and Silbert (1979) indicate that students need to be able to "identify the author's conclusions. . . determine what evidence is presented . . . determine the trustworthiness . . . and identify faulty arguments" (p. 337). Experimental work by Patching, Kameenui, Carnine, Gersten, and Colvin (1983) has demonstrated that instruction in these critical reading skills improves comprehension of low-achieving students.

4. Cognitive mapping is a procedure used to organize what is read. "Story maps organize a story visually so specific relationships of selected story elements are highlighted" (Reutzel, 1985, p. 400). A map of a narrative story could contain the following elements: (a) setting, (b) beginning, (c) reaction, (d) attempt, (e) outcome, and (f) ending (Mandler & Johnson, 1977).

Comprehension monitoring. Comprehension monitoring refers to the student's awareness of her understanding of the text. It is essential that a kid realize when she is failing to understand a text so that she can begin to use problem-solving techniques. When they fail to understand what is written, readers who successfully monitor their comprehension will reread confusing passages, slow their reading rate, refer to reference materials, and even question the text author's skill. Readers who do not monitor their comprehension will either continue to read difficult passages and experience compounded confusion or give up. Here are some ways to develop comprehension monitoring.

1. *Focus on recognizing relevant and irrelevant information.* Ask the student to make a statement about the material being read (predicting upcoming events is a good technique) and then to supply information from the text that supports that statement.
2. *Emphasize the multiple meanings of vocabulary and how the meaning of words is altered by context.* Give examples of text where context alters meaning. Use examples with familiar words to illustrate your point (Beck, McKeown, & McCaslin, 1983).
3. *Impress on the student the idea that he is bringing something to the text, not just passively receiving its message.* This means that the student is continually expected to actively compare what the passage says with what he already knows. Ask questions involving the contrast between a text and information learned previously. Ask the student to identify concepts or operations he finds adequately or inadequately described in the text.
4. *Encourage the student to recognize points in the text that deserve elaboration.* Teach the students to make specific, rather than general, requests for clarification. A student should be able to say things like "I need to know why point A in this passage involves the use of addition, not multiplication" rather than "I need to know more about point A."
5. *Finally, teach the student to stop reading and to think about applying problem-solving or study*

TABLE 9.4
Self-questioning

Problem	Problem-Solving Questions Students Should Ask:
Missing Information	Where did I get lost?
	What kind of information would help me?
	Where can I find out more about this?
Ambiguous Cues	What do the words I'm dealing with mean?
	What cause and effect relationships have been established?
	Exactly which pieces of information pertain to which characters or concepts?
Missing Criteria	If I understand this what would I know (be able to do)?
	What are the passage's guidelines (indicators) for understanding?
	What is a reasonable level of understanding for this kind of passage?

skills when her understanding seems inadequate.

Problem solving. Problem-solving strategies are a particular set of active reading skills a student uses when the tasks are difficult. Monitoring alerts a reader that a task is hard. Tasks are usually difficult because they contain missing (unstated) information or ambiguous cues or because they lack specific criteria for completion (Frederiksen, 1984). Each of these task characteristics can be dealt with by using a self-questioning strategy such as shown in Table 9.4.

Study skills. Study skill interventions teach the student how to search for needed information. They too are a subset of active reading skills. One common study skill technique involves paraphrasing a passage and examining the paraphrased response for key ideas. Teaching the student to sum-

TABLE 9.5
Multipass

Procedure	Purpose	Method
Survey pass	Familiarization	Read chapter title, introduction, headings and subtitles, illustrations and captions, and summary.
Size-up pass	Gain information	Find textual clues. Turn clues into questions. Find answers to questions. Paraphrase answer for yourself.
Sort-out pass	Self-testing	Recognize when additional information is needed, think where to look for answers, search for the answer, and search other sections if necessary.

Source: Drawn from J. B. Schumaker, D.D. Deshler, G. R. Alley, M. W. Warner, & P. H. Denton, "Multipass: A learning Strategy for Improving Reading Comprehension," *Learning Disabilities Quarterly*, 1982, *5*, 295–304.

marize preceding and subsequent discussions that can be used as links to the current passage is also a good idea. The student must learn to use the structure of the text, including illustrations, titles, and headings, to find information. She must also formulate questions and reread the passage for the purpose of answering the question. One system for teaching these skills is *Multipass* (see Table 9.5) (Schumaker, Deshler, Alley, Warner, & Denton, 1982). It is designed primarily for use with content area text books. Like any problem-solving strategy, this procedure must be taught to the point that a student employs it on her own.

SUMMARY

This chapter began by defining comprehension as the act of combining information in text with prior knowledge to construct meaning. Both student skills and text variables influence comprehension. We then discussed causes for comprehension failure, including student deficiencies in prior knowledge, decoding, vocabulary, language, and strategies. This chapter closed with a description of survey- and specific-level procedures and a discussion of instructional recommendations for comprehension strategies.

Study Questions

1. Reading comprehension can best be described as
   a. subskills such as getting the main idea, detecting the sequence, finding facts, and identifying the topic sentences.
   b. an interactive process in which the reader combines information in the text with prior knowledge to construct meaning.
   c. a process in which the reader decodes the words and recognizes what the author intended.
   d. a meaning-driven process in which prerequisites such as prior knowledge and decoding play no part.

2. Readability can be best examined by
   a. reviewing the organization and structure of a text to determine the extent to which the ideas are related and clearly convey meaning.
   b. computing the length of words, the number of words, the frequency of words, and the number of syllables in words for a given passage.
   c. checking to see if the vocabulary is controlled so that students do not encounter words they have not been taught to decode or read by sight.
   d. checking to see if all passages are narrative rather than expository to insure that, in early reading, students can use their knowledge of story maps.

3. Cloze and maze are useful formats for sampling reading comprehension because
   a. like questions after passage reading, they control for prior knowledge.
   b. like paraphrasing, they reveal if the student can arrive at conclusions about the purpose of the passage.
   c. they permit the evaluator to sample a large number of responses and a large sample size increases the reliability of the measure.
   d. students are not permitted to look ahead or back at the passage and a more reliable sample is obtained.

4. One active reading strategy is "right there, think and search, and on my own." The purpose of this strategy is to
   a. focus students' attention on advanced organizers and summaries so they can predict the gist of the story.
   b. encourage students to use the *Mulitpass* strategy so that they can identify missing information and ambiguous passages.
   c. aid students in identifying irrelevant information.
   d. show students that the source of answers may be in the text or in prior knowledge.

5. What decision would you make if the student passed the maze or cloze test and one other measure such as paraphrasing?

6. If the student does not comprehend the survey-level passage and you have ruled out prior knowledge as an assumed cause, what would you look at next?

7. Describe two ways you could check background information (prior knowledge).
   a.
   b.

8. If prior knowledge and decoding cannot account for the failure to comprehend, what is the next most likely assumed cause for failure? How would you check it?

9. If the student cannot pass a word meaning test, what would you consider testing before beginning vocabulary instruction?

10. How would you check a student's strategy use?

Chapter 10

Decoding

To repeat, the domain of reading has been subdivided into decoding and comprehension. Comprehension was covered in chapter 9 and this chapter is about the evaluation of decoding. It begins with a discussion of general reading issues.

FOCUS: READING AND DECODING

Reading Methods

There are many ways to teach reading; some are unique, but most are essentially the same. The similarity among reading methods is obviously the result of the task itself. The task of reading requires you to view print and draw information from it. All reading methods use printed material, and all programs are expected to teach kids to deal with printed material. Everyone seems to want to produce efficient readers who understand and enjoy reading. The disagreement is about how this outcome is to be obtained. This disagreement characteristically centers on methods (how the content is presented) rather than outcomes.

When distinctions are made between methods, they are based on variations in presentation, not on expected student outcomes. Reading approaches have been categorized many ways, including auditory, visual, phonic, linguistic, language-based, and code-emphasis. These labels are not particularly descriptive, and it is safe to say that, for most students, a poorly delivered lesson won't produce as much learning as a well-delivered lesson regardless of its approach. All reading methods deal with language and code as well as auditory and visual skills; so if truly different methods are to be identified, we will need to use other dimensions. In terms of the remedial or special student, some important dimensions we can use to select methods are the degree of structure, the degree to which they can be adapted to small group instruction, the quality of placement tests, the use of controlled (monitored) reading, attention to sequencing, length of daily lessons, and the level of active participation they promote. As a general statement, remedial readers will do better if they work in a structured reading method that follows an empirically validated sequence of skills and in which they actively engage in closely supervised reading. This emphasis

on sequence does not suggest that there's a fixed hierarchy of reading skills; however, there *are* sequences that contribute to efficient acquisition. The requirements of structure, control, sequence, and engaged time need not preclude a meaningful and motivating lesson delivery.

Reading Programs

There might not be a whole lot of difference between the terms *method* and *program* to some of you. We are using *program* here to mean published series, and *method* to mean instructional approach. Many teachers use evaluation to place a student into a program. These teachers will ask things like, "What book should Emily be in?" instead of "What skill does Emily need to be taught?" Consequently, there are many techniques for finding the "best" book for each student. The implied assumption behind these techniques is that there *is* a best book for each student. That's putting a lot of responsibility on book publishers, the test publishers, and the book itself. It isn't putting much responsibility on the teacher.

Teachers should not test for the purpose of placing the student into a book or series of books. They should test for the purpose of placing the student within the sequence of reading skills, the curriculum, and this sequence should contain both subtasks and strategies. *Then* they look for a program (or programs) that includes opportunities for instruction and practice on the skills the kid needs. A competent teacher/evaluator compares both the student and the materials to the curriculum.

Reading Curriculum

A well-designed curriculum features:

1. Generalizable knowledge, skills, and strategies;
2. Efficient sequences that promote positive transfer of learning; and
3. Only essential subtasks and strategies.

In reading, this translates into the development of a course of study that may differ considerably from the one with which you are currently familiar. Take a few minutes to review the reading tasks you are prepared to teach. Many teachers teach decoding rules that work less than 40%, 50% or 70% of the time. Often they teach decoding rules for sounds that occur in low-frequency words. Maybe this time could be spent more efficiently teaching generalizable strategies for predicting the word based on context or teaching a vocabulary that would facilitate use of context. Would you teach sounds in a sequence that promotes or impedes discrimination? How many lessons separate the instruction of *b*, *d*, *p*, *q*, and *g* or *m*, *n*, *h*, and *u*? Have you taught sight words such as *what*, *that*, *them*, *this*, and *these* together? One of the authors has. The result was a group of very confused kids who took twice as long to reach mastery as subsequent groups provided with a more efficient sequence of sight words.

By introducing tasks that are visually or acoustically similar, the probability of mislearning is increased (Carnine, 1981). When mislearning occurs, the time it takes hard-to-teach kids to catch up increases. Yes, you can teach *b* and *d* in the same lesson and not have mislearning. However, your lesson would have to include an intensive investment of time devoted to teaching the critical attributes of each letter/sound as well as the distinguishing differences. Teaching to mastery on one skill before introducing the second skill and separating the *b–d* lessons with instruction on dissimilar skills may be more efficient.

Many reading curricula and many reading programs have been developed without consideration of generalization, efficiency, or essential content. For example, in English there are 100 to 200 possible sound–symbol relationships. However, they are not all equally essential. If we teach all 100 to 200 sound–symbol relationships, we waste our time and the kid's time in several ways. First, it may only take mastery of 20 to 40 generalizable sounds to begin figuring out new words using prior knowledge and context clues. Because this is the case, some teachers are wasting time teaching an additional 60 to 160 sounds before emphasizing context and meaning. Decoding tasks are not inherently meaningful because the sound–symbol relationship is arbitrary. When a task is not meaningful, it requires a lot of drill and practice. Drill and practice on nonessential skills take time away from instruction on essential skills and turn students off.

Prereading

Many tests are available to measure things that aren't really reading but are supposed to be prerequisites for reading. Auditory and visual discrimination are two popular examples of these so-called prereading skills. There is no question that discrimination is necessary for reading. But there are a lot of questions about our ability to teach discrimination and about the types of discriminations that are relevant to reading. When students are asked to discriminate between the sounds of letters, some people say they are doing a prereading task. Others think they are reading. When students are asked to discriminate between animal sounds, some people will say they are doing a prereading task. Others think they are discriminating between animal sounds. Tests that sample geometric shapes or noises are too far removed from the reading curriculum to have instructional utility.

A typical visual discrimination test supplies one letter (word or shape) and then asks the student to recognize it somewhere else, as in examples 1 and 2 below. Each format tests something that is in part visual, and each requires the kid to make a discrimination. However, in all tests of this kind, it is important to recall that the required response, and the content (what is being discriminated) will affect the student's performance. Example 1 is easier than Example 2 because a student may be more successful at discriminating words from nonwords than words from words.

Example 1
Directions: "Put an X over the one that is like the one in the box."

one   ◯ ▭ one △

Example 2
Directions: "Put an X over the one that is like the one in the box."

one   on   only   one   tone

If changes in the content can influence test behavior, then the conclusions drawn from the test should be applied to the content, *not to the kid*. In other words, don't make general statements about someone having good or bad visual discrimination; make statements about what he can or can't seem to discriminate. For example, "Ralph can't tell *a*'s from *o*'s when they are in the middle of words." This kind of statement won't encourage anyone to try to teach visual discrimination but might encourage someone to teach Ralph what the critical differences are between *a*'s and *o*'s.

Auditory discrimination tests that require a student to recognize same and different words or sounds are another matter. Interestingly enough, there is little to indicate that these so-called auditory tasks are all that similar to what students do when they read (Spache, 1976). What these tests can tell is which particular letters or sounds the student confuses with others. The confusion will prevent the student from benefitting from instruction centered on these letters. Therefore, the advantage of the testing is that it tells you which letters you should modify when you teach. For example, if you know the student confuses the visual stimulus ɑ with *o*, you may initially wish to accentuate the stem of the ɑ to make it easier to discriminate from an *o* (i.e., ɑ).

Promising work by Ehri and Wilce (1985), Juel (1985), Lindamood (personal communication, 1986), and Pany (1987) suggests that there is an auditory skill that is teachable (and therefore should be evaluated). This skill is linked to reading success and can be taught as a part of reading instruction. The skill is called *phonemic segmentation*. In a test of phonemic segmentation a student is asked to say the sounds he hears in a word. To do this a student must "hear" and isolate sounds. Here is an example.

Example 3

Directions: "Listen, I'm going to say the sounds in *man*, mmm/ aaa/ nnn. I'm going to say the sounds in *sit*, sss/ iii/ ttt. Now, you say the sounds in *fat*."
Stimulus words: Fat, Fix, And, Mom, Run, Sit, Pup

If nonreaders do poorly on discrimination tests, it may seem that their lack of discrimination skills has resulted in poor reading. However, the opposite could also be true; that is, their poor reading could result in the poor discrimination test scores. Many of the discrimination, coding, and sequence skills we thought of as prerequisites for reading are actually taught during reading instruction and should be part of the reading curriculum. Therefore, students fail tests on these skills *because* they can't read—they don't fail to read because they can't discriminate or sequence.

Decoding

Decoding means breaking the code; using the relationship between printed letters—clusters of letters—and sounds to vocalize words. It is based upon grapheme–phoneme correspondence, or the relationship between print and sound. Decoding may have nothing to do with meaning at all. For example, the word *smek* has no meaning, but you can vocalize it because you can decode it. Decoding has two primary subdivisions: sounds and blending.

The need to teach letter sounds (and cluster sounds) directly to students has been debated. Once again the confusion of *how* to teach may be obscuring a *what*-to-teach issue. Reading teachers have argued the need to teach sounds directly for decades. Some believe that it is best to let students discover the sounds through language-oriented experiences with texts; others think the sounds should be taught directly. While there is growing evidence that *beginning* students benefit from a balanced approach to reading instruction that has both a code and meaning emphasis (Anderson, Hiebert, Scott, & Wilkinson, 1985; Pearson, 1984), for remedial students this debate doesn't really make sense. Kids are considered to be special/remedial because they haven't learned something. Obviously if they haven't learned to use meaning-based skills that is what they need to be taught; if they haven't learned code *that* is what they need to be taught.

Good readers know the sounds letters and clusters of letters make. Some good readers were taught the sounds directly, and others discovered them in the course of their reading experience. Most often, poor readers do not know the sounds. They have not discovered them in the past, and there is no reason to assume they will simply discover them in the future without guidance or direct instruction. It seems incredible that some teachers will continue to extol the virtues of indirect (discovery) learning for students who are so far behind in content that they are being labeled *remedial* or *handicapped*. Surely at some point when a student hasn't discovered the answer we should give him a break and tell him what it is. This guidance will be most effective if it is preceded by specific evaluation.

When nonreaders attack an unknown word, they prefer to use letter cues. They do not seem to use word shapes or other so-called sight characteristics of words. Even if nonreaders did prefer to use sight cues, teaching these cues is ultimately a waste of time because the instruction will not transfer to new words (Samuels, 1976). Students must have knowledge of letter/cluster sounds and how to blend them to read new material. A reading evaluation must include assessment of decoding because this skill is so important that the lack of it accounts for a large portion of nonreaders (Anderson et al., 1985). We do not mean by this that students who can comprehend passages easily should be tested on *all* decoding skills; however, the literature supports the position that students need to decode rapidly in addition to being able to comprehend (Allington, 1983). Without rapid, accurate decoding, students will not be able to use reading as an efficient tool for acquiring large amounts of information. Since the ultimate goal of reading is to construct meaning from text, students who decode slowly, even if they understand what they read, will learn less because they take in fewer idea units per minute than students who read fluently. Thus evaluators need to check rate of decoding even when students pass all measures of comprehension.

Decoding Evaluation Concerns

Once you put aside general concerns about whether to test decoding, there are questions of how to go about it, especially as your focus of concern narrows. We will discuss three topics associated with word and letter–symbol evaluation that sometimes are a source of confusion. These topics are (1) words and sounds in isolation, (2) timing responses, and (3) using nonsense words.

Isolation, Time, and Nonsense. At a specific level, evaluators will sometimes test sounds in isolation, not in a word. Whenever testing any skill in isola-

tion, remember that you are asking the student to do something successful readers seldom do. Testing reading subskills in isolation is a classic example of how testing procedures may differ from teaching procedures. Sounds are best taught within real words, but if they are tested within real words, the other letter sounds may obscure or affect the way the student pronounces the target letter. This may distort your conclusions. (Similarly, passage reading tests are timed to test for skill mastery; however, teaching with timed reading drills is not always a good idea.)

Timing and isolation are not the only testing procedures that are different from teaching procedures. Another technique is to test with nonsense words. Nonsense words are used to sample the student's skill at sounding and blending. Often poor readers need to be tested on short words, not long ones. However, these same readers may already know most short words as sight words. Therefore, to test their knowledge of sounds, you must either risk confusing the results with the complexity of longer words or with the novelty of nonsense words. Real words are replaced with nonsense words in example 4.

Example 4

Real Word	Nonsense Word
cat	jat
run	mun
dig	hig

The risk of obtaining a bad sample because of novelty can be diminished by taking steps to inform the student that, while the words aren't real, you wish her to read them as if they were. If the student reads the nonsense words, you can be sure she is doing so based on her skill at sounding and blending. Although nonsense words make sense for testing, they are useless (or at least needless) for teaching. We recommend using nonsense words to test reading but *never* to teach it.

Reading for Special and Remedial Students

Our discussion of decoding has focused on the content of reading and its relationship to evaluation.

Before beginning the section on survey- and specific-level testing, it is necessary to examine one aspect of reading that is often overlooked: the quality and quantity of instruction provided special and remedial students. To do this we will summarize information from the work of Allington (1983), Haynes and Jenkins (1986), and Ysseldyke, Thurlow, Mecklenburg, and Graden (1984). These authors have noted that the reading instruction provided to low-performing students differs from the reading instruction provided to more able students. Their findings indicate that, all too often, reading instruction for low-performing students is characterized by:

- Little relationship between assessed student need and total allocated time in both special and regular class settings.
- More time on letters, sounds, and words in isolation.
- Less time reading words in text.
- Less silent reading; thus *less* time reading for meaning in text.
- Greater proportion of engaged time spent in reading in regular classrooms than in resource rooms.
- Smaller proportion of time spent in seatwork in regular classrooms than in special education classrooms.
- Greater proportion of direct teacher time spent on reading tasks in regular classrooms than in special education classrooms.

The disparity between what is needed and what is observed is exemplified by the findings of Haynes and Jenkins (1986). They found that in programs where regular classroom teachers and special and remedial teachers shared responsibility for a student's reading instruction, only 50% of the teachers knew the name of the material the other was using and only 27% knew the level of the text the student was reading. They observed that only 15% of the teachers used the same curriculum in both settings. If competing curricula are used, if teachers do not communicate about what they are teaching, and if large portions of time in special education classrooms are spent in independent seat-

work, it is not surprising that few remedial students catch up.

DECISION MAKING

The purpose of evaluation is to guide decision making. The remainder of the chapter describes procedures for deciding what to teach and how to teach it. The "what to teach" decision involves the subskills and content of reading. "How to teach" decisions relate to the treatment recommendations which are briefly previewed in the following paragraphs.

Students with reading problems may require one or more of the following treatment recommendations.

1. Build oral reading rate because comprehension is inhibited by the limited number of words the student can read within typical time limits.
2. Use a balanced approach (phonics and language-based) to teaching both decoding and comprehension.
3. Emphasize decoding (grapheme–phoneme correspondence) to help the student use these skills more automatically.
4. Focus instruction on error patterns such as mispronunciation, insertion, omission, hesitation, repetition, and inattention to punctuation.
5. Monitor decoding but emphasize fluency and teach higher level reading skills (summarizing, questioning, self-monitoring, and predicting).
6. Teach specific "active reading" strategies to improve comprehension.

To select a treatment recommendation, the evaluator needs to answer a few straightforward questions. Examples of questions and kinds of testing procedures are shown in Table 10.1. Notice that the questions address both decoding and comprehension. Procedures for sampling comprehension are found in chapter 9. The comprehension evaluation questions are included here because the purpose of reading is understanding and reading evaluation will include a sample of both comprehension and decoding behavior. This chapter will address questions 1, 3, 4, 5, and 6 from Table 10.1.

TABLE 10.1
Outline for reading assessment

Question	Test or Procedure
1. Is the student's oral reading (accuracy and rate) on grade-level passages acceptable?	Passage-Reading Test, pp. 204–207.
2. Is the student's comprehension of grade-level passages acceptable?	Comprehension Tests—Questions, paraphrase, retelling, cloze, maze, or sentence verification (chapter 9) and Purpose of Reading, Specific-Level Procedure 2, pp. 212–213.
3. Does the student improve reading rate when allowed to reread a passage?	Timed Rereading Test—Specific-Level Procedure 1, pp. 210–212.
4. Do more than half the student's reading errors violate the meaning of the passage?	Use of Context, Specific-Level Procedure 3, pp. 213–214.
5. Are decoding difficulties a result of poor phonic skills?	Phonics Test, Specific-Level Procedure 5, pp. 215–217.
6. Are decoding difficulties a result of consistent error patterns?	Error Pattern Test, Specific-Level Procedure 4, pp. 214–215.
7. Can specific causes of comprehension problems be identified?	Comprehension Checklist (chapter 9).

SURVEY-LEVEL TESTING

The general sample or survey-level testing should begin by collecting errors on reading passages from books used at the student's grade level. In some cases published tests with passages arranged according to levels of difficulty may be used. The advantages of these tests (usually called *reading inventories*) are that they cover many levels of content quickly and they are well organized. The disadvantage is that they may not require the kids to read the kind of material that they need to read in school. The best error samples will be obtained from passages on which a student is from 80% to 85% accurate. Anything higher than 90% will reflect errors of efficiency, such as omitting words, which do not affect comprehension. Anything lower than 75% will reflect desperation and guesses.

Most reading inventories have some system for marking errors and sorting them into categories (i.e., mispronunciations, reversals, repetitions). It is a good idea to review a few of these systems and then devise or select one with which you are comfortable and which you can use consistently. Always

remember that the error (student behavior) varies in importance according to the word misused (content). For example, in the preceding sentence, omission of the word *always* would not be as great an error as omission of the word *misused*.

Passage-Reading Test

Before Beginning.   Assemble materials and equipment before meeting with the student.

1. Collect passages of varying difficulty levels from texts used in class or from published tests. Have a copy for yourself and one for the student. The passages should be about 250 words long. You should be familiar enough with the passages so that you can make judgments about moving to an easier or a harder level if your initial estimate of student skill is in error. In addition to knowledge of difficulty level, you also need to know a criterion for acceptable performance for accuracy and mastery (rate). Suggested criteria for oral passage reading are shown in Figure 10.1.

Passage Reading Summary Form
(used with objective 30m)

DIRECTIONS

For each passage used, record the number of corrects and errors per minute. Also record the accuracy. For each passage, check the rate and accuracy status (pass, marginal no pass, or no pass) for each curriculum level. The status can be found by referring to the interpretation section of objective 30m.

Curr. Level	Form	Expected Rate Correct	Expected Rate Error	Obtained Rate Correct	Obtained Rate Error	Status Pass	Status M. No Pass	Status No Pass	Accuracy Exp. Acc.	Accuracy Obt. Acc.	Status Pass	Status M. No Pass	Status No Pass
8		140	0-7						100-95%				
7		140	0-7						100-95%				
6		140	0-7						100-95%				
5		140	0-7						100-95%				
4		140	0-7						100-95%				
3		140	0-7						100-95%				
2		100	0-5						100-95%				
1		50	0-3						100-95%				

Expected Level (Current Grade Placement) _____

Curriculum Level (Highest level at which
    mastery criterion is met) _____

Levels above (+) or below (−) Expectation _____

Rate Discrepancy at Instructional Level
Obtained Rate _____ ÷ Expected Rate _____ =
    Rate Discrepancy _____

Accuracy Discrepancy at Instructional Level
Obtained Accuracy _____% ÷ Expected Accuracy _____ =
    Accuracy Discrepancy _____

FIGURE 10.1
Passage summary sheet with criteria for acceptable performance. (*Source:* K. W. Howell, S. H. Zucker, and M. K. Morehead, *Multilevel Academic Skill Inventory: Reading, Manual,* p. 10. San Antonio, TX: The Psychological Corporation, 1982. Reprinted with permission.)

FIGURE 10.2
Passage for survey-level test
(Source: K. W. Howell, S. H. Zucker, and M. K. Morehead, *Multilevel Academic Skill Inventory: Reading, Manual,* Card 19. San Antonio, TX: The Psychological Corporation, 1982. Reprinted with permission.)

The yucca is a desert plant. It has long, spiny leaves.

Once a year, it bears beautiful white flowers. The flowers

bloom only at night or on a very dark day. The flowers

produce seeds for more yucca plants.

The yucca could not produce seeds without its partner,

the yucca moth. The yucca moth has only one goal in life.

Its goal is to find a safe place to lay its eggs. The yucca

plant and the yucca moth became partners because each one had

something the other needed.

2. Set up a tape recorder.
3. Get a stopwatch.
4. You will need something to write with to code or score student responses. A calculator may also be useful for determining percentage scores.

In the survey-level test, the evaluator determines the reading level of the student. If there is a discrepancy between the student's current reading level and what is expected in a particular grade level, a sufficient number of relevant *facts* must also be collected so that the evaluator can generate a list of assumed causes for the reading problem. These assumed causes are later verified or disproved through specific-level testing.

This is a two-step process. First, to find the student's current reading level, administer passages at the student's grade and score it. Administer easier or harder passages until you reach the 95–100% accuracy and fluency levels (see Figure 10.1). Sec-

ond, administer easier or harder passages until you reach the 80–85% accuracy level and then take an error sample.

Directions.

1. Select a passage at the reading level closest to your best estimate of the student's reading level.
2. Say to the student: "I want you to read part of this story out loud. Read it as quickly and carefully as you can. If you come to a word you do not know skip it. Please begin." Time the student for one minute and make a slash (/) after the last word read in the one-minute time limit. *Do not stop the student here.*

   As the student reads, mark all errors on your copy of the passage, as shown in Figure 10.2. It is not necessary to note different types of errors when determining rate and accuracy.
3. To establish decoding rate, count the number of words correct and the number of word errors

during the first minute (up to your slash mark). Omissions are not errors. To obtain the student's passage accuracy, find the percentage correct on the entire passage. Divide the words correct by the total number of words read.

4. Compare the student's scores to the criteria suggested in Figure 10.1 or to a criterion you establish using procedures outlined in chapter 8. If necessary, move to an easier or harder passage.

Summarizing Survey-Level Information

The Stimulus–Response Format

To develop a list of assumed causes for specific-level testing, survey-level information needs to be organized systematically. One effective way to summarize responses is to list the passage word (stimulus) on which the student made an error (response) and to comment on each error made. This is illustrated in Figure 10.3. The evaluator can then review the comments and target areas for specific-level testing.

Stimulus	Response	Comment
The Yucca Plant	(omitted)	Doesn't use title for advanced organizer strategy.
yucca	yuca	Vowel conversion error, vocabulary, prior knowledge of desert botany, word not in vocabulary so there is no feedback on decoding error.
plant	pant	Consonant team *(pl)*.
spiny	spinny	Vowel conversion rule, lacks prior knowledge of desert botany.
a	(omitted)	Does not self-monitor for syntax—*year* cannot follow *once*.

FIGURE 10.3
Portion of a stimulus–response summary

Using a Checklist

An example of a content checklist is shown in Figure 10.4. The checklist is composed of content from the reading table of specifications, Table C.1 in Appendix C. By noting each error and then marking the content category it falls into, you can summarize the survey behavior.

Arriving at useful error hypotheses (assumed causes) is essential to the whole evaluative process. The following exercise may help you to formulate good hypotheses. Because this is the task-analytical model, remember that you can't escape the task. In other words, your ability to comment on behaviors or use a table of specifications to derive hypotheses will be related to your knowledge of the reading task.

Exercise 1.   Under "comment," state the type of error made.

Stimulus	Response	Comment
1. stood	stod	
2. hose	hoss	
3. distance	display	
4. these	this	
5. read	road	

Answers:

	Comments
1. stood = stod	This could be the result of a lack of familiarity with vowel teams (*oo*) or a failure to monitor for meaning.
2. hose = hoss	Vowel conversion; does not use final -*e*.
3. distance = display	A guess based on the beginning of the word. Several of these may indicate generally weak decoding skills or simply be the result of trying to read too quickly. When such a guess interferes with passage meaning, you could also assume that the student is not monitoring for comprehension.

Student _____

Grade _____

Date _____

Evaluator _____

	Errors	Total Errors on Each Subtask
8. CVC + e Blending Example: hate, mete, bite, hope, cut		
Sounds		
7. CVC Blending Example: hat, met, bit, hop, cut		
6. Vowel Sounds a, e, i, o, u		
5. Consonant Sounds b, c, d, f, g, h, j, k, l, m, n, p, q, r, s, t, v, w, x, y, z		
4. Same and different word sounds Directions: Teacher says two sounds and asks if they are the same or different.		
3. Same and different letter sounds Directions: Teacher says two sounds and asks if they are the same or different.		
2. Same and different words Example: "Point to the one that looks like the one in the box." [was] saw mas was wos 1 2 3 4		
1. Same and different letters Example: "Point to the one that looks like the one in the box." [a] o e u a 1 2 3 4		

FIGURE 10.4
Content checklist

4. these = this — A sight word substitution. This kind of error may not affect comprehension.

5. read = road — Vowel team, or size configuration substitution. Again there may also be a problem with self-monitoring.

In listing comments, you should have tried to limit yourself to content specific subtasks and strategies. *Content specific* means content subtasks and strategies that are close to the main task. If the main task is to read *cat* and the kid says *cit*, you have many explanations available. Some are specific to the main task (i.e., "doesn't know vowel sounds and is not monitoring for meaning"); others are not (i.e., "lacks intelligence"). Always stick to subtasks that are close. In fact, "assumed causes" and "comments" will often seem simply to state the obvious. For example:

Stimulus	Response	Comment
letter	later	Size, configuration substitution, vowel or double consonant error? Slow; does not use strategy to monitor meaning.
far	fair	Same as above.
error	earrow	Vowel, R-controlled? Slow; does not use strategy to monitor for meaning.
bottom	botom	Double consonant vowel pattern. Slow; does not use strategy to monitor for meaning.
bite	bit	Final -*e* vowel conversion; strategy for monitoring for meaning.
creep	crep	Vowel combination.

A review of the comment section above indicates that the student is not accurate at vowels or vowel conversions and does not use a strategy to monitor for meaning.

Interpretation guidelines. These guidelines are intended to channel your efforts toward one of the following specific-level procedures. Based on the student's performance and the criteria for the passage, respond to the following questions.

Question. Is the student's accuracy (percentage correct) and fluency (rate) on oral reading at or above the criterion for grade level?

Recommendation. If yes, move to a higher level passage and readminister.

If no, move to a lower level until you find the highest level for passing.

Question. Is the student accurate but slow?

Recommendation. If yes, there are at least three assumed causes. You may have to test all three or you may select the one that seems most probable:

- The low rate is caused by a lack of practice reading quickly. Use Specific-Level Procedure 1.
- Rate is impeded by poor use of context clues. Use Specific-Level Procedure 3.
- Rate is impeded by poor use of phonics. Use Specific-Level Procedure 5.

Question. Is the student inaccurate?

Recommendation. If yes, consider the following assumed causes:

- The student does not read for accuracy (e.g., the student believes he is only expected to "get through" the passage—not to read it thoroughly). Use Specific-Level Procedure 2.
- This student has learned error patterns (inappropriate reading strategies) that are impeding accuracy. Use Specific-Level Procedure 4.
- Accuracy is impeded by poor context skills. Use Specific-Level Procedure 3.
- Accuracy is impeded by poor phonics skills. Use Specific-Level Procedure 5.

SPECIFIC-LEVEL TESTING

The transition from the survey to the specific level is made when you begin to select or develop proce-

TABLE 10.2
Facts → Assumed causes → Test

Fact	Assumed Cause	Test
A. Slow but accurate.	• Low rate caused by lack of practice reading quickly.	• Use Specific-Level Procedure 1.
	• Rate is impeded by poor use of passage context.	• Use Specific-Level Procedure 1.
	• Rate is impeded by poor use of phonics; to go more quickly would generate errors.	• Use Specific-Level Procedure 5.
B. Student is inaccurate.	• Not reading for accuracy.	• Use Specific-Level Procedure 2.
	• Poor use of context.	• Use Specific-Level Procedure 3.
	• Learned error patterns.	• Use Specific-Level Procedure 4.
	• Poor use of decoding.	• Use Specific-Level Procedure 5.

dures to verify the assumed causes that you have formulated. The entire process of survey- and specific-level testing is complete when you have summarized your results and have chosen what to teach. This process is illustrated by these steps:

1. Collect the behavior sample. (Survey level)
2. List the assumed cause(s).
3. Select or make up a test(s) to verify the assumed cause(s) and administer. (Specific level)
4. Repeat the procedure or summarize the results.

Seven high-probability assumed causes are outlined in Table 10.2. These are linked to the five specific-level procedures described next. Depending on the information, one or more of these assumed causes may seem more probable than the others, or different assumed causes may be added to those we suggest. *More than one assumed cause may fit a particular student* (e.g., has poor context skills *and* has learned error patterns).

Five Common Specific-Level Procedures

This section describes five procedures to verify (test) the suggested assumed causes. A brief *rationale* for each procedure is followed by *directions* and *interpretation guidelines*. Within these guidelines

are *recommendations* for additional specific-level testing and for teaching if no additional testing is indicated.

As the description of specific-level testing continues, be aware that this discussion is more complex than its application. There are two reasons for this. First, we are supplying explanations and rationale. Second, we are trying to make the thought processes of a skilled evaluator visible. Some of these steps which take paragraphs to describe only take seconds to accomplish.

Figure 10.5 illustrates the decision format that coordinates these procedures. Evaluation questions are in the circles, testing procedures are in the rectangles, and teaching recommendations are in the triangles. You will notice that we have transformed assumed causes into questions. Each procedure is used to answer a question. For example, you will use Specific-Level Procedure 1 when you want to answer this question: If oral reading is accurate but slow, will practice on reading quickly be sufficient?

Specific-Level Procedure 1: Passage Rereading

Rationale.   Given the fact that the student is accurate but slow, it can be assumed that (1) he has a

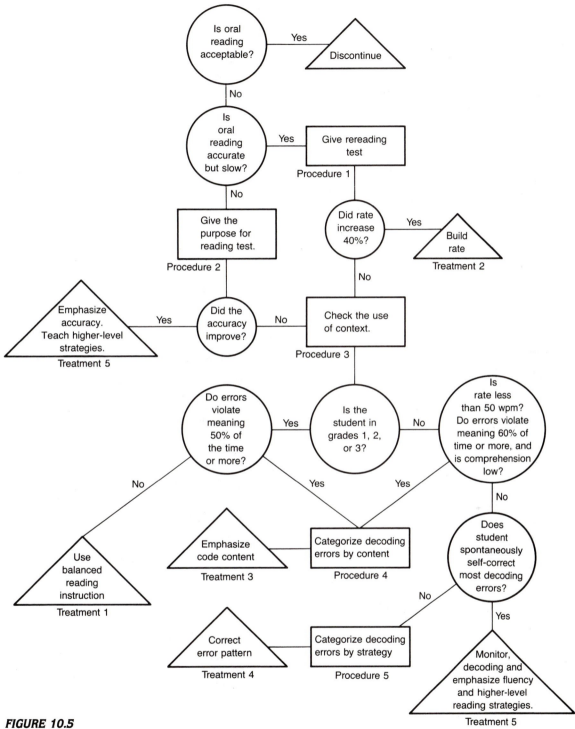

FIGURE 10.5
Decoding evaluation format

211

fluency problem that can be fixed with practice, 2) his rate is impeded by uncertainty about the context, or (3) his rate is impeded by poor phonics. Assumption 3 will be dealt with in the section on phonics. Assumptions 1 and 2 can both be addressed through the rereading procedure. Rereading provides practice and (because he is accurate) allows the student to learn the context during the first reading and use it in the second (talking about the passage after the first reading will help here also). The purpose of this test is to determine if the student's oral reading rate (words correct per minute) increases when he has an opportunity to practice reading the material.

Directions

1. Select the highest level on which the student failed to meet the rate criterion but was 90% accurate.
2. Say to the student, "I want you to read this story aloud. Begin."
3. Note where the student is after one minute but don't stop him. When he finishes reading the passage, point to the beginning of the passage and say: "Now I want you to read it aloud again as quickly and carefully as you can. Are you ready? [pause] Begin."
4. Again, time the student for one minute. Stop the student after the minute is up.
5. Count the number of words correct to obtain rate on corrects per minute on both readings. Do the same for errors.
6. Record the correct words per minute and error words per minute on a summary data sheet such as the one shown in Figure 10.1.

Interpretation Guidelines   Compare the student's rate during initial reading and his rate during the timed rereading. Compute the percentage increase by dividing the initial rate by the rereading rate and subtracting the result from 100.

Question.   Is the student's rereading rate at passage criterion? (See Figure 10.1.)

Recommendation.   If yes, the student's slow rate can most likely be attributed to a lack of fluency instruction. Employ rate-building techniques. (See Teaching Recommendations 1 and 2.)

Question.   Is the student's rereading rate at least 20 to 40% higher than the initial rate?

Recommendation.   If yes, the student's slow rate can most likely be attributed to either the need for fluency instruction (see Teaching Recommendation 2) or poor use of context (to confirm this assumed cause, use Specific-Level Procedure 3).

Question.   Has the student's rate remained the same?

Recommendation.   If yes, the most likely explanation is poor use of decoding (to confirm this assumed cause, use Specific-Level Procedure 5.)

Specific Procedure 2: Checking Purpose for Reading

Rationale.   Use Specific-Level Procedure 2 when you want to answer this question: Will knowing the purpose for reading increase accuracy?

As strange as it may seem, many remedial/special students don't really understand the purpose for reading. This is particularly true of their understanding of the purpose for reading to teachers/evaluators. Often these kids believe their whole goal is to get through the passage—*any way they can!* Their errors are often characterized by frequent nonmeaningful word substitutions that have only the initial sound in common with the stimulus word.

Directions

1. Give a purpose for reading accurately. You may need to do this several times as you must assume that the student has *learned* to read without attention to accuracy. Tell the student that you are interested in finding out how long it

takes her to read the passage *correctly.* Emphasize the importance of accuracy. Note if accuracy improves to acceptable levels.

Interpretation Guidelines

Question. Did the student's accuracy improve to acceptable levels after you emphasized reading for accuracy?

Recommendations. If yes, emphasize reading for accuracy. (See Teaching Recommendation 5— "Teach higher-level strategies.")

If no, the most likely causes are the poor use of context (to confirm this assumed cause, use Specific-Level Procedure 3) or poor use of phonics (to confirm this assumed cause, use Specific-Level Procedure 5).

Specific-Level Procedure 3: Checking Use of Context

Rationale. Use Specific-Level Procedure 3 to answer this question: Does the student use context to decode words?

If you suspect that errors are interfering with reading rate or comprehension, you must find the causes for the errors. One possible cause is that the student is not using context information to decode, leading to errors that violate meaning. Determining if errors do not violate meaning allows an evaluator to rule out failure to use context as a cause.

The steps you follow to collect an error sample in Specific-Level Procedure 3 will also be followed in Specific Procedures 4 and 5.

Directions for Collecting the Error Sample.

1. Select a 250-word passage on which you estimate the student will be about 80% accurate. Use the results from oral passage reading to help make your selection. You will need about 25 errors for students in grade 1; at grade 2 and above, at least 50 errors are recommended.
2. Disregard the student's reading rate for this measure.

3. Point to the passage and say: "I want you to read these words aloud. Take your time and read them as carefully as you can. Try all the words. Begin."
4. If the student is making more than 50% errors, discontinue and select a lower-level passage.
5. Continue moving up or down in passage difficulty until you find a passage on which the student is about 80% accurate.
6. Using the passage you found in Step 5, record the student's errors on your copy of the passage. Write errors directly above the correct form of the words as they appear in the passage. Circle omitted words. Indicate insertions and write in the insertion. Write a *c* next to any errors the student self-corrects. Mark hesitations with an *h.* Underline repeated words. Figure 10.2 illustrates error recording.
7. Note whether the student read with appropriate intonation, attended to punctuation, or made any relevant comments about her reading. You should use a tape recorder to reconfirm your scoring later.

Directions for the Error Category Checklist. While there are many elaborate procedures for analyzing errors, we are using a categorization scheme outlined in an earlier work (Howell et al., 1985). Errors reflecting inattention to context (likely to interfere with meaning) are differentiated from those that are consistent with context (not likely to interfere with meaning). Figure 10.6 can be used to summarize the errors.

1. Make sure you are familiar with the passage; reread it if necessary.
2. For each error, code it as one of the following categories:
   • Category 1: The error response violates the meaning of the passage; i.e., the error does not make semantic or syntactic sense in the context of the passage. (Judge errors in terms of the story as written, not the story as the student may have misread or modified it.)

Category 1 Violates Meaning	Category 2 Does Not Violate Meaning	Category 3 Cannot Classify
Stimulus–Response	Stimulus–Response	Stimulus–Response

Total _____   _____   _____

Category Total _____ ÷ Total Errors _____ = _____% of Errors in Category

FIGURE 10.6
Error category checklist for meaning violations

- Category 2: The error response does not violate the meaning of the passage; i.e., is appropriate or does not disrupt the context of the story.
- Category 3: Any error you are not certain how to classify; include in this type all errors involving proper names.
3. Do not categorize self-corrections.
4. Compute the number of errors in each category and summarize the results by percentage (e.g., 50% category 1, 40% category 2, 10% category 3).

Interpretation Guidelines

Question.   For students in grades 1–3, do 50% or more of the student's errors violate meaning? (Category 1)

Recommendation.   If yes, analyze all errors for error patterns (Specific-Level Procedure 4) or decoding content (Specific-Level Procedure 5).

If no, recommend to the teacher that further instruction contain a balance between code and context (Teaching Recommendation 1).

Question.   For students above grade 3, do 60% or more of the student's errors violate meaning (Category 1) *and* is there evidence of comprehen-

sion problems or slow rate (less than 50 words per minute)?

Recommendation.   If yes, analyze all errors for decoding content (Specific-Level Procedure 5).

If no, monitor decoding but emphasize fluency and higher level reading strategies (Teaching Recommendation 5).

Question.   Did there appear to be consistent patterns of errors such as insertions, omissions, substitutions, or repetitions?

Recommendations.   If yes, assume there are learned patterns of decoding errors (confirm this assumption with Specific-Level Procedure 4).

If no, monitor decoding but emphasize fluency and higher level reading strategies (Teaching Recommendation 5).

Specific-Level Procedure 4: Recognizing Error Patterns

Rationale.   Use Specific-Level Procedure 4 to answer this question: Does the student make consistent strategy errors?

Reading strategies are learned. Often these strategies are the result of our attempts to short-cut the reading task or to avoid difficult material.

Sometimes they work and sometimes they don't. For example, one student may get in the habit of avoiding errors by simply omitting troublesome words, while another may substitute known words and another may mispronounce. As students practice reading they practice using these strategies. Remedial and special students often practice using the wrong strategies and develop what might best be described as poor reading habits. These habits must be countered with direct intervention, as will be described in Teaching Recommendation 4—Correct Error Patterns. However, before this can be done the specific error pattern must be recognized. To do this we will recognize *types* of errors (substitution, insertion, omission) that may or may not relate to the categories of errors (violate meaning, do not violate meaning) we have already discussed.

Directions

1. Follow the seven steps of "Directions for Collecting Error Sample" found under Specific-Level Procedure 3.
2. Categorize the errors according to the error type (e.g., hesitation, mispronunciation, insertion, etc.) by using the Error Pattern Checklist form in Figure 10.7.

Interpretation Guidelines

Question. Do most errors fall into two or three error types?

Recommendation. If yes, correct these error types using Teaching Recommendation 4.

Question. Do errors seem random?

Recommendation. If yes, assume the problem is phonics and analyze errors using the Specific-Level Procedure 5 for Recognizing Code Errors.

Specific-Level Procedure 5: Checking Use of Phonics Content

Rationale. Use Specific-Level Procedure 5 to answer this question: Does the student make consistent phonics and word recognition errors?

If a student does not seem accurate at passage reading or if he is accurate but slow, he may have trouble using phonics. Students who are slow but accurate or who omit or substitute words often are compensating for weak phonics skills by slowing down or avoiding difficult words. Obviously students who are inaccurate because of errors in sound-letter correspondence or blending are having trouble with phonics.

The following discussion will be quite elaborate because phonics itself has so many subdivisions and modifications. However, it is wrong to assume that the number of pages dedicated to phonics implies a higher priority than the other decoding skills we have discussed.

The directions and interpretation guidelines are presented below. Each element of them will be discussed in some depth. You may need to read the subsequent discussion in order to understand the directions and interpretation.

Directions

1. Follow the "Directions for Collecting Error Sample" found under Specific-Level Procedure 3. (If you've already done this once you don't have to do it again—just use the information you already have.)
2. Note the phonetic content associated with each error. Use a checksheet like the one in Figure 10.7 to tally the errors.
3. Identify those phonetic units or strategies that seem to account for a large proportion of errors.
4. Give specific-level tests (CRTs) at accuracy and mastery levels to confirm that instruction is needed on the content areas identified. (A discussion of things to consider and formats to use for this additional testing is found on pages 220–228.)

Interpretation Guidelines

Question. Is the student accurate and fluent using the skill(s) in question?

Recommendations. If yes, teach the use of the skill(s) within passage reading (at the automatic

Error Pattern Checklist: Specific-level Procedure 4

Compare each error in the passage to the checklist (ignore errors on proper names). Make a mark next to the category in which the error seems to fit. Identify the strategic categories in which most errors occur and begin additional testing in those areas. Continue to monitor changes in error patterns.

Error Categories	No. Errors
Mispronunciations	
Errors are substitutions of real words	
Errors are not real words	
Errors are phonetically similar to stimulus word	
Insertions	
Insertions are contextually appropriate	
Insertions are contextually inappropriate	
Omissions	
Omission affects passage meaning	
Omission does not affect meaning	
Hesitation	
Repetition	
Repeats a portion of target word	
Repeats preceding word	
Repeats preceding words or phrases	
Does not attend to punctuation	
Does not pause at punctuation	
Pauses at end of line	
Self-corrects	

Directions for Using the Error Pattern Checklist

Use the Error Pattern Checklist to categorize all decoding errors made on the passage. Ask yourself what the most probable reading strategy explanation is for each error. Check it off by marking the appropriate category. If more than two errors were made on a word, categorize only the first two.

Question	*Recommendation*
1. Are there clear patterns of errors?	If yes, correct the erroneous pattern by targeting it as an instructional objective.

Content Error Checklist: Specific-level Procedure 5

Compare the words in the passage to the student's errors and categorize erors by content area and content subskill. Make a mark next to the subskill indicated by each error. Do not record more than two errors per word. Identify the content areas in which the most errors occurred and begin additional testing in those areas. Continue to monitor changes in error patterns.

Content Categories	No. Errors
Words: errors involving whole words	
Polysyllabic Words	
Contractions	
Compound Words	
Sight Words	
Silent Letters	
Units: errors involving combined letter units	
Endings (Suffixes)	
Clusters	
R-controlled Vowels	
Vowel Teams	
Consonant Digraphs	
Consonant Teams	
CVC Words	
Conversions: errors involving sound modification	
Double Consonant Words	
Vowel +e Conversions	
Sounds: errors involving individual letters and sounds	
Vowels	
Consonants	
Sequence	
Sounds	
Symbols	

Directions for Using the Content Error Checklist

Use the Content Error Checklist to categorize all errors made on the passage. Ask yourself what the most probable content explanation is for each error. Decide what content category the error is from and check it off by marking the appropriate category. If more than two errors were made on a word, categorize only the first two.

Question	*Recommendation*
1. Are there identifiable problems of content?	If yes, conduct specific-level testing of decoding skills reflected in the errors.

FIGURE 10.7

Error analysis (*Source:* Adapted from K. W. Howell, S. H. Zucker, and M. K. Morehead, *MAST: Multilevel Academic Survey Test,* p. 10. San Antonio, TX: The Psychological Corporation, 1985.)

level). Follow Teaching Recommendation 1, Balanced Instruction.

Question. Is the student slow but accurate at using the skill(s) in question?

Recommendation. If yes, teach the use of the skill(s) to the fluency level. Follow Teaching Recommendation 1 but emphasize rate.

Question. Is the student inaccurate at using the skill(s) in question?

Recommendation. If this has been verified by more specific-level testing (see Step 4 of the directions), teach acquisition of the targeted skill(s). See Teaching Recommendation 3.

AN EXAMPLE

Applying Specific-Level Procedures 1-5 lets you rule out competing explanations for student difficulty. Once you verify an assumed cause, you can target skills for instruction. While scoring and summarizing for Specific-Level Procedures 1 and 2 is straightforward, Procedures 3, 4, and 5 require content knowledge for decision making. Here is an example.

Jackie was inaccurate and slow on initial passage reading at the survey level. Using the guidelines presented on page 209, we went directly to Specific-Level Procedure 3. We asked Jackie to read the "Yucca Plant" passage. We knew that we could use the error sample collected in Specific-Level Procedure 3 for Procedures 4 and 5 if her performance warranted further analysis.

We marked Jackie's errors as she read. Some of them are shown in Figure 10.1. Then we organized the errors by category: (a) violates meaning, (b) does not violate meaning, and (c) cannot tell. Fifty-six percent of Jackie's errors violated meaning, 21% did not, and for 23% of the errors we could not tell if meaning was violated. Since there were sufficient meaning violation errors to warrant fur-

Error Pattern Checklist
Compare each error in the passage to the checklist (ignore errors on proper names). Make a mark next to the category in which the error seems to fit. Identify the strategic categories in which most errors occur and begin additional testing in those areas. Continue to monitor changes in error patterns.

Error Categories	No. Errors
Mispronunciations	
Errors are substitutions of real words	3/
Errors are not real words	17
Errors are phonetically similar to stimulus word	1
Insertions	
Insertions are contextually appropriate	
Insertions are contextually inappropriate	
Omissions	
Omission affects passage meaning	6
Omission does not affect meaning	1
Hesitation	1
Repetition	
Repeats a portion of target word	
Repeats preceding word	
Repeats preceding words or phrases	
Does not attend to punctuation	
Does not pause at punctuation	
Pauses at end of line	
Self-corrects	

FIGURE 10.8
Error patterns checklist *(Source:* Adapted from K. W. Howell, S. H. Zucker, and M. K. Morehead, *MAST: Multilevel Academic Survey Test,* p. 10. San Antonio, TX: The Psychological Corporation, 1985.)

ther analysis, we moved to Specific-Level Procedure 4 and completed the Error Checklist shown in Figure 10.8. We looked at each error and categorized it as a mispronunciation, insertion, omission, hesitation, or repetition.

Jackie's problems seem to fall into three principal categories: (a) mispronunciations that are not real words, 17 errors; (b) mispronunciations that are real words, 13 errors; and (c) omissions that affect passage meaning, 6 errors. We could have decided that the patterns were sufficiently consistent to stop testing at this point. We noted, however, that 11 of the 17 mispronunciations were for the one word *yucca.* We also noticed that many of the error words, both real and not real, appeared to violate phonics rules. For this reason we decided to summarize the errors by phonics content by applying Specific-Level Procedure 5. We took out our stimulus–response sheet and added a comments column. These comments are shown in Figure 10.9.

Comments are based on the phonics content we think Jackie missed. Some of her errors were easy to link to a cause; others were not. When she read

pant for *plant* and *boom* for *bloom*, consonant teams seemed to be the explanation of the error. When she read *mother* for *moth*, the explanation wasn't so straightforward. We guessed she used a known word with some letters in common. We also guessed that *moth* is not in her vocabulary (prior knowledge) and that she failed to use a blending strategy. Her difficulty with *yucca* is obviously a

Survey-Level Test: Stimulus, Response and Analysis Summary

Category 1 Error: Meaning Violation

Stimulus	Response	Comment
The Yucca Plant	The Yucca Plant	Doesn't use title for advanced organizer strategy.
plant	pant	consonant team (pl)
spiny	spinny	vowel conversion rule; lacks prior knowledge of desert botany
white	winter	consonant digraphs (wh) or vowel conversion rule — silent e
bloom	boom	consonant teams (bl)
night	night	sight word; lacks word analogy strategy
flowers	tower	consonant teams (fl); word endings (s)
seeds	sed	vowel team (ee); word endings (s)
partner	parking	word endings (er)
moth	mother	added ending of known word *mother*; vocabulary or prior knowledge problem; used known to construct meaning; failed to use soundout-blending strategy.
moth	mother	same as above
goal	girl	vowel team (oa)
eggs	egg	word endings (s)
moth	mother	same as "moth" error above
pollen	polen	vowel conversion; also vocabulary—prior knowledge
dust	dirt	cluster (ust); word analogy strategy—she read *must* (ust) in next word
touch	tach	vowel team (ou)
ovule	ovule	vowel conversion—silent e; also vocabulary—prior knowledge
touches	throws	vowel team (ou), consonant digraph (ch)
ovules	ovules	vowel conversion
hatch	grow	consonant digraph (ch)
enough	even	(ough) clusters
for	from	sight word; r-controlled vowel (or)
plants	pants	consonant team (pl); failure to use meaning to self-correct
safe	saf	vowel conversion; failed to monitor for meaning (no such word)
pollen	polen	same as error above on *pollen*
seeds	sed	same as error above on *seeds*
without	window	consonant digraphs (th); vowel teams (ou)

Total — Category 1 — Meaning Violation

30/53 errors = 56%   ⬭ means omission

FIGURE 10.9
Stimulus–response and comments for Specific-Level Procedure 5

vowel conversion error but it may also be a prior knowledge problem. If she knew there was a desert plant called the *yucca* she could have self-corrected her error based on the context. In a number of cases she could have used meaning to mediate her absence of specific decoding skills, especially vowel conversions and consonant teams. By summarizing

the comments it is possible to see areas of concern and select objectives for further testing.

A summary of phonics content error types is shown in Figure 10.10. As you can see, most of the errors were vowel conversions, CVC + *e*, vowel teams, consonant teams, sight words, and consonant digraphs. Consequently, each of these content

Category 2 Error: No Meaning Violation

Stimulus	Response	Comment
a	(a)	does not self-monitor for syntax; *year* cannot follow *once*
the	these	sight word
the	this	sight word
itself	alone	sight word; syntax error—did not self-monitor for syntax
when	as	sight word; consonant digraph *(wh)*
gathers	gets	consonant digraph *(th)*; word ending *(ers)*
pushes	puts	consonant digraph *(sh)*
lays	lay	word endings *(s)*
there	these	sight word; overreliance on configuration
this	there	sight word; overreliance on configuration
good	great	sight word; vowel team (double sound vowel — *oo*)

Total — Category 2 — No Meaning Violation

11/53 errors = 21%   ⬭ means omission

Category 3 Error: Unknown if Meaning Violation

Stimulus	Response	Comment
yucca	yuca	vowel conversion; vocabulary; prior knowledge of desert botany; word not in vocabulary so there is no feedback on decoding error.
once	every	sight word
yucca	yuca	same as *yucca* error above
yucca	yuca	same as *yucca* error above
yucca	yuca	same as *yucca* error above
yucca	yuca	same as *yucca* error above
yucca	yuca	same as *yucca* error above
yucca	yuca	same as *yucca* error above
yucca	yuca	same as *yucca* error above
yucca	yuca	same as *yucca* error above
yucca	yuca	same as *yucca* error above
yucca	yuca	same as *yucca* error above

Total — Category 3 — Unknown if Meaning Violation

12/53 errors = 23%

FIGURE 10.9
(continued)

Content Error Checklist

Compare the words in the passage to the student's errors and categorize erors by content area and content subskill. Make a mark next to the subskill indicated by each error. Do not record more than two errors per word. Identify the content areas in which the most errors occurred and begin additional testing in those areas. Continue to monitor changes in error patterns.

Content Categories	No. Errors
Words: errors involving whole words	
Polysyllabic Words	24
Contractions	
Compound Words	
Sight Words	9
Silent Letters	
Units: errors involving combined letter units	
Endings (Suffixes)	4
Clusters	1
R-controlled Vowels	1
Vowel Teams	5
Consonant Digraphs	4
Consonant Teams	6
CVC Words	
Conversions: errors involving sound modification	
Double Consonant Words	2
Vowel + e Conversions	14
Sounds: errors involving individual letters and sounds	
Vowels	
Consonants	
Sequence	
Sounds	
Symbols	

FIGURE 10.10

Content error checklist (Source: Adapted from K. W. Howell, S. H. Zucker, and M. K. Morehead, *MAST: Multilevel Academic Survey Test,* p. 10. San Antonio, TX: The Psychological Corporation, 1985.)

areas become an assumed cause for the student's decoding problem. The stimulus—response section of the analysis is now our new set of *facts*. The summary in Figure 10.10 permits us to see where the focus of additional testing should be.

If you were thinking that we now have sufficient information to begin teaching, remember that phonics is a broad category. Which vowel teams, which suffixes, and which digraphs would you teach? Not only is each of these phonics content

areas broad, but there are also strategies for applying the content which Jackie may not be using.

In the next section procedures for assessing more specific content in phonics are presented. These include specific-level tests with a narrower focus than the first five procedures. First, testing letter sounds will be described, then words, and finally, attention.

ADDITIONAL DECODING ASSESSMENT

Testing Letter Sounds

There are many hierarchies of decoding content. Most of them are essentially the same and move in a progression from single letter sounds (vowel and consonants) to sounds associated with clusters of letters (blends and digraphs). These letter and cluster sounds can be tested in words or in isolation. For example, if you are interested in finding out about the student's use of the *a* sounds, you may test by giving a flashcard with only that letter on it and asking, "What sounds does this letter make?" You may also test by giving a word with the letter in it: "Read this word" abate . In this case you would score *only* the kid's use of *a*. If you present the letter in isolation, remember that the letter can make more than one sound. You might say: "This letter makes two sounds, long and short. Give me the two sounds this letter makes." a

If you are interested in the student's skill at converting *a*'s from the long to short sound, you might give a probe such as the vowel conversion sheet shown in Figure 10.11. Once again, in this case you would score only the student's response to the sounded vowel; the *t*'s and *p*'s are carriers that increase the validity of the sample in spite of the fact that real words are not used. Some evaluators test other conversions through the use of diacritical markings. Unless these markings are used in the student's decoding program, such a test will not be useful because it requires knowledge not normally used in reading. While reading this text, for example, you are not depending on diacritical cues.

					tip	tipe	tap	tappe
tip	tupp	tep	topp	tope	tupe	tape	tepe	tipe
tap	tipe	tupe	tepe	top	tope	tupe	tape	tepe
tep	tape	tippe	tuppe	teppe	topp	tope	tupe	tape
tip	tepe	tappe	tipp	tupp	tepp	toppe	tope	tupe
top	tipe	teppe	tapp	tip	tup	tepe	tope	tope
tup	tope	tippe	tepp	tap	tipe	tupe	tep	top
tape	tupe	toppe	tipp	tep	tape	tippe	tupe	tepe
tappe	tap	tuppe	topp	tip	tepe	tappe	tipp	tup
toppe	teppe	tapp	tupp	top	tipe	teppe	tapp	tip
tap	tippe	tuppe	tappe	tupe	tope	tip	tepe	tap

FIGURE 10.11 *(Source:* K. W. Howell, S. H. Zucker, and M. K. Morehead, *Multilevel Academic Skills Inventory—Reading and Language Arts Diagnostic Battery,* p. R-68. San Antonio, TX: The Psychological Corporation, 1982. Reprinted with permission.)

Formats

Sounds can be tested with probe sheets or flashcards. Probe sheets can be used for testing mastery and accuracy, whereas flashcards are useful for accuracy only. The student must give an oral response to the probe if you wish to grade it. Because the oral response is gone in an instant, you must either tape the behavior or score it as the student reads. Simultaneous scoring can be simplified by having your own copy of the probe in a clear plastic binder. Then you can use a transparency pen to write what the student said over each sound missed. After transferring the behavior to the fact sheet, you can wipe the plastic clean. Incidentally, remember to sit behind the kid so that he isn't distracted from the task by your scoring.

The main limitation of flashcards is that they are not practical for timing because you control the student's reading rate with the rate at which you flash the cards. The amount of time it should take a student to read a word on a flashcard is not well established and is difficult to test. The task is quite different from reading a line of print and is probably more analogous to reading highway signs on a curved mountain road at night. Estimates in the literature range to as long as 5 seconds, but actually a proficient reader (which is what you want the kid to be) can decode a single word of nearly any length in about one-half second. As a rule, single units (letters and syllables) should be read with 100% accuracy at a rate of 60 per minute, while words in isolation should be read with 100% accuracy at 80 per minute.

Testing Words

Word Errors

Often students will substitute whole words or parts of words. This is sometimes called *word calling* and is typical of older poor readers. These errors may include whole word substitutions (*is–at*, *in–to*) or partial substitutions (*the-them*, *display–discuss*). Typically when a partial word error is noted, the first or last few letters of the substituted word will be correct.

Take the words missed and present them in isolation. If the student can't decode them accurately and quickly in isolation, she's having sound or blending problems. If she reads previously missed words correctly in isolation, you must check to see if she is making errors that affect her comprehension (Specific-Level Procedure 3). If the errors do affect comprehension, have the student read the passage and tell her to take her time and get every word right. If her accuracy improves, she needs to learn to read words quickly in context. If the errors don't affect her comprehension, you have found an error pattern unique to oral reading. In other words, there would be no problem were there not an oral reading test, so forget the errors.

Blending and Word (Sound) Analogy

When using phonics to decode a word, a student first segments it into units, recalls each unit, and then combines the sounds to say the word. These segmenting and combining activities are called *blending*. Blending is viewed as a separate task from sounding and appears to be linked to linguistic skills associated with knowledge of reading. Knowledge of sounds precedes it; however, blending is of primary importance (Haddock, 1976, 1978; Pearson, 1984; Stanovitch, 1983; Williams, 1984).

Successful readers seldom isolate each individual sound after acquiring a repertoire of sound clusters. A student who knows the "at" in *pat* can use that information in analogous words such as *fat*, *rat*, *mat*, or *bat*. A student who knows "icker" in *sticker* can use that information to decode *flicker* or *bicker*. The technique of word analogy testing can be used to evaluate blending. Decoding by word analogy requires the blending steps of segmenting, recalling units, and combining. It also includes the additional strategy of recognizing a known unit in a new word and segmenting and blending based on segments learned in previous words. Proficient readers use the analogy strategy automatically. Explicit instruction that prepares students to use word analogy strategies appears in a number of reading materials. It is sometimes called *rhyming*. We will describe three assessment procedures that will let you analyze blending with word analogy strategies.

Blending Procedure 1. To see if a student can blend two units, show a letter (or cluster) and supply the sounds of the units before asking for the sound of both together. Example:

Teacher	Student
"This is 'b'."	Pronounces the sound "b"
"This is 'igh'."	Pronounces the sound "igh"
"What is 'b' [pause] 'igh'?"	Pronounces the sound "bigh"

Because the sounds are supplied, this test is evaluating blending of the "b" to "igh." Sounding of "b" and "igh" isn't being tested.

A blending test can be assembled by making up flashcards for each code unit and putting them in order, either by numbering them or fixing them to metal rings (Eeds, 1976). You can make up a table of specifications that corresponds to the order of the cards. By using the table as a record form, you can flip through various code combinations and mark the student's performance on each.

Another technique (Wallen, 1972) is the use of rhythmic word teams. For example:

"This word is ⌈ br | eam ⌉ ." (Pronounce the word.)
"What word is this?" ⌈ bl | eam ⌉

The sound that is supplied ("eam") is *not* being tested. Instead, the production of the "bl" sound and the blending of "bl" to "eam" are being tested. Remember to change the position of the sounds because some students may be able to blend a letter in the initial position but not in the medial or final positions. For example:

To test "B" in the initial place:

"This word is ⌈ t | ap ⌉ ." (Pronounce the word.)
"What word is this?" " ⌈ b | ap ⌉ "

To test "B" in the final place:

"This word is ⌈ ta | p ⌉ ." (Pronounce the word.)
"What word is this? " ⌈ ta | b ⌉ ."

Blending Procedure 2. Another procedure in which the sounds are supplied is the Glass Analysis System (Glass, 1971). This system is ideal for testing blending as well as cluster sounds in both production and identification. It is also an excellent spelling test. In the Glass system, the whole word is shown and the student is given the sound of the word. Next the student is asked to indicate which letter makes each sound in the word and then what sound the letter makes. The system requires students to find letters and clusters within the word. This task (identification of the code units) is a necessary part of blending. Remember that blending is not just putting the sounds together. First the kid must be able to recognize code units within the word. Here is how the Glass system might be used to test the segmenting, sounding, and combining subskills.

	Teacher	Student
Step 1.	"This word is ⌈ Bring ⌉ ." (Show and pronounce the word.) "Say it."	"bring"
Step 2a.	"In the word *bring* which letters make the sound 'br'?"	"B-R"
Step 2b.	"In the word *bring* what letters make the sound 'ing'?"	"I-N-G"
Step 3a.	"In the word *bring* what sound do the letters *B-R* make?"	"br"
Step 3b.	"In the word *bring* what sound do the letters *I-N-G* make?"	"ing"
Step 4.	"Say the word."	"bring"

Once you have followed the sequence, you can easily modify it to incorporate the procedures already discussed. Now that you know the kid knows

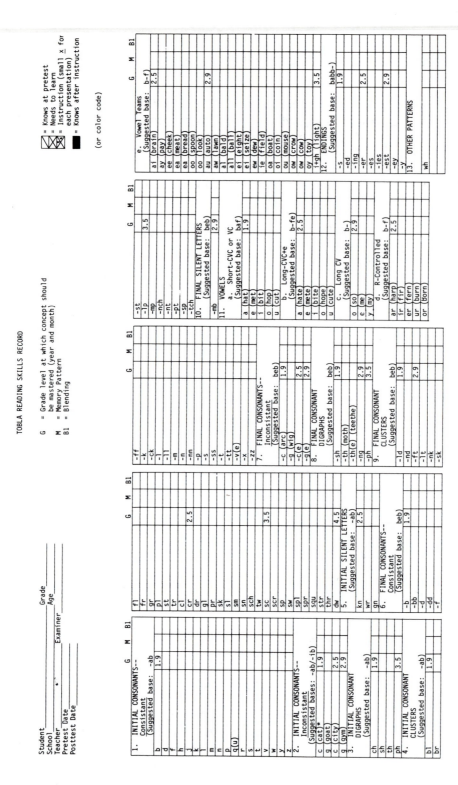

FIGURE 10.12

TOBLA record form *(Source:* Maryann Eeds, *TOBLA: Test of Blending Ability.* Edina, MN: Burgess Publishing, 1976. Reprinted with permission.)

the sounds of "br," "ing," and *bring*, new words can confidently be built using them. For example,

brick		sing
bride	or	fling
broke		swing

Blending Procedure 3. The Glass questions are nicely suited to evaluating blending because they require both subdivision and combination skills as well as blending an analogous word. Since the task of blending requires the student to select units from the word (subdivide it) but then combine these units vocally, the questions can be used to obtain insight into the student's skill at combining. If the student failed at working with rhyming words, for example, you could go through the Glass technique with the words and then combine them, as shown in the example below.

Word A

Stimulus	Response
Step 1. (Show the word "drain.")	
"This word is drain."	
"What word is it?"	"drain"
Step 2. "In the word 'drain,' what letters make the sound 'ain'?"	"A-I-N"
Step 3. "In the word 'drain,' what sound do the letters *A-I-N* make?"	"ain"
Step 4. "Say the word 'drain'."	"drain"
Step 5. (Show the word "train".) "Now say this word."	"train"

Word B

Stimulus	Response
Step 1. (Show the word "trade.")	
"This word is trade."	
"What word is it?"	"trade"
Step 2. "In the word 'trade,' what letters make the sound 'tr'?"	"T-R"
Step 3. "In the word 'trade,' what sound do the letters *T-R* make?"	"tr"
Step 4. "Say the word 'trade'."	"trade"
Step 5. (Show the word "drade.") "Now say this word."	"drade"

Figure 10.12 is a record form for testing blending (Eeds, 1976). Figure 10.12 is broken down according to *content* (i.e., silent letters, final consonants). It is also possible to sequence blending according to the size of the unit in which the subskills are used. By unit size we mean (1) polysyllabic words in isolation, (2) one-syllable words (except CVC), and (3) CVC words. Table 10.3 provides such a sequence designed to mesh with the three testing procedures just described. As with any sequenced set of tests, begin by testing down from the most complex subtask. If the student fails a subtask, move to the next lower one until a subtask is passed.

Sight Words

Evaluating sight words is really no different from evaluating letter sounds. Both are unconsolidated domains of content, and the basic strategy involved in learning them is the recall of grapheme–phoneme correspondence. Just as "a" says "aaa," "boy" says "boy."

Sight words become sight words because they are either frequently used or phonetically irregular. Therefore, some are regular (*man*), while others are irregular (*was*). As students acquire more knowledge of coding rules, more words become regular to them. If you do not know the final-e rule, then *mane* and *cane* are irregular (Carnine & Silbert, 1979). Of course the way you test them is to show them to the student and ask her to read them. If she gives an immediate response (one-half second), then she either knows it as a sight word or has decoded it successfully.

Theoretically, no sight word is any harder to read than any other, just as the sound "b" is not harder to learn than the sound "n." However, ease of learning has nothing to do with ease of usage. Some sight words are more commonly confused than others. This is particularly true of those that begin with *th*—*that, those, these, them, this, thought, throw, threw,* etc. Therefore, when testing sight words at the automatic level, you will want to select a passage with a lot of these items.

High frequency word lists by authors such as Durr and Dolch are available in most reading texts. Eeds (1985) distinguishes between high frequency

words found in basal texts (in which words are selected for their conformity to skill sequences) and
high frequency words found in children's literature.
Most other compilers of word frequency lists have
used basals to establish their samples. Eeds advocates teaching a core of words found in literature
rather than basals. She argues that a goal of reading instruction is reading from all text. The first
220 words of her core list are shown in Figure
10.13. These words appeared most frequently in a

TABLE 10.3
A sequence for testing blending

		Task	Procedures
Components of Phonemic Segmentation	Subtask 11	Blends words in content (Automatic) CAP 80-140 wpm correct, 0-4 errors	Timed reading from text
	Subtask 10	Blends words in isolation at rate (Mastery) CAP 80-100 wpm correct, 0-4 errors	Timed probe sheets
	Subtask 9	Blends words in isolation (Accuracy) CAP 100% correct	Untimed probe sheets or flashcards
	Subtask 8	Blends words in isolation (Accuracy) CAP 100% correct	Procedure 1
	Subtask 7	Blends words in isolation (Accuracy) CAP 100% correct	Procedure 2
	Subtask 6	Blends words in isolation (Accuracy) CAP 100% correct	Procedure 3
	Subtask 5	Produces unit sounds in words (Accuracy) CAP 100% correct	Untimed probe sheets or flashcards "In this word what sound is made by the letter(s) _____?"
	Subtask 4	Supplies spelling of units in words (Accuracy) CAP 100% correct	Untimed probe sheets or flashcards "In this word what letter(s) make the sound _____?"
	Subtask 3	Produces the sound of units in isolation (Mastery) CAP 60-80 spm correct, 0-2 errors	Timed probe sheets
	Subtask 2	Produces the sound of units (Accuracy) CAP 100% correct	Untimed probe sheets or flashcards
	Subtask 1	Identifies the sound of units (Accuracy) CAP 100% correct	Untimed probe sheets or flashcards. "Point to the letter(s) that makes the sound _____."

Bookwords: Final core 227 word list based on 400 storybooks
for beginning readers

the	1334	good	90	think	47	next	28
and	985	this	90	new	46	only	28
a	831	don't	89	know	46	* am	27
I	757	little	89	help	46	began	27
to	746	if	87	grand	46	head	27
said	688	just	87	boy	46	keep	27
you	638	* baby	86	take	45	* teacher	27
he	488	way	85	eat	44	* sure	27
it	345	there	83	* body	43	* says	27
in	311	every	83	school	43	* ride	27
was	294	went	82	house	42	* pet	27
she	250	father	80	morning	42	* hurry	26
for	235	had	79	* yes	41	hand	26
that	232	see	79	after	41	hard	26
is	230	dog	78	never	41	* push	26
his	226	home	77	or	40	our	26
but	224	down	76	* self	40	their	26
they	218	got	73	try	40	* watch	26
my	214	would	73	has	38	* because	25
of	204	time	71	* always	38	door	25
on	192	* love	70	over	38	us	25
me	187	walk	70	again	37	* should	25
all	179	came	69	side	37	* room	25
be	176	were	68	* thank	37	* pull	25
go	171	ask	67	why	37	* great	24
can	162	back	67	who	36	gave	24
with	158	now	66	saw	36	* does	24
one	157	friend	65	* mom	35	* car	24
her	156	cry	64	* kid	35	* ball	24
what	152	oh	64	give	35	* sat	24
we	151	Mr.	63	around	34	* stay	24
him	144	* bed	63	by	34	* each	23
no	143	an	62	Mrs.	34	* ever	23
so	141	very	62	off	33	* until	23
out	140	where	60	* sister	33	* shout	23
up	137	play	59	find	32	* mama	22
are	133	let	59	* fun	32	* use	22
will	127	long	58	more	32	turn	22
look	126	here	58	while	32	thought	22
some	123	how	57	tell	32	* papa	22
day	123	make	57	* sleep	32	* lot	21
at	122	big	56	made	131	* blue	21
have	121	from	55	first	31	* bath	21
your	121	put	55	say	31	* mean	21
mother	119	* read	55	took	31	* sit	21
come	118	them	55	* dad	30	* together	21
not	115	as	54	found	30	* best	20
like	112	* Miss	53	* lady	30	* brother	20
then	108	any	52	soon	30	* feel	20
get	103	right	52	ran	30	* floor	20
when	101	* nice	50	* dear	29	wait	20
thing	100	other	50	man	29	* tomorrow	20
do	99	well	48	* better	29	* surprise	20
too	91	old	48	* through	29	* shop	20
want	91	* night	48	stop	29	run	20
did	91	may	48	still	29	* own	20
could	90	about	47	* fast	28		

*Indicates words *not* on Durr list.

FIGURE 10.13 (*Source:* M. A. Eeds, "Bookwords: Using a Beginning Word List of High Frequency Words from Children's Literature K-3. *The Reading Teacher*, 1985, *38*, p. 420. Used with permission of Maryann Eeds and the International Reading Association.)

after him yes we will next to you must be now put it on	(14)
is a friend better get father first in back can he carry long morning	(28)
don't know if let me go thank this one hard as that stop there	(42)
jump up here wait for her great with us I wonder from his home	(56)
big and little give only two because she says people play run right over	(70)
call each day eat before three would work out keep those lady was new	(84)
about the girl left school while every dog went through an open move your	(98)
began well took door like turn down our watch house hey help them	(112)
climb some more walk all around could cry why did they should start when	

FIGURE 10.14

Core word probe (*Source:* [Content drawn from M. A. Eeds, "Bookwords: Using a Beginning Word List of High Frequency Words from Children's Literature K–3.] *The Reading Teacher,* 1985, *38,* p. 420.)

sample of children's literature that included 30,000 words and 100 books. You may want to compare the Eeds list to lists you are currently using. Words from several sources should be used when a student has a suspected sight word problem. A sample sight word probe based on the Eeds list is shown in Figure 10.14.

Sight words can be tested in context, in phrases, and in isolation. Because some poor readers will typically substitute one sight word for another, it is a good idea to repeat each word on the probe sheet several times. This repetition makes the student use the word more than once, which increases the validity of the test by decreasing the likelihood of lucky guesses. As a rule, only use from 10 to 20 different sight words on any probe sheet. We violated this rule in the development of the probe illustrated in Figure 10.14 because we wanted to sample the domain of core words, not specific sight words. Each is presented only once. CAP for sight words are slightly higher than for sounds but lower than for passage reading. A reasonable criterion is 80 correct with 0–2 errors per minute.

Testing Attention

A commonly stated assumed cause for reading errors is inattention to portions of words. This cause is most often assumed when students make whole

word substitutions of words sharing initial sounds (e.g., *the–their, who–what, is–if*) or when they omit endings (e.g., *-ed, -ing, -ion, -s*). There is a simple procedure to find out if these errors are the result of failure to attend to the whole word or lack of decoding skill.

Select two passages of equal difficulty and underline the characteristically omitted or substituted portion of one in red. Time the student on both and note accuracy and rate. If the accuracy improves considerably but rate maintains when these words are underlined, then the student knows how to decode them but isn't doing so. To remediate this problem, place great emphasis on accuracy and comprehension monitoring. (See Intervention Recommendations 4 and 1.) If accuracy does not improve, or if it improves but rate decreases significantly (more than 20%), teach the words or units themselves.

DECISIONS AND RECOMMENDATIONS

Levels of Student Performance in Reading

The progress of students through the reading curriculum can be categorized into three levels: adequate, remedial, and corrective.

Adequate describes students who are at or above expectations. These students would seldom be referred for a comprehensive reading evaluation.

Remedial describes students who are progressing through the curriculum uniformly but more slowly than expected. These students need to learn the same content as adequately progressing students but they encounter this content later than their more capable peers. While they need the same content as younger students, they also need materials appropriate for their age. In general, they require balanced but extensive instructional interventions (often with a heavy emphasis on building proficiency) to accelerate them through the curriculum sequences.

Corrective describes students who lag behind in the curriculum just as remedial students do, but who *may* present other problems. Corrective students have gaps in their skill development that inhibit their progress. Equally important, they have developed erroneous patterns of working academic tasks. Often, it is not simply a matter of their having learned incorrect strategies for reading but a matter of their having practiced these strategies to automaticity. They require instruction that disconfirms these error patterns rather than instruction which simply teaches correct responses.

Intervention Recommendations[1]

This chapter outlined procedures for (a) sampling and analyzing reading decoding behavior, (b) developing assumed causes for reading problems, and (c) recognizing instructional targets. To complete the initial evaluation process you need to decide which targets to emphasize. Then you can outline a plan for teaching that incorporates what you know about effective reading instruction. This section reviews levels of student progress you are likely to encounter, ways of thinking about organizing instruction for students at these levels, and specific suggestions for delivering instruction. Reading interventions can be categorized into six kinds of instruction: (1) balanced, (2) rate building, (3) code emphasis, (4) error pattern correction, (5) higher-level strategies, and (6) comprehension.

1 Use Balanced Instruction

This recommendation is usually indicated when a student is progressing slowly through an initial, largely code-dominated, reading curriculum. The student will be reading below an expected level. While progress is not adequate, the pattern of errors does not seem to indicate the need to take a radically biased (all code or all language-based) approach. Instead, an intensive, balanced approach is recommended, including direct instruction on phoneme–grapheme correspondence made meaningful through the periodic use of language-based exercises such as student-generated stories, teacher–student shared reading, and teacher readings from more sophisticated texts. Both code strategies and context strategies are taught in a balanced approach.

Teach Code Strategies. Focus on specific grapheme or phoneme problems by highlighting them, referring to them frequently, and reinforcing the student for improvement. Insist on complete accuracy in reading. If necessary, separate the words by pointing to each one and not allowing the student to go on until you move your finger in response to the correct reading of the word. Reduce overuse of context clues in order to increase reliance on code. Do not attack or criticize the use of context, but select passages that deal with novel content and are not redundant, so that fewer context clues will be available. Encourage the student to attempt unknown words by applying his knowledge of code content. Employ an explicit approach to code in which essential sound–symbol relationships are directly taught. Avoid teaching all the sounds in the world. Have the student master a core of high utility sound–symbol relationships along with strategies for using them in new words. High utility sound–symbols are those that appear frequently in text and are regular. Do not teach the student reading terminology (e.g., digraph, blend, CVC) but do teach him sequential, code-based generalizations

---

1. Teaching Recommendations listed are used with permission from The Psychological Corporation and are taken from Howell, Zucker, and Morehead (1985).

for word attack. Use drill and practice to achieve fluency in code content.

Teach Context Strategies.   Focus on the student's skill at using context to predict upcoming events and words in the story. Require the student to explain how he can confirm a prediction and how to provide evidence from the selection to support both predictions and confirmations. Minimize the use of postreading/summary questions. Ask questions PRIOR to reading and emphasize the need to search the passage for answers. Ask passage-dependent vocabulary questions. Allow the student to practice reading with favorite stories, predictable stories, stories chosen by the student, and stories with experiences familiar to the student. Use rereadings. Embed nonsense material in the passage (or delete some important material) and reinforce the student for recognizing it, as a way to reinforce self-monitoring of comprehension. When reading errors do occur, judge their relationships to passage meanings. If the errors jeopardize meaning, talk the student through procedures for using context to correct the error himself. Several of these strategies were described in the section on blending and word analysis on page 222. Teach the student to make summary statements about sentences, then paragraphs, then whole passages.

2   Build Reading Rate

Students who are accurate but slow may have learned reading strategies they cannot employ efficiently because they lack automaticity. Lessons designed to build fluency typically use rapid-paced drill and practice on material on which the student is at least 90% accurate. During these lessons, the student is reinforced for rapid responding and daily improvement in fluency. Errors are typically viewed as rate-induced and are ignored to the extent that error correction procedures are not used (feedback may be given after the student reads the passage, however).

One popular technique for building oral reading rate, suggested by Carnine and Silbert (1979), is summarized below:

1. Select a passage on which the student is accurate.

2. Instruct the student to read for one minute as quickly and accurately as possible and then note the student's rate (e.g., 60 words per minute).
3. Set a target rate for the passage that is 20 to 40% above the initial rate of the student (e.g., 60 wpm × .40 = 24 and 24 + 60 = 84 wpm).
4. Mark the target in the student's book and have her reread the selection just as before (Step 2) as many times as necessary to reach the target.
5. Continue this procedure on various selections until the student's average rate reaches the criterion for her grade level (and accuracy is maintained).

3   Emphasize Code Content

This student does not seem to have adequately mastered basic grapheme–phoneme correspondence. This may mean the student is inaccurate at these skills or that he has not become fluent enough at them to use them automatically when reading.

Reading instruction should be targeted directly on the high frequency errors. Before beginning instruction you may wish to test several specific code objectives to be sure of the exact content or level of proficiency on which the student needs instruction. If you do, begin with the more advanced decoding skills and work backwards to identify weak or missing subskills. As a rule, letter sounds are best taught within words and words within phrases. Extensive drill on words or phonemic units in isolation is generally not recommended, though those procedures are justified if you have tried other methods and failed. Teaching code in context does not preclude explicit skill instruction. Explicit code instruction (synthetic phonics) appears to be superior to implicit or analytic phonics (Johnson & Baumann, 1984). Analytic-implicit phonics approaches, those in which students "see" how words are similar in order to *infer* code, often require that a kid be able to read the words in the practice exercise in which the phonics rules are to be inferred.

In the following analytic exercise, a student is expected to identify which words have the same sounds. To complete Exercise 1, the student would have to be able to read the words. This is silly because if the student can read the words he is not likely to need the practice.

Exercise 1   Circle the words that have the same beginning sound as the word in the box.

| sat | size city cad kit cove cite |
| jet | jug got gem just joy gig |

While good readers make a large number of appropriate analytic code inferences, poor readers do not. Explicit code instruction is efficient and is supported by current research.

In an explicit code lesson, students would be taught a sound and would be asked to read words that require the sound.

Exercise 2

Teacher: "The sound of this letter⬜ⓈⓈⓈ is 'sss'."
            "What sound will you say when you see this letter?" (Hold up "s.")

Students: "sss."

Teacher: "These new words will be in our story. Let's read them together. Remember to say 'sss' when you sound out a word with this new letter."

(Word List on Board)

Sam   sis   mist   sun

A caution: When teaching very specific content (such as vowel teams or word lists), be aware that you are asking the student to perform an essentially meaningless task. The promise that working on these subskills will eventually enable them to make sense of printed matter is a far-removed and hollow one for most remedial students. Therefore, be careful to supply meaning while maintaining a narrow focus on specific subskills. The following recommendations may help students who need direct instruction on specific subskills.

- Be sure of the content you are teaching. Don't isolate (decontextualize) material the student has already learned.

- Be sure the student knows what he is trying to learn (this does NOT mean you should use teaching terminology like "digraphs" or "vowels").

- Provide short, high-intensity practice sessions that require high rates of student response. Avoid long sessions that will bore the student.

- Maintain a quick pace by moving to a new objective as soon as a skill has been learned.

- Reinforce the kid frequently but keep statements of praise or distribution of rewards brief. Tie rewards directly to acquisition of the content (e.g., "good work, you learned the word," not "good work, you're really being good").

- Mix specific lessons with whole-reading experiences such as being read to by the teacher.

- If at all possible, teach students with similar skill deficits in groups, in order to derive the motivational advantage of peers and to promote vicarious learning.

- Modify the presentation frequently but never at the expense of focus on the content.

- Monitor progress and expect rapid improvement. If the student does not acquire the skills in a matter of weeks, you may wish to consider a more balanced approach that emphasizes both code and context.

4   Correct Error Patterns

Student reading errors are the result of many variables, including the level of skills learned, the way the passage was written (and its level of difficulty), and the purpose for which the student is reading. Patterns are learned and past instruction which emphasizes code or meaning frequently leads to different error patterns (Johnson & Baumann, 1984).

When working with a student who clearly illustrates a pattern of reading errors, consider bypassing some specific-level tests and immediately implementing a program for that pattern. Because this means that the information from specific-level testing will not be available, treat the recommendation as a "best guess" and be prepared to modify it if the recommendation does not lead to improved performance. Students whose performance shows evidence of consistent error patterns are typically beyond initial reading instruction but have learned some erroneous strategies for reading passages. These students are not "blank slates." They are employing, often automatically, strategies they have practiced for years. Sometimes kids have a habit of making certain errors that they are actually skilled enough to avoid. Often these error patterns can be recognized and attacked directly. In other cases error patterns are produced by an overreliance on one category of reading cues, and instruction on another category of cues may therefore be appropriate.

Thus, there are two approaches to correcting error patterns: (1) break bad reading habits or (2) correct overreliance on one pattern. You may want to read about both approaches before selecting one.

Direct Intervention on Bad Reading Habits. This technique isn't highly theoretical, just a straightforward set of steps.

1. Identify the pattern of concern.
2. Count the occurrence of the error pattern per 100 words and chart it.
3. Be sure the student can recognize and count the same error pattern (listening to a tape of her reading is useful here).
4. Provide feedback on the occurrence of the error pattern.
5. Reinforce the student for decreasing the number of errors or increasing self-corrections.
6. If the student does not begin to decrease the error pattern in a few days, have her work on one of the following instructional exercises. Some of these exercises are taken from Lovitt's *Tactics for Teaching* (1984).

- Have the student listen to tapes of herself reading and mark (or correct) errors that affect meaning.
- When errors violate meaning, show the student how the words before and after the error can be used to help figure it out.
- As the student listens to her taped reading, show how errors do not help to convey the message of the text by pointing out when they are syntactically wrong, redundant, superfluous, or misleading.

- Ask the student to explain how each error might hurt understanding of the text.
- Read in unison with the student or have her check the reading of other students.
- Make up sentences for the student to read in which all words are very easy except for words typically missed.
- Put problematic words in short phrases on flashcards and drill the student.
- If the student is reading at an appropriate level and comprehension seems adequate, tell her that it isn't necessary to read each word perfectly. Tell her to simply attempt the word and then use context to see if the attempt was correct.
- Accentuate punctuation marks by coloring them. Or overcorrect by having the student pause a set time (e.g., a count of 5) every time there is any punctuation mark.

Correct Overreliance on One Pattern. The following recommendations view oral reading as a process of using code information (grapheme–phoneme correspondence) and context information (syntax and semantics) to determine what words are. Mature readers blend these two kinds of information automatically. Most students take a balanced approach (code and context), but some may rely too heavily on only one kind of information as they read. There are two reasons why problem readers become overdependent on one kind of information: (1) their skills with one kind are so weak that they must compensate, or (2) their past instruction has so heavily emphasized one kind of information that the student automatically employs only those strategies. Because either explanation can account for the same error patterns, it is important to gather more information to ultimately determine which reason best explains a student's difficulty. Ideally, you should collect data continuously during a period of instruction to make this determination (see chapter 15).

When direct instruction on bad reading habits does not seem to work, it may be that the student is actually overreliant on either code information or context information. In these cases, corrective instruction should follow this sequence.

1. Identify an error.
2. Recognize the kind of information (code or context) the student is relying on. To do this, answer the following questions about the types of errors made by a student during oral reading.

Error Type	Questions
Mispronunciations	• Are errors that do not make sense real words? • Do errors on portions of words sound or look dissimilar to the stimulus word?
Insertions	• Do inserted words make sense in the sentence?
Omissions	• Is the student unwilling to attempt words or to guess? • Does the student omit words with graphemes read correctly elsewhere? • Does the student omit function words (e.g., *of, the, it, a*)?
Hesitations	• Does the student hesitate on short, familiar words as well as on longer ones?
Repetitions	• Does the student repeat several of the words preceding a difficult word? • Does the student repeat only words and not portions of words? • Does the student correct only errors that affect passage meaning?

Yes answers indicate errors that result from reliance on context information; no answers indicate errors that result from reliance on code information. If the yes and no answers are about evenly distributed, assume the student is *not* overreliant and use a balanced approach of code and context. (See Teaching Recommendation 1.) If overreliance is evident, first decide which specific skills need to be addressed and then employ the following recommendations.

1. Tell the student that she has made an error.
2. Show how the erroneous strategy led to the error.
3. Show how the appropriate use of the other (nondominant) kind of information would have led to correct reading.
4. Test the student's skill at using this other kind of information.
5. Provide practice to make the use of the appropriate information automatic.
6. Throughout the process, analyze the text to determine if there are adequate opportunities to use appropriate information. Some text may contain only one or two opportunities every 200 to 300 words. To practice, more opportunities will be needed.

5 Teach Higher-Level Strategies

This student is reading below expectations but appears marginally fluent and is either skilled at decoding or able to compensate with other strategies. He needs to develop fluency (increasing his reading rate). The student also needs to be accelerated quickly through a variety of material at different levels of difficulty while he receives instruction on so-called higher-level reading skills. Before examining these higher-level skills, keep in mind that the kid's reading should be closely monitored while these skills are being emphasized. Be alert to developing error patterns that can result from working on less-structured material or material that is above the student's reading level. Do not allow the student to practice reading errors.

Higher-level skills may be conceptualized as interactive skills consisting of (a) comprehension-monitoring skills, (b) interactive and problem-solving skills, and (c) study skills. This may include the teaching of summarizing, questioning, predicting, and clarifying skills as covered in *reciprocal teaching* (Palinscar & Brown, 1984). Instructional recommendations for these higher-level strategies were outlined in chapter 9.

SUMMARY

Reading is an interactive process in which a reader constructs meaning from text. The chapter applied a curriculum-based evaluation approach to reading and linked evaluation findings to instructional approaches that have been shown to be effective. This chapter also described thought processes and activities you would engage in to determine where to begin initial reading instruction. You will need to consider the guidelines in this chapter in conjunction with the evaluation guidelines presented in chapter 9 on reading comprehension, as well as the guidelines presented in chapter 12 on oral language.

Study Questions

1. How should you go about deciding what decoding tasks are essential to teach a student?
2. You have just been told that a child in your reading group tests very poorly on auditory and visual discrimination. How should this affect what you teach her?
3. How is reading instruction for low-performing students different from reading instruction for regular students? Under these circumstances are remedial students likely to catch up?
4. When evaluating reading, should you sample decoding or comprehension skills?
5. Describe the procedure for administering a survey-level decoding test. How accurate should the student be on the test passage?
6. How can you determine whether an accurate but slow reader can benefit from fluency instruction?
7. If a student is inaccurate at decoding and his accuracy improves when a purpose for reading is provided, what would you recommend?
8. If a student reads inaccurately but corrects most of her own errors, what would you recommend?
9. What is the purpose of determining how many errors violate the meaning of a passage?
10. If a student appears to have a decoding problem, what steps should you follow to determine what he should be taught?

Chapter 11

Mathematics

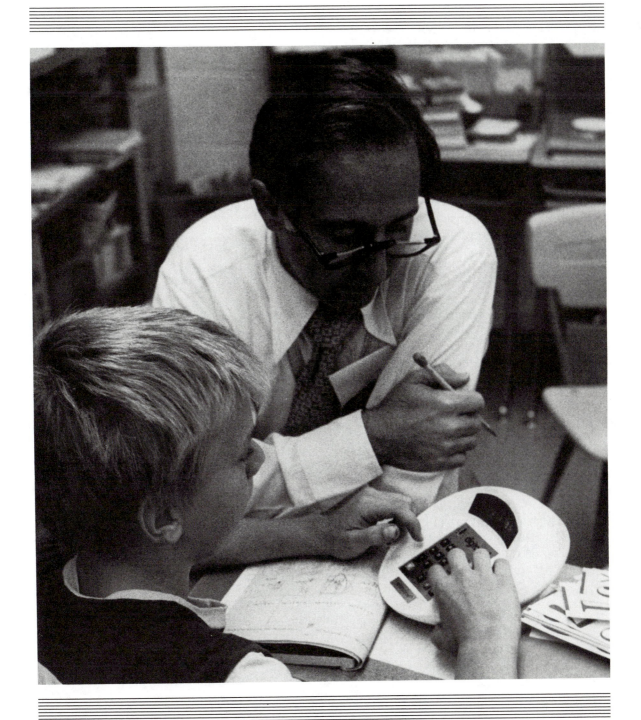

Survey Level to Specific Level
    Error Analysis and Task Analysis
• Specific-Level Testing
    Computation—Basic Facts
        Specific-Level Procedure 1: Checking Accuracy and Fluency on Basic Facts
            Directions
            Interpretation Guidelines
        Specific-Level Procedure 2: Checking Recall and Handwriting
            Directions 2.1
            Directions 2.2
            Interpretation Guidelines
        Specific-Level Procedure 3: Checking Basic Concepts
            Directions
            Interpretation Guidelines
    Computation—Operations
        Specific-Level Procedure 4: Checking Operations Strategies
            Directions
            Interpretation Guidelines
    Applications and Problem Solving
        Specific-Level Procedure 5: Basic Problem-Solving Concepts
            Directions
            Interpretation Guidelines
        Specific-Level Procedure 6: Content Knowledge
            Directions
            Interpretation Guidelines
        Specific-Level Procedure 7: Tool and Unit Knowledge
            Directions
            Interpretation Guidelines
        Specific-Level Procedure 8: Skill Integration
            Directions
            Interpretation Guidelines
Making Instructional Decisions
    Recommendation 1: Teach Accuracy on Basic Facts
    Recommendation 2: Teach Fluency on Basic Facts
        2.1 Handwriting
        2.2 Facts
    Recommendation 3: Teach Specific-Level Computation Skills
    Recommendation 4: Teach Task Strategies
        Verbal Mediation
        Lead Questions
        Select Procedure
        Corrections
        Feedback

Recommendation 5: Teach Specific-Level Application Content and Terms
- Summary

Mathematics is a language used to describe relationships between and among various objects, events, and times. To do that it depends on a system of symbols just as English depends on the letters that recombine throughout this text to convey the various messages we are presenting. Math symbols are used according to certain rules just as words are assembled into sentences according to the rules of syntax. Like any language, in mathematics, the ideas (the messages conveyed) have meaning and can be recognized in other forms—but the symbols are essentially arbitrary. By arbitrary we mean that they are made up—and agreed upon. As long as everyone agrees that " + " is a plus sign, it is. If tomorrow everyone decides that " − " is plus and " + " is take away, we would still be able to explain all the ideas we can explain today. The value of the language resides in the fact that everyone agrees on its symbols—not on the inherent meaning of the symbols themselves. This is an important point to remember when evaluating or teaching math. Evaluation in math centers on the students' knowledge of the symbols used in math and their skill at using these symbols to communicate.

FOCUS: COMPUTATION, APPLICATIONS, AND PROBLEM SOLVING

Computation and Operations

Computation is working problems. For a student to communicate with computation, he must (a) accurately and quickly substitute the various symbols for the quantities being computed, (b) arrange the symbols according to the rules for their use, and (c)

COMPUTATION

Rote	Vocabulary	
	Procedural	*Conceptual*
Has mastery of basic tools (e.g., addition, subtraction, multiplication, division)	Knows how to use basic skills (e.g., step-by-step procedures and algorithms)	Knows why the skills are used (e.g., understands quantitative or qualitative relationships)

FIGURE 11.1
Computation domains (*Source:* Adapted from J. Silbert, D. Carnine, and M. Stein, *Direct Instruction Mathematics.* Columbus, OH: Merrill Publishing, 1981.)

know the correct messages to convey. These three actions lead to the domains (rote, procedural vocabulary, and conceptual vocabulary) presented in Figure 11.1 (Silbert, Carnine, & Stein, 1981).

The three domains should be taught together—though teachers may emphasize one over another depending on a student's needs. The failure to integrate the three can best be seen in errors. For example, a student who produces the following answer

$$\begin{array}{r} 17 \\ +\ 8 \\ \hline 16 \end{array}$$

has failed to carry out a procedure correctly (he has accurately used rote to add the numbers 1, 7, and 8 together but ignored their relative positions). He has also violated the concept of addition by producing an answer that is smaller than the numbers with which he started. Computation involves the uses of facts and of operations, such as addition and subtraction, which may both require factual knowledge.

Application

Most special education teachers allocate time for instruction in computation but do not include adequate time for instruction in problem solving and application (Carpenter, Matthews, Lindquist, & Silver, 1984). To some extent this practice of emphasizing the operation content of computation over the conceptual content may increase the time it takes students to acquire skills and decrease the likelihood that they will maintain proficiency. When computation and operations are taught in isolation, it is difficult to make them meaningful. Meaningless material requires more practice to retain and is more likely to be forgotten than material that is useful in daily tasks.

Application is the content to which computation is applied. Application as a content domain is familiar to us as the *stuff* we think we want to get to "after" students master computation. Application includes measurement of time, temperature, money, length, surface, volume, and weight. Subdomains within these areas include (a) tool use (how do you use a meter stick?), (b) content knowledge (how many centimeters in a meter?), and (c) vocabulary knowledge (what is the definition of *length*?) (Howell, Zucker, & Morehead, 1982).

Figure 11.2 illustrates what we mean by content knowledge, tool use, and vocabulary knowledge. This example contains content lists for the measurement of *time* and *surface*. The lists in Figure 11.2 are not exhaustive. Other content could be included or the same content could be arranged or calibrated differently.

Problem Solving

Problem solving requires the functional combination of computation and application. It has two steps: determining what is called for and carrying it out. When students *determine what is called for* they:

1. Select correct operation(s);
2. Select relevant information, ignore irrelevant information, and note missing information; and
3. Estimate correct answer(s).

When students *carry it out* they:

1. Set up equations and judge which numbers go with which operation.
2. Work equations using procedures which result in correct answers, and
3. Check results after problem solution.

Figure 11.3 illustrates what students would "say" to themselves as they go through each problem-solving step. These steps are linked to math but their relationship to general problem-solving strategies (chapters 3 and 5) should be apparent. Problem solving appears to be the most neglected and the most misunderstood topic in the math curriculum. This is puzzling. It may be that little or no emphasis is placed on problem solving because educators seem to confuse problem solving with working story problems. Because story problems are often just a prose form of computation, problem solving is often approached as if it were simply putting computation into words. As a result, the conceptual part of math is never addressed.

Concept Analysis

Concept analysis is a process through which the defining characteristics of a concept are identified. These characteristics are called *attributes*. Relevant (or critical) attributes are those that are present in all examples of the concept. Irrelevant (noncritical) attributes may or may not be present. Because critical attributes must be present for the concept to exist, they are the defining characteristics of the concept (Carnine, 1983; Thiagarajan, Semmel, and Semmel, 1974). Let's take an easy example. The concept is "square." Think about the critical attributes and a few noncritical attributes. Answers are shown in Figure 11.4.

As you can see, the four different examples of squares shown in Figure 11.4 are all instances of

DOMAINS	SUBDOMAINS		
	Vocabulary Knowledge	*Tool Use*	*Content Knowledge*

Time	*Tools*—definition of function
	Clocks
	Watches
	Calendars
	
	Units—definitions
	Seconds
	Minutes
	Hours
	Months
	Years
	Decade
	Century
	Morning
	Night
	Fall/Autumn
	Winter
	Spring
	Summer
		Uses
		Calendar
		Digital clock–watch
		  Telling time
		  Setting alarm
		  Stop watch
		Analog clock–watch
		  Telling time
		  Setting alarm
		  Stop watch
			Units
			60 seconds = minute
			60 minutes = hour
			24 hours = day
			__ days = month
			12 months = year
			10 years = decade
			10 decades = century
			100 years = century
			
			Concepts
			Early
			Late
			Duration

Surface Measurement	*Terms*
	Area
	Perimeter
	Circumference
	Radius
	Angle
	Line
	Base
	Height
	
	Shapes
	Square
	Rectangle
	Triangle
	Circle
	Polygon
		Kinds of Tools
		Ruler
		Yardstick
		Meterstick
		Tapemeasure
		T-Square
			Units
			Metric
			10 mm = 1 cm
			100 cm = 1 meter
			1000 m = 1 km
			
			Customary
			12 inches = foot
			3 feet = yad
			5280 feet = mile
			640 sq. feet = acre
			
			Algorithms
			Perimeter of a rectangle =
			  (2) length + (2) width
			Perimeter of a triangle = Σ
			  of sides
			Perimeter (circumference)
			  of a circle = $2\pi r$
			Area of a rectangle =
			  length × width
			Area of a triangle = 1/2
			  base × height
			Area of a circle = πr^2

FIGURE 11.2
Application example of subdomains

Problem: Thad, Paula, and Gran read "Where the Wild Things Are" to Christopher. He is 2½ years old. Thad read 26 pages, Paula read 7, and Gran read the rest. There are 38 pages altogether. How many pages did Gran read?

Problem-Solving Skill	Self-Talk
Select correct operation(s)	"Will I add or subtract to solve the problem? I will add how many Thad and Paula read and subtract that from 38."
Select relevant information	"What information do I need to solve the problem? How many pages were read and how many pages were there altogether? Is everything I need to know there? Yes. Is there information I do not need? Yes, Christopher is 2½."
Estimate correct answer	"About how large a number could I get and not exceed 38?"
Set up equation and carry out	"First I'll find the sum of 26 + 7 = _____ and then I'll subtract that sum from 38. 26 + 7 = 33. 38 − 33 = 5."
Check results after problem solution	I have trouble with adding 7's so I'll check as I go. "I'll add my solution to the sum of 26 + 7 and see if it equals 38. 33 + 5 = 38."

FIGURE 11.3
Self-talk in problem solving

the concept. The four nonexamples are not squares. By comparing the examples and nonexamples, you can discover the critical and noncritical attributes. Attribute *d*, for instance, is the only thing preventing our second nonexample from being a square.

There is evidence that identifying defining attributes and teaching them directly will promote concept learning (Engelmann & Carnine, 1982; Mc-

Murray, Bernard, Klausmeir, Schilling, & Vorwerk, 1977). These attributes are identified through the analytical process of (a) establishing examples—instances—of the concept, (b) establishing nonexamples—noninstances—of the concept, and (c) comparing the two groups of examples to identify the attributes.

Table 11.1 lists concepts associated with different computational operations discussed in this chapter. This list of concepts is based on information presented in the book *One Step At a Time* by Bitter, Engelhardt, and Wiebe (1977) and an analysis of math concepts (Howell et al., 1985). The table also gives examples of problems related to these concepts. Most of the concepts are basic to the successful computation of addition, subtraction, multiplication, division, and fraction problems. However, every concept is not necessary for every computation. The "common denominator," for example, isn't necessary for addition.

When a student makes an error in computation, one explanation for the error is that an underlying concept has not been learned. For example, suppose a kid made the following three errors during survey-level testing:

$$
\begin{array}{ccc}
17 & 26 & 18 \\
+4 & +5 & +5 \\
\hline
111 & 211 & 113
\end{array}
$$

What are three possible explanations (assumed causes) for the errors?

1. Concept of place value missing.
2. Defective addition algorithm (procedure).
3. Poor estimation skills.

Because each hypothesis could be true, you need to do specific-level testing to determine what needs to be taught. The purpose of the additional specific testing is to verify one or more of the hypotheses.

Consider those three errors for a minute longer. On the surface, it seems the student doesn't know the answer to 17 + 4, 26 + 5, and 18 + 5. If that's what he doesn't know, then why not drill him on these problems as if they were basic facts by asking him to memorize 17 + 4 = 21, 26 + 5 =

FIGURE 11.4
Analysis of the
concept "square"

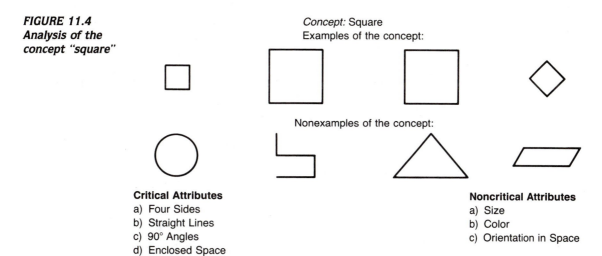

Concept: Square
Examples of the concept:

Nonexamples of the concept:

Critical Attributes
a) Four Sides
b) Straight Lines
c) 90° Angles
d) Enclosed Space
e) Equal Sides

Noncritical Attributes
a) Size
b) Color
c) Orientation in Space

31, and 18 + 5 = 23? The answer is obvious. Knowing that 18 + 5 = 23 without knowing the relevant concepts and algorithms would not help the student figure out what 18 + 6 equals.

When you evaluate in math—even if it's only in computation—you should develop hypotheses about missing concepts and missing strategies as well as the other, more obvious, types of computational errors.

Strategies

Recently a friend of ours observed in several primary classrooms. In one classroom students had been taught several strategies for efficiently working with numbers. One strategy was "counting on" both forward and backward from any number fluently. (An example of counting on forward would be, "Let's start with 6 and count to 10. 6 ... 7 ... 8 ... 9 ... 10." An example of counting on backward would be the same exercise in reverse, i.e., "10 ... 9 ... 8 ... 7 ... 6.") Another strategy used for working with numbers was "counting by" more than the traditional 5's, 10's, and 2's. When introduced to addition and subtraction, these students will be able to use their counting-on strategy to determine answers. When they are introduced to multiplication they can use their "count by a number" strategy to determine answers. Both count on and

count by are very simple strategies that can be generalized to a range of computation problems (Silbert et al., 1981).

In another classroom our friend observed, students were not as fortunate as those who had been taught efficient strategies. These less-fortunate students had been left to generate their own strategies. One 8-year-old was observed counting on his fingers to solve an addition problem. He ran out of fingers and appeared to give up. He got out scissors, plain paper, and tape. He then proceeded to fashion several tubes that he taped to one hand. No, he had not given up on his math problem. Yes, he had made more fingers! While his solution was creative, it was also very inefficient as he spent a good portion of his math period constructing extra fingers, which would have been unnecessary if his teacher had taught him the count on strategy.

Sampling Math Behaviors

Math tests have all the problems of other published tests (see chapter 5): their norms are irrelevant to teaching; their formats and problems don't resemble class assignments; they don't adequately sample the student's behavior; and they don't make it clear why errors are made. To evaluate math we need instruments that sample computation, applications, and problem solving. These instruments need to be

TABLE 11.1
Basic concepts and example problems

Concept	Example Problem	Solution
35. Estimation	Would the answer to 710 + 50 be closer to 700, 800, or 900?	"800"
34. Algorithms for checking problems	"Show me how you would check this answer." $\begin{array}{r}28\\9\overline{)252}\\18\\\hline 72\\72\\\hline 0\end{array}$	$\begin{array}{r}28\\\times\ 9\\\hline 252\end{array}$
33. Algorithms (procedures)	1. $\begin{array}{r}44\\\times 22\end{array}$ 2. $\dfrac{3}{8} \div \dfrac{5}{8} =$	1. $\begin{array}{r}44\\\times 22\\\hline 88\\88\\\hline 968\end{array}$ 2. $\dfrac{3}{8} \div \dfrac{5}{8} = \dfrac{3}{8} \times \dfrac{8}{5} =$ $\dfrac{24}{40} = \dfrac{12}{20} = \dfrac{6}{10} = \dfrac{3}{5}$
32. Set up equation This is a 1-step problem. (In a 2- or more step problem a critical concept would involve which step to complete first as well as how to set up each step.)	There are 5 children in the math group. Today 4 are absent. How many are present? ⓐ 5 – 4 = ▢ b. 4 – 5 = ▢ ⓒ $\begin{array}{r}5\\-4\\\hline ▢\end{array}$ d. $\begin{array}{r}4\\-5\\\hline ▢\end{array}$	There are 5 children in the math group. Today 4 are absent. How many are present? ⓐ correct b. set up incorrectly ⓒ correct d. set up incorrectly
31. Select operation	Thad has 7 miles to walk to get home. He walks 4 days a week. How many miles does he walk in 4 days? a. 7 – 4 = ▢ b. 7 + 4 = ▢ c. $4\overline{)4}$ ⓓ 4 × 7 = ▢	Thad has 7 miles to walk to get home. He walks 4 days a week. How many miles does he walk in 4 days? a. wrong operation b. wrong operation c. wrong operation ⓓ correct

TABLE 11.1
(continued)

Concept	Example Problem	Solution
30. Irrelevant information	Chris catches 14 lobsters and releases 3 because they are too small. Kathy catches 9 and keeps them all. Jack notices that 5 are "in berries" (carrying eggs). How many lobsters do they have? a. (circled) $\begin{array}{r}14\\-\ 3\end{array}$ $\begin{array}{r}11\\+\ 9\end{array}$ b. $\begin{array}{r}14\\-\ 9\end{array}$ $\begin{array}{r}5\\+\ 3\end{array}$ c. $\begin{array}{r}14\\+\ 3\end{array}$ $\begin{array}{r}17\\+\ 9\end{array}$ d. $\begin{array}{r}14\\-\ 3\end{array}$ $\begin{array}{r}11\\+\ 9\\\hline 5\end{array}$	Chris catches 14 lobsters and releases 3 because they are too small. Kathy catches 9 and keeps them all. Jack notices that 5 are "in berries" (carrying eggs). How many lobsters do they have? a. (circled) correct b. set up incorrectly c. wrong operation d. irrelevant information
29. Missing information	Howard and Tom play racquetball 3 days a week. Howard wins 2 of every 3 games they play. Howard is 5'11" tall and Tom is 6'. Tom weighs 150 pounds. How much does Howard weigh?	Can't tell. There is not enough information
28. Decimals	$1.7 \underline{\ \ } 1.8$ $\dfrac{1}{4} = .\underline{\ \ }?$	$1.7 < 1.8$ $\dfrac{1}{4} = .25$
27. Inverse of fractions	$\dfrac{3}{8} \div \dfrac{5}{8} = \dfrac{3}{8} \times \underline{\ \ \ }$	$\dfrac{3}{8} \div \dfrac{5}{8} = \dfrac{3}{8} \times \dfrac{8}{5}$
26. Mixed numbers	$\dfrac{5}{8} + \dfrac{1}{2} = \underline{\ \ \ }$	$\dfrac{5}{8} + \dfrac{1}{2} = 1\frac{1}{8}$
25. Equivalent fractions	$\dfrac{1}{2} = \dfrac{?}{4}$ $\dfrac{2}{4} = \dfrac{?}{8}$	$\dfrac{1}{2} = \dfrac{2}{4}$ $\dfrac{2}{4} = \dfrac{4}{8}$
24. Fraction equal to "one"	$1 = \dfrac{?}{2} = \dfrac{?}{3} = \dfrac{?}{4}$	$1 = \dfrac{2}{2} = \dfrac{3}{3} = \dfrac{4}{4}$
23. Common denominator	$\dfrac{1}{2} + \dfrac{1}{4} = \underline{\ \ \ }$	$\dfrac{1}{2} + \dfrac{1}{4} = \dfrac{3}{4}$

TABLE 11.1
(continued)

Concept	Example Problem	Solution
22. Unity	$1 \times 4 = \underline{?}$ $4 \div 1 = \underline{?}$	$1 \times 4 = \underline{4}$ $4 \div 1 = \underline{4}$
21. Remainders	$17 \div 4 = 4r\,\underline{?}$	$17 \div 4 = 4r\,\underline{1}$
20. Distributive property	$10 \times 6 = 60$ $(2 \times 5) + (10 \times 5) = \underline{?}$	$10 \times 6 = 60$ $(2 \times 5) + (10 \times 5) = \underline{60}$
19. Multiplication/Division by 1 and 0	$\begin{array}{c}8\\ \times 1\\ \hline\end{array}$ $\begin{array}{c}8\\ \times 0\\ \hline\end{array}$ $\dfrac{8}{1} =$	$\begin{array}{c}8\\ \times 1\\ \hline 8\end{array}$ $\begin{array}{c}8\\ \times 0\\ \hline 0\end{array}$ $\dfrac{8}{1} = 8$
18. Associative property	$2 + 2 + 2 = \underline{?}$ a. $4 + 2$ c. $8 + 2$ b. $1 + 2$ d. $2 + 2$	$2 + 2 + 2 = \underline{a}$ a. $4 + 2$ c. $8 + 2$ b. $1 + 2$ d. $2 + 2$

17. Set separation	$xxx - xx = \underline{?}$
	a. xx b. xx
	    x xx
	    xx xx
	c. d. x
	  xxxxx
		$xxx - xx = \underline{d}$
		a. xx b. xx
		    x xx
		    xx xx
		c. d. x
		  xxxxx

16. Union of sets	$xxx + xx = \underline{?}$
	a. xx b. xx
	    x xx
	    xx xx
	c. d. x
	  xxxxx
		$xxx + xx = \underline{a}$
		a. xx b. xx
		    x xx
		    xx xx
		c. d. x
		  xxxxx

15. Sets	Circle the set of Δ's x Δ Δ x x Δ x x	x Δ Δ x x Δ x x
14. Equality	$\underline{\ } + \underline{\ } = 8,$ $\underline{\ } - \underline{\ } = 8,$ $\underline{\ } \times \underline{\ } = 8,$ $\underline{\ } \div \underline{\ } = 8$	$\begin{array}{c}5\\ +\ 3\\ \hline 8,\end{array}$ $\begin{array}{c}24\\ -\ 16\\ \hline 8,\end{array}$ $\begin{array}{c}2\\ \times\ 4\\ \hline 8,\end{array}$ $\begin{array}{c}16\\ \div\ 2\\ \hline 8\end{array}$

246

TABLE 11.1
(continued)

Concept	Example Problem	Solution
13. Expanded notation	763 is equal to — hundreds — tens — ones	<u>7</u> hundreds <u>6</u> tens <u>3</u> ones
12. Zero as a place holder	"Write this number" 7 hundreds 0 tens 3 ones	<u>703</u>
11. Place Value	$\dfrac{27}{+11} = \dfrac{20}{+?} + \dfrac{?}{+1}$ $30 + \quad 8 = ?$	$\dfrac{27}{+11} = \dfrac{20}{+10} + \dfrac{7}{+1}$ $30 + \quad 8 = 38$
10. Regrouping	7 tens and 8 ones can be written as — tens and 18 ones	<u>6</u> tens and 18 ones
9. Addition, subtraction, multiplication, division	$\dfrac{2}{+2} \quad \dfrac{2}{-2} \quad \dfrac{2}{\times 2} \quad 2 \div 2 =$	$\dfrac{2}{+2}=4 \quad \dfrac{2}{-2}=0 \quad \dfrac{2}{\times 2}=4 \quad 2 \div 2 = 1$
8. Multidigit numbers	"Read these numbers" 14 87 172	"Fourteen, eighty-seven, one hundred seventy-two"
7. Mathematical symbols, terminology, and notation	$+, -, \times, \div, =, <, >$	$+$ = add, $-$ = subtract, $\times$ = multiply, $\div$ = divide, $=$ = equals, $<$ = less than, $>$ = greater than
6. One-to-many correspondence	"Draw lines from each ☐ to three 0's" ○ ○ ○ ○ ○ ○ ○ ○ ☐ ☐	

TABLE 11.1
(continued)

Concept	Example Problem	Solution
5. One-to-one correspondence	"Draw a line from each □ to one 0"	
4. Numeral values	"Circle 7 x's" x x x x x x x x x x x x	
3. Groups of 1's, 10's, 100's, 1,000's	"Write this number" 9 thousand 7 hundred 6 tens 3 ones	9000 700 60 3
2. Cardinal numbers (especially "0")	"Count the x's" x x x x x	"1, 2, 3, 4, 5"
1. Number order	"Place these numbers in sequence" 12 7 18	7, 12, 18

Source: Adapted from G. G. Bitter, J. M. Englehart, and J. Wiebe, *One Step at a Time.* St. Paul: EMC Corp., 1977; and K. W. Howell, S. H. Zucker, and M. K. Morehead, *Multilevel Academic Survey Test.* San Antonio, TX: The Psychological Corp., 1985.

sensitive to both a student's procedural and conceptual understandings. While many instruments sample computation, few sample applications and problem solving adequately; fewer still are designed to examine concept knowledge and strategy use.

Strategies

As you may recall from chapters 5 and 8, strategy use can be evaluated through strategy-specific items or error analysis (Lichtenberg, 1984). Current test formats typically elicit answers but do not sample strategy use. To see if a student uses estimation or monitors his own answers, the evaluator will need to use math tests that elicit more than answers. Formats that check problem solving tap strategies a student uses to arrive at a solution. For example, formats for checking strategies are illustrated in Table 11.1 in items 29–35.

The two test formats in Figure 11.5 are meant to sample a student's mastery of the algorithm for addition of a two-digit addend to a one-digit addend with regrouping. In format A all the problems require regrouping. In format B some of the problems do not require regrouping. Which format matches the objective? Yes, format B. The problems that do not require regrouping are non-examples (non-instances) of regrouping. The systematic and judicious use of non-instances forces students to demonstrate their skill at addition as well as their problem-solving skills. The test also includes a diagonal grid for error analysis originally developed by Hoffmeister (1972).

To sample problem-solving skills such as selecting correct operation, selecting relevant information, or setting up equations, one may choose not to have the student actually work the problem but to select how he would work the problem. Examples of stimulus formats that accomplish this are found in Table 11.1, concepts 30–32.

Many objectives, and often entire courses of study, fail to emphasize strategies. When evaluators work from objectives that omit strategic behavior it is easy to select or write test formats that elicit answers rather than evidence of the use of strategies. Because these tests are the tools used to guide remedial instruction, it is not surprising that current research indicates that special and remedial students lack strategies to transfer and generalize new learnings and have difficulty using the knowledge they have (Mann & Sabatino, 1985).

Standards

Criteria for acceptable performance (CAP) are written in the squares of the table of specifications in Appendix C on pages 452–59. In some cases, CAP are listed as "undetermined." This is because the tests resulting from those intersections cover tasks that are too variable, in either content or format, to allow a single statement of CAP. Therefore, before testing those squares, you will need to make or select materials and obtain CAP.

The CAPs listed in the Appendix C tables are reasonable for all students; however, they are *approximate*. The criteria come from a variety of sources including the authors' judgment and experience. Standards for mastery (Column C) were obtained by testing successful elementary students, junior high students, and adults. There is not a very big relationship between CAP and grade level; a fourth grader who has mastered addition will add no more slowly than a high school student who has also mastered it. The criteria seem to be consistently higher than those recommended by White and Haring (1980) and lower than similar criteria recommended by Beck and Albrecht (1981). Obviously the criteria apply only if the student has received instruction in the content (first graders don't learn fractions, so the fraction CAP don't apply to them).

The rate criteria do not apply to students until they can write digits at a rate of 100 correct per minute. If the student cannot write digits at this rate (most first and second graders cannot), a formula can be used to set intermediate aims (see chapter 15). For example, imagine you give a kid a test for adding two addends—two digits to one digit—without regrouping. After she has worked the problems you find that she was accurate but slow because she got a score of 38 digits. There are two obvious assumed causes.

1. She is slow at adding.
2. She is slow at writing digits.

It isn't possible to determine if assumed cause 1 is correct or not until assumed cause 2 has been checked, so you have the student write digits. Writ-

Format A

Name_____ Date_____ Grade_____ Count: correct_____ errors_____ Time: 1 min.

ADDITION - Double Digit With Carrying

48	25	15	78	16	77	17	18	14	26
+38	+78	+29	+13	+49	+15	+54	+49	+37	+19

29	16	17	13	15	17	19	76	17	18
+18	+18	+14	+28	+39	+43	+55	+17	+79	+19

23	36	48	53	64	18	68	15	39	42
+18	+15	+14	+18	+17	+69	+19	+17	+19	+19

16	19	17	19	19	69	17	18	14	15
+18	+18	+18	+19	+18	+16	+68	+23	+36	+48

Format B

Practice Items

45	28	94	76
+ 7	+ 6	+ 8	+ 4
52	*34*	*102*	*80*

28	53	16	94	87	63	60	32	42	51	Digit Count
+ 4	+ 9	+ 8	+ 8	+ 7	+ 9	+ 8	+ 9	+ 2	+ 9	
32	*62*	*24*	*102*	*94*	*72*	*68*	*41*	*44*	*60*	1s (21)

31	58	13	26	74	69	83	49	22	93	
+ 5	+ 2	+ 7	+ 4	+ 7	+ 9	+ 7	+ 0	+ 8	+ 3	
36	*60*	*20*	*30*	*81*	*78*	*90*	*49*	*30*	*96*	non-instance (41)

39	62	78	43	56	24	18	73	83	92	
+ 9	+ 4	+ 3	+ 8	+ 5	+ 9	+ 8	+ 8	+ 5	+ 9	
48	*66*	*81*	*51*	*61*	*33*	*26*	*81*	*88*	*101*	2s (62)

28	49	93	98	15	85	34	45	63	71	
+ 1	+ 6	+ 6	+ 5	+ 7	+ 9	+ 6	+ 5	+ 9	+ 4	
29	*55*	*99*	*103*	*22*	*94*	*40*	*50*	*72*	*75*	non-instance (83)

31	97	19	70	48	65	95	84	36	83	
+ 9	+ 2	+ 5	+ 9	+ 8	+ 8	+ 6	+ 8	+ 6	+ 8	
40	*99*	*24*	*79*	*56*	*73*	*101*	*92*	*42*	*91*	3s (104)

| 1s | non-instance | 9s | non-instance | 8s | 3s 5s | 6s 5s | 4s | number added to itself | 3s |

FIGURE 11.5

Examples of stimulus formats (*Source:* Format A from Precision Teaching Project, Great Falls, Montana, 1977. Format B from K. W. Howell, S. H. Zucker, and M. K. Morehead, *Multilevel Academic Skills Inventory: Math, Manual*, p. 119. San Antonio, TX: The Psychological Corporation, 1982.)

ing digits is called a "tool movement" or "basic movement cycle (BMC)," which means the other skill (working written math) depends upon it (White & Haring, 1980). The relationship of BMCs to larger skills has been expressed in this formula.

$$\frac{\text{Task Mastery Rate}}{\text{BMC Mastery Rate}} \times \text{Current BMC Rate}$$

$$= \text{Intermediate Aim}$$

If the kid writes 75 digits a minute, you can compute her maximum addition rate by using the formula.

This is shown here:

Mastery Rate for
addition facts   =   80 digits
BMC Rate for writes digits = 100 digits
Current writes digits rate   =   75 digits

$$\frac{80}{100} \times 75 = 60$$

The formula tells us that he should be able to respond at a rate of 60 addition digits per minute. However, he only completed 38. Therefore *both* assumed causes seem to be correct. The kid is slow at writing digits (CAP = 100; student = 75) and is slow at basic facts (CAP for intermediate aim = 60; student = 38). By using the formula to determine tool skill, you can also set an intermediate aim for improving his addition without depending on an increase in digit writing. Ultimately, of course, both skills should be taken to the recommended CAP. Remember, this is not lowering the standard for slow students. Obviously, in cases where there are physical ceilings, e.g., a student has no fingers with which to hold a pencil, it is necessary to ask for an alternative response.

CURRICULUM-BASED TESTING

The math curriculum includes computation, applications, and problem solving. In an adequately designed curriculum, these three domains will be inte-

grated to permit teaching for transfer and generalization. For purposes of analysis, these domains are separate taxonomies. To teach tasks in these domains effectively, both concepts and strategies that are components of each task must be specified.

We will first describe procedures for collecting survey-level information. Then we will briefly explore an example of error analysis as it relates to survey-level testing. Following that are specific-level procedures and treatment decisions.

SURVEY-LEVEL TESTING—COMPUTATION, APPLICATIONS, AND PROBLEM SOLVING

The student's classwork is probably the best source of information for initial assessment material. Other sources are tests that sample a range of math tasks. If the survey material (test or class assignment) is too difficult, then the resulting behavior sample will be composed mostly of random responses or desperate guesses. Where one disadvantage of many normed tests is that they lack content validity, one advantage is that they usually have items ranging from easy to difficult. You need this range if you have no idea where a student is currently functioning. Some math texts have chapter reviews in their appendices, and these can be used to assemble a comprehensive survey-level test. Be sure to add problems that sample strategy behavior if the test you select doesn't include them.

Survey-level activities should also include a sample of response rate for basic math facts. Since most survey tests do not sample rate of response, you will need to add this test to your materials. Rate of response to basic facts is such a frequent explanation for other difficulties in math that it warrants attention at the survey level.

Survey-level steps include formulating questions, assembling materials, fact finding, and interpretation. These steps are outlined next.

Step 1   Formulating Questions

Table 11.2 summarizes six key questions you need to explore in math assessment (Howell et al.,

TABLE 11.2
Survey questions and procedures

Question Asked	Method for Finding the Answer
Facts	
1. Is the student fast enough on basic arithmetic facts to use them automatically when necessary?	Administer timed basic facts tests for operations (+, −, ×, ÷)
2. Is the student accurate on basic arithmetic facts?	Administer basic facts tests for operations (+, −, ×, ÷) Examples of basic fact tests are illustrated in Figure 11.5.
Operations	
3. Does the student exhibit patterns of errors in basic operations with whole numbers?	Administer test that samples a variety of computation problems across +, −, ×, ÷. See Figure 11.6 for an example of a survey test of whole numbers.
4. Does the student exhibit patterns of errors in computation involving rational numbers?	Administer test which samples decimals, ratios, percents and fractions. See Figure 11.6 for an example.
Problem Solving	
5. In solving word problems, does the student exhibit incorrect or inconsistent strategies?	Administer a problem-solving test that permits analysis of strategic behavior (not just correct answers).
Applications	
6. Does the student have difficulty with applications of time, temperature, money, and measurements of length, surface, volume, and weight?	Administer a test that samples this content to determine needs for additional testing.

1985). To address these questions, make decisions about conducting additional specific-level testing.

Step 2 Assembling Materials

Assemble materials and equipment before meeting with the student:

1. Select stimulus materials that sample a broad range of computation, applications, and problem-solving objectives. Focus on only objectives typically taught at or near the student's current grade level. For example, if the student has only been taught addition and subtraction, simply cross out problems in multiplication and division. Figure 11.6 shows a survey test designed to sample a broad range of computation skills.
2. Have available scrap paper and extra pencils for the student and a stopwatch for yourself.
3. Plan to collect the survey-level information in one sitting and specific-level samples after you analyze survey-level responses.

Step 3 Administering Tests and Interpreting Results

This step will now be described for each area of math evaluation. High probability causes for failure will be listed in each interpretation section.

Testing Computation

Directions.

1. Select basic fact tests linked to operations on which the student has had instruction.
2. For each fact test, say to the student: "I want you to work these as quickly and as carefully as you can. Don't skip any problems unless you can't do them. When you come to the end of a row, start at the next row. Keep working until I tell you to stop. Please, begin." Start your timing device and time the student for one minute. When the time is up, say, "Stop." Repeat for each set of facts on which the student has had instruction.
3. To establish rate for facts, count the number of problems or digits correct and the number of

$$\begin{array}{r} 2 \\ +3 \\ \hline \end{array} \qquad \begin{array}{r} 8 \\ -6 \\ \hline \end{array} \qquad \begin{array}{r} 3 \\ 6 \\ +2 \\ \hline \end{array} \qquad \begin{array}{r} 39 \\ +4 \\ \hline \end{array} \qquad \begin{array}{r} 46 \\ -3 \\ \hline \end{array} \qquad \begin{array}{r} 51 \\ -28 \\ \hline \end{array}$$

$$\begin{array}{r} 601 \\ 39 \\ +427 \\ \hline \end{array} \qquad \begin{array}{r} 9062 \\ -4185 \\ \hline \end{array} \qquad \begin{array}{r} 8 \\ \times 9 \\ \hline \end{array} \qquad \begin{array}{r} 47 \\ \times 5 \\ \hline \end{array} \qquad 4\,\overline{)24} \qquad 8\,\overline{)37}$$

$$\begin{array}{r} 3075 \\ \times 62 \\ \hline \end{array} \qquad 74\,\overline{)3061} \qquad \frac{4}{20} = \frac{1}{-} \qquad \frac{3}{11} + \frac{2}{11} = \qquad \frac{1}{2} - \frac{5}{18} = \qquad 2\frac{3}{4} \times 5\frac{1}{3} =$$

$$6\frac{3}{4} \div 3\frac{1}{6} = \qquad \begin{array}{r} 2.43 \\ \times\; 2.5 \\ \hline \end{array} \qquad 1.5\,\overline{)24.39} \qquad 7^2 = \qquad \sqrt{144} \qquad \frac{7}{8} = \underline{\quad\quad}\%$$

FIGURE 11.6

Survey level test of computation (*Source:* K. W. Howell, S. H. Zucker, and M. K. Morehead. *Multilevel Academic Skills Inventory: Math. Survey/Placement Test Booklet*, p. 2. San Antonio, TX: The Psychological Corporation, 1982.)

problems or digits incorrect.[1] Omissions are not errors.

4. Compare the student's scores to the criteria suggested in Table C.2 in Appendix C for basic facts or to a criterion you establish.
5. If the student did not meet criterion for rate, sample basic facts again without timing.
6. Say to the student, "Work these problems carefully; take your time; work each one."
7. Count the number correct. Divide by the total.
8. Compare the student's scores to the accuracy criterion suggested in Table C.2 in Appendix C for basic facts.

Interpretation guidelines. Based on the accuracy and rate criteria for basic facts, respond to the following computation questions.

Computation question 1., Is the student's rate on basic facts at or above criterion?

If yes, administer survey tests for operations, applications, and problem solving.
  If no, answer computation question 2.

Computation question 2. Is the student accurate but slow?

If yes, there are at least two causes. Select the one that seems most probable and check it out with a specific-level test.

- The student does not know facts at the automatic level. (Use Teaching Recommendation 2.2.)
- The student does not know facts and/or is a slow writer. (Use Specific-Level Procedure 2.)

Computation question 3. Is the student inaccurate?

If yes, there are at least two causes. Select the most probable for specific-level testing.

- The student doesn't know facts as numerical sentences. (Use Specific-Level Procedure 1.)
- The student doesn't know strategies to complete numerical sentences. (Use Specific-Level Procedure 3.)

Testing Operations

  Directions.
1. Select a test (or analyze classwork) sampling a broad range of problems. The sample should include problem types on which the student has had instruction.
2. Say to the student, "Work each problem; take your time; show your work."[2]
3. Score each item as correct or incorrect.
4. Compare the items correct to expectancies for the student's current grade level. Review your curriculum to determine what the student should be able to do or compare to problem types and curriculum levels shown in Figure 11.7.

Interpretation guidelines. Based on student corrects and errors, respond to the following question.

Operations question. Can the student work items representing objectives for grade-level placement?

If yes, administer items beyond grade level to determine where to begin instruction.
  If no, the student does not know task-specific strategies for working the operation. Check with Specific-Level Procedure 4.

Testing Applications and Problem Solving

  Directions.
1. Select or construct a test sampling a range of problem types. The items should include problems that require one operation for solution and

---

1. A discussion of calibration is found in chapter 8. Some authorities advocate using digits as the unit of measurement while others advocate using whole numbers. There is some evidence that criteria for acceptable responses for basic facts should be based on answers per minute rather than digits per minute (Berquam, 1986).

2. If you were teaching mental computation you would not ask the student to "show work." Reys (1984) notes that mental computation is a key component of *estimation*. However, when testing operations, you will have more to analyze if you have students show work.

Computation Survey Summary

Additonal Testing Guide

	Addition				Subtraction				Multiplication		
CURRIC. LEVEL	ITEM	EX. PASS	PASS	CURRIC. LEVEL	ITEM	EX. PASS	PASS	CURRIC. LEVEL	ITEM	EX. PASS	PASS
3	7. $\begin{array}{r}601\\39\\+427\end{array}$			4	8. $\begin{array}{r}9062\\-4185\end{array}$			8	22. 7^2		
2	4. $\begin{array}{r}39\\+\ 4\end{array}$			3	6. $\begin{array}{r}51\\-28\end{array}$			5	13. $\begin{array}{r}3075\\\times\ \ 62\end{array}$		
2	3. $\begin{array}{r}3\\6\\+2\end{array}$			2	5. $\begin{array}{r}46\\-\ 3\end{array}$			4	10. $\begin{array}{r}47\\\times5\end{array}$		
1	1. $\begin{array}{r}2\\+3\end{array}$			1	2. $\begin{array}{r}8\\-6\end{array}$			4	9. $\begin{array}{r}8\\\times9\end{array}$		

Discrepancy _____
Additional testing _____
No Additional testing _____ (Addition)

Discrepancy _____
Additional testing _____
No Additional testing _____ (Subtraction)

Discrepancy _____
Additional testing _____
No Additional testing _____ (Multiplication)

	Division				Fractions				Dec., Ratios, %		
CURRIC. LEVEL	ITEM	EX. PASS	PASS	CURRIC. LEVEL	ITEM	EX. PASS	PASS	CURRIC. LEVEL	ITEM	EX. PASS	PASS
8	23. $\sqrt{144}$			6	19. $6\frac{3}{4} \div 3\frac{1}{6}$			8	24. $\frac{7}{8} = \_\%$		
5	14. $74\overline{)3061}$			6	18. $2\frac{3}{4} \times 5\frac{1}{3}$			7	21. $1.5\overline{)24.39}$		
4	12. $8\overline{)37}$			6	17. $\frac{1}{2} - \frac{5}{18}$			7	20. $\begin{array}{r}2.43\\\times 2.5\end{array}$		
4	11. $4\overline{)24}$			5	16. $\frac{3}{11} + \frac{2}{11}$			5	15. $\frac{4}{20} = V$		

Discrepancy _____
Additional testing _____
No Additional testing _____ (Division)

Discrepancy _____
Additional testing _____
No Additional testing _____ (Fractions)

Discrepancy _____
Additional testing _____
No Additional testing _____ (Dec., Ratios, %)

Curriculum Level Scale

All items on the survey test are listed below with the most advanced items at the top. The brackets in the left margin indicate the curriculum level at which these items are usually taught. Because curriculum is not a task specific concept, the brackets overlap. The student's curriculum level is the level at which his/her first error occurs (lowest number).

Pass

Item
24
23
22
21
20
19
18
17
16
15
14
13
12
11
10
9
8
7
6
5
4
3
2
1

8
7
6
5
4
3
2
1

FIGURE 11.7
Curriculum level for problem types *(Source:* K. W. Howell, S. H. Zucker, and M. K. Morehead. *Multilevel Academic Skills Inventory: Math, Survey/Placement Test Booklet,* p. 3. San Antonio, TX: The Psychological Corporation, 1982.)

255

no application content, as well as problems that require several steps, and operations or application content. Response formats should be varied to sample problem-solving strategies as well as correct answering. Examples of two response formats and two levels of problem difficulty are shown in Figure 11.8. Include problems from the curriculum you think are appropriate for the student. If he cannot work any, you will have nothing to analyze.

2. Have the student work the problems. If he cannot read, read the problems to him. If he has never been asked to "select procedures for a solution," demonstrate problems in which you are asking him to select the way to work the problem rather than actually working it.

3. Score the problems and compare performance to curriculum-level expectations.

Interpretation guidelines. Based on student corrects and errors, respond to the following application questions.

Application question 1. Is the student's performance within curriculum-level expectations?

*FIGURE 11.8
Problem-solving
formats and
problem complexity*

PROBLEM SOLVING			
Item Types			
Identify Correct Equation		**Produce Correct Equation**	
One Step	*More than One*	*One Step*	*More than One*
1. +	7. +, +	13. +	19. +, −
2. −	8. −, +	14. −	20. −, +
3. ×	9. ×, ×	15. ×	20. ×, ×
4. ÷	10. ÷, +	16. ÷	22. ÷, +
5. +	11. $\frac{n}{n} + \frac{n}{n}$	17. $+ \frac{n}{n}$	23. $\times \frac{n}{n} \div \frac{n}{n}$
6. × %	12. ÷ %, × %	18. × %	24. × %, − %

Examples:

Identify—One Step
Select the answer.

1. Bud has 2 toy airplanes. Sis gives him 3 more. How many airplanes does Bud have all together?

      a. $\begin{array}{r} 2 \\ -3 \\ \hline \end{array}$

      b. $\begin{array}{r} 4 \\ \times 8 \\ \hline \end{array}$

      c. $\begin{array}{r} 10 \\ \times 6 \\ \hline \end{array}$

      d. $\begin{array}{r} 3 \\ +2 \\ \hline \end{array}$

Produce—Two Step
Work the problem.

19. Kim has 6 music books. She gets 4 from Lori and gives 1 to Linda. How many does she have left?

If yes, test at next higher level in curriculum to determine where to begin instruction.

If no, answer application questions 2 and 3.

Application question 2. Does the student exhibit correct strategies?

If yes, test at next higher level.

If no, select one or more of the following assumed causes. All are addressed with Specific-Level Procedure 5.

- Does not know which operation to use;
- Does not recognize relevant, irrelevant, or missing information;
- Does not know how to set up the equation (one-step problems, more than one step);
- Does not know how to work the equation/operation once it's set up;
- Does not know how to estimate problem solutions or doesn't appear to have a clue about what the answers should be;
- Does not know how to check work;
- Is not fluent enough on facts, operations, or problem solving to integrate efficiently.

Application question 3. Does the student succeed at applications—time, temperature, money, measurement?

If yes, test at next higher level.

If no, test these assumed causes at the specific level. All are addressed with Specific-Level Procedures 6, 7, and 8.

- Does not have concept knowledge, vocabulary knowledge, or content-specific algorithm knowledge (i.e., the area of a triangle = 1/2 base times height);
- Does not have adequate tool knowledge (i.e., how to use a ruler, etc.);
- Does not have knowledge of equivalent units (i.e., 10 pennies in a dime, 4 quarters in a dollar, 60 minutes in an hour);
- Is not fluent enough in problem solving to combine with applications;

- Is not fluent enough with application knowledge to combine with problem solving;
- Is not fluent enough in facts, operations, problem solving, or applications to integrate efficiently.

Survey Level to Specific Level

The transition from the survey level to the specific level is made by following these steps.

1. Collect the behavior sample (survey level).
2. List the assumed cause(s). (Select high-probability assumed causes from the survey-level interpretation sections, or analyze tasks and analyze errors.)
3. Select or make up a specific-level to verify assumed causes and administer (specific level).
4. Repeat the procedure or summarize results.

Before describing specific-level procedures, we will explore how error analysis and task analysis (step 2 above) may be applied to survey-level testing to target assumed causes not listed in the survey-level interpretation sections.

Error Analysis and Task Analysis

A math problem is a task that, like any other, places certain requirements on the student. In other words, the nature of the task itself requires the worker to do certain specific things. For example, adding fractions with unlike denominators ($1/6 + 1/4 = \square$) requires skill at adding fractions with like denominators ($2/12 + 3/12 = \square$). Therefore, if a kid fails, one way to find explanations for his failure is to task analyze the problem. The subtasks that result from the analysis will be the same for all students who work the problem. Everyone who computes the solution to "$1/6 + 1/4 = \square$" must do the things listed in Figure 11.9.

If a student does not solve $1/6 + 1/4$ correctly, any of the five subtasks in Figure 11.9, or *their* subtasks, could be used to explain the failure. An alternative explanation for the error could be that the student can complete the subtasks but does not have a strategy for combining them. As explained earlier, strategy problems can often be identified through error analysis.

Add fractions with unlike denominators.
1/6 + 1/4 = 5/12
5. Add fractions with like denominators.
2/12 + 3/12 = 5/12
4. Convert unlike-denominator fractions to like-denominator fractions.
1/6 + 1/4 = 2/12 + 3/12
3. Multiply fractions by a fraction equal to 1, using the factor that produces a denominator equal to the Lowest Common Denominator.
1/6 × 2/2 = 2/12   and   1/4 × 3/3 = 3/12
2. Find factors of the Lowest Common Denominator.

1. Find the Lowest Common Denominator.
6, 12, 18, 24, 30
4, 8, 12, 16, 20, 24

FIGURE 11.9
A task analysis of 1/6 + 1/4

Basic computation, like spelling, is not an area where creative responses are highly prized. Because the responses are highly controlled by the problem, even errors seem to occur by types; these types correspond to the requirements of the problem. Some researchers have studied computational error patterns and proposed categories for them. The categories that are most frequently used are those originally identified by Roberts (1968). They are:

1. Wrong operation,
2. Obvious computational error,
3. Defective algorithm, and
4. Random response.

Enright (1983) has expanded these basic categories to seven error clusters:

1. Regrouping errors,
2. Process substitution errors,
3. Omission errors,
4. Directional errors,
5. Placement errors,
6. Attention to sign errors, and
7. Guessing errors.

As an example, Figure 11.10 shows one of Enright's process substitution errors.

Ashlock (1982) has advised teachers using error analysis to (a) be accepting of the student, (b) collect data—do not instruct, (c) be thorough, and (d) look for patterns. Looking for patterns is obviously the main thing we need to do, but the other three suggestions will have an effect on what we find.

Follow these steps when analyzing errors.

1. Collect an adequate behavior sample by having the student work several problems of each type in which you are interested.
2. Encourage the student to work and talk aloud about it, but do nothing to influence his responses.
3. Record all responses the student makes, including comments.
4. Look for patterns in the responses.
5. Look for exceptions to any apparent pattern.
6. List the patterns you have identified as assumed causes for the student's computational difficulties.
7. Interview the student. Ask him to tell you how he worked the problem to confirm suspected patterns.

For more discussion of error analysis, review chapters 5 and 7.

SPECIFIC-LEVEL TESTING

In this section we will outline eight specific-level procedures for confirming or disconfirming assumed causes that have been derived from interpretation of survey-level work. The specific procedures will be matched to the areas tested at the survey level (computation [basic facts and operations], applications, and problem solving).

Computation—Basic Facts
The student's accuracy and rate at basic facts were already determined during the computation survey procedure. If the student appeared to be inaccurate or accurate but slow, specific-level testing is re-

PROCESS SUBSTITUTION

In this error cluster, the student changes the *process* of one or more of the computation steps and creates a different algorithm that results in an incorrect answer.

Process Substitution 18: *Adds using multiplication process.*

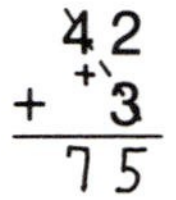

$$\begin{array}{r} 4\,2 \\ +\ 3 \\ \hline 7\,5 \end{array}$$

Process Substitution 19: *(Subtracts instead of adds.) Subtracts smaller digit from larger digit in each column.*

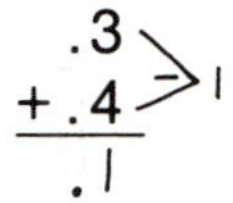

$$\begin{array}{r} .3 \\ +.4 \\ \hline .1 \end{array}$$

Process Substitution 20: *(Doesn't regroup.) Adds bottom addend to each digit in top addend.*

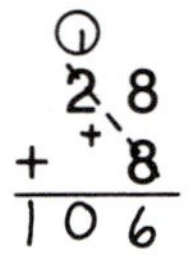

$$\begin{array}{r} 2\,8 \\ +\ 8 \\ \hline 1\,0\,6 \end{array}$$

Process Substitution 21: *Subtracts using multiplication process, and always subtracts smaller digit from larger digit.*

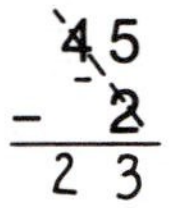

$$\begin{array}{r} 4\,5 \\ -\ 2 \\ \hline 2\,3 \end{array}$$

Process Substitution 22: *(Doesn't regroup.) Adds subtrahend to each digit of minuend.*

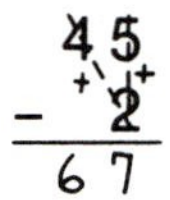

$$\begin{array}{r} 4\,5 \\ -\ 2 \\ \hline 6\,7 \end{array}$$

Process Substitution 23: *Subtracts smaller digit from larger digit in each column.*

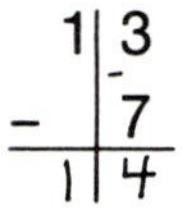

$$\begin{array}{r} 1\,3 \\ -\ 7 \\ \hline 1\,4 \end{array}$$

Process Substitution 24: *Adds instead of subtracts a column of digits.*

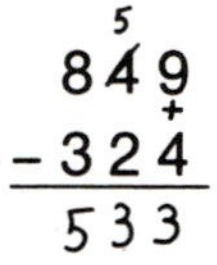

$$\begin{array}{r} 8\,4\,9 \\ -3\,2\,4 \\ \hline 5\,3\,3 \end{array}$$

Process Substitution 25: *Adds digits of minuend, adds digits of subtrahend, and subtracts.*

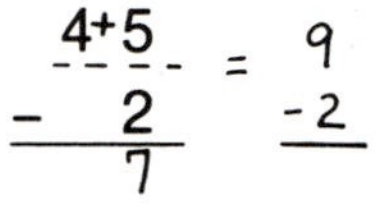

$$\begin{array}{r} 4+5\ =\ 9 \\ -\ 2\ \ \ -2 \\ \hline 7 \end{array}$$

Process Substitution 26: *Multiplies ones column, but adds tens column.*

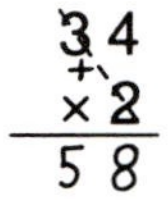

$$\begin{array}{r} 3\,4 \\ \times\ 2 \\ \hline 5\,8 \end{array}$$

Process Substitution 27: *Multiplies ones column, but copies other digit(s) in multiplicand.*

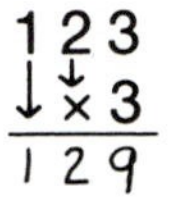

$$\begin{array}{r} 1\,2\,3 \\ \times\ 3 \\ \hline 1\,2\,9 \end{array}$$

FIGURE 11.10

Error analysis *(Source:* B. G. Enright. *Enright® Diagnostic Inventory of Basic Arithmetic Skills.* North Billerica, MA: Curriculum Associates, 1983. Appendix A. Used with permission of Curriculum Associates.)

quired to confirm this finding and collect additional information.

Specific-Level Procedure 1: Checking Accuracy and Fluency on Basic Facts. (Define explanations for errors or low rate encountered on survey-level tests.)

Directions.
1. Construct or select a test sampling basic facts. You will need an instrument for each area you are testing ($+$, $-$, $\times$, $\div$). An example of specific-level tests that permit easy error analysis is shown in Figure 11.5. The probes in Figure 11.5 are the teacher's versions—answers, diagonal lines, and labels would not appear on the student's copies.
2. Say to the student, "Write the answer to each problem. Work carefully."
3. Score the responses. Compare the responses to standards you have established or use ours (100%). Summarize error patterns. Note facts with more than one error.

Interpretation guidelines.

Question. Is the student accurate but slow at basic facts?

If yes, use Teaching Recommendation 2 (fluency building).
   If no, go to Teaching Recommendation 1 (accuracy), use Specific-Level Procedure 2, and consider using Specific-Level Procedure 5.

Specific-Level Procedure 2: Checking Recall and Handwriting. We use a two-part procedure to determine if writing slowly or inadequate recall of facts is the cause of the rate failure on the basic facts survey-level test.

Directions 2.1.
1. Administer a basic facts test for each area of concern ($+$, $-$, $\times$, $\div$). Have the student say the answers rather than write. (Flashcards or a fact sheet are appropriate stimuli.)

2. Say, "Tell me the answer to each problem."
3. Note corrects and errors. Compare the student's performance to your CAP or the one we list in Appendix C. One hundred percent accuracy is an appropriate criterion for facts.

Directions 2.2.
1. Administer a writing-digits or a copying-digits test.
2. Say, "Write/copy numbers from 1 to 100 as quickly and carefully as you can. Please, begin."
3. Time the student for 60 seconds. Say, "Stop."
4. Score the sample and use the procedure for comparing basic movement cycle—writing digits to the skill of math facts.

Interpretation guidelines.

Question. Are the student's oral responses accurate?

If yes, answer the next question and use Teaching Recommendation 2.
   If no, teach basic facts and use Teaching Recommendation 1, or employ Specific-Level Procedure 3.

Question. Can the student write fast enough to demonstrate math fact fluency?

If yes, teach fact fluency (Teaching Recommendation 2.2).
   If no, teach the student to write digits (Teaching Recommendation 2.1).

Question. Is the student having trouble with both accuracy on facts and writing digits?

If yes, teach accuracy on facts (recommendation 1) and writing digits (recommendation 2.1). Also use Specific-Level Procedure 3.

Specific-Level Procedure 3: Checking Basic Concepts. Identify missing or erroneous basic concepts.

Directions.

1. Review concepts 1 through 28 in Table 11.1. Some of these will be appropriate to the content under examination and some will not. Make a checklist of the appropriate concepts to facilitate the evaluation.

2. Use the test in Specific-Level Procedure 1 or write one for target operations or areas of application. Fill in answers before you begin.

3. Point to an item or write one (for example, 3 + 2 = 5). Say to the student, "Tell me how you would figure out the answer to this problem: 3 + 2 = 5." Next say, "Tell me how you are going to remember 3 + 2 = 5."

4. Script the student's response or tape record.

5. Examine the student's written or oral responses for evidence that he understands concepts 1 through 28 from Table 11.1. Note (a) if the concept is appropriate to the target content, (b) if the student seems unaware of the concept, (c) if the student has the concept wrong, or (d) if he has it right.

6. Ask additional questions about those concepts which the student may not have used or may have used incorrectly.

Interpretation guidelines.

Question. Does the student have an adequate repertoire of strategies for figuring out facts and committing them to memory?

If yes, provide practice (Teaching Recommendation 2.2).

If no, *teach* strategies for figuring out facts or strategies for recall, as described in recommendation 1.

Computation—Operations

When the student misses items on the survey-level operations test for whole numbers, decimals, ratios, percents, or fractions, check to see if the student has acquired erroneous strategies for working the operation.

Specific-Level Procedure 4: Checking Operations Strategies. To find erroneous or missing strategies. The specific-level test for operations should contain enough items to obtain an adequate sample and allow error analysis. It may include non-instances (see Figure 11.5) or strategy-specific items (chapter 5).

Directions.

1. Select or construct a test or series of tests sampling the operations or applications content the student missed on the survey-level test.

2. Several testing sessions may be required. Tests can be given during regularly scheduled math classes.

3. Say to the student, "Write the answers to these problems. Please show your work. When you have finished, I will ask you how you have worked some of the problems."

4. After the student completes the problems, ask him to describe what he does when he works a problem. Record his responses.

5. Score the student's answers. Analyze errors using both the student's written work and his descriptions.

6. Compare the student's strategies to task requirements and determine if he has an adequate repertoire of *efficient* strategies for learning facts for recall. (Remember, taping a paper tube to the hand to make an additional finger probably does not meet the requirement for efficiency and generalization inherent in *good* strategies. Also statements like "I will remember" do not qualify as adequate recall strategies.) This sort of testing will be new to most students so be patient. Also be aware that a student's poor language skills may confound your results.

Interpretation guidelines.

Question. Does the student have adequate computation skills for whole numbers and decimals, ratios, percents, and fractions?

If yes, check skills at next curriculum level.

If no, teach specific-level computation skills or task strategies. See Teaching Recommendation 4.

Applications and Problem Solving

If the student does not solve problems within curriculum-level expectations, check student's knowledge of problem solving. Use Specific-Level Procedure 5 and consider evaluating skill at computation.

Specific-Level Procedure 5: Basic Problem-Solving Concepts.

Directions.
1. Select or construct a test to sample each of the following assumed causes:
   - Does not know which operation to use.
   - Does not recognize relevant, irrelevant, or missing information.
   - Does not know how to set up equations for one-step problems; more than one step.
   - Does not know how to estimate problem-solving solutions.
   - Does not know how to check work.

Table 11.1, items 29–35, shows examples of formats for each problem type. Systematically check each across operations (+, −, ×, and ÷) of whole numbers and rational numbers (see Figure 11.12). Include word problems that initially require one-step problems, then two-step problems. Additional examples of stimulus format types are shown in Figure 11.11.

2. Administer items and note the kid's status on each.

   Interpretation guidelines.

   Question.   Does the student demonstrate adequate skill?

If yes, check other skills. Use Instructional Recommendations 4 and 5.

If no, examine errors to decide which of the following explanations seem most likely. (It may be necessary to test them all.) Teach the skill and associated task strategies.

Assumed Causes	Test
The student:	
1) Does not have adequate curriculum-level concept knowledge, vocabulary knowledge, or content-specific algorithm knowledge.	Check knowledge of concepts and vocabulary. Use Specific-Level Procedure 6.
2) Does not have adequate tool knowledge. or	Check tool knowledge and equivalent-unit knowledge. Use Specific-Level Procedure 7.
3) Does not have knowledge of equivalent units or algorithms for specific content of concern.	
4) Is not fluent enough in problem solving to combine with applications.	Review problem-solving fluency. Use Specific-Level Procedure 8.
5) Is not fluent enough with application knowledge to combine with problem solving.	Check fluency of application skills. Use Specific-Level Procedure 8.
6) Is not fluent enough in facts, operations, problem solving, and applications to integrate efficiently.	Check fluency of facts, operations, problem solving, and applications. Use Specific-Level Procedure 8.

Specific-Level Procedure 6: Content Knowledge.

Directions.
1. Select or construct a test to sample concepts and vocabulary for content of concern—time, temperature, money, measurement (linear, surface, volume, weight). Figure 11.12 illustrates the scope of this domain.
2. Administer the test.
3. Score responses. Summarize. Compare to standards established for curriculum level.

Estimate correct answer to word problems.

1. If I work a problem and add 5 to a number, will the answer be bigger or smaller than 5?

2. If I add 50 to a number that is smaller than 50, will the answer be closest to 25, 75, or 150?

3. If I multiply a number that is smaller than 100 by 3, can the answer exceed 200?

4. If I multiply a number that is smaller than 100 by 3, can the answer exceed 300?

5. Do you think the sum of 4360 and 3360 will be closer to 7000 or to 10,000?

6. If I divide a number smaller than 100 by 100, what can you tell me about the answer?

7. If I multiply a number by 4, will I get an odd or even answer?

8. What's the smallest whole number I could multiply by 6 to get an answer greater than 60?

Recognize missing information in word problems.

1. Each child in Mrs. Webb's class has 3 textbooks. How many books are there all together?

2. A chicken lays 3 eggs a day. How many days will it take for her to lay $5 worth of eggs?

3. Lily has 23 marbles. She gives 2 green ones to John and all the blue ones to Julie. How many does she have left?

4. If Syd gives $\frac{1}{5}$ of his fish to Steve and $\frac{1}{5}$ of them to Tom, how many fish do Tom and Steve have together?

Recognize essential and non-essential information in word problems.

... arrived at the hotel 2 hours later.

... put three of them with the others so they would be safe.

... divided them equally among his three friends, Joe, John, and Steve.

... asked Mary to give him half of the pizza that was left.

Check solution to problems using functional algorithm.

3	26	46
+4	− 3	× 6
7	23	276

$$\frac{5}{15} = \frac{1}{3}$$

```
        17
    5 ) 85
        5
        35
        35
```

703	630
+409	× 31
1112	630
7	1890
	19530

```
        426 r 13
   15 ) 6403
        60
        40
        30
        103
        90
        13
```

$$4\frac{1}{3} \div \frac{5}{9} = 7\frac{4}{5}$$

Identify correct equation to solve word problems.

1. Diane has 35 stickers. Maria has 21. How many more stickers does Diane have than Maria?

   a. $\begin{array}{r} 35 \\ +21 \end{array}$ b. $\begin{array}{r} 35 \\ -21 \end{array}$ c. $\begin{array}{r} 21 \\ -35 \end{array}$ d. $21\overline{)35}$

2. Derek has 396 gold coins. He must store them in special boxes that hold 22 coins each. How many boxes will he need.

   a. $\begin{array}{r} 396 \\ -22 \end{array}$ b. $\begin{array}{r} 396 \\ \times 22 \end{array}$ c. $396 \div 22$ d. $22 - 396$

3. For an assignment the teacher asks the class to read pages 133–152 and 382–401 in the textbook. How many pages of reading were assigned?

   a. $(152-133) + (401-382) =$
   b. $133 + 152 + 382 + 401 =$
   c. $(133 + 152) - (382 + 401) =$
   d. $(382 - 133) + (401 - 152) =$

FIGURE 11.11
Stimulus format types for sampling problem solving *(Source:* K. W. Howell, S. H. Zucker, and M. K. Morehead, *Multilevel Academic Skills Inventory: Math, Survey/Placement Test Booklet*, p. 3. San Antonio, TX: The Psychological Corporation, 1982.)

263

FIGURE 11.12
Math summary checklist

Solve All Problems, Integrating Necessary Computation, Applications, and Problem-Solving Skills

Response	Identify	Produce			Appropriate Curriculum Level	
Standard	Accuracy	Accuracy	Mastery	Automatic	No Pass	Pass
Problem Solving—Integrate Subskills						
Check work						
Estimate answer						
Work equation						
Set Up equation						
Determine relevant information						
Determine correct operation/s						

Solve All Problems, Integrating Necessary Computation, Applications, and Problem-Solving Skills

Response	Identify	Produce			Appropriate Curriculum Level	
Standard	Accuracy	Accuracy	Mastery	Automatic	No Pass	Pass
Applications—Integrate Subskills						
Measurement - Scaling						
Weight — Vocabulary						
Tools						
Content						
Volume — Vocabulary						
Tools						
Content						

	Vocabulary
Surface	Tools
	Content
	Vocabulary
Linear	Tools
	Content
	Vocabulary
Money	Tools
	Content
	Vocabulary
Temper-ature	Tools
	Content
	Vocabulary
Time	Tools
	Content

Solve All Problems, Integrating Necessary Computation, Applications, and Problem-Solving Skills

| | Identify | Produce | | Appropriate Curriculum Level | |
| | Accuracy | Accuracy | Mastery | Automatic | No Pass | Pass |

Response Standard

Computation—Integrate Subskills

+	−	×	÷	Operations—Rational Numbers
				Ratios
				Percents
				Decimals
				Fractions

Operations—Whole Numbers

÷
×
−
+

Basic Facts—Integrate Subskills

÷
×
−
+

265

Interpretation guidelines.

Question. Does the student know concepts and vocabulary?

If yes, check other assumed causes for application failure.

If no, teach concepts and vocabulary. Use Teaching Recommendation 5.

Specific-Level Procedure 7: Tool and Unit Knowledge.

Directions.
1. Select or construct a test to sample tool knowledge. Figure 11.2 illustrates the scope of this domain. In linear measurement you will check a student's skill with rulers, tape measures, yard sticks, meter sticks, etc. Across all content you may wish to check his skill with a calculator. (Students who are not fluent on basic facts need to be fluent with a calculator and estimation skills.)
2. Select or construct an instrument that will sample equivalent units or specific algorithms for areas of concern. Have the student state equivalent units in a domain and state algorithms for specific content (i.e., algorithms: "The area of a triangle is equal to 1/2 the base times the height"; "The area of a circle is equal to _____"; equivalent units: "There are __ inches in a foot"; "There are __ feet in a yard"; "There are __ centimeters in a meter)."
3. Administer the test.
4. Score and compare to curriculum-level expectations.

Interpretation guidelines.

Question. Does the student use content-specific tools with ease?

If yes, check other assumed causes for application failure.

If no, teach unknown content. Use Teaching Recommendation 5.

Specific-Level Procedure 8: Skill Integration.

Directions. Essentially, what you will do here is assemble previously collected information or computation and review it in the context of application/problem-solving skills. (If you haven't evaluated computation, you would do that first.) If students are not fluent in facts and operations and applications/problem solving, you will need to teach for fluency and for integration of these skills. As you review, retest any areas where you do not have sufficient data. A checklist for summarizing your judgments is shown in Figure 11.12.

Interpretation guidelines.

Question. Can the student adequately perform tasks in isolation?

If yes, teach for transfer and integration. Use Teaching Recommendation 4.

If no, teach tasks for which problems are identified. Use Teaching Recommendation 5.

Making Instructional Decisions[3]
Once you have confirmed or ruled out assumed causes, you are ready to make treatment decisions. In math, decisions can be easily grouped into a few teaching recommendations: (1) teach accuracy on basic facts, (2) teach fluency on basic facts, (3) teach specific computational skills, (4) teach task strategies, and (5) teach specific-level application content. Since students may have discrepancies in each of these areas you will need to set priorities by combining what you know about task prerequisites and what you know about each kid's interests and values.

After initiating instruction, continue the evaluation process of collecting facts, generating assumed causes, and confirming and ruling out hypotheses. The final section of this chapter outlines teaching

---

3. Teaching recommendations listed are used with permission from The Psychological Corporation and are taken from Howell, Zucker, and Morehead (1985).

recommendations. For additional information on instruction in mathematics, see Silbert et al. (1981), Grouws (1985), Ashlock (1982), Silver (1985), Choate et al. (1987), and Enright (1987).

Recommendation 1: *Teach Accuracy on Basic Facts*

You have a student who is not proficient enough on basic arithmetic facts to use them in higher-level computation and problem solving. There are two approaches to teaching facts: (a) as a series of separate numerical sentences learned in a basic stimulus–response format or (b) through the instruction of underlying strategies. It is no doubt better to teach the underlying strategies until the student is accurate and then to build fluency until he uses them automatically. Of course, it is critical to verify that the student has the prerequisite knowledge and skills needed to learn these basic facts. Consider knowledge of numerals and counting skills to be the primary prerequisites. Addition can be thought of as counting forward and subtraction as counting backward. Multiplication can be thought of as counting forward more efficiently via the method of counting by a given quantity. Division can be thought of as counting backward via the same method. If a student does not seem ready to learn facts, try the following.

Teach him to count by rote (forward and backward from one number to another) at a rate of 100 numbers per minute. Use directions such as: "Count forward (or backward) from ___ to ___. What number are you going to start on? What number are you going to stop on? Begin." For example:

"Count forward from 3 to 9."
"Count forward from 46 to 57."
"Count forward from 77 to 86."
"Count backward from 6 to 3."
"Count backward from 34 to 28."
"Count backward from 54 to 45."

Also, teach the student to supply previous or next numbers at a rate of 100 correct per minute. This can be done by writing random numbers on a sheet

and placing blanks either before or after them. Tell him to fill in the blanks as quickly as possible.

Once the student can count and recognizes numbers, teach addition and subtraction through the use of objects (like blocks) or pictures of objects. Then teach him to transfer these skills to written problems presented in standard form. At this point, substitute operation signs for the verbal directions to "add" or "count forward."

It is important in teaching facts to impress on the student the need to follow the appropriate strategy. Do this by de-emphasizing the production of answers by asking questions about the use of the strategy itself. Here is an example for the problem $4 + 6 = ?$.

Question:	"What kind of problem is this? Look at the sign."
Response:	"Addition."
Question:	"What do we know about the answers to addition problems?"
Response:	"They are bigger than the numbers in the problem."
Question:	"What number will you start with?"
Response:	"6."
Question:	"Why?"
Response:	"I don't have to count as many times."
Question:	"Good. Now solve the problem."
Response:	"$6 + 4$ means $6 + 1 + 1 + 1 + 1$. $6 + 4 = 10$."
Question:	"Good. You followed the steps for adding."

Recommendation 2: *Teach Fluency on Basic Facts*

As we noted earlier, there are at least three explanations for accurate but slow performance on basic facts: the student does not know the facts at the automatic level, the student writes slowly, or the student does not know facts and is a slow writer. The only way to pinpoint the source of the slow rate is to show that the student does know basic facts or is not a slow writer. The simplest way to do this is to have him say the answers to facts. If the student can accurately say 40 or more answers per minute, rule out knowledge of facts and target writing fluency as an objective. If the student cannot say answers fluently, ask him to write the numerals 1 to 99 from memory as quickly as possible. If the student writes fewer than 60 numerals in a minute, then writing fluency or number recall may not be sufficient to demonstrate fact competence. Speed of number recall can be checked by having the student count out loud.

2.1 Handwriting. If assessments indicate that the student simply writes slowly, set a temporary criterion for fluency on facts while you work on increasing writing fluency. Expect the student's rate on basic facts to be about two-thirds the rate on writing numerals. For example, a child who can write numerals at a rate of 45 numerals per minute should have a temporary criterion of about 30 facts per minute.

Slow writers who are capable of increasing their writing rate should generally be taught to do so. Writing slowly can limit the amount of work a student can produce and may contribute to problems completing tasks. Slow production may also impede acquisition of more complex skills because students who attend to handwriting often fail to attend to the critical mathematical attributes of problems. It is important to build writing rate as long as a student does not have a physical handicap that precludes writing. Never put off mathematics instruction while waiting for handwriting fluency to increase.

Lessons designed for building handwriting fluency use brief, intense practice sessions in which the student is encouraged to write faster while maintaining accuracy. Fluency-building routines can be incorporated into daily lessons. Students can be taught to time each other for one minute on a free-writing task or a copying task. Often several very short (10-second) timings on dictated random numbers are better than one long timing. After the timing, the students can check their accuracy and record their progress. They can also be taught to make decisions about the adequacy of their progress. Students who have participated in this kind of

lesson report that they reach fluency criterion quickly and enjoy watching their own growth.

2.2 Facts. Lessons designed to build fluency on facts are typically short (5 to 10 minutes) and use rapidly paced drill over material on which the student is at least 90% accurate. This is often accomplished with flashcards or timed practice sheets. During such lessons, the student is reinforced for rapid responding and daily improvement in fluency. Errors are typically viewed as rate-induced and are ignored to the extent that error correction procedures are not used (feedback may be given after the practice session, however). Peer teaching groups are especially effective and time-efficient. Peers can use cards that contain the problem on both sides, without the answer, so that both students must work each fact. Fluency instruction is intended to make the student automatic at using a skill, which means that the student must be able to recall the fact whenever necessary. This means the student must practice under a variety of different conditions: problems presented orally, in horizontal and vertical written formats, and ultimately on practice sheets with facts drawn from all operations (addition, subtraction, multiplication, division) mixed together.

Recommendation 3: Teach Specific-Level Computation Skills

Unlike reading, computation skills have a relatively clear, highly sequential progression in complexity. Recognizing the subskills of a target task will make instruction in that task far more efficient. Our basic recommendation for teaching computation is to teach subskills and move up or down the hierarchy of computation skills as warranted by the student's performance.

This recommendation to teach specific-level computation skills should be based on evidence that the student has not learned all the subskills in the hierarchy. The list of subskills in Appendix C, Table C.2, includes sequences in computation prerequisites, addition, subtraction, multiplication, division, fractions, and decimals/ratios/percents. Although presented like a ladder, the sequences are actually more like a series of branching, interrelated paths.

Recommendation 4: Teach Task Strategies

Students who are not accurate on facts or operations need to develop a set of computational strategies that can be applied across as many operations as possible. These strategies may be task specific, such as the algorithm for adding or subtracting mixed numbers, or they may be general. Task-specific strategies apply only to a small domain of tasks, while general strategies may apply across several broad domains. The task-specific strategy for adding or subtracting mixed numbers is: "Recognize the problem type; find the common denominator; find the answer; decide if the answer must be converted; convert if necessary." The general strategy for mathematics is to select the operation, recognize the unknown quantity, recognize relevant and irrelevant information, set up the necessary equation(s), estimate the answer, follow the task-specific strategy, correct the work. While you can use the same general strategy for all problems, it will be necessary to recognize the task-specific strategies for tasks your students are working on.

While it is difficult to separate problem-solving skills from computation skills, try to determine where problem-solving skills break down in relationship to basic operations. Two frequent causes of failure to solve application problems correctly are failure to distinguish irrelevant from relevant information and failure to estimate answers.

Once you have identified the missing (or erroneous) strategy, teach the student to use the correct one; de-emphasize the production of answers by asking questions about the use of the strategy itself. (An example of this technique is included in Teaching Recommendation 1.) View problems as opportunities to practice or teach strategy use, not opportunities to find answers. This means focusing on explanations, questions, and feedback on the use of strategies, not answers. The following procedures should help facilitate this approach.

Verbal Mediation. Begin by demonstrating the strategy to the student, describing it aloud as you show how to work the problems. Next have the student practice saying the strategy with you as you guide him through doing the problems himself. Next ask the student to work the problem while saying the strategy aloud without you. Finally, teach the student to say the strategy to himself before beginning to work on a problem.

Lead Questions. Questioning can be an especially powerful device for teaching strategies. Lead questions, described in detail by Stowitschek, Stowitschek, Hendrickson, and Day (1984), are used to guide a student into strategy use by focusing on one or more of the strategic elements of the task before asking the student to actually work the task. Here is an example for the problem 47 + 28.

Strategy	Question	Desired Response
Select operation	"What kind of problem is this?"	"Addition."
Set up operation	"Where will you start adding?"	"7 plus 8."
Relevant vs. irrelevant information	"What does the fact that 7 + 8 will be more than 10 mean?"	"I have to regroup" [or "carry"].
Follow task-specific strategy	"If 7 + 8 is 15, where will you put the 5 ones?"	Student indicates the correct place.
	"Where will you put the 1 ten?"	Student indicates the correct place.

This kind of questioning recognizes that a problem requires a student to make many procedural decisions, not to simply write one answer.

Select Procedure. Sometimes it is effective to have a student select the correct equation for a problem rather than actually work the problem. This focuses her attention on the strategy, de-emphasizes the answer, and requires her to think through the problem from several possible directions.

For example, "Joy has 13 bicycles to fix. 4 are red. Jennifer brings her 10 more. She fixes two each day. What procedure would you use to find out how many days it will take her to fix all the bicycles?"

a.
$$\begin{array}{r} 13 \\ \times\ 10 \\ \hline \end{array}$$ then $3\overline{)130}$

b.
$$\begin{array}{r} 13 \\ +\ 4 \\ \hline \end{array}$$ then $$\begin{array}{r} 17 \\ +\ 10 \\ \hline \end{array}$$ then $2\overline{)27}$

c.
$$\begin{array}{r} 13 \\ +\ 10 \\ \hline \end{array}$$ then $2\overline{)23}$

d $2\overline{)13}$ then $2\overline{)10}$

Corrections. Questions can also be used to correct strategy errors without immediately giving away the answer. This shows the student that he can reason through the problem independently. An ideal sequence presented by Stowitscheck et al. works this way:

1. Demonstrate the strategy.
2. Use lead questions or open questions (ask the student to work on the whole item).
3. When errors occur, change the open question to a multiple-choice question.
4. If an error still occurs, change multiple-choice question to a restricted alternative question.
5. If an error still occurs, repeat the demonstration and start over.

For example, for the problem 8×6:

Device	Teacher	Student Response
Open question	Shows flash-card of 6×8.	"14."
Feedback and multiple choice	"The answer is not 14. Do you have to add or multiply in this problem?"	"Add."
Feedback and restricted alternative	"We don't add, so what do we have to do?"	"I don't know."
Demonstrate	Repeats demonstration with emphasis on operation sign.	

Feedback. Because you are teaching the student how to arrive at an answer, not the answer itself, feedback should be directed at strategy use. Often a student can arrive at a correct answer by using an incorrect strategy (e.g., guessing or working the problem backward). If you give feedback or praise in this case, you run the risk of inadvertently reinforcing the wrong strategy. To prevent this, refer to the correct strategy when giving feedback. For example, "Good for you. You must have paid attention to the sign because you multiplied" [or added, subtracted, etc.].

Recommendation 5: Teach Specific-Level Application Content and Terms

Difficulties in applying mathematics skills in application content are sometimes based on inadequate knowledge of the content rather than lack of proficiency in computation or problem solving. Thus, the direct assessment of specific-level application content may identify skills that should be targeted for direct instruction.

The list of applications skills in Figure 11.12 includes content sequences for time and temperature, money, and measurement of length, surface, volume, and weight (both metric and customary). From this figure you can see the magnitude of the task involved in teaching content-specific information. Content-specific information is to applications and problem solving what prior knowledge is to reading comprehension.

SUMMARY

Chapter 11 began by discussing math. Next it described survey-level procedures, provided some examples of survey material, and listed likely causes for failure at the survey level. Then it briefly discussed error analysis, reviewed specific-level procedures, and linked causes for specific-level problems to instructional recommendations. Our intent has been to illustrate the application of the curriculum-based task-analytical model to this domain. We have emphasized strategic behavior for two reasons. First, a curriculum-based task-analytical model permits analysis of cognitive behavior; second, math instruction in the absence of strategy instruction has little utility.

Study Questions

1. Give an example of each kind of knowledge.
    a. Rote
    b. Procedural
    c. Conceptual
2. A student who has determined that he does not have sufficient information to solve a problem has just
    a. determined what is called for.
    b. carried out the problem.
    c. estimated the answer.
    d. used cluster analysis.
3. Why is teaching story problems not the same thing as teaching problem solving?
4. List some critical and noncritical attributes of a fraction.
5. Why is it important for tests to sample strategic behavior? How can items be constructed to do this?
6. What are two possible reasons that a student can be accurate but slow at basic facts?
7. You have administered a basic facts rate test for a student and you find that she is above criterion. What is your next step?
8. Tell what kind of errors the student made in each problem.

a.	b.	c.	d.
46	243	781	21
+ 32	+ .63	− 48	+ 36
14	3.06	747	7,462

9. What would you do if a student did not know how to recognize relevant and irrelevant information on a survey-level test?
10. An evaluator gives a student a survey-level test and finds that he misses most of the application problems. What kinds of specific-level tests should be given next?

Chapter 12

Language

This chapter is based on material originally produced by
Dr. Theresa Serapiglia (Howell & Kaplan, 1980).

Communication—Pragmatics
- Survey-Level Testing
Collecting the Language Sample
Transcribing the Language Sample
Analyzing the Language Sample
    Syntax
        Syntactic Interference
    Vocabulary
    Pragmatics
    Mean Length of Utterance
- Specific-Level Testing
Syntactic Structures
Vocabulary/Semantics
Communication—Pragmatics
- Assessment Procedures
Before You Begin
Survey Procedure: Language Sample
        Purpose
        Directions
        Interpretation Guidelines
    Specific-Level Procedure 1: Structured Observation of Settings
        Purpose
        Directions
        Interpretation Guidelines
    Specific-Level Procedure 2: Mean Length of Utterance
        Purpose
        Directions
        Interpretation Guidelines
    Specific-Level Procedure 3: Syntax/Morphology Test
        Purpose
        Directions
        Interpretation Guidelines
    Specific-Level Procedure 4: Vocabulary Probe for Word Meanings
        Purpose
        Directions
        Interpretation Guidelines
    Specific-Level Procedure 5: Pragmatic Skills Probe
        Purpose
        Directions
        Interpretation Guidelines
    Specific-Level Procedure 6: Strategy Checklist
        Purpose
        Directions
        Interpretation Guidelines
Instructional Recommendations
    Recommendation 1: Use a Direct Approach

FOCUS: LANGUAGE

This chapter is about oral communication. Written communication (which we will refer to as *written language*) is discussed in chapter 13.

As you begin reading about oral language assessment, keep in mind that an in-depth study of all content domains is well beyond the scope of any text. This chapter provides an introduction to oral language evaluation and a foundation for formulating questions and making decisions. This Focus section will review the importance of language and discuss problems that may cloud an evaluation.

Importance of Language in Schooling

Language is considered by many to be the singularly most important tool for obtaining knowledge and skills, for communicating, and for survival. Children's success in school depends on how well they understand and use language, on their understanding of the language used by the teacher to teach. Schools have a tremendous amount of information to convey to children, most of which is transmitted verbally. Therefore, oral language skills are prerequisite to most instructional activities.

Language is the means by which we engage in extended thinking. Because language and thought are related, language influences and interacts with cognitive processes such as perceiving, conceptual thinking, understanding, remembering, and reasoning. It appears that as cognitive processes become more complex and more abstract, language plays an increasingly important role. Consequently, discrepancies in language development may impair the development of cognitive processes and children with discrepancies in language skills are often unable to benefit fully from regular school programs. These children have difficulty gaining information from verbal and printed messages. They may have problems demonstrating what they know and often are unable to express specific needs for help.

The failure to develop effective language for communication may be devastating and isolating. This failure has far-reaching societal as well as educational implications for a child. The ability to communicate with others is one of the foundations that lets us participate in society. Language is the means by which we are able to label our wants and needs, to express our feelings and emotions, and to form our social interactions. The degree to which a person learns and is able to use language may determine his or her ability to participate in the affairs of life.

OVERVIEW OF LANGUAGE EVALUATION

In language evaluation, as in the other content areas, we are interested in determining what to teach. To do this the evaluator must evaluate to derive specific instructional information. This chapter discusses procedures for assessing syntax and morphology, semantics, and pragmatics, three critical language domains.

There are a large number of theoretical bases from which to assess language. This chapter does not include an in-depth discussion or resolution of these theoretical bases, nor does it focus on the evaluation of the various processes theorists believe children use to understand and produce language. It describes assessment procedures that will enable you to decide what to teach mildly handicapped/remedial students with functional language problems and students who are acquiring English as a second language.

Definitions

While language as a content domain may be analyzed from a number of different perspectives, there are at least four general areas that lend themselves to treatment and are educationally important. They are:

- Syntax and morphology;
- Semantics;
- Pragmatics—communication; and
- Phonology, voice, and fluency.;

This chapter is limited to syntax, semantics and pragmatics. Phonology will not be covered. A content analysis for the targeted domains is shown in Table 12.1.

Syntax and Morphology

Syntax is the rule system that governs order of words in sentences. While there are many acceptable arrangements of words in English sentences, some arrangements are not acceptable. For example, we could say, "The ball is bouncing," "Bouncing is the ball," "Ball bouncing." However, we would not say, "Ball the is bouncing." English syntax rules do not permit this arrangement. The reference for combining noun phrases and verb phrases is shown in Table 12.1, Column I, number 1. While competent speakers may not be able to state syntactical rules that govern word order they demonstrate their knowledge by using the rules correctly.

Morphology is a subset of syntax. Basic units of meaning in English words are called *morphemes* and the rule system that governs how to combine morphemes to make words is called *morphology*. *Free* morphemes stand alone; they are often referred to as *root words*. Examples of free mor-

phemes are *talk*, *group*, and *tie*. There are also *bound* morphemes, which do not stand alone. These are the affixes we add to the beginning or ending of words to modify their meaning. Examples of bound morphemes are *-s*, *-er*, *-ed*, *-ing*, *-un*, *-al*, and *-sur*. When the morpheme *talk* is changed to mean a person who talk*s*, the morpheme *-er* is added to make the word *talker*. When we want to show past tense of *talk* we add the morpheme *-ed*. *Talk* is a free morpheme; *-er* and *-ed* are bound morphemes. Morphology guides how morphemes may be combined to form words and to alter meaning.

Not only are the rules of syntax and morphology consistent within a language, but the chronology or sequence in which typical learners acquire these rules is predictable. For a detailed discussion of syntax and morphology, we encourage you to read Wiig and Semel (1984) and Shames and Wiig (1982).

Semantics

Semantics is the study of meaning within language. It includes:

- Meaning of single words and word combinations;
- Multiple meanings of simple words;
- Figurative language; and
- The influence of content and structure on meaning.

Semantic skill is more than definitions of words in isolation. It is also knowledge and application of the constraints meaning imposes on the ways words are combined. English syntax permits, "The book reads the child." However, semantic rules (meaning rules) preclude that word combination. Books do not read; so the ways the word *book* may be used in a sentence are constrained by both syntax and semantics. A brief analysis of semantics is shown in Table 12.1, Column II, Parts A and B.

Pragmatics

Communication—pragmatics refers to the functions or purposes of language. Think about two people talking. Table 12.2 summarizes an organization for pragmatics suggested by Wiig and Semel

TABLE 12.1
Content analysis of language domains

I *Syntax/Morphology*	II *Semantics/Vocabulary*	III *Pragmatics*
A. Syntax/Morphology	A. Basic	A. One-Way Communication
1. Noun Phrase/Verb Phrase	1. Body Parts	1. Expresses Wants
2. Regular Plurals	2. Clothing	2. Expresses Opinions
3. Subject Pronouns	3. Classroom Objects	3. Expresses Feelings
4. Prepositional Phrases	4. Action Verbs	4. Expresses Values
5. Adjectives	5. Verb Tasks	5. Follows Directions
6. Interrogative Reversals	6. Animals and Insects	6. Asks Questions
7. Object Pronouns	7. Outdoor Words	7. Narrates Event
8. Negatives	8. Family Members	8. States Main Idea
9. Verb *be* Auxiliary	9. Home Objects	9. Sequences Events
10. Verb *be* Copula	10. Meals	10. Subordinates Details
11. Infinitives	11. Food and Drink	11. Summarizes
12. Determiners	12. Colors	12. Describes
13. Conjunction *and*	13. Adverbs	13. Compares and Contrasts
14. Possessives	14. Occupations	14. Gives Instructions
15. Noun/Verb Agreement	15. Community	15. Explains
16. Comparatives	16. Grooming Objects	B. Two-Way Communication
17. *Wh-* Questions	17. Vehicles	1. Considers the Listener
18. Past Tense	18. Money	2. Formulates Messages
19. Future Aspect	19. Gender	3. Participates in Discussions
20. Irregular Plurals	20. School	4. Uses Persuasion
21. Forms of *do*	21. Playthings	5. Resolves Differences
22. Auxiliaries	22. Containers	6. Identifies Speaker's Biases
23. Derivational Endings	23. Days of the Week	7. Identifies Speaker's
24. Reflexive Pronouns	24. Months	Assumptions
25. Qualifiers	25. Emotions	8. Formulates Conclusions
26. Conjunctions *and, but, or*	26. Numbers	
27. Conjunctions	27. Celebrations and Holidays	
28. Indirect and Direct Objects	28. Spatial Concepts	
29. Adverbs	29. Quantitative Concepts	
30. Infinitives with Subject	30. Temporal Concepts	
31. Participles	31. Shapes	
32. Gerunds	32. Greetings and Polite Terms	
33. Passive Voice	33. Opposites	
34. Complex Verb Forms	34. Materials	
35. Relative Adverb Clauses	35. Music	
36. Relative Pronoun Clauses	36. Tools	
37. Complex Conjunctions	37. Categories	
	38. Verbs of the Senses	
	B. Advanced	
	1. Reading Material Vocabulary	
	2. Content Area Vocabulary	
	3. Idioms/Figurative Language	
	4. Multiple Meaning of Words	
	5. Influence of Context on Meaning	

Source: K. W. Howell and J. S. Kaplan, *Diagnosing Basic Skills: A Handbook for Deciding What to Teach.* Columbus, OH: Charles E. Merrill Publishing Co., 1980.

TABLE 12.2
Framework for organizing pragmatics

Function	Uses	Examples
Ritualizing	Greetings, farewells, regulation of turn taking, etc.	"Hello." "How are you?" "See you later."
Informing	Give or request information.	"This chapter is about language." "What is the definition of pragmatics?"
Controlling	Commanding, warning, giving permission, threatening, refusing, offering.	"Summarize what you have read before you continue."
Feeling	Express attitudes/feelings. Respond to attitudes/feelings. Monitor attitudes/feelings of self and others.	"I believe thoughtful teachers can make a difference."
Imagining	Story telling, lieing, speculating, fantasizing.	The authors are excellent spellers.

Source: E. W. Wiig and E. Semel, *Language Assessment and Intervention for the Learning Disabled* (2nd ed.). Columbus, OH: Charles E. Merrill Publishing Co., 1984.

(1984). This listing and Table 12.1, Column III could be used to generate a table of specifications. Most discussions of pragmatics also address skills linked to understanding and applying shifts between being a speaker and a listener. These skills have verbal and nonverbal components. Some nonverbal components are physical proximity, gestures, and eye contact. Verbal components include turn taking, responding, and voice control. Good speakers use their voices to influence outcomes and good listeners interpret the intent of not only words but intonation and volume. In Table 12.1 , Column III, notice that skills associated with the role of listening and being responsive to others are summarized under Part B, two-way communication. While pragmatics is typically thought of as the functions of language between two or more people, pragmatics can also be conceptualized in a frame-

work of inner language or thinking. Inner language is used to cue or prompt, to inform, to question, to control, and so on. To use self-talk to mediate events, one must have adequate inner language. The use of pragmatics or functions of language occurs in a context of four variables (Wells, 1973; Wiig & Semel, 1984):

- Characteristics of participants—sex, age, status;
- Setting—situation for exchange (time and place);
- Topic of communication; and
- Goal, task, or intent of speaker(s).

Social Context of Language

Language has a social framework (Mahoney, 1975). In a social framework the function of language is to initiate and sustain interaction. A kid's language development depends in part on his interaction with his linguistic environment. His development depends on the extent to which the people around him are willing to communicate with him, to respond to what he says and encourage him by their understanding, and to allow him to learn to modify and expand his language. Family members, other adults, and peers are important in the child's social linguistic environment.

Social Rules

The child's understanding of sociolinguistic rules and her familiarity with social contexts are important aspects of language. Students who do not know the social rules of language usage may appear rude or insubordinate (Iglesias, 1985; Saville-Troike, 1976). For example, when the teacher says, "Would you like to do your spelling now?" the child who understands the sociolinguistic rules but does not want to do the assignment may say "Can I do it later?" or just sharpen her pencil a lot. A child who does not understand sociolinguistic rules might only say "no" and be considered unresponsive or rude.

Some children may not participate verbally because the social conditions they're accustomed to are missing (Philips, 1970). Not only are there sociolinguistic rules for turn taking or following directions, there are also different rules for the structure of discourse. In some cultures, stories and messages are *not* organized around a main idea and a sequence of events. They may be organized as associated topics. When a child's discourse style is different from the majority, she may have trouble understanding both oral and written messages. Research indicates that directly teaching children about classroom interaction styles will improve learning (Kawakami & Hupei Au, 1986).

Second-Language Learners

Social rules are not the only influence on the acquisition of language competence. The perceived status of a student's primary language and culture by majority language speakers influences second-language acquisition (Cummins, 1986). In assessing the language environment of second-language learners you may need to note the status of their language in our mainstream society. It is possible to enhance that status within the classroom. Teachers can teach students that all languages are valuable and can model the acceptance of diversity.

General Beliefs, Assumptions, and Misunderstandings

Some children do not develop language as quickly as their peers. Consequently, instruction that is appropriate for their peers may be inappropriate for them. These students must be taught language skills directly and systematically if they are to benefit from educational programming. However, some children are not receiving necessary language evaluation and instruction because their teachers do not attend to language. Certain beliefs and assumptions may encourage us to disregard language problems by attributing them to other causes. Let's look at some of these beliefs and assumptions.

The Child Is Just Quiet and Shy

The belief that the child is just shy and will come around in time may have damaging consequences if in fact she does need instruction and that instruction is not provided. Children who have language discrepancies but who are not behavior problems and who smile when we talk to them are frequently not identified as needing special help; therefore

they are not provided with appropriate language remediation.

School children can get by without speaking much and without being noticed for not speaking, especially in the upper grades. Students are expected to spend a lot of the school day listening and may not be required to give more than short answers. Wilt (1950) studied 568 children in 16 classes and reported that on the average the children he studied spent more than 2½ hours listening during a 5-hour school day, more than twice the amount estimated by their teachers. Teachers may also reinforce nontalking behaviors in the name of discipline.

It's Okay As Long As I Know What He Means

Some teachers respond to the message the child sends and ignore the way in which he sends it. For example, the child may ask, "Her coming, too?" and the teacher may respond, "Yes." Although it is always appropriate to respond to the message, if a child has a language problem, it is also important to notice the way he uses language so that a language intervention may be developed. Sometimes teachers "get used to" hearing certain sentence patterns. As a result, their sensitivity to a child's abnormal language may diminish over time. In addition, teachers are often not aware of the degree to which they fill in the gaps for the child. For example, one teacher we know was so convinced that all children in her special class had adequate language that she recorded a conversation between herself and one of her better students just to prove it to us. When she played back the tape, the conversation went like this:

Teacher: What is your favorite sport? [Pause] Basketball?
Student: Yes, basketball.
Teacher: How long have you been playing basketball? [Pause] Three or four years, hasn't it been?
Student: Yes.
Teacher: Are you glad we're going to be dismissed early today?
Student: Yes.

Teacher:	Do you know why we'll be dismissed early today?
Student:	Mud.
Teacher:	Yes, the rain is so bad that the buses need to get children home before the roads become too muddy.

The teacher had not been aware of the extent to which she had been supplying both the questions and the answers until she listened to the tape.

They'll Grow Out of It

A common misconception is that children's language problems are traces of immature language development they will "outgrow." Many early childhood specialists, including pediatricians, have been known to say, "Don't worry, he'll grow out of it," to parents of 5-year-olds who still aren't talking. This may not be true. It is *not* typical, or acceptable, for a 5-year-old to have a language problem. While some children do outgrow language problems, most don't.

A corollary belief is that as children are exposed to language models every day in school they will learn to understand and use the English language. These language models may or may not be adequate; again, time alone may not solve the problem. A study of the vocabulary and language structure of normal language learners and linguistically different children indicated that language deficiencies were maintained throughout the elementary school years (Serapiglia, 1978). Everyday exposure to the appropriate English language may not be sufficient in itself to enable linguistically different students to acquire adequate syntactic and vocabulary skills.

Language Isn't Learned in School

Most children learn language without purposeful direct instruction at home or at school. Language is usually learned so naturally that we seldom think about it as a remarkable feat. Language development norms indicate that children in typical learning environments master basic language structures between 3 and 5 years of age. Three-year-olds speak in three- to four-word sentences and use speech that is 75% to 90% intelligible. Four-year-olds use more complex sentences and can give an accurate, connected account of some recent experience. Ninety percent of 4-year-olds' speech is intelligible. By the time children with normal language development are 5 years old, they are able to use fully developed complex sentences of about seven to eight words and can carry on meaningful conversations with adults and children. Templin (1957) has stated that children learn to use an estimated vocabulary of about 13,000 words by age 6, 21,000 words by age 7, and 28,300 words by age 8.

Teachers have come to expect a high level of language competence from children when they enter school. It is generally taken for granted that once children reach elementary school, and especially the upper elementary grades, they will have become proficient in language. Children are expected to understand and interpret complex information, instructions, and explanations presented in oral and written form. Furthermore, the language of instruction is not only complex, but it is an academic language that may differ significantly from the language of social communication. Verbal instructions, directions, and explanations provided by both teachers and textbooks are geared to the language level of the majority of the children. Children who are not at this level will have difficulty.

It's the Speech/Language Clinician's Job

Yes and no. It is true that speech/language teachers have been trained in assessment and remediation of language. It's also true that in many school districts speech/language teachers carry a heavy caseload. Their teacher-to-pupil ratio often is anywhere from 1 to 45, to as high as 1 to 95. In some cases, there is no language teacher. It is not realistic to expect that the language teacher can provide all the language instruction necessary. A speech/language teacher may be able to work with a child for only 20 or 30 minutes twice a week. Yet children who need language instruction need lots of it. Language instruction seems to be more successful when it is integrated into the daily school program, which requires the involvement and participation of regular and special teachers. The process discussed in this chapter will provide a structure for language assessment and remediation that may be a vehicle for increased communication and cooperation between the speech/language clinicians and other teachers.

Severity and Causes

Handicapping Conditions

Estimates of the prevalence of speech and language handicaps vary. Determining the extent of the problem is complicated due to definitional problems and the fact that language problems often occur in the presence of other handicapping conditions (Hallahan & Kauffman, 1986). A 1984 report of school-aged children receiving special education and related services under P.L. 94-142 and P.L. 89-313 indicated that, of the general school population, about 2.5% were categorized as speech or language handicapped (American Speech-Language-Hearing Association, 1986). A large proportion of children with language problems (not speech problems) can be found within the traditional handicapping categories. These children are not included in the 1986 2.5% prevalence figure. Here are the estimated percentages of children ages 4 to 17 with oral language disabilities in each special education category (Marge, 1972):

- 100% of the profoundly mentally retarded
- 100% of the severely and moderately mentally retarded
- 80% of the mildly mentally retarded
- 100% of the congenitally deaf and hard of hearing
- 10% of the emotionally disturbed
- 50% of the specific learning disabled
- 95% of the speech handicapped (not included in other categories).

Various physical, sensory, intellectual, and psychological factors have been found to be related to inadequate language development. Many factors that may inhibit language development have been proposed in the literature. Some of these are insufficient stimulation and motivation, improper training, impaired hearing, inadequate intelligence, excessive parental or social pressure, inadequate speech mechanisms, lack of good speech models,

parent overprotection, and emotional trauma. Bilingual conflicts were also once cited; however, typical youngsters seem to benefit from rich multilingual environments and do not seem to suffer from opportunities to experience more than one language. When children from multilingual environments have communication disorders, another factor is probably operating. In addition to the factors listed above, some children do not develop language normally even though there is no apparent reason for their deficit.

Some causative factors—such as impaired hearing, inadequate speech mechanisms, and inadequate social–linguistic environments—need to be considered before or during the assessment process. These factors need to be considered because they are related to treatment programs.

The first of these is impaired hearing. Some indications of a hearing impairment are trouble hearing consonant sounds (which are softer than vowel sounds), voice production problems such as unusual pitch or quality of voice, unusual rhythms, persistent articulation errors, and trouble remembering and understanding long sentences. Children with hearing impairments may have trouble hearing different types of speech sounds. A child may have different hearing efficiency at different times. When a speech or language problem is suspected, be sure that a complete audiological evaluation is part of the assessment. New techniques make hearing evaluations of even young children with severe deficiencies feasible and reliable.

Children Who Do Not Speak English

In addition to the population of handicapped students with language problems, there is a rapidly growing group of school-aged children who are not proficient in English. They have a primary home language other than English or a dialect that is significantly different from the language used in classroom settings. While these kids are not handicapped in a traditional sense, their language differences place them at risk for school failure. Of the students who have a dialect or a primary home language other than English, 75% or *2.5 million* may have language differences great enough to interfere with their school performance (National Coalition of Advocates for Students, 1985). This diversity could be parlayed into a rich foundation on which to base instruction. Unfortunately, it is estimated that in two-thirds of the classrooms of children with limited English proficiency (LEP), instruction is not differentiated to accommodate linguistic differences (U.S. Department of Education, 1984). Approximately 25% of the classrooms in America serve students who are not proficient in English, and this percentage is growing. But consider this: Less than 4% of the teachers in the United States indicate they have any training that would prepare them to differentiate instruction for LEP students (National Coalition of Advocates for Students, 1985). At the time of this writing, in California alone there were more than 5,000 teachers on certification waivers (the state would not certify them for LEP) teaching LEP students. In 1986 the California teacher certification division granted only 550 ESL or bilingual endorsements (Valdez, 1986). This shortage highlights a long overdue need to reassess the role of *all* professionals who work with LEP students.

A LEP child may use nonstandard English codes that are considered inappropriate in social communications outside his linguistic community. The child's nonstandard language code could include syntax, vocabulary, communication strategies, or phonology that is different from that of standard English. It is important to recognize that these codes, while different, are legitimate and are not deficient. Still, the child with competence in the code used in his own environment may also need instruction and practice in standard English as an alternate language code. In that case, the school should provide language instruction and an opportunity to use the conventional forms of English while maintaining an attitude of respect for the child's native language or dialect. Subtle and overt behaviors displayed toward the child's native language and dialect indicate values and attitudes held by the educational community. These values will, in turn, influence the child's language performance. Children who learn that their native language or dialect is not something to be ashamed of and that standard English is worth learning can become proficient in both languages. The child can be competent in both codes and choose whichever is appropriate to the situation. Like millions of other

Americans, he would become a successful language code switcher.

An Explanation. We recognize that by juxtaposing a discussion of LEP students with a discussion of language handicapped students, we risk incurring the disapproval of professionals in the fields of bilingual instruction, English as a second language, proponents of nonstandard English, and special educators. However, it is important to recognize that these constituencies do not demand unique evaluative techniques. Students who do not speak English are not handicapped in a *traditional* sense. As a matter of fact, you have probably noticed by now that we do not believe in handicaps in a traditional sense. Individuals are only handicapped to the extent that environments cannot be organized to accommodate them. Our experience indicates that (a) students who are not competent in social or academic communication are functionally disabled, and (b) the techniques required to correct a lack of competency do not vary. By definition, limited-English-proficient students are not competent in social and academic English communication. While the *source* of difference for both LEP students and special/remedial students is not the same, the evaluation of their language proficiency often is. You can arrive at what to teach handicapped/remedial students and LEP students using the same evaluation procedures. A curriculum-based model of evaluation is appropriate for both.

SPECIFYING THE CONTENT OF ORAL LANGUAGE

Language Domains
As in other fields, the first step in language assessment is to decide what to evaluate. The major components of syntax, semantics, and pragmatics are presented in Table 12.1. The table is a compilation of elements most frequently noted as essential by linguists and language specialists. The content included in the table is content most likely to be appropriate for school-age children who have moderate language problems. It would need to be ex-

tended downward to accommodate children with severe language discrepancies. Specific settings and tasks may alter content and behavioral requirements. Think about the communication demands of settings in which you work as we review the items in Table 12.1.

The content sequence of Table 12.1 is based on studies of typical language development and typical adult language. It is appropriate for children with typical language development as well as for children with language delays. (Children with typical language development would include those who are acquiring English as a second language.) Most children with language delays follow the same sequence of language development; they just do it more slowly (Hallahan & Kauffman, 1986; Lackner, 1968; Lyle, 1965; Miller & Yoder, 1974; Wiig & Semel, 1984). Children who do not follow what is thought to be a typical sequence are called *disordered* (Wood, 1982). Since it is not known whether language skills *must* be learned in a particular sequence, the educational differences between children with language delays and language disorders may not be significant. Unlike other tables in this book, the content of Table 12.1 reads from top to bottom, rather than bottom to top. The order has been reversed to make it clear that each item of content is *not* necessarily a prerequisite to the next higher skill. So don't assume that because a child passes a higher-level skill she has mastered all lower-level skills. In general, however, skills with higher numbers are more complex than skills with lower numbers.

The tasks reflected in Table 12.1 include both receptive and expressive skills. Receptive tasks are those in which students identify, understand, or comprehend. Expressive tasks are those in which students produce a verbal response. The nature of the assessment tasks and the confidence with which the results of the receptive and expressive assessment can be interpreted are different. One important distinction between the assessment of receptive and expressive language is that expressive language is overt and directly observable while reception is covert and can only be inferred from a related overt response.

Criteria for acceptable performance (CAP) are not listed within the table because information relating to CAP for language skills is not available. However, there is a standard for language use that has been established by general consent and is universally recognized. That standard is conventional adult speech. Adult speakers of standard English virtually never say, "I goed there," "Him and her are coming," "The boys is playing," "He gots a big dog," or "I out the window saw them." Therefore, the criteria for all skills, while not formally determined, approach 100% accuracy. This means that even a few errors indicate a need for specific-level assessment. At the same time, a child's performance must be compared to that of his peers and analyzed in the context in which it is observed. Now let's briefly discuss each of the content areas.

Syntactic Structures

Again, syntax comprises rules relating to the structures of language. Teachers must have knowledge of the syntactic structure of the English language to determine which structure a child is able to use and which structure she has not yet mastered. On first observation it may appear that there are an infinite variety of types of sentences one can produce using English syntactic structures. While there is an infinite variety of ideas to express, actually there is a finite number of structures speakers use to produce sentences. These structures are combined to produce basic sentences at lower levels of language functioning. At higher levels of language functioning, speakers expand basic sentence patterns to produce more mature, complex sentences using syntactic structure to modify, coordinate, substitute, and subordinate. The basic sentence, "The boy ran," has been expanded in Table 12.3 to illustrate the use of the prepositional phrase, adjective, and adverb to modify. The use of a conjunction coordinates the elements of the thought. The relative adverb clause subordinates one idea to another.

Important syntactic structures listed in Table 12.1 are defined in Table 12.4 (pp. 286–287). Few of us have committed those structures to memory, so Table 12.4 can be a helpful reference. These content areas can be combined with behavior and conditions to form tables of specifications.

While tables will not be presented for all language areas, Table 12.5 (pp. 288–289) provides an

TABLE 12.3
The expansion of a sentence using syntactic structure

Sentence	Additional Syntactic Structure Used
The boy ran.	
The boy ran up the hill.	Prepositional phrase
The freckle-faced boy ran up the hill.	Adjective
The freckle-faced boy ran up the hill immediately.	Adverb
The freckle-faced boy ran up the hill immediately, but he stopped suddenly.	Conjunction
The freckle-faced boy ran up the hill immediately, but he stopped suddenly when he got to the top.	Relative adverb clause

example. The behaviors listed in the Table of Specifications for Syntactic Structures (Table 12.5) are (a) *imitates sentences,* (b) *produces sentences with prompts or in controlled situations,* and (c) *produces spontaneous sentences.* When the content and behavior are combined, they form tasks. For example when *pronoun* is the content and *imitates* is the behavior, the task requires the kid to imitate sentences that include pronouns. There is evidence to support the idea that a child's ability to imitate is closely related to his current level of linguistic competence and to his comprehension of utterances. Modeling with imitation is a valuable language-training procedure for children with language problems (Kauffman & Hallahan, 1981; Wood, 1982). *Notice the absence of tasks requiring the kid to identify the syntactic structure by name or to state the rules for the use of syntactic structure.* The labels for the structures and rules are specified for *teachers, not children.* For example, children may use *he, she,* and *it* appropriately without knowing the label *pronoun. Do not teach the labels!*

Vocabulary/Semantics
Vocabulary, the meanings of individual words, is a component of semantics. Individual words are not simply labels used in isolation, but represent relationships. Semantics takes into account meaning, underlying concepts, and the relationship of words and sentences to contexts and ideas. Vocabulary and semantic content is unlike the content for syntactic structures. Where there is a finite number of syntactic structures commonly used in English, the individual words and the contexts in which they are used are almost limitless. One can continue learning and using new vocabulary and developing new meanings for previously learned words throughout life. Vocabulary content is not similar from person to person. The vocabulary that each child will need is related to the context and environment in which he lives. Children who live in rural areas, urban areas, or institutions will have different vocabulary content.

A list of vocabulary categories has been suggested in Table 12.1. This listing is representative of words commonly used by children in early stages of word development. In addition to these basic vocabulary categories, it is imperative to include words in the initial assessment that have immediate utility for the child in everyday functioning as well as the vocabulary content that is necessary for learning. This prerequisite vocabulary must be taught if the student is expected to benefit from lessons. Update the semantic content of Table 12.1 as vocabulary demands change.

Communication—Pragmatics
The student does not use basic syntactic structures and vocabulary as an end in itself. Children and adults use language for a reason, usually to communicate. Language is used to affect the behavior and attitudes of others and to regulate activities and attention. These functions are referred to as *pragmatics.*

Table 12.1 lists common communication functions. The overall goal of pragmatics instruction is to increase the child's repertoire of communication strategies for use in critical communication situations. The teacher should identify critical communication situations that arise for particular children and add them to the content listing.

SURVEY-LEVEL TESTING

The steps one uses during a language evaluation, including the survey procedures about to be described, are outlined later in this chapter under the heading Assessment Procedures. The following discussion supplies necessary background for the procedures. Many teachers and speech/language clinicians believe that language assessment should be conducted with norm-referenced, standardized tests. They are assuming that language functioning can only be adequately determined by normative testing under conditions in which the stimulus, time, and circumstances are held constant. Muma (1973, 1978) has addressed the issue of standardization of language assessment and has concluded that assessment under standardized conditions is actually contradictory to what we know about language behavior. It places too great a restraint on the student's responses, making the responses less representative. The assumption that all speakers should respond to the same stimuli and circumstances in the same way is untenable (Bernstein, 1970; Gerber & Bryen, 1981; Shames & Wiig, 1982). For these reasons a language-sampling procedure for language assessment is recommended and described here.

Collecting the Language Sample

The first question asked at the survey level is, "Does the kid have a receptive or expressive problem?" Direct, purposeful observation of the child's language in everyday situations may tell you if there is a problem. We will describe a somewhat structured approach for use as a survey-level test if you suspect a language problem. This approach is called the *language-sampling procedure*. This method for determining the child's current level of functioning in language consists of obtaining a sample of her language behavior and transcribing and analyzing it. As a rule, if a child is able to produce complete sentences 50% of the time, the language-sampling technique can be used for assessment method.

The language sample should be representative of the child's language performance. To be completely representative, the sample would have to include a large number of sentences from the child in a large number of situations. As with any testing procedure, reliability will tend to increase with the number of items. We recommend collecting approximately 50 sentences. The number of utterances people have used for a language sample varies from a minimum of 10 sentences in the *Basic Inventory of Natural Language* (Herbert, 1979) to 100 sentences in the *Developmental Sentence Scoring Procedure* (Lee & Koenigsknecht, 1974) and the *Language Sampling, Analysis, and Training* (Tyack & Gottsleben, 1974). Wiig and Semel (1984) have noted that an even greater number of utterances may be needed to obtain a reliable and valid sample.

Various factors have been identified that affect children's natural language production. These factors should be considered in language sampling. It is the responsibility of the evaluator to create an environment that will encourage the child's performance and elicit the best possible sample. Prepare the environment carefully ahead of time. Pay close attention to all details of the testing situation such as timing and setting up equipment. Choose a setting that is familiar to the child for the language assessment. As an evaluator, you can use any space in which you and the child feel comfortable as long as you keep extraneous distracting factors to a minimum. You may want to sit at a level even with the child. Sometimes it helps to sit on the floor with younger children.

When acting as an evaluator, you must be willing to subordinate your interests to those of the child and to follow what the child thinks. You must respond to the child with vocabulary and grammatical forms she understands; you should not be instructive or corrective. If the kid perceives the situation as threatening, it could significantly limit her responses or confine them to those which she is confident she can produce. Let your face and voice show the child that it is safe and that you are interested in what she says.

Collect the language sample in at least three typical language situations. Have objects, devices, toys, photographs, and pictures immediately available. Younger children may require these tangible objects to stimulate conversation. The stimulus materials used by Lee and Koenigsknecht (1974) for young children were a doll family, a transport truck with small cars inside, a barn with farm animals, pictures, and the retelling of "The Three Bears" with the aid of pictures. You can present the stimulus materials one at a time as appropriate, but do not try to elicit responses by asking questions about the objects; simply use them to promote conversation. A useful technique with younger children is to allow them to play in an activity area and record their language as they play and interact with other children. In this case it is necessary to have a tape recorder with automatic volume control that can pick up the child's voice within a particular range. It may also be appropriate to evaluate the

TABLE 12.4
Language syntactic structures—A brief description

1. *Noun Phrase/Verb Phrase*
   A noun phrase may consist of a noun alone, a determiner and a noun, a pronoun, or a clause.
   A verb phrase may consist of a main verb alone, an auxiliary plus a verb, a verb plus a noun, adjective, or adverb.

2. *Regular Plurals*
   Indicate more than one.
   Nouns plus *-s* ending.

3. *Subject Pronouns*
   Noun substitutes.
   Singular pronouns—*I, you, he, she, it*
   Plural pronouns—*we, you, they*

4. *Prepositional Phrases*
   Phrases composed of a preposition followed by a noun phrase
   Commonly used prepositions are *in, to, for, at, on, from, of, with, by*

5. *Adjectives*
   Modify nouns
   Example: The boy threw the *red* ball.

6. *Interrogative Reversal Form for Questions*
   Sentence order is reversed, using simple auxiliaries.
   Example: Is she coming home?

7. *Object Pronouns*
   Singular pronouns—*me, you, him, her, it*
   Plural pronouns—*us, you, them*

8. *Negatives*
   Not and *n't* in contractions.

9. *Verb* be *as an Auxiliary*
   Forms: *am, is, are, was, were, be, being, been*
   Examples: He *is* running. They *are* laughing.

10. *Verb* be *as Copula*

Forms: *am, is, are, was, were, be, being, been,* any form of the *be* verb used to link a subject noun to a predicate.
Example: I *am* happy.

11. *Infinitives*
    to plus verb.
    Example: I want *to* eat a hamburger.

12. *Determiners*
    a, an, the, that, this, these, those

13. *Conjunction* and *to Join Elements*
    Example: I bought shoes *and* a hat *and* gloves.

14. *Possessive Nouns and Pronouns*
    Possessive nouns
    Singular pronouns—*my, mine, your, our, hers, his*
    Plural pronouns—*ours, yours, theirs*

15. *Noun/Verb Agreement*
    Noun and verb agree in number.
    Example: He *is* going. They *are* going.

16. *Comparatives*
    Regular comparatives with *-er* and *-est*
    Expanded irregular comparatives: *good, better, best*

17. Wh- *Questions*
    Questions beginning with *wh-*
    who, whose, what, where, which, when, why, how

18. *Past Tense*
    Regular past tense is formed by adding the suffix *-ed*
    Irregular past tense examples: *ran, saw, came*

19. *Future Aspect*
    going to, may, can, will, should

20. *Irregular Plurals*
    Example: *women, children, mice*

21. *Forms of do*

child's language as she interacts with a parent or other familiar adult.

For older children, have ready a list of topics that may be of interest. These can include familiar events, school and community activities, visits they have made, what they like to do after school, whom they play with, what shows they watch on TV, current events, and brothers and sisters. One topic that has a high probability of success is the child's dog, other pets, or animals in general. Pictures, photographs, filmstrips, and films may be used to stimulate discussion. You may ask the child to relate an episode or happening, retell a story, complete a partially told story, or explain how or why something happens. It helps to have some degree of familiarity with these topics yourself. As evaluators

TABLE 12.4
(continued)

   do, did, done
   Example: He will *do* the work. He *did* the work. He has *done* the work.

22. *Auxiliaries*
   Simple auxiliary constructions.
   has, have, had, can, could, would, should, might, must, ought, will, shall
   Example: I *can* go. He *has* a pony.

23. *Derivational Endings for Nouns*
   -er, -ist
   Examples: *painter, organist*

24. *Reflexive Pronouns*
   myself, yourself, himself, herself, itself

25. *Qualifiers*
   very, much, more, most, less, least, too, so, quiet, almost, just, little, pretty, somewhat

26. *Conjunctions* and, but, or
   and, but, or used to coordinate sentences
   Example: My aunt came *and* she brought me food.

27. *Conjunctions*
   Used to coordinate sentences: *after, before, because, if, since, so*
   Example: He ran away from home *because* he wanted to see the world.

28. *Indirect and Direct Objects*
   Relationship
   Example: Show the bus driver the dog. *Bus driver* is the indirect object. The *dog* is the direct object.

29. *Adverbs*
   Modify verbs, adjectives, complete sentences, and other adverbs. Primarily formed by adding the derivational suffix *-ly.*
   Example: *happily.*

Some adverbs do not change their form. Examples are *up, out, near, after, fast, in, around, here, there, always*

30. *Infinitives with Subjects*
   Example: I want *you to come* home.

31. *Participles*
   Verb occupying an adjective position.
   Example: She got sick *eating* pizza.

32. *Gerunds*
   Verb occupying a noun position.
   Example: *Throwing* things in school is bad.

33. *Passive Voice*
   The subject is acted upon by the object.
   Example: The cat is chased by the dog.

34. *Complex Verb Forms*
   Using multiple auxiliary constructions.
   Example: I *would have been* grounded for three days.

35. *Relative Adverb Clauses*
   Clauses embedded in sentences introduced by the words *where, when, why.*
   Example: The boy rode the horse home *when* he heard the signal.

36. *Relative Pronoun Clauses*
   Clauses embedded in sentences introduced by the words *who, which, what, that.*
   Example: The girl *that* wore the big white hat went home already.

37. *Complex Conjunctions*
   Used to subordinate sentences: *while, whether, until, unless, except for, although, however.*
   Example: She couldn't leave the mountain *unless* her horse came back.

we watched episodes of popular television programs so we could hold up our end of the conversation.

The question-answer format should be avoided if possible. If you do fall back on the use of questions, be sure that any questions you ask are more likely to elicit a whole sentence than a short phrase or one-word answer. Direct questions such as "What is the boy doing?" will frequently elicit a single word response such as "running." A language sample composed of "yes," "Tuesday," "blue," "maybe," and "Ralph" would be hard to analyze. Open-ended questions like "What happened at recess and how did the fight get started?" may elicit longer responses. If the child produces a high percentage of phrases or partial sentences, you may need to change *your* language. Use phrases such as "Tell me about it" or "Tell me more."

Arrange the situation to elicit higher-level structures and vocabulary. Provide the opportunity for the child to use the various structures listed in Table 12.1. Have him discuss something that a group did, something that happened in the past or will happen in the future to elicit plurals and past and future

TABLE 12.5
A table of specifications for language syntactic structures

Student's Name _____

Evaluator's Name _____

Date _____

	Imitates Sentences	Produces Sentences with Prompts or in Controlled Situations	Produces Spontaneous Sentences
1. Noun Phrase/Verb Phrase			
2. Regular Plurals			
3. Subject Pronouns			
4. Prepositional Phrases			
5. Adjectives			
6. Interrogative Reversals			
7. Object Pronouns			
8. Negatives			
9. Verb *be* Auxiliary			
10. Verb *be* Copula			
11. Infinitives			
12. Determiners			
13. Conjunction *and*			
14. Possessives			
15. Noun/Verb Agreement			
16. Comparatives			
17. *Wh-* Questions			

tense. The use of puppets can provide versatility in the use of language structure for the young child. You may direct the child to ask the puppet something to elicit interrogative reversals and *wh-* questions. Having the student tell the puppet to do something will elicit prepositions, and telling the puppet not to do something will elicit negatives.

Some children will be unresponsive. It may help to have another child present on these occasions. It may also be useful to provide a game that can be a stimulus for communication between youngsters. Record both children and transcribe the language

sample for the target student only. It can be difficult and challenging to take useful language samples from more seriously handicapped youngsters in conversational settings. In situations like these someone should monitor the child throughout the day and record all the language the child produces. In this way you will have a sample of the child's language behavior in functional, natural situations.

The more skilled you are in creating situations, the more information you will be able to derive from the language sample and the less assessment

TABLE 12.5
(continued)

		Produces	
	Imitates Sentences	*Produces Sentences with Prompts or in Controlled Situations*	*Produces Spontaneous Sentences*
18. Past Tense			
19. Future Aspect			
20. Irregular Plurals			
21. Forms of *do*			
22. Auxiliaries			
23. Derivational Endings			
24. Reflexive Pronouns			
25. Qualifiers			
26. Conjunctions *and, but, or*			
27. Conjunctions			
28. Indirect and Direct Objects			
29. Adverbs			
30. Infinitives with Subject			
31. Participles			
32. Gerunds			
33. Passive Voice			
34. Complex Verb Forms			
35. Relative Adverb Clauses			
36. Relative Pronoun Clauses			
37. Complex Conjunctions			

you will need to do at the specific level. Conversely, the less information you obtain from the language sample, the more you will need to do at the specific level.

The social situation is one of the most powerful determinants of verbal behavior. Labov (1969) has reported two complete interviews with a young black boy to illustrate this point. The first interview was conducted by a friendly white interviewer who put an object on the table in front of the boy and said, "Tell me everything you can about this." The child's responses were defensive and monosyllabic. The second interview was conducted by a black man who was familiar with the child's neighborhood. The interviewer brought along potato chips and the child's best friend. The three of them sat on the floor and discussed normally taboo topics. The child's language was strikingly different: the supposedly nonverbal child became quite adept at language.

Transcribing the Language Sample

Tape record the language sample. You may also try to write down the child's utterances directly at the time in addition to taping the language sample. Writing the sentences at the time they are produced will certainly expedite the transcription and analysis process; however, there are several dangers involved. First, writing down a child's responses may inhibit his language performance. Second, you may not be able to write fast enough or remember what the child actually says, and it is essential in this procedure to record *exact* utterances. Novice language evaluators tend to change what the child actually says to correspond more closely to conventional English. It is extremely difficult for adults to even copy unconventional phrasing. The student may say, "He running," and the evaluator may write, "He's running." Compare the sentences written during the time the language sample was taken with the sentences on the tape to eliminate this type of error. Never let an uninformed typist transcribe the language sample. While conducting research, Dr. Theresa Serapiglia once recorded the language of a number of students with language

problems, and her unwary typist systematically corrected all the students' errors as she transcribed the samples.

Make tally marks to indicate the approximate number of sentences a child has uttered during the conversation so that you know when you have obtained the 50 sentences. After you have taken the language sample, judge if the language the child produced during the session is comparable to the language she produces in other circumstances. If you do not know the child well, ask someone who does. If you judge that the language is not typical, take an additional language sample.

Transcribing the language sample is a critical part of the assessment process and must be done with precision. It should be transcribed and analyzed by the person who took the sample as soon as possible after it is taken. This allows that person to analyze the sample before forgetting much valuable information about inflection and voice. Each transcribed sentence must be evaluated by comparing it with the stimulus materials and conversational context. For example, the child's utterance may be transcribed as, "She is running up the hill." It is only possible to evaluate the use of the pronoun *she* if the evaluator can compare the pronoun to the stimulus to determine if in fact the child was referring to a female. Likewise, the use of the verb phrase *is running* and preposition *up* can only be evaluated by comparison to the stimulus or event being related. Using pictures or a short story as a stimulus allows the evaluator to make those comparisons more readily.

A child may be intelligible to one listener and not to another, depending on the listener's familiarity with that child. The standard for judging intelligibility should be that of an objective, unfamiliar listener. Again, utmost care must be taken to transcribe what the child said, not what you thought you heard. Here is an extreme example in which the evaluator "heard" what was in her mind rather than what was on the tape. The teacher had just evaluated the daughter of close personal friends and reported at a group training session that the child's language was adequate. The group asked the teacher to play the tape to review the evidence. The first question the evaluator asked was, "Where does your Dad work?" The answer the evaluator heard was, "My Daddy works in a garage." The others listening to the tape heard a series of sounds with an intonational pattern but were not able to hear even one intelligible word. The evaluator replayed the taped response several times before she was able to recognize and acknowledge that in fact the child's response was unintelligible, but that she knew that the father worked in a garage and thought she heard that response.

None of us speaks in sentences all the time, and though we do not expect children to speak in sentences all the time, single word utterances are not included for analysis. Obviously, a sentence does not need to be correct to be included in the sample. Sentences may contain incorrect grammar, vocabulary, and word order such as "Her gonna go?" or "Why dog barking?" Only different utterances are counted; repetitions of utterances are not counted. If the child repeats the same sentence several times, use only the first of the series. If the sentence is so garbled that it is unintelligible, it should not be included in the sample. The number of partial sentences and one-word responses should be tallied and recorded. The number of repetitive utterances and the number of unintelligible utterances can be noted, as well as the number of hesitations and disfluencies.

Decisions are made during the transcription process. One decision to be made is where each sentence stops and the next one begins. The most useful indication of the beginnings and endings of sentences is the child's intonational patterns and pauses. Some children use *and* frequently to begin sentences. You should recognize that *and* in that case is not joining thoughts to form compound sentences, but is used as a filler at the beginning of a sentence. Other conjunctions such as *because* and *so* may be overused by children to start sentences. As with the case of *and*, you should not consider these words to be conjunctions joining two sentences, but fillers. A child may produce a long, rambling sentence by stringing together several noun phrases such as "There is a boy and a truck and a dog and a ball and a tree and a flower and a cloud and the sun." In sentences like this, count only two repeated elements.

Analyzing the Language Sample

Syntax

Once the sample has been transcribed, you are ready to begin analysis. The first step in analysis is to identify those sentences with syntactic errors or omissions. Read over each sentence and determine if the sentence sounds like one that an adult speaker with conventional usage would say. It may help to rewrite the sentence in conventional form, using information you remember about the context of the sentence. For example, the child's sentence may be, "I gots three pencils," and you determine that the child attempted to say "I have three pencils." Next identify the type of error. If you know the content, you may be able to do this from memory, but it is easier to tally the errors directly onto a table like Table 12.1 or Table 12.4. This will save time. Score the response as correct if the student has produced the target syntactic structure; if not, leave it blank. It is important to recognize that a sentence may be correct but lack desired syntactic sophistication. Because of this, it is often a good idea to search the language sample for evidence of each target skill. When you find that the student has not produced the structure, you will have to go back and use specific-level questions and statements to elicit the syntactic structures.

In Table 12.6 the first utterance has an error in subject pronoun and an error in past tense. Sentence two contains an interrogative reversal error that was identified with the aid of a comment about the student's intonational pattern. Sentence three has no syntactic errors, but is very simple. The numbers after each utterance are taken from Table 12.1.

Syntactic Interference. Evaluators need to determine if omissions or errors in syntax are related to interference points between other languages or dialects and English. Following is a summary of (a) the syntactic interference points between Spanish and English and (b) the syntactic features of Black nonstandard English that differ from standard English (Hopper & Naremore, 1978). The syntactic interference points between Spanish and English are:

TABLE 12.6
Language transcription examples

What was said	What should have been said	Error type (Keyed to Table 12.1)
1. After wash her hair what did her do?	What did she do after she washed her hair?	3, 18
2. I could do that Connie? [intonation indicates question]	Could I do that, Connie?	6
3. I ran.	This morning before school I went out running.	Not complex

1. The -s ending is often omitted in plurals, possessives, and third person singular verbs. Also, past tense endings may appear to be absent. ("They play there yesterday.") Comparative endings on adjectives are not used. Spanish employs added words rather than suffixes to show comparatives. ("His shirt is more pretty.")
2. Negative commands may be expressed by *no* instead of *don't.* ("No go there.")
3. Articles may be absent from speech. ("She is teacher.")
4. Spanish employs *to have* in many idioms for which English uses *to be.* ("I have hunger," or "He has six years.")
5. *Do* may be absent from questions. ("You like ice cream?")

Syntactic features of nonstandard Black English that differ from standard English are listed below.

1. The expression of possession is different. ("Joe book.")
2. Negation is expressed by a double negative or *ain't.* ("I ain't got no car.")
3. Subject–verb agreement differs. ("We is here.")
4. The -s ending is omitted from the third person singular verbs. ("She laugh.")

5. The word *is* is not necessary in present tense. ("He here.")
6. *If* constructions are changed. ("I find out do she want to stay.")
7. *-ed* past tense may be omitted. ("He walk.")
8. Future tense of verbs may be expressed differently. ("He 'gon go.")
9. *Be* expresses habitual action. ("He be sick.")

While this chapter does not deal extensively with articulation problems, they are so alarming to teachers that we'll briefly mention dialect and culturally different speech codes. The major differences between standard English and nonstandard Black English and the major interference points for Spanish speakers learning English have been summarized by Hopper and Naremore (1978). Phonological interference points between Spanish and English are:

1. Initial and final voiceless plosives are not aspirated in Spanish. *Coat* may sound like *goat. Pig* may sound like *pick.*
2. Spanish has neither voiced nor voicelsss "th," so the child may substitute "d" for voiced "th," giving *dis* instead of *this*; "s" may substitute for voiceless "th," giving *sing* instead of *thing.*
3. Spanish makes no distinction between "b" and "v."
4. Spanish has the "s" sound but not the "z," "zh" (as in *treasure*), "sh" (as in *shop*), and "j" (as in *jump*).
5. "r" and "l" may be substituted for one another.
6. The vowel sounds in the English words *pig, fat,* and *sun* are not used in Spanish. (*Pig* may become *peeg, fat* may become *fet,* rhyming with *set,* and *sun* may sound as though it rhymed with *John.*)

Phonological interference points between Black English and standard English are as follows:

1. "r" and "l" may be omitted before consonants in the last sound in a word.

2. Consonant clusters at the end of words will be shorter.
3. Final consonants will be weaker.

Vocabulary

It is difficult to make good survey decisions about a child's functional level in vocabulary by analyzing a language sample alone. Sometimes it is obvious in the sample that a child's vocabulary skills are deficient because of his limited word choice or the use of such fillers as "that thing," "you know that thing," or "that riding thing." Other times you come away with the feeling of just not being sure. In that case, specific-level assessment will be needed.

Pragmatics

The language sample may also be used to determine the child's skills in communication, though an interview of her teacher or family may help. While performance standards for communication are not precise, the child's peer group can be used as a comparison standard. Using the pragmatic content in Table 12.1, scan the language sample or inquire during the interview for evidence of successful use of each function. Here is an excerpt from a child's language sample.

"I seen them on television. And this other guy got robbed and the other guy got mad. And he, and he, well there was a bad guy. The car was all torn up. The lady said,

'Give me the money.' They bombed the vices. They cops, do you know?"

In this sample the child does not appear to be telling events in sequence or using subordination as an aid in organizing his material. Since he has not used subordination to decide what to feature and what to subordinate, his story lacks order. You would record this information on Table 12.1 as No Pass (NP) for "Sequence Events" (Part A, item 9) and "Subordinate Details" (Part A, item 10) This indicates that specific-level testing may be needed in those areas.

Mean Length of Utterance

A traditional method for assessing children's language development is to determine the average length of their utterances. After the language sample has been transcribed onto the transcription sheet, the evaluator can determine the mean length of the child's utterances (MLU). Figure 12.1 is an example of calculating the MLU. Count the number of words and divide by the total number of sentences. Count each word only once. If the child repeats, as in the utterance, "I ... I am going to see the dolphins," or "That ... that dolphin has a ball," count the words *I* and *That* only once. If the child corrects his sentence, as in sentence two in Figure 12.1, count the corrections, not the words the corrections replace. Do not count filler expressions such as "you know" or "ah, ah" as in sentence four.

FIGURE 12.1 Calculating the mean length of utterance

Sentence	Repetitions and Fillers not Counted	Number of Words per Sentence
1. That ... that dolphin has a ball.	that	5
2. And, uh, the dolphin the fat dolphin has a big nose.	and, uh, the dolphin	7
*3. And, uh, it's the ball I liked.	and, uh	6
4. Pretty soon he swam uh uh away under the water.	uh, uh	8
5. And, uh, we bought drinks and sandwiches and chips and salad.	and, uh, and, and	7
	Total Words	33
	MLU	6.6

*Count "it's" as "it is."

Count contractions as two words. Do not count more than two *and's* plus the words that *and* connects (as indicated by sentence five in Figure 12.1). Do not count stereotypic starters like those in sentences two, three, and five, "and uh."

In cases in which the child's mean length of utterance is low compared to developmental norms and there are no errors in syntactic structures, one appropriate language goal would be to increase the child's mean length of utterance. Developmental norms indicate that the approximate mean number of words per utterance is from 2 to 3.5 words for 2- to 3-year-olds, 4 to 6 words for 4- to 5-year-olds, 6 to 7 words for 6-year-olds, and 7 to 8 words for 7- to 8-year-olds (Templin, 1957).

When analyzing the language samples of children who are functioning at higher levels in language, the mean number of words per sentence and the number of different kinds of structures included in the sentences should be considered simultaneously. A low number of words per sentence is a signal that the student is probably not incorporating various language structures into his sentences and is not producing mature, expanded sentences.

Some caution is needed here. Listeners are inclined to credit speakers who have a high mean length of utterance with advanced language performance when the primary characteristic of their language is actually verbosity. Verbose speakers use stylistic devices to modify, qualify, repeat, and pad the main argument. Listeners often credit speakers like this with saying something intelligent (Labov, 1969). However, have you ever felt overwhelmed and impressed with a person's speech, only to wonder later what he really said? We notice this phenomenon most frequently in election years.

SPECIFIC-LEVEL TESTING

Syntactic Structures

The survey-level language-sampling process is rarely sufficient because the child does not have the opportunity to produce all the syntactic forms. Specific-level assessment should be conducted to systematically assess those syntactic structures that were either not produced in the language sample or about which you have conflicting or insufficient information. This method uses direct statements and questions designed to prompt the child to respond with particular structures. Caution is necessary because often kids will respond in ways that are unexpected, but not necessarily incorrect. For example, "Tell me what you did yesterday" is a request designed to elicit a response that includes a verb in the past tense. If the child responds by saying, "Boyd and me like to play ball," the response is not incorrect because it's not the target response. It is simply not the target response. Language is so complex that expecting a child to respond to particular stimuli with particular responses is not realistic.

To determine if the child can imitate an utterance, model a sentence and ask him to repeat it. If he is speaking in phrases you should also ask him to expand his response to determine if he is able to speak in complete utterances. You can ask him to "Say the whole thing" or "Tell me some more."

Determine if the child can produce spontaneous sentences with or without the use of cues and prompts. The child's progress can be assessed on a continuous basis by evaluating his use of prompts and recording the progression from dependence on explicit models and prompts to approximating the target with more subtle prompts and finally to producing spontaneous sentences without prompts. The child's reliance on explicit prompts over a long period may indicate that the level of difficulty of the target is too high.

Vocabulary/Semantics

Compose vocabulary lists as appropriate. Be sure they coincide with the words you know to be functional and meaningful to the child in her situation. Determine if she can identify the vocabulary by asking her to identify the objects, persons, and events when given the vocabulary orally. Ask her to label the objects, body parts, and concepts presented to assess expressive vocabulary.

Once the child has mastered the basic vocabulary, it is also essential that her knowledge and use of vocabulary be assessed on those particular words that she needs in order to comprehend a particular unit of instruction or reading material. To accomplish this you must first identify those vocabulary words that will be used. Review the material and select those words that may cause difficulty. You may assess a student's comprehension of the vocabulary by asking her to identify persons, things, or events you have labeled, or by responding to stimuli in which the vocabulary words are used in familiar and unfamiliar contexts. This can be done by asking the student to match synonyms to the sentences in which they make sense. Assess expressive vocabulary by asking her to give definitions, synonyms, and meanings and to use the target words in sentences in familiar and unfamiliar contexts (Barrett, Huisingh, Jorgensen, & Zachman, 1983).

Communication—Pragmatics

Create communication situations appropriate to the individual to assess specific pragmatics. The assessment can be conducted over a period of time using either simulated or real-life events. Follow a procedure similar to the one used to obtain the survey sample except you must structure opportunities for the student to display specific skills. For example, if you want to sample "gives instructions" (Table 12.1, section III, number 14), you would need to create a situation where the student is required to give directions. This situation could be a game or a lesson in a cooperative peer group. In this kind of situation you could also observe whether the student "considers the listener."

When interviewing a parent or teacher, be sure to ask about each content item. One of the authors once asked a teacher if his 10-year-old student had any communication problems. The teacher said no. However, when asked about each item, the teacher indicated the student could actually pass only items 1 and 6.

ASSESSMENT PROCEDURES

Before You Begin

Assemble materials and equipment before meeting with the student. You need to:

1. Determine if the student produces complete sentences 50% of the time. If not, you will need to go directly to specific-level testing in all areas.
2. Decide on settings for conversation and assemble any stimulus materials you may need. Select settings with the goal of eliciting a large number of natural responses. Plan to sample in at least three settings.
3. If you plan to include other students and if you plan to sample across several settings—more than one class, recess, lunch, at home, or on the bus—schedule appointments ahead of time.
4. Set up a tape recorder. Record student responses so you can refer to them.

Survey Procedure: Language Sample

Purpose. To find out if there is a discrepancy between the student's performance and what is required for communication competence.

Directions.
1. Elicit a 50-sentence (or more) sample.
   a. One-word utterances or short phrases are not counted as part of the 50-sentence minimum but are included in the transcription.
   b. Sentences with incorrect grammar are counted as part of the 50-sentence minimum, e.g., "Him gonna cry?" or "Why Lee Lee barking?"
   c. Structure the conversation to elicit plurals, past and future tense, vocabulary, etc. Use tables of specifications to guide you. See pages 285–290 for a discussion on how to elicit a variety of responses.
2. Use props (pictures, comics, games, toys) and other students to create a context for conversation. Avoid asking questions.
3. Transcribe the sample.
4. Analyze and tally errors using tally sheets or tables of specifications based on Table 12.1. Summarize errors across syntax and morphology, semantics, and pragmatics.
   a. Determine sentence boundaries.
   b. Analyze each sentence in the context of the conversation.

c. Do not analyze unintelligible responses; just total them.
d. Count only the first utterance of a repetition. Analyze and record only two repeated elements in a sentence where there are strings of the same element.
e. Tally the number of partial and one-word responses, repetitions, hesitations, disfluencies, and unintelligible responses.

5. Note any areas where errors or omissions occur. The CAP is acceptable adult speech.

Interpretation guidelines. It is important to remember that language is a complex process. Rarely does any student need instruction in only semantics, or only syntax/morphology, or only pragmatics. Therefore, it is a good idea to answer all of the following questions on the basis of the survey-level sample and to use each specific-level procedure that is indicated.

Question. Is the student's language competence at acceptable levels?

If yes, cease evaluation, check referral, or repeat the survey-level procedure in another setting. Use Teaching Recommendation 1.
If no, move to the next question.

Question. Does the classroom setting appear to inhibit communication?

If yes (or if you are unsure), observe the classroom (Specific-level Procedure 1).
If no, check the next question.

Question. Does the student say enough for you to focus on a problem?

If yes, check the next question.
If no, test mean length of utterance (Specific-level Procedure 2).

Question. Are there consistent error patterns in one or more domains—syntax/morphology, semantics, or pragmatics?

If yes, test error patterns (Specific-level Procedures 3, 4, and 5).
If no, ask the next two questions.

Question. Are there errors in fluency, phonology, and/or voice?

If yes, refer student to a specialist for further evaluation.
If no, check the next question.

Question. Does the student fail to communicate in spite of adequate prerequisite skill?

If yes, test communication strategy (Specific-Level Procedure 6).
If no, repeat analysis by returning to the first of these questions.

Specific-Level Procedure 1: Structured Observation of Settings

Purpose. To find out if the setting inhibits communication.

Directions.
1. Design an observation checklist or prepare to record and analyze communication transactions within the classroom. For a review of general observation procedures, see chapter 7, pages 126–131. Look for (a) frequency of opportunities for students to receive comprehensible information, (b) frequency of opportunities for students to produce responses, (c) quality of communication environment specific to meaningfulness of messages and acceptance of communication attempts of students with discrepant skills, and (d) appropriateness, frequency, and quality of corrective feedback. The checklist in Figure 12.2 can be used to organize observations and analyze data.
2. Collect setting data.
3. Summarize and analyze.
4. Compare setting to the standard for a language learning environment.

FIGURE 12.2
Checklist for structured observation

Opportunity to Learn Language	Yes	No
1. Is the presentation understandable—semantics and syntactic structure at correct level?	___	___
2. Is the presentation meaningful—linked to prior knowledge or interest of student?	___	___
3. Is there visual support for verbal input—pictures, graphs, role playing, objects, gestures, etc.?	___	___
4. Is the student given frequent opportunity to respond?	___	___
5. Is there monitoring for understanding?	___	___
6. Are corrections linked to critical attributes of skill and to meaningfulness?	___	___
7. Are there multiple models (peers and teachers) available?	___	___
8. Is the classroom structured to increase frequency of communication?	___	___
9. Do peers and teacher have strategies for engaging a shy student who would remain silent if given a choice?	___	___
10. Are peers and teacher comfortable communicating with the student or do they look away or move away when student initiates contact?	___	___
11. If student is acquiring English as a second language, is the primary language and culture of the student valued?	___	___
12. Is there collaboration with other classes, activities, and the home to insure focus, quality, and frequency of opportunity?	___	___

Interpretation guidelines. If the setting seems to inhibit communication, use Teaching Recommendation 2.

Specific-Level Procedure 2: Mean Length of Utterance

Purpose. To find out if the student's overall sentence length is deficient.

Directions.
1. Use the language sample. Count the number of words in each utterance (sentence).
   a. Do not count repetitions and fillers.
   b. Count contractions as two words.
   c. Count self-correction but not words correction replaces.
2. Count the number of sentences.
3. Divide by the number of sentences.
4. Compare to standards for mean length of utterance (page 294).

Interpretation guidelines. Build fluency and sophistication using Teaching Recommendation 7 as well as 2, 3, and 8.

Specific-Level Procedure 3: Syntax/ Morphology Test

Purpose. To find patterns of syntax errors and omissions.

Directions.
1. Develop a probe that will permit the student to initiate and produce the structures in question.
2. a. For a *produce* response ask a question or show specific pictures to elicit the structure. Elicit about 10 responses for each form of concern. If the student cannot produce responses, move to imitate.
   b. For an *imitate* response say to the student, "Say this, 'The boy walked to town.'" Include syntactic/morphological

structures of concern. Again, provide about 10 items for each form.

3. Record and transcribe the responses.
4. Analyze, tally, and summarize the responses using Table 12.1.

Interpretation guidelines. Teach specific structures using Teaching Recommendations 3 and 6.

Specific-Level Procedure 4: Vocabulary Probe for Word Meaning

Purpose.   To find patterns of vocabulary errors or omissions.

Directions.
1. Select or develop a test to sample classes of words the student does not seem to know. The words may be drawn from materials used in the classroom, vocabulary used for instruction, and vocabulary used for social interaction. Review chapter 9 for additional considerations. Include formats that let you sample single meanings, multiple meanings, and meaning based on context. Limit the length of the question or stimulus to ensure that the student has a chance to show you what he knows. Start with oral production and move to recognition–identification tasks only if the student fails to produce definitions.
2. Say to the student, "What is a _____?" for a production response. Say, "Point to the _____," for an identification response.
3. Record the responses.
4. Transcribe, score, and summarize the responses. Use a tally that follows your table of specifications or Table 12.1.
5. Identify categories of words with which the student has difficulty.

Interpretation guidelines. Use Teaching Recommendations 4 and 6.

Specific-Level Procedure 5: Pragmatic Skills Probe

Purpose.   To find patterns of pragmatics errors or omissions.

Directions.
1. Based on Table 12.1, create situations that permit you to sample skills. Include situations in which the student must decide when to use the skill as well as situations in which he is asked simply to use the skill.
2. Record student responses during the situation.
3. Transcribe, analyze, and summarize the responses.
4. Judge if the responses are adequate for the student's communication settings.

Interpretation guidelines. Use Teaching Recommendations 5 and 6.

Specific-Level Procedure 6: Strategy Checklist

Purpose.   To find out if the student is competent in communication.

Directions.
1. Develop a strategy checklist based on your observations of communication demands and on language literature or use the one shown in Figure 12.3.
2. Conduct the observation-interview and record status of each item. This checklist is best filled out by a group of individuals who are familiar with the student.
3. Summarize and analyze information and note status on strategy checklist.
4. Disregard items marked "yes." List items marked "no" as instructional objectives. Continue to test items marked "unsure."

Interpretation guidelines. Use Teaching Recommendations 8 and 1 for those skills missed on the checklist.

Instructional Recommendations
For students whose language competence is below expectations, the following instructional recommendations are indicated.

FIGURE 12.3
Checklist for communication strategies

Strategy	Yes	No	Unsure
Does the student:			
Have a purpose-intent for communication?	_____	_____	_____
Think about communication intent?	_____	_____	_____
Plan ways to accomplish intent?	_____	_____	_____
Monitor to see if intent is being met?	_____	_____	_____
Recognize when a problem occurs?	_____	_____	_____
Analyze problem for solution?	_____	_____	_____
Recognize when assistance is needed?	_____	_____	_____
Recognize resources for solution?	_____	_____	_____
Seek appropriate help?*	_____	_____	_____
Adjust responses as result of analysis?	_____	_____	_____
Recognize when intent is met?	_____	_____	_____
Verify intent is met through alternative message?	_____	_____	_____
Actively plan to incorporate new language skills into old?*	_____	_____	_____

*A language learner's willingness to *risk* is a major factor in acquiring communication competence (Wong-Fillmore, 1986).

1. Use a direct approach to teach syntax/morphology, semantics, and pragmatics in communication contexts.
2. Modify settings to increase opportunities for communication.
3. Teach syntax and morphology.
4. Teach semantics.
5. Teach pragmatics.
6. Focus instruction on error patterns within specific domains—syntax and morphology, semantics, and pragmatics.
7. Increase the number and richness of ideas.
8. Teach control strategies for monitoring and modifying communications with others and for inner language. Include instruction on how the student can increase opportunities for communication input/output.

Recommendation 1: Use a Direct Approach

Direct refers to emphasis across language domains as well as instruction for acquisition of new skills and instruction for fluency, generalization, and maintenance. This direct teaching is rich with models and meaningful opportunities to use "new" skills. *Direct* does not imply meaningless drill or absence of context. What it does mean is instruction focused on objectives and optimal use of learning time. In a direct approach, you decide when the context of "natural communication" does not afford sufficient opportunities for examples and practice and when it does. Introduce a new language skill in isolation when natural opportunities are infrequent. However, this isolation is not the isolation of a "black box"; it is the isolation of a teacher-generated communication opportunity. In a direct approach you recognize that the student must become an active, not passive, receiver of language learning.

Recommendation 2: Modify Settings to Increase Opportunities for Communication

People acquire language competence in warm and supportive environments in which there are high expectations for communication from all members of the group. In settings that enable and support all students there is both encouragement to communicate and direct instruction when information is required (Westby & Rause, 1985).

Recommendation 3: Teach Syntax and Morphology

Teaching sentence structure and word formation requires knowledge of the content and allocation of instructional time. Interventions may vary from *low context* to *high context* and from *recognize–identify* responses to *produce* responses. Wiig and Semel (1984) point out that there are some general principles for selecting instructional formats and for designing instruction.

1. Unfamiliar word and sentence formation rules should be introduced and sequenced according to normal developmental sequences or established orders of difficulty.
2. The word selections featured in phrases, clauses, and sentences used for intervention should be highly familiar. They may be selected from vocabulary lists for age or grade levels at least 3 years or grades below the child's current vocabulary age or grade level.
3. Sentence length in number of words should be kept to an absolute minimum. This may be achieved by limiting sentence length to 5 to 10 words and phrase or clause length to 2 to 4 words. Minimum sentence length will depend upon the syntactic complexity of the units for which the rules apply.
4. Pictorial or printed representations of words, phrases, or clauses should be given for all spoken sentences. Pictures of referents for content words with referential meaning may be used in association with printed representations of nonreferential or function words.
5. Unfamiliar word or sentence formation rules should be introduced in at least 10 illustrative examples. The examples should feature different word selections.
6. Knowledge of word or sentence formation rules should be established first in recognition and comprehension tasks and then in formulation tasks.
7. The knowledge and control of word and sentence formation rules should be established first with highly familiar word choices. It should then be extended to contexts with higher level or less familiar vocabulary or with unfamiliar concepts.
8. The knowledge and use of word and sentence formation rules should be tested in at least 10 examples that feature vocabulary not previously used. (pp. 436, 437)

Recommendation 4: Teach Semantics

Vocabulary instruction was discussed in chapter 9, pages 169–170. Those recommendations also ap-

ply to vocabulary instruction for oral language. In this section we will describe a few additional approaches to increasing word knowledge with the recognition that research on teaching vocabulary indicates that teachers do not allocate enough time for it (Jenkins & Dixon, 1983). The lesson formats we will discuss include examples, synonyms, morphemes, definitions, and semantic features. For additional information on these formats, review Carnine and Silbert (1979) and Johnson (1983).

Examples. Teach new words by example when the student does not have a synonym for the word, does not know the morpheme, or lacks the vocabulary to acquire a definition. Concepts are frequently best defined by examples and nonexamples that focus on critical attributes. (See Concept Analysis, chapter 11.)

Synonyms. If a student already knows the meaning of a synonym, introduce a new word by linking it to the old. For example:

Teacher:	*"Sclerosis* [new word] means *hardening* [known word]. What is another word for *hardening?"*
Student:	"Sclerosis."
Teacher:	"Yes, *sclerosis* means hardening. When arteries harden, we can say *hardening of the arteries* or *blank* of the arteries. What's another way to say *hardening of the arteries?"*

To insure that the student knows that the new word is not exclusively linked to the words used in the example, be sure to change the example. In the case of *sclerosis,* to insure that it's not linked to arteries only, you would practice a sentence in which you meant hardening of plant cell walls.

Teacher:	"Plants become woody when *hardening* of the cell walls occurs. Use your new word in this sentence. Plants become woody when *blank* of the cell walls occurs."
Student:	"Plants become woody when sclerosis of the cell walls occurs."

FIGURE 12.4
Semantic features—
Vehicles (*Source:*
Adapted from D. D.
Johnson, "Three
Sound Strategies for
Vocabulary Develop-
ment." *Ginn Occasional
Papers: Writings in
Reading and Language
Arts.* Columbus, OH:
Ginn & Co., 1983.)

| | | Concept: Vehicles | | | | | | | |
| | | Features | | | | | | | |
Words	Carries Things	Land	Air	Sea	Windows	Wheels	Wings	Fuel
Tricycle	+	+	–	–	–	+	–	–
Bicycle	+	+	–	–	–	+	–	–
Automobile	+	+	–	–	+	+	–	+
Truck	+	+	–	–	+	+	–	+
Bus	+	+	–	–	+	+	–	+
Train	+	+	–	–	+	+	–	+
Tanker	+	–	–	+	?	–	–	+
Airplane	+	+	+	–	+	+	+	+
Helicopter	+	+	+	–	+	+/–	–	+
Space shuttle	+	+	+	–	?	+	+	+
Wagon	+	+	–	–	–	+	–	–
Rickshaw	+	+	–	–	–	+	–	–

Key: +   Applies to concepts
      –   Does not apply to concepts
      ?   May apply to concepts
     +/–   Sometimes applies to concepts

Morphemes.   Opportunities for generalization occur when something can be used many ways. When
units of meaning are taught and then the student is
given opportunities to use that information to define new words, it is likely that he will learn more
words. For example; Teach the student that *re-*
means "do again." Next teach that *unite* means
"join." Ask, "What does *reunite* mean?" The answer: "Join again."

Definitions.   When teaching definitions, do not ask
students to go to the dictionary and look something
up. Teach the meaning of the word by defining it as
you did in teaching morphemes. Check the learning
by asking questions that verify that the student has
a *deep* understanding of the word's meaning and
recognizes critical components of the definition. An
example from Carnine and Silbert (1979, p. 315)
illustrates this kind of definition teaching.

> Teacher: "Respite means *short rest.* John
> worked hard all day. Then he went home and
> slept for ten hours. Did he take a respite? . . .
>
> Ann worked hard all morning. At twelve she
> stopped and ate a quick lunch and then went

back to work. Did she take a respite? How do
you know?"

Semantic Features.   This format for enriching the
meaning of new words is often effective. First, students are engaged in a discussion. Old words are
linked to new by defined words, and classification is
used to clarify and expand word knowledge. Figure
12.4 illustrates a semantic features list. Semantic
features can be used to augment more traditional
vocabulary instruction such as examples, synonyms, morphemes, and definitions. However, do
not expect students to *discover* the meaning of new
words through semantic feature analysis. New
word meanings must be taught (Archer, May,
1986).

Recommendation 5: Teach Pragmatics
Instruction in pragmatics requires integration of
skills in syntax and semantics as well as application
of knowledge of specific language functions. Another way of describing pragmatics is to link it to
code recognition and application. One code is used
when seeking help from a friend and another code
when seeking help from a stranger. Role playing is
a good format for pragmatics. Students can practice a variety of roles as they learn critical information linked to a variety of communication purposes.

Lesson information includes (a) purpose of the skill with a variety of examples of situations in which the student needs the skill and (b) critical components of the skill. During initial acquisition, lesson format should include models or demonstrations and opportunities for guided practice. This practice includes verbal rehearsal of what the student will *think* as well as rehearsal of what he will *say* and *do*. Next there is guided practice across settings, and finally, independent practice. Since all pragmatics require that the communicator recognize what skill is needed under which conditions, practice across settings is essential.

Recommendation 6: Focus Instruction on Error Patterns

During instruction be prepared to address errors; however, when a student is making consistent errors a more intense approach may be required. It has been said if an error occurs in the first 30 attempts during new learning and if the error is corrected, only a few corrections will be required. However, if an error goes uncorrected and is practiced (learned), it could take thousands of corrections to change the learned response (Englemann, 1979). This is especially true if opportunities to make the response occur frequently in uncontrolled situations. If there is a content area in which this is true, it is language.

Instruction that focuses on error correction needs to be immediate and frequent. Opportunities to make the specific errors of concern need to be built into instruction. Corrections should be based on the cause of the error. The following *causes* of errors are the most likely:

1. Failure to see how things are different—discrimination;
2. Failure to see how things are the same—generalization;
3. Missing information.

A discrimination error occurs when a student carries an old rule into a new situation. When the student learns that you add -*s* to make English words plural and does not know words for which the rule does not apply, she may make discrimina-

tion errors. The solution is to teach the discrimination. For example, say to the student, "We say two boys, four hats, ten pencils . . . but we say six sheep. We say one sheep, two sheep, three sheep . . . but we say one boy, two boys, three boys."

A generalization error occurs when the student fails to see how two things are the same. A correction for this kind of error would include information of the critical ways things are similar. A student who can ask for help in one classroom and not another needs to be taught that the ways of seeking assistance are similar across situations.

In both discrimination and generalization errors, some information is missing. However, there are occasions when a student makes errors because she just doesn't know. When correcting this error, simply supply the information.

Recommendation 7: Increase the Number and Richness of Words (Ideas)

To increase the number and richness of ideas, the child has to incorporate additional structures into her natural speech. Structures such as adjectives, adverbs, prepositional phrases, and coordinating elements are targets to be included at lower levels, while structures such as complex verb forms and clauses are included to increase the number of words per utterance at upper levels. The long-range goal is to increase the mean length of the child's utterances by including various language structures; the short-range objective is that the child produce sentences using specified structures. An example of an objective at a lower level is, "The child will produce sentences using *prepositional phrases*." The format of higher-level objectives stays the same, but the language structures specified change, e.g., "The student will produce sentences using the *relative adverb clauses*."

Recommendation 8: Teach Strategies

The discussions of strategy instruction in chapters 9, 10, and 11 adequately outline formats for teaching general and specific strategies. Strategy instruction in language parallels strategy instruction in other domains.

SUMMARY

This chapter defined oral language and explored some beliefs, assumptions, and misunderstandings about language acquisition. It also discussed in detail what to consider when conducting an evaluation of language. We have linked these consid-erations to explicit procedures for conducting survey- and specific-level tests. The specific-level procedures described match the most probable causes for language difficulties. Guidelines for in-terpreting test results were linked to instructional recommendations.

Study Questions

1. Semantics is
   a. the study of meaning within language.
   b. the rule system that governs order of words in sentences.
   c. important to speech and language personnel but not to teachers.
   d. the study of the functions and purpose of language.
2. Discourse style refers to
   a. syntax and semantics as they are developed in the young child.
   b. effective communication for school use.
   c. a language-sampling procedure used to examine pragmatics.
   d. the social/cultural influence on ways ideas are organized.
3. A direct approach to language instruction recognizes that
   a. language cannot be taught but is naturally acquired.
   b. there is emphasis across domains of need as well as across levels of proficiency.
   c. instruction in syntax takes precedence over other areas of need.
   d. instruction occurs in natural rather than structured environments.
4. Prevalence estimates of language problems
   a. vary because definitions vary and the extent to which children with other handicaps have language problems is difficult to determine.
   b. suggest that most handicapped students do not have language problems but have more serious problems which, unlike language, interfere with schooling.
   c. have been reduced since P.L. 94-142 and the introduction into schools of free and ap-propriate educational services.
   d. are not important because parents and teachers are quick to observe if a problem ex-ists.
5. How would you collect a language sample?
6. What would you do if you suspected that a student's classroom environment inhibited communication?
7. What would you do for additional testing if, after you analyzed the language sample, you believed that an assumed cause for the difficulty was semantics?
8. If the primary concern is that the student doesn't talk much, how would you go about deciding if he talked enough?
9. If the primary error pattern in the oral language sample is syntax, how would you con-duct specific-level testing?
10. If the student performed well in the situations where you sample her language but the referring teacher continues to express concern about such communication skills as follow-ing directions, asking questions, expressing wants appropriately, and understanding how to be a listener, what would you do?

Chapter 13

Evaluating Written Communication

Portions of this chapter are based on material originally
produced by Dr. Joseph Kaplan (Howell & Kaplan, 1980).
The expansion of this material has been influenced significantly
by the work of Dr. Stephen Isaacson, State University of
New York at Geneseo.

_____ *Chapter Outline* _____

Authorities suggest there are three aspects of written communication: (1) purpose, (2) process, and (3) product (Isaacson, 1985). This discussion of written communication will focus on these three and link them to curriculum-based assessment.

FOCUS ON WRITING

Components of Written Communication— Some Definitions

Purpose

Purpose in written language is analogous to *pragmatics* in oral language. Britton (1978) has dis-

cussed three purposes of written language: *expressive*, *poetic*, and *transactive*. Table 13.1 summarizes the definitions of these three purposes. Evaluators cannot judge whether a written communication is adequate if they don't know what the writer intended and what conventional form is typically used with that kind of message. It is also useful to know what effect the communication has on the recipient.

Process

The process of writing seems to have the four stages (Isaacson, 1985): *planning*, *transcribing*, *reviewing*, and *revising*, shown in Table 13.2. Planning includes a prewriting stage in which the writer formulates a purpose for writing, decides what to write, selects a style that is likely to accom-

TABLE 13.1
Writing purposes

Function	Attributes
Expressive	Close to the self
	Addressing speaker's consciousness
	May be relatively unstructured
Poetic	Patterned verbalization of feelings and ideas
	Not restricted to poems
Transactive	Instructs
	Performs
	Persuades

plish the purpose, and organizes the message. Planning also occurs during writing and includes planning for development of a message as well as planning for manipulation of mechanics of writing. The focus of planning is to accomplish the identified purpose. As writers of this text we planned our content and how to present it to you. We also planned our format: how many chapters, chapter subdivisions, paragraph length, sentence complexity. Some planning occurs before writing; other planning takes place during writing. On large projects, allocation of time also requires planning.

Transcription in written communication is the process of putting a message into print. Some people dictate messages into tape recorders for secretaries to commit to print. Others write with pencil and paper or use a keyboard to transfer messages to a written form. There are even computers that translate voice messages into print. No matter what the medium, transcribing requires the simultaneous integration of a number of skills. These skills are the mechanics and conventions of writing. For students in schools today, mechanics includes handwriting, spelling, capitalization, punctuation, and grammar. Computer software that can proof for misspelling may someday replace handwriting with keyboard skills. However, until all students have the same access to computers that they now have to pencils, handwriting and spelling will remain major components of transcribing.

Reviewing, a third component of the writing process, appears to interact with planning. Good writers frequently look back over their work to check how things are going just as good readers look back to check understanding. Reviewing is often thought of as the first stage of the last component: revising. As writers review their work they revise it.

Revision may include changes in style, content, word selection, and sentence complexity. If the

TABLE 13.2
Process in writing

Planning	Transcribing	Reviewing	Revising
Prewriting	Modes	Monitor	Modify to Meet
Formulate purpose	Dictation	Match of message	Purpose
Match style to	Typing	to purpose	Style
purpose	Computer keyboard	Accuracy of	Content
Organize message	Pen or pencil	mechanics	Word selection
			Sentence complexity
During writing	Mechanics		Organization
Develop message	Handwriting (Typing		
Manipulate	etc.)		Correct Errors in
mechanics	Spelling		Mechanics
	Capitalization		Handwriting
	Grammar		(Typing, etc.)
	Form—Margins,		Spelling
	heading, etc.		Capitalization
			Grammar
			Form—Margins,
			heading, etc.

message is as clear or vague or as concise or wordy as the writer intends, then the revision stage may focus only on corrections in spelling, punctuation, grammar, and appearance. Revisions in appearance may include adjustments in handwriting, type style, margin size, page color, heading size, and a variety of other features. Good writers are aware that the physical organization of a written message influences how it is received and whether it is understood. Good writers adjust organization to meet the needs of the audience.

Product

Products are the result of purpose and process. These products are analyzed to determine how well a student has mastered writing. Isaacson (1984, 1985) has noted that theories of written language offer five components of written products: *fluency, syntactic maturity, vocabulary, content,* and *writing conventions* (which includes mechanics). Each can be directly observed. Isaacson's descriptions of these components and suggested procedures for evaluating each one are summarized in Table 13.3. Because ease of evaluator acquisition and ease of use are factors that should be weighed along with reliability, validity, and overall value, we have added an estimate of utility to Isaacson's original summary. Some of the procedures Isaacson suggests are easy for an evaluator to learn and others are not.

Strategies

Writing strategies are not a separate component but are imbedded in purpose, process, and product. They include (a) procedures for deciding what to do and (b) procedures for how to do it. As in reading, math, and oral language, there are both general strategies and task-specific strategies. A general strategy is characterized by the question, "What should I be doing?" A task-specific strategy is characterized by the spelling question, "Can this word be correctly spelled by sounds?" Both questions fit into the category of deciding what to do. The writing subdomains of purpose and process primarily feature strategies for deciding what to do. The subdomain of product features strategies for deciding how to do it.

CURRICULUM ISSUES

Purpose and Process

Effective writing skills, along with competence in reading, are expressions of literacy. The failure to acquire reading and writing as functional extensions of language accounts for the greatest number of referrals to special and remedial education (Hallahan & Kauffman, 1986). No one argues the importance of writing instruction; however, what to teach and how to teach are hotly debated.

Before getting to how writing should be taught, maybe a page or two needs to be spent on whether it should be taught at all. Bridge and Hiebert (1985) report that students spend very little time in writing activities. They also report that the miniscule percentage of time spent in writing is spent copying verbatim from workbooks or teacher-prepared worksheets. They note that students seldom compose written messages and almost never write for an audience other than the teacher. While Bridge and Hiebert's work is limited to one school district, their findings correspond to previous studies of classroom practice (Applebee, 1981; Petty & Finn, 1981). There is compelling evidence that the little time allocated for writing instruction is not even spent on mechanics or the writing process. It is spent on copying tasks, which are at best a form of handwriting practice and at worst busy work assigned to keep students occupied. This bleak picture of "no time for writing" gets bleaker considering how time is spent out of school. Fielding, Wilson, and Anderson (1985) questioned 158 fifth-grade students about how they spent time outside of school and found a glaring absence of writing activities. The point is that a discussion of writing instruction is fatuous if writing is not taught in schools or used by students outside of school.

This means your authors are in something of a bind with this chapter. It takes several pages (which you will have to pay for) to do a good job explaining written communication. In some ways it is hard to justify spending about 15% of the content discussion in this text on something teachers only teach about 2% of the time. However, writing is one of the "3 Rs" and failure at it can be disabling

TABLE 13.3
Components of written communication products

Component	Evidence	Direct Measures	Efficiency Rating					
			Training Time			Scoring Time		
			Low	Medium	High	Low	Medium	High
Fluency	Production of simple sentences and elaboration into compositions of gradually increasing length	Total number of words	X					
		Ratio of correct word sequences	X			X	X	
Syntactic maturity	Production of sentences of increasing complexity	Total number of sentences by type: fragment, simple, compound		X			X	
		Total number of T-units per sentence			X		X	
		Length of T-units per sentence			X		X	
Vocabulary or semantic maturity	Fewer repetitions of favored words and use of more sophisticated words	Total number of unusual words (teacher's best guess about unusual)	X				X	
		Proportion of mature words (from a word frequency list)	X				X	
		Proportion of unrepeated words	X					X
Content	Attention to organization of thought, originality, and style	Text cohesion			X			X
		Holistic rating		X			X	
		Analytic rating			X			X
Conventions	Mechanical aspects of writing such as margins, grammar, spelling, and punctuation	Proportion of errors in each category		X			X	

Source: Drawn from works by S. Isaacson, 1984, 1985.

to communication and stigmatizing to students. In addition, *it can be taught*. Obviously efforts to teach written communication should be preceded by a thorough evaluation.

Debate on How to Teach

Today tremendous emphasis is placed on what is called *the writing process*. *Process* in this context includes the previously discussed purpose, process, product, and strategies. Proponents of the writing process appear to be reacting to what they describe as an overemphasis on skill instruction. Advocates of the writing-process approach contend that skill approaches focus primarily on mechanics. They state that skill instruction neglects more complex tasks linked to print communication such as planning, reviewing, and revising. These critics believe that skill approaches fail to produce writers who can apply mechanics—the conventions of written language—meaningfully or for practical functions. While we agree that writing should be an integrated activity, we think it is a mistake to advocate a curriculum that ignores mechanics. Emphasizing the process of writing at the expense of mechanics is an unbalanced approached. Just as good readers use a balanced integration of grapheme–phoneme knowledge and complex strategic behaviors to understand written language, effective writers combine mechanics with sophisticated writing strategies to produce written language. Good writers use conventions of print to convey a message that in turn produces a desired effect (Frose & Straw, 1981). To reduce a discussion of written communication to an argument on whether the writing process is more important than mastery of mechanics misses the point. Mechanics are necessary tools required by the process of writing. But there is much more to writing than mechanics. Evaluators of written communication must be able to analyze a student's application of purpose, process, product, and strategies to effectively determine where to begin instruction.

Writing and Reading

It is often claimed that gains in reading competence influence gains in writing competence and that competence in writing influences reading. The nature of the writing–reading relationship is still being explored. Tierney and Leys (1984) have pointed out that the magnitude of the relationship seems to vary with the age of the writer and the kind of measure employed to assess the interaction. It is probably safe to say that there are good readers who are not good writers, but there are probably no good writers who are not also good readers. Good writing includes reading your own text for planning and review and often reading the text of others as an informational source. Eckhoff (1983), Geva and Tierney (1984), and Bereiter and Scardamalia (1984) have all observed that what a person reads influences his or her writing style. If you read something stilted, your writing is stilted. Armbruster (1984b) has pointed out that school texts are often poorly organized, obscure, and insensitive to their audience. She has suggested that students be taught to rewrite poor texts. She believes that analysis and revision of a poorly written text provides kids with practice in critical reading and critical writing. Armbruster is suggesting that by teaching kids to become critics and editors we will teach them strategies they can use to improve their reading comprehension and their writing skills. Since the style of what you read influences how you write, it is important for evaluators to analyze the materials a student reads. Curriculum-based assessment does not occur in a vacuum. Determining the extent to which a student uses particular written material as a model for writing is an important component of assessment.

Product (Mechanics)

Handwriting and spelling appear under Mechanics in both Tables 13.2 and 13.3. Some of you may be wondering why we would choose to elaborate on spelling and handwriting. It is because these mechanical aspects of writing are the most immediately alarming to teachers and, therefore, the sources of most requests for remedial help. It's certainly not because your authors consider either subject to be more important than the purpose and process of written language. In fact, one of us can't spell well at all (it's his vowels) and uses a rather primitive style of printing. We all know someone who is successful and cannot spell, or whose handwriting is illegible.

If success in the real world isn't contingent upon achievement in spelling and handwriting, why include this section? We could say that the reason is the same as the reason given by people who climb mountains, "because it's there." Spelling and handwriting are taught in schools all over this country. One day a week, most elementary and middle school students have to write their names or copy material. Spelling and writing are part of the curriculum. Teachers and students seem to be stuck with them, for better or worse. Until schools outlaw spelling tests and every student is issued a tape recorder, a typewriter, or a portable computer that takes dictation, teachers need to be aware of the problems students may encounter in both subjects. Even if spelling and handwriting were not in the curriculum we'd probably still address them anyway. They seem to account for more bias in grading than any other variable.

Handwriting[1]

"No subject in the curriculum is as neglected or as poorly taught, above the first three grades, as handwriting. And in no other subject are the results of instruction less impressive" (Cole, 1956, p. 97). While these sentiments may still be accurate, handwriting, despite its neglect in the public schools, has still managed to generate some controversy. Here are some commonly asked questions about handwriting.

To Write or Not to Write? Many teachers ask themselves this question when confronted by a student's seemingly unsolvable handwriting problem. At such times, teachers tend to engage in a lot of rationalizing, such as: "Why bother?" "Writing is just a means to an end." "Kids don't have to write to be able to communicate." The student with an "unsolvable" handwriting problem is often taught a substitute skill such as typing—keyboarding or using a tape recorder. This is based on the reasoning that the student needs to communicate her thoughts and, since writing is only one means to-

ward this end, it should not be thought of as the end itself. The authors agree. In fact, we would be the first to recommend that kids with severe difficulties with writing be allowed to express themselves in another manner, i.e., the tape recorder, typewriter, or computer, at least until their problems have been solved. But eventually somebody is going to have to teach them how to write legibly or face the difficult realization that they never will be taught.

As we suggested, there does not appear to be an absolute relationship between success in the work world and legibility in handwriting. However, we must admit that being able to write legibly does make your life easier. In the real world a kid will sign her name on countless forms. She'll need to take notes in classes. She'll write lists and directions to places, leave notes for friends, and take messages over the phone. These are just a few of the instances in which she'll have to use handwriting. Therefore, every student who is physically able should be taught handwriting in school to the extent that she is competent enough to communicate in that medium. While computers are changing the need to use handwriting, they are not an available option for everyone everywhere.

Cursive or Manuscript? Do teachers need to teach both and, if so, which should be taught first? While both are usually taught, with manuscript preceding cursive (Barbe, 1974), there is still some controversy about whether both should be taught. One argument against cursive is based on perception studies that show that the farther handwritten forms depart from the vertical, the less legible they become (Hildreth, 1964). The joining of letters, increasing of their slant and elongation, as well as the addition of loops, all serve to decrease the legibility of cursive writing. There is also wide variation among individuals' writing in cursive, while manuscript writing tends to vary less among people. This makes manuscript more standard and less open to interpretation, thus facilitating communication. Another argument against cursive is that increases in speed lead to decreased legibility. It appears that manuscript deteriorates less than cursive under the pressure of speed. Research suggests that, while manuscript and cursive may be performed at simi-

---

1. This section is drawn from Howell & Kaplan, 1980.

lar rates, legibility decreases more quickly in cursive than in manuscript (Hildreth, 1964). There do not appear to be any significant differences in writing rates between the two styles when experience and practice are comparable for those people tested. Instead, handwriting rates are thought to be more closely related to the quality of instruction, the duration of practice, and the individual traits of the writer than they are to the writing style taught.

Proponents of manuscript argue that the letter forms are more easily mastered by young children, enabling them to express themselves in writing at an earlier age. They also maintain that there is a greater need for manuscript writing in society than cursive (with the exception of a signature). There are, however, arguments presented against manuscript. Many children prefer cursive because they consider it "real" or "grown up" writing, while manuscript is considered "baby" writing. Banks and other institutions won't accept printed signatures because they are too easy to forge. And some educators feel that cursive writing is easier to learn, especially for the handicapped student, because it supposedly cuts down on the number of letter and word reversals.

Success in cursive writing is *not* contingent upon prior instruction in manuscript (Lovitt, 1973; Staats, Brewer, & Gross, 1970). This means that manuscript is *not* a prerequisite to cursive. Therefore, if a student is having difficulty, the style decision should be made early and adhered to.

For the most part, it is safe to say that teachers teach both spelling and handwriting the way it was taught to them. They generally do not attend to the data that show that there is no prerequisite relationship between manuscript and cursive. In addition, they are usually so inflexible in their expectation that all students write in a preferred style that they will frequently refuse to accept manuscript writing from older students. This means that if you, as a special education teacher for example, decide to teach an older student manuscript because it is easier for her, you will be placing her at odds with the tradition of many teachers.

Spelling

As they do with handwriting, teachers tend to teach spelling the way it was taught to them. Conse-quently, most spelling lessons consist of memorizing word lists even though there are years of evidence showing that this isn't the best way to teach students to spell words. Whatever "spelling" is, it certainly is not one independent skill or ability. Nothing correlates particularly highly with spelling. There isn't any syndrome or set of characteristics that typify bad spellers. Hardly anyone ever says a kid is suffering from "dysspellia," because the only characteristic that separates spellers from nonspellers is the number of words they spell correctly.

To spell well a student must determine how the word is pronounced, if it is spelled like it is pronounced, and how it is spelled if it isn't spelled like it's pronounced (Spache, 1940). As an oversimplification, spelling can be viewed as the flip side of phonetic decoding. When you ask a student to decode, you show him letters and ask for sounds. When you ask a student to spell, you give him sounds and ask for letters. Therefore the predictability of the sound—letter correspondence in words is an important concern.

Misspellings fall roughly into two categories: phonetic and nonphonetic misspellings. Phonetic misspellings can be read as the stimulus word, for example, writing *o-r-d-r* for *o-r-d-e-r*. Nonphonetic misspellings can't be read, as in *a-t-u-s* for *o-r-d-e-r*. The type of misspelling a student makes is critical. The phonetic speller is actively using phonetic clues (though they are the wrong ones), while the nonphonetic speller does not seem to be attending to letter sounds.

A confounding factor in spelling instruction is the observation that many successful spellers simply "see" the word in their minds and copy it onto their papers. Poor spellers seem to lack this skill, which is sometimes referred to as *revisualization* or *visual memory*. (When presented with an uncertain word, they may write it out to find out if it looks right. When they do this, they may be comparing the word they wrote to their memory of the word's appearance, or they may simply be checking their spelling by reading what they wrote.) It appears that revisualization as a skill cannot be taught directly as it is a byproduct of other skills such as decoding. Good spellers can do it and bad spellers can't, but teaching it doesn't make bad spellers any better.

There do seem to be some prerequisites to good spelling. One of the most important spelling prerequisites is the skill to discriminate accurately (attend to and perceive) what is heard. If a kid thinks the word *dropped* is pronounced "drop" because she has difficulty perceiving or attending to the endings of spoken words, she will probably write *d-r-o-p* in those instances where *d-r-o-p-p-e-d* would be correct. If she has difficulty discriminating the medial consonant sounds in words, she might perceive *ankle* as *angle* and write it in the wrong context; e.g., "The angle bone is next to the foot." One way to test for this prerequisite is to have the student repeat each spelling word dictated to make sure he heard it accurately. As an evaluator, whenever you come across a misspelled word in the student's written work, ask him what word he was trying to write. If he mispronounces the word, you may have a speech or regional accent problem to address instead of a spelling problem.

Since spelling is only important in written communication, you must always be aware of the effect of handwriting on a student's spelling performance. Students who have not mastered the skill of handwriting are unable to concentrate on the process of spelling. In other words, handwriting should be an automatic skill like operating an automobile. If the average driver had to stop and think about the mechanics of using the brake every time he turned a corner, it would interfere with his concentration on the most important facet of driving, navigating safely through traffic. Similarly, thinking about how each letter is written tends to interfere with spelling, whether the student is engaged in revisualizing a word or sounding it out.

Should you suspect that poor performance in writing is interfering with the student's spelling, ask him to spell words verbally before writing them. Make comparisons between his verbal and written spelling. On occasion, one may find students whose spelling errors (on the same words) drop markedly when they are told to spell verbally first. Similarly, some students cannot spell some words verbally unless they first attempt to write them. In survey-level testing, give students the option of spelling the word verbally or in writing, to observe the student's preferred response mode. (By the way, preferred response modes are learned

and not evidence of fixed auditory or visual abilities. See the discussion of aptitude treatment interaction in chapter 15.)

Phonetic Skill. The most obvious prerequisite to spelling is the ability to recall the letters that make sounds. This phonetic skill is so similar to what is expected while reading that reading and spelling instruction can be used nicely to reinforce each other. Unfortunately, for some mysterious reason educators in this country teach different spelling and reading words at the same grade level. This is not done in other countries, where the same word list is often used for both skills. However, in the United States books with different word lists are provided. We assume this is because the procedure allows publishers to sell two different books when one would suffice. At any rate, a decoding table of specifications can be used to test spelling by simply asking, "What letter(s) makes this sound?" and proceeding through the table. In addition, some phonetic generalizations occur reliably enough that students may be able to use them to attack unfamiliar words. These generalizations are outlined in Table 13.4. Of course, these generalizations cannot be used at the automatic or even mastery levels, but they may help a student reach accuracy.

Another critical phonetic skill is reading and spelling clusters. Spelling is a lot like blending in that it requires the student to break the word down, translate it into code, and reassemble it. During the analysis of the word it is best to attend to clusters within the word as opposed to the individual letters. In the word *string*, for example, the student could focus on each letter or on the clusters *str* and *ing*. The Glass Analysis System described in the blending portion of chapter 10 is an excellent evaluative and instructional technique for spelling.

Phonetic Segmentation. Current studies indicate that a skill more basic than recalling sound–letter or sound–cluster correspondence is a listening discrimination skill called *phonetic segmentation* or *sound isolation.* This skill is not the kind of discrimination in which you distinguish *ankle* from *angle*; it is a skill in which students determine the number of sounds or phonemes in a word and separate them into phonemic units. Phonemic segmentation is not

TABLE 13.4
Phonics generalizations applied to spelling

1. Double the letters *f, l, s,* or *z* in most one-syllable words when preceded by a short vowel. Examples are *cliff, sniff, bluff, whiff, cuff, puff, fell, tell, swell, ball, spill, fill, spell, brass, press, cross, miss, fuss, pass, buzz, fizz, jazz.* Exceptions are *bus* and *gas.*

2. The silent *e* at the end of a word makes a short vowel long. Examples are *pin* and *pine, dim* and *dime, hat* and *hate, mat* and *mate, rat* and *rate, cub* and *cube, plan* and *plane, cap* and *cape, at* and *ate, mad* and *made, mop* and *mope, kit* and *kite, rod* and *rode, hid* and *hide, rip* and *ripe, fad* and *fade, cut* and *cute, tub* and *tube, can* and *cane, hop* and *hope, not* and *note,* and *fin* and *fine.*

3. When you hear *k* after a *short* vowel, spell it *ck;* when you hear *k* after a *long* vowel or consonant, spell it *k.* Examples are *neck, dusk, flank, track, hunk, slack, stuck, deck, rink, milk, check, tuck, task, fleck, lack, coke, make, rock, knock,* and *stink.* Use *c* at the end of polysyllabic words when you hear *ik.* Examples are *attic, plastic, metric, cosmic, classic, Atlantic, optic, frantic.*

4. When you hear *j* after a short vowel, you usually spell it *dge.* After a long vowel or consonant you use *ge.* Examples are *age, gadget, lodge, huge, strange, cage, nudge, stage, page, bridge, change, hinge, edge.*

5. When you hear *ch* after a short vowel, use *tch.* When you hear *ch* after a long vowel or consonant, use *ch. Ch* is always used at the beginning of a word. Examples are *chop, bench, batch, pinch, church, witch, blotch, pitch, porch, crutch, lunch, sketch, fetch, patch.* Exceptions are *rich, which, much, such, sandwich.*

6. When you have a one-syllable word with a consonant at the end of a word that is preceded by a *short* vowel and the suffix begins with one vowel, double the consonant. If any one of these conditions is not met, don't double. Examples are *ship* and *shipper, ship* and *shipping, hot* and *hottest, slop* and *sloppy, mad* and *madder, rob* and *robber, star* and *starry, fat* and *fatter, fog* and *foggy, wit* and *witness, grin* and *grinning, mad* and *madly, cold* and *colder, farm* and *farming, dust* and *dusty, rant* and *ranted, boat* and *boating, weed* and *weeding, blot* and *blotter, grim* and *grimmest, rest* and *restless, flat* and *flatly, slim* and *slimmer, feed* and *feeding,* and *win* and *winning.*

7. A word ending in a silent *e* drops the *e* before a suffix beginning with a vowel, but does not

change before an ending beginning with a consonant. Examples are *hope* and *hoping, dive* and *diving, write* and *writing, tune* and *tuneful, shine* and *shiny, time* and *timer, hope* and *hopeless, take* and *taking, sore* and *soreness, flame* and *flaming, fame* and *famous, care* and *caring, hide* and *hiding, hope* and *hoped, lone* and *lonely, use* and *useful, sure* and *surely, close* and *closely, make* and *making, life* and *lifeless, like* and *likeness, shade* and *shady, noise* and *noiseless,* and *tire* and *tiresome.*

8. Double the consonant when adding a suffix after a short vowel. Examples are *capped, caper, capping, moping, mopping, mapped, filling, filed, filing, filled, taping, tapping, taped, tapped, tapper, hopped, hoped, hopping, hoping.*

9. In words ending in *y* preceded by a consonant, the *y* changes to *i* before any ending except *-ing* or *-ist.* In words ending in *y* preceded by a vowel, keep the *y.* Examples are *cry* and *crying, rely* and *reliance, pray* and *prayer, worry* and *worrying, joy* and *joyful, enjoy* and *enjoyment, say* and *saying, sleepy* and *sleepiness, glory* and *glorious, delay* and *delayed, merry* and *merriest, study* and *studying, lonely* and *loneliness, pay* and *payable, carry* and *carried, stray* and *strayed, fly* and *flier, supply* and *supplied, healthy* and *healthier, spy* and *spying, funny* and *funniest, tiny* and *tiniest, injury* and *injurious.*

10. When adding *ble, dle, fle* to a word, consider the initial vowel sound. A long vowel or consonant simply needs *ble, dle, fle.* A short vowel continues to need all the help it can get. Examples are *buckle, freckle, puddle, ruffle, stable, rifle, stifle, staple.*

11. While most nouns form the plural by adding *s* to the singular, nouns ending in *s, x, sh,* and *ch* form the plural by adding *es.* A noun ending in *y* preceded by a consonant forms the plural by changing the *y* to *i* and adding *es.* Examples are *cats, dogs, kisses, boxes, fishes, churches,* and *candies.*

12. An apostrophe is used to show the omission of a letter or letters in a contraction. The possessive of a singular noun is formed by adding an apostrophe and *s.* The possessive of a plural noun ending in *s* is formed by adding an apostrophe. Examples are *cannot* and *can't, will not* and *won't, I had* and *I'd, I will* and *I'll, had not* and *hadn't, Jim's car, the dog's bone, the groups' scores.*

syllabication. In a syllabication task students would tell how many syllables there are in *man*. In a phonemic segmentation task they would isolate and name the phonemes—"m-a-n." In the word *man*, there are one syllable and three distinct phonemes. Research in phonemic segmentation indicates that it is a skill linked to both reading and spelling and that it can be taught (Liberman & Shankweiler, 1985; Pany, 1987; Read & Ruyter, 1985; Williams, 1984). Research has not yet confirmed whether phonemic segmentation is truly a prerequisite for spelling, a facilitative skill, or part of spelling itself. A complete spelling evaluation of young children and poor spellers needs to include a test of phonemic segmentation skills. However, very few instruments currently available sample phonemic segmentation skills in the context of spelling assessment.

A sequence for evaluating the student's skill at spelling-related phonetic skills is shown in Figure 13.1. The steps should be applied to words the student has previously misspelled. These words are found during the survey-level testing.

Rules. The major controversy in the field of spelling has been whether instruction should focus on learning each and every word by rote or applying a few phonics generalizations (rules) to many words. For years spelling was taught by rote memorization with the result that each word required a separate act of learning. This practice was based on the idea that the English language is nonphonetic and does not readily lend itself to the teaching of phonics generalizations. However, research conducted during the 1950s disputed this notion and eventually led to the current philosophy that students need to learn the phonetic patterns in words and how to apply them. Hanna and Moore (1953) and Deverell (1971) analyzed the phoneme–grapheme correspondences in the 3,000 words most commonly taught in spelling programs in the United States and reported these findings: (a) 80% of all the phonemes in the spoken words are predictably represented by graphemes (letters) when the words are written; (b) consonant sounds and blends are regularly spelled more than 90% of the time; and (c) nearly three-fourths of the vowel sounds present no serious spelling problem, since the vowel speech sounds are spelled regularly from 57% to

1. *Word Reproduction:* Given words dictated one at a time by the examiner, the student will correctly repeat each word with ____% accuracy taking no more than ____ seconds per word.

2. *Syllable Isolation:* Given words dictated one at a time by the examiner, the student will correctly say each word with an obvious pause between syllables (clusters). This will be done with ____% accuracy taking no more than ____ seconds per word.

3. *Sound Isolation:* Given syllables (clusters) dictated one at a time by the examiner, the student will correctly say each sound (phoneme) in a syllable with an obvious pause between sounds. This will be done with ____% accuracy taking no more than ____ seconds per syllable.

4. *Sound–Symbol Correspondence:* Given sounds (phonemes) dictated one at a time by the examiner, the student will correctly write the letters (graphemes) that make each sound. This will be done with ____% accuracy taking no more than ____ seconds per sound.

5. *Operational Knowledge:* Given the directions to do so, the student will correctly say and describe all of the steps necessary to phonetically spell unknown words. This will be done with ____% accuracy taking no more than ____ seconds.

FIGURE 13.1
Informal phonetic spelling inventory

99% of the time in the vocabulary analyzed. From these data it was concluded that "in spite of its many imperfections, the English system of writing is in origin and in its main features phonetic, or alphabetic" (Hanna & Moore, 1953, p. 330).

The findings of Spache (1940) that "good" spellers tended to have greater skill in phonics and better auditory discrimination appear to support the notion that English is phonically regular enough to warrant teaching phonics generalizations in the spelling curriculum. The situation seems to parallel the old proverb about giving a man a fish versus a fishing rod. Teachers can teach each word to a student or they can give him a tool with which he may learn to spell words on his own. Please note, however, that there is a significant difference between a phonic generalization and a low utility rule that works less than half the time. The rules included in Table 13.4 have high utility and work frequently enough to be worth teaching. Not all rules are this useful.

Morphographs. In addition to being able to apply phonics generalizations and to spell irregular words, students need to master a specific content domain within language that permits writers to geometrically increase the number of words they can spell. This domain is really a way of subdividing spelling by organizing the content into units of meaning—morphographs—rather than words. Morphographs are the building blocks of all words. Some morphographs are words, some are affixes (the parts you use at beginnings and endings of words), and some are bases (the parts you use with affixes to form words) (Dixon, Englemann, & Olen, 1981; Wiig & Semel, 1984). In Table 13.5 we list morphographs that can be easily combined to form a number of words. Once the spelling of a morphograph has been learned, one can apply phonics rules to combine it with others to make numerous new words that have been previously

TABLE 13.5
Example of morphographs in English

Affixes	Nonword Bases	Words
be-	tain	born
de-	astro	gain
dis-	cant	listen
-ed	stance	talk
-ing	ject	tear
re-	gress	time
un-	lief	grade
-s	ceed	act
-ship	spect	grace
pro-	quire	
-ion	vise	
-ive	semble	
-or	sist	
in-		
ad-		

taught. Take a few minutes to see how many new words you can make by combining the morphographs in Table 13.5 with words. Dixon and colleagues (1981) suggest that if teachers teach a few phonics rules with high utility morphographs, even very poor spellers will become successful. Students who have mastered basic phonic skills—sound–symbol correspondence and phonemic segmentation skills—will benefit from instruction in morphographs. These students are usually found in grades 4 through 12.

We have discussed both handwriting and spelling in some detail and have risked leading you away from the larger topic of written language. Our intent—*purpose*—has been to emphasize how large a domain writing is by describing two skills within the subskill of mechanics. We also believe that handwriting and spelling are significant to kids who don't "do" them well.

ASSESSMENT PROCEDURES

In the rest of this chapter we will discuss procedures for sampling and analyzing written communication. Because written communication is a complex process composed of large skill domains, we will to some extent deviate from the format previously used. After the interpretation guidelines for survey-level testing, we will present two levels of specific-level assessment. We will describe specific-level procedures designed to narrow the focus of assumed causes. We will not provide specific-level procedures for all assumed causes of writing difficulties. The process of evaluation is outlined in Figure 13.2.

Survey-Level Testing

The purpose of survey-level testing is to collect a general sample of a student's work that can be used to note facts and generate assumed causes for difficulty. An evaluator may analyze existing samples of student work or structure opportunities to write. There are a number of ways to obtain samples of written work. One is to collect existing samples

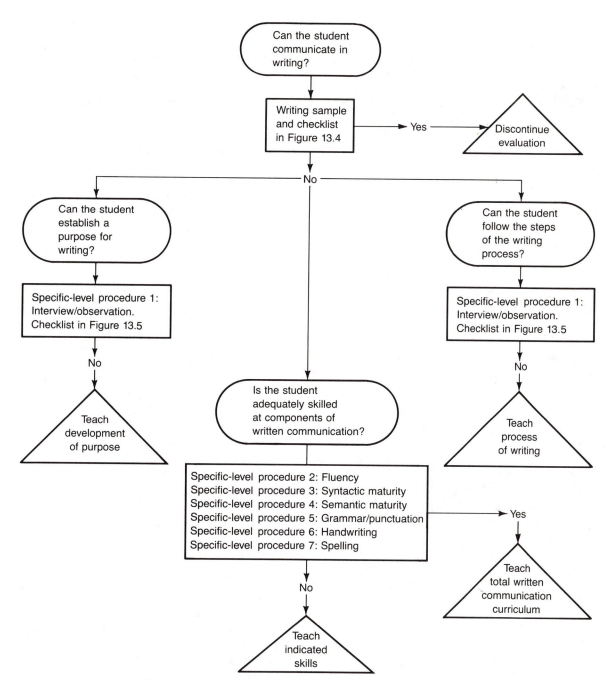

FIGURE 13.2
Evaluating written communication

Prompt A	Prompt B
"What is the best and the worst thing about lunch?" (Hutchinson, 1987)	"Families are special people. I'd like to learn about who is special in your life. Who are the members of your family? Do you have brothers or sisters? What do you like to do with your mom or your dad? What do you like best about your family times together?

FIGURE 13.3
Pre-writing prompts

from a variety of assignments that have different purposes for writing.

If samples are not readily available, then you can provide the student with a topic. The topic stimulus can be a picture(s), a description of an age-appropriate situation, or a question. Since a student's prior knowledge and current interest in the topic are critical, it is important to consider stimuli that permit wide variations in experience or require little previous experience. The disadvantage of using samples from a structured assignment is that the *purpose* is somewhat removed from a need generated by kids. (However, since most writing in schools probably isn't linked to student-generated needs to communicate, one more contrived assignment isn't really that atypical.)

Prompts should be as free from cultural bias as possible. Consider the two prompts in Figure 13.3. In prompt A, it does not matter where a student has lunch or what they have for lunch. In prompt B, however, if they do not live with both a mom and a dad and have brothers and sisters, they may have trouble with this "story starter." Many young children are uncomfortable and self-conscious about less-than-traditional family arrangements. Since large numbers of children do not come from traditional families, this prompt seems dated at best. Even if the student were a good writer, the topic could be culturally and conceptually difficult to address. A second problem with prompt B is that it is

lengthy. If a student has difficulty listening and difficulty remembering more than a few sentences, she may miss part of the prompt. Constructing a good prompt can be difficult. For this reason some evaluators use pictures. Again, for a picture to facilitate writing it must prompt ideas, not impede them.

Perhaps a greater problem associated with collecting samples of written communication is deciding how to score them and establishing standards for comparison. First, the content must be determined. A next step is to establish standards. Some standards are *absolute* (e.g., criteria for punctuation/capitalization). Whether a writer is 5 or 50, declarative sentences begin with capitals and end with periods in conventional English. If the content parallels Isaacson's (Table 13.3), an evaluator must establish local standards by age group for *fluency, syntactic maturity, semantic maturity,* and *content* as well as some aspects of mechanics. This is no small task. While written communication is not the same process as oral communication some value can be obtained from reviewing oral language content lists, especially specifications for syntax, semantics, and pragmatics. In written communication, as in oral communication, simple sentences are mastered before compound or complex.

Procedures

Question.   Can the student communicate effectively in writing across a variety of purposes? Is there a discrepancy between performance and what is acceptable?

Method for Determining the Answer.   Written language sample(s). Figure 13.4.

Directions.
1. Collect at least two samples from two occasions. Provide a verbal or pictoral writing prompt or collect samples from previous writing tasks.
2. Encourage the student to do his best and allow time for planning, transcribing, reviewing, and revising.

Component	Adequate	Not Adequate	Not Observed
Content			
Organization of thought			
Emphasis linked to intent			
Transition and bridges from idea to idea			
Paragraph structure focuses intent			
Theme well developed			
Unity—cohesion of text			
Development of thought			
Relevance of ideas to intent			
Logic			
Subordination of ideas			
Fluency			
Product length adequate for intent			
Time to construct message acceptable			
Syntactic maturity			
Sentence complexity appropriate for message			
Semantic maturity			
Vocabulary appropriate for message			
Conventions—Mechanics			
Format (margins, headings, etc.)			
Handwriting			
Spelling			
Grammar			
Punctuation			
Capitalization			

FIGURE 13.4
Checklist for scoring survey-level written communication samples (*Sources:* Adapted from B. S. Bloom, J. T. Hastings, and G. F. Madaus, *Handbook on Formative and Summative Evaluation of Student Learning,* New York: McGraw-Hill, 1971; and S. Isaacson, "Assessing Written Language." In C. Simon (Ed.), *Communication Skills and Classroom Success: Assessment Methodologies for Language-Learning Disabled Students.* San Diego, CA: College Hill Press.)

3. Using established criteria and content specifications, score and summarize the student's responses. Pass the sample on to a second rater to increase reliability. Figure 13.4 illustrates how the content in Table 13.3 can be used to create a checklist for summarizing student performance.
4. Using Figure 13.4, note areas needing additional attention. Areas recorded as "adequate" are disregarded; those marked "not adequate" or "not observed" will require specific-level testing.

Specific-Level Testing

Interpretation Guidelines and Specific-Level Procedures
The evaluation should follow the outline in Figure 13.2. To answer the following questions use one or

more of the specific-level procedures (to be presented below).

Can the student establish a purpose for writing?	Specific-Level Procedure 1
Can the student follow the steps of the writing process?	Specific-Level Procedure 1
Is the student adequately skilled at components of written communication?	Specific-Level Procedures 2–7

If the survey-level exercise indicates problems with the writing process, use Specific-Level Procedures 1–4. If the problem seems to be mechanical, skip to Specific-Level Procedures 5, 6, and 7. Directions for each specific-level procedure and interpretation guidelines follow. Remember that the student may have problems in more than one area.

Specific-Level Procedure 1: Interview/Observation. Most behaviors for written communication purposes and processes are cognitive. While one cannot verify that they are occurring, there are indicators an evaluator can look for and questions to ask that will shed light on whether a student is aware of particular strategies.

Directions.

1. Develop a checklist of the characteristics of *purpose* and *process* based on an analysis of writing, or use the one shown in Figure 13.5.

Content	Adequate	Not Adequate	Not Observed
Purpose			
Recognizes variety of functions of written language and links to composition style			
Descriptive			
Narrative			
Expository			
Persuasive			
Adjusts writing to audience			
Matches style to goal			
Process			
Planning			
Takes time before writing to decide what to do			
Transcribing			
Graphic representation legible on first draft			
Graphic representation adequate on final draft			
Reviewing			
Looks over work during writing to see how its going			
Revising			
Changes text after drafts to obtain intent			

FIGURE 13.5
Checklist for purpose and process strategies in written communication

2. Through observations and questions, rate the student on each item.
3. Note areas of instructional need.

Interpretation guidelines.

Question. Are there indicators that the student uses *purpose* and *process* of writing effectively?

If yes, review data from product analysis and select instructional targets (Specific-Level Procedures 2-7).

If no, teach the skills or strategies marked "not adequate" or "not observed" in Figure 13.5.

Specific-Level Procedure 2: Fluency Test—Ratio of Correct Word Sequence. This procedure was outlined by Videen, Deno, and Marston (1982). They compared numerous written communication measuring systems to this approach, which focuses on correct sequence of words. Implicit in this system is the notion that a correct sequence reflects not only fluency but syntax maturity. Figure 13.6 illustrates Videen, Deno, and Marston's procedure for assessing fluency of written composition. While it does not analyze all the components of writing, it takes very little time and correlates with a number of more time-consuming procedures used to measure written products.

Directions.
1. Obtain samples of the student's writing. Use the samples from the survey level or you may obtain others. If there seems to be variability in the student's production, look at more than two samples.
2. To score the samples give credit for (a) appropriate beginning word, (b) each subsequent word that is correct in sequence and spelling, and (c) appropriate ending word. Appropriate sequence means the word conforms to both semantic and syntactic constraints. It makes sense, in that place, in that sentence. (Practice scoring using the example in Figure 13.7.)
3. Summarize data.

Sample Scored Sentence:
^ Jack ^ and ^ Paula ^ and ^ Mary ˬ last ^ week ^ to ^ shell ˬ peacans. ˬ

Key:	Carets above words indicate correct counts.
	Carets below words indicate incorrect counts.

1. A correct caret is placed before "Jack" to indicate a correct starting word.
2. An incorrect caret is placed before "last" to indicate that "Mary last" is not a correct sequence in this sentence. A word like *met* was probably omitted and would have been correct.
3. An incorrect caret is placed before and after "peacans" because it is misspelled. It cannot be counted as a correct sequence after "shell" nor can it be counted as a correct ending word, which the last caret would indicate, because it is misspelled.

Score:	The correct-incorrect ratio is: *correct 8/11* and *incorrect 3/11.*

FIGURE 13.6
Examples of scoring using correct word sequence count

4. Compare to established standards. To determine standards for this task you could compare your students' scores to scores of students whom classroom teachers judge to be competent writers; however, we have observed that since inaccuracy in word sequence is not acceptable to most recipients of written messages, an absolute standard of 1:1 is advisable. To emphasize the quality of fluency in this procedure, establish the number of words expected in written communication at specific grade levels and combine that standard with the standard for correct sequence.

Interpretation guidelines.

Question. Is the student fluent?

If yes, move to next procedure.

FIGURE 13.7
Practice for scoring
ratio of correct
word sequence

Directions: In the sentence below see if you can determine the correct word sequence
count.

| Bird | had | fly | away | and | left | his | fether | in | sandbox. |

Correct sentence: A bird had flown away and left his feather in the sandbox.

Thoughts:
(1) It looks like a starting word was omitted, like "a."
(2) "Had fly" is not a correct sequence because "fly" is an incorrect tense ("flown").
(3) "Fly away" is not a correct sequence because "fly" is incorrect in this sentence.
(4)⎱
(5)⎰ "Fether" is a misspelling and cannot be correct after "his" or before "in."
(6) It looks like a word was omitted (e.g., "the").
You should have marked the sentence like this. The numbers are keyed to the thoughts/
rationale for marking.

‸ Bird ^ had ‸ fly ‸ away ^ and ^ left ^ his ‸ fether ‸ in ‸ sandbox ^ .
   1   2 3   4   5   6
Score: Ratio of corrects: 5/11   Ratio of incorrects: 6/11

If no, does the problem appear to be a syntax problem or a spelling problem? Go to specific-level procedure 3 for syntax and 7 for spelling. If syntax and spelling are ruled out, teach fluency.

Question. Are all other content areas on the checklist (Figure 13.4) adequate?

If yes, teach written communication skills following a validated sequence.

If no, carry out the specific-level procedures for areas not passed in Figure 13.4.

Specific-Level Procedure 3: Syntactic Maturity. One way to judge syntactic maturity is to use T-units. A T-unit is a minimal terminal unit, such as a main clause plus attached subordinate clauses. It is most conveniently conceptualized as a "thought unit." To summarize syntactic maturity, calculate the mean length of each T-unit and rate each sentence. The T-unit procedure has been described by Loban (1963), Hunt (1965), and Isaacson (1985).

The sentence-rating procedure is taken from Polloway and Smith (1982) and Isaacson (1985). A T-unit is a group of words that can stand alone. Any main clause and all dependent clauses compose the thought unit. After calculating T-units, tally the number of sentence fragments, simple sentences, compound sentences, compound run-on sentences, and complex sentences. Figure 13.8 illustrates how to calculate the mean T-unit to summarize sentence complexity.

Limitations of the T-unit procedure. Not everyone agrees with the underlying assumptions of the T-unit. As early as 1968, Christensen expressed concern that mature writers may not use more words than less able writers. Arguing that good communicators often say more with less, he pointed out that long clauses are often the mark of inept writers. The authors tend to agree, believing that increases in the T-unit illustrate increases in syntactic maturity but not necessarily communicative sophistication.

Directions.

1. Collect samples of the student's written communication or analyze the sample obtained in the survey-level procedure.
2. Score the sample using the procedures illustrated in Figure 13.8. Find mean T-unit length and rate sentence complexity.
3. Compare the student's performance to his previous performance or to a standard you have established or found in the literature.

Interpretation guidelines.

Question. Is the student's syntax mature?

If yes, check other assumed causes for problems in written products.

If no, teach specific-level skills for expanding and increasing sentence complexity.

Directions:

1. Count the total number of words in the sample.
2. Count the total number of T-units in the sample.
3. Divide the total number of words by the total number of T-units. The quotient will be the mean length of T-unit.
4. Rate each sentence as a fragment, simple, compound, compound run-on (more than 2 independent clauses), or complex sentence.
5. Summarize T-units and sentence types. Compare to a standard and decide if and where improvement is needed. (Fragments and run-on sentences would be intervention targets.)

Practice Example: Score this passage:
Howard rides his bicycle and Thad rides in a seat on the back. They wear hats to shade their eyes. They go to the park and they go down the big slide.

Key: Howard rides his bicycle / and Thad rides in a seat on the back. / They wear hats to shade their eyes. / They go to the park / and they go down the big slide./

Number of words   32
Number of T-units   5
32 (words) ÷ 5 (T-units) = 6.4 (mean length of T-unit)

An Example

Definition:
T-unit = One group of words that will stand alone with all subordinate clauses.

Practice

Sentence	T-units	Type of sentence
Thad likes to run.	1	Simple sentence
While Thad likes to run, he also likes to swim.	1	Complex sentence: one independent and one dependent clause
Thad likes to run and he also likes to swim.	2	Compound sentence: 2 independent clauses
When Thad collects shells	0	Sentence fragment
Thad collects shells and he builds sand castles and he splashes Christopher and he also reads to Tonya.	4	Compound run-on sentence.

FIGURE 13.8
Calculating mean T-Unit and rating sentence complexity

Specific-Level Procedure 4: Semantic Maturity.[2] This test is similar to the semantic test in chapter 12. A limitation is that counting words and comparing them to a word frequency list is time consuming. It may be more efficient to simply judge whether word choice is adequate.

Directions.
1. Obtain samples of written work or analyze samples from survey.
2. Use the procedure described by Isaacson (1985).
   a. Obtain a graded list of frequently used words (e.g., Barrett et al., 1983).
   b. Note words used by the student that are listed above the student's present grade/age level.
   c. Count the total number of words in the sample.
   d. Calculate the percentage of "mature words."
3. Summarize the student's performance and compare to standards.

Interpretation guidelines.

Question. Is the student's vocabulary skill adequate?

If yes, check other skills.
   If no, teach vocabulary. Refer to recommendations in chapter 9 and chapter 12.

Specific-Level Procedure 5: Grammar/Punctuation. The purpose of the checklist is to focus on content subdivisions within grammar, punctuation, and capitalization. Figure 13.9 illustrates these skills. You could add handwriting and spelling to a checklist but we have chosen to treat them separately.

Caution. This procedure focuses on production skills. Do not overlook a need to probe behavior at

_____
2. This section is drawn from Isaacson, 1985.

the recognition–identification level. As with other behaviors, some kids may not be able to spontaneously produce the response but they may recognize correct/incorrect usage. Since most basal series and most tests sample recognition behavior in written communication, the authors did not think it necessary to describe how to do this. Instruction for students who recognize the correct/incorrect form will be different from instruction for students who do not.

Directions.
1. Collect at least five representative samples of a student's written communication.
2. Tally errors in the categories shown in Figure 13.9.
3. Summarize the student's performance.
4. Compare to a standard for acceptable work. Since errors in mechanics are seldom acceptable, we use a 100% criterion.

Interpretation guidelines.

Question. Is the student's grammar acceptable?

If yes, answer next question.
   If no, teach and check aspects of mechanics. Mark "not adequate" or "not observed." Probe specific skills in isolation at the produce or identify levels.

Question. Are capitalization and punctuation skills acceptable?

If yes, check handwriting (Specific-Level Procedure 6) and spelling (Specific-Level Procedure 7).
   If no, teach capitalization and punctuation and check handwriting and spelling. Probe skills marked "not adequate" or "not observed" in isolation at the produce or identify levels.

Specific-Level Procedure 6: Handwriting.

Directions.
1. Collect at least three representative samples of the student's writing. Include work that

	Error Tally	Skill Adequate	Skill Not Adequate	More Data Needed
Grammar				
Sentence forms				
Simple				
Compound				
Complex				
Compound/complex				
Sentence types				
Declarative				
Interrogative				
Exclamatory				
Imperative				
Other				
Capitalization				
First name in sentence				
Name of person				
Title				
Days of week				
Month				
Street names				
Towns, cities, states, countries				
Personal pronoun "I"				
Buildings, companies, products				
Geographical names				
Family relationship used for name				
First word of quotation				
Other				
Punctuation				
Period				
End of sentence				
Initials and abbreviations				
Question Mark				
End of sentence				
Exclamation point				
Exclamatory sentence				
Emphasis				

FIGURE 13.9
Checklist for grammar, punctuation, and capitalization (continued on pp. 326–327)

	Error Tally	Skill Adequate	Skill Not Adequate	More Data Needed
Comma				
Items in a series				
Month, year				
City, state				
Day, month				
Direct address				
After year in sentence				
After state or country in sentence				
After introductory word in sentence				
Before conjunction joining independent clause				
Surround appositive				
Set off dependent clause				
Set off adverbial clause				
After greeting and closing in letters				
Apostrophe				
Contractions				
Possessions				
Semicolon				
Separation of series				
Other				
Colon				
Salutation of letter				
Expression of time				
Appositives				
Other				
Hyphen				
Compound word or phrase				
Prefix when base is capitalized				
Other				

FIGURE 13.9
(continued)

requires copying, writing from memory, and writing in the context of another task such as reading questions and formulating an answer. Include a timed task. Have the student use mode (cursive or manuscript) being taught.

2. Mark and analyze errors on *each* sample.
3. Complete a recording sheet like the one shown in Figure 13.10 for each sample. (If you cannot score the sample because it is completely illegi-

ble, you may want to see question A below before proceeding.)

4. Total the number of errors you record in each category (alignment, letter size, letter formation, etc.).
5. Divide this total by the total number of symbols written for each task. This computation will give you the proportion of errors per symbol for each sample.

	Error Tally	Skill Adequate	Skill Not Adequate	More Data Needed
Quotation marks				
Direct quotations				
Single with direct				
Block quotations (no marks)				
Dialogue				
Title				
Special use of words				
Parentheses				
Interruptions				
Technical information within text				
Italics				
Titles				
Words used as words				
Foreign words				
Stress				
Ellipses				
Omissions				
Dash				
Interruptions				
Other Usage				
Number words/digits				
Spell if 1 or 2 words				
In a list, use digits if any numbers contain 3 digits				
Spell any number at the beginning of a sentence				

FIGURE 13.9
(continued)

6. Note if writing becomes less legible at end of longer tasks.
7. Note if writing is less legible in context of another task like reading or math.
8. Identify the areas of most concern.

Interpretation guidelines.

Question A. Is the handwriting illegible?

If yes, check to see if there is a difference between manuscript and cursive. Repeat the procedure using samples from alternate handwriting style—manuscript if cursive is illegible; cursive if manuscript is illegible.

If no, check questions B, C, and D.

Question B. Does the student have an alignment, letter size, spacing, letter formation, spatial

Student _____ Grade _____ Evaluator _____ Date _____

Task _____

POWER/TIMED   COPY (NEAR/FAR) /MEMORY   TOTAL NO. OF SYMBOLS _____

ALIGNMENT	SIZE	SPACING	LETTER FORMATION	ORIENTATION	ADDITION	SUBSTITUTION	OMISSIONS
See Spot	See Spot	Se eSpot	See Spot	See Spot	Seee Spot	SEE Spot	Sec Spot

FIGURE 13.10
Handwriting recording form (error analysis)

orientation, omission, addition, or substitution problem across tasks or within one kind of task?

If yes, teach to area of concern and check questions C and D.
 If no, check questions C and D.

Question C. Is the writing less legible at end of longer tasks?

If yes, fatigue is confirmed as a problem, examine grip and provide practice.
 If no, check question D.

Question D. Is the writing less legible in the context of other tasks like reading, math, or written communication (i.e., less legible on the survey writing samples) than on specific-level tasks in isolation?

If yes, teach for writing fluency.

Specific-Level Procedure 7: Spelling.

Directions.
1. Construct and administer a spelling test that will permit you to collect about 75 errors. Be sure that the test provides an opportunity for each type of spelling error. Use the error types identified by Spache (1940) shown in Table 13.6.
2. Score and categorize the errors.
3. Summarize the errors by category using the format illustrated in Figure 13.11.
4. Identify areas of concern.
5. Use an informal phonetic spelling inventory (Figure 13.1).

Interpretation guidelines.

Question A. Do there seem to be identifiable error patterns?

If yes, provide error correction instruction. Also check questions B, C, D, and E.
 If no, check questions B, C, D, and E.

TABLE 13.6
Common spelling errors

1. Omission of a silent letter (e.g., *wether* for *weather*, *reman* for *remain*, *fin* for *fine*)
2. Omission of a sounded letter (e.g., *requst* for *request*, *plasure* for *pleasure*, *personl* for *personal*, *juge* for judge)
3. Omission of a doubled letter (e.g., *suden* for *sudden*, *adress* for *address*, *sed* for *seed*)
4. Doubling (e.g., *untill* for *until*, *frriend* for *friend*, *deegree* for *degree*)
5. Addition of a single letter (e.g., *darck* for *dark*, *nineth* for *ninth*, *refere* for *refer*)
6. Transposition or partial reversal (e.g., *was* for *saw*, *nickle* for *nickel*, *bron* for *born*)
7. Phonetic substitution for a vowel (e.g., *prisin* for *prison*, *injoy* for *enjoy*)
8. Phonetic substitution for a consonant (e.g., *prixon* for *prison*, *cecond* for *second*, *vakation* for *vacation*)
9. Phoentic substitution for a syllable (e.g., *purchest* for *purchased*, *financhel* for *financial*, *naborhood* for *neighborhood*, *stopt* for *stopped*)
10. Phonetic substitution for a word (e.g., *weary* for *very*, *colonial* for *colonel*)
11. Nonphonetic substitution for a vowel (e.g, *rad* for *red*, *reword* for *reward*)
12. Nonphonetic substitution for a consonant (e.g., *watching* for *washing*, *inportance* for *importance*)

Source: G. D. Spache. (1940). "Characteristic Errors of Good and Poor Spellers," *Journals of Educational Research, 34,* 182–189.

Question B. Does the student use phonic generalizations?

If yes, check questions C, D, and E.
 If no, confirm the ones he knows and teach ones he doesn't.

Question C. Does the student recognize when he misspells a word and know how to find correct spelling?

If yes, check questions D and E.
 If no, teach proofing skills.

Stimulus	Response	Error Type from Table 13.6 (listed as it occurred)
1. keeper	*kepr*	3, 2
2. stories	*strz*	2, 9
3. team	*tem*	1
4. teach	*tesh*	1, 12
5. cowboy	*kboy*	8, 2
6. why	*y*	2, 1
7. funny	*funy*	3
8. that's	*thets*	apostrophe
9. kite	*kit*	1
10. sorry	*sry*	2, 3
11. line	*lin*	1
12. air	*ar*	1
13. became	*becm*	2, 1
14. mile	*mil*	1
15. bigger	*bigr*	3, 2
16. birds	*brdz*	2, 8
17. animal	*aml*	6, 2
18. I'll	*Il*	apostrophe, 3
19. tribe	*trb*	2, 1
20. truck	*truk*	2
21. eight	*at*	7, 1
22. won	*on*	2
23. merry	*mry*	2, 3
24. helper	*helpr*	2
25. fair	*fr*	2, 1
26. send	*sen*	2

FIGURE 13.11
Categorization of spelling errors

Question D. Does the student have a problem spelling in the context of another task (survey-level writing task) that didn't show up in specific-level assessment?

If yes, teach for fluency.
   If no, check question E.

Question E. If the student is at or above third grade, does he use morphographs effectively?

If yes, address other problems.
   If no, check the morphographs he knows and begin instruction on high utility ones he doesn't know. Use morphographs listed in Table 13.5 to formulate beginning assessment.

INSTRUCTIONAL RECOMMENDATIONS

In this chapter we will not discuss instructional recommendations in any detail. The emphasis in earlier chapters should serve as a model for organizing interventions. Previous recommendations fall into these intervention groups: (a) teach content—planning, reviewing, mechanics, semantics, spelling, etc.; (b) intervene on errors; and (c) teach strategies. Within these three interventions, fluency and generalization should be addressed. Because writing is an active, constructive process, student involvement is paramount. This involvement is characterized by self-monitoring. Even something as mechanical as handwriting can be improved with self-monitoring. Students who monitor their work will review what they need to do, check what they have done, and judge the adequacy of their responses.

Students need frequent meaningful opportunities to write. They also need explicit instruction in the purpose, process, and product development of written communication. Even after they master individual components, they will probably need instruction in how to integrate these complex skills to achieve their desired effects.

SUMMARY

Chapter 13 defined written communication as a complex process that includes purpose, process, and product. It provided a detailed description of two components found in both process and product —handwriting and spelling. The authors discussed evaluation issues in writing and addressed concerns regarding the absence of writing instruction in schools. We then outlined procedures for analyzing written communication.

_____ *Study Questions* _____

1. Planning occurs
   a. before and during transcription.
   b. before transcription.
   c. before the purpose has been formally established.
   d. primarily in the reviewing stage.
2. How do planning, reviewing, and revising interact with one another?
3. Why has so much time been spent discussing spelling and handwriting in this chapter? Are they the most important aspects of written communication?
4. Is it better to teach writing as a process or to focus on mechanics?
5. How many correct word sequences are in these sentences?

   My friend has a poodle. He soft and pretty.

6. How is a student's fluency determined?
7. Calculate the mean T-unit length for these sentences.

   Yesterday we went to look at some land. While we were there, we saw a rattlesnake, which did not bite us. We went away from there and we left it alone.

8. You have calculated the semantic maturity of a student's writing sample, and find that he is below his peers in this area. What should you teach?
9. What are the indicators that a student needs further instruction on the writing *process*?
10. What should you do if you administer a spelling evaluation and the student seems to exhibit no identifiable error patterns?

Social Skills

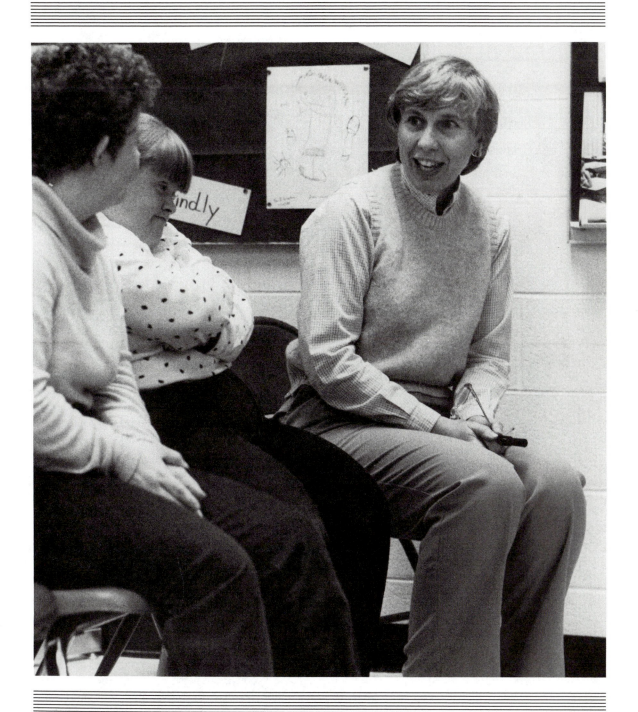

FOCUS ON SOCIAL SKILLS

Let's begin this discussion by making the point that the distinction between academic and social behavior is fairly arbitrary. In spite of the fact that methods for the two domains are often presented in separate courses, the authors believe that the same principles of learning and treatment apply to both. Academic behaviors and social behaviors both respond to the same sorts of interventions. The critical distinction between the two is not found in the topography of the behaviors or the nature of their treatment, but in the minds of the teachers and researchers who work with them. We can briefly encapsulate the problem by stating that teachers believe they are hired to produce academic behaviors and to *control* social behaviors. As a result, they typically develop curriculum, plan lessons, and schedule instructional time for academics, but not for social behavior. Teachers seldom set aside a time to teach students how to behave socially; instead they expect "good" social behavior and react to "bad" social behavior. In some ways social behavior is like oral language in that students are expected to be proficient at it when they enter school.

The typical chapter on evaluating social behavior advises you to (a) select a behavior to change, (b) count it, (c) chart it, (d) intervene on it, and (e) observe the data for evidence of the intervention ef-

fect. Although continuous data collection and analysis have become linked to the evaluation of social behavior, they are equally applicable to academics. Therefore the authors have placed that discussion in chapter 15. Teachers who focus on academics could benefit from some information about monitoring and data collection; those who focus on social behavior could benefit from knowledge of the design and delivery of instruction.

Some Groundwork

In this chapter we will assume you already know:

1. That social behavior is learned and determined in part by prior experience;
2. That it is influenced by the context (situation) in which the individual is behaving; and
3. That it can be changed through the application of various interventions including those that fall under the heading of *behavior management*.

Over the years the term *behavior* has almost become synonymous with conduct. However, in this chapter the term *behavior* is used to describe *either* academic *or* social actions. *Social behavior* takes place between individuals. It may include interpersonal events, such as communication, play, and cooperation. It may also include withdrawal, aggression, and antisocial acts. Social behavior can be interpreted so broadly that it includes nearly all behavior.

Throughout the chapter we will use terms like *inappropriate* and *appropriate*. The authors recognize that these terms are relative and subjective so we won't even try to define them (you know it when you see it). *Maladaptive behavior* refers to behavior that interferes with the social, academic, or physical growth of the student or his peers. *Overt behaviors* are those requiring muscular movement, such as standing up or speaking. *Covert behaviors* are those involving cognitive activity, such as thoughts and feelings. Overt behaviors should be described in terms that are not open to interpretation and are easily understood by people who are not familiar with the student or his behavior. For this reason, all statements regarding the student's overt behavior are put to the *stranger test* (a test of reliability). This simply means that a stranger reading the behavioral statement should be able to see and count the same number of occurrences the evaluator sees and counts. The process of writing a behavioral statement that passes the stranger test is referred to as *pinpointing*, and the resultant statement is called a *pinpoint*.

While inappropriate behavior is called *maladaptive*, appropriate or positive behavior is referred to as *target behavior*. Target behavior is the behavior that the teacher wants the student to engage in after instruction is finished. A *target pinpoint* is really nothing but an objective. Because social behaviors are seldom described in task-analytic terms, we will use the label *prerequisite* for *subtask* throughout most of this discussion. *Prerequisites* are the essential skills, knowledge, beliefs, expectations, or perceptions that a student must have to engage in a target pinpoint. *Type 1* prerequisites consist of skill and knowledge. *Type 2* prerequisites consist of beliefs, expectations, and perceptions.

Control versus Therapy

Many treatments designed to change children's social behaviors don't work. By "don't work," we mean that the changes don't last. Although you may change the student's social behavior in one setting, that change often doesn't maintain or generalize to other settings. There are at least two explanations for this. The first is that the intervention used was not properly designed in that it didn't incorporate efforts to make sure that the change would generalize. The second is that the selection of the pinpoint (the behavior to be changed) was incorrect. If the wrong behavior is selected, any intervention is useless. Just as in academic areas, one must use great care when deciding *what to teach* a student about social behavior.

As you recall, a central component of any evaluative effort is comparison: To evaluate is to compare. Therefore it is important to consider what an evaluator is comparing the student (or her behavior) to. When one evaluates academics, the standard of comparison is a preexisting set of learning outcomes or academic objectives. In social behavior, this prespecified set of learning outcomes does not exist because there is no widely accepted social behavior curriculum. Obviously, curriculum-based evaluation is hard to do without a curriculum. (Because there isn't an agreed-upon curriculum in social behavior, this text won't supply tables of specifications.) Without a curriculum, comparisons (and consequently, evaluations) get sloppy.

The operational definition of maladaptive behavior in most classrooms is "whatever irritates the teacher." If all teachers were equally tolerant, this wouldn't be a problem, but they aren't. When Walker and Rankin (1983) gave teachers a list of maladaptive behaviors and asked them to note which ones they would not accept in their classroom, one teacher marked 51 as unacceptable while another marked 8. This variability in teacher tolerance introduces tremendous confusion into the educational system's efforts to deal with social behavior.

Because few school programs have articulated objectives for social skills, interventions in the area are almost always reactive. This means that no work is done in social skills until a student does something adequately offensive to alarm a teacher. In response, the offending behavior is stated in observable terms and counted prior to intervention. Next, a series of interventions is tried until the behavior is increased or decreased. The purpose of all this seems to be to control the student's behavior at a level that is acceptable to the teacher or class. The weaknesses of this system stem from the facts that (a) all teachers do not have the same personal standards, (b) all classrooms do not require the same social behaviors, and (c) the behavioral requirements of classrooms are frequently quite different from the requirements of the everyday world. Consequently, controlling the student in one class doesn't guarantee her adjustment in another or outside. Because this focus on "situational control" is not educationally legitimate, the entire program (including its evaluation) becomes suspect.

Control

Control is something others do to bring a person into alignment with the requirements of a current situation regardless of that person's wants. Control is imposed from the outside and is effective only as long as the outside pressure is present (or thought to be). While education also begins as an external intervention, its purpose is to teach the skills a person needs to (a) remain in control of herself and (b) advance toward her own social objectives without (c) violating socially imposed restrictions or (d) consuming an inordinate amount of community resources.

It is easy for teachers to confuse control and education, particularly considering that control of a child is often a legitimate educational objective. However, while the focus of education should always be beyond the walls of the classroom, many teachers lose sight of this principle when faced with the prospect of routinely dealing with groups of children. While evidence of this loss of perspective is abundant, one particularly interesting example was reported in the study just mentioned (Walker & Rankin, 1983). In an effort to develop a scale for recognizing potential mainstreaming sites, the authors asked classroom teachers to rank order a list of problematic behaviors. Of the behaviors ranked, teachers responded that "poor attendance" was the least problematic, being ranked lower than all others (including profanity, nervous tics, and wearing a brace). One interpretation of these results is that many teachers would rather have a kid completely gone than to have him there while being disruptive.

The authors have encountered further evidence of the control-specific orientation many teachers take to social behavior. In one of our graduate classes (made up of currently practicing special education teachers), we started the social behavior unit by asking for examples of "behaviors you would like to learn to change." The responses included "stop getting out of seat," "stop talking out," "stop cheating," and "stop hitting." Every example supplied by the class had two things in common. First, they were all behaviors that, if allowed to occur, would threaten the teacher's control of the class. Second, they were all behaviors targeted for *deceleration*. The class of 30 teachers did not think of a single thing they wanted students to do—only things they wanted stopped. No one suggested "increasing appropriate social contact," "increasing assertiveness," "increasing use of questions," or increasing anything else. This premium on doing away with behaviors is consistent with the goal of classroom control but is antithetical to the concepts of education and instruction. *Teaching is giving, not taking away.*

By focusing on controlling student behavior, teachers make themselves the agents of control. As long as this is the case, students will have problems in the outside world. As educators, we really have two options: We can spend the rest of our lives with the students or we can teach them to control themselves. Given the other option, teaching self-control sounds like a good idea.

Self-Control

To reach the objective of self-control one must do two things. First, plan for generalization by seeing that every lesson in social behavior leads the student out of the special class. Second, teach the student the skills necessary to walk into any situation and discover how she should behave if she wishes to stay, and how she can get out if she wishes to leave. To do these things "appropriately," the student must learn to (a) analyze each setting, (b) discover the critical aspects of that setting (the cues that tell how to behave there), (c) decide what to do, (d) do it, and (e) monitor and adjust her behavior according to the circumstances.

So-called normal individuals can do these five things. Somehow they've learned to find the cues in the environment and use their adaptive skills to either select behaviors consistent with those cues, or avoid places where they can't adjust. The behavior-disordered individual hasn't learned these things. If she hasn't spontaneously learned these skills in the past, there's really no reason for us to expect that she will in the future. Yet that's exactly what educators expect when all they do is control the kid in one setting after another, expecting that she's somehow going to "pick up" normal social behavior. One would do better to *teach* analyzing, monitoring, problem solving, and adaptation skills directly. This means incorporating these skills in the curriculum.

Social Skills Curriculum

Figure 14.1 lists content areas that might be used to make up a social skills curriculum. These are the general areas in which students probably should be skilled if they are to behave appropriately across settings. The reason language is listed first is that a large proportion of the cues that tell how to behave in any situation are linguistic.

Another content area to include in a social skills curriculum is relaxation. People considered successful can relax in stressful situations. This skill at relaxation allows them to function better. Behavior-disordered individuals sometimes can't do this even though one can teach people to recognize when they are stressed and to relax (Kaplan, 1982).

Self-monitoring/evaluation is the skill to track one's own behavior. If you have self-monitoring skills, you are in a good position to begin to control yourself. Teachers often complain that they don't have time to take data on students; a good solution

1. Language
2. Relaxation
3. Self-monitoring/Evaluation
4. Problem solving
5. Recognition of target thoughts and behaviors
6. Knowledge of cognitive/behavioral change techniques

FIGURE 14.1
Social behavior content areas

to that problem is to teach them to take data on themselves. Self-monitoring will not automatically change behavior, but it is a prerequisite for self-initiated change.

Problem solving is probably the pivotal domain of content for a social skills curriculum. While problem-solving and thinking skills training has been widely discussed (Derry & Murphy, 1986), some main points need to be summarized. Students who have problems in social behavior don't solve problems well (Schumaker, Pederson, Hazel, & Meyer, 1983). Given problems, they generate fewer solutions (meaning they literally have less freedom to act); given solutions, they pick the worst ones (often picking options with which they are familiar over more effective ones). While many people imagine disruptive students to be clever and cunning adversaries, the truth is that students with behavior problems are often confined within a very limited set of behavioral options because they automatically select "inappropriate" responses from the very narrow range of behaviors with which they are familiar. Their poor problem-solving skills prevent them from pushing aside the first options they recall (the inappropriate ones they have practiced so often in the past) so that they can recognize more acceptable responses.

In addition to language, relaxation, and problem solving, students need to be aware of behavior and cognitive change techniques if they are to control their own behavior. They should know a few simple principles like reinforcement, punishment, extinction, and positive self-talk. Then they will be in a position to use these techniques on themselves.

Once students have intervention skills, they need to recognize target thoughts, feelings, and behaviors that need to be changed. This includes recognizing what is appropriate and what is not appropriate to different situations.

These six content headings could be used to develop a behavioral curriculum, as explained in chapter 3. Again, in the absence of a prespecified curriculum, teachers tend to react to the students' inappropriate behaviors. Consequently, efforts to work with social behavior are piecemeal. This is bad because interventions that are not coordinated into a system of delivery are less effective (Gagné, 1985). Suppose a math teacher decided to cover addition, fractions, counting, and square roots (all things his students couldn't do correctly) in a single lesson. And next imagine that the way he decided to teach these various tasks was by merely giving the students occasional feedback on their errors—no initial explanation and no corrective feedback. Such a lesson is similar to the social behavior "instruction" many students receive when they are simply reprimanded for talking out, getting out of seat, or whatever other violations happen to come up throughout the day.

Task Analysis and Social Skills

To many of you, the material on curriculum presented in chapters 2 and 3 may seem to be strictly related to academics. However, things like tables of specifications and objectives pertain just as much to social behavior. Table 14.1 is a table of specifications for the task "begin play." As you can see, the table has a content axis and a condition axis. (Conditions are particularly relevant to social behavior because it tends to be situation-specific.)

While it is true that concepts such as content, conditions, and tables of specifications are important to the discussion of social skills, the idea of *strategies* is particularly important. A math lesson that merely presents isolated answers is less efficient than one that presents the strategies for arriving at the answers. Similarly, behavior change programs that provide feedback on various social errors or reinforcement for appropriate behavior, while commonplace, represent poorly conceptualized instruction. These attempts at social-skill training focus only on facts like "out of seat" or "on time" and ignore the underlying strategies that consolidate the domain of social skills. These include specific techniques for obtaining attention; reading environmental cues; adjusting posture,

TABLE 14.1
Table of specifications for "begin play"

Objective: Glenna will begin play in various situations without disrupting others.

| | Conditions | | |
Behavior and Content	Role Play in Class	With Familiar Students at Recess	With Strangers after School
Begin play if allowed or repeat sequence if rejected			
Ask permission to play			
Select a person to ask about playing			
Determine if additional players can be used			
Decide if you know how to play it			
Decide if you want to play it			
Identify an ongoing game			

CAP: Without disrupting others.

speech, and facial expression; joining groups; leaving groups; and initiating contact with strangers. They also include general strategies for setting personal goals, arranging resources, plotting a course of action, monitoring progress, and adjusting behavior.

A Model of Social Behavior

If there were a widely accepted social behavior curriculum, then evaluators could evaluate by comparing the student to the objectives of that curriculum. Without a curriculum, they must compare the student to their own standards or to various models of behavior. Many such models exist, though they vary in complexity and function. To coordinate the material in this chapter, we have come up with our own nifty model (Figure 14.2). This model isn't very complex and is not even original, but it seems functional.

According to this model, the world is composed of "things" and things can be divided into two categories—those that the kid can't do and those that he can do. Next, the things that the kid can do are divided into two subcategories—those that he does do and those that he doesn't do. (We admit it's simplistic.)

Given this model, the questions that you ask yourself when you evaluate a student are (a) "Is this kid behaving inappropriately because he *can't* do the appropriate behavior?" or (b) "Is the student behaving inappropriately because he *chooses* the wrong thing to do?" These are two very different conditions.

In a way it sounds as if we are saying that there are two types of behavior-disordered students in classrooms, one type who can't behave appropriately and another who is selecting not to. We aren't. The same student may have both problems. We've never seen a kid with a social behavior difficulty who had only one problem behavior. Most kids have many problems, some of which they can't deal with appropriately and some of which they can. Keeping in mind that we are talking about types of problems, not types of kids, let's look at the two types a little more closely by using an analogy.

You are currently reading a book (this one). If you are a student, some of you are reading this chapter 10 minutes before the test (got ya!) and

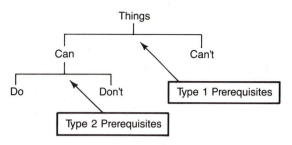

FIGURE 14.2
The basic model for evaluating social behavior

others are reading it weeks ahead of time. As you read some of you are seated in chairs, others on couches, and some are probably in bed or on the floor. None of you are sitting on the ceiling, because you *can't*. The environment (gravity) prohibits you from sitting on the ceiling.

When we say that a student *can't* do the appropriate thing, we mean that he lacks the skills to do it or to overcome the environmental influences that militate against it. When we say that a student *doesn't* do the appropriate thing we mean that he has selected, from among the things he can do, the wrong one. Now we have to be careful here because some of you may think this means the student has consciously, and with intent to irritate you, selected an inappropriate way to behave. While this is sometimes true (in which case the student is reacting to you as much as you are reacting to him), more often selecting an inappropriate behavior is *not* the same as deciding to behave inappropriately.

People often select behaviors automatically (Kirsch, 1985). If you recall the discussion of automaticity, it said that automatic responses occur without the use of working (conscious) memory. So here's the question. When you started to read this chapter did you say this to yourself, "Well I'd rather not stand while I read so I guess I'll lean, sit, or lie down. Research shows that those who lie down to study (particularly in bed) learn less—so I'll sit. I could sit on the floor or in a chair or on the couch. I never sit in *that* chair because that's where I throw my stuff when I walk in at night. The couch is OK but gets more like a bed the longer I sit in it. So I'll pick the floor. In fact I'll pick the floor next to the window so I get the best light and can see if anyone more interesting than this book is walking by."

While each of you had many options from which to choose (many places to sit), we doubt that many of you recall consciously choosing where to sit. You did choose, but it was not the kind of rational and considered choice you might employ when selecting an investment or new job. Just as you are not "aware" of all of the choices you make, kids with behavior problems are largely unaware of the ones they make or how they make them. Because they are unaware of the strategy they use to select the behavior, feedback that their choices are wrong is not apt to alter the strategy they used.

Can versus Can't

The evaluation starts with the question, "Is the kid behaving inappropriately because she can't do the appropriate behavior?" This question attributes the inappropriate behavior to a missing prerequisite. A student may not be able to engage in a behavior because (a) she doesn't have the skills to do so, or (b) something in the environment is inhibiting her. If either case is true the evaluator has found an example of missing Type 1 prerequisites because he has found a student who does not have the skill or knowledge to carry out appropriate behavior.

Do versus Don't

In our model (Figure 14.2) the student who can do a behavior must still select whether or not to do it. The selection depends upon Type 2 prerequisites such as beliefs, expectations, and perceptions. Let's go back to the discussion of choosing a place to sit. When you walk into a bank to apply for a loan you still don't sit on the ceiling because you still can't. You *can* sit on the floor, but you don't sit there either because your perceptions of the situation, desire to get the loan, and beliefs about appropriate behavior tell you to select a chair.

Selections are based upon covert things like interests, perceptions, expectations, fears, and desires. These things form a selection strategy that the student uses to pick responses. When people have options, they select one and don't select the others by using selection strategies related to what they're thinking at the time, what's important to them, and what's not important. These thoughts, as

well as the way people go about changing and working with what they know, are learned. Because different people have different learning histories, they have different ideas and beliefs about the world. As a result, they select different things to do. If, for some reason, our thinking changes, we make different selections. To evaluate selection strategies, evaluators must work within the domain of covert behaviors. This is considerably more difficult, and chancy, than working with the overt explanations associated with Type 1 prerequisites.

Applied Behavior Analysis. One way to find Type 1 and Type 2 prerequisites is to use applied behavior analysis (Kerr & Nelson, 1983). This is a system through which one attempts to specify the antecedents and consequences of naturally occurring behaviors. The assumption behind applied behavior analysis is that behavior is affected by context. That means that an understanding of the environment is necessary. This is particularly true within "high impact environments" such as the school and family (Bower, 1972).

Behavior is interactive. It takes place between the individual and the current environment. So if you want to evaluate social behavior you can't just attend to the individual; you must also attend to the social environment. For example, suppose Victorio has the problem "hitting peers." How is his environment supporting this undesirable behavior? To answer this question the evaluator observes Victorio and writes down what is seen, in the format shown in Figure 14.3.

Imagine that in observing Victorio you find that he hits (a) in the classroom, (b) during free time, (c) in the mornings, (d) when there's low structure, and (e) when his peers are saying negative things about him. Next you look around to see what happens after he hits somebody and you find that (a) the peer runs away, (b) the negative comments stop, and (c) the teacher puts Victorio in time out (removes him from the reinforcement of the classroom). If the behavior is maintaining (Victorio is continuing to hit peers), it is assumed that the antecedents and consequences are in "balance."

Sometimes the environment may actually prohibit appropriate behavior. As stated earlier, the criterion for appropriate social behavior, unlike

FIGURE 14.3
Applied behavioral analysis of Victorio's hitting behavior

Antecedents S^1	Behavior R	Consequences S^2
1. Classroom 2. Free time 3. Morning 4. Low structure 5. Peers give negative comments	Student hits peer	1. Peer runs away 2. Negative comments stop 3. Teacher puts kid in time out

academic skills, is not the *median* of successful students. In this culture, the social criterion is the *norm*. Consequently, a teacher should not expect any student to exhibit social behavior that isn't like the class average. (Our feelings about individuality require us to elaborate on this for a moment. We are *not* suggesting that all students *should* behave in the same way. We are simply stating that it is unrealistic for teachers to expect them to do otherwise.)

The environmental frequency of a behavior places ecological boundaries (ceiling or floor) on that behavior. These may not be at the same level as the teacher's expectation. For example, imagine a

student named Karen. Karen originally talks out in class 3 times per minute. The absolute floor for this behavior would be zero times per minute. The teacher expects Karen to talk out no more than .03 times per minute. Excluding Karen's behavior and that of another kid with the same pinpoint, talk-outs occur in the classroom 1.5 times a minute. These levels are shown in Figure 14.4.

As you can see in Figure 14.4, Karen's behavior has moved toward the teacher's expectation but has not passed the ecoiogical floor. For this behavior, or any other social behavior, the ecological floor is as far as the change should go. At this point (.03 on the chart), the environment actually begins to work

FIGURE 14.4
Karen's "talk out" behavior decreasing to the ecological floor

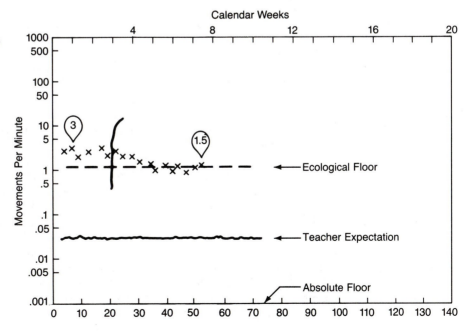

against the behavior change. A teacher can cause the student to go beyond the ecological floor by calling upon increasingly powerful interventions, but consider what incidental lessons he would be teaching! First of all he would be teaching the student to deviate from her peers, which is often the special student's biggest problem in the first place. Second, he would be teaching the student to disregard the primary environmental cue defining appropriate behavior (the behavior of others). Therefore, he would be decreasing the likelihood of his intervention generalizing to any other setting. If the "normal" student gets out of seat six times in a period, the special education/remedial kid should be allowed to do that too.

Behavior that is abnormal, even if it is in the direction with which we are most comfortable, is still abnormal. If a teacher wants Karen to conform to his expectations, he should first move her to the class average, and then move the whole class to a more appropriate level. This level must be determined through careful observations of target settings, not through teacher judgment alone. As a general rule, it appears that special education teachers have more tolerance for inappropriate behavior than do regular education teachers (Algozzine, Herr, & Eaves, 1976). Therefore, moving students to the special teacher's level of tolerance will not promote generalization to other classes. The unique techniques, materials, peer groups, and attitudes of special teachers can actually inhibit generalization.

The generalization and maintenance of behavior change should always be uppermost in the evaluator's or teacher's mind when setting criteria or selecting interventions. If one uses procedures that will not generalize, then he is guilty of merely controlling the student for his own comfort. We aren't particularly fond of the way many schools try to make all students behave in an "average" way. But we think that using behavioral technology to make them average is considerably less of a trespass than using it to make teachers comfortable.

Applied behavior analysis and a task-analytical approach are used to determine if the student lacks Type 1 prerequisites and therefore "can't" engage in proper behavior. If she can't behave appropri-

ately because she lacks the skills needed to deal with her environment, then obviously the teacher should teach her these skills. But what about the student who can behave appropriately but doesn't? According to the model in Figure 14.2, one must also consider those factors that lead students to select inappropriate things to do. This requires a move away from the conventional consideration of overt behavior and movement cycles. As a result, some rationale for this move needs to be provided.

Rationale and Caution for a Cognitive Approach to Social Behavior

Some students know what to do and have the necessary skills to do it but still misbehave because their belief systems encourage them to select maladaptive behaviors. They may automatically reject attempts at communication, distrust representatives of authority, and accept without question the opinions of those who enjoy status in their peer group. These students seem to react impulsively without thought of the consequences of their behavior. Anxiety, fear, anger, or just plain confusion may influence their selection of behaviors. These students need to learn new selection strategies before one can realistically expect them to engage in the target behavior consistently. To teach these strategies one must evaluate the student to determine which Type 2 prerequisites she needs to develop.

We began this chapter by stating that the effects of behavioral interventions frequently don't last and don't generalize. In the "operant" or "behavioral" camp, behaviors are viewed as the result of stimuli in the environment. A behavior learned in the presence of one set of stimuli may not occur as often in a setting where these stimuli aren't present. Therefore the best way to explain the presence or absence of a behavior is to analyze the environment, as was illustrated with the example of Victorio in Figure 14.3. This procedure makes sense if kids respond directly to the environment.

There is major evidence, however, that humans *don't* respond directly to the environment. That evidence is the fact that we don't all act the same way in the same environment. If behavior is only the re-

FIGURE 14.5
(a) Applied behavior analysis of Victorio's hitting behavior

Antecedents S^1	Behavior R	Consequences S^2
1. Classroom 2. Free time 3. Morning 4. Low structure 5. Peers give negative comments	Student hits peer	1. Peer runs away 2. Negative comments stop 3. Teacher puts kid in time out

(b) Applied cognitive-behavioral analysis of Victorio's hitting behavior

Antecedents S^1	Behavior R	Consequences S^2
1. Classroom 2. Free time 3. Morning 4. Low structure 5. Peers give negative comments	*Thought* "If I let them talk to me that way I'm a sissy." Student hits peer.	1. Peer runs away 2. Negative comments stop 3. Teacher puts kid in time out

sult of the situation, then why don't all kids act the same way in the same class? The answer is that they don't respond to the environment itself but to their cognitive representations of the environment (Mahoney, 1977). Said another way, people don't behave according to what is going on, but according to what they *think* is going on. These thoughts and feelings are the result of the interaction of environmental stimuli with learned perceptions, expectations, and beliefs. Perceptions, expectations, and beliefs are cognitive behaviors developed during our individual pasts. Ignoring the issue of innate personality differences (teachers can't alter innate things too well anyway), the best explanation for individualistic behavior is unique learning histories. Because people have learned different things and their behavior is partially the result of their learning, they behave in different ways (Shuell, 1987).

Take a second look at Victorio. Figure 14.3 is reproduced in Figure 14.5a. This is an example of applied behavior analysis. In Figure 14.5b an additional component, a thought, has been added to the analysis. Victorio has learned the belief that inactivity in the presence of insults is the sign of a sissy. Since he thinks a sissy is something bad, Victorio doesn't remain inactive; he pummels his peer. If he

had the belief "sticks and stones may break my bones but words will never hurt me," he might select a different response to the situation. His beliefs comprise part of the selection strategy by which he chooses what to do. If this idea (that prior learning produces beliefs, expectations, and perceptions that in turn determine behavior) is correct, it follows that efforts to change behavior should include efforts to change what the student believes, how he perceives what is happening, and what he has come to expect. Obviously, these efforts would have to be preceded by an evaluation of the student's perceptions and expectations.

The Theory
We are working on the premise that every student has a selection strategy that he applies to make choices from available responses in the environment. This selection strategy is obviously not "real" in any physical or stable sense. It is the functional manifestation of the jumbled mass of prejudices, interests, fears, and desires acquired over the kid's lifetime. There are at least three labels applied to the cognitive behavior that comprises the selection strategy. They are perception, expectation, and be-

lief. While the authors don't maintain these three are in any way independent of each other or have any absolute reality, the terms themselves are useful for clarifying the theory.

Perception

Perceptions function as a template between awareness and the outside world. Perception allows people to notice those things that prior experience has taught are worth attention. For example, have you ever purchased a car only to discover on the way home from the dealer that the roads are suddenly crowded with exactly the same make, model, and color? Just as prior experience can cause you to notice the presence of cars you didn't notice before, it can cause you to miss other things. Sometimes a student can't do the correct thing because she is so busy attending to those things she has learned to perceive that she doesn't even see other options. To select an option, a student must first perceive it. There is some evidence that behavior-disordered individuals do not perceive the same numbers or types of options perceived by others. One explanation for this can be found in the so-called "availability heuristic" (Tuersky & Kahneman, 1973). The availability idea states that people are most apt to select options that are easy for them to recall. This ease of recall is thought to be a function of past experience. If in the past a kid has experienced one type of option frequently (or dramatically), that is the type of option she will most easily recall. Consequently, that is the type of option she will be most apt to select. Aggressive behavior is a good example of this. If a student has seen force applied frequently or dramatically to solve problems, then she is best prepared to recognize (perceive) forceful solutions to problems. When she experiences a new situation she may search for options, but because of her specially trained perception she only recognizes the ones involving force. Because she fails to "see" nonforceful options, she has fewer choices to make and therefore less freedom to act.

Recognition of options is a Type 2 prerequisite skill that can be taught. Because the absence of the skill may cause a student to be unable to select appropriate behaviors, it must be considered in the behavioral evaluation. One way to assess a student's ability to identify options is to present partially finished stories and ask her to supply as many endings as she can. For example, "John is downtown at night and has lost his money. List as many ways as you can think of for him to call his friends."

If the student cannot supply solutions to hypothetical problems or if all of her solutions are unrealistic or illegal, her problem could be in the solutions she perceives rather than in her skill at carrying them out.

Expectations

Every introductory psychology course teaches that the quality of a reinforcer is determined by the student. That is to say, what is reinforcing (or punishing) to one student may not be reinforcing (or punishing) to another. When a teacher takes $20 out to buy "reinforcers" at the first of the school year, he is really buying *potential* reinforcers. He hopes the kids will like what he buys, but they may not.

If a kid decides to work for candy, she carries out the work on the *expectation* that the candy will be received. This expectation is the result of past experiences in which candy was received after work was done. When a teacher follows a response with a pleasant stimulus, the probability of the response recurring is linked to the student's expectation that more responses will lead to additional pleasant stimuli.

If we take the strict operant model (Figure 14.6a) and insert perceptions and expectations, the model looks like Figure 14.6b. This amended model (Figure 14.6b) says that behavior will be chosen from among the perceived ecologically available responses. The selection will also be based upon the expected consequences of choosing each of the perceived responses (Rotter, 1982).

Beliefs

A belief is an idea an individual takes as fact. In other words, what a person believes is as real to him as what he is seeing and hearing at any given moment. Beliefs have been raised to factual status by the past experiences of the individual. These past experiences were themselves affected by perceptions and expectations, so of course it isn't possible

FIGURE 14.6
(a) The operant model

Stimulus ⟶ Response ⟶ Stimulus

(b) The operant model including perceptions and expectations

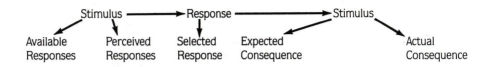

| Stimulus | ⟶ | Response | ⟶ | Stimulus | |
| Available Responses | Perceived Responses | Selected Response | Expected Consequence | | Actual Consequence |

to clearly distinguish beliefs from perceptions and expectations. However, a belief can be viewed as a rule which the person now applies to all situations regardless of current perceptions and expectations. A delinquent may believe, for example, that "cops can't be trusted" and hold that belief at all times. To others, that belief may seem appropriate in some situations and inappropriate in others, but the delinquent will continue to hold it as fact in all situations. Prejudices are examples of beliefs. They are acquired through learning and can be diminished by teaching other, incompatible beliefs.

Just as teachers can teach strategies for arriving at correct answers to academic problems, they may change a student's social skills through systematic instruction. For this instruction to be effective, they must pinpoint the perceptions, expectations, or beliefs that need to be changed or expanded. In other words, once again the teacher must decide *what to teach*. Frankly, we have some concern about presenting this material. There are three reasons for this concern: uncertainty about its practicality, risk of diluting the curriculum, and fear of misapplication.

Application. First of all, there isn't much sense in evaluating what you can't change. Few teachers or school psychologists are at present sufficiently informed in the area of cognitive intervention to design a systematic change program to alter a student's selection strategies. But some teachers are prepared, and there is an evolving behavioral technology that deals with cognition that all teachers should know about (see Kaplan, 1982). This "behavioral" approach to cognition appears to the au-

thors to be the logical next step for psychology to take. Our uneasiness results from our uncertainty about whether or not this next step should be a theoretical or an applied one.

Curriculum. Our second concern is based on the knowledge that special education has a long unfortunate history of misplaced faith in ideas about the unseen. We have spent decades directing treatments at the hypothesized cognitive or perceptual characteristics of kids (see Appendix A). Frequently our pursuit of the "psycholinguistic," "psychobehavioral," "psychomedical," and "psychoeducational" has led us far away from the skills we have an ethical responsibility to teach. So why do it again by suggesting that teachers consider the cognitive strategies by which kids select behaviors? The answer is that most teachers, most of the time, are already directing their attention to the covert behaviors of students. While "education" has many meanings, it certainly implies an effort to teach students to believe, to expect, and to perceive things differently than those who are uneducated. We accept this when the task is long division; it is harder to accept when the topic is making friends.

Misapplication. If some of you are getting nervous with all this talk about changing thoughts and beliefs—good! It is important to understand the implications education has for the lives of students. This discussion is easier when we limit it to apple-pie issues like littering or drug abuse. Suppose instead that we advocated changes in beliefs about abortion, tax fraud, religious orientation, or sexual activity. These more provocative issues spark controversy over the role of schools and the rights of individuals. Such controversy is easy to recognize when the topics are so clearly inflammatory. But it is imperative that educators recognize that all actions in school have social implications. (For example, the seemingly innocuous practice of sequencing elementary social studies lessons so that they cover local, county, state, national, hemispheric, and finally global issues has been criticized for making students regionally oriented and not citizens of the world.)

Our third concern is that teachers/evaluators will inappropriately attempt to impose their own belief systems on students. This would constitute a major misapplication of educational technology. We have made the point several times throughout this text that behavior is situational. That is to say, its appropriateness varies from setting to setting and it must be judged with its context in mind. Now we are saying that covert events like thoughts, beliefs, and perceptions are behaviors. If this is true then it follows that these covert behaviors must also be judged in reference to their context. Because "context" in this case includes the psychological as well as the geographic environment of the individual, it should be clear that there is no one "correct" way to think about or to perceive things. This has several implications for the current discussion.

A teacher's responsibility is to increase a student's behavioral options along with her control over these options. *The objective, therefore, is not to purge the student of "inappropriate thoughts" but to build a potentially useful repertoire of beliefs and perceptions along with systems for controlling them.* Remember that the student's current set of covert responses have been learned and have a reinforcement history. Because they may be quite appropriate in a nonschool setting, effective efforts to remove them could get the kid into trouble. (The idea that "words can never hurt me" may be fine for chemistry class but dead wrong in a particular home.) Ultimately the goal must be to present alternative ways of thinking, to teach the student how to test the environmental consequences of cognition, and to teach her how to exercise self-control.

EVALUATING SOCIAL BEHAVIOR

Teachers often view their student's problematic social behavior as a manifestation of emotional disturbance requiring the attention of a psychiatrist or psychologist. Actually most misbehavior exhibited in the classroom is learned and is specific to the classroom. (It is interesting to note that about 70% of classroom misbehavior occurs during transitions between lessons [Arlin, 1979]. This tells us that by simply improving management of transitions teachers can dramatically cut down on the misbehaviors they frequently blame on the child's emotional state.)

When children do not behave as teachers would like them to, it is often because they are lacking one or more of the prerequisite skills or selection strategies necessary for them to behave appropriately. One would not expect a student to compute long division successfully without mastering multiplication, division, and subtraction facts. Similarly, one should not expect her to be on time for class if she doesn't know what time the late bell rings, what the penalty for being tardy is, or how to make class a rewarding experience. *No amount of psychotherapy or token reinforcement is going to get a student to behave the way you want her to if she doesn't have the prerequisites necessary to behave that way.* It therefore becomes the evaluator's responsibility to find out what prerequisites a student needs in order to behave appropriately. The process used to make this decision is basically no different from that used in academics although there will be two variations in the process.

First, like reading comprehension, social behavior does not have a set of ordered prerequisites. Social behavior prerequisites seldom have the kind of functional or developmental relationship to one another that is necessary for building a sequence so we will not attempt to provide ordered lists of skills. Second, we have included an additional form to be used at the survey level that we call the "analysis sheet." It is used to help identify facts about the student's behavior.

The entire social behavior evaluation procedure is illustrated by the flowchart in Figure 14.7. During the fact-finding stage the evaluator describes the student's maladaptive behavior in terms that are easily understood and not open to interpretation. To assure that the behavior can be measured reliably, the stranger test is applied. To assure that it is not trivial, the "so-what" test is applied. (The so-what test is applied by reading the maladaptive behavior and asking yourself, "Is this really important enough to work on?") If the statement passes the stranger and so-what tests, it becomes a pinpoint or "fact." If it doesn't pass the tests, the evaluator rewrites it.

The evaluator then begins the task-analyzing stage by pinpointing the target behavior. Descriptions of target behaviors that do not pass the stranger and so-what tests are also rewritten. Once acceptable target pinpoints are produced, they are ready to be task analyzed. All of the prerequisites essential to the successful completion of the target pinpoint are listed in the prerequisite column on the analysis sheet. At this time each of the prerequisites is tentatively classified as Type 1 or Type 2.

The hypothesizing stage begins when the evaluator decides which, if any, prerequisites the student is lacking. Prerequisites that the evaluator knows the student has are not listed as assumed causes, while those he knows the student lacks are listed as instructional objectives. Those prerequisites about which the evaluator is in doubt are treated as assumed causes and targeted for specific-level testing.

The final stages, validating and decision making, take place at the specific level. Validating begins when the evaluator designs and administers probes to determine which of the assumed causes are actually valid (which prerequisites the student is lacking and needs to be taught). The results of this specific-level testing are then used to decide what to teach the student.

An Example

Social skills are sufficiently unique to justify going through a sample social skill evaluation before moving on to the sections on survey- and specific-level testing/observation.

Jay was a 7-year-old repeating the first grade.

According to his teacher, he was "always hurting somebody." She tried a number of interventions, including removing Jay from the classroom (to stand in the hall or sit in the office) and making phone calls to Jay's parents. The calls home were stopped when Jay came to school with a bruised face the next day. She suspected that these bruises were inflicted by one of Jay's parents and that such abuse was not unusual. (Such suspicions should always be reported to authorities.)

Jay's physically aggressive behavior had been a problem since he first entered school. He was constantly being separated from the other children to keep him from hitting, biting, pushing, or squeezing them. His academic performance suffered as a consequence of the behavior, which continued into his second year in first grade. Jay was eventually referred to a school psychologist for testing to determine his eligibility for a self-contained class of behavior-disordered (BD) students. He met the criteria and was immediately placed in the BD program. This solved the regular classroom teacher's problem, but it didn't help Jay. It also created a problem for the BD teacher because Jay's hitting didn't stop in the new surroundings. So the BD teacher attempted to diagnose Jay's problem by using the task-analytical model.

There were enough behavioral data available from Jay's 3 years in school to simplify any survey-level assessment. The maladaptive pinpoint (hits peers) was easy to select and count, and everyone (especially the peers) agreed that it passed the so-what test as a target pinpoint. Jay's new teacher decided that the target pinpoint should be "interact positively with his peers." To satisfy the stranger test, this was defined as (a) the absence of unprovoked physical acts inflicting pain, and (b) the presence of socially acceptable physical interactions, e.g., touching without inflicting pain. These target pinpoints were then task analyzed by Jay's teacher. She listed all of the prerequisites on an analysis sheet, as seen in Figure 14.8.

Jay's new teacher and his former teacher met to discuss each of the listed prerequisites. At first, Jay's former teacher was reluctant to meet. She protested, "If I knew what Jay's problem was, I

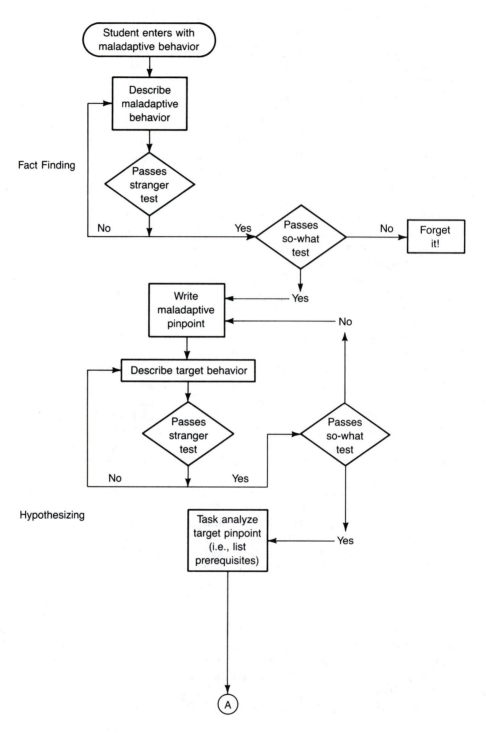

FIGURE 14.7
Using the TA model to determine if a student has the prerequisite skills necessary for appropriate behavior

Student enters with maladaptive behavior

Describe maladaptive behavior

Fact Finding

Passes stranger test

No   Yes

Passes so-what test   No   Forget it!

Yes

Write maladaptive pinpoint   No

Describe target behavior

Passes stranger test

No   Yes

Passes so-what test

Hypothesizing

Task analyze target pinpoint (i.e., list prerequisites)   Yes

A

348

FIGURE 14.7
(continued)

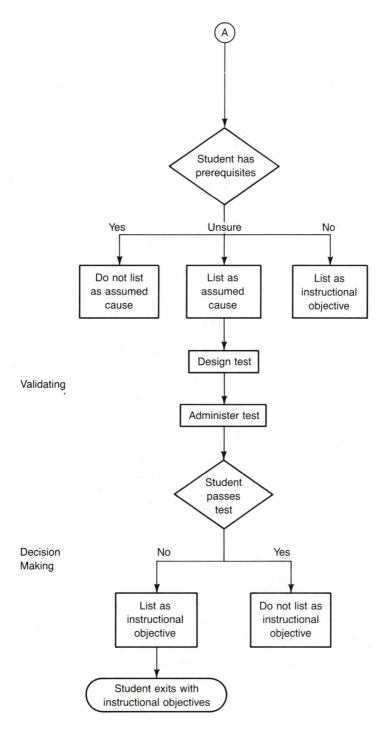

Validating

Decision
Making

Behaver: __Jay__ Manager: __Rice__
Diagnostician: __Kaplan__ Date: __November 1987__
Target Behavior: __Jay will interact positively with peers (no unprovoked hitting or other acts of physically aggressive behavior; instead, he will touch, pat, hold peer without inflicting pain).__

Type	Prerequisites of Target Behavior	Status (as determined by interviewing previous teachers)
1	1. Knows how to engage in positive interactions with peers (knows that you are supposed to touch peers without hurting them).	1. This is really the target behavior; everything he does indicates he doesn't know this. And considering suspected corporal punishment at home plus considerable amount of time separated from appropriately behaving peers, it's likely Jay may not have learned how to interact positively with peers — need to test.
1	2. Knows difference between positive and negative interactions (able to recognize when he is hurting peer and when he isn't).	2. When he's interacting with peer, even if he's not hitting or squeezing, he's always rough — uses more force than necessary — has never been observed interacting in gentle, soft, or even neutral way — need to test.
1	3. Knows and recognizes the consequences of engaging in positive and negative behaviors.	3. Knows what happens when he misbehaves but since he seldom, if ever, behaves properly with his peers, he has not had much opportunity to experience positive consequences — need to test.
1	4. Knows that it is more acceptable to interact positively with peers than negatively.	4. No information — need to test.
1	5. Controls his own behavior.	5. The teacher reports no problems with nonsocial behaviors such as motor tasks or self-care. Interestingly, Jay interacts fairly well with adults by avoiding them or being passive around them. No need to test.
1	6. Is not simply doing what the other kids do.	6. Jay's negative interactions are six times higher than the average in his special class! No need to test.
2	7. Wants to interact positively with peers.	7. Current teacher has no information on this at all — previous teacher assumes he doesn't. Need to test.
2	8. Considers the consequences of positive interactions rewarding and those of negative interactions aversive.	8. Since previously applied consequences for negative interactions do not appear to have any effect on his behavior, maybe Jay does not consider them aversive. No information about positive consequences since teacher has had little occasion to use any. Need to test.

FIGURE 14.8

wouldn't have asked for somebody else to work with him!" She was told that her inability to modify Jay's behavior by herself didn't mean she had nothing to contribute toward his treatment program. She was an "expert" on Jay's behavior and so could provide valuable data to others. By the end of the meeting, she tended to view Jay in a different light. She no longer saw him as a "bad seed" in need of exorcism, and it was largely through her cooperation that each prerequisite was evaluated.

Figure 14.8 illustrates the hypothesizing stage of Jay's diagnosis. During the meeting held in Jay's old classroom, all the prerequisites were listed on the blackboard and all his former teacher's comments regarding the status of each were written alongside. Where there was any doubt about a prerequisite, it was listed as an assumed cause and singled out for specific-level testing. Informal specific-level assessments were then designed and constructed. The conclusions drawn from the assessments are shown in Figure 14.9, which we recommend that you read thoroughly. Upon completion of this assessment by the BD teacher, it was determined that (a) Jay could not describe or act out appropriate behavior on cue; (b) he was unable to categorize examples of behavior; (c) he did know the consequences of specific behaviors; (d) he could not say what others thought of his behavior—only how they acted around him; and (e) it was not clear if he wanted to get along with others or only wanted to avoid negative contingencies.

Given those determinations, it was obvious that Jay needed to be *taught* the concept of appropriate and inappropriate behavior. As things were, the consequences teachers were delivering in response to his misbehavior probably made little sense to him. Social reinforcers such as the attention of peers weren't making any sense at all. Jay did not *know how* to interact positively with his peers, nor did he know that it's more socially acceptable to interact positively with peers than to interact negatively. Therefore, he could not benefit from feedback about his behavior. Treatment programs designed to teach these prerequisites were developed by the BD teacher. After considerable time and effort, Jay was able to interact positively with his peers. Negative interactions were kept at a minimum and eventually disappeared altogether.

SURVEY LEVEL

If a school is taking an affirmative stance on teaching social skills, then it has a functional curriculum in social skills in place. With such a curriculum an evaluator will be able to recognize objectives for pivotal skill areas (such as problem solving and self-monitoring) and select or develop screening tests for them. This is exactly the same curriculum-based evaluation procedure employed with academics.

Unfortunately it is more likely that the school will not have a social skills curriculum. This will put the evaluator in a position analogous to that of a teacher trying to decide who needs remedial reading without the aid of reading tests. As a result, most evaluations of social behavior are initiated by a referral (complaint) from a teacher or parent troubled by something the student is doing. (The person initiating the call for assistance will usually indicate if that problem falls within a broad category such as peer relations, assertiveness, aggression, or self-help. These general referrals always require clarification. One of us was once asked to see a student for his "out-of-seat" behavior. Because the kid always stayed in his seat in the author's office, he went to the classroom to observe and found that while the student was often out of his seat, so was everyone else. The problem was what he was doing when out of seat—bumping into things and flapping his arms—not being out of seat.) This initial focus on misbehavior feeds the exaggerated concern with control already discussed. The first order of business when evaluating social skills is to change this orientation by switching the focus from maladaptive behaviors to target behaviors.

The Survey-Level Procedure

There are two steps in the survey-level procedure: selecting a target and taking data to note discrepancies.

Step 1: Select the Target.   To convert the initial referral into a more specific and manageable starting point, you must do two things:

1. Define the maladaptive and target behaviors in behavioral terms.
2. Apply the so-what test.

FIGURE 14.9
Jay's fact sheet

FACT SHEET

Behaver: _Jay_   Manager: _Rice_

Diagnostician: _Kaplan_   Date: _November 1987_

Maladaptive Behavior: _Jay hits, kicks, squeezes, pushes a peer on the average of 12 times per day._

Target Behavior: _Jay will interact positively with peers (no unprovoked hitting or other acts of physically aggressive behavior; instead he will touch, pat, hold peer without inflicting pain)._

PREREQUISITES OF TARGET BEHAVIOR (Assumed Causes for Maladaptive Behavior)	SPECIFIC TEST	CONCLUSION
1. Jay must know how to engage in positive interactions with peers.	1a. Given a situation Jay was asked to tell about the appropriate thing to do.	1a. Jay was not able to describe or produce appropriate behavior.
	1b. In role playing Jay was given a situation and asked to act out the appropriate thing to do.	
2. Jay must know the difference between positive and negative interactions.	2a. The teacher had other students act out appropriate interactions and Jay was asked to identify if they were appropriate or inappropriate.	2a. When behaviors were modeled for him, he was unable to identify and categorize them.
	2b. Jay was shown pictures of kids' faces with different expressions such as fear and happiness. He was asked to label the interactions in the pictures as positive and negative.	
3. Jay must recognize consequences of engaging in positive and negative behaviors.	3. The teacher asked Jay to describe what would happen to him if he engaged in maladaptive	3. Jay explained that others would stay by him and not run away. He wouldn't get into trouble—was not

punished. They didn't yell at him. He seemed to know the consequences of specific behaviors.

4. Jay could indicate which behaviors would cause him to get into trouble and which wouldn't—but he could not predict which behaviors the teachers or peers wanted him to engage in. He indicated no understanding of link between positive behaviors and social acceptance. All he's aware of is the simple cause-and-effect relationship (hit kid and Jay gets into trouble).

5. Jay responded the same as in 4 above. He would say he wanted to have a friend in order to avoid trouble. His actual wants could not be determined.

6. Throughout the evaluation Jay has seemed aware of consequences. He certainly expressed a desire to avoid negative consequences on tests 3, 4, and 5. However, he never showed any understanding that a positive interaction would be rewarding in itself or that he might receive anything of interest for behaving well.

behaviors (obviously, the term "maladaptive" was not used—examples were given).

4. The teacher asked Jay which of several behaviors she and the other students liked the most.

5. Jay was asked several questions such as "Which would you rather have, someone to play with or someone to fight with?"

6. Review of his comments and behavior on the previous tests.

4. Jay must know that it is more socially acceptable to engage in positive interactions with peers than in negative interactions.

5. Jay must want to interact positively with peers.

6. Jay must consider the consequences of positive interactions rewarding and of negative interactions aversive.

As you recall, maladaptive behaviors are those you want to get rid of and target behaviors are those you want to have more of. The two should be mutually exclusive, meaning that the student can't do them both at the same time and that the more you see of one the less you'll see of the other. They should also be stated in observable terms. For example, if Joey makes negative statements about himself, they can be counted. Some people may think that Joey has "poor self-concept," but this is not measurable. What makes one person's self-concept good and another's poor is open to interpretation and therefore may be debated. Pinpoints should be stated in terms that are not open to interpretation and therefore may not be debated. To describe a student's maladaptive behavior as lazy, bad, disobedient, or disrespectful is not factual. If you make such descriptions, what you have done is put a label on a group of behaviors. The problem is that different people will put different labels on the same group of behaviors. Therefore, we urge you to stick to the facts.

Specificity is particularly important for the target behavior. It is important because one cannot analyze anything that is not described in behavioral terms. Suppose an evaluator wrote a target behavior, e.g., "Joey will be a good boy" or "Janey will do good work." Who can task analyze those target behaviors? One needs statements describing exactly what the kid will do or look like when the target has been reached.

If you pay attention to the following rules, you should have no trouble pinpointing maladaptive and target behaviors. First, try to use verbs instead of adjectives. Words like *hits*, *smiles*, *cries*, and *talks* convey more meaning than *rough*, *happy*, *sad*, or *motor-mouth*. Second, avoid adverbs. For example, *talks a lot*, *hits hard*, *smiles inappropriately*, and *laughs loudly* may be interpreted variously by different people. Third, stay away from value judgments. Don't use constructs such as *lazy*, *dumb*, *generous*, *considerate*, *conscientious*. Again, stick to the cold, hard facts and describe the behavior (or absence of behavior) that you can observe. For the target behavior you'll have to use your imagination since it is unlikely that you will have observed the student engaging in such behavior. Describe what behavior *you would like to observe*. While not man-datory, if you think it would help you to task analyze the target behavior, write it as a performance objective with conditions and criteria for acceptable performance. Table 14.2 provides instances and not-instances of maladaptive and target pinpoints.

Once you have stated the target and maladaptive behaviors in measurable terms, sit back in your chair. Relax, read over both statements, and ask yourself, "So what?" Is this behavior really worth the time and attention of a teacher and a student? If it isn't, we recommend either forgetting it completely or returning to the person who made the referral to see if there wasn't something more notable that was left out.

To apply the so-what test, you can ask others—including the student and peers—if they think the target is important. We also recommend asking yourself if the pinpoint falls into the domain of control or instruction. If it is only a control problem, then you should be aware that the time and effort you spend bending the student to the constraints of the current setting will most likely be of no benefit to him after the school day has ended.

Step 2: Collect Data and Note Discrepancies. Once the behaviors (target and maladaptive) have been specified, they need to be measured. At the survey level we recommend that you do this through direct observation of the target and maladaptive pinpoints.

Tips on conducting an observation are presented in chapters 8 and 15. It is best to collect data as unobtrusively as possible while still collecting it yourself. It is not a good idea to ask the referring teacher to collect the data, as he is a pivotal factor in the student's environment. If you are the teacher, see if you can get an aide or another teacher to volunteer some time to collect the data you need.

Some general points about observation deserve to be repeated.

1. It is better to observe a behavior for several short periods than one long one.
2. It is important to observe the circumstances under which the behavior occurs.
3. Use the median score from at least 3 days of observation as your best estimate of the kid's current status.

TABLE 14.2
Instances and not-instances of maladaptive and target pinpoints

Maladaptive Pinpoints Instances	Target Pinpoints Instances
1. Calls out without raising hand.	1. Raises hand and waits to be called.
2. Does not complete assignments by due date.	2. Completes 100% of work by due date.
3. Is not in seat when late bell rings.	3. Is in seat before late bell rings.
4. Hits peers without physical provocation.	4. Sits next to peers without hitting them.
5. Makes verbal responses that are irrelevant to questions asked.	5. Makes comments related to topics being discussed.
6. Repeats questions he has already asked.	6. Asks the same question only once.
7. Says "I don't have to" or "I don't want to" when given a directive.	7. Complies with directive first time given, every time given.
8. Makes inaudible statements.	8. Speaks in a voice audible to all parts of the room.
9. Makes self-deprecating remarks (e.g., "I'm dumb," "I'm stupid," "I'm a retard").	9. Lists 10 good things about himself in one minute.
10. Plays with younger children during recess.	10. Plays with children his own age during recess.

Not-Instances	Not-Instances
1. Is aggressive.	1. Is considerate of others. [What does "considerate" mean?]
2. Is off task.	2. Is on task. [Open to interpretation.]
3. Is immature.	3. Is mature. [Construct]
4. Calls out inappropriately.	4. Requests permission to speak appropriately. [What does "appropriately" mean?]
5. Is anxious.	5. Is mellow/calm. [Compared to what?]
6. Cannot accept criticism.	6. Accepts punishment. [Open to interpretation]
7. Is immature.	7. Exercises self-control.
8. Uses back talk.	8. Speaks respectfully.
9. Is tardy.	9. Is on time. [Open to interpretation]
10. Is dirty.	10. Has good hygiene.

4. If the pinpoints never occur you will need to prompt them by testing. In this case the tests may come in forms like role-playing, questioning, or interviews.

Once you have collected data on the student's use of the target and maladaptive behaviors, examine them in terms of a standard. As you recall, the standard for social behavior is the class average, as determined through the collection of an ecological baseline. If the student's behavior is no different from that of others in the environment, select a new pinpoint or devise a group intervention.

Step 3: Hypothesizing. In the task-analytical model, a maladaptive behavior is assumed to occur because something is keeping the target behavior from replacing it. Therefore the operational question is not "Why is the kid screwing up?", it is "Why isn't the kid doing it right?" As with any other task, it is assumed that the student is failing at the social task because of a missing component prerequisite (subtask) or strategy.

Obviously, social skill tasks vary from one another as much as academic tasks. "Asking for assistance" may be as different from "arriving on time" as "multiply fractions" is from "do long division." However, most social skills do share the common set of prerequisites illustrated in Table 14.3. Because sequences of prerequisites have not been articulated for social skills (as they have been for academics), it is more efficient to run through this common list prior to actually task analyzing any social skill. This list is based in part on the work of Kaplan (1982). As Kaplan has noted, some of these prerequisites are merely desirable and not essen-

tial. If one or more of the prerequisites in Table 14.3 seems to be missing, treat it as the assumed cause for student failure (an assumption to be verified shortly with specific-level probes). The status of the prerequisites should be judged by as many people who know the student as possible.

SPECIFIC LEVEL

Once a target behavior has been properly identified and several prerequisites for it have been specified, additional specific-level testing is necessary to determine which particular prerequisite(s) the student may be missing. Beginning with a list of prerequisites like the one in Table 14.3, note the ones marked unsure and test each one. This usually means developing specific probes, as few "knows the consequences of engaging in the target behav-

TABLE 14.3
Prerequisites

If a student does not engage in a target behavior, ask yourself if...

Type 1 (Do behaviors)	Status (yes - no - unsure)
1) ...the student can discriminate the target and maladaptive behaviors from each other and from other behaviors.	_____
2) ...the student can monitor his own behavior well enough to know when he is engaging in the target or maladaptive behavior.	_____
3) ...the student can monitor the environment well enough to recognize events that should prompt the target behavior or inhibit the maladaptive behavior.	_____
4) ...the student knows what behavior is expected of him.	_____
5) ...there are personal factors (e.g., allergies or seizures) or environmental factors (e.g., missing resources or the behaviors of others) that prohibit the target behavior or mandate the maladaptive behavior.	_____
6) ...the student has the skills/knowledge to engage in the behavior successfully.	_____
7) ...the student knows the consequences of engaging in the target behavior.	_____
8) ...the student knows the consequences of engaging in the maladaptive behavior.	_____

ior" tests already exist. Table 14.4 provides brief descriptions of specific-level tests for each of the common prerequisites found in Table 14.3. These procedures will be described in the following pages. They include questioning (open, multiple choice, and restricted alternative), role-playing, cue sort, and structured interviews.

Questions

Often the simplest way to find out something is to ask. How reliable is it to simply ask? Up to a point it is safe to assume that any test can be made more reliable by adding a few more items (though this won't necessarily affect its validity). This means that if you observe a behavior 20 times you are surer of it than if you observe it only once. Therefore, if you need to ask questions of a student, ask them several times in a variety of settings and cir-

cumstances. If the student tends to give consistent responses, you may take this as evidence of reliability. If the responses are inconsistent, you don't know if the kid is changing or if the question is poor. Either way you need to do additional testing. There are several types of questioning techniques you can use and you may switch from one to another according to the responses you get (Stowitschek et al.,1984). Let's go through these types using this example.

Knows consequences of
engaging in the target behavior.

Open Question. This is the least constraining form of question. To use it, ask "What will happen to you if you get to class on time?" Because correct answers could include everything from "I'd feel good"

TABLE 14.3 (continued)

Type 2 (Select behaviors)	Status (yes - no - unsure)
9) . . .the student generates solutions to problems that include the target behavior.	_____
9.1 . . .the student perceives the target as an option.	_____
9.2 . . .the student is willing to allocate the resources necessary to carry out the target option.	_____
10) . . .the student wants to select the target behavior.	_____
10.1 . . .the student considers the consequences of engaging in the target behavior rewarding.	_____
10.2 ..the student considers the consequenes of engaging in the maladaptive behavior aversive (or less rewarding than engaging in the target behavior).	_____
10.3 . . .the student values the target behavior more than the maladaptive behavior.	_____
10.4 . . .the student does not consider the target behavior aversive.	_____
11) . . .the student holds beliefs that promote the target behavior and are incompatible with the maladaptive behavior.	_____
12) . . .the student expects to carry out the target behavior successfully.	_____

Directions:
1) In the Status column, mark each prerequisite as yes, no, or unsure.
2) Prerequisites marked yes are ignored.
3) Prerequisites marked no are listed as potential instructional objectives.
4) Prerequisites marked unsure are set aside for specific-level testing.

TABLE 14.4

Prerequisites Type 1 (Do behaviors)	Specific-level probes
1) ...the student can discriminate the target and maladaptive behaviors from each other and from other behaviors.	Give the student a list of behaviors, a series of pictures, or role-playing examples and ask her to indicate the target and maladaptive behavior.
2) ...the student can monitor her own behavior well enough to know when she is engaging in the target or maladaptive behavior.	Ask the student to record her own behavior or to think back over an interval and state whether or not she engaged in the behaviors of interest.
3) ...the student can monitor the enviroment well enough to recognize events that should prompt the target behavior or inhibit the maladaptive behavior.	Ask the student how she can tell what to do or give the student statements of the behavior and various scenes (through pictures, descriptions, or role playing) and ask her to match scenes to behaviors.
4) ...the student knows what behavior is expected.	Ask her. Say, "What do I want you to do?" or "What should you be doing?" If the student is unable to produce the desired response, give some choices and ask her to identify which one is correct. Say, "Should you be in your seat, or should you be out of your seat?"
5) ...there are personal factors (e.g., allergies or seizures) or environmental factors (e.g., missing resources or the behaviors of others) that prohibit the target behavior or mandate the maladaptive behavior.	Look for any evidence of personal or environmental factors that might trigger the maladaptive behavior or prevent the student from engaging in the target behavior. Investigate the room temperature, allergies to food or clothing, sensitivity to noise, and any others. Take a sample of the behavior of the other students to see if her current status is typical.
6) ...the student has the skills/knowledge to engage in the behavior successfully.	Conduct an assessment using criterion-referenced measures to check necessary skills. Task analyze the behavior first if it is fairly complex; e.g., an academic assignment.
7) ...the student knows the consequences of engaging in the target behavior.	Ask her. Say, "What happens to you when you. . .?" If she is unable to produce the desired response, give some choices and ask her to identify which one is correct. Say, "Do you get to go to recess?" or "Do you get to read?"
8) ...the student knows the consequences of engaging in the maladaptive behavior.	Ask her. Say, "What happens to you when you. . .?" If she is unable to produce the desired response, give some choices and ask her to identify which one is correct. Say, "Do you miss recess?" or "Do you have to stay after school?"

TABLE 14.4 (continued)

Prerequisites Type 2 (Select behaviors)	Specific-level probes
9) . . .the student generates solutions to problems that include the target behavior.	
9.1 . . .the student perceives the target as an option.	Supply the student with various restatements of the problem or of analogous problems, involving other people. Ask, "What could they do to get what they want?"
9.2 . . .the student is willing to allocate the resources necessary to carry out the target option.	Use a forced-choice questioning format, e.g., "Which would you rather have *(the problem solved)* or *(the resource required)*?
10) . . .the student wants to select the target behavior.	
10.1 . . .the student considers the consequences of engaging in the target behavior rewarding.	Give her a list of rewards including ones you have used in the past and are presently using with her and ask her to sort them according to value (which she likes the most to the least). Use the ABC technique to determine thoughts about receiving various rewards.
10.2 . . .the student considers the consequences of engaging in the maladaptive behavior to be aversive (or less rewarding than engaging in the target behavior).	Give her a list of punishers including ones you have used in the past and are presently using with her and ask her to sort them according to value (which she finds the most aversive to the least). Use the ABC technique to determine thoughts about receiving various punishers.
10.3 . . .the student values the target behavior more than the maladaptive behavior.	Give her a list of behaviors (including the target behavior) and have her sort them according to their importance *to her.* If she cannot complete this type of exercise, ask a series of restricted alternative questions such as, "Which would you rather do, work by yourself or with a group?"
10.4 . . .the student does not consider the target behavior aversive.	Give her a list of behaviors including the target behavior and ask her to sort them according to which she least prefers to do (list them in order of preference from least to most preferable).
11) . . .the student holds beliefs that promote the target behavior and are incompatible with the maladaptive behavior.	Use the control investment technique or other forms of structured interview.
12) . . .the student expects to successfully carry out the target behavior.	Ask her. Say, "Is there any reason why you can't. . .?"

to "Whatever the teacher wants to happen," you must be prepared to interpret the responses or to seek clarification of them.

Multiple Choice. This type limits possible responses to the choices supplied.

> "If you get to class on time, will you . . .
>   (a) get sent to the office?
> correct → (b) get to come to class?
>   (c) get to take an extra 2 weeks off this summer?
>   (d) get out of work?

The choices may be presented verbally or in the form of cartoons/pictures. The complexity of the item can be increased or decreased by altering the number and wording of the alternatives. The disadvantage of multiple choice is that it doesn't allow responses not supplied.

Restricted Alternatives.   If a student typically selects a certain alternative you can rule that one out by removing it from competition.

> "If you get to class on time you will *not* get out of work; what will you get?"

Role-Playing

Role-playing may or may not involve the student being evaluated. Sometimes you can use peers to role-play scenes, much as you would present cartoons, for the student to analyze. At other times you may ask the student to play a part in a hypothetical situation so that you can see how knowledgeable the student seems to be. Often initial attempts at role-playing fail because students are uncomfortable with it. Therefore, you may need to use it routinely if you are going to use it at all. When using role-playing, keep the directions specific and the scenes short. Also be sure to specify the sort of behavior expected, for example, "Show me how *I want* students to arrive at class."

Cue Sorts

Cue sort techniques (Stephenson, 1980) are particularly useful for Type 2 prerequisite tests. To use a cue sort, give the kid several terms, cartoons,

or pictures, each on a separate card. These cards should include the content you are interested in and a range of plausible distractors (e.g., if you are interested in the consequence "get to come to class," you would include it along with others like "get extra points" or "go to the office").

Once the kid has the cards, you ask her to sort them according to some categorical system. For example, "Put the cards in two piles—one for what might happen if you come to class on time and one for what might happen if you are late." You then grade the responses by noting how well the sorting matches the actual consequences.

Cue sorts are uniquely suited for gaining insight into a student's beliefs and perceptions. For example, you can give a student a stack of cards with various behaviors on them and ask him to put the behaviors in order according to those his teacher would find least acceptable. Next ask him to order the same cards according to his own idea of acceptability, and then again according to what he thinks his best friend would find acceptable. Differences in the sortings reflect the student's beliefs about the behaviors as well as his perceptions of his teacher and his friend.

An example cue sort is shown in Figure 14.10. The student was first asked to sort the 10 words according to "What you like to do" and "What your teacher likes you to do." Next the teacher was asked to sort the cards in terms of what he wants the student to do. Some conflict in perceptions is apparent.

Structured Interview

Like cue sorts, structured interviews are reserved for Type 2 prerequisites. The purpose of the structured interview is to get the student to talk within a given format. If this format is carefully structured, the things the student says can be used to draw inferences about covert thoughts/feelings. As always, it is important to note that these inferences may not always be correct and that generalizations from overt behavior (in this case, talk) to covert status (in this case, thought or feeling) should always be treated with some caution. However, if an evaluator asks a student "What is 6×8?" and the student says "48," few of us would question the inference

FIGURE 14.10
A sample cue sort

Kid's Sorting		Teacher's Sorting
What do you like to do?	What does the teacher want you to do in class?	What do you want the kid to do in class?
play	be quiet	learn
be happy	be serious	be happy
mess around	work	think
laugh	think	work
learn	learn	be serious
talk	talk	be quiet
think	laugh	talk
work	mess around	laugh
be quiet	be happy	play
be serious	play	mess around

that "the student knows how to multiply" even though the inference is based on verbal behavior. That's because the inference is supported by the narrow framework imposed by the rules of the multiplication problem itself. If a similar framework could be developed for social behavior, inferences here would also be easier to defend.

Figure 14.2 presented a model that has been used throughout this chapter to structure our discussion of social behavior. Having a model of this kind helps you *and* the authors to organize and clarify our thinking. This is the basic idea behind a structured interview. The students are given a model they can understand so that they can organize and articulate their thoughts within a framework. Here are two models that are easy to explain and use with most students.

ABC. The ABC procedure is based on a therapeutic model developed by Ellis (1971). *A* stands for Antecedents, *B* for Beliefs, and *C* for Consequences (this is another way of stating the Stimulus-Response-Stimulus model). If *B* includes thoughts and *C* includes feelings, then a chain can be set up that sounds like this: *stimuli* (a) are interpreted through *beliefs* (b) to produce *feelings* (c). This model asserts that how you feel is controlled by what you think. In Figure 14.11, two individuals are presented with the same antecedent stimuli, the requirement that they attend a meeting. Joe thinks, "I won't get my important other work done," so he feels frustrated and resentful about the requirement. Ken thinks, "This is a good excuse to put off some work," so he feels relieved and cheerful.

The ABC model can be used to get insight into the relationship between a student's thoughts and feelings in this way. First you set up a situation in which most people would think or feel predictably. For example, let's say you tell the kid, "You get to school without your notebook, and a friend tells you there is to be a big biology test today." Then you give her two clearly different thoughts: (a) "There's no way I can pass without my notes—I'm in trouble!" (b) "I can borrow Blanche's notes and study between class—I'll make it!" Next you ask her to describe how she might feel when thinking

FIGURE 14.11

Antecedent	Belief	Consequence
Both individuals have work to do but their boss has called them and told them to attend a meeting.	Joe: "I won't get my important work done."	Joe feels bad.
	Ken: "This is a good excuse to put off this work."	Ken feels good.

FIGURE 14.12

A	B	C
Left biology notes at home.	I'm in trouble!	Bad, worried, upset
	I'll make it!	Good, concerned but hopeful.

each thought (Figure 14.12). This takes a little practice, even for older, articulate students, so you shouldn't expect too much immediately in the way of revealing responses. Also you have to remember that there aren't a lot of feelings to list. Therefore, students may supply the same responses for very different stimuli. A "first date" or a "run-over pet" might both lead a perfectly well-adjusted kid to say, "I feel sick to my stomach."

After the student seems to have the idea of matching feelings to thoughts, you can reverse the exercise and give situations and feelings. Now the student must come up with thoughts. For example: "You are walking out of the school in the afternoon; you feel nervous and uneasy; what might you be thinking?" Whether the student is supplying thoughts or feelings, you want to keep an ear open for things that sound (a) out of context or (b) inflexible.

Statements that are out of context are those which seem to have little relationship to the situation, thought, or feeling supplied. They are often naive and unrealistic. For example, you tell the student he's having a birthday party and he thinks his dad is going to give him $50, and he says he feels "sleepy." In the parlance of special education teachers, such a student is known as a "space cadet" because of his "spacy" responses. However, such off-the-topic and slightly irregular responses may not be totally random. A series of ABC exercises may reveal that this student's irregular thoughts and feelings are consistently linked to specific situations (e.g., spacy responses are always associated with social situations like birthday parties). This information can be used to select topics or situations about which the student must learn.

Inflexible statements are the key to dogmatic belief systems. If the student seems unable to give anything but stereotyped responses to certain pre-

sentations, it may mean he is unaware of other options. This lack of awareness can be the result of a belief that overshadows his current perceptions about what is currently going on. Such beliefs limit the student's options because they mask them. The stereotyped "delinquent" beliefs that authority is bad and that force is the most effective solution to conflict are the easiest for teachers to spot. That's because these beliefs lead kids into aversive contact with the teacher. Nevertheless, other beliefs such as "I should be taken care of" or "the others are better than I" are just as common and show up frequently in ABC exchanges.

We've already alluded to one problem with the ABC model. The model as we've presented it assumes that stimuli in the environment cause thoughts which, in turn, spark feelings. However, there are an infinite number of environmental stimuli producing a finite number of thoughts that lead to comparatively few feelings. Consequently, any number of stimuli may evoke the same thought, and any number of thoughts can lead to the same feeling. The linear relationship between environment, thought, and feeling is not well established, and is certainly not predictable (in fact the authors don't even believe it exists). However, remember that we are not presenting the model as a factual representation of the human psyche—but as a convenient format for conducting a structured interview. This model is based on a problem-solving paradigm. That is, it assumes that you can trouble shoot inappropriate behavior or cognition problems much like an engineering error. The basic premise is that students have problems making appropriate choices because they fail to recognize each option and consider it in terms of its effect.

Control/Investment. The control/investment model is shown in Figure 14.13. This model is particularly

**If Control is Disproportionate to Investment,
We Experience Anxiety**

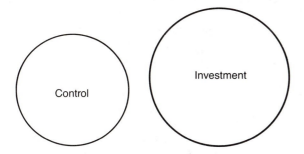

FIGURE 14.13
Control/investment model

effective when presented to the student along with a group of peers. The two circles represent the student's perceived control and perceived investment in a situation. The model is presented like this: "In any situation we each have some investment and some control. For example, when we go to a hospital for surgery, we have lots of investment in what the surgeon will do to us, but once we're asleep we have no control over what will be done. To the degree that our investment exceeds our control (is disproportionate to it), we experience anxiety."

Once again we are not implying that this simple model enjoys the status of a biblical truth. It does, however, explain some common experiences. Many of us suffer from inflated investment. It is the result of the anxiety-producing habit of adding tangential factors to an otherwise clear-cut decision. The practice can turn a trip to the grocery store into a life-and-death venture.

Have you ever started to go to the store, then realized that you have no cash, the banks are closed, you're afraid to cash a check without knowing your balance, and you've messed up your bank book? The anxiety you start feeling is greater than the carton of milk you were going to buy would seem to have deserved. That's because you've inflated the trip to the store into a confrontation with your budget.

The other side of inflated investment is inadequate or incorrectly perceived control. Lots of times

people will allow an anxiety-producing situation to go on indefinitely when acquiring a few simple skills would help them control the situation. This is true of people who fear mechanics but don't learn about cars, or who bounce checks but won't organize a bookkeeping system.

Evaluators can employ the model by giving the students examples from their own experience (e.g., the more you know about spelling the less you fear spelling tests). Once a student understands the model, one can begin to use it to assess her cognition. This is done by asking her to identify the things that are most important to her. Next ask her to estimate the extent to which she can affect (control) these important things. If there is a discrepancy between the value she puts on something and the control she has (or thinks she has) over it, this discrepancy can be resolved two ways; she must deflate her investment or expand her control.

How much control a person has over a situation depends on her skills and knowledge. Therefore, if it appears that the student lacks control, a Type 1 evaluation is called for. If it turns out that she has needlessly inflated her investment or overestimated her control, then the evaluator should try to recognize the beliefs leading to the inflation. Often this can be accomplished by asking the student to tell her what she thinks is the worst (or best) thing that can happen to her in the circumstances being discussed (this can be facilitated by using multiple-choice or restricted alternative questions). Some stereotypic beliefs are quite common and easily recognized. Kaplan (1982) has listed a variety of beliefs that will influence a student's feelings of investment or control in various situations, including:

1. I must be good at everything I do.
2. Everyone should treat me fairly.
3. Anyone who walks away from a fight is a punk.
4. School is dumb.

Once identified, the various perceptions, expectations, and beliefs that are compatible with maladaptive behaviors can be countered with those that seem to promote target behaviors. This activity, changing the way students think, is obviously serious business.

A NOTE ON TYPE 2 INTERVENTIONS

The authors have already discussed some concerns about evaluating cognitive behaviors. We have used the techniques just presented but have no data to show that they are better or worse than procedures you could make up yourself. For that matter, we have no data to show that they are better than doing nothing. Sometimes, when working with a student, an obviously unrealistic expectation or inaccurate perception will pop out through one of these models. In these cases, it seems clear that the inappropriate expectation/perception should be changed. Often the best change technique is to promote (through reinforcement) cognitive behaviors that are incompatible with the inappropriate ones.

Cognitive changes are not always monumental readjustments of personal philosophy. More often they are simple corrections of an inaccurate expectation. A consultant friend of ours (Karna Nelson) used this process with a teacher who had a troublesome new student. After being given assignments, the kid frequently just put them away, saying, "I'll do it tomorrow." The teacher was puzzled. When Karna task analyzed "immediately begins work," the prerequisite "thinks work should be done immediately" emerged. As a test the teacher asked, "How long do you think you have to do an assignment?" to which the student replied, "a week." Baffled, the teacher asked, "Why do you think that?" and the kid explained, "In my last school we had contracts, and it didn't matter when we worked as long as the contract was met in a week." This simple explanation took the two teachers a lot of time to find, but they didn't find it at all until they sat down and analyzed the target behavior "immediately begins work." The intervention took only a few minutes and involved explaining the differences between the new class and the old one. In this case the student was behaving inappropriately not because of complex missing skills, entrenched beliefs, or mysterious emotional peculiarities. Instead, he was behaving inappropriately because he held the rational expectation that two special classrooms would have the same rules. If he lacked anything, it was the skills necessary to determine the rules of the new setting.

This is not a text on cognitive interventions (see Kaplan, 1982, if you want one), so we're going to leave the topic with a final caution. For *any* academic, social, or cognitive behavior, once you have selected a pinpoint and started an intervention, you *must* monitor the effect of the intervention. This is the main point of chapter 15. When dealing with cognitive pinpoints, poor therapists will often persist with an intervention that conforms to their idea of mental health but does not produce healthy change in the client. Sometimes this persistence will even produce damage. If a teacher cannot document positive change in the client, then it's time for the *teacher* to change.

As for the validity of these cognitive procedures, reread the cautions expressed earlier. Each of these techniques is derived from the application of logic to the often less-than-logical domain of behavior disorders. Therein lies the ultimate uncertainty of the system. A very wise psychiatrist once advised the authors that logic can be applied successfully only to human-made things. To apply these techniques, one must assume that the perceptions, expectations, and beliefs of students are human-made in the sense that they have been learned during past social interactions. This assumption remains and will remain unproven. Therefore, attempts to alter selection strategies oblige us to adhere to the highest ethical standards and to proceed with caution.

SUMMARY

This chapter has been different from those which preceded it because it deals with the global domain of "social behavior." Some of the major points presented were:

- Social behavior and academic behavior are not that different.

- Efforts to develop social skills curriculum are needed.
- Social skills should be taught, not controlled.
- Attempts to deal with social skills must address covert as well as overt behaviors.

In addition to these points, a variety of specific procedures were covered and some examples were provided. We intentionally omitted extensive discussions of data collection, observation, and charting from this chapter not because we think they are unimportant, but because we think they are important for academics as well as social skills (see the next chapter). Throughout the chapter we attempted to illustrate the application of a curriculum-based, task-analytical approach to social skills and to caution against its misapplication.

Study Questions

1. Contrast *control* and *therapy*.
2. List several content areas that might be addressed by a social skills curriculum.
3. Which of the following task elements is particularly important to the development of tables of specifications in social behavior?
    a. Content
    b. Criterion
    c. Condition
    d. Behavior
4. Define and give an example of each of the following:
    a. Type 1 prerequisite
    b. Type 2 prerequisite
5. What is the distinction between a target and a maladaptive pinpoint? Why is it important to develop both?
6. Which of the following are examples of target pinpoints?
    a. On task
    b. Speaks respectfully
    c. Hits peers without provocation
    d. Is in seat before bell rings
    e. Lists 10 good things about self
7. Explain how you could use a cue sort to gain insight into a student's thoughts about the opinions of others.
8. What problem with the ABC procedure was mentioned in the chapter?
9. Explain how inflated investment can cause anxiety.
10. If monitoring shows that a type 2 intervention is not working, what should you do?

Chapter 15

Deciding How to Teach

There are two general types of evaluation, *summative* and *formative*, teachers and psychologists can use to measure changes in child behavior (Bloom et al., 1971). The traditional measures (achievement and aptitude tests) are included in the category of summative evaluation, i.e., evaluation that occurs after teaching and learning have taken place. Summative evaluation is designed to measure the end result (product) of instruction and to identify the students who have and have not met the objectives of instruction. Testing that occurs at the end of a unit of teaching for purposes of grading is also summative. In contrast, formative evaluation measures learning as skills are being formed. Where summative evaluation is used to describe the outcomes of instruction, formative evaluation is used to measure progress towards objectives.

The term *formative evaluation* is unfamiliar, and the technology used often seems esoteric at best. However, the authors believe the topics covered in this chapter are of critical importance to special/remedial education. Because of its importance (and an unfortunate lack of interest in it), we have decided to clearly label our coverage of it and to set it aside in this last chapter. As the reader you may bypass it with ease if you wish but we encourage you not to. This chapter deals with evaluative procedures that can make your teaching 5 to 10 times more effective (Fuchs, Deno, & Mirkin, 1985; White, 1986)! In our opinion, formative evaluation, in the form of data-based program modification (DBPM) (Deno & Mirkin, 1977), is the most promising solution to the problem of selecting effective treatments for special/remedial students.

INDIVIDUALIZING INSTRUCTION

This text has focused primarily on the recognition of what a student should be taught. As a result, the content chapters (chapters 9 through 14) dealt with data collection, which isn't of much use for deciding *how* to teach. However, certain issues related to treatment selection need to be addressed. This discussion will not be new to the professional literature but it may be surprising to some of you. In it we contend that one of the most popular approaches to individualizing instruction—matching students to treatments on the basis of their "learning styles"—is unvalidated and probably fallacious. We will follow this discussion with an alternative known as *data-based program modification*.

Before going any further, a few comments about the tone of the next few pages seem in order. The topic under discussion is the usefulness of psychological tests for treatment selection. Therefore, the tone is about to become somewhat "psychological." We haven't focused on psychological testing in this text, other than in Appendix A, so this discussion will seem a bit more theoretical. To make it easier to follow, here are a few important definitions:

1. *Psychology*—The study of the mind, including its structure and activity.
2. *Aptitude or Ability*—The natural (unlearned) capacity, or inclination, to learn a particular skill, or benefit from a particular instructional approach. In psychological theory certain levels of aptitude/ability are thought to be necessary for learning to take place. Terms like *aptitude/ability* refer to the capacity a student has; *skill* refers to the way that capacity is used.
3. *Cognition*—Thinking; a cognitive test attempts to summarize how a person thinks.
4. *Perception*—Receiving information from the environment through one of the five senses. A perception test attempts to summarize how a person gets information.
5. *Variables*—Any student characteristic can be a variable. Variables can be roughly categorized as skills (like reading, spelling, problem solving) or abilities (like memory capacity, auditory discrimination, or visual perception). Skills are thought to come about through the interaction of the person and environment. Skills are thought to be learned and easily altered (changed) through instruction. Ability variables are thought to be part of the person, innate, and not easily altered through instruction.
6. *Sensory modality*—The so-called channel through which information about the environ-

ment is received or discriminated, e.g., auditory (hearing), visual (seeing).

7. *Psychological test*—A test that attempts to measure a theoretically defined trait (such as cognitive capacity or sensory modality) rather than a learned skill such as problem solving or reading.

8. *Process* (learning process)—The way a person deals with information. The way one learns, as opposed to the *product*, which is *what* one learns.

Psychological testing is used to operationally (functionally) define characteristics of the human mind that are predicted by theory. Because psychological theory works to explain how learning takes place, some authors attempt to use it to explain how instruction should be carried out. Often these attempts seem successful, particularly when they focus on alterable variables such as problem-solving skills, attention skills, and memory skills (Frederiksen, 1984; Siegler, 1983; Wagner & Sternberg, 1984). Unfortunately, many of these attempts are also unsuccessful—particularly those that attempt to draw treatment implications from the study of unalterable student abilities.

In any case, whenever psychological tests are used they must exhibit the same levels of reliability *and* validity required of skill tests as explained in chapter 4.

The Problem

Once an evaluator/teacher has decided what a student needs to be taught, he or she must select how to teach it. There are many different approaches, programs, techniques, and methods available for presenting any objective and it is widely recognized that students vary in how well they respond to these different treatments. Therefore the evaluator must make a choice. Special educators and school psychologists have consistently elected to base these treatment choices on measures of student abilities or aptitudes. Many special educators and psychologists have attempted to describe types of learners, as defined by various cognitive or perceptual aptitude measures, and to match these learners to complimentary types of instructional programs.

This system of treatment selection is dangerous because:

1. It is based on the use of cognitive/perceptual measures that are:
   a. time consuming to give,
   b. poorly validated,
   c. generally unreliable, and
   d. not curriculum-based.
2. By emphasizing measures of learning process over measures of learning product, it focuses teacher attention on various hypothesized student abilities/aptitudes and distracts from the curriculum.
3. It disregards easily altered factors that cause treatments to vary in effectiveness, such as the teacher's effectiveness and the student's prior knowledge.
4. It doesn't work.

The problem as outlined here is not news to anyone who has had a chance to attend to the professional literature. In the text that preceded this one (*Evaluating Exceptional Children*, Howell, Kaplan, & O'Connell, 1979), an argument was made against the use of cognitive and perceptual tests for the selection of treatments. At that time, we debated the inclusion of the argument as it seemed a bit out of date; in the late 1970s it looked as if the practice of deriving treatment recommendations from theoretical interpretations of summative test scores was finally on its way out. But it wasn't. Today we are faced with the same decision and, unfortunately, the decision must be to include the argument again. We'd hoped things would have changed more than they have in the last decade, but they haven't.

The fields of special education and school psychology have generated a major controversy revolving around evaluators' attempts to recognize and cash in on patterns of human learning and perception. If "patterns of human learning and perception" is an unfamiliar phrase, we can translate it into "special educationese" and call it the "recognition of individual strengths and weaknesses." When peculiarities in student cognition or perception are "diagnosed" and treatments "prescribed," the process is referred to as *diagnostic–prescriptive teaching, psychomedical evaluation,* or *psychoeducational evaluation* (Mann, 1975).

During the 1960s, a large number of evaluative tools were developed with the intention of measuring aptitudes. The most frequently mentioned aptitudes corresponded to the sensory modalities: visual, auditory, and kinesthetic. While the idea of modality preference is not new (Galton, 1883), it experienced a revival with the widespread interest in learning disabilities. Out of the area of learning disabilities came a preoccupation with testing instruments such as the Marianne Frostig Developmental Test of Visual Perception (1963), the Illinois Test of Psycholinguistic Abilities (ITPA) (1968), the Detroit Test of Learning Aptitude (1967), and the Weschler intelligence tests (1974). These instruments were intended to measure aptitudes related to instruction. Underlying each was the assumption that psychological processes or perceptual characteristics relevant to instruction could be measured in children (Mann, 1975). Many people who believed in these instruments also felt that instruction could be tailored to individuals on the basis of the test scores.

The isolation and training of abilities were popular topics in psychology in the eighteenth century. At that time mental entities such as passion, courage, and intelligence were discussed as if they were recognizable and discrete human characteristics (Heidbreder, 1961). For example, Itard (1932), who some call "the father of special education," attempted to train the abilities of the Wild Boy of Aveyron by immersing him in hot water. These attempts to sharpen his student's "senses" seem absurd and cruel now but they stemmed from the idea that sensory abilities can be exercised and developed (like a muscle)—an idea that is still popular in some schools today. In the last century this was referred to as "faculty psychology" (Mann, 1975). In the field of education, faculty psychology accounted for practices such as memorizing verse in order to develop a disciplined mind.

There are three platforms on which the idea of ability assessment must stand. They are (a) the quality of the model's assumptive basis, (b) the tools the model relies upon, and (c) the model's educational utility. The second and third factors are easy to attack if you are aware of current research on evaluative instruments and educational interventions (Forness & Kavale, 1983; Lakin, 1983). The problem is that instrumentation and interventions change. This means that an analysis of diagnostic–prescriptive teaching from only the second and third points becomes quickly dated. For example, in the early 1970s, Hammill and Larsen (1974a) criticized ability measures such as the Frostig and Detroit because of their low reliabilities. However, by revising their tests or developing new ones with higher reliabilities, authors are able to revive interest in the procedure without addressing its apparently faulty assumptive underpinning.

Therefore, teachers need to prepare themselves to evaluate the new tests that are constantly appearing on the scene not only in terms of their technical adequacy but also their assumptive basis. An entire generation of students went from first to eighth grade before criticism of the ITPA became sufficiently widespread to put it out of use in all but the most arrested school programs.

Aptitude–Treatment Interactions

While tools and outcomes may vary, the basic assumptions of a model can't change too much without redefining the whole model. The diagnostic–prescriptive model depends on several assumptions, one of which is the existence of persistent and predictable aptitude by treatment interactions (ATI) (Cronbach, 1967; Glaser, 1972). ATI is the idea that individuals with certain abilities (aptitudes) will behave differently in certain programs (treatments) than in others. The idea is widely accepted because it is logical, but using an idea is always harder than accepting it.

Cronbach (1957) first used the term *aptitude–treatment interaction* (ATI) to describe a process by which certain aptitudes might tend consistently to predict the achievement of a student in a given instructional setting. He stated that:

An aptitude, in this context, is a complex of personal characteristics that accounts for an individual's end state after a particular educational treatment, i.e., that determines what he learns, how much he learns, or how rapidly he learns. (1967, p. 23)

For some reason, school psychology and special education elected to define *personal characteristics* in terms of innate abilities rather than more alterable variables such as a student's prior knowledge or acquired interests.

Although belief in ATI is widespread, the empirical evidence of its existence is not so abundant (Berliner & Cahen, 1973; Bracht, 1970a; Lloyd, 1984; Salomon, 1972). Two reviews of ATI research in the late 1960s indicated that attempts by teachers to use ATIs in their classrooms were premature (Bracht, 1970b; Cronbach & Snow, 1969). Ironically these reviews were published at the very time that special educators were filling pages of evaluation reports with aptitude scores.

Educators have acknowledged the idiographic (individual) nature of learning for a long time. For example,

The best method for one cannot be the best for all. There is not one mind reproduced in millions of copies, for all of which one rule will suffice; there are many differing minds, each of which needs, for its adequate education, to be considered to some extent by itself. (Thorndike, 1917, p. 67)

This quotation is representative of modern statements by many special educators even though it was written in 1917. The age of the statement and the frequency with which it's paraphrased today point out the failure of the educational community in reaching one of its most cherished goals—individualization. Calls for individualizing instruction, tailoring programming to student characteristics, and meaningfully matching students to treatments have filled the journals, teacher lounges,

and inservices agendas for generations; they have become the hallmark of special education. Unfortunately, attempts to answer these calls through psychoeducational evaluation have fallen flat (Glass, 1983; Lloyd, 1984).

Obviously all students do not respond to instruction in the same way. The blame for these inconsistencies has often been laid on the influence of one or more personological variables (variables within the person). These variables are referred to as *aptitudes* or *abilities*. Some educators have claimed that instruction can be adjusted to account for the influence of aptitudes (Dunn, 1983; Dunn, Dunn, & Price, 1981; Kaufman & Kaufman, 1983; Willis, 1985). The principal thrust of these claims is that certain types of students will learn more efficiently if they are treated in ways indicated by their scores on aptitude measures. ATI is not to be confused with selecting different objectives for students at different skill levels or with assuming that some treatments are more efficient than other treatments. But when special educators test for an individual's ability strengths and weaknesses, they are attempting to use ATIs. For example, "auditory learner" is an aptitude statement; "phonetic program" is a treatment statement; "auditory learners need phonetic programs" is an ATI statement (Dinsmore & Isaacson, 1986).

Looking for ATI

Prior to the widespread interest in ATI, most educational research was of the horse-race variety. That is, groups of students were placed in different methods and then observed to see which method was best. Figure 15.1 shows a typical study comparing phonic reading program A with whole-word

FIGURE 15.1
A typical method comparison study

	Program Variables	
A (Phonics)		*B (Whole Word)*
Total Students 1,000		Total Students 1,000
Average Pretest = Grade 2		Average Pretest = Grade 2
Average Posttest = Grade 3.5		Average Posttest = Grade 3
Average Gain = 1.5 Years		Average Gain = 1 Year
BEST		WORST

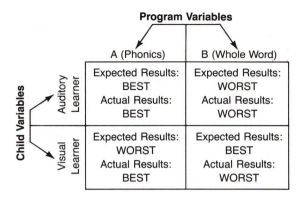

Program Variables

		A (Phonics)	B (Whole Word)
Child Variables	Auditory Learner	Expected Results: BEST Actual Results: BEST	Expected Results: WORST Actual Results: WORST
	Visual Learner	Expected Results: WORST Actual Results: BEST	Expected Results: BEST Actual Results: WORST

FIGURE 15.2
A typical ATI study

program B. In this example the phonic program wins.

One problem with this kind of study is that even though phonic programs are best for most students, there are always a few students who will not do well in phonics. So interactive studies were evolved to look at both program variables and child variables. Figure 15.2 illustrates a typical ATI study, the results of which *do not* indicate an ATI taking place between auditory/visual learners and phonic/whole-word programs. There are two explanations for this failure: (a) the aptitudes weren't accurately measured, or (b) the treatments weren't really different. Some authors, such as Waugh (1975), were early critics of diagnostic–prescriptive teaching. However, the use of ATI-based instruction flourished through the '70s and into the '80s under the tutelage of some teacher trainers who apparently ignored the absence of validation. Today the use of ATI, while clearly refuted by authors such as Arter and Jenkins (1979), Kavale (1981), Glass (1983), Lloyd (1984), and Ulman and Rosenberg (1986), continues to be advocated by teachers and psychologists who attempt to tailor instruction to left or right brains, avoid deficits in simultaneous processing ability, or continue the search for auditory and visual learners.

The frustration many educators feel over this continuing distraction from more legitimate instructional concerns has been well articulated by Lakin (1983).

It is a professional disgrace, given the wealth of evidence made available in the past decade, that . . . [this] position still may be seen as controversial in some quarters. Not only has the diagnostic–prescriptive approach lacked substantiated effectiveness in teaching children but, also, its general acceptance in special education circles has encouraged the creation of many essentially worthless, though profitable, enterprises of psychometry and "treatment." Its demise as an educational paradigm is long overdue as the research cited so clearly shows . . . it is outrageous that these essentially useless "professional" practices are allowed to persist. (p. 237)

Why It Doesn't Work
The fact that ATI-based treatment selection can't be proven to work doesn't mean the idea of ATI is wrong. It does, however, mean it isn't functional. Researchers continue to try to find ATIs. But their efforts are confounded by several problems.

Poorly Defined Aptitudes. In dealing with aptitudes, there has been a tendency in special education to define them with the test designed to study them. The reasoning goes something like this: "I believe there is such a thing as form constancy. Therefore I have devised a paper-and-pencil test involving tasks logically related to form constancy. I can now tell when a kid has a form constancy problem because the kid will score low on my test."

There is ample evidence indicating that researchers, both inside and outside special education, have indeed tailored the definition of aptitudes to fit their own needs or frames of reference. For evaluators, the problem is finding aptitude measures that are good evaluative tools. Such measures must be both reliable and highly predictive of future learning.

Poorly Defined Treatments. Definitional problems in the ATI field are not limited to aptitudes. Even if a teacher were able to recognize an "auditory learner," the match to treatment is unlikely as there is no scale available that will tell the teacher just how "auditory" or how "visual" any given program is. This is because treatments have frequently been defined in broad terms. As Shulman (1970) noted, "ATIs are likely to remain an empty phase as long as aptitudes are measured by micrometers and environments by divining rod" (p. 374). In the case of treatments, many of the measurement problems inherent in the assessment of abilities should not exist, because treatments seem open to view in ways in which cognitive processes are not. But treatments may not be as simple as they seem. Classroom treatments are particularly hard to define as any number of influences (such as the teacher's mood, the sequence of the instructional material, the amount of time available, and other characteristics) may alter them from day to day (Rhetts, 1974).

Unstable Interactions. Many researchers seem to assume that student abilities don't change although treatments do. In reality, it is quite possible that aptitudes are not stable at all and that the relationship of abilities to treatments may vary a lot more than anyone would ever wish. Any given task, learning multiplication facts, for example, may depend on a variety of abilities from the time the task is first attempted until it is mastered (Tobias, 1976). This means that learning a task could require auditory abilities at one time and visual abilities at another. The assumption that human abilities directly correspond to such arbitrary tasks as *r*-controlled vowels and addition of mixed fractions is incredibly simplistic.

Performance Data. Finally, the ultimate problem with ATI has to be that it currently is used as a summative procedure. Because diagnostic–prescriptive teaching depends on the use of one-shot performance testing, it requires the tests to have spectacular predictive strength and *no* summative test has ever demonstrated such strength. Performance measures tell us what a student can do now—that's it. They may be powerful enough to significantly predict outcomes for large groups of students on globally defined tasks but those of us interested in treating individuals will always be disappointed by them.

Why ATI Is Still Around

The ATI issue is intriguing and the promise it holds for instruction is great. It is not difficult to understand the interest shown in ATI by researchers. What is difficult to explain, however, is the wide-spread rush of special educators to put into classroom practice something that cannot even be reliably produced in the laboratory. One explanation is that ATI and its attendant psychological jargon have allowed special educators to sound and feel different from regular educators (Pugach, 1987). Another is that special teachers really aren't interested in the idea of ATI at all; a quick survey will probably reveal that few are even familiar with the term. It is equally unlikely that many can state the basic assumptions upon which ability testing relies (though most would probably accept them as fact [Arter & Jenkins, 1979]). Their interest lies in the fact that ATI, as it has been presented to the field of special education, offers a cookbook path to instruction that is extremely appealing to practitioners. It emphasizes finding "types" of students by using various tests. These types of students are then matched to programs that seem logically to complement their particular label. In reality, teachers should be skeptical of any program titled *Methods for _____* (fill in your favorite label). Similarly, they should demand validation studies for testing instruments that try to summarize (or profile) children's cognitive or perceptual functioning.

AN ALTERNATIVE TO PREDICTION

Special educators have become bogged down in attempts to use ATI to predict which students will do best in which programs. In many cases, these predictions have far surpassed the reliability of existing testing instruments and the validity of learning theories. As the science of ATI evolves, it is possible that both the reliability and validity of interaction prediction will improve. In the meantime, educators should be asking if there is an alternative strategy for matching students to methods—and there is.

At present, the best way to match a student to a method is to pick the best available treatment (it can even be argued that the best way to make this initial treatment selection is simply to ask the student [Elliott, 1986]), place the student in it, and see how she does. In the past, this technique was not used because the tools were not available to *quickly* evaluate the effectiveness of the placement. The risk of misplacing a student for months or even weeks wasn't acceptable. Due to advances in formative evaluation and applied behavioral analysis, this is no longer the case. It is now possible to place a student in a program and evaluate the validity of the placement in a matter of days. Essentially, this procedure is ATI backwards. Instead of looking for aptitudes to interact with treatments, the teacher looks for treatments to interact with aptitudes. The result is a movement away from attempts to measure and define abilities and toward the exact measurement of student behavior, tasks, and treatments.

Data-Based Program Modification (DBPM)

Again, once an evaluator has decided what a student should be taught, he must decide how to teach it. As already explained, attempts to predict preferred treatments from measures of student learning style appear to be successful only about 25% of the time (Arter & Jenkins, 1979; Ulman & Rosenberg, 1986). What can be done to assure that students are learning the most material in the least amount of time? The answer lies in the application of DBPM procedures. In abbreviated terms, DBPM evaluation employs the repeated administration of specific-level tests to monitor the student's progress in treatments.

Look at the chart in Figure 15.3. If the dots represent measures of a skill the teacher wants the student to learn, and the line represents how fast the student should be learning the skill, would you

continue to use the same treatment or would you change? If you said you would change, you just made a correct data-based program modification decision (Howell & McCollum-Gahley, 1986).

The idea that student progress should be monitored and that adjustments in instruction based on this monitoring will lead to improved progress is not new (Bloom et al., 1981; Eaton, 1978; Fuchs, Deno, & Mirkin, 1985). However, the data collection, recording, and analysis procedures about to be described have failed to take hold even in special education. There seem to be at least four reasons for this. First, with the exception of a few notable supporters such as Lovitt, White, Eaton, Deno, and Mirkin, advocates of these procedures have often been content to report their findings only to each other and have failed to aggressively inform the educational community. Second, DBPM seems radical to many administrators and they do not adequately support the efforts of teachers to use it (Beck, 1981). Third, the procedures are initially time consuming and difficult to apply. Finally, the highly technical tone of DBPM seems to affront teachers who believe they hold a "humanistic" view of teaching.

Each of these problems has solutions. The first seems to be taking care of itself as a new generation of researchers have begun to advertise their findings among a wider audience. The second problem, lack of administrative support, may be affected by linking DBPM procedures to issues such as accountability, minimal competency testing, and outcome-based instruction (all of which have become administrative buzz words). The time-consuming nature of DBPM, the third problem listed, may eventually be remedied by the increased use of computers to run software programs like *Aimstar* (Hasselbring & Hamlett, 1983). However, the real solution for this problem will come when researchers fine-tune these techniques so that they are more accessible to teachers, and when administrators provide an environment that supports teachers who are willing to expend extra effort for increased student learning. As for the fourth problem, the authors suggest that a careful examination of DBPM will reveal it to be highly humanistic. Behind the charts and decision rules about to be described, you will find an

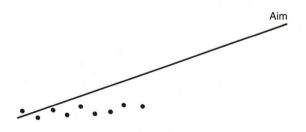

Aim

FIGURE 15.3

overriding commitment to the idea that kids should be involved in their own education and that treatments should be tailored to their personal preferences. These data collection procedures are designed to allow students to communicate with teachers and to allow teachers an opportunity to respond and be accountable.

THE CONCEPT OF PROGRESS

As an introduction to the topic of data-based program modification, recall the chapter 1 description of special education. In that chapter special education was characterized as the application of exceptional teaching techniques for the purpose of increasing the rate of student learning (Figure 1.3). Special/remedial students were shown to be behind in the curriculum because of their failure to progress adequately in regular instruction. These students emerge from instruction less skilled than others because of their lower rates of learning or progress through the curriculum.

If the special student's chief problem is inadequate progress, then instructional interventions that improve progress will solve that problem. Because student progress through the curriculum is directly determined by the instruction received, information about progress, and the impact of various program modifications on it, is essential. The procedures for collecting this information are more easily understood if the distinction between performance and progress is clear.

Performance

Performance is how well a person can do something right now. A person's current performance on a task can be shown by his position on the vertical (behavior) axis of charts like the ones shown in this chapter. A performance level can be determined with as little as one measurement of the target behavior. The performance level is noted by simply giving a test (or taking an observation) and recording the student's score. In Figure 15.4 the score reported is 40. (Note that the vertical axis always represents levels of skill or behavior, while the horizontal axis always represents the passage of time.)

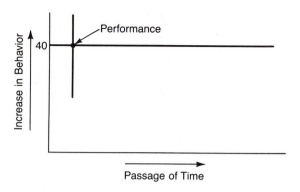

FIGURE 15.4

Evaluation involves the comparison of levels of behavior to a standard. Without a standard (also called *criterion* or *aim*), the level of performance has little meaning and cannot be used for decision making. With a standard and a measure of performance, one can note the difference between the two and use this discrepancy to make some decisions.

For example, if the performance standard (criterion) is 80 correct per minute and the student works at a rate of 40 per minute, his level of performance relative to the standard can be displayed as shown in Figure 15.5. In this case, there is a discrepancy between the performance and the standard that can be summed up by saying:

> "The kid is *40* behind and needs to move along the behavioral axis by going from 40 to 80."

A performance discrepancy tells where the student is (40) and where he should be (80). It gives no information about where the student is actually going, so an evaluator can't tell if he is getting better, worse, or staying the same. It only tells that instruction is needed on this skill. For this reason, performance data are sometimes referred to as

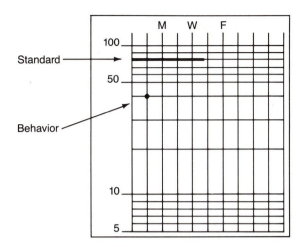

FIGURE 15.5

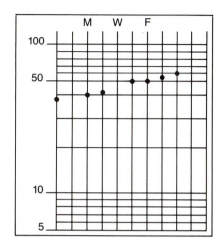

FIGURE 15.6

"static data," meaning they do not show movement. These are the kinds of data educators are most familiar with as they are derived from single administrations of a test.

Progress (Behavior Change)

A student's progress on a task is determined by simultaneously summarizing changes along *both* the vertical (behavior) and horizontal (time) axes of the chart. It is not possible to note progress without also noting performance because progress is a change in performance over time. Therefore, progress cannot be determined with a single data point. Several data points are needed to determine progress, and while no fixed number is required, the validity of progress statements increases with the number of data points upon which they are based.

Figure 15.6 shows several data points. Each data point represents a performance score obtained by giving the same test at different times. Because identical or equivalent tests/observations were repeated each day, the differences in performance from day to day can be attributed to learning. As seen in Figure 15.6, there is clearly acceleration up the chart. This movement in a particular direction is called *trend*. Students with different trends are learning (progressing) at different rates.

Like performance, progress has little meaning without an aim or standard. If the standard is an increase of 40 per minute in one week (5 instructional days) and the student only increases 20, then he is progressing at a rate which is lower than desired. As seen in Figure 15.7, this lower rate of progress produces a performance deficit of 20 per minute in only one week.

If the student's behavior remains at 40 for the entire week, no progress (change in behavior) is

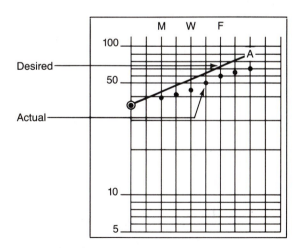

FIGURE 15.7

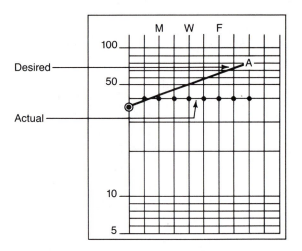

FIGURE 15.8

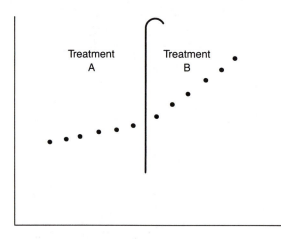

FIGURE 15.10

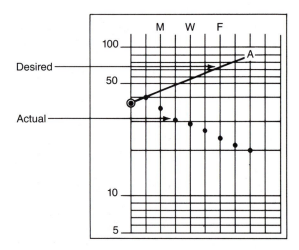

FIGURE 15.9

noted (Figure 15.8). If the student's behavior decreases, then he is "progressing" away from the standard. In this context progress only means change, not necessarily improvement (Figure 15.9).

Because learning is indicated by a change in performance across time, it can be seen in the progress of the student toward a performance objective. This information is important because progress data are uniquely suited to deciding *how* to teach. Progress data tell you where the student is and,

more importantly, where he is going. This type of data is "dynamic," showing both the direction and magnitude of change. Educators are not especially familiar with this type of data and in the past have been forced to judge the quality of progress informally.

The Value of Trend

DBPM requires accurate, continuous measurement of student behavior. The resulting data can be analyzed for evidence of acceptable or unacceptable growth (progress) toward a specific objective, and comparisons can easily be made between a student's growth in different treatments.

Figure 15.10 shows a student's reading behavior in two treatments. Each dot represents a timed oral reading test showing the number of words read in one minute. In this case, the student is in each treatment for one week, and the superiority of treatment *B* over treatment *A* is obvious because the trend in the data is steeper.

In Figure 15.11a, the score for one test is supplied. Whether or not the student is improving or getting worse can't be determined from this one summation of her total performance.

In Figure 15.11b three possible posttest scores have been added. As a teacher, if you obtained posttest A, you would no doubt be pleased; posttests B and C would not cause you to celebrate.

FIGURE 15.11

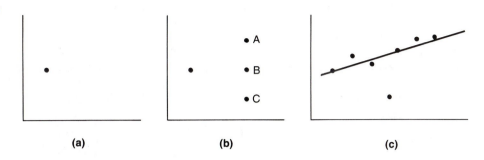

(a)   (b)   (c)

Figure 15.11c contains a score as low as score C in Figure 15.11b. However, the low score in Figure 15.11c isn't particularly disturbing because the overall *trend* illustrated in the figure is positive. Given the data in Figure 15.11c, you could make decisions on the overall movement of the behavior, not a single data point. This is called *trend analysis*.

THE NEED FOR DECISION MAKING

The key to any formative evaluation system is frequent data collection. Educators interested in making decisions about student programs should be able to see that the more frequently they test/observe, the more often they can make data-based decisions. If we schedule our data collection daily, then we can make daily decisions. If, however, we only monitor learning monthly, we can only make informed decisions once a month. The best data decisions will be made from systems that include frequent curriculum-based monitoring because they will produce the most sensitive data.

Data decision rules are guides to interpretation that tell what to do when certain patterns of data occur. Many teachers are used to applying some set of decision-making "rules" to their instruction. These rules are seldom absolute, but do provide guidance. An example of a data-based rule with which most teachers are familiar is the "3 times in 3 days" rule attributed to Fernald (1943). This rule says if a kid works a task correctly three times a day for three days in a row, he has learned the task and should move on.

Another familiar rule is the "instructional level" rule often used to select readers for students. While designated levels vary, it is common to hear that if a student reads from material in which he is above 90% accuracy it is too easy for instruction, and below 80% is too hard. Therefore, the interval from 80% to 90% represents the "instructional level" that falls between the so-called independent and frustration levels.

There are a lot of other decision rules around, and each one depends on some type of data. In the examples above, the data required for the first rule were "correct and incorrect behavior each day," while the data required for the second rule were "accuracy of passage reading." As one might expect, the more sophisticated the data collection system, the more sophisticated the decisions that can be made with that system. Because the highest level of sophistication is characteristically reserved for the most problematic students, special/remedial educators may use data collection and interpretation procedures that would seem needlessly complex to regular classroom teachers.

If every time teachers taught people something they learned it as quickly and as thoroughly as possible, then there would be no need for collecting data and making data decisions. However, this is not the case. The techniques used for one student at one time on one task may not work as well at another time for another student. Even the same student may respond differently across tasks or time. The whole idea behind individualized instruction (and special education) is that instruction can and should be altered to produce better results. These changes should not be made in objectives or criteria, but in the way the student is taught.

Many educators believe the skill to modify instruction at the appropriate time is the mark of true teaching. This "feel" for when a student is being frustrated or bored allows some teachers to pick from among the various techniques available those that will be most effective. While all teachers have the same techniques available, only the very best know how to alter them at the critical instant to maintain optimal learning.

Because exceptional teaching means modifying instruction, special and remedial teachers must have skills in two areas: instructional modification and decision making. Instructional modification skills allow them to adjust and implement a wide range of treatments, methods, programs, and techniques. Decision-making skills allow them to decide when these adjustments are needed by individual students. One set of these skills is of limited use without the other. Obviously, there is no advantage to knowing that it is time to switch methods if one only knows how to use one method. Similarly, knowing how to teach many different ways isn't particularly valuable if one can't decide which way to teach.

DATA

Data-based program modification obviously requires the use of data. The kind of data collected and the procedures used to collect them will have a lot to do with how the system works. This section deals with types of data, collection procedures, and data summary. It will cover certain key concepts including the differences between behavior, products, and status and the difference between absolute and proportional change.

Sources of Data

Evaluators may collect data on changes in a student's behavior, the products those behaviors produce, or the status of the student. These sources of data were described in chapter 7. Here are their definitions, as a review.

- *Behavior*—Covert or overt action. Overt action involves muscular movement (e.g., standing up or raising hand). Covert action involves thinking/feeling (e.g., solving a problem or feeling embarrassed).
- *Product*—The effect or result of a behavior (e.g., pages read, problems completed, or windows cleaned).
- *Status*—The condition or location of a person. Some examples of condition are on-task, happy, angry, appropriate/inappropriate. Location status includes on time, out of seat, in class.

The functional distinction between a behavior and its product is hard to define. Small, discrete products like answers written and words read might just as well be treated as if they were the behaviors write answer and say word. However, larger, more complex products like assignments finished or pages read should always be treated as products. That is because most pages and lessons increase in difficulty so the learning required by one page isn't equal to the next. Also, these targets are composed of many small behaviors. Products, like behaviors, are conveniently measured by counting each one and reporting the number produced during a period of time.

Behaviors produce products and lead to changes in a student's status. Because of this it is usually best to collect data on behavior, as it is the central concern. However, sometimes it is easier to collect data on a student's status or product completion. For example, imagine that you are concerned with the amount of time a student seems to be moving around the class. You could watch the student to count the behavior "gets out of seat" or periodically check out-of-seat status. Setting up spot checks and noting the status is probably more efficient then setting aside intervals of observation time exclusively to watch for behavior. Counting a behavior often requires more vigilance and takes more effort than noting a student's status or checking the products produced.

TABLE 15.1

Count	Time	Formula	Rate per Minute
15 correct	1 minute	15/1	15 correct per minute
8 errors	2 minutes	8/2	4 errors per minute
67 problems	15 minutes	67/15	4.47 correct per minute
20 errors	1 minute, 20 seconds (1.3 minutes)	20/1.3	15.4 errors per minute
4 pages	60 minutes	4/60	.07 pages per minute

Types of Data

Rate

Behaviors can vary along several dimensions, including frequency, duration, intensity, and situational appropriateness. To simplify this discussion (and what you do in the classroom), deal only with rate and duration (both of which were discussed in chapter 8). Rate refers to the frequency of an occurrence during a time interval. It is found by counting the correct or error occurrences and dividing that count by time. By convention, most educators use minutes as the interval of time. The formula for rate is:

$$\frac{\text{Count}}{\text{Time (in minutes)}} = \text{Rate}$$

When recording rate of students' behavior or the products they produce, count the occurrences and note the time (in minutes). This will allow you to calculate the rate. Obviously this is easier to do if you always watch for one minute because the rate will then be the same as the count (e.g., 15 occurrences in one minute equals a rate of 15 per minute). Portions of a minute, 15 seconds for example, are converted to a decimal (e.g., 15 seconds = .25 minutes). This is made easier by rounding the time figures off to a single place and remembering that .1 minute is equal to 6 seconds. Examples are shown in Table 15.1.

Always count *both* correct and error behavior to obtain information about the student's accuracy. In doing so, record the separate rates, not the total. In other words, record 20 corrects and 5 errors per minute—not 25.

Duration

Duration refers to the length of an event (in time). Duration data are usually reported by noting the time interval (in minutes) between the beginning and the end of the event. For example, a behavior may last for 15 seconds (.25 minutes), or a student may be out of seat for 1.8 minutes. Duration data are used primarily to summarize student status (e.g., 5.5 minutes "late for class," or 11 minutes "working on math").

Data Collection Procedures

Continuous

Data may be collected continuously (during the whole time the evaluator is with the student) or at specific intervals (this was also discussed in chapter 8). Continuous data collection gives the best overall picture of what the student is doing, but it requires constant vigilance and as a result is too difficult for many behaviors and kinds of status. Continuous data collection can be used for behaviors and status that are so obvious that they automatically come to the teacher's attention. For example, behaviors like "throwing up" or "asking the teacher for help" will always be noticed so they are easily recorded continuously. "Late for class" is an example of an easily monitored status. Products can often be recorded continuously, particularly if they are written products, as they can simply be counted at the end of a session. To take continuous data, have a portable device for recording frequency of occurrence (to be converted to rate) or beginning and ending times (to be converted to duration).

Interval

When a behavior or status is hard to detect (e.g., eye contact with peer), one cannot afford to watch for it continuously. In this case, specific time intervals (e.g., 5 minutes) can be set aside to attend to and record an occurrence. These intervals can be spread over the entire day and added together to give a more representative image of what the student is doing.

Perhaps the most efficient interval procedure is to set a timer that will periodically signal you to attend to the student. If the student is engaged in the target behavior or in the targeted status when the signal goes off, you note it on a record sheet or counter.

Types of Charts

Monitoring and decision making are greatly improved if the data collected can be visually displayed. This is usually accomplished by charting the data on either an equal interval chart or ratio chart.

Looking at the charts in Figures 15.12 and 15.13, you can see that the scales (distances between numbers on the vertical axis) are different on ratio charts than on equal interval charts. On an equal interval chart the frequency (horizontal) lines are all the same distance apart; this is not true on the ratio chart. On an equal interval chart the distance between 2 and 4 is the same as the distance between 50 and 52. On a ratio chart the distance between 2 and 4 is the same as the distance between 50 and 100. This is because the ratio of 2 to 4 is the same as the ratio of 50 to 100, as shown here:

$$4/2 = 2$$
$$100/50 = 2$$

In ratio terms this means 4/2:100/50.

Ratio charts have some advantages and some disadvantages. Their primary disadvantage is that few educators are familiar with them. Their primary advantage is that they display learned changes in behavior more accurately than equal interval charts. This is because the ratio chart recognizes that in some cases the same amount of behavior change does not indicate the same amount of learning. For example, two students (Deb and Carl) are both working on their addition facts. On the first session Deb can only do 5 facts per minute while Carl can do 30. One week later Deb can do 10 facts and Carl can do 35. Who has learned the most? Most teachers will recognize that Deb has actually learned the most because her skill at addition has doubled while Carl's has only improved by 15%. This is easier to understand intuitively than it is to put into words. It means that, while learning is indicated by changes in behavior, equal changes in behavior do not necessarily indicate equal learning.

Let's follow Deb and Carl to a set of charts. Figure 15.14a is an equal interval chart and 15.14b is a ratio chart. On 15.14a the changes made by Carl and Deb are the same. On 15.14b, their increases, while the same in absolute terms (+5), look very different. They look different because the ratio (proportion) of change is the best indicator of how much learning has occurred (Deb has improved 100% and Carl only 15%). The equal interval chart actually distorted the picture of their learning. The logarithmic scale of the ratio chart allows behavior change to be displayed without this distortion, regardless of the frequency at which the change occurs (White, 1986).

Scores derived from measures of product completion usually do not follow ratio patterns. This is because products (other than the very simple products like writing digits and saying words discussed earlier) tend to vary in difficulty. For example, successive lessons in a text build upon each other, making later lessons harder than earlier ones. If the program is properly structured this increase in complexity tends to offset the student's increasing skill, so that the 23rd math assignment may actually be as hard to finish as the 3rd one. What this all means is that product completion is best viewed as an equal interval phenomenon.

Scores derived from measures of status are also charted on equal interval graphs. This is especially true when a student's status is changing not because of learning, but in response to a behavior management intervention. It is hard to argue, for example, that a student who knows how to sit at

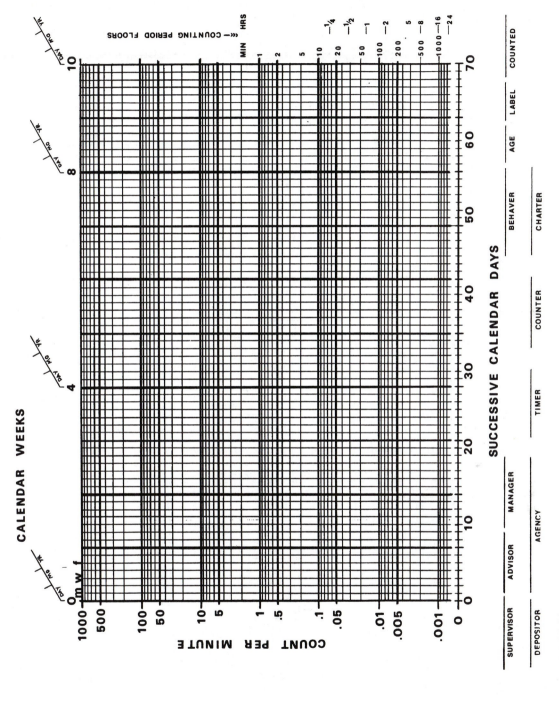

FIGURE 15.12
6-cycle ratio chart

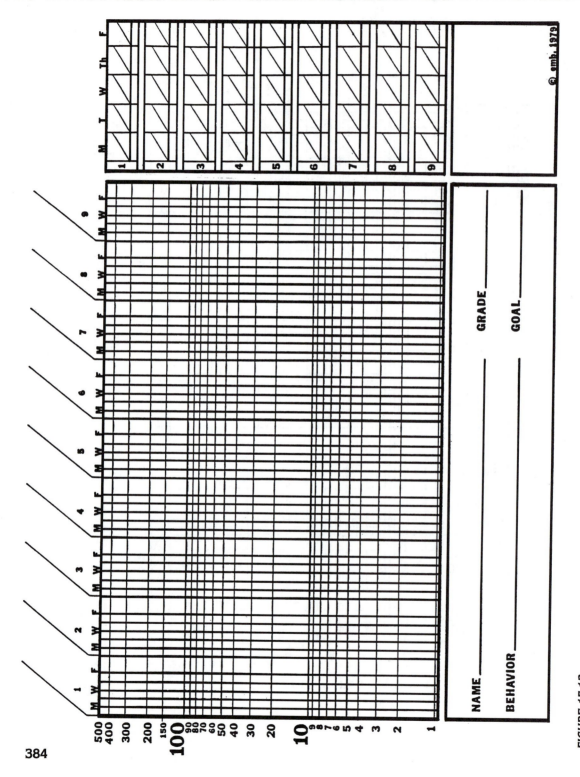

384

FIGURE 15.13
2.5-cycle ratio chart (Source: Berquam, 1986.)

FIGURE 15.14

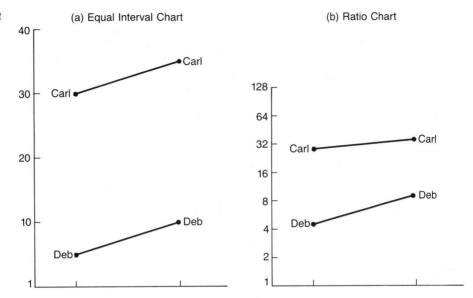

his desk during formal instruction but doesn't, needs to "learn" to do it. A program to change his out-of-seat behavior to in-seat behavior may involve the application of reinforcers or punishers but little if any instruction. In this case, successive minutes in seat are not more complex and therefore duration scores are not influenced by increases in difficulty or skill proficiency.[1] Therefore, equal in-

terval data are produced. Table 15.2 shows the preferred chart for displaying each type of data discussed.

Collecting Data
Formative evaluation will be most successful when:

1. The teacher initially counts only priority behaviors.
2. The teacher identifies strategies to make timing and recording behavior easier.
3. The teacher evaluates the recorded data frequently (preferably daily).

1. Any status affected by fatigue will become harder as time passes. This means a logarithmic chart will need to be used but in this case the chart must treat each successive minute as if it were *harder*. This is the inverse of the chart shown in Figure 15.16. These behaviors are usually *highly* physical and therefore beyond the scope of this discussion.

TABLE 15.2

	Source of Data	Type of Data	Recommended Chart
1.	Behaviors (e.g., says words, writes answers, requests help)	Rate (correct and error)	Logarithmic
2.	Products (e.g., pages completed, friends made, objectives met)	Rate Percentage accurate	Equal interval Equal interval
3.	Status (e.g., in seat, happy, on task).	Duration	Equal interval

4. Curriculum-based testing or observation is used.
5. The system remains a tool for teaching rather than a "cause." Specific programs of formative evaluation should only be used as long as they help the student.

Strategies to facilitate timing and recording behaviors include:

1. Group timings. This works best with written activities. For example: time one-minute handwriting samples, one-minute math fact sheets, one-minute spelling tests.
2. Students can record time started and stopped. (This can easily be done with a rubber stamp of a clock on worksheets. Direct them to look at a wall clock and mark the hands on their papers.)
3. A kitchen timer or prerecorded tape can be used to time sessions.
4. Students can work together to time and record data for each other. This can work well with flashcard drills.
5. Students can read into a tape recorder. Teachers can later check correct and error rates.
6. Mechanical counters. Single and dual tally counters are available, as well as beads and golf-score counters.
7. Teachers should count for a fixed period of time each day. Counting for different intervals confuses the data pattern because such factors as endurance, boredom, and latency of response may enter into the data analysis.
8. One-minute timings are easy to chart because the raw score is the same as rate per minute.
9. Aides, peers, student teachers, and volunteers can be trained to help develop materials and to count and record behaviors.
10. Teachers should count when the behaviors are likely to occur and when other distractions will be minimal.

An Example

One of the authors and two other teachers in Arizona evolved a data-based teaching program for math facts.[2] This program was used in an open classroom setting; 78 kids studied, timed, and charted math facts by themselves. Many of the students were mainstreamed special education students.

The teachers were concerned that their students were weak in computational mathematics. The pinpoints for the program were addition facts 0–20, subtraction facts 0–20, multiplication facts 0–9, and division facts 0–9. Each student was expected to reach a rate of 50 to 60 correct answers (written) per minute in all four areas. Because the program was a drill program, students were not placed into it unless (a) they could write digits at a rate of 60 to 80 per minute and (b) they were somewhat accurate on the facts and already were doing about 15 problems per minute. (Students who are not at least 25% of the way to criterion probably need direct instruction and not drill.)

Data Collection. This is how the program worked. Each student was given a file folder. Inside the folder, charts were stapled to one flap and a sheet of clear plastic was stapled to the other. Every day the teachers would place up to four probe sheets in the folder (addition, subtraction, multiplication, or division, depending on the student's skill). There were many equally difficult forms of these probes so the students could not simply memorize them. Every day immediately after the noon recess, when the kids returned to the class, a 10-minute tape of instrumental music would play over the room's intercom system. The beginning of the music was a cue for the students to pick up their file folders. A bell would sound on the tape at one-minute intervals, allowing the students to time themselves. Each probe sheet would be placed under the plastic sheet and worked by writing on the plastic with an overhead projector pen. When the student was ready, he would listen for a bell and then work for one minute. When the next bell sounded on the tape, the student would stop working and check what he had done. The answers to each probe sheet were on the back of the sheet, allowing self-checking. Once

2. Special thanks to Ms. Teresa Cook and Ms. Connie Ann Nygaard.

TABLE 15.3
Steps for data collection/recording

Step 1: *Select source of data.*
    Behavior: What student does
    Product: What student accomplishes
    Status: Condition of student

Step 2: *Select type of data.*
    Rate: Average number per minute
                  (best for behavior and products)
    Duration: Length in minutes
                  (best for status)

Step 3: *Select data collection procedure.*
    Continuous: Entire time student is present
                  (best for products or noticeable behaviors)
    Interval: Preselected times
                  (most efficient)

Step 4: *Select type of chart.*
    Equal interval: For products and status
    Logarithmic: For behaviors

Step 5: *Collect and chart data.*

the rates of corrects and errors were found and the students had recorded the results on the appropriate charts, they would erase the plastic, get out the next probe, and listen for another bell to start their next timings. The students knew they had 10 minutes to take the four probes, check their own work, and record their own progress.

Data Interpretation. Students and teachers would review the charts daily. If the students found that their charts were not showing adequate progress toward their aim, then they would contract with the teacher for a program change. Many programs were available for the students to use, including instruction (peer instruction, programmed texts, math fact games, homework) and consequence changes (free time, parent-delivered rewards, class privileges, and redeemable points). The students would select one of these programs and use it for a few days to see if their charts showed improvement.

Results. All students in the program (regardless of handicapping condition) reached mastery on the fact probes, most within 3 to 5 weeks. Many students progressed at this rate in all four areas at the same time.

It is important to note that by properly designing the program, the teachers were able to collect formative data with minimal daily effort or time. There is no question that programs like this take time to develop. The teachers spent additional time to design a program, but once it was implemented, it ran smoothly and efficiently. When time is saved in the classroom, it should be student time.

Table 15.3 lists the steps required before an evaluator can begin to interpret data. Each step needs to be carried out carefully. The last half of this chapter deals with the interpretation of progress data. The next few pages will describe how to summarize data on a chart. The summaries of progress and performance are necessary for decision making. As you will see, each summary exer-

FIGURE 15.15

	Time in Minutes	Count Correct	Error	Rate per Minute (Count/Time) Correct	Error
Monday	10	40	20	40/10 = 4	20/10 = 2
Tuesday	1.5	8	5	8/ 1.5 = 5.3	5/ 1.5 = 3.3
Wednesday	20	10	5	10/20 = .5	5/20 = .25
Thursday	1	40	20	40/ 1 = 40	20/ 1 = 20
Friday	7	24	17	24/ 7 = 3.4	17/ 7 = 2.4

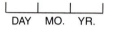

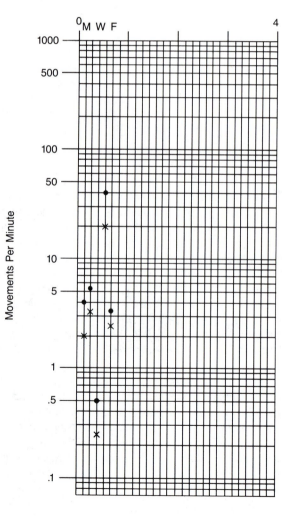

cise is meant to obtain an overall impression of either where the student is—or where he is going. Individual data points on the chart quickly lose value in this process. In fact, the first rule of formative evaluation is:

> Never make a decision from
> a single datum point

DISPLAYING DATA

Charting

Step 1. Convert Data
If charting rate of behavior, label the vertical axis of the chart "rate (count) per minute." If charting duration, label the axis "minutes." For rate, divide the count obtained for both correct and errors by the number of minutes of the test or observation. Five days' worth of rate data illustrating common charting problems is shown in Figure 15.15. On Tuesday note that fractions of minutes are treated as decimals and on Wednesday that behaviors occurring less often than once a minute require a chart that goes below 1.

Step 2. Mark Floors and Ceilings
On the chart note any permanent constraints on the data such as floors (least possible scores) or ceilings (highest possible scores). For accuracy and duration data, the floor is 1. Rate floors are found by dividing the length of the observation (in minutes) into 1. For example, the floor of a 2-minute timing is $1/2 = .5$. Floors are marked with dashed lines *not* crossing the Sunday line, as shown in Figure 15.16.

Ceilings are marked with a dashed line crossing Sunday lines and are either equal to the total available opportunities or the total opportunities allowed by the available time. For example, the ceiling for a behavior that takes 6 seconds to complete would be 10 per minute ($60/6 = 10$). The ceiling for accuracy is 100%.

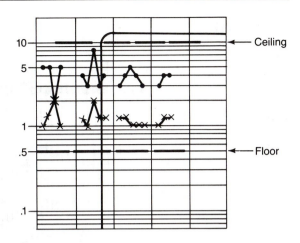

FIGURE 15.16

Step 3. Mark Aims
Performance aims are the same as CAP for the objective being monitored. Mark aims with a wavy line. If a performance aim and aim date (date by which the aim is to be met) can both be specified, don't bother with a wavy line; instead mark the intersection of the aim rate and aim date with an *A*. Use an upright *A* for acceleration (correct) behaviors and an upside down *∀* for deceleration (error) objectives, as seen in Figure 15.17.

Step 4. Chart Data
Refer to Figure 15.18 for conventional charting rules.

Determining Current Performance
Whenever an evaluator collects a lot of different pieces of data, she needs to summarize those data to make them more manageable. If she has read chapter 4 and Appendix B, then she knows all about ways of summarizing score distributions with means, standard deviations, percentiles, and other quantitative mechanisms.

When repeated measures of a behavior are charted, the median score of *the last three recorded days* is used to summarize performance. By

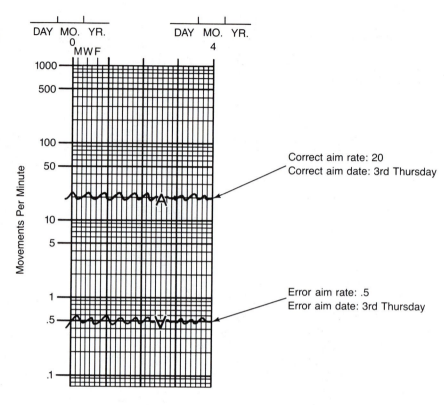

**FIGURE 15.17
Marking objectives
on the chart**

Correct aim rate: 20
Correct aim date: 3rd Thursday

Error aim rate: .5
Error aim date: 3rd Thursday

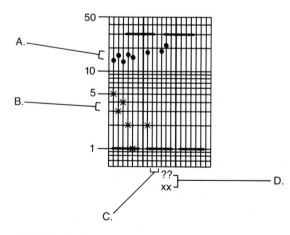

A. Acceleration behaviors (corrects) are charted as dots (•).
B. Deceleration behaviors (errors) are charted as x's (X).
C. On days when timings do not occur, don't chart anything.
D. Zero behavior is usually marked below the floor with a question mark (?).
Note: Don't connect the dots or x's; it will only confuse the picture.

**FIGURE 15.18
Charting rules**

390

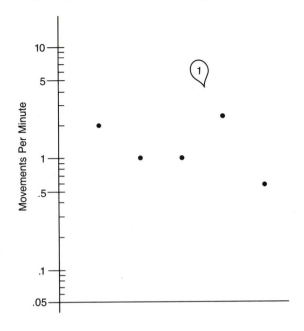

FIGURE 15.19

convention the median is marked on the chart in a teardrop, or bubble, as shown in Figure 15.19. Remember to look for the median *score*, not the median day.

In Figure 15.19 the median rate of 1 was found by noting the scores of the last three days—1, 2, .7—and ranking them from highest to lowest:

2
1 ◄────── median
.7

This is more easily done by simply looking at the data and noting the highest, lowest, and middle (median) dot found during the last three days. If the same score is obtained on two days it is counted twice. Therefore, the median of 5, 10, and 5 is 5.

Determining Current Progress (Trend)

Up until now our focus has been on recording performance (or lack of it) in the form of dots, x's, question marks, ceilings, floors, and teardrops. But formative evaluation is about progress. Remember that formative evaluation doesn't even begin until you, as the evaluator, are in a position to disregard individual data points. You need to be able to put dots on the chart to find a trend—but once you've found it the dots are of no further interest. There are two ways to note the trend of a set of data: best fit estimation and median slope calculation.

Best Fit

This is the least exact way to find a trend; it is also the easiest and most common. The procedure is simple. Take a set of data points, eyeball the data, and draw a line through those that seem to fit. Obviously this is easier with low variability data, as seen in Figure 15.20a, than with high variability data like those shown in Figure 15.20b. It is also

FIGURE 15.20
Best fit lines

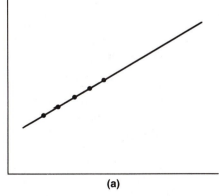

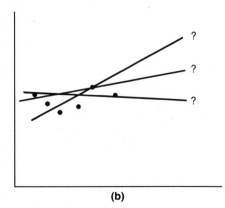

(a)   (b)

easier to do with lots of data points than with only a few. For most students on most behaviors, best fit lines are adequate for decision making.

Median Slopes

The second and more exact way to find a trend is to employ the median slope technique developed by White (1972). This technique is harder to explain than to do and once mastered takes only about 10 seconds to carry out. Each step described below is illustrated in Figure 15.21.

Step 1.   Divide data in half *along time axis*.
Step 2.   Divide data in quarters *along time axis*.
Step 3.   *Switch to the frequency axis*. For each half of the data, find the frequency line on which the median score falls.
Step 4.   For each half of the data find the intersection of the quarter line and the median frequency line.
Step 5.   Connect the two quarter/median intersections to draw the trend.

Here are some hints to follow when finding median slopes.

Medians.   The median of each half of the data is still the middle score of each half. Visually it is the dot (or X) that has as many marks below it as above it.

18
18
18
17 = median
12
12
8

When there is an even number of data points, assume the median is halfway between the middle two. For example, the median of 8, 15, 17, and 18 would be 16.

Dividing Data.   To divide the data in half or quarters use data, not actual days. This means splitting the data charted, not the calendar days covered.

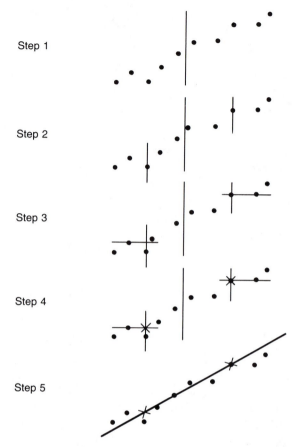

FIGURE 15.21
Finding the median slope

Half and Quarter Lines.   When dividing the data, the half line will intersect a dot in cases where there are an odd number of data. *In these cases the dot is no longer used during calculations.* It is *not* a problem if the quarter lines strike dots; in these cases the dots are used.

A Common Mistake.   The most common error people make when calculating a median slope is to draw a line intersecting the median score of each half. The median scores are used only to find the median frequency line. It is the median frequency/quarter intersects that should be connected.

The median slope technique is used to recognize trends in data. These trend lines are summaries of *central tendency* and, once extended, become our best guess of where a student will be at some future date. Therefore by extending the line to a performance aim we can anticipate when an objective will be met.

Determining Expected Progress

The student's actual progress is shown in the trend. Formative evaluation begins with this recognition of trend, as its focus is the comparison of actual progress to expected progress. To make this comparison, find expected progress, in the form of progress aims. The procedure for doing this is simple.

In Figure 15.22 a student's current performance (as indicated by the median of 3 days of data) is connected to an aim (as indicated by the *A*). The line between the current performance and the aim is

called the *minimum 'celeration line*, *objective*, or *aim line*. It is a progress objective and visually represents the path a student must follow to get from where he is now to where you want him to be at the end of instruction. The hardest part of finding the aim line is deciding on the aim date. The aim rate, or performance level, is specified as CAP in the instructional objective and should have been established earlier through a standardization process like the one described in chapter 8. The aim date, however, must be selected using one of the following procedures. In all cases the idea here is to attempt to specify the day one expects the student to reach the performance criterion. This means thinking about how long it should take to teach a task. A thorough discussion of these procedures can be found in Deno and Mirkin (1977).

Curriculum-Determined Aim Dates

Ideally a curriculum will specify when a student is expected to learn each objective. However, few curricula are that specific; even if they are, the date sequence becomes a moot point for special/remedial students as they are already behind. However, it is possible to recognize how many objectives they must complete in order to catch up and how long that should take.

Product Completion

The procedure for product completion is outlined in Figure 15.23; read through that figure now.

In the example the student can catch up in one year by completing one chapter test every six instructional days. This does *not* mean that his problem will be solved by bombarding him with assignments. It means that he needs sufficient instructional support to complete the assignments at a faster pace than others. *This approach should only be used if the assignments involved are meaningful.*

Behavior Change

This procedure is better than product completion because it does not place blind faith in the relevance of every assignment in the text. Instead it uses the assignments as indicators of expected behavior change. It is outlined in Figure 15.24.

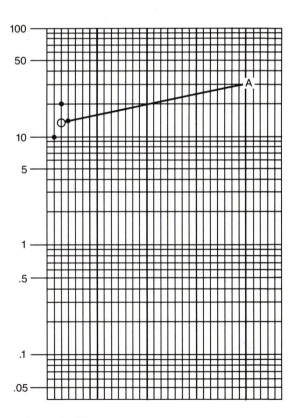

FIGURE 15.22

Step	Example
1. Identify products to be completed that represent desired learning outcomes.	End-of-chapter tests passed in math.
2. Determine how many of these products the student has already finished. This will be the current level of performance. Mark this on an equal interval graph.	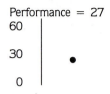

3. Decide how many products he would have finished if he were progressing adequately and subtract his current performance from that to find the product discrepancy.

Ideal products completed   40
− Current products completed   −27
Product discrepancy   13

4. Decide how long you have to work with the student to make up the discrepancy and the number of products other students will finish in that time. Add this number to the product discrepancy.

If there is one year (40 weeks) to catch the student up and the rest of the class will cover 20 new chapters in that year, she must complete 20 + 13 = 33 chapters.

5. Add the products to be completed (33) to those already done (27). This gives you the performance aim.

$$\begin{array}{r} 33 \\ +27 \\ \hline 60 \end{array}$$ products to be finished
products already finished
Total products completed by the end of instruction

Performance aim = 60
Aim date = 40 weeks from the start of school

6. Find the minimum 'celeration line by marking the intersection of the performance aim and the aim date. Connect the two points with a line.

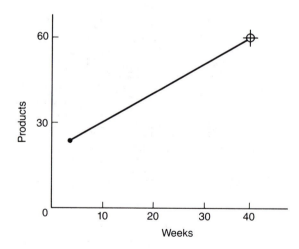

or

Divide the number of products to be done (obtained in step 4) by the available time to find out how many must be completed per week.

33/40 = .83 chapters a week. With five instructional days a week this figures out to .17 chapters a day (.83/5 = .17), or one chapter every six instructional days.

FIGURE 15.23
Using product completion to set an aim date

Step	Example
1. Carry out the product completion procedure described above to determine what chapter test he needs to be working on now and which one he needs to be working on at the end of instruction.	Current chapter = 27 Target chapter = 60
2. Determine what objectives/skills will be taught in the intervening chapters.	
3. Divide the objectives into groups that represent reasonably consolidated domains of content and that should be taught during a 4- to 6-week period (short-term objectives).	In this case the student is learning fractions. The fraction content is illustrated by the table of specifications. With one year (40 weeks of instruction) available, a minimum of six 4- to 6-week periods of instruction can be delivered so the table is carved up into six reasonably consolidated domains.
4. Devise a test covering the content of each domain.	Test titles: 1. Converting Fractions 2. Adding and Subtracting Fractions With Common Denominators 3. Adding and Subtracting Mixed Numbers Without Common Factors Between Uncommon Denominators 4. Multiplying and Dividing Fractions With Common Denominators—No Conversion Required 5. Multiplying Mixed Numbers With Conversions 6. Dividing Mixed Numbers With Conversions
5. Set performance criteria for each test in the form of an aim rate and intersect it with the aim date of 6 weeks. Mark the intersection with an *A*. Connect the lower left-hand corner of the chart (0 performance on the first day) to the *A* to find the minimum 'celeration line. (Few students will actually enter a unit at zero performance so the aim line can be adjusted in most cases.)	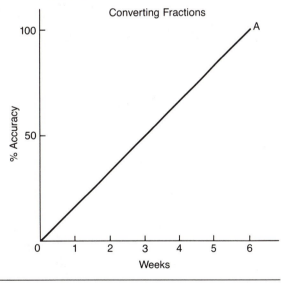

FIGURE 15.24
Using behavior change to set an aim date

Normative Aim Dates

In many cases it is too difficult to use curriculum to determine aim dates. One alternative is to use a standard rate of progress, called standard 'celeration. This rate of progress was originally specified by Liberty (1975) and is essentially a normative standard. The standard rate of progress is ×1.25 (25% improvement each week) and was derived from a study of 361 precision teaching programs. Each program contained at least 5 data points

Step	Example
1. Find the student's initial level of correct and error performance and mark it on a ratio chart.	10 correct / 4 errors
2. Multiply the initial correct level by 1.25 (or your own established rate) and divide the error level by 1.25 to get the predicted change for one week.	Initial performance predicted for one week. $10 \times 1.25 = 12.5$ $5 \div 1.25 = 4$
3. Mark the predicted performance on the chart 7 days after the initial performance.	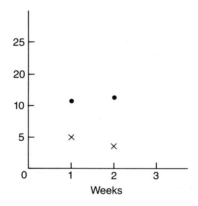
4. Draw a straight line connecting the initial and predicted marks. Extend this line to the performance aims to find the aim date. *This can only be done on a ratio chart.*	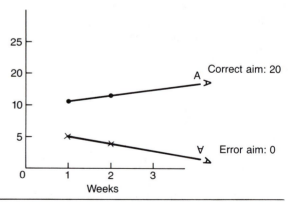

FIGURE 15.25
Using the standard 'celeration line

(with an average of about 11). The results showed that:

1. 50% of the students were able to change × 1.33 per week or better for acceleration targets.
2. 50% of the students were able to decrease unwanted behavior ÷ 1.46 per week.
3. 53% of the students could grow at a rate of × 1.25 per week or better.
4. 66% of the students decelerated unwanted behavior at a rate of ÷ 1.25 per week.

Because of this study, × 1.25 per week (25% change each week) has become accepted as a reasonable expected level of behavior change (White & Haring, 1980). It means that a student who can do 10 problems one week should be able to grow to 12.5 the next, 15.6 the next, 19.5 the next, 24.4 the next, and so on.

There are some dangers associated with the 1.25 standard. While it is widely accepted, it has not been vigorously validated through replication studies across age levels, content areas, and teaching conditions. In the authors' experience it is often too low, especially for errors. For example, in one of our university classes we expect students to define key terms at a rate of 30 correct per minute. Last semester every student in the class moved from 1 to 30 in 4 weeks. In most cases errors vanished within the first week. This is a progress rate of × 2.3 (230% improvement each week) for corrects. If the × 1.25 standard 'celeration rate had been applied it would have taken 14 weeks—more than 3 times as long—for our students to reach the "definitions correct" aim. Progress levels of × 1.5, × 2, and × 3 are not uncommon for many skills and for many special/remedial students. The math fact program described early in this chapter produced average improvement rates of × 1.54 for special students, which seems common for basic facts (Howell, 1978). Therefore, we recommend the use of the standard 'celeration line only when no other procedure is available and when it will be treated as an initial guess, not an absolute prediction. If at all possible, consider establishing your own standard 'celerations by averaging the trends of successful students on the tasks you will be teaching. Accept your own minimum 'celeration as long as it exceeds 1.25—do not accept anything lower. The steps for using standard 'celeration are illustrated in Figure 15.25.

Student-Determined Aim Dates

This procedure has great advantages but also has some risk. If unable to find an aim date and unwilling to risk a normative guess by using standard 'celeration, one can use the student's own progress to find the aim date. This is done by collecting several days of data *during instruction* (this is *not* a baseline, or no instruction, period) and then finding the median slope for those data. The median slope may then be extended to the aim rate. Once the student's current trend is extended to the aim rate, it becomes a student-determined minimum 'celeration line and the point where it intersects the rate becomes the aim date (Figure 15.26). The risk is obvious: If the student is not learning optimally when the line is drawn it will underestimate possible progress. However, it does have the advantage of indicating a sort of "progress floor." Because the line is based on the student's own progress, it is reasonable to demand this level or more during subsequent learning on the same task. As long as the student-determined aim line (sometimes called a *can-do line*) is viewed as the minimal acceptable progress, it can be adjusted later if greater progress is demonstrated. An adjustment procedure will be presented shortly.

This procedure has tremendous instructional advantages over the other two. A teacher can contract with the student to give a reward every day his performance exceeds his own aim line. This procedure puts him in "competition" with himself as opposed to a norm or a behavioral criterion. Because the median slope line typically splits the data in half, the student will be rewarded about 50% of the time without any change in progress. This means that a contract based on this line is both individual and highly positive.

Envelopes

An envelope is simply a pair of dotted lines drawn parallel to the median slope. Envelopes should be

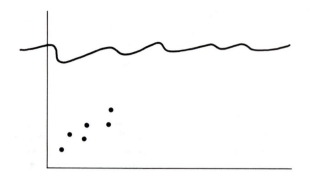

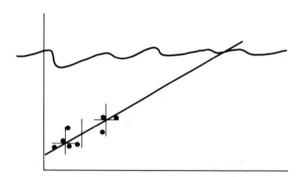

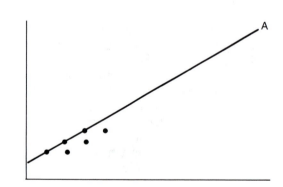

Steps
1. Mark the aim rate and collect several (5 or more) days of data as instruction is taking place.
2. Calculate the median slope and extend it to the aim rate.
3. Mark the aim and treat the median slope as a minimum 'celeration line.

FIGURE 15.26
Finding a student-determined aim date

drawn so that 80% or more of the data points used to calculate the median slope fall between the dotted lines. Look at the examples in Figure 15.27 and notice how data points that are extremely deviant from the others have simply been ignored when drawing the envelope. Also, notice that the envelope lines are parallel and do not converge as they move up the chart. This will only be true on a logarithmic graph.

Envelopes are interesting because their "width" is determined by variability in both time and behavior. If the envelope is compared to a time reference, such as the eighth Wednesday in Figure 15.27c, the width becomes behavioral and we can say "on the eighth Wednesday, I expect her to score between 20 and 80." If we compare the envelope to a behavior reference, such as 100 per minute in Figure 15.27d, we can say "she will reach 100 per minute between the tenth and twelfth week." Envelopes illustrate clearly the dual nature of learning: Learning is indicated by changes in behavior across time.

Using Envelopes to Make Predictions
Once the envelope has been drawn, it can be extended into the future just like the median slope; like the median slope it can be used to make predictions. Look at the data in Figure 15.28. The median slopes and the envelopes have been extended for the correct and error rates. While the slopes remain the best predictor of the student's arrival at the aim, the envelopes indicate the earliest and latest dates that that arrival can be expected. Note that while the correct and error slopes reach their aims on the same day, the variability in errors causes one to be less certain of the prediction made for the error slope. The prediction for the correct trend could be off by as much as one week without prompting concern about changing the program. The error prediction could be off by as much as three weeks because there is three times as much variability in those data.

The bounce, or variability, in the data is due in part to error of measurement (chapter 4 and Appendix B). Because the envelope encompasses this error, it describes a student's status more accurately than the median slope or an individual data point. For example, look at Figure 15.29, which

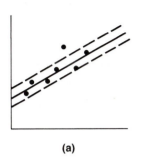 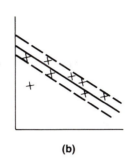 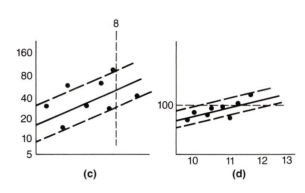

(a)   (b)   (c)   (d)

FIGURE 15.27
Envelopes

shows the intersection of the envelope with an aim rate. Notice that on the third Tuesday, the student scores above the aim rate. Does this mean he has met his aim? As an evaluator you can't be sure because the bounce in the data is partially produced by error, which means that the student may have scored above criterion more or less by accident. So you may not want to risk stopping instruction because of this single data point. To guarantee that the student is at aim, you need to monitor him for at least as many days as the width of the envelope indicates. As a rule, a student is not said to have met aim until he is above it on his worst day. Because aims themselves are seldom absolute, teachers should begin to teach a new task after the student's first score exceeds the aim rate, but con-

tinue to monitor the original skill for the width of the envelope to be sure of the decision.

If you decide to use envelopes and to define mastery as the point where the envelope has passed the aim (rather than data points passing the aim), you will need to consider the influence of ceiling effects. This topic is discussed in relation to probe construction in chapter 8. There must be more items on a probe sheet (or opportunities during a time interval) than criteria calls for or a ceiling effect will influence data. Variability cannot be completely removed. Therefore, once the edges of the envelope bump into the ceiling or floor of the test, the data will become distorted. To avoid this distortion provide room for variability by assuring that the ceiling is at least the width of the envelope above the aim

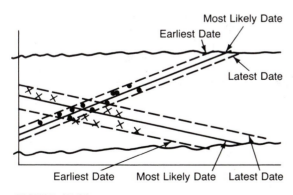

FIGURE 15.28

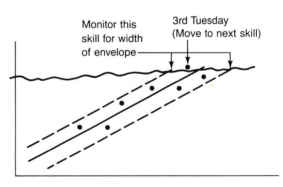

FIGURE 15.29

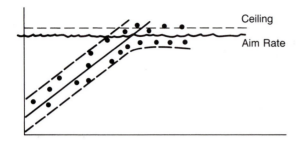

FIGURE 15.30

rate. This is shown in Figure 15.30. In Figure 15.30 the variability (envelope) is wider than the space between the aim rate and ceiling; therefore the data have begun to flatten out and the student cannot reach criterion unless the ceiling is raised.

Using Envelopes to Adjust Aim Dates

Owen White (1983) has suggested using envelopes to adjust aim dates. Because the minimum 'celeration line may underestimate what the student can actually do, White has suggested using the top boundary of the envelope as a new minimum 'celeration line once the lower boundary reaches the original minimum 'celeration line. This procedure is illustrated in Figure 15.31.

DECISION MAKING

A framework for decision making was constructed in chapter 6 (see Table 6.1). We pointed out that, while some decisions can be based on summative evaluation, others, particularly those addressing the modification of treatment, can only be based on progress data. To review briefly, educators make what-to-teach and how-to-teach decisions. How-to-teach decisions can be made in two areas: curriculum and instruction. Curriculum decisions focus on the level of objective to be taught and the context (degree of isolation) in which it will be taught. Instructional decisions address the format of instruction, the incentives employed, and the delivery of instruction. The remainder of this section will show how formative data can be used to guide decisions

about changes in format, incentive, and delivery. These changes should be thought of as exercises in fine tuning rather than the major reconstruction of lessons. Obviously no one wants to tear everything apart to start completely over; if teachers have to do so too often they'll burn out. However, change is necessary and the considerable value of formative evaluation is that it alerts one early enough that small adjustments can head off big problems.

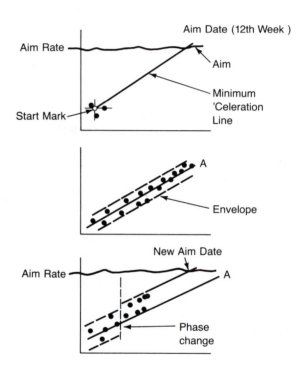

Step 1: Draw original minimum 'celeration line using any of the procedures described in this chapter.

Step 2: Begin teaching and draw the envelope—if the data begin to move above the minimum 'celeration line (as they do at the point indicated by the arrow), carry out Step 3.

Step 3: Draw a new envelope and extend the top boundary of the envelope to the aim rate line (keeping it parallel to the minimum 'celeration line) to select the new aim date.

FIGURE 15.31
Using an envelope to adjust an aim date

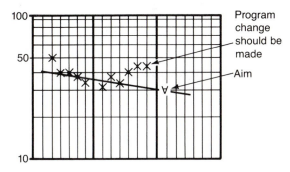

FIGURE 15.32
The three-day rule

Deciding When to Change

A program should be changed when it isn't working. The more quickly this change takes place the more student time will be saved. If an informal data collection system is being used, teachers/evaluators should set up a routine schedule of program review (every 2 weeks is recommended) and make decisions to retain or alter current treatments.

More formal formative systems have the power to alert one immediately if change is indicated. Some authors suggest that changes be made in a program if, for any 3 consecutive days, the data are *below* (for acceleration) the aim line. For deceleration targets, changes should occur if 3 consecutive days are *above* the line (McGuigan, 1980). Figure 15.32 shows an example of the 3-day rule applied to error rates.

If a student is below the acceleration aim line or above the deceleration aim line for 3 days in a row, the chances are less than 6% that he will reach his aim without a change in the instructional program (White, 1984; White & Liberty, 1976). Other authors have allowed 7 to 10 days of inadequate performance prior to initiating changes and still obtained superior student growth (Fuchs, Deno, & Mirkin, 1984).

Data decision guidelines are provided in Table 15.4. This table is almost identical to Table 6.2 in that the numbers and decisions are the same. The only difference is that pictures of progress data have been supplied to illustrate the kind of student learning that indicates which decision to use. These data decision rules should be employed every 2

weeks in an effort to assure optimal student progress.

Monitoring and Adjusting Instruction

Because there are so many incentive and delivery variables and because student responses to them are often personal and temporary, it is not possible to match particular patterns of data to specific delivery changes. Therefore, as a teacher it is sometimes necessary to make small changes in programs and to monitor and adjust the treatment until you find an effective lesson. This means comparing the effects of a new treatment to those produced by a previous treatment.

Comparing Programs

Decisions about instruction can be made by approaching them as if they were research questions to be resolved through the analysis of formative data. This is called *single-subject research* (Tawney & Gast, 1984).

In single-subject (one-student) research, the investigator asks questions about topics that do not lend themselves to the group experimental designs encountered in most educational research. In typical experimental/control group design studies, the effect of a treatment is judged by comparing the treatment group to the control group. In single-subject research, each student functions as his own "control" because he is placed in first one treatment and then the other. The changes noted in student performance and progress as the treatments switch are then examined. This procedure shows which treatment is best for an individual student and allows the teacher to fine-tune instruction.

In the monitoring/decision-making model described in this chapter, a teacher would either place a student in one program and then change him to another or place the student in two programs at the same time. The ways the student learns in each treatment are then compared to judge the relative effect of the two treatments. The resulting changes can be described in terms of their direction and significance.

Direction. Changes in direction are either up (positive) or (down) negative. If progress data are being

TABLE 15.4
How to teach decisions

Questions	Decisions (Numbers correspond to Table 6.1)		Indicating Data Description	Chart
Am I working on the correct objective?	B.1.1	Stay with current objective.	Student is not at aim, but makes some correct responses.	Record / Floor
	B.1.2.a	Move to a more complex objective.	Student is at or above CAP.	Aim
	B.1.2.b*	Move back to an easier objective.	Student makes no correct responses and has made no progress after several sessions.	Record / Floor
	B.1.2.c	Expect faster learning (move aim date forward).	Student is below CAP but progress is greater than expected.	A
Is the context appropriate?	B.1.3.a	Teach the skill in the context of larger tasks. Explain the relevance of the task. Make the lesson "applied." (Ex: Do subtraction in a checkbook.)	Student has the necessary background information to derive meaning from the context. (Ex: knows what a checkbook is, what it is used for, or is resisting lessons and seems bored.)	A
	B.1.3.b*	Teach the largest manageable unit of the objective in isolation. Use "rote" instruction. If student is accurate, employ fast-paced repetitive drill. Set daily performance aims and reinforce improvement. Put the skill in context as soon as possible.	Student is lacking the background necessary to use context or is confused by context.	A
Is my instruction appropriate?	B.2.1	Stay with current format, incentive, and delivery.	Student is progressing toward aim as expected.	

*Employ only as a last resort.

TABLE 15.4
(continued)

Questions		Decisions (Numbers correspond to Table 6.1)	Indicating Data Description	Chart
Should the emphasis be on accuracy, fluency, generalization, or maintenance?	B.2.2.a	Accuracy instruction. Extensive explanation, modeling, demonstration, guided practice with correction and feedback. Little independent work.	Student is less than 83% accurate.	
	B.2.2.b	Fluency instruction. Emphasize rate. Give extensive drill and practice with frequent timings. Make sure accuracy is maintained.	Student is above 83% accuracy, but is slow.	
	B.2.2.c	Generalization instruction. Reduce extrinsic reinforcement, teach self-monitoring. Present the task in novel contexts, expect student to adjust responses to fit changes in the situation.	Student is accurate or accurate and fast.	
	B.2.2.d	Maintenance instruction. Stop active instruction. Review periodically, monitor retention. Use skill in context of higher skills. Move to variable schedules of reinforcement.	Student is at or above aim.	
Should the lesson be made more interesting?	B.2.3.a	Change type or schedule of reinforcement. Use preferred activities or student-selected rewards. Consider increasing or decreasing the frequency of reinforcement. Change when reinforcement is delivered to make it more or less predictable. Change type of reinforcer.	Was improving, but is getting worse or beginning to resist lessons.	Decreasing Progress or Increasing Variability

403

TABLE 15.4
(continued)

Questions	Decisions (Numbers correspond to Table 6.1)	Indicating Data Description	Chart
	B.2.3.b — Provide meaning. Explain relevance of task. Work skills in the context of higher-level skills. Begin and end lessons by explaining how the skill can be used. Allow student input into the kind of instruction received. Allow student to chart own progress. Make lessons applied.		or Lack of Attendance
Should the delivery be modified?	B.2.4 — Change setting, or delivery. - Questioning - Feedback - Pace - Explanations - Length of lessons - Size of group - Lesson sequence - Type of practice	Below aim, but seems to have prerequisite skills. Is making inadequate progress in spite of appropriate objective, context, emphasis, and incentives.	

FIGURE 15.33

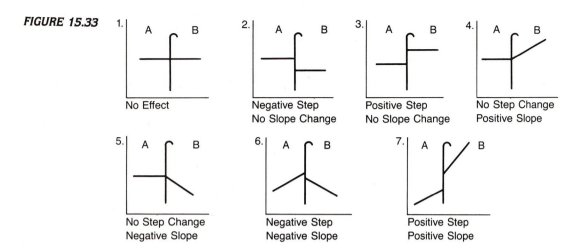

1. A   B
No Effect

2. A   B
Negative Step
No Slope Change

3. A   B
Positive Step
No Slope Change

4. A   B
No Step Change
Positive Slope

5. A   B
No Step Change
Negative Slope

6. A   B
Negative Step
Negative Slope

7. A   B
Positive Step
Positive Slope

examined, then a change in direction is called a *slope change*. If performance data are examined, then changes in direction are called *step changes*. The series of illustrations in Figure 15.33 shows various configurations of step and slope changes as students go from program *A* to program *B*.

It is important to note that step and slope changes are independent of each other. Therefore, program changes that have the effect of increasing a student's total performance (positive step) may not always increase their progress.

Significance. The whole point of monitoring and comparing treatment is to determine which method is the best for a particular student at a particular time on a particular task. Changes in behavior across time can be summarized numerically but these data are often difficult to interpret. The easiest way to summarize and interpret data for individual students is to represent them visually on a chart. On charts that have both behavior and time axes, the steepest line represents the most behavior change per time unit. Therefore, as a rule, the best program change is the one that brings about the steepest slope. To judge significance ask "Did this program change save time?" because the students with steepest slopes arrive at performance aims the soonest.

Because charts have two dimensions, the effect of a phase change can be noted in two ways. Figure

15.34 shows a chart with two treatments (separated by the hooked vertical "phase change" line) and two learning slopes. The dotted lines represent predicted growth in each treatment. Obviously, phase *B* is superior; the effect of the phase change from *A* to *B* can be seen by selecting either a date or behavior frequency for comparison. The net effect of the phase change on the 12th Sunday is 20%, meaning the student will be 20% ahead on that day if left in treatment *B*. The net effect at the 100% performance aim is 2 weeks, meaning the student will arrive at 100% two weeks earlier if left in treatment *B*. The phase change illustrated in Figure 15.34 is significant if you (as the teacher) believe that saving 2 weeks of instruction is significant.

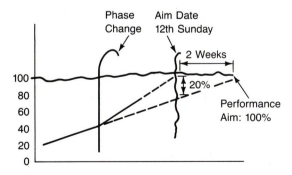

FIGURE 15.34

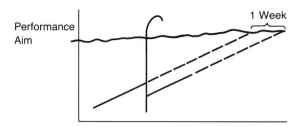

FIGURE 15.35

The chart in Figure 15.34 shows the slope effect of a phase change. A step change can also alter the time required to arrive at a behavioral level, as seen in Figure 15.35. In this case, the student was better off in phase A.

SUMMARY OF FORMATIVE EVALUATION

How to Do It

This chapter began with the assertion that one-shot (summative) psychological and educational tests, particularly those designed to assess ATI, are not adequately powerful to predict which of the many available treatments will be ideal for a particular student. It then presented an alternative to prediction known as *data based program modification*. To describe procedures for carrying out formative evaluation, topics related to data collection, data display, progress summary, and decision making were covered. The decision-making procedures described included the application of data decision rules and the comparison of programs.

Because this discussion has been a long and convoluted one, you may find the procedural outlines in Tables 15.3 and 15.5 useful as a reference. Table 15.4 is a summary of treatment decisions. Table 15.5 outlines how these decisions can be used for formative evaluation.

How Well It Works

The data decision rules outlined in this chapter are based largely on the work of White (1984)

and others. While they have not been widely researched, the results that are available seem to demonstrate clearly that teachers who periodically review formative data and base treatment decisions on them are more effective (White, 1986). For example, Haring, Liberty, and White (1970–1980) found that a group of teachers using similar rules were 2.2 times more successful at selecting appropriate treatment modifications then teachers who did not use the rules. Fuchs, Deno, and Mirkin (1984) found that teachers who employed formative evaluation and data-based program evaluation produced statistically and educationally superior student progress.

Fuchs and Fuchs (1986), in a meta-analysis, reviewed 21 studies and concluded that cumulative effects are obtained when data display, decision rules, and behavior modification are combined during teaching. In this case the average performance of students receiving data display, decision rules, and behavior modification was 37% higher than that of students who weren't. This study looked at 3,835 student programs, 83% of which involved handicapped learners. Of these, 38% focused on reading, 19% on reading and math, 14% on math, and the remainder on areas such as preschool skills, spelling, and high school content.

There is little doubt in our minds that formative evaluation is the most powerful tool currently available to teachers. It is the sort of high-tech excep-

TABLE 15.5

1. Set aim (performance/date), as explained on pages 389–397.
2. Find student's current performance, as explained on pages 389–390.
3. Connect current performance and aim, as explained on page 393.
4. Select the best available treatment and begin instruction.
5. Collect and chart every time you teach—a minimum of 3 times a week.
6. Review data on each student every 2 weeks by asking, "Should I change my instruction?"
7. If change is indicated, employ the data decision rules (Table 15.4).

tional teaching procedure that makes special education truly special. We also recognize that it is time-consuming. In part this is because researchers and publishers have failed to popularize the tools required to use it and teachers attempting to do so must therefore be prepared to develop some of their own materials. We would like to say we have found a quick and easy gimmick that will help hard-to-teach students. We haven't. We have found that in education, just as in any other field, the hardest problems necessitate the greatest effort.

A FINAL WORD (CAUTION)

Evaluation has its basis in comparison. Consequently it tends to accentuate differences within and between individuals. It is wise to remember that every difference is not a meaningful one. In short, just because something can be measured doesn't mean it needs to be measured. In addition, if measurement should reveal a difference, it doesn't follow that the difference must be important.

Current testing techniques have received extensive criticism because of misapplications. The most important of these misapplications centers around significance statements. For example, an IQ score of 69 may be significantly less than the average score of 100. But is it significantly less than an IQ score of 71? No. Yet the result of scoring above or below 70 on an IQ test can have serious ramifications for the student. These ramifications are the result of placing too much significance on a small range of IQ scores.

Many tests are powerful enough to give information about direction. That is, if two students take the test, it will tell which student is performing above the other. But few currently available tests will tell us if the student is performing *significantly* above the other. In spite of this, some educators seem obsessed with making significance statements about children, and they frequently offer test scores to support these statements.

G. V. Glass (1974) has written about an evaluative paradox which can be paraphrased as follows. Learning can be directed most efficiently by evaluating frequently. However, learning flourishes most spontaneously in an environment which is nonjudgmental. If there is any way out of this apparent paradox, it must certainly be to control the way we are judgmental. Special educators, more than any other group of teachers, must constantly remind themselves that it is possible for children to be different without being either good or bad.

Study Questions

1. Contrast treatment selection through aptitude-treatment-interaction and data-based program modification according to each of the following:
   a. Procedure for deciding how to teach
   b. Source of information used for decision making
   c. Type of measures used
2. Contrast performance and progress.
3. What two pieces of information are needed to specify a progress aim?
   a.
   b.
4. Students who are 100% accurate
   a. can still do better.
   b. cannot improve beyond that level in one or more aspects of performance.
   c. have reached a progress expectation.
   d. have reached fluency.

5. The line that connects a student's current performance to the aim is called _____.
6. To find what a student's performance is at any given time, take _____ days of data, then find the intersection of the _____ rate and the mid _____.
7. For the following data:
   a. Chart corrects and errors according to standard charting conventions on a ratio chart (a copy of the chart in Figure 15.12 or 15.13 may be used).
   b. Indicate the aims.

   Aim date: 8th Wednesday
   Correct aim rate: 80
   Error aim rate: 5

   c. Calculate and draw the median slope.

Day	Length of observation	Correct	Error
Mon.	1 min	30	12
Tue.	5 min	200	50
Wed.	5 min	175	45
Thu.	10 min	400	70
Fri.	2 min	90	15
Mon.	5 min	250	35
Tue.	1 min	60	5
Wed.	3 min	200	8
Thu.	10 min	750	50
Fri.	1 min	90	4

8. How often should the data decisions be employed?
9. How does a delivery decision differ from a format decision?
10. How might you respond to a teacher who complains that data-based program modification requires too much teacher time?

APPENDIXES

Appendix A

Issues

CLASSIFICATION

Labels

One of the most common reasons for evaluating students is to classify them to comply with the requirements of various funding agencies or to document the existence of a handicapping condition when documentation is necessary to qualify the student for special services. In this case, the evaluation is for the purpose of specifying the "kind" of student being treated. This sort of evaluation seldom supplies information about the treatment the student needs. The reason for this is simple. All students in the categories currently used (e.g., "mentally retarded") are not the same. Therefore, regardless of the numerous books and courses titled "Methods for the Mentally Retarded," knowing that a student has been categorized as mentally retarded doesn't tell you what or how to teach. The currently used disability categories lack educational relevance because that they are not *educational* categories. They are quasimedical categories that were originally based on the supposed cause of the student's problem.

Classification, when properly used, is a process that aids the development of theory by promoting understanding between interested parties. Researchers are able to classify according to any number or combination of variables. In special education, students are routinely classified according to source variables (student characteristics that supposedly explain why a child isn't learning) (Reynolds & Balow, 1972). Traditional source variables correspond to the current disability categories. These problems are thought of as the sources of educational failure because those who believe in them are working under the assumption that failures to learn can be traced to the student.

The use of source variables for classification was supported in part by the fact that, with certain severe conditions, classification and treatment are nearly synonymous. Because the field of special education grew out of treating severely handicapped individuals, the confusion may have been with us from the start (Quay, 1973). Classification may lead to accurate treatment statements when the individual being classified is severely biologically handicapped. For example, phenylketonuria (PKU) is a pathological condition that usually results in intellectual retardation due to the accumulation of phenylalanine (a substance found in many foods including *NutraSweet*) within the bloodstream of the child. The implication of accurately classifying an individual as having PKU is straightforward; don't feed the child things that contain phenylalanine. But even in this case, the condition doesn't always result in retardation (Baumeister & Muma, 1975), and it certainly does not determine which reading program will work most effectively.

When the problem is the academic deficiency of a mildly handicapped student the variables for classification are less specific. There is no one variable that explains reading failure. In fact, there is no one definition of reading. Yet educators have tended to treat students who fail academically as if they had enzyme deficiencies. That is, they have sought to label students using kid characteristics and then to make treatment statements from the label. This practice can succeed only when the label is precise and sensitive to treatment. Of course, our educational labels are far from precise; a "gifted child" in one school district may be a "slow learner" in another. This is because the categories of exceptionality, while based on theories of causation (see pages 416–418 in this appendix), are almost always defined with normative tests (see pages 52–53), which compare students to each other rather than to a functional standard. Anyone who performs differently in the group (for whatever reason) looks exceptional when measured normatively.

The use of normative tests to define deviance involves basic normative assumptions. In operation, these assumptions dictate that any subgroup of the population is deviant. That is to say, the more "special" a small group is the more deviant they are in the normative sense. This situation was initially acceptable because of our widely held belief that the schools are the tool by which the American culture is maintained and that American society is a cultural melting pot. Mercer (1973) spoke to this issue when she observed that "clinical assessment has reinforced the 'melting pot' process by defining persons who have not 'melted' as subnormal" (p. 9). Normative comparison tends to isolate and stigmatize any subgroup that is truly different from the norm. Two obvious ways in which kids may differ from the norm are by race and wealth. With the increased social awareness of the 1960s, commonplace discriminatory practices of all kinds came under attack. Because both race and wealth have been viewed by the Supreme Court as suspect classifications, court cases have held that the use of middle-class norms is inappropriate for making educational placement decisions about minority students (*Larry P. v. Riles*, 1979; *Diana v. State Board of Education*, 1970, 1973; *Hobson v. Hanson*, 1967). In response, some districts began to stop using general ability testing because the practice was legally too risky (Deno, 1971).

In 1979 we observed that:

The legal, social, and educational price being paid for the use of traditional normative testing for the purpose of classification will almost certainly continue to rise. As it does, it will be interesting to see at what point this use is simply discontinued because of the confusion and misunderstanding this practice breeds. (Howell et al., 1979, p. 22)

Rueda, Figueroa, Mercado, and Cardoza (1985) have reported that this point has apparently been reached in the state of California (which is not to imply that there is no confusion left in that state), where the *Larry P. v. Riles* case has curtailed the use of IQ testing (Galagan, 1985). As a result of that litigation, the proportion of students classified as educably mentally retarded has dropped dramatically. It appears that the demise of IQ testing in California has led to the reclassification of EMR students into the LD and language impaired categories. While many educators may applaud the demise of IQ testing, it is sobering to note that IQ testing was not discontinued because of widespread dissatisfaction expressed by educators. It was legislated and litigated out of existence by "outside" agencies. This is not a good example of education policing its own practices.

Saying too Much and too Little at the Same Time

The problem with classifications and labels is that they may lack meaning, or worse yet, that they have more meaning than they should. Lack of spe-

cific meaning is not limited to educational labels but is a characteristic of all words. Korzybski (1948) describes a kind of word game in which the players attempt to supply the meaning for words by first giving a definition and then defining the words in the definition without reusing key words. In a short time the players find their vocabularies exhausted as they reach a level at which they "know" but can't "tell" the definition. Korzybski says the game takes from 10 to 15 minutes. If the game is played by special educators using labels such as *mentally retarded*, *learning disabled*, or *behavior disordered*, it takes about 5. In other words, these categories are all defined in terms of other categories.

At the other extreme (and ironically at the same time), a label may have too much meaning. This is referred to as *surplus meaning* (Cromwell, Blashfield, & Strauss, 1975), and it comes about when a term is used to describe things that cannot be directly or accurately measured. Once a term is used vaguely, it can be applied to many situations. A person who hears the term may not know to which situation it refers because the term has too many meanings. Surplus meaning can obscure understanding.

The term *mental retardation* (or even *retardation*) is the classic example of a term with too little and too much meaning. The term has various definitions. Most include the key words *permanent*, *limitation*, *intelligence* (*intellectual capacity*), *central nervous system*, and *incompetence*. The circularity of the term can be seen by playing Korzybski's game with a dictionary: the term *mental* relates to the term *intelligence*, and *intelligence* relates to the term *ability*. The term *retardation* relates to the term *limitation*, which relates to a lack of *capacity*. *Capacity*, by referring to *ability*, completes the circle back to *mental*.

The surplus meaning of a term like *retarded* is also obvious. It means *slow to develop*, but it carries with it the image of incurable incompetence. We once sat in on a staffing in which the school psychologist's report contained the unfortunate comment that the child was "retarded in the area of reading." The parent, seeing that comment, never got beyond the word *retarded* and reacted to the statement as if his child had been labeled mentally deficient.

An interesting pattern in many special education texts that deal with learning disabilities has been to try to clarify terms by presenting synonyms for them. Thus we get terms like *minimal brain dysfunction*, *dyslexia*, and *perceptually impaired*. This technique actually increases the surplus meaning. For a term to be used specifically, it is best to reduce the use of synonyms, not to promote their use.

While any number or combination of variables can be used to classify individuals, they do not all have equal treatment utility. For this reason, systems of classification have been proposed outlining the relative importance of different variables. Cromwell et al. (1975) proposed criteria for the classification of children. These criteria would go a long way toward bridging the gap between classification and treatment. As you read them, consider the labels you are currently learning about or working with. Do they meet these conditions? The criteria first require that labels be agreed upon by individuals working with them (teachers, psychologists, and parents). Next, they must describe a specific group of children and apply equally to all members of the group. Finally, any classification system should be logically consistent, have clinical utility, and be so simple to deal with that it will be used. These variables and criteria can be arranged into a rational system for classifying children, but unfortunately, even the best systems are seldom actually put into practice (Haring & Schiefelbusch, 1976; Shinn, 1986).

Labels seem to (a) confuse treatment, (b) negatively stigmatize clients, (c) inhibit the work of professionals, and (d) cost a lot of money (Hagerty & Abramson, 1987). The damage caused by labeling is most popularly discussed in terms of negative stigma. Labels put the burden of educational failure on the child. It can never be pleasant for a child to be called "retard" or "sped" by peers. However, problems with self-concept and personality constructs are difficult to prove and are therefore under constant debate (Heller, 1982). As special educators we should perhaps focus more attention on what labels do to our own effectiveness as teachers.

ORIENTATIONS TO SPECIAL EDUCATION

The Doctors Do not Understand my Illness

There are many different ways to think about special/remedial students and how they should be treated. For purposes of this discussion two competing models will be polarized by defining them in stark, mutually exclusive terms. In operation these two models may never be seen in the absolute forms presented here, but the assumptions that follow from them and the premises on which they are based should be easily recognized in the literature, child study team meetings, and evaluation reports we encounter every day.

Psycho-medical vs. (alias medical, psycho-educational, traditional, diagnostic-prescriptive, internalistic)	*Task-Analytical* (alias behavioral, functional, direct behavior analysis, contextualistic)

It is important to be familiar with both the psycho-medical and task-analytical models because each has its particular limitations and strengths. Efforts have been made to take the two models and blend them, but they are legitimately at odds with each other in several respects and therefore cannot be easily compromised. Besides, when two philosophies are in fact combined all you're really doing is producing a third and different one: The original two don't go away. Rather than expend time trying to reconcile two different points of view, it is sometimes better to switch from one to the other according to need. An efficient evaluator must be able to pick and choose between models, as well as procedures, according to need. Some models are better for one purpose than for another. The psycho-medical model, for example, is said to be better suited for the severely handicapped.

The two models are briefly contrasted in Table A.1. The model characteristics that are not easily compromised revolve around the source of failure, variables measured, and direction of treatment.

We won't elaborate on each element of the table but will spend some time on the basic premise

TABLE A.1
Two Models of Evaluation

		Psycho-medical Model *(Psycho-educational)*	*Task-Analytical Model* *(Behavioral)*
1.	The basic premise is . . .	if a student fails at a task it is because the student has something wrong with cognitive or perceptual abilities.	if a student fails at a task it is because he or she has not mastered an essential component of that task.
2.	The source of failure is assumed to . . .	reside within the student	reside within the interaction between the student and the environment.
3.	Evaluation begins by focusing on . . .	the student.	the task on which the student is failing.
4.	The tests used . . .	try to measure cognitive or perceptual abilities.	try to measure skill or knowledge.
5.	The most frequently used tests are . . .	norm-referenced tests based on logically developed theories of learning.	criterion-referenced tests based on empirically validated sequences of tasks.
6.	The evaluator draws conclusions about . . .	the student's cognitive or perceptual strengths and weaknesses.	the student's skills or knowledge.
7.	Treatment is directed at . . .	changing or accommodating the student's cognitive or perceptual abilities.	changing the student's task-related behavior.
8.	Instruction involves . . .	presentations that address cognition or perception.	presentations that are directly related to a sequence of tasks.
9.	Instruction treatments are selected . . .	making predictions from tests of student ability.	monitoring the student's progress and adjusting instruction.

(point 1) as all other material in the table flows from it. At first this may seem to be setting up a simple inside/outside dichotomy about blame for student failure. That's not the case. Whereas the psycho-medical approach does place the burden on the student, the task-analytical model does not really relieve the student of the burden. The task-analytical model does not say that the problem lies outside of the student, but rather that it lies within the interaction of the student and the outside. Therefore, the student has something to do with it because this interaction could not take place without him or her. It is possible then that the dichotomy is best understood in terms of the discussion of *interactions* presented in chapter 1. The psycho-medical model tends to focus on only one element of the learning interaction—the kid. The task-analytical model focuses on the interaction itself.

Causation

Mental retardation is an excellent agent for examining the incursion of psycho-medical reasoning into education. The first people to be truly interested in the handicapped were medical personnel who worked with the most obviously and severely disabled clients. While their interest was indisputably directed at helping their clients they could not really be called "educators" as few of them had instruction as their primary focus. Unfortunately during the first part of this century educators were primarily concerned with *excluding* these students from school. Early medical investigators could easily identify persons with abnormal physiological attributes such as epilepsy and Down syndrome. These pathological attributes were studied until a sizable body of information developed pertaining to the medical etiologic correlates of mental retardation. This led to a biological definition of retardation that had a distinctly medical orientation (Blanton, 1975). The biological definition raised retardation to the status of a label. The label "MR" came to describe a condition that (a) resided within the individual and not the environment and (b) was stable and not subject to treatment. This definition has supported the pervasive belief that the retarded person cannot be taught because retarda-

tion is permanent (Dunn, 1968). Because of the profound influence of the medical orientation many educators came to view retarded people as people who could not acquire advanced knowledge and skills. At the same time the economic and social realities of supporting them did spark interest in their custodial care. Educators soon were expressing interest in tools that would easily identify students who might be expending instructional resources with no hope of becoming educated. The belief was that, once identified, the educational alternatives available to these students could be limited according to their intellectual potential. The thrust of this new activity was educational, not medical. The result was an educational definition of retardation that became operational in a typically educational fashion—*testing* (Frankenberger & Harper, 1986; French, 1986).

The population of students who score extremely low on IQ tests includes a relatively high proportion of students with other handicaps, including physical and sensory problems. These gross physical and sensory defects lent support to the idea that the IQ test could identify permanently handicapped people. However, as the use of the test expanded, the conclusions based on scores of 25 or 40 began to be applied to scores of 65 or 80. The current definition of mental retardation used by the American Association on Mental Deficiency includes a provision for significantly subaverage intelligence as measured by an IQ test. This should include about 2.3% of the total population. Of relevance to this discussion, however, is the observation that as many as 80% of those considered retarded exhibit no gross pathology (Heber, Garber, Harrington, Hoffman, & Falender, 1972). More recently, Hallahan and Kauffman (1982) have placed this figure at about 90%. Of the remaining 10% of those called *retarded* (those who do exhibit pathology), the majority fall into only a few principal syndromes, such as Down syndrome. In view of this, it is remarkable that the image of mental retardation projected in many courses and texts on the subject is centered around pathological symptoms such as chromosome aberrations. The fact that the majority of students labeled *retarded* have no medical problems but do come from low-income settings,

FIGURE A.1

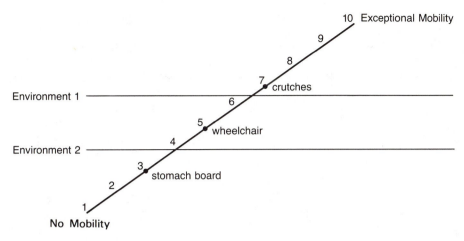

norities, and linguistic minority backgrounds seems to argue for an environmental cause of *retardation* in at least 80% of the cases.

Today a student with no medical indications of abnormality may be classified as retarded through the use of the IQ test. In fact, Mercer (1973) found that 99% of the students labeled retarded she studied had been given an IQ test, while only 13% had been given a medical examination to determine the source of their failure to learn. The irony is that while the evaluation procedures employed to recognize retardation have completely eliminated the need for medical evidence, the label *retarded* retains medical connotations such as the idea that it is caused by an internal condition. Many educators still view the student who is labeled *retarded* as one who can't be educated due to some lack of internal capacity.

The task-analytical model takes a different view of deviant behavior using an *applied behavior analysis approach.* The model originally saw student behavior as the *R* (response) in Skinner's classic $S_1 \rightarrow R \leftrightarrow S_2$ model. The straight Skinnerian view is that responses are a product of antecedent (S_1) and consequent (S_2) environmental events. Behavioral psychologists have more recently expanded this model to include prior learning as a mediator between the student and the environment (Chi & Glaser, 1985; Mahoney, 1977). In this view, a response is determined in part by the environmentally based task and in part by the knowledge

brought to the task by the student. This allows the model to account for different people doing different things under apparently similar conditions (see chapter 14 on Social Skills). More direct to our discussion is the special point that this model includes environment as well as individuals in its description of behavior.

An example of this interactive idea can be found in the distinction often drawn between a *handicap* and a *disability.* The solid line in Figure A.1 shows the range of "ability to move." At the lower end of the line are individuals without any mobility; at the upper end are those with complete, even exceptional, mobility. Along the line are individuals using stomach boards (a mobility level of 3), wheelchairs (level 5), and crutches (level 7). Two different environments (represented by the horizontal, solid lines) intersect this mobility line. Each environment is capable of accommodating different levels of mobility. Let's say that the buildings in environment 1 have doorways that are 23" wide, meaning that people with crutches can move freely within it but people in wheelchairs (which are 25 inches wide) cannot. Environment 2 has wider doors and can handle a mobility range from 4 to 10, allowing both wheelchairs and crutches free access. The question then is "Where does a *handicap* reside?" A person in a wheelchair is more disabled than a person on crutches, but in environment 2 this difference in mobility does not matter because buildings in this environment have been designed with sufficiently wide doors. Therefore the wheelchair-bound individual, while disabled in both environments, is only handicapped in environment 1. Handicaps, therefore, are found in the *interaction* of the person's abilities with the environment.

Alterable Variables

A person working in the psycho-medical model may argue that the best evaluation will focus on the *primary* cause of the handicap, which they could insist is the individual's disability. However, the proponent of the task-analytical view would respond from a purely functional perspective by pointing out that if the purpose of the evaluation is to alter the quality of the student/environment interaction it should focus on those variables (environmental or personal characteristics) that are the easiest to alter.

As pointed out earlier, the educational evaluation that is most useful to teachers is the one that targets variables teachers can control. For an evaluative system to have high *instructional utility*, it must deal with instructional variables by addressing areas that instruction can influence. If that is done then the results of the evaluation can be used in the classroom. If the evaluation addresses variables that are beyond the ability (or duty) of teachers to change, then the results cannot be used in the classroom and teachers should not be held accountable for them. Personological characteristics such as age, racial/ethnic background, IQ score, cognitive/perceptual functioning, brain damage, hemispheric dominance, and others commonly addressed in psycho-medical evaluations are often difficult to change; in fact, they have been called *unalterable* variables (Bloom, 1980). Instructional variables such as teacher questioning techniques, grouping, materials, lesson pace, feedback, and use of correction procedures are more easily altered and therefore of greater instructional utility (Bickel & Bickel, 1986; Brophy, 1983; Goodman, 1985).

Summary

The idea of functional assessment implies a focus on things that can be changed. If learning is interactive it is obvious that the curriculum and instructional elements of this interaction are more easily modified than the student element. The order in which tasks are presented and the sort of feedback a teacher gives are easier to change than a student's IQ. Teachers modify the environment to produce learning—we don't open up kids' heads and go in with soldering irons to correct their minimal brain dysfunction. (Talk about parental permission problems!) To be functional we must focus on things we can control.

Searching for causes is not the primary goal of special educators; fixing the problem is. For those who consider themselves practitioners, the goal is not to just *understand* but also to *serve* the handicapped. Although these two goals are logically related, limitations in time and resources will cause one to be chosen over the other. Classification based on causes is a legitimate stage of theory development, but it has limited value to the area of behavioral intervention (Hunt & Lansman, 1975). To those who would try to aid the handicapped, treatment is more important than simple classification. However, a brief review of the field of special education will reveal an overwhelming preoccupation with classification and its tools as well as a pervasive confusion of classification and treatment.

TRAINING PROCESSES

Which Curriculum Should We Teach?

"Process deficits" refers to hypothesized irregularities in the way a student's neurological system handles information. The term has a variety of different meanings, but is most closely associated with the so-called psycholinguistic model of treating learning disabilities. This model evolved out of an earlier theory of language acquisition. The process dysfunction idea was popularized by Samuel Kirk through the development of the Illinois Test of Psycholinguistic Ability (ITPA). The utility of process remediation has been hotly debated and generally refuted (Arter & Jenkins, 1979; Lloyd, 1984; Kavale & Glass, 1982; Zigmond & Miller, 1986).

In chapter 3 we argued that tasks have many facets (so many you were required to learn a lot of terminology just to keep them all straight). In the past, texts in special education did the opposite; they presented complex explanations of student learning and glossed over descriptions of the curriculum. That is because a different view of curriculum was held in the past. (It is still held in some quarters today [Pugach, 1987].) The process deficit view holds that the foundation of the curriculum is a set of cognitive and perceptual information-processing skills. These skills include things like visual perception, auditory discrimination, sequential memory, attention skills, sequential and simultaneous processing, and others. The idea is that those processing skills/abilities are prerequisites to academics and that students who fail in academics often do so because they lack the facility at processing needed to even begin academics. Therefore, evaluators attempted to evaluate these processing skills in isolation (independent of academics) and teachers tried to teach them prior to teaching academics and so-

cial skills. In this system a student referred for a reading problem might be given a fairly general reading test followed by specific tests that ask him to trace geometric shapes or recall dictated numbers. Similarly, the student's remedial program might include exercises in matching geometric shapes, listening to animal sounds, or even walking balance beams because the assumption is that the student has failed reading because of a process deficit. These lessons are meant to remediate the underlying process deficits—not to teach reading itself.

How is the task-analytical model different? We talk about cognitive skills like problem solving and hypothesized information-processing mechanisms like short-term memory too. The difference can be seen in Figure A.2. In the process view of curriculum, the entire sequence is underpinned by nonacademic cognitive and perceptual abilities such as memory and attention. (These are usually described as if they were specific to sensory modalities, such as "auditory memory" or "attention to

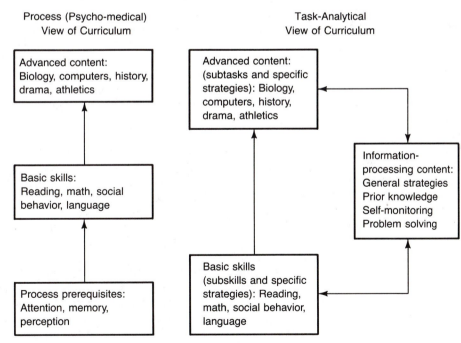

FIGURE A.2   Process (Psycho-medical) View of Curriculum   Task-Analytical View of Curriculum

visual stimuli.") Therefore, advocates of the model maintain that these processes must be trained, often in isolation, prior to training basic skills or higher-level content.

In the task-analysis view, information-processing skills (general strategies, prior knowledge, self-monitoring, problem solving) are not viewed as prerequisites for the academic/social curriculum: They are part of that curriculum. In other words, self-monitoring and problem solving are the same as reading, math, biology or drama. The task-analytical orientation tells instructors that they should be teaching how to process the information contained in the curriculum rather than just the curriculum itself.

Teachers make an error in *either* model when they attempt to isolate the information-processing content from the skills the student needs. Process-oriented teachers have often made the mistake of believing that their lessons in auditory discrimination, sequential memory, or simultaneous processing were teaching reading. They weren't. Teachers in the task-analytical model will be making the same mistake if they focus on things like vowel sounds to the exclusion of larger problem-solving strategies. Skills like reading and information processing must be blended for either to be taught effectively.

SPECIAL EDUCATION AND THE NORMAL CURVE

In the distribution of academic skills, special education students are at the extremes. The handicapped student is at the bottom; the gifted student is at the top. For the purpose of this example, we can disregard the gifted child because, if we consider gifted to be high on the distribution of academic skills, that child can already do what normal children can do. (There are, of course, gifted students who score low on distributions of academic skills. These students are considered gifted according to some other criterion such as adaptive behavior, IQ scores, or measures of talent.) But the handicapped special students are behind and they must be caught up to be normal.

There are only two ways to help someone catch up if she is behind. One is to make her go faster. The other is to make the kids who are ahead go slower. Both systems would work, but the second doesn't seem likely to obtain wide acceptance. Catching up is hard to do as long as the analog for academic achievement is a normal curve. The normal distribution *requires* a lower half. In the past, special education has developed numerous efficient means of instruction (Goodman, 1985), but these methods were quickly adopted by regular education. So instead of selectively accelerating the slow students, new technology has advanced the entire curve. As long as the mean of a normal distribution is considered to be the desired level of academic ability, there will always be special students even if their skills are adequate.

STATISTICAL "SIGNIFICANCE"

Being Sure Isn't Always Being Right
Educational and statistical significance may be most clearly contrasted by describing a research study. In this particular study, two groups of fairly low-functioning students who had been labeled *retarded* were trained to remember words in a foreign language. The training sessions took place over several days and involved only 10 words. Each group of students was taught differently. In the end, one group's average definition accuracy was 3.78 words while the other group's mean accuracy was 4.32 words. When a test for the statistical significance between group means was employed, the difference between the groups (.54 words) was found to be significant. The determination that these results would only happen by chance 5 times out of 100 justified a final conclusion by the study's author that one method was better than the other.

Figure A.3 shows the distribution of scores for the two groups just described. Note that while Group B's average score is higher than Group A's, the two distributions overlap almost completely and that no students in either group recalled all 10 words while several in both groups couldn't recall any words. Theoretical issues aside, the question

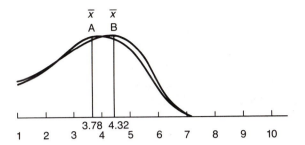

FIGURE A.3

remains, "How educationally significant are these statistically significant findings?" They seem to say teachers should choose to employ method B rather than method A. But what real benefit is that when, after days of training, the average student in both groups was still less than 50% accurate. In our minds data showing that one group of low-functioning students scored half a word better (on words they'll probably never use) after hours of training is not evidence of educational significance regardless of its statistical status. Tests of statistical significance tell us only how much confidence we can place in the results of the study—they do not assure us that these results are meaningful.

Many educators and psychologists believe that once statistical significance is found the problem is solved. This is wrong. Statistics are simply tools; they are not as important as the questions they help answer. Unfortunately few authors acknowledge this in their presentations; in fact Zucker and Meyen (1975) are the only ones we ever saw do it! As a result, the confusion of statistical and educational significance is widespread.

Statistical significance is reported in terms of probabilities (.05 means the probability of getting the same results by accident is only 5 out of 100).

Probabilities are funny things. How high a probability we would like to have depends on the importance of the decision we are going to make. For example, one of the authors was once chased into a log cabin at Admiralty Cove, Alaska, by a Brown bear. While waiting for the bear to stop sniffing at the door, he happened to notice a pamphlet on bears conveniently left in the cabin by the Park Service. The document, titled "The Bears and You," said that the chance of being injured by a bear in Alaska was about 1/50 of the chance of being injured in an auto accident. As there are no cars at Admiralty Cove and the author has a quick statistical mind, he determined that his chance of being killed by this particular bear was zero ($0 \div 50$). However, even this low a probability level did not convince your author to go outside. Instead, he mumbled, "You can prove anything with statistics" and pushed a table in front of the door.

Now let's look at significance from an evaluation point of view. We once attended a staffing for a student who turned out to speak Spanish. Records from his previous year in a school with bilingual programs indicated the kid was doing well in all academic areas. But the student's current teacher had given him a popular math test on which items are presented verbally. The student scored more than two standard deviations below the mean on the math test, so the teacher referred him for remedial math. Statistically, a score of two standard deviations below the mean should only happen 3 times in 100 ($p < .03$). Is the student educationally behind in math, given a low score of such statistical improbability? No. The fact that he could not understand the test (as it was given in an unfamiliar language) certainly overshadows the fact of a low score. The math score, while significantly low in a statistical sense, didn't represent this student's math skills so the results have no significance for math instruction.

Appendix B

Survival Statistics

INTRODUCTION

The following discussion deals with the differences between NRT and CRT score modifications. To have this discussion, we will present a great deal of measurement content, including some pivotal statistics. The computational steps for each statistic will be presented along with an example. Practice exercises will also be made available so that you can follow the computational steps yourself. If this content is new to you (or old but painful), we encourage you to try these practice computations.

UNIT 1: DISTRIBUTIONS

Scores

The terms *obtained* or *raw score* refer to the score derived directly from a test/observation. These raw scores may need to be translated or modified to make them more meaningful. For instance, suppose you are taking a course during which you are given an exam. Later you ask the instructor how you did on the test and are told, "You got a score of 23." How do you feel? Without knowing how many points were possible, how others did on the test, or the grading scale, you probably will feel confused. Knowing an isolated score provides you with insufficient information.

Distributions of Scores

An NRT score derives its meaning from its reference to the norming population. The raw score on an NRT is meaningless. To make the raw score meaningful it must be placed within the context of the norming population. Visually this can be accomplished by presenting the scores of the entire popu-

Raw Scores	Students Obtaining Score
30	/
29	/
28	//
27	////
26	///
25	////////
24	////
→ 23	///
22	//
21	/
20	/
19	/
18	
17	
16	
15	

FIGURE B.1
Frequency distribution

lation as a frequency distribution (Figure B.1) or as a "curve" (Figure B.2).

How good was a score of 23? Well, when we look at the frequency distribution we can see that a score of 23 is quite low compared to the scores obtained by most of the other students. The score of 23 now has meaning because we have placed it within the context of the norming population. Stated differently, we have "referenced" the score to the norming population. Because the concept of normative comparison is important we will go through it once more. In Figure B.1, the group's scores were first summarized according to the way they distributed from highest to lowest. A mark for each student obtaining a score was made next to it, giving an overall impression of how the class did on the test. If you got a score of 23, it seems you did poorly on the test when compared to the other students. It is important to remember that we have *no*

FIGURE B.2
A score curve

2 3 4 5 6 7 8 9 10 11 12 13 14 15 16 17 18 19 20 21 22 23 24 25 26 27 28 29 30

information about your actual knowledge; we only know that you scored lower than most other students. We are able to make this observation because we have placed your score within the context of the norming sample's distribution of scores.

Normal Distributions

Normative evaluation is conceptually linked to the idea of a normal distribution, sometimes called a *normal* or *bell-shaped curve*. The assumption underlying this idea is that the probability of a high score occurring is the same as that of a low score occurring. For example, suppose that 10 people were asked to flip a coin 10 times. The number of heads for the group might be summarized as in Figure B.3. Hardly anyone would be expected to get all heads or all tails. The probability of flipping a head is the same as flipping a tail, so most people would be expected to get about 50% heads and 50% tails. As the number of people flipping coins increases, the distribution of heads should begin to take on the appearance of Figure B.4. Ultimately, if enough people flip enough coins, the picture of the number of heads obtained will approximate a normal curve.

Many normative tests are constructed so that the scores are forced to normally distribute themselves. Most IQ tests, for example, have an arbitrarily designated mean of 100. More people should, therefore, score 100 on an IQ test than any other score, and as many should score above 100 as below it. The normal distribution makes the assumption that the probability of a high or low score is the same. That is, a head is as likely as a tail; a high IQ is as likely as a low IQ. However, as it turns

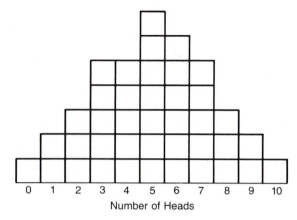

FIGURE B.4
Forty flips of a coin

out, nature plays with loaded dice. To return to the IQ example, any given person is *not* as likely to get a high or low score on an IQ test. Such influences as poor diet, traffic accidents, or substandard education may affect the general abilities that IQ tests attempt to measure. Because some of these influences are more likely to affect one subgroup of society (low-income families, for example), that group's average IQ score may not be 100. Therefore, a true distribution of intelligence might look more like a bimodal curve or like the skewed curve in Figure B.5. A bimodal curve is one which has two peaks, indicating subgroups of students within the distribution are scoring differently from each other. The normal curve is not guaranteed. It is a statistical concept that implies a uniform and predictable relationship among the instances of whatever trait is being studied. In reality, however, many traits are not normally distributed. The number of fingers that people have is not randomly distributed; most

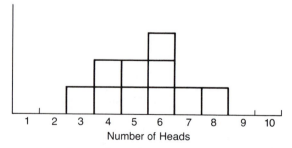

FIGURE B.3
Ten flips of a coin

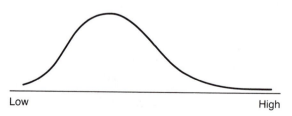

FIGURE B.5
A skewed (lopsided) curve

would have 10, only a few would have none, and even fewer would have more than 10.

Pictured frequency distributions, like the one in Figure B.1, can be helpful for illustrating the performance of classes or other small groups, but they get unwieldy for whole schools or districts. Because it is inconvenient to construct visual norms for every test, statistical procedures are used to translate the raw scores into a different type of score to convey information about both the student's behavior and its relationship to the behavior of the other students in the norm sample. It is this process of converting the *raw score* into a useful form that gives us most of the statistical content taught in evaluation texts.

It is not necessary to represent every distribution visually to tell where a student falls within that distribution. (If it were, normative decisions would be prohibitively cumbersome.) Instead, it is possible to label portions of the distribution and to simply report that portion in which the student's score falls. This allows us to know where the student is within the context of a typical norming sample. A teacher does this in reporting that a student has scored "above average" or "below average." When making such statements, the teacher is simply halving the distribution (at the mean) and reporting which half the student is in. Procedures of this type are simple and seem to convey some meaning, but obviously students who are below average do not all have the same score. Because small score differences may be meaningful, a finer subdivision of the distribution is necessary. These subdivisions are derived from calculations that use various parameters that describe distributions.

The Center.   The *mean* is one parameter used to describe the center of a distribution. The mean is known as a measure of central tendency. It is the best predictor of how any individual will behave on an NRT (Figure B.6.). Two distributions may differ from each other by having different means. If the average score of one group is 100 and the average score of another is 75, then the two groups have behaved differently on the test used. (When reading research articles you may have come across a reference to the t-test. This is a procedure used to determine if differences between group means are

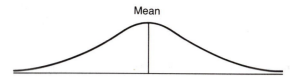

FIGURE B.6
The mean

statistically significant.)

If you are asked to guess the IQ of a stranger, your best bet is to guess 100 because on most IQ tests 100 is the mean. The mean is the average of the total of all scores. It is calculated by adding all the scores together and dividing by the number of scores. Other indicators of central tendency include the median (middle score) and the mode (most frequently occurring score).

Practice Computation

Computing the Mean

$$\text{Mean} = \frac{X}{n} = \bar{X}$$

Drama Test (maximum score 30)

Students	Raw Scores
1.	25
2.	25
3.	24
4.	23
5.	22
6.	22
7.	22
8.	21
9.	20
10.	18
11.	18
12.	18
13.	15
14.	9
15.	6
	288

Step 1.   List the scores in any order, but list each student's score.

Step 2.   Add up the scores. Sum = 288.

Step 3. Divide the sum of the scores by the total number of scores. 288 ÷ 15 = 19.2. Conclusion: The mean is 19.2.

Find the mean for the following geology test scores. Check your Answer in Table B.1.

Students	Raw Scores	Students	Raw Scores
1.	50	11.	28
2.	45	12.	28
3.	42	13.	24
4.	39	14.	23
5.	38	15.	21
6.	30	16.	20
7.	30	17.	15
8.	29	18.	10
9.	29	19.	10
10.	29	20.	9

The Width. The mean, median, and mode are all indicators of the center of a distribution and can be used to cut the distribution into two halves. A distribution of scores can also be segmented according to its variability. This is usually accomplished by calculating the standard deviation of the distribution. This procedure allows us to recognize the degree to which the scores in a distribution do or do not clus-

ter around the center. If the scores are tightly clustered, as are the scores of Group A in Figure B.7a, then a raw score of 18 indicates behavior that is extremely different from the others taking the test. The score of 18 is said to be at the extreme lower end of the group's variability. However, the same score for Group B (Figure B.7b), while still below average, is well within the group of scores. This means 18 is not as deviant for Group B as for Group A. Notice that both groups of 30 students taking the same test had the same average performance, but their variability was different. This could be the result of any number of factors, including the instruction they have received.

To make comparisons more sensitive, we slice the distribution into smaller and smaller pieces. By using variability as a parameter we can report where a student's score falls in the distribution with greater accuracy. For example, a student who is two standard deviations below the mean has scored relatively lower than a student who is only one standard deviation below the mean. In a normal curve (the ideal distribution illustrated in Figure B.6), 68% of all scores fall within ± 1 (one) standard deviation (SD) of the mean; 95% fall within ± 2 (two). If the category of *mentally re-*

FIGURE B.7

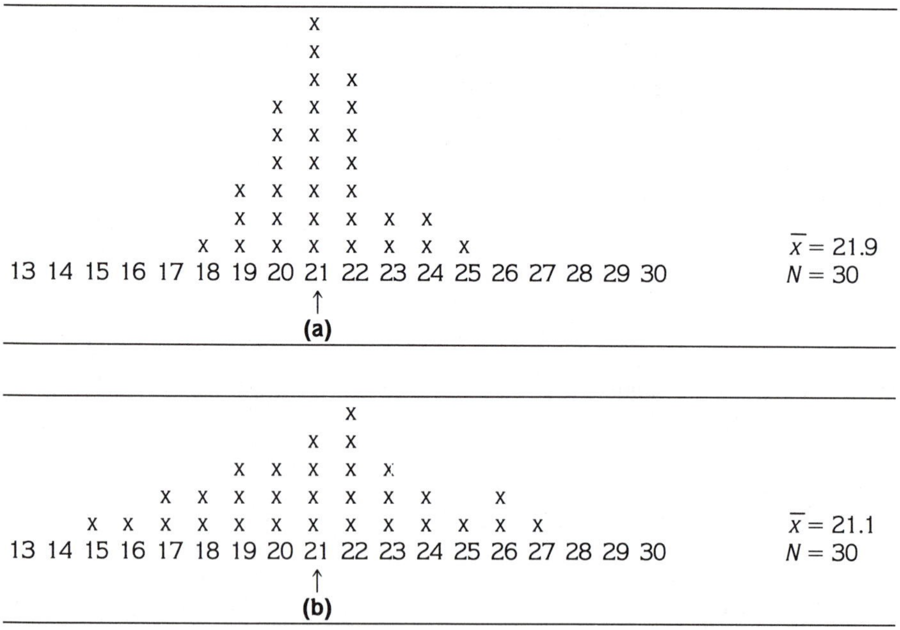

$\bar{x} = 21.9$
$N = 30$

(a)

$\bar{x} = 21.1$
$N = 30$

(b)

tarded is limited to individuals with IQ scores lower than 2 standard deviations below the mean, then (assuming IQ is normally distributed) 2.3% of the population should be retarded.

Normal IQ		High IQ		Low IQ		Total IQ
−2 to +2 SD		+2 SD		−2 SD		
95.4%	+	2.3%	+	2.3%	=	100%

The standard deviation describes a group's variability. If all students taking a test made the same score on the test, there would be no variability. The more the students deviate (spread out) around the mean, the more variability there is in their scores. The significance of variability differences between two groups is typically judged with an *F*-test. Here are the formula and computational steps for calculating the standard deviation. As you follow them note that squaring scores, as required by the formula, tends to place greater value on extremely high and low scores.

Practice Computation
    Computing the Standard Deviation

$$SD = \sqrt{\frac{\Sigma x^2 - \frac{(\Sigma x)^2}{N}}{N - 1}}$$

Drama Test (maximum score 30)

	Raw Scores	Scores Squared
1.	25	625
2.	25	625
3.	24	576
4.	23	529
5.	22	484
6.	22	484
7.	22	484
8.	21	441
9.	20	400
10.	18	324
11.	18	324
12.	18	324
13.	15	225
14.	9	81
15.	6	36
$\Sigma x = 288$		$\Sigma x^2 = 5{,}962$

Step 1. List the scores in any order, but list each student's score.
Step 2. Add up the scores. Sum = 288.
Step 3. Square each score in a list next to the student's score.
Step 4. Add up all the squared scores. Sum of the squares = 5,962.
Step 5. Square the sum of the scores calculated in Step 2. $288^2 = 82{,}944$.
Step 6. Divide the number derived in Step 5 by the number of students. $82{,}944 \div 15 = 5{,}529.6$.
Step 7. Subtract the number derived in Step 6 from the number derived in Step 4. $5{,}962 - 5{,}529.6 = 432.4$.
Step 8. Divide the number derived in Step 7 by the number of students minus one.
$$\frac{432.4}{15 - 1} = \frac{432.4}{14} = 30.89$$
Step 9. Find the square root of the number derived in Step 8. $\sqrt{30.89} = 5.56$.
Conclusion: The standard deviation is 5.56.

Calculate the standard deviation for the geology test scores and check your answer with Table B.1.

Students	Raw Scores
1.	50
2.	45
3.	42
4.	39
5.	38
6.	30
7.	30
8.	29
9.	29
10.	29
11.	28
12.	28
13.	24
14.	23
15.	21
16.	20
17.	15
18.	10
19.	10
20.	9

TABLE B.1
Summary of drama test scores (maximum score 30)

	Raw Scores	z-Scores	t-Scores	Percentile	Percentage
1.	25	1	60	97	83
2.	25	1	60	97	83
3.	24	.9	59	87	80
4.	23	.7	57	80	77
5.	22	.5	55	67	73
6.	22	.5	55	67	73
7.	22	.5	55	67	73
8.	21	.3	53	53	70
9.	20	.1	51	46	67

Mean ---

	Raw Scores	z-Scores	t-Scores	Percentile	Percentage
10.	18	− 2	48	33	60
11.	18	− 2	48	33	60
12.	18	− 2	48	33	60
13.	15	− 8	42	20	50
14.	9	− 18	32	13	30
15.	6	− 24	26	6	20
Sum = 288		Mean = 19.2		SD = 5.56	

Summary of geology test scores (maximum score 50)

	Raw Scores	z-Scores	t-Scores	Percentile	Percentage
1.	50	2	70	100	100
2.	45	1.5	65	95	90
3.	42	1.3	63	90	84
4.	39	1	60	85	78
5.	38	.9	59	80	76
6.	30	.2	52	72.5	60
7.	30	.2	52	72.5	60
8.	29	.1	51	60	58
9.	29	.1	51	60	58
10.	29	.1	51	60	58
11.	28	0	50	47.5	56
12.	28	0	50	47.5	56
13.	24	− .3	47	40	48
14.	23	− .4	46	35	46
15.	21	− .6	44	30	42
16.	20	− .6	44	25	40
17.	15	− 1	40	20	30
18.	10	− 1.5	35	12.5	20
19.	10	− 1.5	35	12.5	20
20.	9	− 1.6	34	5	18
Sum = 549		Mean = 27.45		SD = 11.53	

UNIT 2: STANDARD SCORES

If the information that a student is $+1$ SD from the mean is not sufficiently specific, the raw score can be translated into a new standard score. By using the mean and standard deviation of the distribution, a standard score can be devised for each raw score. This conversion of raw scores to a more easily interpreted form helps us use test results. Standard scores are useful for comparing a student's relative performance on two different tests that may have been given to two different norming populations (and that would therefore have different means and standard deviations) as well as for most other uses (Anastasi, 1982).

Z and T

Standard scores include percentiles, z-scores, t-scores, stanines, and others you may have heard of. While a raw score of 11 may be high on one distribution and low on another, a standard score of 11 always labels the same portion of every distribution. A t-score of 50, for example, is always the average score of any distribution. Therefore, we know, without looking at the distribution, that a t-score of 70 is further above average than a t-score of 51, regardless of the raw score obtained. Standard scores provide greater precision because they use the standard deviation to slice the distributions into fractions. In fact, the number of slices is only limited by the decimals a person wants to allow in the scores (and even these can be removed with t-scores).

Two common types of standard scores are the z-score and t-score. They report where the student is in the distribution with reference to both the mean and standard deviation. The z-score is calculated by subtracting the mean score ($\bar{x}$) from the student's score (x) and then dividing the results by the standard deviation. If Ed got a raw score of 8 on a history test where the mean was 12.9 and the standard deviation was 3.48, Ed's z-score is -1.41.

$$z = \frac{x - \bar{x}}{SD} = \frac{8 - 12.9}{3.48} = -1.41$$

The t-score is essentially the same as the z-score, except the result is multiplied by 10, 100, or 1000 to clear the decimal, and added to 50 to get rid of any negative numbers. The formula for calculating t-scores is:

$$t = 10\left(\frac{x - \bar{x}}{SD}\right) + 50$$

So Ed's t-score is:

$$t = 10\left(\frac{8 - 12.9}{3.48}\right) + 50 = 36$$

All of the scores on Ed's history test have been translated to standard scores in Figure B.8.

Calculating standard scores may seem like a lot of work but they have some advantages. Converting the scores on two different normed tests to standard scores enables an evaluator to compare a student's performance in the two areas. For example, suppose Ed took a biology test the same day he took the history test. And then suppose that for some reason his teacher wished to determine in which course Ed was doing the best (in relation to the other students). On the history test Ed got a raw score of 8; on the biology test he got a raw score of 15. However, there were 75 problems on the biology test and only 25 on the history test. On which test did he get the best score? By converting the two different test scores to standard scores, the teacher takes into account the mean and standard deviation for each test and therefore can compare Ed's scores (Figure B.9). The results indicate that Ed did better on the history test. But remember that his score on either normative test is related only to the performance of the other students. That Ed got a better standard score on the history test doesn't mean he knows more history than biology.

Percentage and Percentile

Two other ways of reporting scores are percentages and percentiles. The two are different but often confused. *The percentage score is one way to report a student's accuracy.* Percentage and rate

FIGURE B.8
History test t- and z-scores

Raw Score (x)	z-score $z = \dfrac{x - \bar{x}}{SD}$	t-score $t = 10\left(\dfrac{x - \bar{x}}{SD}\right) + 50$
20	2.04	70
17	1.18	62
16	.89	59
16	.89	59
15	.60	56
15	.60	56
14	.32	53
14	.32	53
14	.32	53
13	.03	50
12	− .26	47
12	− .26	47
11	− .55	45
11	− .55	45
10	− .83	42
10	− .83	42
8	− 1.41	36
4	− 2.56	24
Sum = 232	$\bar{x}$ = 12.9 SD = 3.48	

are commonly used to report CRT results. A percentage is the obtained score, divided by the total possible score. On Ed's history test, he scored 8 out of 25 points so he was accurate on 32% of the items and wrong on 68% of them (8 ÷ 25 = .32(100) = 32%).

A percentile does not tell if the student was accurate or not. The percentile tells how a student scored in relation to other students, and so it is used to report NRT results. Neither percentage (%) nor percentile (%ile) are as useful as z- and t-scores for describing a student's position in a distribution because the mean and standard deviation are not used to calculate them. Percentiles are determined in two ways. Sometimes they are determined by rank ordering the students and finding out what percentage of the total number of students scored the same as, or lower than, the student you are interested in. In Ed's case, 2 students scored the same as or lower than he did. There are 20 students all together, so his percentile score would be 2 ÷ 20 = 10th percentile.

Rounded percentiles can be obtained by segmenting the entire range of scores into 100 slices. In the example of the history test, there are 18 scores, so each slice covers .18 of a score (18 ÷ 100 = .18) and each score has 5.6 slices in it. Because the top score of 20 is at the hundredth percentile, the next score (17) has a rounded percentile of 94 (100 − 5.6 = 94.4) and the next score (16) has a rounded percentile of 89 (94.4 − 5.6 = 88.8).

FIGURE B.9

	History Test (25 items)	Biology Test (75 items)
Ed's score (x)	8	15
mean $(\bar{x})$	12.9	52.7
SD	3.48	14.5
z-score	− 1.4	− 2.6
t-score	36	24

Practice Computation

Translating Raw Scores into z-Scores

$$z = \frac{X - \bar{X}}{SD}$$

Drama Test (maximum score 30)

	Raw Scores	z-Scores
1.	25	1
2.	25	1
3.	24	.9
4.	23	.7
5.	22	.5
6.	22	.5
7.	22	.5
8.	21	.3
9.	20	.1
10.	18	− .2
11.	18	− .2
12.	18	− .2
13.	15	− .8
14.	9	− 1.8
15.	6	− 2.4
	288	

Step 1. List the raw scores in any order, but list each score.

Step 2. Compute the mean. 288 ÷ 15 = 19.2.

Step 3. Compute the standard deviation.

$$\sqrt{\frac{5962 - \frac{82944}{15}}{15 - 1}} = 5.56$$

Step 4. Subtract the mean computed in Step 2 from a raw score. For example, 25 − 19.2 = 5.8.

Step 5. Divide the number derived in Step 4 by the number computed in Step 3. 5.8 ÷ 5.56 = 1.04.

Conclusion: The raw score 25 is equal to z-score of 1.04 (rounded to 1).

Step 6. Repeat the process for each raw score.

Now translate the raw scores on the geology test into z-scores and check your results in Table B.1.

Geology Test Scores

Students	Raw Scores	Students	Raw Scores
1.	50	11.	28
2.	45	12.	28
3.	42	13.	24
4.	39	14.	23
5.	38	15.	21
6.	30	16.	20
7.	30	17.	15
8.	29	18.	10
9.	29	19.	10
10.	29	20.	9

Translating z-Scores to t-Scores

$$t = 10 \left(\frac{X - \bar{X}}{SD} \right) + 50$$

Drama Test (maximum score 30)

	Raw Scores	z-Scores	t-Scores
1.	25	1	60
2.	25	1	60
3.	24	.9	59
4.	23	.7	57
5.	22	.5	55
6.	22	.5	55
7.	22	.5	55
8.	21	.3	53
9.	20	.1	51
10.	18	− .2	48
11.	18	− .2	48
12.	18	− .2	48
13.	15	− .8	42
14.	9	− 1.8	32
15.	6	− 2.4	26

Step 1. List the raw scores in any order, but list each score.

Step 2. Translate the raw scores to z-scores.

Step 3. Multiply each z-score by 10. (.5)10 = 5.

Step 4. Add 50 to the score derived in Step 3. 5 + 50 = 55.

Conclusion: The z-score .5 is equal to the t-score 55.

Step 5. Repeat the process for each z-score.

Now translate the z-scores on the geology test into t-scores and check your results in Table B.1.

Geology Test Scores

Students	Raw Scores	Students	Raw Scores
1.	50	11.	28
2.	45	12.	28
3.	42	13.	24
4.	39	14.	23
5.	38	15.	21
6.	30	16.	20
7.	30	17.	15
8.	29	18.	10
9.	29	19.	10
10.	29	20.	9

Translating the Scores to Percentiles

Drama Test (maximum score 30)

	Raw Score	Percentile	Percentile Score	Rounded Percentile
1.	25	100	96.7	97
2.	25	100	96.7	97
3.	24	86.6	86.6	87
4.	23	79.9	79.9	80
5.	22	73.2	66.5	67
6.	22	73.2	66.5	67
7.	22	73.2	66.5	67
8.	21	53.1	53.1	53
9.	20	46.4	46.4	46
10.	18	39.7	33	33
11.	18	39.7	33	33
12.	18	39.7	33	33
13.	15	19.6	19.6	20
14.	9	12.9	12.9	13
15.	6	6.2	6.2	6

Step 1. List the scores in order from largest to smallest. List all scores.

Step 2. Divide 100 by the number of scores. 100 ÷ 15 = 6.67.

Step 3. Round off the number in Step 2 to one decimal. 6.67 = 6.7.

Step 4. Assign a value of 100 to the first score on the list. The first score (25) would have a value of 100.

Step 5. Subtract the number obtained in Step 3 from 100 and assign it to the second number on the list.

Score	Percentile
25	100
25	93.3
24	86.6

Continue subtracting down the entire list.

Step 6. When several scores are the same, average their percentiles together. The result is rounded to the nearest tenth and becomes the percentile score. For example, since the first two raw scores are 25, their percentiles (100 + 93.3) are averaged to 96.7. This becomes the percentile score.

Score	Percentile	Percentile Score
25	100	96.7
25	93.3	96.7

Step 7. Round off the percentile score from Step 6.

Score	Percentile	Percentile Score	Rounded Percentile
25	100	96.7	97
25	93.3	96.7	97

Conclusion: A student who scored 25 on the drama test is at the 97th percentile.

Now translate the raw scores on the geology test into percentiles and check your results in Table B.1.

Geology Test Scores

Students	Raw Scores	Students	Raw Scores
1.	50	11.	28
2.	45	12.	28
3.	42	13.	24
4.	39	14.	23
5.	38	15.	21
6.	30	16.	20
7.	30	17.	15
8.	29	18.	10
9.	29	19.	10
10.	29	20.	9

Computing Percentages

Drama Test (maximum score 30)

	Raw Score	Percentage
1.	25	83
2.	25	83
3.	24	80
4.	23	77
5.	22	73
6.	22	73
7.	22	73
8.	21	70
9.	20	67
10.	18	60
11.	18	60
12.	18	60
13.	15	50
14.	9	30
15.	6	20

Step 1. List the raw scores.
Step 2. Divide each raw score by the total possible score. $25 \div 30 = .83 = 83\%$
Conclusion: A student who scores 25 out of 30 has received 83%.

Now translate the raw scores on the geology test into percentages and check your results in Table B.1.

Geology Test Scores

Students	Raw Scores
1.	50
2.	45
3.	42
4.	39
5.	38
6.	30
7.	30
8.	29
9.	29
10.	29
11.	28
12.	28
13.	24
14.	23
15.	21
16.	20
17.	15
18.	10
19.	10
20.	9

Criterion-Referenced Test Scores

Criterion-referenced tests/observations are used to determine a student's performance relative to a behavioral standard, or criterion for acceptable performance.

Designing CRTs involves two steps. First, a behavioral objective is written including a statement of the behavior that the students will use to indicate their learning and to what criterion they will use it. Second, the materials necessary for the students to exhibit the behavior are assembled. The criterion given in the objective is the behavioral standard that will be used to make decisions about the status of the student.

Because the criterion-referenced probe is based upon a behavioral objective, the raw score on the test can be read as a behavioral statement. As long as the conditions and behavior specified in the objective are relevant, the raw score does not require conversion or translation to be meaningful. For example, if an objective says "Given a sheet of mixed addition and subtraction facts 0–20, the student will write the answers at a rate of 40 correct with 0 errors" and Mary Lee writes 20 problems, then the raw score of 20 is all that is needed to see that she has not reached the criterion. As long as the teacher knows that writing answers is relevant and that the criterion (40 correct, 0 errors) is relevant, the raw score is relevant.

The meaning of a normative standard is based on the "power" of the argument that students should behave like other students. A behavioral standard must be based on the power of evidence showing that the behavioral criterion in the objective is relevant and functional. The teacher's belief in the criterion must be supported by more than personal opinion.

Grade Equivalency Scores

Anyone who has ever listened to the reading of two students who both scored at the same grade level on a reading test is probably already suspicious of the term "grade level." Most kids are in the grade they are in because of age, not specific skills. And age may have little or nothing to do with skill acquisition. Therefore, it seems ridiculous to use a term such as *grade level* to describe a student's academic skills. But it is done all the time.

Grade level is a normative idea based on the average performance of various sample populations. As they are currently determined and *scaled* for tests like the *California Test of Basic Skills*, grade equivalency scores can only be used for normative comparison. Their application is limited by the sample on which they are based, the other limitations inherent in all normative comparisons, and the imposition of a 10-month fixed scale of growth. If Bridget scores at the sixth-grade level on a test, then she is scoring at the 50 percentile of the sixth graders in the original sample. (Outlandish as it may sound, it is possible that none of the students in that sample could do a sixth-grade assignment; the NRT scores tell us nothing about a student's actual functioning.) Those sixth graders and Bridget may have nothing else in common at all. Perhaps the greatest injustice done to remedial students is to treat them as if they were in the grade that their grade equivalent scores correspond to. A ninth-grade student who scores at the first-grade level undoubtably doesn't learn like a first grader, care about what first graders care about, or even read in the same way.

Here is an oversimplified example. Suppose the list of words in Figure B.10 makes up a reading test, and each word is given a score of one point. Todd and Elizabeth take the test. The average score for a first graders is 1; second graders, 2; and so forth. In this case both Todd and Elizabeth would be considered third-grade readers. Armed with this knowledge their teacher might then place them in a third-grade book containing the sentence "They originally ate at the cafe." Even with the same test score, these students would read the sentence differently because grade level does not supply specific information about what a student can or cannot do.

	Todd	Elizabeth
ate	X	X
they	X	-
house	-	X
originally	X	-
interpretation	-	X
nevertheless	-	-
	3	3

"They originally ate at the cafe."

FIGURE B.10

Another problem with grade equivalent scores is the matter of *scales*. Learning does not necessarily occur on an equal-interval scale, although grade-equivalent scores treat it as if it did. The amount of math a student learns between the second grade and the third grade is not the same as the amount learned between the eleventh and twelfth grades. Similarly, the third-grade reading level is not half as difficult as the sixth-grade reading level. In fact, for some basic reading and math skills the student is not exposed to any really new material after about the fourth grade, making the amount of decoding and computation covered each year progressively less. Because of this, saying a student decodes at the tenth-grade level is like saying that a student is at the second-grade level in high school economics. It doesn't make sense because high school economics isn't even taught in the second grade. Yet many popular achievement tests provide norms for primary content all the way into high school.

A final problem with grade equivalency scores is the way they are presented by test publishers. Many tests designed for and normed on students of a limited age-span report grade equivalencies higher or lower than the norming sample. In other words, a test designed for use on students in grades 6, 7, 8, and 9 may be normed only on students in those grades. Yet the test manuals may report grade equivalency scores for the test that range from first to twelfth grade. Those equivalency scores that are not based on actual norms are projected through a process called *interpolation*, which is not the same as norming.

The frequency with which grade equivalency scores are used to pick programs for students or to evaluate programming is probably due to their apparent simplicity. But as Tallmadge and Horst (1974) have pointed out, "This apparent simplicity is entirely illusory, and there is ample evidence to contraindicate the use of grade equivalent scores or grade equivalent gains for *any purpose whatever* in educational evaluation" (p. 70). This caution does not just pertain to the evaluation of children but also to program and teacher evaluation (Glass, 1974). The International Reading Association has even called for a moratorium on the use of such scores.

UNIT 3: SUMMARIZING RESULTS

Earlier these steps of measurement were presented:

1. Define the thing to be measured.
2. Make it observable.
3. Assign numbers to it.
4. Summarize the results.

Definition was addressed through the comparison of CRTs and NRTs in chapter 4, and the assignment of numbers was just addressed through the discussion of scores. Making the thing observable was focused on in chapter 5, which covered the qualities of good tests/observations. This final section of Appendix B addresses the issue of summarizing test/observation results.

Discrepancies

The original model of evaluation was S ←→ B. The
$$\downarrow$$
$$D$$
previous discussions of scores and standards have dealt with the derivation of the B (the behavior) and the S (the standard). Ultimately, however, the essence of evaluation is the comparison of the standard and behavior to find a discrepancy. A useful summary supplies the direction and magnitude of the student's discrepancy to allow us to judge its significance. It is the magnitude of the discrepancy (how far from the standard one is) and its direction from the standard (above or below it) that determine the decisions we make. For example, if the standard for reading is the class average of 50 and a student (Tom) scored 45, we know the direction of his discrepancy is down (negative) and the magnitude is 5. Should Tom, who is currently getting 15 minutes of tutoring in reading, be stepped up to 30 minutes? Deciding whether or not a -5 reading discrepancy warrants an extra 15 minutes of instructional time depends on the teacher's view of significance.

Significance

Normative discrepancies are linked to the concept of the normal distribution, as are most educational statistics. As a result their significance is frequently judged on the basis of "statistical significance." Statistical significance in this case refers to the application of procedures for determining the probability of any event happening by accident. The analysis used to judge the statistical significance of an occurrence is most commonly based on the assumption that the distributions involved are normal. If the reading test Tom's class takes results in scores that routinely fluctuate by ± 10 points, then Tom's -5 discrepancy could simply be an accident. Knowing this, his teacher is unlikely to think it is significant enough to justify the extra 15 minutes of reading instruction. A discrepancy of -15, however, might seldom occur by accident and therefore be considered significant. Statistical significance is usually reported in terms like $p < .05$. This means that statistically the chances are less than 5 out of 100 that the same score will occur by accident. Five times out of 100, while considered improbable enough to be called statistically significant, is still one accident out of 20. Given the hundreds of measurements and decisions that occur daily in the classroom, it is obvious that many of those that are statistically significant will be accidental and have no educational significance. Statistical significance was described in greater detail in Appendix A.

CRT Discrepancies

Raw scores on normed tests take on different meanings according to the norming populations to which they are compared. Similarly, the differences in criteria found in objectives make the raw scores on criterion-referenced tests take on different meanings. While the raw score on a CRT does represent a basic unit of behavior, the implications of that score for decision making are not always clear. To determine educational significance a teacher must ask, "How much teaching is needed to remove the discrepancy?"

If we want to evaluate a student's skill in an area we must have predetermined standards of performance in that area. If we have both the standard and a measure of the student's performance, we can note any discrepancy between the two. The discrepancy between actual and expected behavior is what we are supposed to correct through teaching. A small discrepancy signals the need for a small change in behavior, and therefore less teaching, than a large discrepancy. As a result, discrepancy scores are more meaningful to teachers than raw scores.

Criterion-referenced probes are designed to accurately describe the student's behavior relevant to task-specific standards (as opposed to norms). When CAP has not yet been reached, the discrepancy between the standard and the student's performance can be described in absolute or ratio terms. An "absolute discrepancy" is determined by subtracting the smaller number from the larger.

Standard		Performance		Absolute Discrepancy
75	−	60	=	+ 15
Performance		Standard		Absolute Discrepancy
75	−	60	=	− 15

If the standard is larger than the performance, label the discrepancy + to show that the behavior must increase. If the standard is smaller, label the discrepancy − to show that the behavior must decrease. A ratio discrepancy is determined by dividing the larger of the two by the smaller. For decision making, ratio discrepancies are superior to absolute ones. Discrepancy ratios (Deno & Mirkin, 1977) are a good way to summarize the current performance (or progress) of a student in different areas so priorities for instruction can be set. The discrepancy ratio is the criterion-referenced equivalent of a standard score (z-score, t-score, percentile). It allows you to compare the student's behavior in different content areas to decide in which he or she needs the most help.

The steps to determine the ratio are simple.

1. Establish the standard. The standard is CAP.
2. Measure the performance. Performance is the student's current functioning as determined through direct observation or testing.
3. Divide the larger of the two by the smaller to find the magnitude.
4. Indicate the direction the behavior must change to reach the standard. × means the behavior must increase; ÷ means it must decrease.

Standard		Performance		Ratio Discrepancy
75	÷	60	=	× 1.25
Performance		Standard		Ratio Discrepancy
75	÷	60	=	÷ 1.25

Figure B.11 shows Ralph's performance and CAP for several skills. The discrepancy ratio has been calculated for each of these skills. He is most behind in "talks out" because the magnitude of the discrepancy for that behavior shows that he needs to alter his behavior by a factor of 6.7.

The direction of change needed to remove the discrepancy is placed in front of the number. For a behavior you wish to *increase*, the ratio should be preceded by a plus sign (+) or times sign (×). For a behavior you want to *decrease*, the ratio is preceded by a subtract sign (−) or divide sign (÷). The times sign means the current performance must be increased by the proportion shown in order to rectify the discrepancy. In Figure B.11,

FIGURE B.11
Discrepancy ratios
for several behaviors

	*Summary of Ralph's Current Level of Performance**					
	Decoding		*Math Facts 0-9*			*Talks Out*
	CVC + e words	*+*	*−*	*×*	*÷*	*In Class*
CAP	70	50	50	50	50	.03
Student performance	35	50	45	32	27	.2
Absolute discrepancy	− 35	0	− 5	− 18	− 23	+ .17
Discrepancy ratio	× 2	× 1	× 1.1	× 1.6	× 1.9	÷ 6.7

*All data in movements per minute.

Ralph's CVC + *e* behavior is currently 35 problems per minute. If it increases (is multiplied) by a factor of 2, it will be at 70 and there will be no discrepancy. Ralph's "talks out" behavior occurs .2 times per minute (an average of once every 5 minutes). The average level of talking out in his class is .03 times per minute. His "talks out" behavior must decrease (divide) by a factor of 6.7 to meet the standard. Therefore it is labeled ÷ 6.7.

UNIT 4: DETERMINING THE RELIABILITY AND VALIDITY OF CRTs

This unit presents procedures for calculating coefficients of reliability and validity for CRTs. In covering this topic, we have selected, and in some cases modified, procedures for classroom use.

Each procedure yields a coefficient that can be used to make judgments about the quality of tests or items. The requirements for the reliability and validity of tests and test items are as follows:

Below   .50 =   Unacceptable (Throw it out)
Between   .50 and .90 = Somewhat acceptable (Consider revision)
Above   .90 =   OK

Calculating Reliability
Two methods of estimating reliability are described in this section. The methods have been selected primarily for their ease of application.

Method 1
One simple technique for estimating the internal consistency of a CRT is to determine the percentage of agreement among the items (Becker & Englemann, 1976). To present this technique, it has been divided into three phases.

The agreement between two items can be determined by following these steps.

Computational Steps, Phase A

Step 1. Administer the items to a group of students.
Step 2. Record the responses as seen in Table B.2, indicating for each student if the item is correct (1) or incorrect (0).
Step 3. Count the number of students who got the same score on both items A and B (8).
Step 4. Divide the number of students determined in Step 3 by the total number of students who took the test.
          8 ÷ 10 = 80%.
          Conclusion: There is 80% agreement between items A and B.

The agreement among all items can be calculated by following these steps.

Computational Steps, Phase B

Step 1. Administer the items to a group of students.
Step 2. List all possible item pairs.
          A-B, A-C, A-D, B-C, B-D, C-D.

TABLE B.2
Reliability method one

		Items			
		A	B	C	D
Students	1	1	1	1	1
	2	1	0	1	1
	3	1	1	1	1
	4	0	0	0	0
	5	1	1	0	1
	6	0	0	1	1
	7	1	1	1	1
	8	1	1	0	1
	9	1	1	1	1
	10	1	0	1	1

Step 3. Calculate the agreement between each pair.

A-B = 8/10 = 80%
A-C = 7/10 = 70%
A-D = 9/10 = 90%
B-C = 5/10 = 50%
B-D = 7/10 = 70%
C-D = 8/10 = 80%

Step 4. Average together the percentages obtained in Step 3.

$$\frac{80 + 70 + 90 + 50 + 70 + 80}{6} = 73\%$$

Conclusion: There is 73% agreement among the items on the test.

The average agreement of each item can be calculated by following these steps.

Step 1. Calculate the agreement for every possible combination of items.
A-B = 80%
A-B = 70%
A-D = 90%
B-C = 50%
B-D = 70%
C-D = 80%

Step 2. List the total percentage of agreement for each item with every other item.

Item A		Item B	
A-B = .80		A-B = .80	
A-C = .70		B-C = .50	
A-D = .90		B-D = .70	
Total:	2.4		2

Item C		Item D	
A-C = .70		A-D = .90	
B-C = .50		B-D = .70	
C-D = .80		C-D = .80	
Total:	2		2.4

Step 3. Divide each total in Step 2 by the number of items minus 1 ($N - 1$) to find the average.

Item A	Item B
2.4 ÷ 3 = 80%	2 ÷ 3 = 67%
Item C	Item D
2 ÷ 3 = 67%	2.4 ÷ 3 = 80%

Conclusion: Items B and C need revision. If B and C were revised, items A and D would probably be raised. Therefore, there is no need to revise them yet.

Method 2
A second technique is to give the test to a group of kids and then observe the results to see if any items stand out as being too hard or too easy. This technique can be used on NRTs and CRTs.

Observational Steps

1. Administer the test to a group of students.
2. Record the responses, as seen in Table B.3.
3. Sum the number of items correct for each student, and the number of students who got each item correct. For example, student 5 got eight items correct. Item F was done correctly by nine students.
4. Examine the table for items that stand out as being too hard or too easy. Item C was missed by seven students. Item H was missed by no students.
5. Observe the table for items that do not seem to discriminate between high and low students.

TABLE B.3
Reliability method two

		Items										*Student Total Correct*
		A	B	C	D	E	F	G	H	I	J	
Students	1	1	1	1	1	0	1	0	1	1	0	7
	2	1	1	0	1	1	1	0	1	1	1	8
	3	1	0	0	1	1	1	1	1	1	1	8
	4	0	1	0	1	1	1	1	1	0	1	7
	5	1	0	0	1	1	1	1	1	1	1	8
	6	1	1	0	0	0	0	1	1	0	0	4
	7	0	0	0	0	0	1	0	1	0	1	3
	8	1	1	1	0	1	1	1	1	1	1	9
	9	1	1	1	0	1	1	1	1	1	1	9
	10	1	0	0	1	1	1	1	1	1	1	8
Item Total Correct		8	6	3	6	7	9	7	10	7	8	

Item D was missed by both high-scoring and low-scoring students.

Calculating Validity

For any CRT there are two validity questions to be answered. (1) Does the test discriminate between preinstruction and postinstruction students? (2) Does the test discriminate between masters and nonmasters of the task? These same two questions can be asked about each test item. Each question can be answered by using one of the methods shown in Figure B.12.

All methods for calculating the validity of CRTs use both pre- and posttest data. All four methods for determining validity incorporate an element of instruction. First, the test is given, then instruction takes place, then the test is given again. The effectiveness of the instruction will influence the validity of the test, just as the validity of the test should influence the effectiveness of instruction.

The following procedures for determining CRT validity are examples of the so-called threshold loss technique. This technique looks at the probability of assigning masters or nonmasters of a task to an inappropriate group (e.g., a nonmaster to a mastery group or a master to a nonmastery group). Of the many techniques available, these procedures seem easiest to compute and interpret (Berk, 1980).

Test Validity Method 1 and Item Validity Method 1 compare pretest and posttest scores to contrast masters and nonmasters.

Test Validity Method 1

This method answers the question: How well does the test discriminate between students who have or have not had instruction at the task?

Formula: $1 - \left(\frac{\bar{x}_1}{\bar{x}_2}\right) = \text{test validity}$

where $\bar{x}_1$ = mean pretest score
$\bar{x}_2$ = mean posttest score

Computational Steps (using data in Table B.4)

Step 1. Administer the test to a group of uninstructed students (pretest).

Step 2. Administer the test to a group of instructed students (posttest).

Step 3. Calculate the mean pretest score.

$$\bar{x}_1 = \frac{10}{8} = 1.25$$

Step 4. Calculate the mean posttest score.

$$\bar{x}_2 = \frac{33}{8} = 4.13$$

FIGURE B.12
Test and item
validity formulas

Test Validity	Item Validity
Method 1	*Method 1*
$1 - \left(\dfrac{\bar{x}_1}{\bar{x}_2}\right) =$ $\bar{x}_1$ = Mean pretest score $\bar{x}_2$ = Mean posttest score	A = Number of instructed students who got the item correct B = Number of uninstructed students who got the item correct $(A/N_1) - (B/N_2) =$ N_1 = Number of instructed students N_2 = Number of uninstructed students
Method 2 $\dfrac{(P_2 + F_1)}{N} =$ F_1 = Uninstructed nonmasters F_2 = Instructed nonmasters P_1 = Uninstructed nonmasters P_2 = Instructed nonmasters $N = F_1 + F_2 + P_1 + P_2$	*Method 2* $(C/P) - (D/F) =$ C = Number of masters who got the item correct D = Number of nonmasters who got the item correct P = Number of masters F = Number of nonmasters

Step 5. Divide the number in Step 3 by the number in Step 4.
1.25 ÷ 4.13 = .30
Step 6. Subtract the number in Step 5 from the number 1.
1 − .30 = .70

Conclusion: Because .70 lies in the acceptable range, the test is sufficiently valid for the purpose of discriminating between uninstructed and instructed groups of students. In fact, if student 3 were excluded from the computation (because that student had met CAP on the pretest and therefore may have actually had instruction), the validity would be even higher.

Item Validity Method 1

This method answers the question: How well do the individual test items discriminate between students who have or have not had instruction at the task? It is an adaptation of a technique by Brennan (1972) which has been proposed by Crehan (1974).

Formula: $(A/N_1) - (B/N_2) =$ Item validity

where A = Number of instructed students who got the item correct
B = Number of uninstructed students who got the item correct
N_1 = Number of instructed students
N_2 = Number of uninstructed students

Computational Steps (using data in Table B.4)
Step 1. Administer the test to a group of uninstructed students (pretest).
Step 2. Administer the test to a group of instructed students (posttest).
Step 3. Count the number of instructed students.
8.
Step 4. Count the number of uninstructed students.
8.
Step 5. Select an item. In this example use item C.
Step 6. Count how many of the students in the instructed group got item C correct.
8.

TABLE B.4
Data for determining the validity of a CRT

		A	B	C	D	E	CAP = + 4 *Student Totals*
				Items			
Uninstructed	1	0	0	0	0	1	1
Students	2	0	0	0	0	0	0
(pretest)	3	1	1	1	0	1	4
	4	0	1	0	0	0	1
	5	0	0	0	0	0	0
	6	0	0	1	0	1	2
	7	0	0	0	0	1	1
	8	0	0	1	0	0	1
Item totals		1	2	3	0	4	Total pretest score = 10 Mean pretest score = 1.25
Instructed	1	1	0	1	1	1	4
Students	2	1	1	1	1	0	4
(posttest)	3	1	1	1	1	0	4
	4	1	1	1	1	0	4
	5	1	0	1	1	0	3
	6	1	0	1	1	1	4
	7	1	1	1	1	1	5
	8	1	1	1	1	1	5
Item totals		8	5	8	8	4	Total posttest score = 33 Mean posttest score = 4.13
Item validity Method 1		.87	.38	.62	1.00	0	
Item validity Method 2		.87	.62	.62	.75	.25	

Step 7.   Count how many students in the uninstructed group got item C correct.
3.

Step 8.   Divide the number obtained in Step 6 by the number obtained in Step 3.
$8 \div 8 = 1$.

Step 9.   Divide the number obtained in Step 7 by the number obtained in Step 4.
$3 \div 8 = .38$.

Step 10.   Subtract the number obtained in Step 9 from the number obtained in Step 8.
$1 - .38 = .62$

Conclusion: This item is marginally valid for the purpose of discriminating between students who have or have not had instruction. The validity of each item has been calculated and listed in Table B.4. Of the five items, B and E should be omitted.

Test Validity Method 2

Test Validity Method 2 and Item Validity Method 2 both assume that CAP has been set for the test. Remember that CAP is determined by standardizing the test on a population of students who are successful at the task. If CAP has not been meaningfully determined, then these methods are useless. Ideally, the way to set CAP is to establish a cutting score below which the student won't progress successfully to the next task. For example, suppose subtask A is an essential subtask of task B. If CAP for subtask A is 80%, then a student who scores 70% on subtask A should not succeed at task B. (Because CAP is often situation- and task-specific, you should always report its source.)

Once CAP has been established, then those who score above it are said to have mastered the task. One way to summarize the test validity is by looking at the proportion of students which the test classifies as nonmasters before instruction and masters after instruction.

Test Validity Method 2 answers the question: How well does the test discriminate between instructed students who have or have not mastered the task? A procedure for answering this question has been described by Crehan (1974).

Formula: $\dfrac{(P_2 + F_1)}{N}$ = Test validity

where F_1 = Uninstructed nonmasters
F_2 = Instructed nonmasters
P_1 = Uninstructed masters
P_2 = Instructed masters
N = $F_1 + F_2 + P_1 + P_2$

Computational Steps (using data in Table B.4)
Step 1.   Administer the test to a group of instructed students. Determine how many students are in the group.
8.
Step 2.   Administer the test to a group of uninstructed students. Determine how many students are in the group.
8.
Step 3.   Determine the number of uninstructed students who did not meet CAP.
7.
Step 4.   Determine the number of instructed students who did meet CAP.
7.
Step 5.   Add the numbers obtained in Steps 3 and 4.
7 + 7 = 14.
Step 6.   Add the number in Step 1 to the number in Step 2.
8 + 8 = 16.
Step 7.   Divide the number obtained in Step 5 by the number obtained in Step 6.
14 ÷ 16 = .88

Conclusion: The validity of the test (its ability to discriminate masters from nonmasters) is acceptable.

One problem with all the procedures described here is that they do not tell how often similar results might be obtained by chance. (For a discussion of this issue, see Swaminathan, Hambleton, and Algina, 1974).

Item Validity Method 2

This method answers the question: How well do the individual test items discriminate between masters and nonmasters of the task? This technique also assumes that a CAP level has been established for the test. The method described by Johnson (1951) and Brennan (1972) compares the proportion of students above CAP and below CAP to the number passing the item.

Formula: $(C/P) - (D/F)$ = Item validity

where C = Number of masters who get the item correct
D = Number of nonmasters who get the item correct
P = Number of masters
F = Number of nonmasters

Computational steps (using data in Table B.4)
Step 1.   Administer the test to a group of students. (This group can include both instructed and uninstructed students.)
Step 2.   Determine the number of students who have met CAP.
8.
Step 3.   Determine how many students are below CAP.
8.
Step 4.   Select an item. In this example use item C.
Step 5.   Count how many of the students who met CAP got item C correct.
8.
Step 6.   Count how many of the students who did not meet CAP got item C correct.
3.

Step 7. Divide the number in Step 5 by the number in Step 2.

$$8 \div 8 = 1.$$

Step 8. Divide the number in Step 6 by the number in Step 3.

$$3 \div 8 = .38$$

Step 9. Subtract the number in Step 8 from the number in Step 7.

$$1 - .38 = .62.$$

Conclusion: Item C is acceptable but needs revision.

Computation Practice. This exercise is for practice in calculating the reliability and validity of CRTs. Try following each of the procedures outlined previously. The list provided below should help you recall each of the methods used to determine the reliability and validity of CRTs. Refer to the appropriate pages to view the sequential order of computational steps to do each of the procedures. The raw data are supplied in Table B.5. All of the calculations will be done with both the pre- and posttest scores; therefore, $N = 20$.

Answers to the exercise follow Table B.5, and the results of the calculations are summarized in Table B.6.

- Reliability: Method 1
  Computational Steps, Phase *A, B,* and *C*
- Reliability: Method 2
  Observational Steps
- Test Validity: Method 1
  Computational Steps

TABLE B.5
Student scores for practice computation

| | | | | | Items | | | | Total |
		A	B	C	D	E	F	G	Scores
Pretest									
	Blake	0	0	0	1	1	0	0	2
	Debbie	0	0	0	0	0	0	0	0
	Joe	0	0	1	0	0	0	0	1
	Marybeth	0	0	0	0	0	0	0	0
	Connie	0	0	1	0	0	0	0	1
Students	Kathi	0	0	0	0	0	0	0	0
	Mada Kay	1	1	0	1	1	1	1	6
	Ken	0	0	0	0	0	1	0	1
	Karna	0	0	0	0	0	0	0	0
	Win	0	0	0	0	0	0	0	0

Total pretest score = ____
Mean pretest score = ____

| | | | | | Items | | | | Total |
		A	B	C	D	E	F	G	Scores
Posttest									
	Blake	1	1	0	1	1	1	1	6
	Debbie	1	1	1	1	1	0	1	6
	Joe	1	1	0	1	1	1	1	6
	Marybeth	1	1	1	1	1	1	1	-
	Connie	1	1	0	1	1	1	1	6
Students	Kathi	1	1	1	1	1	1	1	-
	Mada Kay	1	1	1	1	1	1	1	-
	Ken	1	1	0	1	1	1	1	6
	Karna	1	0	1	1	1	0	1	5
	Win	1	1	1	0	1	0	0	4

Total pretest score = ____
Mean pretest score = ____

- Item Validity: Method 1
  Computational Steps
- Test Validity: Method 2
  Computational Steps
- Item Validity: Method 2
  Computational Steps

Answers to Practice Exercise

Reliability
Method 1: Internal consistency (agreement among items)

Phase A

A-B $\frac{19}{20} = 95\%$	B-D $\frac{17}{20} = 85\%$	C-G $\frac{12}{20} = 60\%$
A-C $\frac{13}{20} = 65\%$	B-E $\frac{18}{20} = 90\%$	D-E $\frac{19}{20} = 95\%$
A-D $\frac{18}{20} = 90\%$	B-F $\frac{17}{20} = 85\%$	D-F $\frac{15}{20} = 75\%$
A-E $\frac{19}{20} = 95\%$	B-G $\frac{18}{20} = 90\%$	D-G $\frac{19}{20} = 95\%$
A-F $\frac{16}{20} = 80\%$	C-D $\frac{11}{20} = 55\%$	E-F $\frac{15}{20} = 75\%$
A-G $\frac{19}{20} = 95\%$	C-E $\frac{12}{20} = 60\%$	E-G $\frac{18}{20} = 90\%$
B-C $\frac{12}{20} = 60\%$	C-F $\frac{9}{20} = 45\%$	F-G $\frac{17}{20} = 85\%$

Phase B

Percentage		Frequency		
.95	×	5	=	4.75
.90	×	4	=	3.6
.85	×	3	=	2.55
.80	×	1	=	.80
.75	×	2	=	1.50
.70	×	0	=	0
.65	×	1	=	.65
.60	×	3	=	1.80
.55	×	1	=	.55
Total		20	=	16.2

$$\frac{16.2}{20} = .81$$

Average Agreement = 81%

Phase C
Average Agreement of Item

A	=	.87	E	=	.84
B	=	.84	F	=	.74
C	=	.58	G	=	.86
D	=	.83			

Reliability
Method 2: Observing the data. It can be seen that item C is not a good item as many pretest students got it correct and many posttest students got it wrong. It can also be seen that student 7 scored well above the others on the pretest.

Test Validity Method 1

Step 3	= 1.1
Step 4	= 6
Step 5	= .18
Step 6	= .82
Conclusion	= .82

Test Validity Method 2

Step 1	= 10
Step 2	= 10
Step 3	= 9
Step 4	= 8
Step 5	= 17
Step 6	= 20
Step 7	= .85
Conclusion	= .85

Item Validity Method 1
(Only item F will be discussed here as an example.)

Step 3	= 10
Step 4	= 10
Step 5	= Item F
Step 6	= 9
Step 7	= 2
Step 8	= .9
Step 9	= .2
Step 10	= .7
Conclusion	= .70

Item Validity Method 2
(Item F only)

Step 2	= 9
Step 3	= 11
Step 4	= Item F
Step 5	= 9
Step 6	= 2
Step 7	= 1
Step 8	= .18
Step 9	= .82
Conclusion	= .82

TABLE B.6
Summary of computational exercise

						CAP = 6			

		A	B	C	D	E	F	G	*Total Scores*
Pretest	1	0	0	0	1	1	0	0	2
	2	0	0	0	0	0	0	0	0
	3	0	0	1	0	0	0	0	1
Students	4	0	0	0	0	0	0	0	0
	5	0	0	1	0	0	0	0	1
	6	0	0	0	0	0	0	0	0
	7	1	1	0	1	1	1	1	6
	8	0	0	0	0	0	1	0	1
	9	0	0	0	0	0	0	0	0
	10	0	0	0	0	0	0	0	0
Item Totals		1	1	2	2	2	2	1	*Mean pretest score* = 1.1
Posttest	1	1	1	0	1	1	1	1	6
	2	1	1	1	1	0	1	1	6
	3	1	1	0	1	1	1	1	6
Students	4	1	1	1	1	1	1	1	7
	5	1	1	0	1	1	1	1	6
	6	1	1	1	1	1	1	1	7
	7	1	1	1	1	1	1	1	7
	8	1	1	0	1	1	1	1	6
	9	1	0	1	1	0	1	1	5
	10	1	1	1	0	1	0	0	4
Item Totals		10	9	6	9	8	9	9	*Mean pretest score* = 6

Test Validity Method 1	.82						
Item Validity Method 2	.82	.91	.08	.82	.71	.82	.91
Test Validity Method 2	.85						
Item Validity Method 1	.90	.80	.40	.70	.60	.70	.80
Reliability (Average Agreement)	.87	.84	.58	.83	.84	.74	.86

Appendix C

Tables of Specifications

TABLE C.1
A table of specifications for decoding

| | | Behavior Difficulty | | | |
| | | Identify | | Produce | |
		A. Accuracy (% data) Materials: target unit and 3 distractors (usually on flash cards)	B. Accuracy (% data) Materials: flash cards or untimed probe sheet	C. Mastery (Rate data) Materials: probe sheet	D. Automatic (rate or %) Materials: passage from book
Complex Words	21. *Irregular sight words* Example: was, what, who	21a. CAP: 100% Accuracy	21b. CAP: 95% correct or better	21c. CAP: 60-80 correct per minute. 0-2 errors per minute	21d. CAP: 80-140 words correct per minute. 0-2 sight word errors per minute or 95% sight words correct.
	20. *Polysyllabic words*	20a. No test	20b. CAP: 95% correct or better	20c. CAP: 60-80 correct per minute. 0-2 errors per minute	20d. CAP: 80-140 words correct per minute. 0-2 polysyllabic word errors per minute or 95% polysyllabic words correct per minute.
	19. *Contractions* Example: didn't, I've, let's	19a. CAP: 100% correct	19b. CAP: 95% correct or better	19c. CAP: 60-80 correct per minute. 0-2 errors per minute	19d. CAP: 80-140 words correct per minute. 0-2 contraction errors per minute or 95% contraction words correct per minute.
	18. *Compound words* Example: airport, into, doghouse	18a. No test	18b. CAP: 95% correct or better	18c. CAP: 60-80 correct per minute. 0-2 errors per minute	18d. CAP: 80-140 words correct per minute. 0-2 compound word errors per minute or 95% compound words correct per minute.

Content Difficulty

TABLE C.1
(continued)

		Behavior Difficulty			
		Identify		Produce	
		A. Accuracy (% data) Materials: target unit and 3 distractors (usually on flash cards)	B. Accuracy (% data) Materials: flash cards or untimed probe sheet	C. Mastery (Rate data) Materials: probe sheet	D. Automatic (rate or %) Materials: passage from book
Modifications	17. *Silent letters* Example: knife	17a. No test	17b. CAP: 100% correct	17c. CAP: 60-80 correct per minute. 0-2 errors per minute	17d. CAP: 80-140 words correct per minute. 0-2 silent letter errors per minute or 95% silent letter words correct per minute.
	16. *Affix morphographs (prefix, suffix)* (Suggested base: babb-) s, ed, ing, er, est, ly, ness, ful, pre, re, de, in, pro, con	16a. CAP: 100% correct	16b. CAP: 100% correct	16c. CAP: Words: 60-80 correct per minute. 0-2 errors per minute. Isolation: 60 correct per minute. 0-2 errors per minute.	16d. CAP: 80-140 words correct per minute. 0-2 endings/suffixes word errors per minute or 95% endings/suffix words correct per minute.
	15. *Plurals* Example: cats, kittys, copies	15a. No test	15b. CAP: 100% correct	15c. CAP: Words: 60-80 correct per minute. 0-2 errors per minute.	15d. CAP: 80-140 words per minute. 0-2 plural word errors per minute or 95% plural words correct per minute.
Clusters (Syllables)	14. *Clusters/Syllables* Example: ash, ab, im, op, able, eck, ing, ion	14a. CAP: 100% correct	14b. CAP: 100% correct	14c. CAP: Words: 60-80 correct per minute. 0-2 errors per minute. Isolation: 60 correct per minute. 0-2 errors per minute.	14d. CAP: 80-140 words correct per minute. 0-2 cluster word errors per minute or 95% cluster/syllable words correct per minute.

Content Difficulty

TABLE C.1
(continued)

| | | Behavior Difficulty | | | |
| | | Identify | | Produce | |
		A. Accuracy (% data) Materials: target unit and 3 distractors (usually on flash cards)	B. Accuracy (% data) Materials: flash cards or untimed probe sheet	C. Mastery (Rate data) Materials: probe sheet	D. Automatic (rate or %) Materials: passage from book
Teams	13. *r-Controlled Vowels* (Suggested base: b-f) ar, er, ir, or, ur Example: barf, berf, birf	13a. CAP: 100% correct	13b. CAP: 100% correct	13c. CAP: Words: 60-80 correct per minute. 0-2 errors per minute. Isolation: 60 correct per minute. 0-2 errors per minute.	13d. CAP: 80-140 words correct per minute. 0-2 *r*-controlled vowel errors per minute or 95% *r*-controlled vowel words correct per minute
	12. *Vowel Teams (digraphs)* (Suggested base: b-f) ai, ay, ee, ea, oo, au, aw, ei, ew, ie, oa, ou, ow, oy, ue Example: baif, fayf, beef.	12a. CAP: 100% correct	12b. CAP: 100% correct	12c. CAP: Words: 60-80 correct per minute. 0-2 errors per minute. Isolation: 60 correct per minute. 0-2 errors per minute.	12d. CAP: 80-140 words correct per minute. 0-2 vowel teams/ digraph errors per minute or 95% vowel teams/digraph words correct per minute.
	11. *Consonant digraphs* (Suggested bases: *ta* for initial and *ak* for final) sh, th, ng, ph, wh, ch Example: tash, shak, phak, taph	11a. CAP: 100% correct	11b. CAP: 100% correct	11c. CAP: Words: 60-80 correct per minute. 0-2 errors per minute. Isolation: 60 correct per minute. 0-2 errors per minute.	11d. CAP: 80-140 words correct per minute. 0-2 consonant digraph errors per minute or 95% consonant digraph words correct per minute.
	10. *Consonant teams* (Suggested base: -ab) bl, br, fl, fr, gr, pl, st, cl, cr, dr, gl, pr, sk, sl, sm, sn, sch, tw, sc, scr, sp, sw, spl, spr, squ, str, thr, dw. Example: blab, brab, flab	10a. CAP: 100% correct	10b. CAP: 100% correct	10c. CAP: Words: 60-80 correct per minute. 0-2 errors per minute. Isolation: 60 correct per minute. 0-2 errors per minute.	10d. CAP: 80-140 words correct per minute. 0-2 consonant team errors per minute or 95% consonant team words correct per minute.

Content Difficulty

TABLE C.1
(continued)

| | | Behavior Difficulty ——————————————————————→ | | | |
| | | Identify | | Produce | |
		A. Accuracy (% data) Materials: target unit and 3 distractors (usually on flash cards)	B. Accuracy (% data) Materials: flash cards or untimed probe sheet	C. Mastery (Rate data) Materials: probe sheet	D. Automatic (rate or %) Materials: passage from book
Conversions	9. *Vowel conversions* Example: hap, hape, happe, hep, hepe, hepp, heppe, hip, hipe	9a. CAP: 100% correct	9b. CAP: 100% correct	9c. CAP: Words: 60-80 correct per minute. 0-2 errors per minute. Isolation: 60 correct per minute. 0-2 errors per minute.	9d. CAP: 80-140 words correct per minute. 0-2 vowel conversion errors per minute or 95% conversion words correct.
	8. *CVC + e Blending* Example: hate, mete, bite, hope, cute	8a. CAP: 100% correct	8b. CAP: 100% correct	8c. CAP: 60-80 correct per minute. 0-2 errors per minute.	8d. CAP: 80-140 words correct per minute. 0-2 CVC + *e* blending errors per minute or 95% CVC + *e* blending words correct per minute.
Sounds	7. *CVC Blending* Example: hat, met, bit, hop, cut	7a. CAP: 100% correct	7b. CAP: 100% correct	7c. CAP: 60-80 correct per minute. 0-2 errors per minute.	7d. CAP: 80-140 words correct per minute. 0-2 CVC blending errors per minute or 95% blending words correct per minute.
	6. *Vowel Sounds* a, e, i, o, u (short and long)	6a. CAP: 100% correct	6b. CAP: 100% correct	6c. CAP: 60-80 correct per minute. 0-2 errors per minute.	6d. CAP: 80-140 words correct per minute. 0-2 vowel sound errors per minute or 95% vowel sound words correct per minute.

Content Difficulty

TABLE C.1
(continued)

| | Behavior Difficulty ⟶ | | | |
| | *Identify* | | *Produce* | |
	A. Accuracy (% data) Materials: target unit and 3 distractors (usually on flash cards)	B. Accuracy (% data) Materials: flash cards or untimed probe sheet	C. Mastery (Rate data) Materials: probe sheet	D. Automatic (rate or %) Materials: passage from book
5. *Consonant Sounds* b, c, d, f, g, h, j, k, l, m, n, p, q, r, s, t, v, w, x, y, z	5a. CAP: 100% correct	5b. CAP: 100% correct	5c. CAP: 60-80 correct per minute. 0-2 errors per minute.	5d. CAP: 80-140 words correct per minute. 0-2 consonant sound errors per minute or 95% consonant sound words correct per minute.
4. *Same and different word sounds* Directions: Teacher says two sounds and asks if they are the same or different	4a. CAP: 100% correct responses (Mastery identification would require immediate responses)	4b. No test	4c. No test	4d. No test
3. *Same and different letter sounds* Directions: Teacher says two sounds and asks if they are the same or different	3a. CAP: 100% correct responses (Mastery identification would require immediate responses)	3b. No test	3c. No test	3d. No test
2. *Same and different words* Example: "Point to the one that looks like the one in the box." was̲ saw mas was wos	2a. CAP: 100% correct responses (Mastery identification would require immediate responses)	2b. No test	2c. No test	2d. No test
1. *Same and different letters* Example: "Point to the one that looks like the one in the box." a̲ o e u a	1a. CAP: 100% correct responses (Mastery identification would require immediate responses)	1b. No test	1c. No test	1d. No test

Content Difficulty

TABLE C.2
A table of specifications for computation

D. **Multiplication and Division**	Behavior Difficulty ──────────────────────────────────→			
	Identify	Produce (in writing)		
	A. *Accuracy* (% data) Materials: target unit and 3 distractors	B. *Accuracy* (% data) Materials: flash cards or untimed probe sheet	C. *Mastery* (rate data) Materials: probe sheet	D. *Automatic* (rate or % data) Materials: assignments from textbook, content area exercises, or published test
Example				
20/708̄	13. Multiply and divide numerals with zeros as place holders	13a. no test	13b. CAP 98% or better	13c. CAP undetermined	13d. CAP 100%
873 ⨯ 96	12. Multiply and divide two or more digits by two digits	12a. no test	12b. CAP 98% or better	12c. CAP 40 digits correct 0 errors	12d. CAP 100%
	11. Multiplication and division algorithms	11a. CAP 100%	11b. CAP 100%	11c. no test	11d. CAP 100%
$8 \times 100 = 800$	10. Multiply by 1, 10, 100, 1000	10a. CAP 100%	10b. CAP 100%	10c. CAP 80 digits correct 0 errors	10d. CAP 100%
22r2 3/68̄	9. Divide two digits by one or two digits to get an answer with a remainder	9a. no test	9b. CAP 98% or better	9c. CAP undetermined	9d. CAP 100%
9 3/27̄	8. Divide two digits by one digit to get a two-digit answer (no remainder)	8a. no test	8b. CAP 98% or better	8c. CAP 50 digits correct 0 errors	8d. CAP 100%
22 3/66̄	7. Divide two digits by one digit to get a two-digit answer (no remainder)	7a. no test	7b. CAP 98% or better	7c. CAP 40 digits correct 0 errors	7d. CAP 100%
38 ⨯ 2	6. Multiply two digits by one digit with regrouping	6a. no test	6b. CAP 98% or better	6c. CAP 30 digits correct 0-2 errors	6d. CAP 100%
32 ⨯ 2	5. Multiply two digits by one digit without regrouping	5a. no test	5b. CAP 98% or better	5c. CAP 40 digits correct 0-2 errors	5d. CAP 100%
8 ⨯18 ÷ 0 =	4. Multiplication and division by zero and one	4a. CAP 100%	4b. CAP 100%	4c. no test	4d. CAP 100%
	3. Multiplication facts (0-10) and division facts (problems in which the division result falls between 0-10)	3a. CAP 100%	3b. CAP 100%	3c. CAP 40 problems correct 0 errors	3d. CAP 100%
5, 10, 15, 20 20, 15, 10, 5	2. "Count by" forward and backward	2a. no test	2b. CAP 100%	2c. CAP undetermined	2d. CAP 100%
⨯, ÷, •, /, ̄⌐	1. Multiplication and division symbols and notation	1a. CAP 100%	1b. CAP 100%	1c. no test	1d. CAP 100%

TABLE C.2
(continued)

C. Fractions (Note that CAP are in *problems* not *digits*, per minute.)

| | | Behavior Difficulty → | | | |
| | | Identify | Produce (in writing) | | |
Example		A. *Accuracy* (% data) Materials: target unit and 3 distractors	B. *Accuracy* (% data) Materials: flash cards or untimed probe sheet	C. *Mastery* (rate data) Materials: probe sheet	D. *Automatic* (rate or % data) Materials: assignments from textbook, content area exercises, or published test
$2\frac{1}{4} \div 1\frac{3}{5} =$	24. Divides two mixed numerals when the result requires conversion to simplest form	24a. no test	24b. CAP 95% or better	24c. CAP 5 problems correct 0 errors	24d. CAP 100%
$8 \div \frac{1}{4} =$	23. Divides whole numerals by fractions	23a. no test	23b. CAP 95% or better	23c. CAP 6 problems correct 0 errors	23d. CAP 100%
$\frac{3}{4} \div \frac{1}{5} =$	22. Divides fractions without cancellation when the result requires conversion to simplest form	22a. no test	22b. CAP 95% or better	22c. CAP 4 problems correct 0 errors	22d. CAP 100%
$\frac{3}{4} \div \frac{1}{2} =$	21. Divides fractions with cancellation	21a. no test	21b. CAP 95% or better	21c. CAP 6 problems correct 0 errors	21d. CAP 100%
$2\frac{1}{3} \times 1\frac{1}{4} =$	20. Multiplies two mixed numerals	20a. no test	20b. CAP 95% or better	20c. CAP 2 problems correct 0 errors	20d. CAP 100%
$\frac{1}{4} \times \frac{2}{3} =$	19. Multiplies fractions when the result requires conversion to simplest form	19a. no test	19b. CAP 95% or better	19c. CAP 15 problems correct 0 errors	19d. CAP 100%
$\frac{1}{3} \times \frac{1}{4} =$	18. Multiplies fractions when the result does not require conversion to the simplest form	18a. no test	18b. CAP 95% or better	18c. CAP 35 problems correct 0 errors	18d. CAP 100%
$3\frac{1}{4} + 4\frac{1}{2} =$	17. Adds and subtracts mixed numerals without common denominators when the result requires conversion to the simplest form	17a. no test	17b. CAP 98% or better	17c. CAP 6 problems correct 0 errors	17d. CAP 100%
$\frac{11}{12} + \frac{3}{5} =$	16. Adds and subtracts fractions without common factors in the denominators when the result requires conversion to simplest form	16a. no test	16b. CAP 98% or better	16c. CAP 4 problems correct 0 errors	16d. CAP 100%

TABLE C.2
(continued)

C. Fractions (Note that CAP are in *problems* not *digits,* per minute.)

		Behavior Difficulty →			
		Identify	Produce (in writing)		
		A. *Accuracy* (% data) Materials: target unit and 3 distractors	B. *Accuracy* (% data) Materials: flash cards or untimed probe sheet	C. *Mastery* (rate data) Materials: probe sheet	D. *Automatic* (rate or % data) Materials: assignments from textbook, content area exercises, or published test
Example					
$2/5 + 2/10 =$	15. Adds and subtracts fractions when one denominator is evenly divisible by another and the result requires conversion to the simplest form	15a. no test	15b. CAP 98% or better	15c. CAP 8 problems correct 0 errors	15d. CAP 100%
$2\frac{3}{7} - \frac{1}{7} = 2\frac{2}{7}$	14. Subtracts a fraction from a mixed numeral when the sum does not require conversion to simplest form	14a. no test	14b. CAP 98% or better	14c. CAP 16 problems correct 0 errors	14d. CAP 100%
$2\frac{3}{8} - 1\frac{2}{8} = 1\frac{1}{8}$	13. Subtracts two mixed numerals with fractions (simplest form) of like denominators	13a. CAP 100%	13b. CAP 98% or better	13c. CAP 16 problems correct 0 errors	13d. CAP 100%
$2 - \frac{1}{4} = 1\frac{3}{4}$	12. Subtracts a fraction from a whole number (0-9)	12a. CAP 100%	12b. CAP 98% or better	12c. CAP 35 problems correct 0 errors	12d. CAP 100%
$1\frac{3}{8} + \frac{1}{2} = 1\frac{7}{8}$	11. Adds fraction to a mixed numeral when one denominator is evenly divisible by another and the sum does not require conversion to simplest form	11a. CAP 100%	11b. CAP 98% or better	11c. CAP 15 problems correct 0 errors	11d. CAP 100%
$\frac{3}{8} - \frac{2}{8} = \frac{1}{8}$	10. Subtracts fractions with like denominators when the result does not require conversion to the simplest form	10a. CAP 100%	10b. CAP 98% or better	10c. CAP 30 problems correct 0 errors	10d. CAP 100%

TABLE C.2
(continued)

C. Fractions (Note that CAP are in *problems* not *digits*, per minute.)		*Behavior Difficulty* →			
		Identify	*Produce (in writing)*		
		A. *Accuracy* (% data) Materials: target unit and 3 distractors	B. *Accuracy* (% data) Materials: flash cards or untimed probe sheet	C. *Mastery* (rate data) Materials: probe sheet	D. *Automatic* (rate or % data) Materials: assignments from textbook, content area exercises, or published test
Example					
$\frac{3}{8} + \frac{1}{8} = \frac{4}{8} = \frac{1}{2}$	9. Adds fractions with like denominators when the sum requires conversion to simplest form	9a. CAP 100%	9b. CAP 98% or better	9c. CAP 30 problems correct 0 errors	9d. CAP 100%
$\frac{2}{4} = \frac{1}{2}$	8. Renames fractions (0-9) to simplest form	8a. CAP 100%	8b. CAP 100%	8c. CAP 35 problems correct 0 errors	8d. CAP 100%
$\frac{7}{2} = 3\frac{1}{2}$	7. Renames improper fractions (0-9) to mixed numerals	7a. CAP 100%	7b. CAP 100%	7c. CAP 30 problems correct 0 errors	7d. CAP 100%
$\frac{1}{3} + 2\frac{1}{3} =$	6. Adds two mixed numerals with fractions (simplest form) of like denominators when the result does not require conversion to simplest form	6a. CAP 100%	6b. CAP 100%	6c. CAP undetermined	6d. CAP 100%
$\frac{2}{5} + \frac{1}{5} =$	5. Adds fractions (simplest form) with like denominators	5a. CAP 100%	5b. CAP 100%	5c. CAP 50 problems correct 0 errors	5d. CAP 100%
$\frac{3}{8}$ $\frac{1}{8}$ $\frac{5}{8}$	4. Places three fractions (simplest form) with like denominators in sequence	4a. CAP 100%	4b. CAP 100%	4c. CAP 75 digits correct 0 errors	4d. CAP 100%
$\frac{1}{2}$ = ◐	3. Matches fractions (simplest form) to subdivided objects	3a. CAP 100%	3b. CAP 100%	3c. CAP undetermined	3d. CAP 100%
=, −, /	2. Fractions, symbols, and notation	2a. CAP 100%	2b. CAP 100%	2c. no test	2d. CAP 100%
⊕	1. Subdivides sets and/or objects	1a. CAP 100%	1b. CAP 100%	1c. CAP undetermined	1d. CAP 100%

TABLE C.2
(continued)

B. Addition and Subtraction

		Behavior Difficulty			
		Identify	Produce (in writing)		
		A. *Accuracy* (% data) Materials: target unit and 3 distractors	B. *Accuracy* (% data) Materials: flash cards or untimed probe sheet	C. *Mastery* (rate data) Materials: probe sheet	D. *Automatic* (rate or % data) Materials: assignments from textbook, content area exercises, or published test

Subtraction

Example					
8742 − 968	10. Three or more digits from three or more digits with or without regrouping	10a. no test	10b. CAP 98% or better	10c. CAP undetermined	10d. CAP 100%
42 −24	9. Two digits from two digits with regrouping	9a. no test	9b. CAP 100%	9c. CAP 40 digits correct 0 errors	9d. CAP 100%
44 −22	8. Two digits from two digits without regrouping	8a. no test	8b. CAP 100%	8c. CAP 60 digits correct 0 errors	8d. CAP 100%
23 − 9	7. One digits from two digits with regrouping	7a. no test	7b. CAP 100%	7c. CAP 60 digits correct 0 errors	7d. CAP 100%
40 −10	6. Two digits ending in zero from two digits ending in zero	6a. no test	6b. CAP 100%	6c. CAP 70 digits correct 0 errors	6d. CAP 100%
23 − 2	5. One digit from two digits without regrouping	5a. no test	5b. CAP 100%	5c. CAP 70 digits correct 0 errors	5d. CAP 100%
4 −0	4. Subtraction of zero from a digit and a digit from itself	4a. CAP 100%	4b. CAP 100%	4c. CAP 80 digits correct 0 errors	4d. CAP 100%
4 −4	3. Subtraction facts 1-20	3a. CAP 100%	3b. CAP 100%	3c. CAP 40 problems correct 0 errors	3d. CAP 100%
− 1 =	2. Subtraction symbols and notation	2a. CAP 100%	2b. CAP 100%	2c. no test	2d. CAP 100%
	1. Separates sets	1a. CAP 100%	1b. CAP 100%	1c. CAP undetermined	1d. CAP 100%

TABLE C.2
(continued)

B. Addition and Subtraction

		Behavior Difficulty →			
		Identify	*Produce (in writing)*		
		A. *Accuracy* (% data) Materials: target unit and 3 distractors	B. *Accuracy* (% data) Materials: flash cards or untimed probe sheet	C. *Mastery* (rate data) Materials: probe sheet	D. *Automatic* (rate or % data) Materials: assignments from textbook, content area exercises, or published test

Addition

Example		A	B	C	D
8742 + 968	10. Three or more digits to three or more digits with or without regrouping	10a. no test	10b. CAP 98% or better	10c. CAP undetermined	10d. CAP 100%
23 +87	9. Two digits to two digits with regrouping	9a. no test	9b. CAP 100%	9c. CAP 60 digits correct 0 errors	9d. CAP 100%
23 +23	8. Two digits to two digits without regrouping	8a. no test	8b. CAP 100%	8c. CAP 80 digits correct 0 errors	8d. CAP 100%
23 + 9	7. Two digits to one digit with regrouping	7a. no test	7b. CAP 100%	7c. CAP 70 digits correct 0 errors	7d. CAP 100%
23 + 2	6. Two digits to one digit without regrouping	6a. CAP 100%	6b. CAP 100%	6c. CAP 80 digits correct 0 errors	6d. CAP 100%
3 4 +2	5. Three or more single digits in a column	5a. CAP 100%	5b. CAP 100%	5c. CAP undetermined	5d. CAP 100%
2 +0	4. Zero and one as addends	4a. CAP 100%	4b. CAP 100%	4c. CAP 40 problems correct 0 errors	4d. CAP 100%
2 +2	3. Addition facts 1-20	3a. CAP 100%	3b. CAP 100%	3c. CAP 40 problems correct 0 errors	3d. CAP 100%
+1 =	2. Addition symbols and notation	2a. CAP 100%	2b. CAP 100%	2c. no test	2d. CAP 100%
	1. Combines sets	1a. CAP 100%	1b. CAP 100%	1c. CAP undetermined	1d. CAP 100%

TABLE C.2
(continued)

A. Numbers

| | Behavior Difficulty → | | | |
| | Identify | Produce (in writing) | | |
	A. *Accuracy* (% data) Materials: target unit and 3 distractors	B. *Accuracy* (% data) Materials: flash cards or untimed probe sheet	C. *Mastery* (rate data) Materials: probe sheet	D. *Automatic* (rate or % data) Materials: assignments from textbook, content area exercises, or published test
18. Write digits	18a. no test	18b. CAP 100%	18c. CAP 100 correct 0 errors	18d. CAP 100%
17. Count unordered objects, events, or characteristics	17a. no test	17b. CAP 100%	17c. CAP undetermined	17d. CAP 100%
16. Count ordered objects	16a. no test	16b. CAP 100%	16c. CAP undetermined	16d. CAP 100%
15. Rote count (oral) from one number to another (forward and backward)	15a. no test	15b. CAP 100%	15c. CAP ½ (.5) seconds for each number	15d. CAP 100%
14. Determine the number of ones, tens, and hundreds in a numeral (greater than 100)	14a. CAP 100%	14b. CAP 100%	14c. CAP undetermined	14d. CAP 100%
13. Put three numerals in sequence (10 or greater)	13a. CAP 100%	13b. CAP 100%	13c. CAP 50 correct 0 errors	13d. CAP 100%
12. Determine the number of ones and tens in a numeral (1-100)	12a. CAP 100%	12b. CAP 100%	12c. CAP 5 seconds per trial 10 out of 10 trials correct	12d. CAP 100%
11. Put three numerals in sequence (10 or greater)	11a. CAP 100%	11b. CAP 100%	11c. CAP 50 correct 0 errors	11d. CAP 100%
10. Recite numerals (10 or greater)	10a. CAP 100%	10b. CAP 100%	10c. CAP 100 correct 0 errors	10d. CAP 100%

TABLE C.2
(continued)

A. Numbers

| | Behavior Difficulty → | | | |
| | Identify | | Produce (in writing) | |
	A. *Accuracy* (% data) Materials: target unit and 3 distractors	B. *Accuracy* (% data) Materials: flash cards or untimed probe sheet	C. *Mastery* (rate data) Materials: probe sheet	D. *Automatic* (rate or % data) Materials: assignments from textbook, content area exercises, or published test
9. Match, select, and read numerals (10 or greater)	9a. CAP 100%	9b. CAP 100%	9c. CAP undetermined	9d. CAP 100%
8. Numerals in sequence (0-10)	8a. CAP 100%	8b. CAP 100%	8c. CAP ½ (.5) seconds per trial 10 out of 10 trials correct	8d. CAP 100%
7. Match sets to numerals (0-10)	7a. CAP 100%	7b. CAP 100%	7c. CAP 40 correct 0 errors	7d. CAP 100%
6. Count subsets (0-10)	6a. CAP 100%	6b. CAP 100%	6c. CAP undetermined	6d. CAP 100%
5. Count tangible objects (0-10)	5a. CAP 100%	5b. CAP 100%	5c. CAP undetermined	5d. CAP 100%
4. Match, select, and read numerals (0-10)	4a. CAP 100%	4b. CAP 100%	4c. CAP undetermined	4d. CAP 100%
3. Recite numerals (0-10)	3a. no test	3b. CAP 100%	3c. CAP 3 seconds 0 errors	3d. CAP 100%
2. Determine equal and unequal sets	2a. CAP 100%	2b. CAP 100%	2c. CAP undetermined	2d. CAP 100%
1. Determine which sets have the most (least)	1a. CAP 100%	1b. CAP 100%	1c. CAP undetermined	1d. CAP 100%

NOTES: 1. All rate data are in "movements per minute," although 1-minute timings are *not* always necessary.
2. Movements may be defined as *digits* (e.g., 22 + 23 = 45, giving a score of *2* correct) or as problems (e.g., 2½ + 2¾ = 5¼, giving a score of *1* correct).
3. All mixed numbers and fractions used to determine CAP for subtable C used the digits 0–9. Therefore, a problem with 9⅝ might have been used but 9⁵⁷/₈₂ would *not* have been used.

Appendix D

Study Question Answers

Chapter 1
1. See Glossary.
2. d
3. a
4. d
5. c
6. b
7. The way you think about special students and academic/social problems will determine the results of your evaluation.
8. (a) 1
   (b) 2

Chapter 2
1. See Glossary.
2. c
3. a
4. d
5. b
6. b, d
7. (a) Within words
   (b) While dressing
   (c) Internal observations of class
   (d) Using real money
8. Fewer items are needed for highly consolidated domains.
9. Testing is only a way to collect behavior. Evaluation involves thought, comparison, and judgment.

Chapter 3
1. See Glossary.
2. c
3. a
4. c
5. b
6. d
7. c
8. Behavior—Write
   Content—Commas
   Conditions—In sentence containing a series or list
   Criteria—100% accuracy
9. (a) 2
   (b) 2
   (c) 2

Chapter 4
1. See Glossary.
2. b
3. c
4. a
5. (a) Norm-referenced test
   (b) Criterion-referenced test
   (c) Criterion-referenced test
   (d) Norm-referenced test
   (e) Norm-referenced test
   (f) Criterion-referenced test
   (g) Norm-referenced test
   (h) Criterion-referenced test
6. a
7. c
8. d
9. c
10. Does it measure the content you wish to teach?
    Does it have behavioral criteria?
    Are the response domains appropriate?
    Is it keyed to objectives?
    Do the items resemble real life situations? (fidelity)

Chapter 5
1. See Glossary.
2. b
3. b
4. (a) Consult the research to see if there are existing criteria.
   (b) See how well kids who have mastered the skill can do it.
   (c) Ask an expert.
5. a
6. (a) Ask the student to explain how he works.
   (b) Do an error analysis.
   (c) Use strategy-specific items.
7. d
8. Students will attain different levels of proficiency. For example, a student in a third-grade classroom where the CAP on a skill is 75% accuracy will not be as proficient as a student in a classroom where the CAP is 100% accuracy. Which student would you rather have in your fourth-grade class?

Chapter 6

1. See Glossary.
2. b
3. d
4. d
5. d
   c
   a
   b
6. d
7. Task and instruction

   The task and the instruction are things which we can alter to produce learning. There isn't much we can do as teachers to change the characteristics of the student. Emphasizing student characteristics takes the responsibility for learning off the teacher and places it on the student. From this we get ideas such as, "If he's not learning, it's because he has a short-term memory problem," rather than, "If he's not learning, I'd better change the way I teach."

Chapter 7

1. See Glossary.
2. b
3. a, b, d
4. e
5. (a) Overt behavior
   (b) Overt behavior
   (c) Covert behavior
   (d) Status
   (e) Covert behavior
6. c
7. a
8. (a) 1. The student does not know the strategy for doing long division.
   2. The student does not know his subtraction facts 0–20.
   3. The student does not know his division facts 0–20.
   (b) 1. The student does not know that she should not be out of her seat.
   2. The student knows she should not be out of her seat, but is not able to *decide*

to stay in her seat at the automatic level (in the presence of classroom distractors).

3. The student does not want to stay in her seat.
(c) The student does not know *igh*.
(d) The student thinks that the problem is solved as a column addition problem; he has added 6, 2, and 4.

Chapter 8

1. See Glossary.
2. a
3. c
4. b
5. c
6. c
7. a
8. The probe should contain words with *ea* in them. Twenty percent of the words could be "noninstances," that is, words without *ea*. There should be at least 90 words.

Chapter 9

1. b
2. a
3. c
4. d
5. Discontinue testing; continue to monitor.
6. Check speed or rate of decoding.
7. (a) You could supply the background information and look for a change in comprehension.
   (b) You could sample comprehension in other content areas. If the student did well with other content, you could assume that background information was missing for the passage used in the survey-level test, but that when background information is known, the student comprehends.
8. Check vocabulary. Sample words in context and in isolation if necessary. Use tests 1-4 described on pages 184–187 as needed.

9. Check language.
10. To check strategy use, construct a strategy checklist like the one shown in Figure 9.6. Interview the student while he reads. Rate your estimate of his strategy use and plan interventions accordingly.

Chapter 10

1. Teach the student decoding rules that consistently work (don't have a lot of exceptions) and that the student doesn't already know.
2. It shouldn't. She still needs to be taught to read.
3. The evidence suggests that low-performing students spend *less* time reading than regular students. Under these circumstances, it is unlikely that remedial students will ever catch up.
4. You should sample both.
5. Have the student read a passage that is close to your best estimate of her reading level. See how many words she can correctly read in one minute. Note the presence of errors and their type. A passage that the student reads with 80–85% accuracy will yield the best sample of errors.
6. Administer a timed rereading. If the student's rate on the rereading is at least 20% higher than his initial rate, he can probably benefit from fluency instruction.
7. Emphasize accuracy and teach higher-level strategies.
8. Monitor decoding and emphasize fluency.
9. To determine whether the student is making use of context to decode.
10. Collect a sample of his errors and categorize them according to decoding content. Recognize error patterns and teach the content that the student doesn't know.

Chapter 11

1. (a) $6 \times 4 = 24$
   (b) "First I add the ones, then I add the tens."

(c) "When I subtract, my answer should be smaller than the number I started with."
2. a
3. Story problems are just a particular kind of math problem which calls for a specific set of problem-solving behaviors. Teaching problem solving involves instructing in a set of general strategies that apply in many situations; for example, checking work, deciding what information is needed, reinforcing yourself for doing a good job, etc.

4.

Critical	*Noncritical*
1. Represents part of a whole	1. Size
2. Has a numerator and a denominator	2. The style in which the numbers are written
3. Is a ratio statement	3. The length of the line between the numerator and the denominator.
4. Represents division	

5. Unless tests sample strategic behaviors, it is impossible to get information about a student's strategy usage. Items that sample strategies should require the student to decide which *procedure* to employ, rather than to produce the correct answer.
6. (a) The student does not know facts to the automatic level.
   (b) The student writes slowly.
7. Move on to the next objective.
8. (a) The student subtracted (selected the wrong operation).
   (b) The student did not line up the decimal point correctly.
   (c) The student subtracted 1 from 8 in the ones column.
   (d) The student guessed.
9. Develop a specific-level test that measures this skill. If the assumed cause is verified (the student can't do it on the specific-level test either), then it should become an instructional objective.
10. Tests that sample the subtasks and strategies needed for application.

Chapter 12

1. a
2. d
3. b
4. a
5. To collect a language sample follow the steps outlined on pages 285–290. Collect a 50-sentence sample. Be sure to structure a situation in which you can elicit a representative sample of the student's language. Analyze the sample, note and categorize errors, and decide on areas of concern for specific-level testing.
6. If you suspect that the classroom environment is inhibiting language, observe in the classroom. Use a checklist like the one shown in Figure 12.2. Be prepared to consult with the classroom teacher to help her increase opportunities for communication if this is the source of the problem.
7. Develop a test to sample classes of words the student does not seem to know based on your analysis of errors and omissions. Use the guidelines provided in Specific-Level Procedure 4 on page 298.
8. Check the mean length of utterance to determine if the amount of language is adequate. Follow guidelines in Specific-Level Procedure 2, outlined on page 297.
9. Develop a probe which will require the student to initiate and produce the structures for which there is a concern. Follow the guidelines for Specific-Level Procedure 3 outlined on pages 297–298.
10. Observe or sample language in additional settings or probe pragmatics (the concerns mentioned by the teacher are in the domain of pragmatics). Follow Specific-Level Procedure 5 outlined on page 298 if you probe pragmatics. Follow language-sampling procedure if you collect a sample in a different setting.

Chapter 13

1. a
2. The student compares the product to his plan when he reviews. If his product does not match his plan, he either revises his product, modifies his plan, or both.
3. They are not the most important aspects; however, they are the aspects that teachers emphasize most.
4. Teach it as a process.
5. ˆMy ‸ friend ‸has ˆ a ˆ poodle.ˆ ˆHe ‸ soft ˆ and ˆ pretty.ˆ
   Corrects: 8/11
   Incorrects: 3/11
6. Count the number of words he can write in a given time period.
7. Yesterday we went to look at some land. (1 T-unit) While we were there, we saw a rattlesnake, which did not bite us. (1 T-unit) We went away from there and we left it alone. (2 T-units)
   4 T-units, 31 words, Mean T-unit length: 7.75 words per T-unit.
8. Vocabulary and meaning
9. If the student does not plan, review, or revise his work appropriately, he needs instruction in the process.
10. Check whether the student:
    (a) employs phonic generalization;
    (b) recognizes when a word is misspelled;
    (c) has a problem spelling in the context of another task; or
    (d) uses morphographs correctly.

Chapter 14

1. Control brings a student's behavior into alignment with a particular setting whereas therapy addresses behavior across settings and times.
2. Relaxation
   Problem solving
   Self-monitoring/evaluation
   Recognition of target thoughts and behavior
   Knowledge of cognitive/behavioral change techniques
3. c
4. (a) Type 1: Knowledge and skill, e.g., reading skill, or knowledge of social situations.
   (b) Type 2: Perceptions and beliefs, e.g., viewing reading as meaningless skill, or enjoying getting into fights.
5. A maladaptive behavior is one which the teacher wishes to get rid of; the target behavior is one the teacher wishes to promote. The two should be mutually exclusive so that build-

ing the target decreases the maladaptive. Both need to be recognized in order to assure that the behavior change is worthwhile and appropriately focused.

6. d, e

7. By having a student sort words or pictures according to different directions. For example, "Put the ones your teacher likes the most first or put the ones you like the most first."

8. Thoughts may not cause feelings.

9. By making a problem seem more important than it should, therefore making the risk seem higher.

10. Change the intervention.

Chapter 15

1. *ATI*
   (a) Predict from aptitude measures
   (b) One-shot testing
   (c) Norm-referenced aptitude test scores

   DBPM
   (a) Recognize effective treatments
   (b) Repeated measures
   (c) Criterion-referenced skill tests

2. A performance score says where a student is; progress scores tell where he is going.

3. (a) Aim rate
   (b) Aim date

4. a

5. Minimum 'celeration, objective, or aim line.

6. 3, mid, date

7. To be correct the data should look like this.

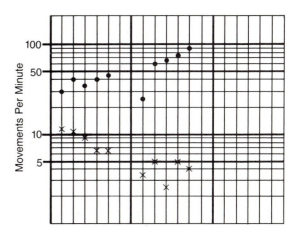

8. Every two weeks, or whenever the data falls below the aim line for three consecutive days.

9. Delivery involves teacher actions such as pace, questioning, correction, and feedback. Formats refer to *lesson design*. These include acquisition, fluency, and generalization/maintenance.

10. By reminding them that it is student time we are trying to save, and that time spent in DBPM increases the learning rates of the student.

References

Algozzine, B., Herr, D., & Eaves, R. (1976). Modification of biases held by teacher trainees toward the disturbingness of child behaviors. *Journal of Educational Research, 69,* 261-264.

Allington, R. L. (1983). The reading instruction provided readers of differing reading abilities. *The Elementary School Journal, 83,* 548-559.

American Psychological Association. (1983). *Standards for educational and psychological tests.* Washington, DC: Author.

American Speech-Language-Hearing Association. (1986). Personal communication from Director of Professional Practices Division, C. A. Kamara.

Anastasi, A. (1982). *Psychological testing* (5th ed.). New York: Macmillan.

Anderson, R. C., & Armbruster, B. (1984). Content area textbooks. In R. C. Anderson, J. Osborn, & R. Tierney (Eds.), *Learning to read in American schools* (pp. 217-226). Hillsdale, NJ: Erlbaum.

Anderson, R. C., Hiebert, E. H., Scott, J. A., & Wilkinson, I. A. G. (1985). *Becoming a nation of readers.* Washington, DC: U.S. Department of Education, National Institute of Education.

Anderson, R. C., Osborn, J., & Tierney, R. (1984). *Learning to read in American schools: Basal readers and content texts.* Hillsdale, NJ: Erlbaum.

Anderson, R. C., & Pearson, P. D. (1984). A schema-theoretic view of basic processes in reading comprehension. In D. Pearson, R. Barr, M. Kamil, & P. Mosenthal (Eds.), *The handbook of reading research.* New York: Longman.

Applebee, A. N. (1981). *Writing in the secondary schools.* Urbana, IL: National Council of Teachers of English.

Archer, A. (1986). Personal communication. San Diego, CA.

Arlin, M. (1979). Teacher transitions can disrupt time flow in classrooms. *American Educational Research Journal, 16,* 42-56.

Armbruster, B. (1984a). Commentary. In R. J. Tierney & M. Leys, *What is the value of connecting reading and writing?* Reading Education Report No. 55. Urbana-Champaign: University of Illinois.

Armbruster, B. (1984b). The problem of "inconsiderate text." In G. G. Duffy, L. R. Roewhler, & J. Mason (Eds.), *Comprehension instruction perspectives and suggestions* (pp. 202-217). New York: Longman.

Arter, J. A., & Jenkins, J. R. (1979). Differential diagnosis—prescriptive teaching: A critical appraisal. *Review of Educational Research, 49,* 517-555.

Ashlock, R. B. (1982). *Error patterns in computation: A semi-programmed approach* (3rd ed.). Columbus, OH: Merrill.

Baker, L., & Brown, A. (1984). Metacognitive skills and reading. In P. D. Pearson (Ed.), *The handbook of reading research* (pp. 363-364). New York: Longman.

Baldauf, R. B. (1982). The effects of guessing and item dependence on the reliability and validity of recognition based cloze tests. *Educational and Psychological Measurement, 42,* 855-867.

Barbe, W. (1974). Instruction in handwriting: A new look. *Childhood Education, 50,* 207-209.

Barrett, M., Huisingh, R., Jorgensen, C., & Zachman, L. (1983). *Teaching vocabulary, Volume 1, Grades K-4*. Moline, IL: LinguiSystems.

Bateman, B. D. (1971). *Essentials of teaching*. Sioux Falls, SD: Dimension.

Baumeister, A. A., & Muma, J. R. (1975). On defining mental retardation. *The Journal of Special Education, 9*, 293-306.

Beck, I. L., McKeown, M. G., & McCaslin, E. S. (1983). Vocabulary development: All contexts are not created equal. *The Elementary School Journal, 83*, 178-181.

Beck, I. L., Perfetti, C. A., & McKeown, M. G. (1982). Effects of long-term vocabulary instruction on lexical access and reading comprehension. *Journal of Educational Psychology, 74*, 506-521.

Beck, R., & Albrecht, P. (1981). Great Falls Precision Teaching Project, Great Falls, MT.

Becker, W. C., & Englemann, S. (1976). *Teaching 3: Evaluation of instruction*. Chicago: Science Research Associates.

Bensoussan, M., & Ramraz, R. (1984). Testing EFL reading comprehension using a multiple-choice rational cloze. *The Modern Language Journal, 68*, 230-239.

Bereiter, C. (1985). Toward a solution of the learning paradox. *Review of Educational Research, 55*, 201-226.

Bereiter, C., & Scardamalia, M. (1984). Learning about writing from reading. *Written Communication, 1*, 163-188.

Berk, R. A. (1979). The relative merits of item transformations and the cloze procedure for the measurement of reading comprehension. *The Reading Teacher, 11*, 129-138.

Berk, R. A. (1980). A consumers' guide to criterion-referenced test reliability. *Journal of Educational Measurement, 17*, 323-349.

Berk, R. A. (1986). A consumers' guide to setting performance standards on criterion-referenced tests. *Review of Educational Research, 17*, 137-172.

Berliner, D. C. (1984). The half-full glass: A review of research on teaching. In P. L. Hosford (Ed.), *Using what we know about teaching*. Alexandria, VA: Association for Supervision and Curriculum Development.

Berliner, D. C., & Cahen, L. S. (1973). Trait treatment interaction and learning. In F. N. Kerlinger (Ed.), *Review of research in education* (Vol. 1). Ithaca, NY: Peacock.

Bernstein, B. (1970). A sociolinguistic approach to socialization: With some reference to educability. In F. Williams (Ed.), *Language and poverty: Perspectives on a theme*. Chicago: Markham.

Berquam, E. (1986, April). *Skip it!* Port Angeles, WA.

Bickel, W. E., & Bickel, D. D. (1986). Effective schools, classrooms, and instruction: Implications for special education. *Exceptional Children, 52*, 489-500.

Biemiller, A. (1978). Relationships between oral reading rates for letters, words, and simple text in the development of reading achievement. *Reading Research Quarterly, 13*, 223-253.

Bitter, G. G., Englehart, J. M., & Wiebe, J. (1977). *One step at a time*. St. Paul: EMC Corp.

Blanton, R. L. (1975). Historical perspectives on classification of mental retardation. In N. Hobbs (Ed.), *Issues in the classification of children*. San Francisco: Jossey-Bass.

Bloom, B. S. (1980). The new direction in education research: Alterable variables. *Phi Delta Kappan, 61*, 382-385.

Bloom, B. S. (1984, May). The search for methods of group instruction as effective as one-to-one tutoring. *Educational Leadership, 41*, 4-17.

Bloom, B. S., Hastings, J. T., & Madaus, G. F. (1971). *Handbook on formative and summative evaluation of student learning*. New York: McGraw-Hill.

Bloom, B. S., Madaus, G.F., & Hastings, J. T. (1981). *Evaluation to improve learning*. New York: McGraw-Hill.

Boulding, K. (1972). The schooling industry as a possible pathological section of the American economy. *Review of Educational Research, 42*, 129-143.

Bowen, E. (1984, December 3). A debate over dumbing down. *Time, 124*, 68.

Bower, E. M. (1972). Education as a humanizing process and its relationship to other humanizing processes. In S. E. Golann & C. Eisdorfer (Eds.), *Handbook of community mental health*. Englewood Cliffs, NJ: Prentice-Hall.

Bracht, G. H. (1970a). Experimental factors relating to aptitude treatment interactions. *Review of Educational Research, 40*, 627-645.

Bracht, G. H. (1970b). The relationship of treatment tasks, personological variables, and dependent variables to aptitude treatment interactions (Doctoral dissertation, University of Colorado, 1969). *Dissertation Abstracts International, 30*, 4268A. (University Microfilms No. 70-5820, 215).

Bradley-Johnson, S., Graham, D. P., & Johnson, M. (1986). Token reinforcement on WISC-R performance for white, low-socio-economic, upper and lower elementary-school-age students. *Journal of School Psychology, 24,* 73-79.

Brennan, R. L. (1972). A generalized upper-lower item discrimination index. *Educational and Psychological Measurement, 32,* 280-303.

Bridge, C. A., & Hiebert, E. H. (1985). A comparison of classroom teachers' perceptions of their writing instruction and textbook recommendations on writing practices. *The Elementary School Journal, 86,* 155-172.

Britton, J. (1978). The composing processes and the functions of writing. In C. R. Cooper & L. Odell (Eds.), *Research on composing: Points of departure* (pp. 13-28). Urbana, IL: National Council of Teachers of English.

Brophy, J. E. (1983). Classroom organization and management. *The Elementary School Journal, 83,* 265-285.

Brown, A. L., & Bryant, B. R. (1984). Critical reviews of three individually administered achievement tests. *Remedial and Special Education, 5,* 53-60.

Bruning, J. L., & Kintz, B. L. (1968). *Computational handbook of statistics.* Glenview, IL: Scott Foresman.

Brunswick, E. (1943). Organismic achievement and environmental probability. *Psychological Review, 50,* 255-272. As cited in Cole, M., Hood, L., & McDermott, R. P. Concepts of ecological validity. *Newsletter of the Institute for Comparative Human Development, 2,* 34-37.

Campbell, N. R. (1940). *Final report, Committee of the British Association for Advancement of Science on the problem of measurement.* London: British Association.

Carnine, D. W. (1981). Reducing training problems associated with visually and auditorily similar correspondences. *Journal of Learning Disabilities, 14,* 276-279.

Carnine, D. W. (1983). Direct instruction: In search of instructional solutions for educational problems. In D. Carnine, D. Elkind, A. D. Hendrickson, D. Meichenbaum, R. L. Seiben, & F. Smith (Eds.), *Interdisciplinary voices in learning disabilities and remedial education* (pp. 1-66). Austin, TX: Pro-Ed.

Carnine, D., & Silbert, J. (1979). *Direct instruction reading.* Columbus, OH: Merrill.

Carpenter, T. P., Matthews, W., Lindquist, M. M., & Silver, E. A. (1984). Achievement in mathematics: Results from the national assessment. *The Elementary School Journal, 84,* 485-495.

Carroll, J. B. (1963). A model for school learning. *Teacher's College Record, 64,* 723-733.

Carver, R. P. (1982). Optimal rate of reading prose. *Reading Research Quarterly, 18,* 56-88.

Carver, R. P. (1983). Is reading rate constant or flexible? *Reading Research Quarterly, 18,* 190-215.

Chas, M. I., & Woodson, E. (1974). The issue of item and test variance for criterion-referenced tests. *Journal of Educational Measurement, 11,* 63-64.

Chi, M. T. H., & Glaser, R. (1985). Problem-solving ability. In R. J. Sternberg (Ed.), *Human abilities: An information-processing approach.* New York: W.H. Freeman.

Choate, J. S., Bennett, T. Z., Enright, B. E., Miller, L. J., Poteet, J. A., & Rakes, T. A. (1987). *Assessing and programming basic curriculum skills.* Boston: Allyn & Bacon.

Christensen, F. (1968). The problem of defining a mature style. *English Journal, 57,* 572-579.

Cole, L. (1956). Reflections on the teaching of handwriting. *Elementary School Journal, 57,* 95-99.

Crehan, K. D. (1974). Item analysis for teacher-made mastery tests. *Journal of Educational Measurement, 4,* 255-262.

Cromwell, R. L., Blashfield, R. K., & Strauss, J. S. (1975). Criteria for classification systems. In N. Hobbs (Ed.), *Issues in the classification of children* (Vol. 1, pp. 4-25). San Francisco: Jossey-Bass.

Cronbach, L. J. (1957). The two disciplines of scientific psychology. *American Psychologist, 12,* 671-684.

Cronbach, L. J. (1967). How can instruction be adapted to individual differences? In R. M. Gagné (Ed.), *Learning and individual differences* (pp. 353-379). Columbus, OH: Merrill.

Cronbach, L. J., & Snow, R. E. (1969). *Final report: Individual differences in learning ability as a function of instructional variables.* Stanford, CA: Stanford University.

Cummins, J. (1986). Empowering minority students: A framework for interaction. *Harvard Educational Review, 56,* 18-36.

Cziko, G. A. (1983). Commentary: Another response to Shannahan, Kamil, and Tobin: Further reasons to keep the cloze case open. *Reading Research Quarterly, 18,* 361-365.

Danks, J. H. (1982, September). *Text comprehension processes in reading: Final report.* (NIE Grant Research Rep.). Kent, OH: Kent State University.

Das, J. P., Kirby, J. R., & Jarman, R. F. (1979). *Simultaneous and successive cognitive processes*. New York: Academic Press.

Davies, I. K. (1973). *Competency based learning: Technology, management and design*. New York: McGraw-Hill.

Deno, E. (1971). Some reflections on the use and interpretation of tests for teachers. *Focus on Exceptional Children, 2*, 1-11.

Deno, S. L., & Mirkin, P. K. (1977). *Data based program modification: A manual*. Reston, VA: The Council for Exceptional Children.

Derry, S. J., & Murphy, D. A. (1986). Designing systems that train learning ability: From theory to practice. *Review of Educational Research, 56*, 1-39.

DeSanti, R. J., & Sullivan, V. G. (1984). Inter-rater reliability of the cloze reading inventory as a qualitative measure of reading comprehension. *Reading Psychology: An International Quarterly, 5*, 203-208.

Deshler, D. (1985, June). Presentation. Kyrene School District, Tempe, AZ.

Deverell, A. F. (1971). The learnable features of English orthography. In B. B. Bateman (Ed.), *Learning disorders* (Vol. 4) (pp. 129-160). Seattle: Special Child Publications.

Dick, W., & Hagerty, N. (1971). *Topics in measurement: Reliability and validity*. New York: McGraw-Hill.

Diederich, P. B. (1967). Pinhead statistics. In F. T. Wilhelms (Ed.), *Evaluation as feedback and guide* (pp. 260-277). Washington, DC: National Education Association.

Dinsmore, J. A., & Isaacson, D. K. (1986). Tactics for teaching dyslexic students. *Academic Therapy, 21*, 293-300.

Dixon, R. & Englemann, S. (1979). *Corrective spelling through morphographs: Teacher's presentation book*. Chicago: Science Research.

Dixon, R., Englemann, S., & Olen, L. (1981). *Spelling mastery: A direct instruction series*. Chicago: Science Research.

Dunn, L. M. (1968). Special education for the mildly retarded: Is much of it justified? *Exceptional Children, 35*, 5-22.

Dunn, R. (1983). Learning style and its relation to exceptionality at both ends of the spectrum. *Exceptional Children, 49*, 496-506.

Dunn, R., Dunn, K., & Price, G. E. (1981). Learning styles: Research vs. opinion. *Phi Delta Kappan, 62*, 645-646.

Durkin, D. (1978-1979). What classroom observations reveal about reading comprehension instruction. *Reading Research Quarterly, 14*, 481-533.

Eaton, M. D. (1978). Data decisions and evaluation. In N. G. Haring, T. C. Lovitt, M. D. Eaton, & C. L. Hansen (Eds.), *The fourth R: Research in the classroom* (pp. 167-190). Columbus, OH: Merrill.

Eckhoff, B. (1983). How reading affects children's writing. *Language Arts, 60*, 607-616.

Eeds, M. (1976). TOBLA: Test of Blending Ability. Edina, MN: Burgess International.

Eeds, M. A. (1985). Bookwords: Using a beginning word list of high frequency words from children's literature K-3. *The Reading Teacher, 38*, 418-423.

Ehri, L. C., & Wilce, L. C. (1985). Movement into reading: Is the first stage of the printed word learning visual or phonetic? *Reading Research Quarterly, 20*, 163-179.

Eisner, E. W. (1982). *Cognition and curriculum*. New York: Longman.

Elliott, S. N. (1986). Children's ratings of the acceptability of classroom interventions for misbehavior: Findings and methodological considerations. *Journal of School Psychology, 24*, 23-35.

Ellis, A. (Ed.). (1971). *Growth through reason: Verbatim cases in rational-emotive therapy*. Palo Alto, CA: Science and Behavior Books.

Engelhardt, J. M. (1977). Analysis of children's computational errors: A qualitative approach. *British Journal of Educational Psychology, 47*, 149-154.

Englemann, S. (1979, August). Direct instruction workshop. Eugene, OR.

Englemann, S., & Carnine, D. (1982). *Theory of instruction*. New York: Irvington.

Enright, B. E. (1983). Enright Diagnostic Inventory of Basic Arithmetic Skills. North Billerica, MA: Curriculum Associates.

Enright, B. E. (1987). ENRIGHT SOLVE Action Problem Solving Series. North Billerica, MA: Curriculum Associates.

Farr, R. C. (1969). *Reading: What can be measured?* Newark, DE: International Reading Association Research Fund.

Fernald, G. M. (1943). *Remedial techniques in basic school subjects*. New York: McGraw-Hill.

Fielding, L. G., Wilson, P. T., & Anderson, R. C. (1985). *A new focus on free reading: The role of trade books in reading instruction*. (Working paper). Urbana-Champaign: University of Illinois, Center for the Study of Reading.

Forness, S. R., & Kavale, K. A. (1983). Remediation of reading disabilities part one: Issues and concepts. *Journal of Learning Disabilities, 11,* 141-152.

Frankenberger, W., & Harper, J. (1986). Participation of psychologists in multidisciplinary team evaluations. *Psychology in the Schools, 23,* 53-58.

Frederiksen, N. (1962). Proficiency tests for training evaluation. In R. Glaser (Ed.), *Training research and education.* Pittsburgh: University of Pittsburgh Press.

Frederiksen, N. (1984). Implications of cognitive theory for instruction in problem solving. *Review of Educational Research, 54,* 363-407.

Frederiksen, N. (1986). Toward a broader concept of human intelligence. *American Psychologist, 41,* 445-452.

French, L. A. (1986). MR testing and evaluation: New dimensions and old concerns. *Psychology in the Schools, 23,* 64-76.

Frose, V., & Straw, S. B. (1981). *Research in the language arts: Language and schooling.* Baltimore: University Park Press.

Fuchs, D., Fuchs, L. S., Dailey, A. M., & Power, M. H. (1985). The effect of examiner's personal familiarity and professional experience on handicapped children's test performance. *Journal of Educational Research, 78,* 141-146.

Fuchs, L. S., Deno, S. L., & Mirkin, P. K. (1984). The effects of frequent curriculum-based evaluation on pedagogy, student achievement, and student awareness of learning. *American Educational Research Journal, 21,* 449-460.

Fuchs, L. S., Deno, S. L., & Mirkin, P. K. (1985). Data-based program modification: A continuous evaluation system with computer software to facilitate instruction. *Journal of Special Education, 6,* 50-57.

Fuchs, L. S., & Fuchs, D. (1986). Effects of systematic formative evaluation: A meta-analysis. *Exceptional Children, 53,* 199-208.

Gaffney, J., & McCloone, B. (1984, March). *Prior knowledge assessment procedures.* Workshop module presented at the Arizona Council for Exceptional Children, Tucson, AZ.

Gagné, R. M. (1985). *The conditions of learning and theory of instruction* (4th ed.). New York: Holt, Rinehart & Winston.

Galagan, J. E. (1985). Psychoeducational testing: Turn out the lights, the party's over. *Exceptional Children, 52,* 288-299.

Galton, F. (1883). *Inquiries into human faculty and its development.* London: J. M. Dent & Co.

Garnett, K. (1986). Telling tales: Narratives and learning disabled students. *Topics in Language Disorders, 6,* 44-56.

Gerber, A., & Bryen, D. N. (1981). *Language and learning disabilities.* Baltimore: University Park Press.

Gersten, R., Woodward, J., & Darch, C. (1986). Direct instruction: A research-based approach to curriculum design and teaching. *Exceptional Children, 53,* 17-31.

Geva, E., & Tierney, R. J. (1984). *Text engineering: The influence of manipulated compare contrast selections.* Paper presented at the annual meeting of the American Educational Research Association, New Orleans.

Glaser, R. (1972). Individuals and learning: The new aptitudes. *Educational Researcher, 1,* 5-12.

Glass, G. G. (1971). Perceptual conditioning for decoding: Rationale and method. In B. B. Bateman (Ed.), *Learning disorders* (Vol. 4) (pp. 75-108). Seattle: Special Child Publications.

Glass, G. V. (1974). Teacher effectiveness. In H. J. Walberg (Ed.), *Evaluating educational performance.* Berkeley, CA: McCutchan Publishing.

Glass, G. V. (1977). Integrating findings: The meta-analysis of research. In L. S. Shulman (Ed.), *Review of Educational Research, 5,* 351-379.

Glass, G. V. (1983). Effectiveness of special education. *Policy Studies Review, 2,* 65-78.

Goodman, L. (1985). The effective schools movement and special education. *Teaching Exceptional Children, 17,* 102-105.

Gronlund, N. E. (1973). *Preparing criterion-referenced tests for classroom instruction.* New York: Macmillan.

Grouws, D. A. (1985). The teacher and classroom instruction: Neglected themes in problem solving research. In E. A. Silver (Ed.), *Teaching and learning mathematical problem solving: Multiple research perspectives* (pp. 295-308). Hillsdale, NJ: Erlbaum.

Guilford, J. P. (1965). *Fundamental statistics in psychology and education.* New York: McGraw-Hill.

Guthrie, J. T. (1973). Reading comprehension and syntactic responses in good and poor readers. *Journal of Educational Psychology, 65,* 294-299.

Haddock, M. A. (1976). Effects of an auditory and an auditory-visual method of blending instruction on the ability of prereaders to decode synthetic words. *Journal of Educational Psychology, 68,* 825-831.

Haddock, M. A. (1978). Teaching blending in beginning reading instruction is important. *The Reading Teacher, 31*, 654-658.

Haertel, E. (1985). Construct validity and criterion-referenced testing. *Review of Educational Research, 55*, 23-46.

Hagerty, G. J., & Abramson, M. (1987). Impediments to implementing national policy change for mildly handicapped students. *Exceptional Children, 53*, 315-323.

Hallahan, D. P., & Kauffman, J. M. (1982). *Exceptional children: Introduction to special education.* Englewood Cliffs, NJ: Prentice Hall.

Hallahan, D. P., & Kauffman, J. M. (1986). *Exceptional children* (3rd ed.). Englewood Cliffs, NJ: Prentice Hall.

Hambleton, R. K., & Novik, M. (1973). Toward an integration of theory and method for criterion-referenced tests. *Journal of Educational Measurement, 10*, 159-170.

Hammill, D. D., & Larsen, S. C. (1974a). The relationship of selected auditory perceptual skills and reading ability. *Journal of Learning Disabilities, 7*, 429-435.

Hammill, D. D., & Larsen, S. C. (1974b). The effectiveness of psycholinguistic training. *Exceptional Children, 41*, 5-14.

Hammill, D. D., & Larsen, S. C. (1978). The effectiveness of psycholinguistic training: A reaffirmation of position. *Exceptional Children, 44*, 402-414.

Hanna, P. R., & Moore, J. T. (1953). Spelling—From spoken word to written symbol. *Elementary School Journal, 53*, 329-337.

Hansen, C. (1978). Story retelling used with average and learning disabled readers as a measure of reading comprehension. *Learning Disability Quarterly, 1*, 65.

Haring, N. G., & Eaton, M. D. (1978). Systematic instructional procedures: An instructional hierarchy. In N. G. Haring, T. C. Lovitt, M. D. Eaton, & C. L. Hansen (Eds.), *The fourth R: Research in the classroom* (pp. 23-40). Columbus, OH: Merrill.

Haring, N. G., Liberty, K. A., & White, O. R. (1970-1980). Field initiated research studies of phases of learning and facilitating instructional events for the severely/profoundly handicapped. (Available from the U.S. Office of Special Education, Project No. 413CH60397A, Grant No. G007500593)

Haring, N. G., & Schiefelbusch, R. L. (Eds.). (1976). *Teaching special children.* New York: McGraw-Hill.

Hasselbring, T., & Hemlett, C. (1983). *Aimstar.* Portland, OR: ASIEP Education.

Haynes, M. C., & Jenkins, J. R. (1986). Reading instruction in special education resource rooms. *American Educational Research Journal, 23*, 161-190.

Heber, R., Garber, H., Harrington, S., Hoffman, C., & Falender, C. (1972). *Rehabilitation of families at high risk for mental retardation.* Progress report. Madison: University of Wisconsin, Rehabilitation Research and Training Center in Mental Retardation.

Heidbreder, E. (1961). *Seven psychologies.* New York: Appleton-Century-Crofts.

Heller, K. A. (1982). Effects of special education placement on educable mentally retarded children. In K. A. Heller, W. H. Holtzman, & S. Messick (Eds.), *Placing children in special education: A strategy for equity.* Washington, DC: National Academy Press.

Herbert, C. H. (1979). *Basic inventory of natural language.* San Bernardino, CA: C.H.E.C. Point Systems.

Hildreth, G. (1964). Manuscript writing after sixty years. In V. D. Anderson et al. (Eds.), *Readings in the language arts.* New York: MacMillan.

Hoephner, R. (1974). Published tests and the needs of educational accountability. *Educational and Psychological Measurement, 34*, 103-109.

Hoffer, K. (1983). Assessment and instruction of reading skills: Results with Mexican-American students. *Learning Disability Quarterly, 6*, 458-467.

Holdaway, D. (1979). *The foundations of literacy.* Sidney, Australia: Ashton Scholastic.

Hopper, R., & Naremore, R. C. (1978). *Children's speech: A practical introduction to communication development* (2nd ed.). New York: Harper & Row.

Hosseini, J., & Ferrell, W. R. (1982). Measuring metacognition in reading by detectability of cloze accuracy. *Journal of Reading Behavior, 14*, 263-274.

Howell, K. W. (1978). Using peers in drill type instruction. *Journal of Experimental Education, 46*, 52-56.

Howell, K. W. (1983). Task analysis and the characteristics of tasks. *Journal of Special Education Technology, 6*, 5-14. [Note: This article, which appeared in 1985, has a 1983 publication date.]

Howell, K. W. (1985). A task analytic approach to social skills. *Remedial and Special Education, 2*, 24-30.

Howell, K. W. (1986). Direct assessment of academic performance. *School Psychology Review, 15*, 324-335.

Howell, K. W., Kaplan, J. S., & O'Connell, C. Y. (1979). *Evaluating exceptional children: A task analysis approach.* Columbus, OH: Merrill.

Howell, K. W., & Kaplan, J. S. (1980). *Diagnosing basic skills: A handbook for deciding what to teach.* Columbus, OH: Merrill.

Howell, K. W., & McCollum-Gahley, J. (1986). Monitoring instruction. *Teaching Exceptional Children, 19,* 47-49.

Howell, K. W., Zucker, S. H., & Morehead, M. K. (1982). Multilevel Academic Skills Inventory: Math. San Antonio, TX: Psychological Corp.

Howell, K. W., Zucker, S. H., & Morehead, M. K. (1985). MAST: Multilevel Academic Survey Test. San Antonio, TX: Psychological Corp.

Hunt, E., & Lansman, M. (1975). Cognitive theory applied to individual differences. In W. K. Estes (Ed.), *Handbook of learning and cognitive processes* (Vol. 1). New York: Erlbaum.

Hunt, K. W. (1965). *Grammatical structures written at three grade levels.* (NCTE Research Rep. No. 3). Urbana, IL: National Council of Teachers of English. (ERIC Document Reproduction Service No. ED 113 735).

Hutchinson, T. (1987). Personal communication. San Antonio, TX.

Iglesias, A. (1985). Communication in the home and classroom: Match or mismatch? *Topics in Language Disorders, 6,* 29-41.

Isaacson, S. (1984). Evaluating written expression: Issues of reliability, validity and instructional utility. *Diagnostique, 9,* 96-116.

Isaacson, S. (1985). Assessing written language. In C. S. Simon (Ed.), *Communication skills and classroom success: Assessment methodologies for language-learning disabled students.* (pp. 403-424). San Diego, CA: College-Hill Press.

Itard, J. M. G. (1932). *The wild boy of Aveyron.* New York: Appleton-Century-Crofts.

Jenkins, J. R., & Dixon, R. (1983). Vocabulary learning. *Contemporary Educational Psychology, 8,* 237-260.

Jenkins, J. R., & Pany, D. D. (1978). Standardized achievement tests: How useful for special education? *Exceptional Children, 44,* 448-453.

Johnson, A. P. (1951). Notes on a suggested index of item validity: The U-L index. *Journal of Educational Psychology, 42,* 499-504.

Johnson, D. D. (1983). Three sound strategies for vocabulary development. Ginn Occasional Papers: *Writings in reading and language arts* (Number 8). Co-

lumbus, OH: Ginn & Co.

Johnson, D. D., & Baumann, J. F. (1984). Word identification. In P. D. Pearson (Ed.), *Handbook of reading research* (Part 3) (pp. 583-608). New York: Longman.

Johnson, D. D., Levin, K. M., & Pittleman, S. D. (1984). *A field assessment of vocabulary instruction in the elementary classroom* (Program Rep. 84-3). Madison: University of Wisconsin, Wisconsin Center for Education Research.

Johnson, M. (1967). Definitions and models in curriculum theory. *Educational Theory, 7,* 127-140.

Juel, C. (1985, December). *Support for the theory of phonemic awareness as a predictor in literacy acquisition.* Paper presented at the National Reading Conference.

Kaplan, J. S. (1982). *Beyond behavior modification: A cognitive-behavioral approach.* Portland, OR: ASIEP Education.

Kauffman, J. M., & Hallahan, D. P. (1981). *Handbook of special education.* Englewood Cliffs, NJ: Prentice-Hall.

Kaufman, A. S., & Kaufman, N. L. (1983). Kaufman Assessment Battery for Children. Circle Pines, MN: American Guidance Service.

Kavale, K. (1981). Functions of the Illinois Test of Psycholinguistic Abilities (ITPA): Are they trainable? *Exceptional Children, 47,* 496-510.

Kavale, K. A., & Glass, G. V. (1982). The efficacy of special education interventions and practices: A compendium of meta-analysis findings. *Focus on Exceptional Children, 15,* 1-16.

Kawakami, A. J., & Hupei Au, K. (1986). Encouraging reading and language development in cultural minority children. *Topics in Language Disorders, 6,* 71-80.

Kelley, T. (1927). *Interpretation of educational measurements.* Yonkers, NY: World Book.

Kerr, M. M., & Nelson, C. M. (1983). *Strategies for managing behavior problems in the classroom.* Columbus, OH: Merrill.

Kintsch, W. (1974). *The representation of meaning in memory.* Hillsdale, NJ: Erlbaum.

Kintsch, W., & Greene, E. (1978). The role of culture-specific schematic in the comprehension and recall of stories. *Discourse Processes, 1,* 1-13.

Kintsch, W., & Keenan, J. M. (1973). Reading rate as a function of the number of propositions in the base structure of sentences. *Cognitive Psychology, 5,* 257-274.

Kirsch, I. (1985). Response expectancy as a determinant of experience and behavior. *American Psychologist, 40,* 1189-1202.

Korzybski, A. (1948). *Science and sanity: An introduction to non-Aristotelian systems and general semantics* (3rd ed.). Lakeville, CN: Institute of General Semantics.

Labov, W. (1969). The logic of nonstandard English. In J. E. Alates (Ed.), *Monograph series on language and linguistics* (No. 22). Washington, DC: Georgetown University Press.

Lackner, J. R. (1968). A developmental study of language behavior in retarded children. *Neuropsychologia, 6,* 301-320.

Lakin, K. C. (1983). A response to Gene V. Glass. *Policy Studies Review, 2,* 233-239.

Langer, J. A. (1982). Facilitating text processing: The elaboration of prior knowledge. In J. A. Langer & M. T. Smith-Burke (Eds.), *Reader meet author: Bridging the gap* (pp. 149-162). Newark, DE: International Reading Association.

Lee, L. L., & Koenigsknecht, R. (1974). *Developmental sentence analysis: A grammatical assessment procedure for speech and language clinicians.* Evanston, IL: Northwestern University Press.

Lennon, R. T. (1962). What can be measured? *The Reading Teacher, 5,* 326-327.

Lerner, (1971). *Children with learning disabilities: Diagnosis and teaching strategies.* Boston: Houghton Mifflin.

Liberman, I. Y., & Shankweiler, D. (1985). Phonology and the problems of learning to read and write. *Remedial and Special Education, 6,* 8-17.

Liberty, K. A. (1975). *Data decision rules.* Unpublished working paper, University of Washington, Child Development and Mental Retardation Center, Experimental Education Unit, Seattle.

Liberty, K. A., Haring, N. G., & White, O. R. (1980). Rules for data-based strategy decisions in instructional programs: Current research and instructional implications. In W. Sailor, B. Wilcox, & L. Brown (Eds.), *Methods of instruction for severely handicapped students.* Baltimore: Paul H. Brookes.

Lichtenberg, D. (1984). The difference between problems and answers. *Arithmetic Teacher, 31,* 44-45.

Lindamood, P. (1986). Personal communication. Tempe, AZ.

Linsley, J. (1978). The highest-energy cosmic rays. *Scientific American, 239*(1), 60-70.

Lloyd, J. W. (1984). How shall we individualize instruction—Or should we? *Remedial and Special Education, 5,* 7-15.

Lloyd, J. W. & Loper, A. B. (1986). Measurement and evaluation of task-related learning behaviors: Attention to task and metacognition. *School Psychology Review, 15,* 336-345.

Loban, W. D. (1963). *The language of elementary school children* (NCTE Research Rep. No. 1). Champaign, IL: National Council of Teachers of English.

Lovitt, T. C. (1973). *Applied behavior analysis techniques and curriculum research.* Report submitted to the National Institute of Education.

Lovitt, T. C. (1984). *Tactics for teaching.* Columbus, OH: Merrill.

Lund, K. A., Foster, G. E., & McCall-Perez, F. C. (1978). The effectiveness of psycholinguistic training: A reevaluation. *Exceptional Children, 44,* 310-319.

Lyle, J. G. (1965). A comparison of the language of normal and imbecile children. *Journal of Mental Deficiency, 5,* 40-51.

MacGinitie, W. H. (1984). Readability as a solution adds to the problem. In R. C. Anderson, J. Osborn, & R. Tierney (Eds.), *Learning to read in American schools* (pp. 141-151). Hillsdale, NJ: Erlbaum.

Mager, R. F. (1962). *Preparing instructional objectives.* Belmont, CA: Fearon.

Mahoney, G. J. (1975). Ethological approach to delayed language acquisition. *American Journal of Mental Deficiency, 80,* 139-148.

Mahoney, M. J. (1977). Reflections on the cognitive-learning trend in psychotherapy. *American Psychologist, 32,* 5-13.

Mandler, J. M., & Johnson, N. S. (1977). Remembrance of things passed: Story structure and recall. *Cognitive Psychology, 9,* 111-151.

Mann, L. (1975). Psychometric phrenology and the new faculty psychology: The case against ability assessment and training. *Journal of Special Education, 9,* 261-268.

Mann, L., & Sabatino, D. A. (1985). *Foundations of cognitive process in remedial and special education.* Rockville, MD: Aspen.

Marge, M. (1972). The general problem of language disabilities in children. In J. V. Irwin & M. Marge (Eds.), *Principles of childhood language disabilities.* New York: Appleton-Century-Crofts.

McGuigan, C. A. (1980). Analysis and use of performance data. In C. L. Hansen (Ed.), *Child assessment: The process and the product* (pp. 105-130). Seattle: Program Development Assistance Center.

McMurray, N. E., Bernard, M. E., Klausmeir, H. S., Schilling, J. M., & Vorwerk, K. (1977). Instructional design for accelerating children's concept learning. *Journal of Educational Psychology, 69*, 660-667.

Mehan, H. (1981a). The competent student. *Anthropology and Education Quarterly, 11*, 131-152.

Mehan, H. (1981b). Social construction in psychology and sociology. *The Quarterly Newsletter of the Laboratory of Comparative Human Cognition, 3*, 71-77.

Mercer, J. R. (1973). Crosscultural evaluation of exceptionality. *Focus on Exceptional Children, 5*, 8-15.

Messick, S. (1980). Test validity and the ethics of assessment. *American Psychologist, 35*, 1012-1027.

Meyer, B., & Rice, G. E. (1984). The structure of text. In D. Pearson, R. Barr, M. Kamil, & P. Mosenthal (Eds.), *Handbook of reading research* (pp. 319-351). New York: Longman.

Miller, J. F., & Yoder, D. E. (1974). An ontogenetic language teaching strategy for retarded children. In R. L. Schiefelbusch & L. L. Lloyd (Eds.), *Language perspectives: Acquisition, retardation and intervention*. Baltimore: University Park Press.

Moore, D. S. (1985). *Statistics: Concepts and controversies*. New York: W. H. Freeman.

Moos, R. H. (1973). Conceptualizations of human environments. *American Psychologist, 28*, 652-655.

Muma, J. (1973). Language assessment: Some underlying assumptions. *ASHA, 15*, 331-338.

Muma, J. R. (1978). *Language handbook—Concepts, assessment, intervention*. Englewood Cliffs, NJ: Prentice Hall.

National Coalition of Advocates for Students (1985). *Barriers to excellence: Our children at risk*. Boston: Author.

Olson, M. A. (1976). Criterion-referenced reading assessment in a large city school district. *Journal of Reading Behavior, 8*, 387-396.

Osborn, J. (1984). The purpose, uses, and contents of workbooks and some guidelines for teachers and publishers. In R. C. Anderson, J. Osborn, & R. J. Tierney (Eds.), *Learning to read in American schools: Basal readers and content texts* (pp. 45-111). Hillsdale, NJ: Erlbaum.

Osgood, C. E. (1953). *Method and theory in experimental psychology*. New York: Oxford Press.

Palinscar, A. S., & Brown, A. L. (1984). Reciprocal teaching of comprehension-fostering and comprehension-monitoring activities. *Cognition and Instruction, 1*, 117-175.

Pany, D. (1987, January). *Phonemic segmentation*. Presentation. Kyrene School District, Tempe, AZ.

Patching, W., Kameenui, E., Carnine, D., Gersten, R., & Colvin, G. (1983). Direct instruction in critical reading skills. *Reading Research Quarterly, 18*, 361-365.

Pearson, D., Barr, R., Kamil, M., & Mosenthal, P. (1984). *Handbook of reading research*. New York: Longman.

Pearson, P. D. (Ed.). (1984). *Handbook of reading research*. New York: Longman.

Pearson, P. D., & Johnson, D. (1978). *Teaching reading comprehension*. New York: Holt, Rinehart & Winston.

Petty, W. T., & Finn, P. J. (1981). Classroom teachers' reports on teaching written composition. In S. Haley-James (Ed.), *Perspectives on writing in grades 1-8* (pp. 19-33). Urbana, IL: National Council of Teachers of English.

Philips, S. (1970). Acquisition of roles in appropriate speech usage. *Monograph Series on Language and Linguistics* (No. 23). Washington, DC: Georgetown University Press.

Pikulski, J. J., & Pikulski, E. C. (1977). Cloze, maze, and teacher judgment. *The Reading Teacher, 30*, 776-770.

Polloway, E. A., & Smith, J. E. (1982). *Teaching language skills to exceptional learners*. Denver: Love.

Posner, G. J., & Strike, K. A. (1976). A categorization scheme for principles of sequencing content. *Review of Educational Research, 46*, 665-690.

Postman, N., & Weingartner, C. (1969). *Teaching as a subversive activity*. New York: Dell.

Prater, M. A. (1986). Personal communication. Anaheim, CA.

Prieto, A. G., & Rutherford, R. B. (1977). An ecological assessment technique for behaviorally disordered and learning disabled children. In *Behavioral disorders* (Vol. 2, pp. 169-175). Lancaster, PA: Lancaster Press.

Propst, I. K., & Baldauf, R. B. (1981). Psycholinguistic rationale for measuring beginning ESL reading with matching cloze tests. *RELC Journal, 12*, 85-89.

Pugach, M. (1987). The national education reports and special education: Implications for teacher preparation. *Exceptional Children, 53*, 308-314.

Pyrczak, F. (1976). Context-independence of items designed to measure the ability to derive the meanings of words from their context. *Educational and Psychological Measurement, 36*, 919-924.

Quay, H. C. (1973). Assumptions, techniques and evaluative criteria. *Exceptional Children, 40*, 165-170.

Raphael, T. E., & Pearson, D. P. (1985). Increasing students' awareness of sources of information for answering questions. *American Educational Research Journal, 22,* 217-235.

Rasool, J. M., & Royer, J. M. (1986). Assessment of reading comprehension using the sentence verification technique: Evidence from narrative and descriptive texts. *Journal of Educational Research, 79,* 180-184.

Read, C., & Ruyter, L. (1985). Reading and spelling skills in adults of low literacy. *Remedial and Special Education, 6,* 53-60.

Resnick, L. B., & Weaver, P. (Eds.). (1979). *Theory and practice of early reading* (Vol. 1, 2, and 3). Hillsdale, NJ: Erlbaum.

Reutzel, R. (1985). Story maps to improve comprehension. *The Reading Teacher, 38,* 400-404.

Reynolds, M. C., & Balow, B. (1972). Categories and variables in special education. *Exceptional Children, 38,* 357-366.

Reys, R. E. (1984). Mental computation and estimation: Past, present, and future. *The Elementary School Journal, 84,* 547-557.

Rhetts, J. E. (1974). Task, learner, and treatment variables in instructional design. *Journal of Educational Psychology, 66,* 339-347.

Rigney, J. W. (1980). Cognitive learning strategies and dualities in information processing. In R. Snow, P. A. Federico, & W. Motaguel (Eds.), *Aptitude, learning and instruction* (Vol. 1). Hillsdale, NJ: Erlbaum.

Roberts, G. H. (1968). The failure strategies of third grade arithmetic pupils. *The Arithmetic Teacher, 15,* 442-446.

Robinson, F. P. (1946). *Effective study.* New York: Harper & Brothers.

Rogoff, B. (1978). Spot observation: An introduction and examination. *Quarterly Newsletter of the Institute for Comparative Human Development, 2,* 21-26.

Rosenshine, B. V. (1983). Teaching functions in instructional programs. *Elementary School Journal, 83,* 335-352.

Rotter, J. B. (1982). *The development and application of social learning theory: Selected papers.* New York: Praeger.

Royer, J. M., & Cunningham, D. J. (1981). On the theory and measurement of reading comprehension. *Contemporary Educational Psychology, 6,* 187-216.

Royer, J. M., Lynch, D. J., Hambleton, R. K., & Bulgareli, C. (1984). Using the sentence verification technique to assess the comprehension of technical text as function of subject matter expertise. *American Education Research Journal, 21,* 839-869.

Rueda, R., Figueroa, R., Mercado, P., & Cardoza, D. (1985). *Performance of Hispanic educable mentally retarded, learning disabled, and nonclassified students on the WISC-R, SOMPA, and S-KABC.* Final report: Handicapped-Minority Research Institute. Los Alamitos, CA: SWRL Educational Research and Development.

Salomon, G. (1972). Heuristic models for the generation of aptitude-treatment interaction hypotheses. *Review of Educational Research, 42,* 327-343.

Samuels, S. J. (1976). Modes of word recognition. In H. Singer & R. B. Ruddell (Eds.), *Theoretical models and processes of reading* (2nd ed.). Newark, NJ: International Reading Association.

Samuels, S. J. (1983). Diagnosing reading problems. *Topics in Learning and Learning Disabilities, 2,* 1-11.

Samuels, S. J., & Kamil, M. L. (1984). Models of the reading process. In P. D. Pearson (Ed.), *Handbook of reading research* (pp. 185-224). New York: Longman.

Sattler, J. M. (1982). *Assessment of children's intelligence and special abilities* (2nd ed.). Boston: Allyn & Bacon.

Saville-Troike, M. (1976). *Foundation for teaching English as a second language: Theory and method for multi-cultural education.* Englewood Cliffs, NJ: Prentice-Hall.

Schooley, D. E., Schultz, D. W., Donovan, D. L., & Lehman, I. J. (1975). *Quality control for evaluation systems based on objective-referenced tests.* Working paper, Department of Education, Lansing, MI.

Schumaker, J. B., Denton, P. H., & Deshler, D. D. (1984). *Learning strategies curriculum: The paraphrasing strategy.* Lawrence: University of Kansas.

Schumaker, J. B., Deshler, D. D., Alley, G. R., Warner, M. W., & Denton, P. H. (1982). Multipass: A learning strategy for improving reading comprehension. *Learning Disability Quarterly, 5,* 295-304.

Schumaker, J. B., Pederson, C. S., Hazel, J. S., & Meyer, E. L. (1983). Social skills curriculum for mildly handicapped adolescents: A review. *Focus on Exceptional Children, 4,* 1-16.

Serapiglia, T. (1978). Comparison of the syntax and vocabulary of bilingual Spanish, Indian, and monolingual Anglo-American children. *Working Papers on Bilingualism, 16,* 75-91.

Shames, G. H., & Wiig, E. H. (Eds.). (1982). *Human communication disorders: An introduction.* Columbus, OH: Merrill.

Shinn, M. (1986). Does anyone care what happens after the refer-test-place sequence: The systematic evaluation of special education program effectiveness. *School Psychology Review, 15,* 49-58.

Shuell, T. J. (1987). Cognitive conceptions of learning. *Review of Educational Research, 56,* 411-436.

Shulman, L. S. (1970). Reconstruction of educational research. *Review of Educational Research, 40,* 371-397.

Siegler, R. S. (1983). How knowledge influences learning. *American Scientist, 71,* 631-638.

Silbert, J., Carnine, D., & Stein, M. (1981). *Direct instruction mathematics.* Columbus, OH: Merrill.

Silver, E. A. (1985). *Teaching and learning mathematical problem solving: Multiple research perspectives.* Hillsdale, NJ: Erlbaum.

Singer, H., & Ruddell, R. B. (1985). *Theoretical models and processes of reading* (3rd ed.). Newark, DE: International Reading Association.

Spache, G. D. (1940). Characteristic errors of good and poor spellers. *Journal of Educational Research, 34,* 182-189.

Spache, G. D. (1976). *Investigating the issues of reading disabilities.* Boston, MA: Allyn & Bacon.

Special Education Assessment Coalition. (1981). *Special education assessment matrix.* Monterey, CA: CTB/McGraw Hill.

Staats, A. W., Brewer, B. A., & Gross, M. C. (1970). Learning and cognitive development: Representative samples of cumulative-hierarchical learning and experimental longitudinal methods. *Monographs of the Society for Research in Child Develoment, 35* (8, Serial No. 141).

Stanovitch, K. E. (1983). Individual differences in cognitive processes of reading II. Text-level processes. *Annual Review of Learning Disabilities, 1,* 66-71.

Stephenson, W. (1980). Newton's fifth rule and Q methodology: Application to educational psychology. *American Psychologist, 35,* 882-889.

Stowitschek, J. J., Stowitschek, C. E., Hendrickson, J. M., & Day, R. M. (1984). *Direct teaching tactics for exceptional children.* Rockville, MD: Aspen.

Swaminathan, H., Hambleton, R. K., & Algina, J. (1974). Reliability of criterion-referenced tests:

Decision-theoretic formulation. *Journal of Educational Measurement, 11,* 263-267.

Swezey, R. W. (1981). *Individual performance assessment: An approach to criterion-referenced test development.* Reston, VA: Reston Publishing.

Tallmadge, G. K., & Horst, D. P. (1974). *A procedural guide for validating achievement gains in educational projects.* Washington, DC: U.S. Department of Health, Education and Welfare, Office of Education.

Tawney, J. W., & Gast, D. L. (1984). *Single subject research in special education.* Columbus, OH: Merrill.

Taylor, R. L. (1984). *Assessment of exceptional students: Educational and psychological procedures.* Englewood Cliffs, NJ: Prentice-Hall.

Templin, M. C. (1957). *Certain language skills in children: Their development and interrelationships.* Minneapolis: University of Minnesota Press.

Tenenbaum, H. A. (1983). Effects of oral reading rate and inflection on comprehension and its maintenance (Doctoral dissertation, University of Florida). *Dissertation Abstracts International, 45,* 1086A.

Thiagarajan, S., Semmel, D. S., & Semmel, M. I. (1974). *Instructional development for training teachers of exceptional children.* Bloomington, IN: Center for Innovation in Teaching the Handicapped.

Thorndike, E. L. (1917). *Education: A first book.* New York: Macmillan.

Thorndike, R. L., & Hagan, E. (1969). *Measurement and evaluation in psychology and education* (3rd ed.). New York: John Wiley.

Tierney, R. J., & Leys, M. (1984). *What is the value of connecting reading and writing?* (Reading Education Rep. #55). Urbana-Champaign: University of Illinois.

Tobias, S. (1976). Achievement treatment interactions. *Review of Educational Research, 46,* 61-74.

Torgesen, J., & Kail, R. J. (1980). Memory processes in exceptional children. In B. K. Keogh (Ed.), *Advances in special education: Basic constructs and theoretical orientations* (Vol. 1) (pp. 55-99). Greenwich, CT: JAI Press.

Tucker, J. A. (1985). Curriculum-based assessment: An introduction. *Exceptional Children, 52,* 199-204.

Tuersky, A., & Kahneman, D. (1973). Availability: A heuristic for judging frequency and probability. *Cognitive Psychology, 5,* 207-232.

Tyack, D., & Gottsleben, R. (1974). *Language sampling, analysis, and training: A handbook for teachers and clinicians.* Palo Alto, CA: Consulting Psychologists Press.

Ulman, J. D., & Rosenberg, M. S. (1986). Science and superstition in special education. *Exceptional Children, 52*, 459-460.

U.S. Department of Education, Office of Special Education. (1984). *The condition of bilingual education in the nation.* Washington, DC: Author.

Valdez, C. (1986, February). *Effectiveness of bilingual education as related to teacher training.* Keynote address, Arizona Association for Bilingual Education, Tucson, AZ.

Videen, J., Deno, S., & Marston, D. (1982). *Correct word sequences: A valid indicator of proficiency in written expression* (Research Rep. No. 84). Minneapolis: University of Minnesota, Institute for Research on Learning Disabilities.

Wagner, R. K., & Sternberg, R. J. (1984). Alternative conceptions of intelligence and their implications for education. *Review of Educational Research, 54*, 179-223.

Walker, H. M., & Rankin, R. (1983). Assessing the behavioral expectations and demand of less restrictive settings. *School Psychology Review, 12*, 274-284.

Wallen, C. J. (1972). *Competency in teaching reading.* Chicago: Science Research Association.

Wang, M. C., Reynolds, M. C., & Walberg, H. J. (1986). Rethinking special education. *Educational Leadership, 44*, 26-31.

Waugh, R. P. (1975). The I.T.P.A.: Ballast or bonanza for the school psychologist? *Journal of School Psychology, 13*, 201-208.

Waugh, R. P. (1978). *Research for teachers: Teaching students to comprehend.* Portland, OR: Northwest Regional Educational Laboratory.

Wells, G. (1973). *Coding manual of the description of child speech.* Bristol, England: University of Bristol, School of Education.

Westby, C. E., & Rouse, G. R. (1985). Culture in education and the instruction of language learning disabled students. *Topics in Language Disorders, 5*, 15-28.

White, O. R. (1972). *A manual for the calculation and use of the median slope—A technique of progress estimation and prediction in the single case.* Working Paper No. 16, Regional Resource Center for Handicapped Children, University of Oregon.

White, O. R. (1983, March). Data decision rules. Paper presented at the Precision Teaching Winter Conference, Orlando, Florida.

White, O. R. (1984). Performance-based decisions: When and what to change. Paper presented at Precision Teaching Winter Conference, Park City, Utah.

White, O. R. (1986). Precision teaching—Precision learning. *Exceptional Children, 52*, 522-534.

White, O. R., & Haring, N. G. (1980). *Exceptional teaching.* Columbus, OH: Merrill.

White, O. R., & Liberty, K. A. (1976). Evaluation and measurement. In N. G. Haring & R. Schiefelbush (Eds.), *Teaching special children.* New York: McGraw-Hill.

Wiig, E. H., & Semel, E. (1984). *Language assessment and intervention for the learning disabled* (2nd ed.). Columbus, OH: Merrill.

Williams, J. P. (1984). Phonemic analysis and how it relates to reading. *Annual Review of Learning Disabilities, 2*, 91-96.

Williams, R. N., & Zimmerman, D. W. (1984). On the virtues and vices of the standard error of measurement. *Journal of Experimental Education, 52*, 231-233.

Willis, G. W. (1985). Successive and simultaneous processing: A note on interpretation. *Journal of Psychoeducational Assessment, 4*, 343-346.

Wilt, M. E. (1950). A study of teacher awareness of listening as a factor in elementary education. *Journal of Educational Research, 43*, 626-636.

Wong-Fillmore, L. (1986, February). *Language learning research: Its implications for the effective instruction of American Indian and Spanish Speaking Children.* Paper presented at the Arizona Association for Bilingual Education, Tucson, AZ.

Wood, M. L. (1982). *Language disorders in school-age children.* Englewood Cliffs, NJ: Prentice-Hall.

Yavorsky, D. K. (1977). *Discrepancy evaluation: A practitioner's guide.* Charlottesville: University of Virginia, Evaluation Research Center.

Ysseldyke, J. E., Thurlow, M. L., Mecklenburg, C., & Graden, J. (1984). Opportunity to learn for regular and special education students during reading instruction. *Remedial and Special Education, 5*, 29-37.

Zigmond, N., & Miller, S. E. (1986). Assessment for instructional planning. *Exceptional Children, 52*, 501-509.

Zucker, S. H., & Meyen, E. L. (1975). Attitudinal stability of teachers of exceptional children. *Journal of Experimental Education, 43*, 94-96.

Zukav, G. (1979). *The dancing wu li masters.* New York: Bantam.

Glossary

Ability training Treatment that attempts to change cognitive or perceptual characteristics of the student. See *Aptitude–treatment interaction*.

Academics A term usually referring to the *basic skills* (e.g., reading, arithmetic), but which may also refer to content areas such as science, social studies, or even drama and physical education. A distinction is often made between academic behavior and *social behavior*.

Accuracy The level of correct performance required by a task.

Acoustically similar Sounding almost like (e.g., /b,p,d,t/, /f,v/, /k,p,g/) (Carnine & Silbert, 1979, p. 75).

Acquisition The initial phase of learning. In order to enter acquisition, a student must have all required subskills. The goal of acquisition is accuracy. See *Format*.

Active reading Use and integration of a variety of skills and information sources to derive meaning from text. Active readers use relevant prior knowledge, decoding skills, language knowledge, and context to understand what they read. They monitor their own understanding and problem-solve when they fail to understand.

Aim An objective expressed in terms of proficiency level and a target date.

Aptitude–treatment interaction (ATI) The belief that individuals with certain abilities will behave differently in certain treatments than individuals who lack those abilities. Efforts to use ability measures to select treatments are common but generally ineffective.

Assertiveness As used in popular psychology, "assertiveness" refers to the strong but nonaggressive declaration of opinion or need. In this context, being assertive is positive and healthy. It does *not* mean being pushy.

Assumed cause The hypothesized explanation for failure or success at a task.

Automatic response An accurate response performed at a high rate with distractions present. Automatic responses are often thought to occur without conscious thought. Automaticity is generally considered to be the highest level of proficiency.

Basic movement cycle (BMC) See *Basic skills*.

Basic skills Sometimes referred to as *tool skills*, basic skills include elementary reading, mathematics, and communication tasks. They are the skills one must use repeatedly to carry out complex tasks.

Behavior In a classical sense, "behavior" refers to any muscular activity or movement. Special education refers to two categories of behavior: overt and covert. Overt behavior involves movement that can be detected and confirmed reliably by observers without the use of specialized equipment. Covert behavior may be self-reported or detected by inference from overt behaviors (such as biofeedback recordings or psychological test scores). Covert behaviors include thoughts and feelings.

When special educators use the term "behavior," they are often referring exclusively to social behavior, as in the explanation "She has a behavior problem." This gives the erroneous impression that *academic* and *social behaviors* are somehow different, when, in fact, both respond to the same learning processes.

Behavior disorder (BD) A label applied to individuals who engage in any of a variety of inappropriate or deviant behaviors. The term "behavior disorder" has gained wide acceptance as an alternative to *emotional disturbance*.

Behavior modification While this term could apply to any effort to change any behavior, it is used almost exclusively to describe the use of contingency management programs arranged by educators to address specific student behaviors. See *Contingency*.

Behavioral model See *Medical model*.

Best-fit line A line drawn through a set of data that best represents both the central tendency of the data and changes in data patterns.

Bilingual interference The idea that meaning, syntax, or phonology from one language may negatively influence a second language.

Blending A decoding strategy in which the reader isolates letter sounds and cluster sounds within words and combines them to say the word (e.g., in the word "sister," a student would isolate "sss," "iii," "sss," and combine to say "sis," etc.).

Bound morpheme Unit of meaning that cannot stand alone (e.g., affixes like *re-*, *de-*, *-ing*, and *-er* do not stand alone).

Calibrate To adjust the size of a task by removing or adding content.

CAP See *Standard* and *Criterion*.

CEC See *Council for Exceptional Children*.

'Celeration A generic term for changes (acceleration or deceleration) in behavior. On a graph it may be represented by a line drawn through data.

Child-study team Also called a multidisciplinary team. A group mandated by *PL 94-142*, composed of a student's teacher and parents, an administrator, and an evaluator (usually a school psychologist). The team's purpose is to determine the need for special education services. In some districts, this group also writes the *IEP*, although a separate meeting is suggested for this purpose. The meeting is often called a *staffing*. When appropriate, the student may also attend the meeting.

Classification The evaluative process of labeling or naming things to facilitate communication and understanding. In special education the term may refer to the label placed on a student (e.g., "MR" or "LD"). See *Decisions*.

Clinical teaching "An alternative test-teach-test-teach process" (Lerner, 1971, p. 103).

Cloze A procedure used to sample reading comprehension. The student is asked to fill in the blanks in a passage where every *n*th word has been deleted. Students who understand what they read are able to make good guesses about what the omitted word should be (e.g., "In a book, words _____ defined in a glossary"). Cloze is also used with oral language to check language comprehension.

Cluster Groups of letters that can be sounded together to make one sound (e.g., in "sister," "sis" is a cluster of letters that can be sounded together). See *Blending*.

Code emphasis An approach to reading instruction that focuses on skills for decoding words. See *Decoding*.

Comprehension See *Reading comprehension*.

Comprehension monitoring Self-checking for understanding during reading. For example, a student might say to himself, "What does this mean? Do I need to reread, should I slow down?" It is a student's awareness of his understanding of the text.

Comprehensive evaluation The evaluation required by *PL 94-142* prior to a *child-study team* meeting. It typically includes estimates of skill and ability along with a *developmental* history and behavioral observations.

Computation Rote skills, procedures, and concepts students use to (1) add, (2) subtract, (3) multiply, (4) divide, and (5) calculate fractions, decimals, ratios, and percentages.

Concept analysis Process through which defining characteristics are identified. Defining characteristics include critical and noncritical attributes (e.g., in the letter *b* the critical attributes are its shape and orientation. Noncritical attributes include size and typeface).

Condition The circumstances, or situation, specified in an objective. See *Objective*.

Consolidated domain A group of tasks that share strategic operations. In a highly consolidated domain, many items can be worked by learning a few strategic steps.

Content A topic being taught (e.g., vowels, questioning, Pima history, and Alaskan glaciers).

Content domain See *Content*.

Contingency The arrangement between a behavior and its consequences. The contingency is the thing that links a behavior to the stimulus that follows it. It is the expectation that the contingency will function that raises (in the case of an expected reward) or lowers (in the case of an expected punisher) the probability of someone doing something.

"Contingency management" is the process of consciously designing and employing contingencies to change behavior. It is frequently used synonymously with *behavior modification*, though *behavior modification* is much more general.

Control See *Therapy*.

Correlation The relationship between two measures of student behavior (not necessarily causative). *Correlation coefficients* are used to describe parameters of measurement such as reliability and validity. They are typically reported as fractions falling between −1 and +1.

Correlation coefficient A fraction falling between +1 and −1, usually labeled *r*. The significance of the correlation depends on many things, such as the size and composition of the population used to obtain it. The seriousness of the decision being made should be the primary determinant of any ideal level. However, levels above .85 are usually demanded for measures used to make treatment decisions for individuals.

Council for Exceptional Children (CEC) The largest organization of special educators. The Council has state branches and a large national structure. Its annual convention has been attended by as many as 10,000 people. The organization promotes several publications and lobbies on behalf of special education at the state and national levels. The address of CEC is 1920 Association Drive, Reston, Virginia 22091–1589; Phone, (703) 620-3660.

Covert behavior Unseen or currently unmeasurable behavior such as thinking/feeling.

Criterion (Criterion for Acceptable Performance, or CAP) The standards in an *objective*. The criterion tells how well (accurately, frequently, or to what quality) a behavior should be carried out by a student who has finished instruction on a task. See *Objective*.

Criterion-referenced test Test or observation that compares an individual's behavior to a performance standard or criterion.

Critical thinking skills Sometimes referred to as "problem-solving skills," this domain is largely ill-defined. Critical thinking skills are supposed to be needed when working tasks that require inference, synthesis, or creative solutions. Teachers often refer to critical thinking skills as those that exceed rote recall or literal understanding. Their use implies the active application of *strategies* for solution, understanding, or

memory. Individuals with these skills are supposedly better prepared to control their own learning and to achieve more sophisticated understanding of content than those without critical thinking skills.

Curriculum The content and behaviors (*objectives*) taught in a class. It is *not* synonymous with the published materials used in a class or the teacher's approach to delivery of instruction.

Curriculum alignment The process of matching evaluation procedures and instruction with the curriculum to assure that you are testing what you teach and teaching what you test.

Curriculum-based evaluation Evaluation materials and procedures that are directly tied to the objectives being taught. See *Curriculum alignment*.

Data decision rules The use of empirically validated guidelines (rules) in the interpretation of *data*. The rules are linked to patterns of data and are employed at some fixed interval (often every 2 weeks). Teachers use these rules to decide if they should move ahead in the curriculum, move back to an easier task, alter their instruction, alter their use of *contingencies*, or continue with their current program.

Data-determined 'celeration See *Median slope*.

Day lines Vertical lines on a chart.

Decisions Evaluation is a process of decision making. This includes decisions about placement and classification, as well as treatment. Treatment decisions involve the determination of what to teach and how to teach it.

Decoding The sounding and blending of letters and words. Decoding and comprehension are the two primary subdivisions of reading. "Translating printed words into a representation similar to oral language, e.g., reading 'I am hot' for the words *I am hot*" (Carnine & Silbert, 1979, p. 30).

Decoding rules A rule that when applied should assist a reader in figuring out a word. For example, "when a word ends in 'e,' the vowel says its name and the 'e' is silent. *Mope*. 'O' says its name and 'e' is silent."

Delivery Includes various teacher actions during instruction. Delivery change is one type of "How to teach" decision. See *Decisions* and *Treatment*.

Development The result of aging in a particular environment. It is *not* the same as maturation, which is simply aging. Two people of the same age may develop differently because of the different environments in which they have lived (or their different interpretations of the same environment).

Diagnosis In special education, *diagnosis* may have any of several meanings. It may refer to a statement of the student's physical or psychological status, or it may refer to the category of handicapping condition into which the student is placed. Diagnosis may also refer to a statement of what and how the student should be taught. The three definitions do not necessarily relate to each other.

Direct evaluation Evaluation that measures the performance of students in the materials that they are using or on the tasks they are learning. Direct evaluation is not possible without curriculum-test alignment.

Direct instruction This term originally referred to instruction limited to content (concepts, skills, discriminations) linked in a causative way to an *objective*. In that sense, direct instruction involved teaching only the target *task* or its immediate *subtasks*.

Direct instruction has also come to mean the use of various "behavioral" techniques during instruction. These include the consistent use of scripts, prompts, cues, correction procedures, and teacher responses.

A third definition emphasizes the relationship of tasks to each other as well as concept analysis and curriculum design.

Discrepancy The difference, in absolute or ratio terms, between what a student is doing and what he or she should be doing.

Discrimination Recognizing how things are different.

DSM III The *Diagnostic and Statistical Manual of Mental Disorders, Volume 3*, put out by the American Psychiatric Association.

Dynamic data Data that describe performance over a period of time. See *Formative evaluation*.

Dyslexia "Dyslexia" is used to describe individuals who have difficulty dealing with symbols. In special education, it is associated very closely with *learning disabilities* and reading problems. Originally a medical/psychological term, its transition into education has resulted in tremendous overuse. Today it is not particularly useful.

Efficacy In social service and particularly special education, this term refers to the "goodness" of a program. If the program is effective and cost efficient, it has efficacy.

Emotional disturbance (ED) Sometimes called "emotional handicap (EH)." See also *Behavior disorder*.

Envelope Best-fit lines drawn to incorporate the range of responding or variability in data.

Error analysis The process of examining incorrect responses in order to gain insight into a student's use of inappropriate *strategies*.

Evaluation The process by which investigators come to understand things and by which they attach relative value to things. Evaluation cannot take place without comparison of behavior to a standard.

F-AC-T (sheet) Used to summarize a task-analytical evaluation. It has columns for Fact/Assumed Cause/Test/Decide.

Fatigue point The point at which a reduction in physical stamina is reflected in a skill (i.e., tired hand—poor handwriting).

Feedback Feedback comes after a student has done something. It is the information that tells him if what he did was wrong or right. Whereas this information may also be reinforcing and even instructional, *reinforcement*, correction, and feedback are not necessarily the same.

Fidelity The degree to which a test, or test items, is realistic or lifelike. See *Validity*.

Fluency In evaluation, fluency is a proficiency dimension defined by the rate of student response. Fluency may also refer to the instruction used to improve a student's skills from accuracy to mastery. (See *Mastery*.)

Format Lessons can be categorized into three formats (*acquisition, fluency,* and *generalization*/maintenance), each designed to produce a different behavioral outcome. See *Decisions*. Format can also refer to the type of item (true/false, completion) used on a test. See *Identify* and *Produce*.

Formative evaluation Evaluation that occurs as skills are being developed. Formative data are called "dynamic" because they show movement. See *Progress*.

Free morpheme Unit of meaning that can stand alone; a word (e.g., "courage," "male," "tent").

Frequency data The number of times a behavior occurs during a time interval (usually minutes).

Frequent evaluation Ongoing or continuous assessment.

Generalization The process of using a skill learned in one environment or under one condition under new conditions or in a new environment.

Generalize In special education, this term is usually used in a behavioral sense. A behavior is said to generalize if it transfers (switches) from one situation (set of stimuli) to another. Special students are often characterized as those who do not generalize, meaning that they learn to do something for one teacher in one class but can't do it anywhere else.

Generalization is harder if the two settings in question are very different. This is why special evaluation procedures should be similar to classrooms if their results are to be generalized to instruction. (Classrooms should also be similar to the real world.)

Handwriting Penmanship skills necessary to write letters and digits.

Identify A response domain. Test items which require the student to select the answer from a set of distractors. See *Produce*.

Idiographic evaluation The use of procedures which are tailored to the individual or which compare the individual to himself over time.

IEP (Individual Education Plan) The control component of *PL 94-142*, the plan is required for all special education students and contains a complete outline of the services they are provided. The IEP contains long-term goals, specific short-term *objectives*, statements of current educational performance, statements describing the resources to be used to meet the goals and objectives, and dates for initiation and review of the program.

The IEP is written in conjunction with parents, teachers, the school administration, and in some cases, the student. Any party who disagrees with the plan may appeal it to a review board or to the courts. The plan is *not* a contract for service. See *Child-study team*.

Individualized instruction Making decisions about student instruction on a one-to-one basis. Individualized instruction implies tailored lessons on selected objectives in the curriculum. It does *not* mean one-to-one instruction. (A teacher may employ individualized instruction by deciding to teach a student in a group or by the use of unique instruction.)

Intermediate aim A reference point on the way to an aim. For example, if the aim (criterion) is to have a student be 100% accurate in 6 weeks, an intermediate aim could be to have her 50% accurate in 3 weeks.

Interrogative A question.

Labeling A classification process. Not useful in treatment.

Language sample The recorded transcription of oral communication. Often used in survey-level assessment of language.

Learning Relatively permanent modifications in thought or behavior that result from environmental events (instruction) but not from conditions such as pathology, maturation, or fatigue. Learning is operationally defined (indicated) by a change in behavior over time.

Learning disabled The single most frequently redefined term in special education. *Learning disabled* usually refers to someone who doesn't learn when no one can tell why. The explanations for this failure range from brain damage to bad teaching. Learning disabilities represent the largest (in terms of number of clients) category of educational handicap. It is a mild handicap designation and is definitionally linked to the lack of progress in school.

Learning mode (modality, channel) *Mode* or *modality* refers to the medium of presentation of a lesson. The term would be useful if it referred to lecture, tutoring, or self-instruction; however, in special education it usually refers to so-called stimulus–response categories. The categories are sometimes called *channels*, particularly by those who believe in *process deficits* and remediation. The common stimulus modes (channels) referred to are the auditory and visual channels. Some educators believe that learners have stable preferences for one of these modalities over the other, and attempt to use these preferences during instruction. This idea has questionable utility. Learning is more clearly influenced by the structure, organization, presentation, and grouping practices of the teacher.

Least Restrictive Environment A term from *PL 94-142*, LRE refers to the placement of students. Given two equally instructional settings, the student should be placed in the one which is least restrictive. That is, the placement should be the most like the placement to which the treatment is to generalize (usually the regular classroom).

Maintenance Continued mastery of a skill after instruction has ended.

Master See *Mastery*.

Mastery See *Rate* and *Fluency*. Mastery is a proficiency dimension. Mastery criteria go beyond accuracy in that they require the student to work correctly and quickly. Rate statements, usually in terms of a rate per minute, are used in mastery objectives. Percentage statements are used in accuracy objectives.

Maze A procedure used to check reading comprehension. Students are asked to select correct words in passages in which words have been omitted. Like *cloze*, every *n*th word is omitted. Unlike cloze, the correct word and several incorrect words are presented above or below the blank where the word was omitted (i.e.,

"In a book, words _____ defined in a glossary"). is, are, phonemes

Mean The average score. A measure of central tendency.

Measurement The assignment of numerals to objects or events according to rules (Campbell, 1940).

Median The middle-most score. A measure of central tendency.

Median slope A line drawn through a series of data points to summarize their trend.

Medical model The *medical model* assumes that causes of behavior problems reside within the client; that is to say, *the client* is sick. In contrast, the so-called behavioral model used in most social service assumes that behavior grows out of the interaction of the person and the environment. In the medical model, therapy is directed at the internal cause of the problem (surgery and medication are examples of this treatment). Teachers do not administer that kind of treatment. They attempt to alter people's behavior by manipulating the environment through instruction.

Minimal competency The idea that students must reach a certain level of proficiency before graduating from a program or grade level.

Minimum 'celeration The minimal amount of change considered acceptable. Calculated by comparing current progress rate to the aim rate.

Mode The most frequent score. A measure of central tendency.

Morpheme Smallest unit of meaning in the English language, i.e., *born* is a morphograph, it has meaning; *orn* is not a morphograph, it does not have meaning. *-ed* is a morphograph, it has meaning; *e* is not. (Dixon & Englemann, 1979)

Morphograph See *Morpheme.*

Morphology Rule system for combining units of meaning to make words. We can add *-ed* to *talk* to indicate that someone spoke in the past.

No-effect point The intersection of a projected 'celeration line from the previous phase with the 'celeration line of the intervention phase. Identifies the point at which the intervention is causing no effect.

Norm-referenced test An evaluation that compares an individual's behavior to the behavior of others.

Objective Objectives are statements of the expected behavioral outcomes that will result from instruction. They contain behavioral descriptors, conditions for the behavior, content descriptions, and *criteria.*

Observation A process of summarizing student behavior that samples time and situations rather than items. During observation the evaluator waits for the behavior rather than prompting it with items as in *testing.*

Off-Task A general term implying that the student isn't doing what he or she is supposed to be doing. A student could be "off" one task by being "on" another. The appropriate task is usually defined by the observer or teacher. See *Status.*

On-Task See *Off-task.*

Paraphrasing A procedure used to sample reading comprehension. A student reads a passage and tells what she read in her own words. Specific criteria for judging the adequacy of a student's paraphrase have been developed by Schumaker et al., (1984).

Percentage Number correct divided by the total possible correct.

Performance A measure of behavior taken on one occasion.

Phonemic segmentation Segmenting sounds in oral language. May be a prerequisite to phonetic segmentation. See *Phonetic segmentation.*

Phonetic misspelling Misspelling of a word that can be read (e.g., *ordr* for *order*).

Phonetic segmentation Isolating sounds within a word (e.g., "man"—"mmm aaa nnn"). A subtask of *blending.*

Phonics Sound–symbol relationships in words. See *Decoding.*

Placement See *Classification.*

PL 94-142 See *Public Law 94-142.*

Pragmatics The purposes or functions of language (e.g., to inform or to control).

Precision teaching An evaluative system that summarizes changes in performance over time through direct and daily measurement of behaviors. *Precision teaching* refers directly to a behavioral teaching procedure based on repeated measures of the *objective* behavior, charting, and standardized instruction. It is used in general to describe a variety of *formative evaluation* (data-based program modification) systems.

The basic ideas of precision teaching are (a) objectives must be written to include movement, (b) movements can be counted and recorded on ratio charts, (c) *trends* in objective learning can be recognized and summarized, and (d) the trends of learning under different instructional conditions can be interpreted to select the most efficient instruction.

Prior knowledge Considered a prerequisite for comprehension. The background information necessary for understanding a written or spoken message (e.g., if a student has never heard of the ocean, he may not understand a story about hunting for sunken ships in the Caribbean). It is relevant, previously learned information used by good readers to understand what they read.

Probe A criterion-referenced test or observation procedure.

Problem-solving See *Strategy*; *Critical thinking skills*.

Process of written communication A process with at least four components—planning, transcribing, reviewing, and revising (Isaacson, 1985).

Process remediation (process deficit) In this sense, a process is an unlearned sequence of activity leading to a product. This activity takes place within the individual at an unconscious level and is not directed by the person. If a person who is poked in the finger with a needle withdraws the finger and says "ouch," a process of this kind has taken place. It is assumed that learning takes place through certain neurological, psychological, perceptual, and learning processes and that if one of these processes is damaged (or impaired), learning will not take place. Process remediation is directed at repairing or developing a process as opposed to teaching a particular lesson.

These learning processes are hypothetical and their remediation is based on theories of learning. Different theories describe different processes and different remediation activities. Process remediation directed at various so-called *learning modalities* was very popular in special education during the 1960s and early 1970s. The theoretical basis and remedial utility of process remediation remains unvalidated.

Process deficits refers to hypothesized irregularities in the way a student's neurological system handles information. The term has a variety of meanings but is most closely associated with the psycholinguistic model of treating learning disabilities. This model evolved out of an earlier theory of language acquisition. The process dysfunction idea was popularized by Samuel Kirk through the development of the Illinois Test of Psycholinguistic Ability (ITPA). The utility of process remediation has been hotly debated (Arter & Jenkins, 1979; Glass, 1977; Hammill & Larsen, 1974b, 1978; Kavale, 1981; Lund, Foster, & McCall-Perez, 1978).

Produce A response domain. Test items that require the student to generate the answer. See *Identify*.

Produce format See *Produce*.

Proficiency Criterion level necessary to satisfactorily perform the next skill in a skill sequence.

Proficiency domain A range of response defined by level of accuracy or rate (e.g., "reads words at a rate of 140 per minute"). Proficiency domain is rate.

Prognosis Prediction.

Progress data Information obtained by taking repeated measures of a behavior across time. Progress data are typically used in *formative evaluation* and in conjunction with *data decision rules*.

Projective testing During projective testing, the evaluator has the client do something and then interprets the client's behavior according to a theory. Typically, the only link between what the client does and the evaluator's conclusion is the theory. For example, a student may be asked to copy geometric shapes, and the evaluator may draw conclusions about her emotional status from her work. While drawing and emotions may seem unrelated, the evaluator has a theory that ties the two together. The psychologist uses the theory to generalize conclusions beyond the tasks the student completes (Anastasi, 1982; Sattler, 1982).

The tests themselves don't supply conclusions. This is not a situation in which a particular test score automatically implies a particular treatment. During placement evaluations, psychologists and others are employed to render judgments. They may choose to base their judgments on test scores, observations, interviews, or all three. But ultimately, the responsibility for the judgment rests with the person—not the test (American Psychological Association, 1983).

Proportional scale A scale that measures growth in a multiplicative fashion and indicates rate of improvement more accurately than an equal-interval scale.

Psychoeducational evaluation Assessment of processing abilities (also referred to as "psychomedical evaluation").

Psychoeducational evaluation philosophy If the pupil hasn't learned, there must be something wrong with him.

Psychotic See *Behavior disorder*.

Public Law 94-142 *(PL 94-142) PL* stands for public law; *94* refers to the Ninety-Fourth Congress; and *142* means this was the 142nd law that Congress passed.

PL 94-142 says students with handicaps should be given an education. Beyond that, it is difficult to say what it means because of the various regulations it has spawned and court decisions it has led to. Special educators have probably erred by overstating the impact of the law to secure resources and respect for the field. It would have been better to say "it is correct and practical to educate handicapped students" rather than to say "it is the law." Laws can disappear through funding cuts, legislation, or litigation.

Purpose of written communication   Why we write; the functions of written language (i.e., expressive, poetic, transactive) (Isaacson, 1985; Britton, 1978).

Rate   The number of responses divided by the time a behavior was observed. Rate is a form of data, or behavior summary, that takes into account the frequency with which a behavior occurs and the length of time during which it occurs (usually in minutes). Other types of data include accuracy (percentage), duration, and intensity. See *Criterion*.

Raw score   The number of responses.

Reading   An interactive process in which the reader brings what he knows about the world to the printed page. What is known is used to construct meaning from what is written. See *Reading comprehension*.

Reading comprehension   Understanding text. Students combine what they know with what is printed to construct meaning. This process occurs as a student reads. Students draw upon decoding skills, vocabulary knowledge, language, and prior knowledge to make sense of what is written.

Reading method   An instructional approach, not a program that is a published series.

Reading program   A published series rather than a method.

Reinforce (reinforcer)   See *Behavior*. A reinforcer is something that follows a behavior and raises the probability of the behavior reoccurring. A reinforcer need *not* seem to be pleasant to the person giving it, only to the person receiving it. If a kid does not like M&M's, then they aren't reinforcers for that kid. Positive reinforcement takes place when you are given something you want.

Reliability   How consistently a test measures what it measures.

Remedial   A term applied to *curriculum* and occasionally to the students placed in that curriculum. Remedial instruction presents students with curriculum that typical students received at a younger age. It usually follows the same sequence but at a later time.

Response class   Behaviors that are so closely related that intervening on one will change the others within the class.

Response domain   The type of behavior required to answer a test item. See *Identify* and *Produce*.

Retelling   A procedure used to sample reading comprehension. A student reads a passage and says what she read. Unlike paraphrasing, where a student must use her own words, a student may simply restate what she read.

Score   A numerical summary of behavior. Standard scores, gain scores, and grade equivalency scores and others are described in Appendix B.

Semantic maturity   Skill in selecting individual words for a particular message.

Semantics   The study of meaning within language. It includes (a) meaning of single words and word combinations, (b) multiple meanings of words, (c) figurative language, and (d) the influence of content and structure on language.

Semilogarithmic   A chart with equal intervals on one axis and ratio intervals on the other. See *Six-cycle chart*.

Sentence types

Complex sentence   A complete idea that includes one independent clause (e.g., "Kim writes well") and one dependent clause (e.g., "when she plans reviews and revises her work").

Compound run-on sentence   More than two complete ideas joined by connecting words (e.g., "Eddie runs fast and Eddie drives fast and Eddie talks fast and Eddie likes cars").

Compound sentence   Two complete ideas joined by a connecting word (e.g., "Kim composes music and she enjoys playing the piano").

Sentence fragment   Incomplete idea (e.g., "My grandchildren are").

Simple sentence   Complete idea that consists of a single subject and a single predicate (i.e., in "Eddie runs fast," *Eddie* is the subject, and *runs fast* is the predicate).

Sentence verification   A procedure used to sample reading comprehension. A multiple-choice format is used in which students select a sentence that means the same as an original sentence from the passage. Incorrect sentences may include similar sentence structures or similar vocabulary.

Six-cycle chart   A semilogarithmic chart used to chart changes in behavior without distorting the data. See *Semilogarithmic*.

Slice Segmenting a behavior to raise the frequency. Taking complex behavior and counting its components. See *Calibration*.

Slope (trend) See *Precision teaching*. *Slope* refers to the slope of the student's learning as seen on a chart, with time on one axis and content or skill on the other. Slope is another term for progress, trends, or learning. The student with the greatest slope is progressing the fastest and learning the most. He is covering the most content in the smallest amount of time.

Social behavior Social behavior includes those actions that are taken in response to, or in consideration of, others. It includes almost everything except self-stimulating behavior and addiction (though these may have social components, also). For some reason, social behavior is usually separated from *academic* behavior during teacher training.

Sociolinguistic rules Cultural guidelines for communication. Knowledge of what can be said, to whom, and in what context.

Sound analogy strategy Refers to strategy where a student uses known sounds to decode new words (e.g., "if I can decode *rich*, I can use that information to decode a similar word, *which*." This is sometimes referred to as a "rhyming strategy") (Carnine & Silbert, 1979).

Specific level Evaluation designed to test a particular assumption. A specific-level test is always a *criterion-referenced test*. Specific-level tests are *calibrated* to match short-term instructional objectives. See *Survey level*.

Speech Mechanical aspects of language (e.g., phonology, voice, and fluency).

Staffing See *Child-study team*.

Standard The norm or *criterion* to which a student's behavior is compared during evaluation. Without a standard, evaluation is not possible.

Standard 'celeration 'Celeration of $\times 1.25$.

Standard error of measurement A boundary of confidence that can be placed around a test score. Standard error is calculated from the standard deviation and reliability of the test.

Standardization Process of establishing a behavioral criterion, or norm.

Static data Data that describe performance at only one time.

Status A person's condition or location—not his behavior.

Step change The immediate effects of a phase change.

Story map A technique used to assist readers in understanding what they read. Often a map is a diagram that illustrates how events are sequenced, how ideas are related, and what aspects of characters are important. It is a graphic representation of events and concepts in a story.

Strategy A learned (though not necessarily consciously employed) procedure for dealing with a situation or problem. The term refers to any of a variety of activities employed to aid your own attention, memory, academic production, or social competence. See *Task*.

Structured instruction See *Direct instruction*.

Subskill See *Task analysis*.

Subtask An essential component of a task that, when mastered, enables the learner to perform the task successfully.

Summative evaluation Evaluation that takes place at the end of a unit or section of instruction. Summative and formative evaluation can be contrasted like this: Summative evaluation takes place at the end of a lesson or project and tells the evaluator what has happened. Formative evaluation takes place during the lesson or project and tells the evaluator what is happening. Summative evaluation "sums up" the activity. It is after the fact, like end-of-the-year testing. Formative evaluation is ongoing and yields information that can be used to modify the program prior to its termination.

Survey level Evaluation designed to collect a general sample of student behavior. Survey-level evaluation is designed to locate areas of difficulty, but it lacks the specificity required to guide treatment. *Assumed causes* are developed from survey-level information. See *Specific level*.

Syntactic interference The influence of the syntax of one language or dialect on another language or dialect.

Syntax Rule system that governs the order of words in a sentence.

Syntax maturity Skill in combining words to convey a message.

Table of specifications A grid composed of intersecting sequences of content, behavior, conditions, or criteria. Tables of specifications are used to generate objectives and test items and to assure *Curriculum alignment*. See *Curriculum-based evaluation*.

Task Any behavior or set of behaviors. The things that we teach are sometimes called *concepts* or *tasks*. It is hard to separate these clearly. Superficially, a task is an action and a concept is an idea; however, we know the concept has been learned only if the task can be completed and, if designed properly, the task can't be completed without knowing the concept. Therefore, a task could be just about anything.

Before a task can be dealt with, it must be made "behavioral" by stating it in the form of a performance *objective*. Several objectives form a *curriculum*.

In education, the objective is typically called a task. All tasks are composed of two things—essential subtasks and a task *strategy*. Essential subtasks are simply the other tasks a person *must* be able to complete in order to complete the main task. In a cumulative sense, a task is "harder" than its subtasks (though an individual subtask may have taken longer to learn). A subtask is essential if the task cannot be done without it.

A task may have several subtasks (the number depends on how finely the task is subdivided). The task strategy is the procedure by which these subtasks are combined to produce the task. If a student is skilled at all essential subtasks but does not know the strategy needed to combine them, he cannot do the task.

Task analysis The process of isolating, sequencing, and describing the essential components of a task. Effective instruction is guided by task analysis. Task analysis is the process of clarifying the task, recognizing its essential subtasks, recognizing the task strategy, and sequencing the elements for instruction. Teachers use task analysis to avoid attempting to teach things students cannot learn (due to a missing subtask) or things they already know.

Task-analytical model Diagnosing a child's learning problem by applying the cycle of fact finding, task analyzing, hypothesizing, and validating.

Terminal objective A performance objective that describes the behavior required of the learner at the end of a period of instruction.

Test curriculum match See *Curriculum alignment*.

Test format The way test stimuli are presented (e.g., multiple choice, fill in the blank, matching).

Testing A process to determine how a child functions in reality by asking her to perform a selected sample of behaviors.

Text structure The organization of written material; the way ideas are related to convey a message. Some text structures interfere with a reader's comprehension while other text structures facilitate comprehension. Headings, transition statements, alerting state-ments, and summaries are often used by writers to organize a message so that it is easily understood.

Text variables The features of written material that contribute to or interfere with a reader's comprehension. Text variables include organizers such as headings, introductory comments, and summary statements. They also include vocabulary complexity and sentence length. See *Text structure*.

Tool skills Skills that are essential subtasks of many *basic skills*. For example, "saying sounds" is a tool skill necessary for all oral language tasks, and "writing digits" is a tool necessary to write out a phone number or balance a checkbook.

Treatment An intervention. In education, the systematic manipulation of the environment to produce a desired change in behavior. See *Decisions*.

Treatment modality See *Learning mode*.

Trend See *Slope; Precision teaching*.

Trial A trial is a single stimulus–response presentation. In arithmetic, each problem on a worksheet is a trial. In language training, each request for an object is a trial. A trial has a clear beginning (teacher direction) and ending (student response).

T-unit A group of words that can stand alone and make sense. T-units are used in analysis of sentence complexity. The number of units that can stand alone within a sentence is one indicator of sentence complexity.

Validity How well a test describes reality and measures what it's supposed to measure.

Verbal mediator Once students are able to verbalize a procedure, they are able to literally "talk" their way through a situation to its solution. In the literature this is sometimes called *verbal mediation*.

Visually similar Look-alike (e.g., *b/d/p/q/g, m/n/u/h, v/w, n/r*) (Carnine & Silbert, 1979, p. 73).

Writing mechanics Grammar, punctuation, capitalization, handwriting, and spelling.

Writing process approach A teaching focus that emphasizes writing as a communication act. Proponents suggest that currently there is too much emphasis on skill instruction and not enough on planning, transcribing, reviewing, and revising.

Written communication Written language; written expression.

Name Index

Subject Index

Italicized page numbers indicate definitions.

WE VALUE YOUR OPINION—PLEASE SHARE IT WITH US

Merrill Publishing and our authors are most interested in your reactions to this textbook. Did it serve you well in the course? If it did, what aspects of the text were most helpful? If not, what didn't you like about it? Your comments will help us to write and develop better textbooks. We value your opinions and thank you for your help.

Text Title _____ Edition _____

Author(s) _____

Your Name (optional) _____

Address _____

City _____ State _____ Zip _____

School _____

Course Title _____

Instructor's Name _____

Your Major _____

Your Class Rank _____ Freshman _____ Sophomore _____ Junior _____ Senior

_____ Graduate Student

Were you required to take this course? _____ Required _____ Elective

Length of Course? _____ Quarter _____ Semester

1. Overall, how does this text compare to other texts you've used?

_____ Superior _____ Better Than Most _____ Average _____ Poor

2. Please rate the text in the following areas:

	Superior	Better Than Most	Average	Poor
Author's Writing Style	_____	_____	_____	_____
Readability	_____	_____	_____	_____
Organization	_____	_____	_____	_____
Accuracy	_____	_____	_____	_____
Layout and Design	_____	_____	_____	_____
Illustrations/Photos/Tables	_____	_____	_____	_____
Examples	_____	_____	_____	_____
Problems/Exercises	_____	_____	_____	_____
Topic Selection	_____	_____	_____	_____
Currentness of Coverage	_____	_____	_____	_____
Explanation of Difficult Concepts	_____	_____	_____	_____
Match-up with Course Coverage	_____	_____	_____	_____
Applications to Real Life	_____	_____	_____	_____

3. Circle those chapters you especially liked:
   1   2   3   4   5   6   7   8   9   10   11   12   13   14   15   16   17   18   19   20
   What was your favorite chapter? _____
   Comments:

4. Circle those chapters you liked least:
   1   2   3   4   5   6   7   8   9   10   11   12   13   14   15   16   17   18   19   20
   What was your least favorite chapter? _____
   Comments:

5. List any chapters your instructor did not assign. _____

6. What topics did your instructor discuss that were not covered in the text?_____

   _____

7. Were you required to buy this book? _____ Yes _____ No

   Did you buy this book new or used? _____ New _____ Used

   If used, how much did you pay? _____

   Do you plan to keep or sell this book? _____ Keep _____ Sell

   If you plan to sell the book, how much do you expect to receive? _____

   Should the instructor continue to assign this book? _____ Yes _____ No

8. Please list any other learning materials you purchased to help you in this course (e.g., study guide, lab manual).

   _____

9. What did you like most about this text? _____

   _____

10. What did you like least about this text? _____

   _____

11. General comments:

   May we quote you in our advertising? _____ Yes _____ No

   Please mail to: Boyd Lane
                     College Division, Research Department
                     Box 508
                     1300 Alum Creek Drive
                     Columbus, Ohio 43216

   Thank you!